No class of fact or academic
division of knowledge is
the copyrighted property
of one profession –
the field of a profession
is not an area set apart.
It is the bringing to bear
of a certain plexus of
knowledge and skill
on some accomplishment
humanly desirable.

HENRY V. HUBBARD

Educational Planning

Educational Planning

Frank W. Banghart

Director, Educational Systems and Planning Center
Florida State University

Albert Trull, Jr.

Architectural Facilities Planning
Florida State Department of Education

The Macmillan Company New York
Collier-Macmillan Limited London

Printed in the United States of America

The Macmillan Company
866 Third Avenue, New York, New York 10022
Collier-Macmillan Canada, Ltd., Toronto, Ontario

Library of Congress catalog card number:
74-163613

Printing: 1 2 3 4 5 6 7 8 Year: 3 4 5 6 7 8 9

The quotation on the endpapers is from Henry V. Hubbard, *Planning and the Planning Profession: The Past Fifty Years, 1917–1967,* edited by Russell Van Nest Black (Washington, D.C.: American Institute of Planners, October 1967), p. 23.

Prologue

Educational planning, especially comprehensive educational planning, is a new field for educational decision-makers (see the outline illustration in the Contents), following the work of urban, social, transportation, economic, military, industrial, and government planners. The influences and needs of these other planners are compelling educators to re-examine existing educational programs and the effect of education in solving urban problems. The mounting failures of our institutions of education are producing serious doubts about the ends that education is supposed to serve, about the nature of the educational process as a whole, and about the professionalism and skills of our educators. These doubts, in turn, are creating a new awareness of the significance of educational planning.

The failure to attack problems and utilize opportunities has sharply exposed the theoretical foundations of educational planning. Most school districts make good plans only partially, if at all. Most of the planning systems used are limited to relatively short-range objectives (i.e., data gathering, curriculum planning, the developing of educational specifications, and annual budgeting). Only in rare instances has planning been used for comprehensive purposes and extended to long-range goals.

The purpose of comprehensive educational planning is to develop a long-range guide that will use the best available resources to attain educational objectives and permit continuous evaluation of the problems of the planning process itself. To illustrate how these tasks can be performed, a seven-phase educational planning model is presented in this book.

The possible contents of such a model have become more and more abundant: economists, sociologists, architects, engineers, geographers, political scientists, and many others have developed theories, with supporting validation, related to human activities and their physical requirements. For this reason, the illustrations and examples used in this book focus primarily on physical planning.

No attempt is made to furnish a neat cataloguing of planning disciplines. The boundaries between disciplines are becoming blurred as they attempt to define urban activities, and in turn educational activities. The proposed seven-phase model is meant to be used as a framework, rather than a catalogue. Within this framework, the various disciplines can be combined to provide new ways of solving old and emerging educational problems. These disciplines may also provide a means for analyzing information from many different sources and for understanding and planning a comprehensive educational system that emphasizes school plant planning. The first objective of this book is to provide an understanding of planning procedures.

This book also attempts to synthesize the new approaches with the old approaches to the educational planning process. The works of Webber, Burgess, and others on urban processes and values; of Chapin and McLaughlin on urban activity systems; of Isard, Tiebout, and others on economic structures; of Lichfield and Hill on evaluative methods; and of Harris, Ackoff, and others on simulation have remained unknown to most educational planners, because these works are scattered through many different sources and written in the technical languages of different disciplines. Because of a mistaken view that theory is irrelevant to the practical educator, it is necessary to bring these interdisciplinary developments to the attention of the educational planner. This is the second objective of this book.

Despite great advances in recent times, formidable problems remain in relating theory to practice. Obvious relationships are not yet established: the relationship between urban activity analysis and curriculum, between decision theory and practical data-processing, and between these and educational management, teacher in-service training, classroom size, site conservation, student-community relationships, pollution, ghetto creation, and so on. Seemingly disparate, these problems and processes are interrelated, for they are different aspects of one urban system. Identifying and describing them have been immensely aided by new analytical techniques such as systems analysis, operations research, general systems theory, and cybernetics. The development and application of these techniques have uncovered a universal framework for processing populations, organizations, and programs in large complex systems through communication and control. Thus, the third objective of this book is to reveal the general tools of analysis, evaluation, and control usable in comprehensive educational planning processes, and especially those related to the planning of physical environments conducive to learning.

This book presents neither new theoretical statements nor a practical step-by-step manual of how to plan. Rather, this seven-phase model attempts to provide a framework by which educational planners and others may use new tools or develop new approaches for solving the planning problems of an educational environment.

The purpose of comprehensive educational planning is to help ensure the accomplishment of the educational goals set by today's society for tomorrow's achievements. No claim is made that the characteristics of educational planning described in this book apply to every educational problem. However, a systematic approach to the major phases of planning, along with appropriate steps for solving a particular problem, should be most useful. This approach allows new methods to be fused with traditional ones into an effective framework for action.

Certain basic phases have been identified as necessary for any planning process. This is true regardless of the specific problems being considered, or the degree of depth and thoroughness being sought, or the level of quality desired. The seven major phases are the seven parts of this book:

Part One	Defining the educational planning problem
Part Two	Analyzing the planning problem area
Part Three	Conceiving and designing plans
Part Four	Evaluating plans
Part Five	Specifying the plan
Part Six	Implementing the plan
Part Seven	Monitoring the plan in action

Each part requires a certain number of procedures or steps. Their number and kind depend on the problems, their function, their distribution in time and space, their relationship to the environment, and the personal elements of the planner's classification system. This book does not presume to dictate all of the steps. Additional steps may be added and variations on those listed may be found. For most planning tasks, however, the steps as shown are sufficient for the building of a unique model for the solving of each educational problem.

Contents

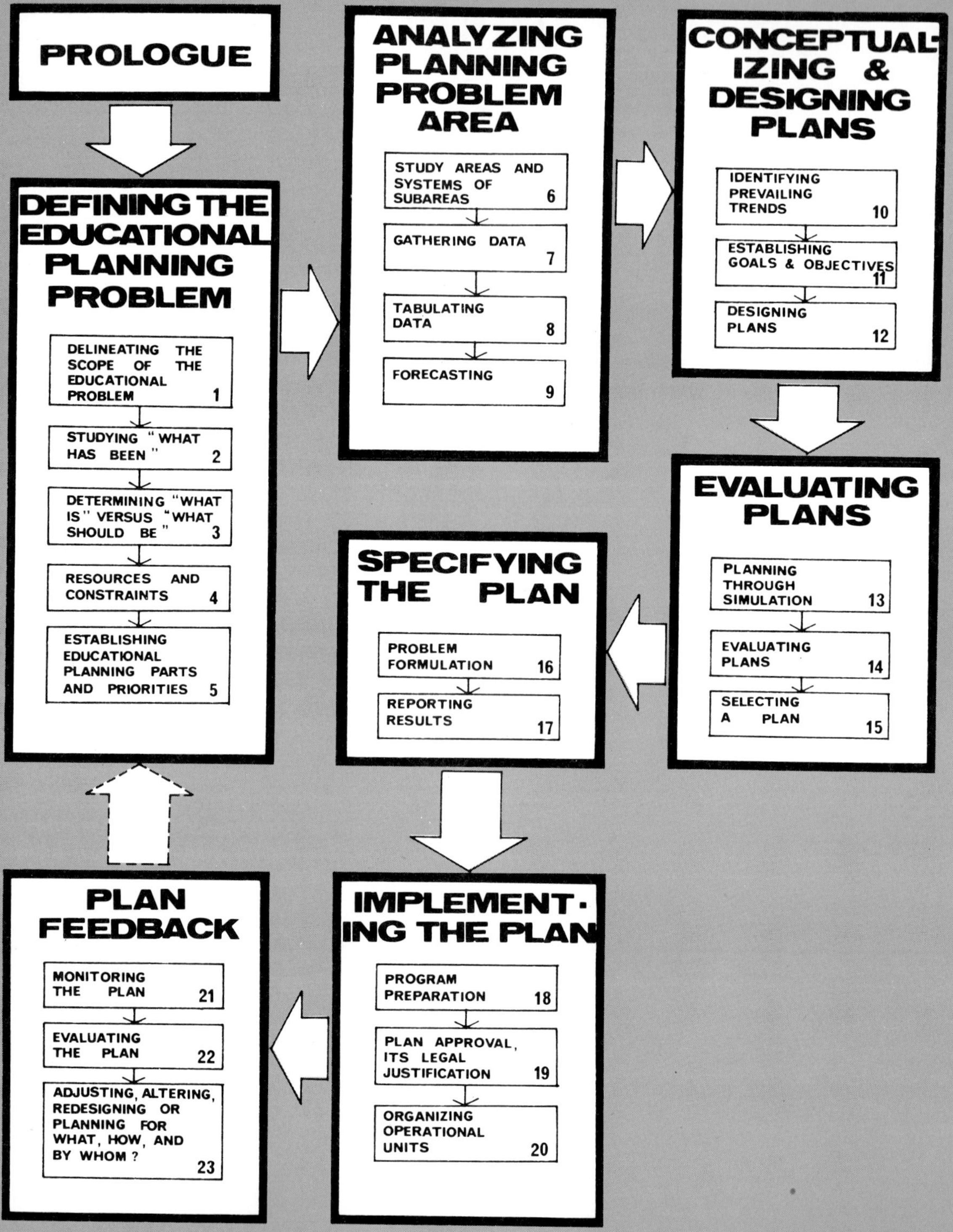
PROLOGUE
DEFINING THE EDUCATIONAL PLANNING PROBLEM
DELINEATING THE SCOPE OF THE EDUCATIONAL PROBLEM 1
STUDYING "WHAT HAS BEEN" 2
DETERMINING "WHAT IS" VERSUS "WHAT SHOULD BE" 3
RESOURCES AND CONSTRAINTS 4
ESTABLISHING EDUCATIONAL PLANNING PARTS AND PRIORITIES 5
ANALYZING PLANNING PROBLEM AREA
STUDY AREAS AND SYSTEMS OF SUBAREAS 6
GATHERING DATA 7
TABULATING DATA 8
FORECASTING 9
CONCEPTUALIZING & DESIGNING PLANS
IDENTIFYING PREVAILING TRENDS 10
ESTABLISHING GOALS & OBJECTIVES 11
DESIGNING PLANS 12
EVALUATING PLANS
PLANNING THROUGH SIMULATION 13
EVALUATING PLANS 14
SELECTING A PLAN 15
SPECIFYING THE PLAN
PROBLEM FORMULATION 16
REPORTING RESULTS 17
IMPLEMENTING THE PLAN
PROGRAM PREPARATION 18
PLAN APPROVAL, ITS LEGAL JUSTIFICATION 19
ORGANIZING OPERATIONAL UNITS 20
PLAN FEEDBACK
MONITORING THE PLAN 21
EVALUATING THE PLAN 22
ADJUSTING, ALTERING, REDESIGNING OR PLANNING FOR WHAT, HOW, AND BY WHOM? 23

Part One

Defining the educational planning problem

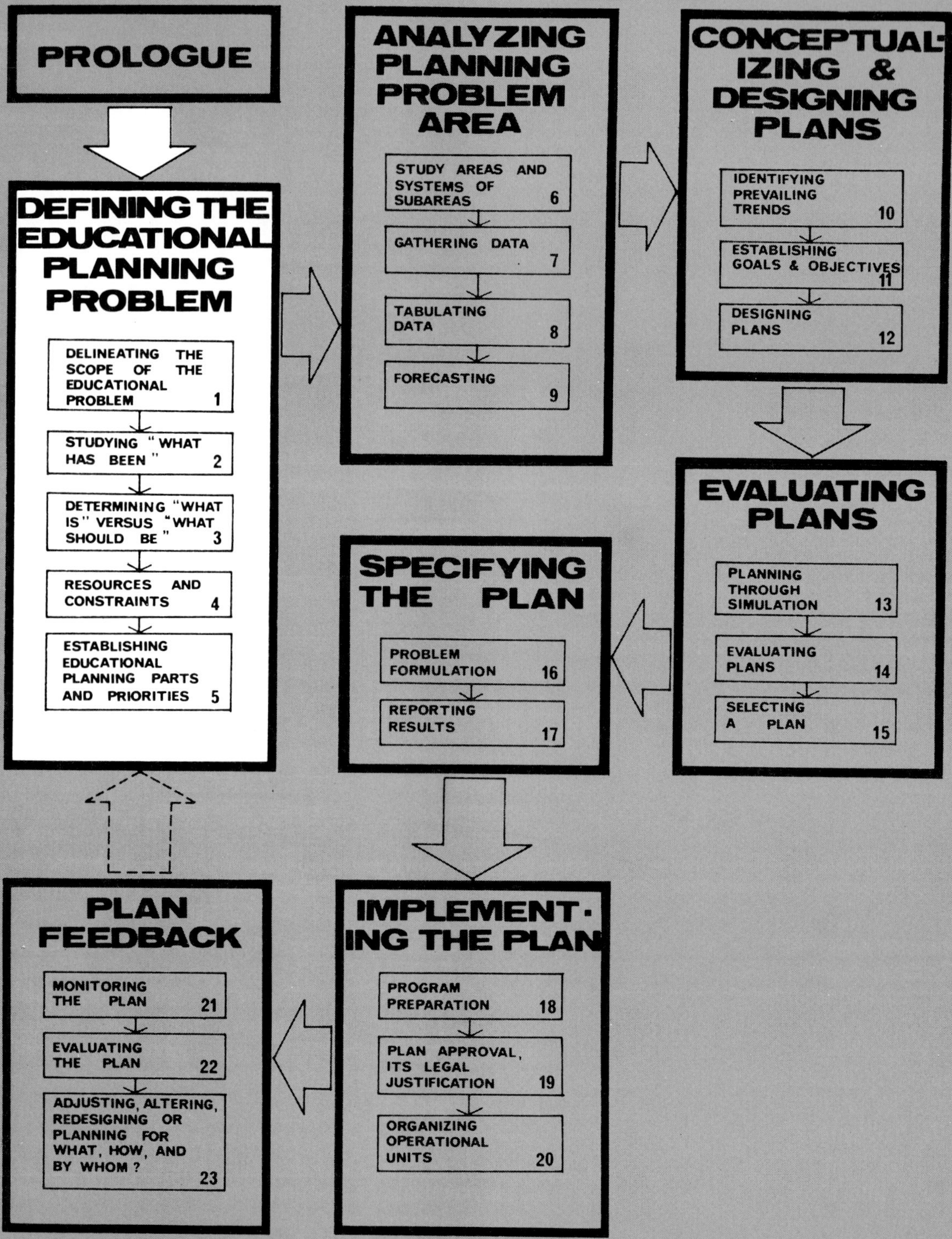
PROLOGUE
DEFINING THE EDUCATIONAL PLANNING PROBLEM
DELINEATING THE SCOPE OF THE EDUCATIONAL PROBLEM 1
STUDYING "WHAT HAS BEEN" 2
DETERMINING "WHAT IS" VERSUS "WHAT SHOULD BE" 3
RESOURCES AND CONSTRAINTS 4
ESTABLISHING EDUCATIONAL PLANNING PARTS AND PRIORITIES 5
ANALYZING PLANNING PROBLEM AREA
STUDY AREAS AND SYSTEMS OF SUBAREAS 6
GATHERING DATA 7
TABULATING DATA 8
FORECASTING 9
CONCEPTUALIZING & DESIGNING PLANS
IDENTIFYING PREVAILING TRENDS 10
ESTABLISHING GOALS & OBJECTIVES 11
DESIGNING PLANS 12
EVALUATING PLANS
PLANNING THROUGH SIMULATION 13
EVALUATING PLANS 14
SELECTING A PLAN 15
SPECIFYING THE PLAN
PROBLEM FORMULATION 16
REPORTING RESULTS 17
IMPLEMENTING THE PLAN
PROGRAM PREPARATION 18
PLAN APPROVAL, ITS LEGAL JUSTIFICATION 19
ORGANIZING OPERATIONAL UNITS 20
PLAN FEEDBACK
MONITORING THE PLAN 21
EVALUATING THE PLAN 22
ADJUSTING, ALTERING, REDESIGNING OR PLANNING FOR WHAT, HOW, AND BY WHOM? 23

Introduction

The first phase of any planning exercise is the definition of the problem. What is the problem? How is it to be studied? What degree of refinement and detail is to be considered? What time interval is required? Providing approaches to these and other questions is the purpose of Part One.

One problem-formulation technique is the following five-point process:

Step 1 Delineating the scope of the educational problem
Step 2 Studying "what has been"
Step 3 Determining "what is" versus "what should be"
Step 4 Identifying resources and constraints
Step 5 Establishing educational planning priorities

These five steps are described in detail in Chapters 1 through 5 in Part One.

1 Delineating the scope of the educational problem

A problem is caused when an activity or event deviates from what is desired. The procedures used to regain the desirable orientation determine the scope of the problem and hence the information that will allow decision-makers to solve the problem.

Activities or events may be grouped in many ways. (See Figure 1.1.) Regardless of how it is done, such grouping makes it possible for the planner to identify the parts of the problem and to decide what elements must be considered in arriving at a solution. Grouping also reduces the complexity of the problem by making clear the relationships between the elements. Such an ordering of the elements also provides hints for potential solutions. It further provides the planner a direction for planning. Finally, this kind of grouping provides a convenient organization of the data for constant reference and for future use.

Many problems are enormously complex and it is clearly necessary to subdivide them into several parts. This book is about the understanding of these parts as independent elementary units (their structure and function), their organization into a whole, and the functioning of the whole. In this case the problem is educational planning, and the order of presentation is as follows:

1 The need for educational planning.
2 The meanings of educational planning.
3 The nature of educational planning.

THE NEED FOR EDUCATIONAL PLANNING

Why is educational planning necessary? What is the mission of educational planning? Whom does educational planning serve and benefit? How does the educational planning process operate? What types of tasks are suitable for the educational planning process? What relationships exist between educational, urban, transportation and economic planning, and other planning?

The need for planning arose with the intensified complexities of modern technological society. Problems such as population, manpower needs, ecology, decreasing natural resources and haphazard application of scientific developments—all place demands on educational institutions for solution. If educational organizations are to meet these problems, then planning becomes a necessity and planning competence becomes mandatory. However, often the communities that these educational establishments serve are unwilling to recognize the need for planning. They, in effect, are demanding solutions while simultaneously rejecting a method by which these solutions could be found.

> General agreement as to the need of a physical plan is yet to be reached. Until the public decides that development according to plans is preferable to development control by market forces alone, any work or discussion of the planning process and its details would be an academic exercise.[1]

Many of the problems faced today are a result of man's effort to improve one aspect of his life at the cost of another. These seesaw maneuvers and isolated "improvements" are detrimental and, in the long run, become part of the problem. Planners in various fields, especially educational planners, are recognizing the need for inclusive planning that considers the social and physical, as well as economic, aspects of any given problem. Solving problems in this three-pronged manner is becoming an important task in educational planning.

Educational planning, as it relates to curriculum planning, physical planning, financial planning,

[1]George M. Raymond, "The Planning Profession: A House Divided," *Pratt Planning Papers*, no. 4, **2**:3 (1964).

FIGURE 1.1

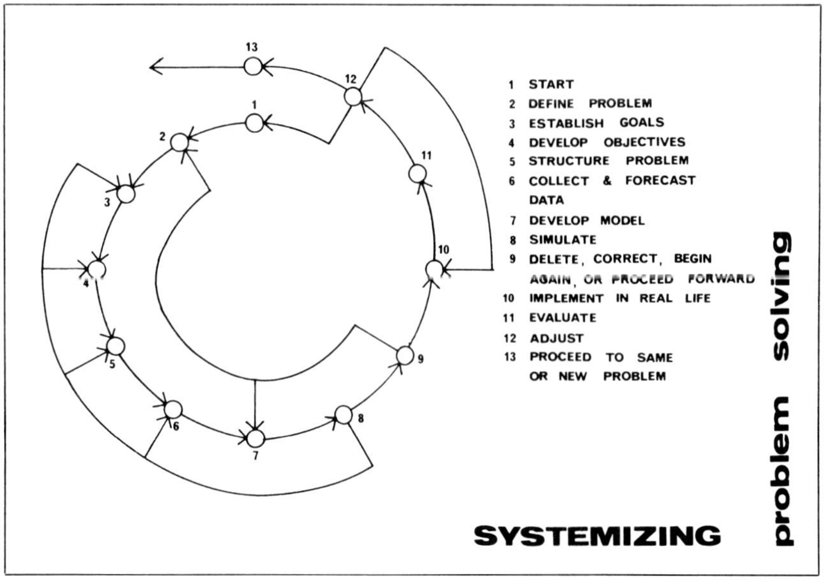

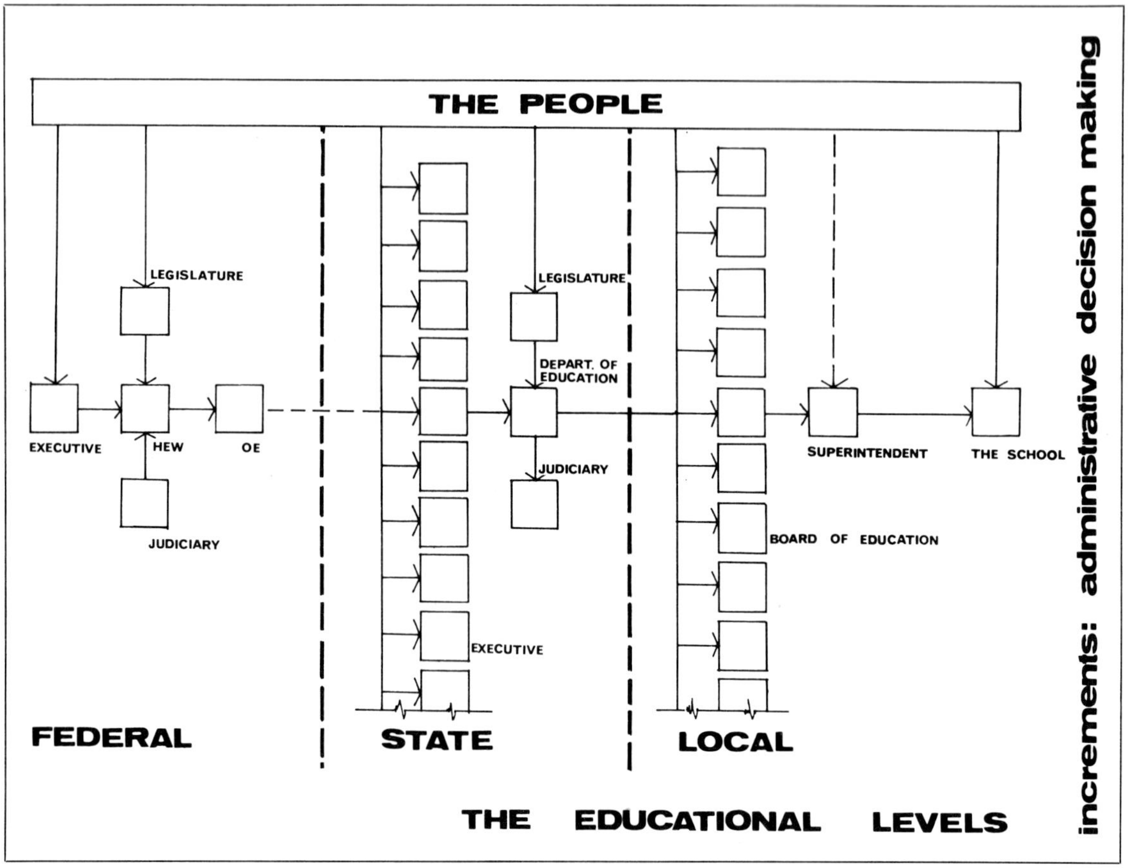

FIGURE 1.2

administrative planning, and so on, has been by and large uncoordinated and incremental. (See Figure 1.2.) In many cases, the result has been a detriment to individual learning and a waste of resources. Such compartmentalization of educational activities has created stumbling blocks for those trying to improve existing programs.

To rigidly maintain isolated processes is to deprive the individual and society of optimal educational yields. To cope with social and physical problems and to overcome the inadequacies of educational planning as it exists today, the following format of planning activities is proposed:

1 Educational planning in general terms: research; development of theory and techniques; drawing up state, regional, and school district plans in broad quantitative terms.
2 Educational planning in physical terms: middle-range and long-range plans (five-, ten-, fifteen-, and twenty-year intervals) of school buildings, layout of school buildings and their proper setting, establishing environmental criteria for learning activities, aesthetic questions, and technological research.
3 Educational planning in social terms: surveys that reflect the people's wants, curriculum planning, instructional strategies, manpower and social needs surveys, and physical designs that enhance personal and social interaction.

4 Educational planning in administrative terms: developmental control, decision-making, management and operation, inventory control, transportation planning and school plant surveys.

We have now become aware of the possibility of rearranging the entire urban environment as an educational organism. Coupled with this possibility is a shift from education solely as a preparation for work to education as a leisure-time activity. This forecast will make the knowledge industry the number one consumer of goods and services. These trends emphasize that flexibility is needed if the educational institutions are to facilitate the rapidly changing character of urban society. These trends also require new tools for coordinating all facets of urban life around learning activities. One tool that can be employed is planning. By its very nature, educational planning serves an integrating function and can be of prime importance in the future of urban development.

THE MEANINGS OF EDUCATIONAL PLANNING

The meanings of educational planning are discussed under three headings: Characteristics, Dimensions, and Constraints. The discussion of characteristics attempts to delineate the distinguishing traits of educational planning activities. In a further endeavor to describe the field of planning, the dimensions sections denote the extent and range of planning activities possible for educational systems. Consideration is given to the various limiting factors, or constraints, associated with educational planning.

Characteristics of educational planning

To understand the meaning of educational planning requires a definition of characteristics that might be identified as unique. The field of educational planning is of relatively recent origin. Because it is eclectic, borrowing from various disciplines, the question is raised whether educational planning *per se* consists of a body of knowledge in its own right. In other words, is there a specific discipline called *educational planning*, or is it merely a general term to be used to describe architectural planning, transportation planning, or other planning techniques when applied to the educational field? Educational planning's lack of uniquely identifying characteristics has troubled its membership for some time. In recent years, however, a theoretical framework has been developed that seems to cut across the various disciplines; a technology is beginning to evolve that does not vary, suggesting the emergence of a unique educational planning discipline.

Educational planning is first of all a rational process. It is characterized by the organized development of society's learning activities. Educational planning is concerned with social goals, means and ends, processes and controls. It is conceptual designing on which decisions and actions by groups may be made. "Preparing to do" is called *planning*, and "communicating what is to be done," is called a *plan*.

Educational planning is a dynamic concept, borrowing heavily from the theoretical framework of cybernetics (the science of communication and control), which ensures that a plan is not so rigidly constructed as to make deviation impossible. Rather, the objective is explicitly stated, and reasonably detailed procedures are established. As the process nears completion, procedural modifications are made as information is fed back to the decision-maker and the plans are updated.

We have entered into a period of complexity that will not permit a random process of problem solving. Educational planners are acutely aware of the need to establish principles by which human beings can deliberately influence the shaping of their own destinies. Furthermore, to qualify themselves as shapers of events, the educational planners must possess three unique areas of special knowledge. These areas include:

1 A comprehension of contemporary scientific methods and an ability to use them with facility.
2 A knowledge of comparative values and value systems, in order to facilitate rational decisions about community goals.

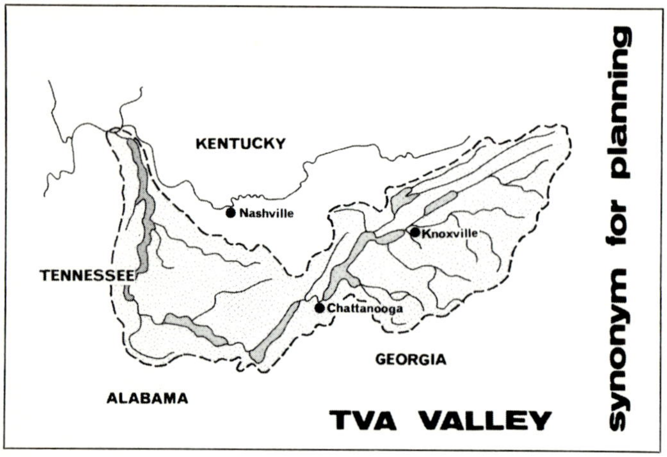

FIGURE 1.3

3 An understanding of continuities and discontinuities, trends, and directions of change in human affairs so as to apprehend emerging possibilities.[2]

Planning, obviously, involves a variety of activities. Although writers have assigned diverse meanings to those activities, two characteristics are prominent throughout: procedures and direction. That is to say, ". . . planning is a series of related steps organized around and moving towards the accomplishment of an objective."[3] Describing the meaning of planning in the language of development, David Lilienthal, former director of the Tennessee Valley Authority, wrote in 1944, "Unified development is, in substance, the valley's synonym for planning."[4] (See Figure 1.3.)

George B. Galloway, a former planning practitioner, has elaborated on these concepts in stating that, ". . . it [planning] is organized foresight plus corrective hindsight." It ". . . pertains to all the problems of government, economy and society. It involves the cooperation of all the social, physical and natural sciences."[5]

Other writers have grappled with the problems of the meaning of planning, and at least one has expressed the idea that the problem might involve the distinction between reporting and "doing." Description and research are both part of scientific activity and contribute in their own distinctive ways to educational planning.

> . . . description contributes to the selection of units of the scientific model, to the location of its boundaries, to the determination of the system states in which it is to be found, and to the development of empirical indicators for measuring the values of the theoretical units employed.
> . . . research is more than question asking. A piece of research tests an hypothetical prediction. The prediction, in turn, has antecedents in an explicit or implicit theoretical mode. The research test of the prediction always provides a feedback to the model from which it is derived, either to substantiate the model's continued viability or to require its modification.[6]

On the other hand, Robert B. Mitchell focused on the meaning of planning by distinguishing between plan-making and planning. Plan-making is an institutional way of reaching decisions, and planning is

> . . . the guiding process in a long chain of decision making by people over a long period of time. Occasional crystallization into plans is only part of the process. Planning is thus a consciously guided program of a whole range of public and private actions leading to development or redevelopment. What is produced is essentially a plan for the nature, rate and process of change. Because its base has broadened to involve

[2]A. Benjamin Handler, "What Is Planning Theory?," *Journal of the American Institute of Planners*, no. 3, **23**:145 (1957).

[3]Mary McLean (ed.), *Local Planning Administration* (3rd. ed.; Chicago: The International City Managers' Association, 1959), p. 41.

[4]Ibid.

[5]Ibid., p. 42.

[6]Robert Dubin, *Theory Building* (New York: Free Press, 1969), p. 6.

physical, social and economic planning [and educational planning as well] it can take over techniques of analysis from other fields.[7]

This is not to assert that educational planning should be dependent on developments in other disciplines, but rather, by a process of its own, follow the scientific steps of hypothesis, analysis, and thesis in order to develop its own systems. Educational planning should revolve around the method of analysis and plan-making, decision-making, the setting of objectives and goals, and community organization and structure and their relation to community life.

Harvey S. Perloff and Benjamin Handler conceptualized the meaning of planning as a blending of procedure and content. This meaning emphasizes the necessity of regarding planning as the perception of the whole. This conception of planning includes people, physical objects, ecological forces, and their interrelationships. Handler points out that interrelationships between city and region and between city and the federal government must also be considered. He also adds that any definition of planning must include such characteristics as economics, politics, social factors, budgeting, and patterns of living. All of these factors demand that the educational planner be more than eclectic. Even though he draws from fields such as economics, psychology and mathematics, the educational planner must develop his own set of tools to handle his unique planning procedures, objectives, and goals.[8]

The meaning of planning involves several component processes, such as the objectives to be attained; an efficient procedure for attaining them; the appropriate allocation of the resources required to attain the objectives; and a conception of the proper form to achieve the objectives, such as the manipulation of the physical environment. However, a totally accepted, specific definition of planning has yet to be formulated. It must not be a simple and arbitrary definition, but an assessment of activity relationships; thus, the definition should be structural or functional. That is, the meaning of planning is determined by the intrinsic events of the problem at hand and its extrinsic influences.[9]

Planning is a deliberate, organized, continuous process of identifying different elements and aspects of an organism, determining their present state and interaction, projecting them in concert throughout a period of future time, and formulating and programming a set of actions and plans to attain desired results. "The process itself is the actuality." Planning involves internal actions and events subject to complete or partial control within the organism, and those external to the organism over which it has little or no control. Although this distinction is not absolute for certain considerations and occurrences, it serves to identify what the organism can bring about on its own initiative. A wide range of probabilities and judgements must be developed for these different actions and events, some of which are physically tangible, others comparatively intangible, some subject to meaningful quantification, others difficult or impossible to measure at present in numerical terms.[10]

Planning is concerned with the conservation of resources. It attacks problems like waste, duplication, misuse of resources and poor timing in the management of resources. Planning helps keep incompatible activities apart from one another, times and locates public investments in education to match private investments, protects natural resources and reserves sites and spaces for future needs. Planning in the most general sense can refer only to any imaginative preparation for the future by an individual or group, which is what learning is all about. The essence of planning and learning is its concern for the educational environment of the human community. Therefore, the planner must know the values, the goals, and the social structure of the community in order to serve it. Harvey Perloff, a planning educator, used planning as a generic term that describes ways in which people, acting through organized entities, endeavor to solve problems and to approximate the vision of the future that they hold.[11]

[7]Handler, p. 145.
[8]Ibid., p. 146.

[9]James E. Lee, "The Role of the Planner in the Present," *Journal of the American Institute of Planners*, no. 3, **24:**151–157 (1959).
[10]Melville Branch and Ira M. Robinson, "Goals and Objectives in City Comprehensive Planning," *Town Planning Review*, no. 4, **38:**262 (1968).
[11]McLean, p. 41.

Dimensions of educational planning

To understand the meaning of planning, one must consider its dimensions, which include the range and aptitude of the various characteristics associated with planning as they have been described. In this section, nine dimensions associated with the educational planning process have been selected and are briefly considered. The consideration of these nine dimensions gives reasonable assurance of a comprehensive and efficient plan.

SIGNIFICANCE

Every problem has some significance. The degree of significance, however, depends on the social importance of the proposed educational objective. To achieve this objective, the decision-maker must have access to clear-cut guidelines and the proposed criteria for evaluation. Once the decision has been made and the proposed objective reached, any educational observer can then evaluate the contribution made by planning and hence judge its significance by the criteria that were established during the planning process.

FEASIBILITY

Assuming the plan is significant and offers the planner sufficient guidelines based on analytical studies and appropriate procedures, the next relevant question is whether the plan is feasible. Several factors will determine the feasibility of the plan, not the least of which is the appropriate political authority. Along with political authorization, technical feasibility and cost estimates are other aspects that should be given realistic consideration.

RELEVANCE

The increased use of technology and sophisticated planning techniques has augmented the concept of relevancy. Planning places heavy emphasis on processes closely associated with attaining objectives. The concept of relevance is absolutely essential to the appropriate implementation of an educational plan. Matters to be resolved involve organizational realism, the degree of relevance associated with the process, the assurance that the plan will converge more specifically on the solution of the problem as time goes by and that the plan is indeed near the optimal process for attaining the specified objectives.

DEFINITIVENESS

All conceivable contingencies, obviously, cannot be built into the educational plan. Great care, however, should be taken to identify the maximum number of contingencies to be given prior consideration. The growing use of techniques such as simulation, whereby the actual plan is run in advance by the use of artificial data, helps to anticipate as many contingencies as possible. The concept of definitiveness minimizes the occurrence of unexpected events that could divert resources from the planned objective.

PARSIMONIOUSNESS

The principle of parsimony in educational planning states that the plan should be outlined in the simplest manner. With so many components required for overall planning, the act of being prudent develops a sensitivity to the infinite numbers of interactions among the various components. The application of this principle permits more time for exploring other alternatives associated with each subphase of the overall planning and aids in the development of guidelines that afford the decision-maker the most efficient choice among the various solutions.

ADAPTABILITY

The educational plan should be dynamic rather than static; it should be constantly undergoing change as information is fed back into the system. As the plan nears completion, the deviations from the educational plan should become smaller until finally the activities converge specifically on the attainment of the original educational objectives. Through the use of a variety of processes, the adaptable or flexible plan can be designed to avoid the unexpected.

TIME

Associated with time are several important factors. One aspect of time deals with the natural cycle of the subject matter under planning. Another is the immediate need to change an unbearable situation (e.g., busing students to achieve appropriate racial mixing). Yet another time factor is the limitations of educational planners in predicting the future. Walt LeBaron, an educational futurist, according to Perry Rosove of Systems Development Corporation, deals with problems centered ". . . around validation and reliability of trend analyses and the extant theories of psychological and social causation."[12]

Finally, time affects our ability to evaluate present educational needs in relation to those of the future.

MONITORING

Monitoring involves the establishment of educational criteria to assure that the various components of the plan are working effectively. Measurements of performance are made throughout the duration of the plan, but the tolerance limits associated with variances in the plan are given due consideration. It is assumed that if the plan is appropriately adaptable, certain amounts of controlled variation will take place. To assure smooth operation, procedures should be established to allow the educational planner to determine the reasons for the variations within the educational planning system.

SUBJECT MATTER

The final dimension of planning is the subject matter of what is being planned. Seven subjects have been identified by William P. McClure as affecting educational planning. They are as follows:

1 Goals and objectives, or what we desire as outputs from the educational process, which becomes the most fundamental of all subject matters.
2 Programs and services, or how we organize patterns of learning activities and their supportive services.
3 Human resources, or how we help and improve their performance, their interaction, their specialization, their behavior, their competence, their growth and their satisfaction.
4 Physical resources, or how we utilize facilities, or plan their pattern of distribution, of how extensive do we get, and of what utility value do the resources possess especially with relations to other physical resources.
5 Finance, or how do we cost out the expenditure and plan for revenue which shape in large measure the character of how we utilize human and physical resources of the school system.
6 Governmental structure, or how do we organize and manage the operation and control of educational programs and activities.
7 Finally, social context, or what source elements must we consider in the educational system, which in reality is only a miniature social system that includes various elements of the entire social system of the community.[13]

Constraints on educational planning

Constraints play various roles in defining the meaning of educational planning. The major constraints include politics, economics and time. As a general rule, constraints affect the educational planning process more at the small end of the scale rather than at the large end; that is, if constraints arise in the educational planning process in a local-regional plan of geographical dimensions, the constraints will be greater at the local level than they will be at the regional level.

[12]Don K. Richards, "Initiation of Planning in the Utah State Education Agency, Part VII," *Comprehensive Planning in State Education Agencies*, ed. Bernard S. Furse and Lyle O. Wright (Salt Lake City: Utah State Board of Education, 1968), pp. 40–41.

[13]William P. McClure, "Planning Adjustments in the Educational System," *Educational Planning in the United States*, ed. Stanley Elam and Gordon I. Swanson (Itasca, Ill.: F. E. Peacock Publishers, 1969), p. 116.

Educational planning, or for that matter any kind of planning, is intimately involved with politics and policies resulting from politicking. This relationship has been characterized by F. Stuart Chapin (a teacher and researcher of urban planning), who wrote, "Thus, in a very fundamental sense the planning process must play an important role in supplying policy alternatives and pressing for decisions from the earliest and broadest level of policy formulation on down to the more detailed levels of policy determination."[14] To this John M. Pfiffner and R. Vance Presthus have added:

> The distinction which is sometimes made between "policy" and "planning," the one being value-loaded and the other a mere technique, seems to suffer from a failure to see that means and ends are but part of a continuum.... As long as means are related to ends and the latter in turn are concerned with values, planning and policy are also related.[15]

Policy precedes planning whenever educational planning at any given level is carried on within a framework in which the educational policies are established at the next higher administrative level. Educational planning, likewise, can precede educational policy, because planning involves a decision and a choice among alternative courses of action. In selecting a course of action, educational planning becomes a policy for the next lower administrative unit. This relationship between educational planning and educational policies is best expressed by the hierarchical structure of most educational administrations, because in the past, the practice of the administration has been to establish the relationship of planning to politics. Administrative decision-making is influenced by, and in turn influences, a whole range of activities involved in the formulation of educational policy. The meaning of this relationship to educational planners is that their business is the public's business and they are contributing to the determination of public policy. The moment public policy is insulated from public scrutiny, educational planning is doomed to fail.[16]

[14]McLean, p. 43.
[15]Ibid.
[16]Ibid., p. 44.

The constraints placed on educational planners by educational policy are somewhat unique because guidelines have not always been clearly defined.

> Unlike other professions, such as engineers, doctors, etc., the planner has no clearly defined area of technical expertise which is universally recognized. He must constantly devise models or methods to deal with value choices which, as yet, are not totally technically bounded.[17]

Educational planning involves people from various disciplines, and the problem of economics in time and cost is a major constraint. The essence of economic constraints stresses the importance of producing a plan that brings together, in proper relation, all the costs required to attain educational objectives. Achieving those objectives within the constraints of cost effectiveness depends on the detailed planning from each operating department within the educational and community establishments. If, for an example, the recreational program of the community and the recreational departments of the school fail to coordinate their programs within the limitations of the resources available, their programs may cost more than the amount necessary, at the same time adding nothing to community or educational objectives. (See Figure 1.4.) In order for educational planning to be effective and economical in time and cost, it must coordinate its efforts with its many hierarchical levels, as well as with the community.

Detailed programs for educational action can be fitted to each other and at the same time promote realization of overall community objectives, thus ensuring that one program will not conflict with another. The growing sensitivity to the needs for costing out specific programs in terms of their relative payoff for the community emphasizes the problem of coordination.

The constraints of needing political and/or legal permission are also placed on the educational planner and his planning process. However, the fact remains that the educational planning process must be extremely adaptable and flexible to be continuous. If not, planning becomes sporadic, producing disruptive

[17]Richard Bolan, "Emerging Views of Planning," *Journal of the American Institute of Planners*, **33**:233 (July 1967).

FIGURE 1.4

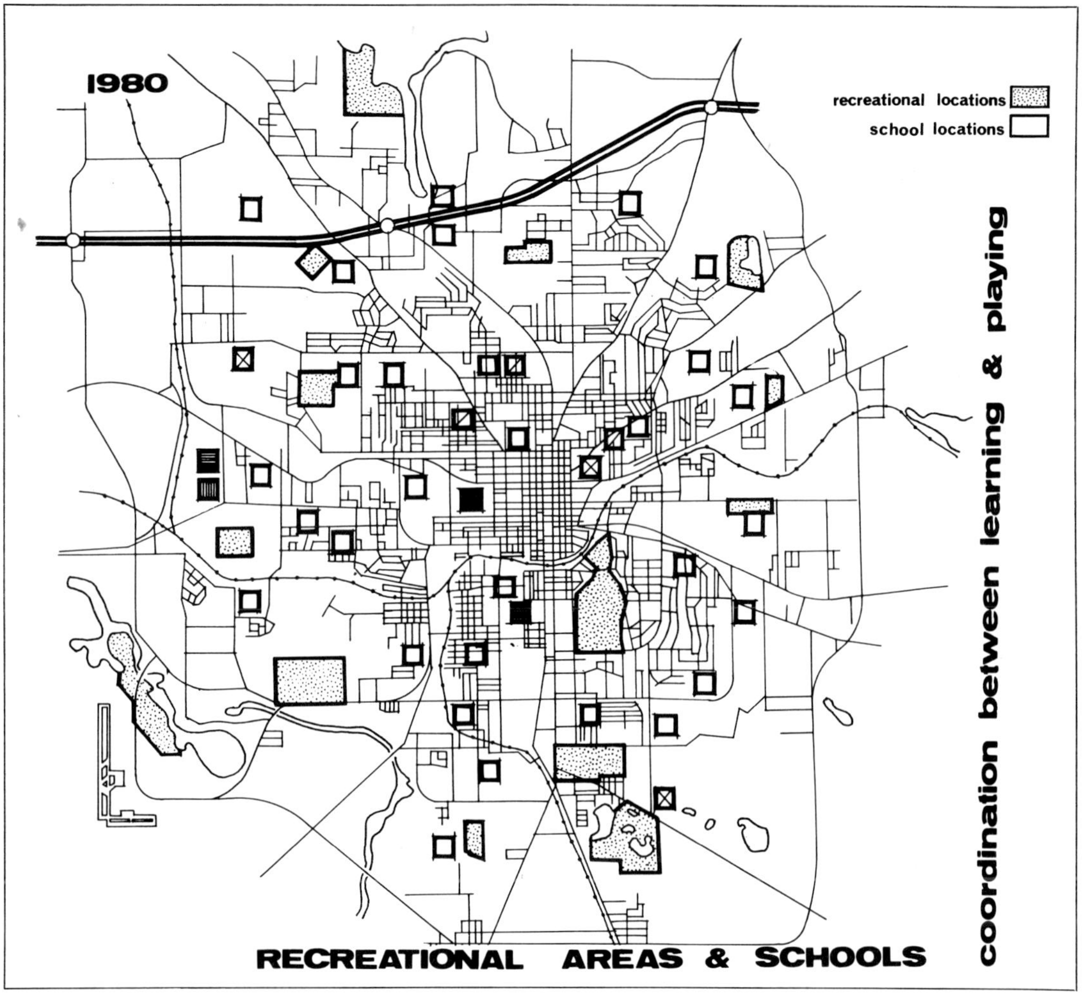

consequences that lead to ineffective education. Chapin wrote,

As policy decisions are reached of a broad and general nature, planning solutions can be developed in generalized form. As these solutions are reviewed and decisions are reached of a more detailed order, the planning process picks up from there to carry the solution to a more detailed stage. Thus, both policies and plans are progressively refined to the point where an acceptable plan proposal emerges. But as conditions alter the applicability of earlier findings and proposals, policies and plans are reviewed and often modified. This explains the emphasis in the field on planning rather than on plans.[18]

[18]McLean, p. 46.

The operational definition of education planning, especially comprehensive educational planning, in this book is as a process that does the following:

1 It produces valid information in the form of alternative courses of action, together with the predicted consequences of each alternative to aid the educational decision-maker in formulating and administering educational policies to achieve established educational objectives.
2 It serves as a guideline for monitoring educational activities designed especially for achieving established educational objectives and defines a criter-

ion of performance to measure the degree of success in achieving the goals.

3 It provides a coordinating link among long-range goals and intermediate programs and a detailed operating plan for implementing annual programming in concert with both intermediate and long-range frameworks.
4 It furnishes the basis for re-examination and refinement of educational objectives and programs through the process of replanning.
5 It provides a means for continuous review and hence flexibility among such constraints as the interdependence of planning and public policy, of economics and available resources and of educational needs and need fulfillment.
6 It establishes an inventory of needs to determine the logical process for gathering, evaluating and projecting information.
7 It fits comprehensive planning of other public agencies who contribute to the development and welfare of the community.
8 It incorporates appropriate tools such as the following:
   a. Planning-programming-budgeting systems;
   b. Systems analysis and systems synthesis;
   c. Network scheduling;
   d. Management information system;
   e. Modeling and simulation;
   f. Environmental analysis and need assessment;
   g. Cost-benefit and cost-effectiveness analyses;
   h. Management and control systems; and
   i. Educational planning techniques or operations research.

THE NATURE OF EDUCATIONAL PLANNING

Planning, unlike other professions, has no clearly circumscribed area of technical knowledge that is universally recognized. Instead, it is seen as a manifestation of the growing tendency toward the conscious organization of human activities. In this process a continuous search for efficiency in its broadest sense characterizes the natural purposes of planning, the materials with which planning works, the role of planners and some planning properties.

The natural purposes of educational planning in achieving efficiency in the problem-solving process requires a minimum of three aims. They are

1 To ascertain the truth.
2 To determine a course of action.
3 To persuade.

Searching for truth means finding facts acceptable to others. This means, then, that premises and their reasoning must withstand close examination. Under such conditions, each set of facts possesses its own specific system for testing what is the truth. To date, no composite test by experience or examination has been developed to help the educational planner in searching for the truth.

The second natural purpose of planning, determining a course of action, looks to the future. This, in fact, is the essence of planning. Therefore, the actual results of planning are partly formed by many unforeseen or unforeseeable factors. Frequently it is not possible to know conclusively whether or not the result sought has been attained and to what extent the result is due to planning activities. This is probably why the making of correct decisions without responsibility is difficult. Such then is the hazardous nature of planning.

The third purpose of planning, persuading, requires reasoning. Reason must appeal to personal attitudes, predilections, prejudices and emotions, which govern actions. Such a task is immensely difficult. The mental state of others must be discerned if one is to convince them that something is valid from their point of view. These attitudes must be met by rational expression, which may still be fallacious. Persuasion involves extraordinary mental processes such as those found in teachers, administrators, and others whose tasks in large measure require persuasion.

The materials that planners work with are precise in nature, limited in nature and speculative in nature. Precise material or information consists of observations from which a conclusion may be drawn by scientific methods. Limited information consists of material of poor quality or limited extent. Also included is material of doubtful validity or of tentative character. The speculative material consists of impressions and probabilities not susceptible to mathematical expression, including the possibility of the existence of unknown factors and their possible effect.

The planner's role has at least four dimensions. First is the type of task: technical or administrative. Technical skills include researching, programming, designing, budgeting, drafting legal controls, and so on. The second type is concerned with implementing plans, coordinating planning activities, politicking, and so on.

The second dimension of the planner's role is the client whom the planner serves. In some cases, the client may be the entire community, a client seldom served by educational planners. A second type of client is a specific group, especially a group whose work is isolated. Regardless of client-type, however, each problem must be analyzed and its value to the group or to the community as a whole weighed accordingly.

A third dimension of the planner's role is his sponsor, public or private. The public sector, by the very nature of its work, possesses the greatest number of educational planners. For the private sector, there exist a much smaller number of educational planners, who, in general, possess specialized knowledge and skills. When specialized information is required, they supplement the services of educational planners working for the public organization.

Finally, the orientation of the problem the educational planner undertakes to solve helps to characterize the nature of educational planning. In education, two specific orientations exist: (1) those activities directed toward the social processes, such as the psychology of learning, curriculum planning, teacher training, team teaching or individualized instruction; and (2) those activities directed toward the physical environment. These activities include the equipment used for learning, such as television, books, computers; the types of housing used for learning; and the community in which the housing is located.

The properties of planning are the properties that define the process. Planning is a process of determining appropriate goals and objectives, of obtaining and analyzing pertinent information about the problems involved in reaching those goals, and of obtaining agreement on steps that can solve those problems and achieve the objectives that were first set. Consequently, educational planning must always possess such properties as rationality, comprehensiveness, depth of design and, above all, continuity. Educational planning, therefore, must fit the task and must reflect any limitations, whether they be of resources or time.

SUMMARY

The subject of Chapter 1, "Delineating the Scope of the Educational Problem," is in most other planning processes known only as "defining the problem." Our presentation has centered on the problems of educational planning, the need for it, its nature, and its meanings. Using the described techniques does not require a problem so general and all-encompassing as educational planning, but may also be applied to limited and well-defined problems, such as planning a school building or planning a course of studies. Regardless of the problem's scope, however, no problem can be adequately solved unless its background is furnished to the educational planner. Can the problem be specifically identified and described quantitatively and qualitatively? Can the variables and their interrelationships be separated for study without losing the sense of the total problem? Can solutions be found more effectively and efficiently by several specialists? Can the solution time be plotted in network fashion, such as the management network PERT, for more effective results? Can the solution arrived at be accepted and acted on within a reasonable time?

Chapter 1 is not intended to be a guide to the ideal solution of any one problem. Rather, Chapter 1 describes one way of studying the problem carefully using the substeps—the need, the nature, and the meaning—as a guide. The suggested guide leads us in a logical and coherent fashion to "studying 'what has been' the problem."

2 Studying "what has been"

Primitive Beginnings in Planning
Egyptian City Planning
Assyrian City Planning
Babylonian City Planning
Aegean Contributions to Planning and Education
Planning and Education by the Romans
Byzantine Influence on Planning and Education
Romanesque Influence on Planning and Education
Gothic Influence on Planning and Education
Renaissance Planning and Education
Baroque Planning and Education
The Industrial Age and Education
The Garden City Concept
The Meaning of Planning and Education Today

The history of educational planning cannot be expected to deal definitively with the planning of education as such, because neither "planning" nor "education" has ever existed as it does today. However, the ups and downs and forward movements of planning and of education have paralleled the social progress made by men and, consequently, have left a legacy of how problems were solved. This legacy represents more or less an orderly development of "what has been" in planning and helps to give the educational planner a hint to the shape of the future. History gives a better understanding of the past, whereas planning provides a shape for the future.

Planning is future oriented, and involves a comprehensive analysis of the present, as well as the historical forces that have fostered it. The principles of planning are said to have been ". . . discovered as the occasion for their use arose, necessity being the mother of invention."[1] However, students of planning feel that "without a long running start in history we shall not have the momentum in our own consciousness to take a sufficiently bold leap into the future. . . ."[2]

To get a sufficient perspective of the immediate tasks of planning ". . . it will be well to take a fresh look at man's historic development as shaped and

[1]Harold Koontz and Cyril O'Donnel, *Principles of Management* (New York: McGraw-Hill, 1964), p. 15.

[2]Lewis Mumford, *The City in History* (New York: Harcourt, Brace and World, 1961), p. 3.

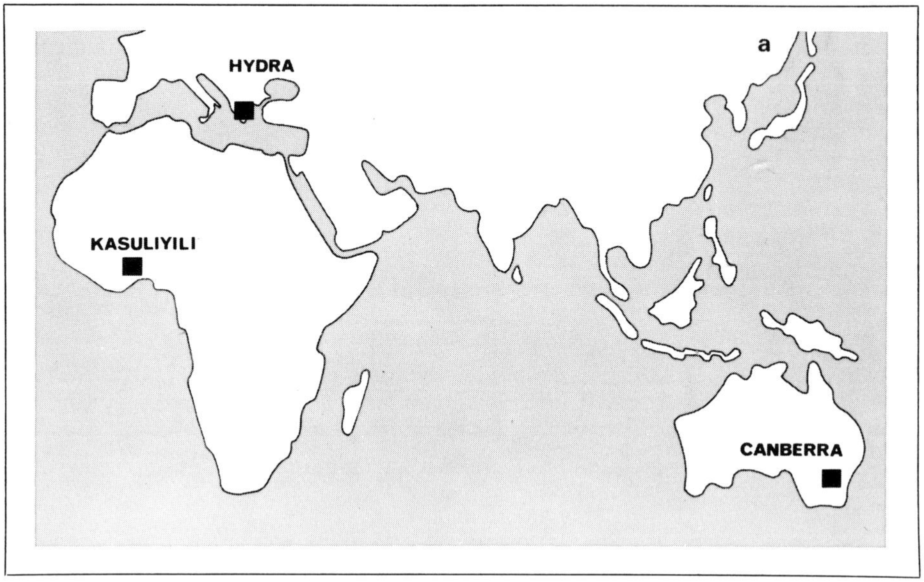

FIGURE 2.1
Map of unplanned, partially planned, and totally planned communities

(b) An unplanned town

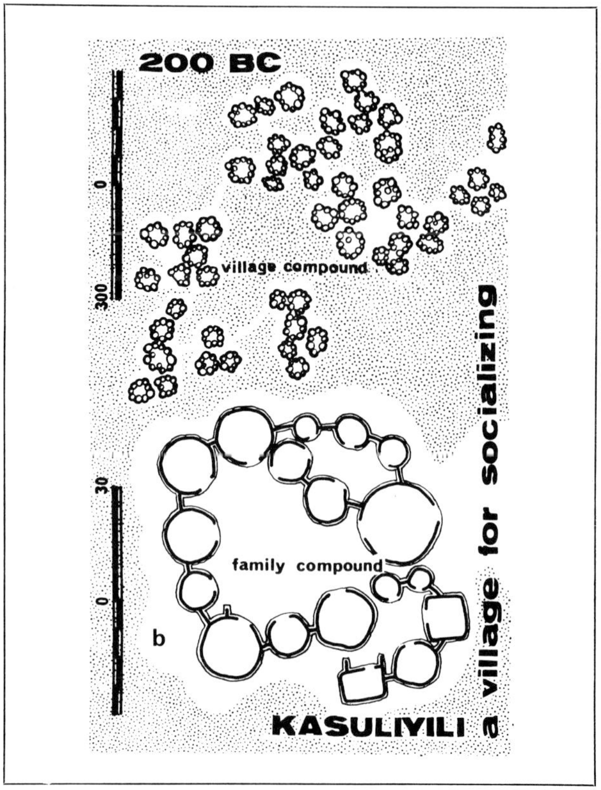

molded by the city."[3] Since the onset of civilization, the city has been the focal point of human activities (see Figure 2.1), including education. A study of these activities, the structures developed to accommodate them, and their place within their own social and physical settings will help to indicate some possible new directions that are being overlooked in current educational planning. By establishing a new image of order that embraces the activities and purposes of man, the development of educational planning can then be established to fit within the development of the city's total comprehensive planning.

Today, many planning projects that receive federal aid must include a long-range educational plan. As a result, school boards are asked more frequently to relate educational plans to areawide planning. The location of new school facilities must be related to population projections and residential development. School programs must be related to community programs. In fact, education is affected by, and in turn affects, most activities within the community. Educational planning, therefore, has by political

[3]Ibid, p. 4.

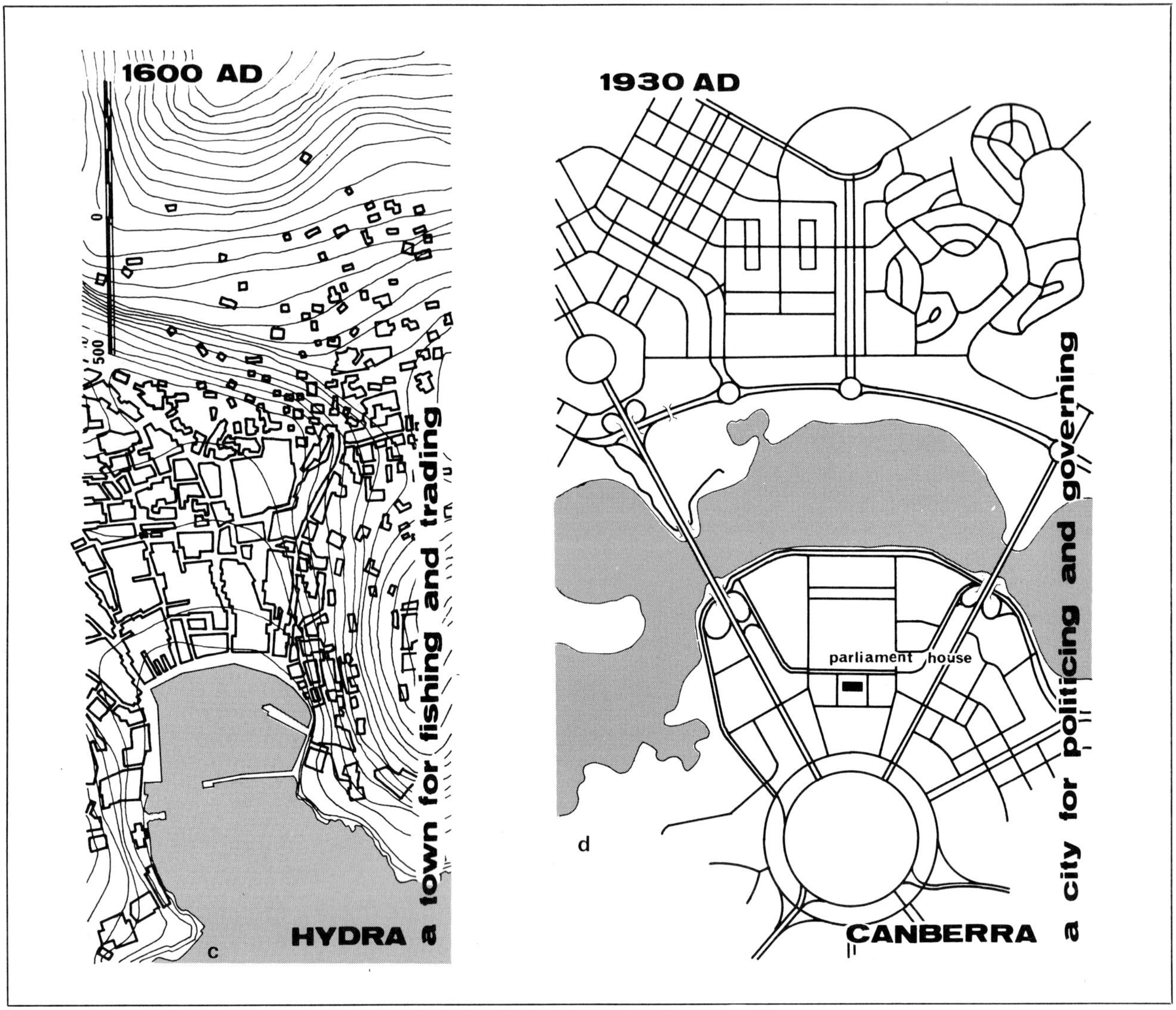

(c) A partially planned town *(d) A totally planned city*

action become a part of a city's total comprehensive planning process. A detailed examination of the development of the city should aid in the understanding of the planning process.

The uniqueness of each city contributes to the character of its membership, and vice versa. The physical setting, the people, their activities, and their purposes are significant to the development of the city's individuality. (See Figure 2.2.) First, and most important in early planning, was the physical location of the city. The topography, the surrounding landscape, the climate, the nearby resources and the natural modes of access to the site influenced the directions that the city took. The second significant factor was the people and their characteristics. These characteristics were determined by social, political, religious and working attitudes. These same factors are still at work, and the extent of their influence can

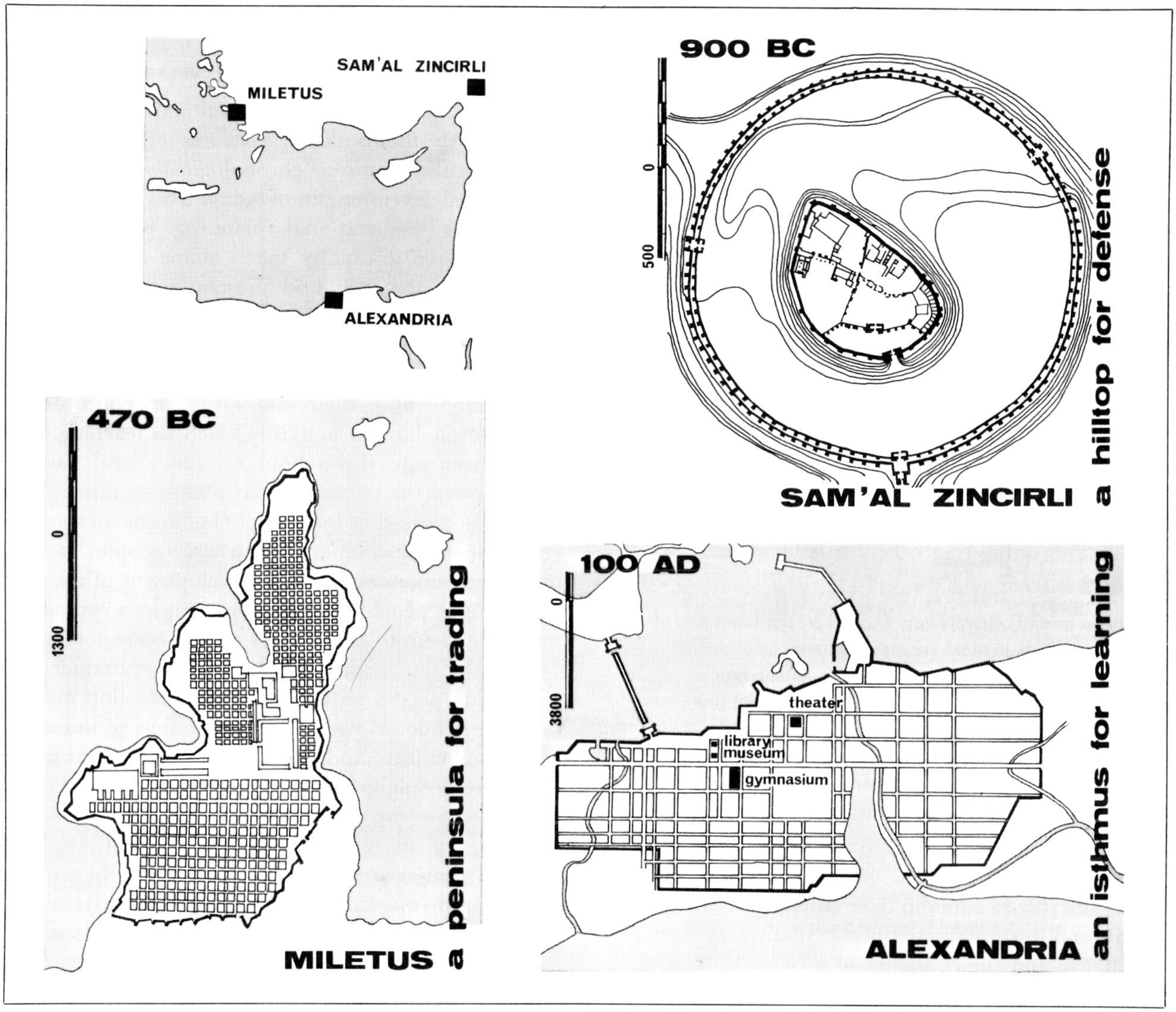

FIGURE 2.2

Map of three early cities with unique settings

be observed as they determine the character of today's city.[4]

To define the city one must look for its organizing nucleus, trace its boundaries, follow its social lines of force, establish its subsidiary centers for association and communication and analyze the differentiation and integration of the groups and institutions.[5]

[4]Ludwig Hilberseimer, *The Nature of Cities: Origin, Growth, and Decline, Pattern and Form, Planning Problem* (Chicago: Paul Theobald, 1955), pp. 115–116.

[5]Mumford, p. 43.

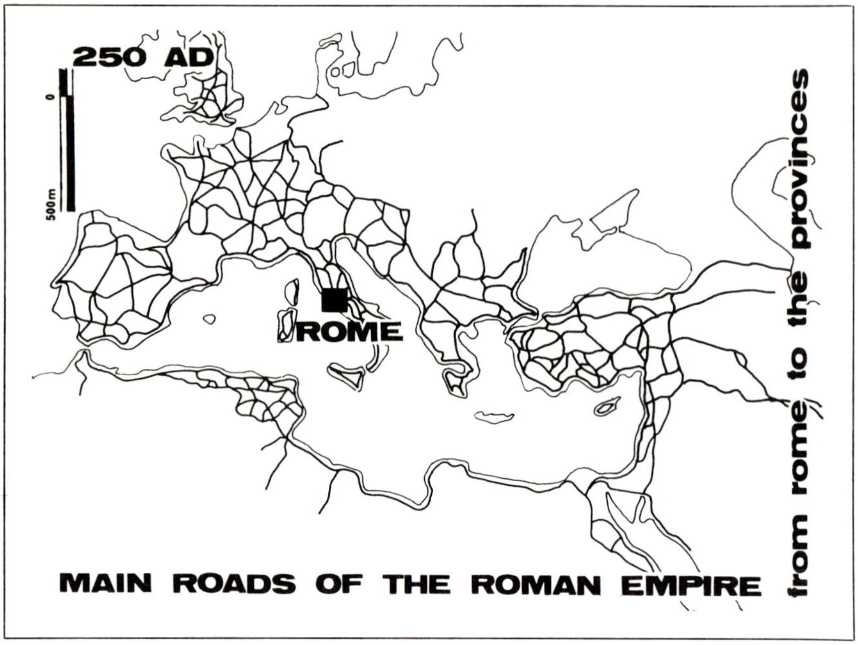

FIGURE 2.4

an ambivalent character that it has never wholly lost. It ". . . combined the maximum amount of protection with the greatest incentives to aggression; it offered the widest possible freedom and diversity yet imposed a drastic system of compulsion and regimentation."[13]

A place for the manifestation of human creativity and output, the city has been the expediter, the place where things happen. (See Figure 2.4.)

> The city effected the mobilization of manpower, a command over long distance transportation, and intensification of communication over long distances in space and time, an outburst of invention along with a large scale development of civil engineering . . .[14]

With the advent of a higher civilization came the master managers of power. A population density confined to smaller areas than previously encouraged organization and, consequently, domination. The power of controlling a population was extended by political maneuvers to gain control of an even larger population.

> Urban communities, engrossed in the new expansion of power forfeited [their] sense of limits: the cult of power exulted in its own boundless display: it offered the delights of a game played for its own sake, as well as the rewards of labor without the need for daily drudgery, by forcible collective seizure and wholesale enslavement. The sky was the limit. We have the evidence of this sudden case of exaltation in the increasing dimensions of the great pyramids; as we have the mythological representation of it in the story of the ambitious Tower of Babel, though that was curbed by a failure of communication which an over-extension of linguistic territory and culture may in turn have repeatedly brought about.[15]

The city, as a container, stood as a symbol of ever-threatening aggression and extreme self-protection. A thriving city, with its tools and mechanical equipment, its hoards of gold, silver and jewels heaped high in palace and temple, its well-filled granaries and storehouses and its surplus of men and women, was a visible object that invited collective aggression. Thus, the physical form and institutional life of the city were ". . . shaped in no small measure by the irrational and magical purposes of war."[16] Monu-

[13]Ibid., p. 46.
[14]Ibid.

[15]Ibid., p. 52.
[16]Ibid., p. 45.

FIGURE 2.5

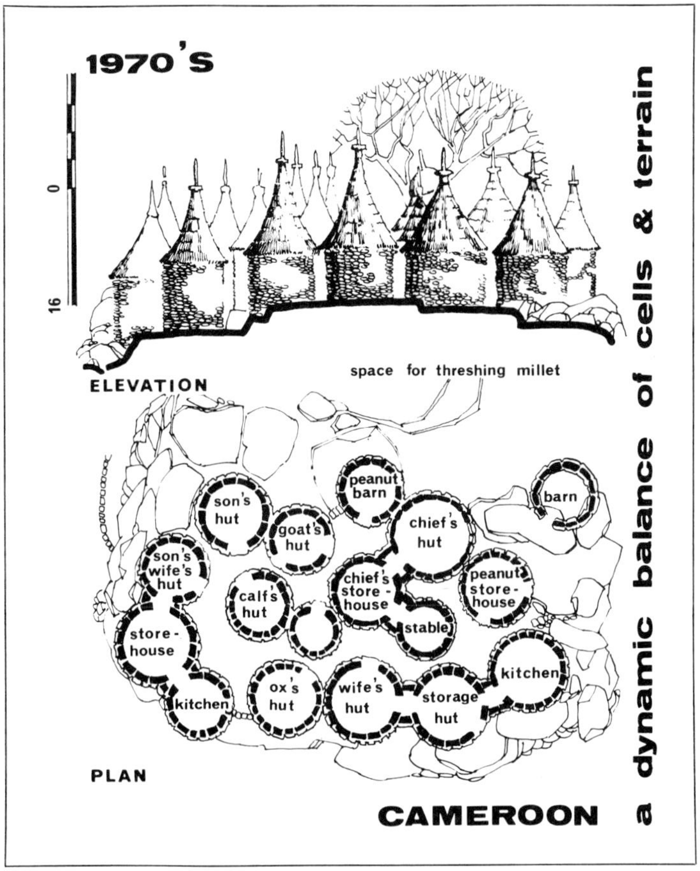

ments and tablets from the Egyptian and Mesopotamian cultures depict the irrationalities of war and power. These remains show their monarchs performing considerable feats, mutilating, torturing and killing with their own hands their chief captives. This type of leadership was supported by the city's deity and his magic potentates, and ". . . the temple became both the starting point and the object of aggressive action."[17]

From the earliest records of the city, evidence of competition and conflicts has been found. The city, even at its origin, experienced intensive struggle and conflict from within: ". . . a thousand little wars were fought in the marketplace, in the law courts, in the ball game. . . ." In fact, "to exert power in every form was the essence of civilization."[18]

Now all organic phenomena have limits of growth and extension which are set by their very need to remain self-sustaining and self-directing : they can grow at the expense of their neighbor only by losing the very facilities that their neighbor's activities contribute to their own life. Small primitive communities accepted these limitations and their dynamic balance just as natural ecologic communities register them.[19] [See Figure 2.5.]

The city, however, is not just all struggle and conflict. A city is a container that holds a mixture of many peoples, with their many-faceted interests,

[17]Ibid., p. 44.

[18]Ibid., p. 52.

[19]Ibid.

a

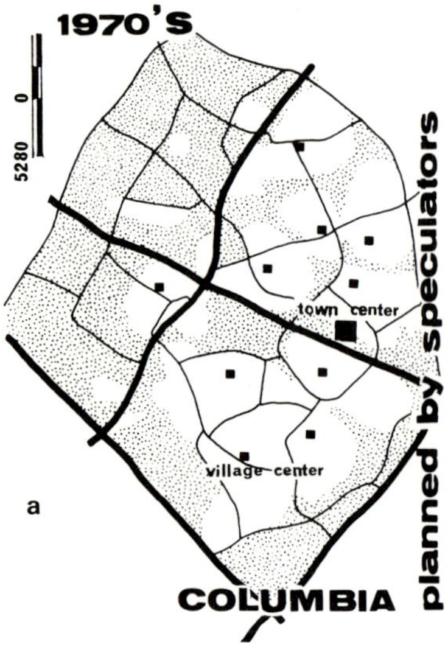

b

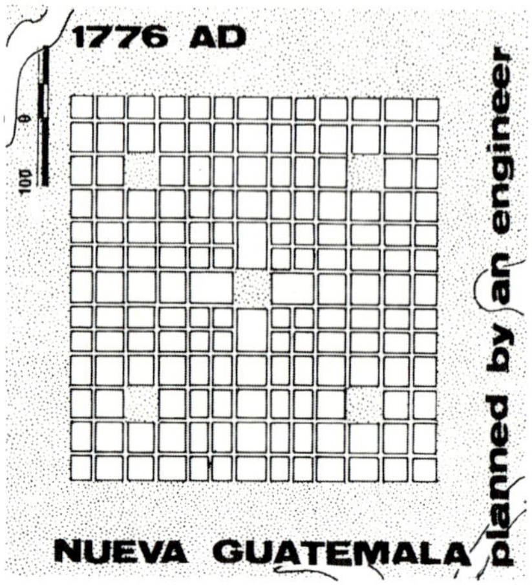

c

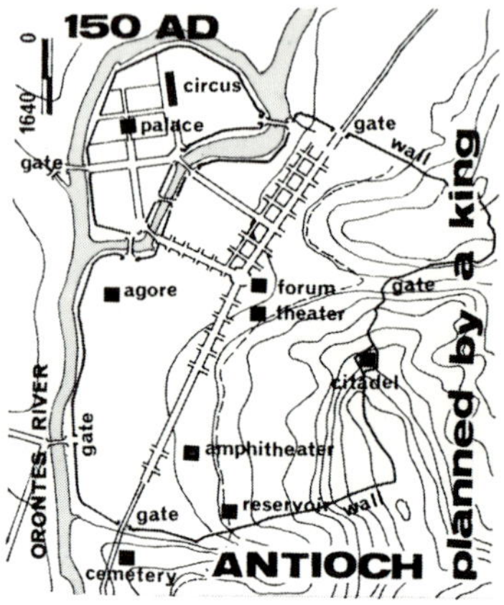

e

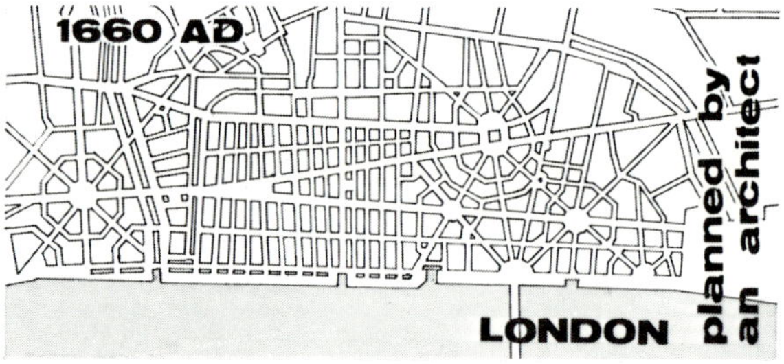

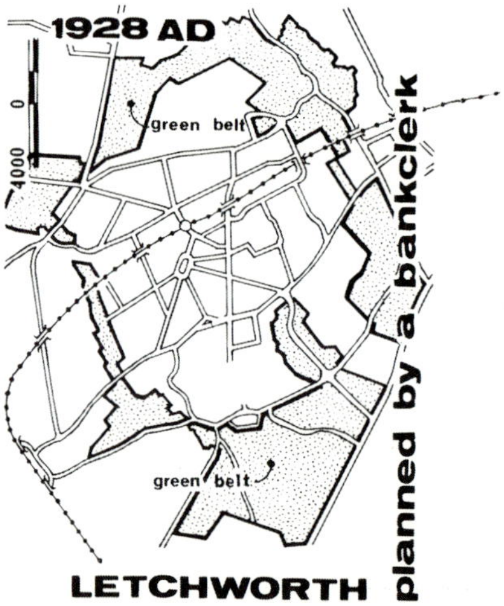

The city is the perfect community

. . . and building cities is the duty of kings.

THOMAS AQUINAS

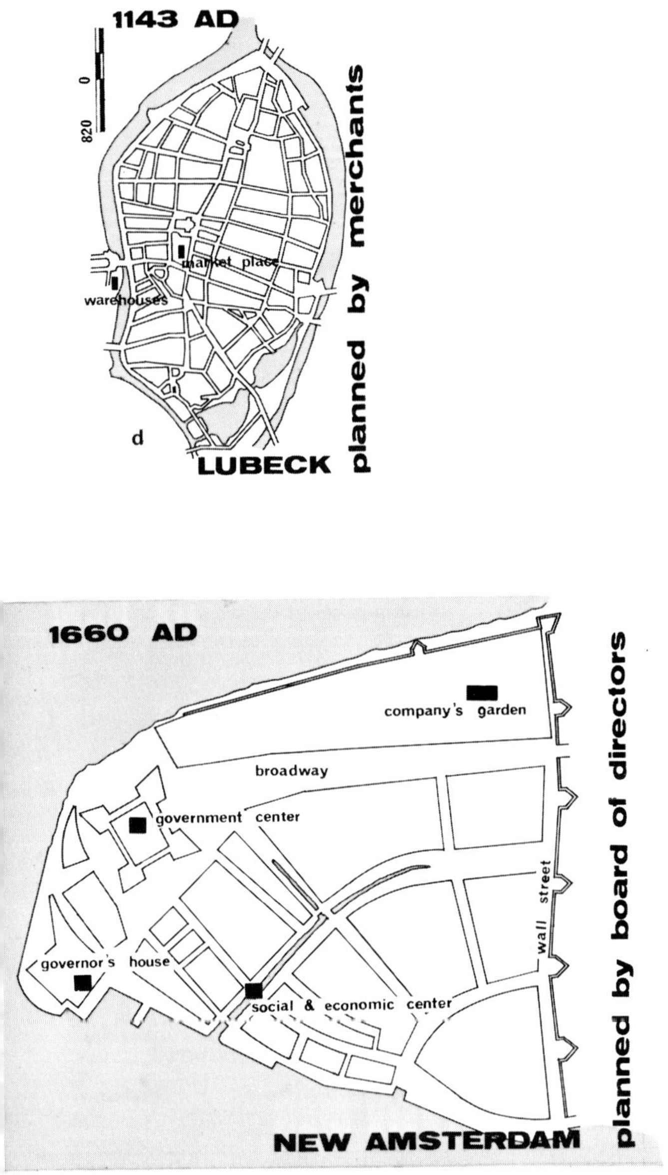

FIGURE 2.6

carrying on a great variety of activities. As a complicated network of people, activity and physical structures, "the city is not so much a mass of structures as a complex of interrelated and constantly interacting functions—not alone a concentration of power, but polarization of culture."[20]

Cities have been founded for many purposes, as Christopher Tunnard points out:

> Cities have been founded for purposes of defense, religion, politics, hygiene, cooperation, and colonization; others have their origin in smuggling, slavery, piracy, amusement or caprice. Sometimes beginnings are to be found in miracles, moral precepts and dreams. City builders may have been motivated by exploitation, emulation, esthetics, improvement, megalomania; . . . towns have been planned by kings, dictators, and empresses, bank clerks and boards of directors; by painters, sculptors and architects; by duly-elected representatives of the people; by merchants, princes of the church and pilgrim bands, and above all by speculators and gamblers.[21] [See Figure 2.6.]

Regardless of their origin, cities are dynamic organizations with an innate capacity for change. Cities will continue to change their base of existence, as they have been forced to do in the past. First forming around abbeys, temples, or at trade-route junctions, these agglomerations, even though they themselves were formed by the social, political, or cultural forces in the town, became subcenters to new centers. The marketplaces of many cities are excellent examples of the incorporation of such clusters.

> It is no accident that the word *forum* comes from the word *forus*, meaning "outside." . . . merchants and artisans established them outside earlier settlements and formed the market quarter. Even the finally magnificent Roman forum was originally a market square on the edge of the town. [See Figure 2.7.] St. Mark's Square, which has become the center of all that we consider beautiful, was in all probability a marketplace outside the earlier community of Venice, then called Olivalo. . . .[22]

[20] Ibid., p. 85.
[21] Christopher Tunnard, *The City of Man* (New York: Scribner, 1953), p. 16.
[22] Ibid., p. 17.

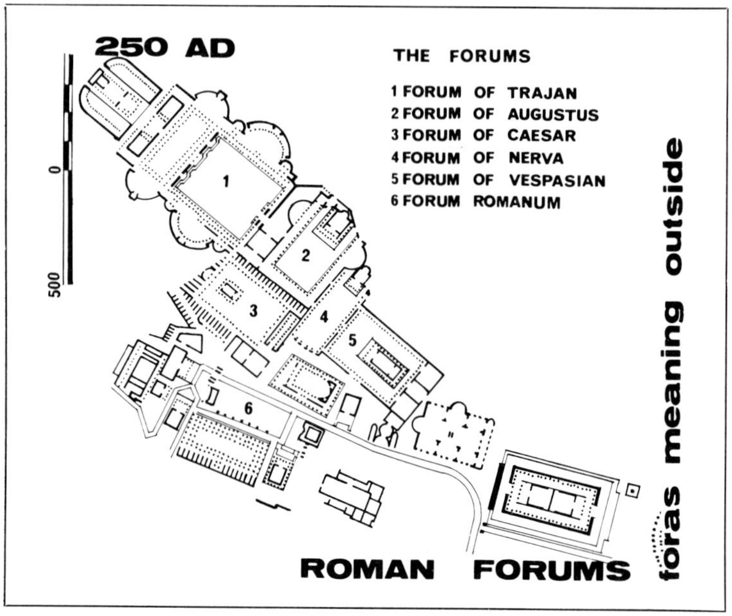

FIGURE 2.7

The planning of cities and the influence it had on learning will be examined in detail in the remainder of this chapter. There are many criteria for relating a city to an age, to a period, or to an area. Arthur Korn developed a thesis about the existence of three types of historic cities. The Asiatic towns of Egypt, Mesopotamia, India, and China based their economics on the inundations of a river. (See Figure 2.8.) These agricultural communities were ruled by a learned branch of priests or kings. Another kind of historic city was the city-state (Greek or Roman), composed of an elite people who depended on slave labor for their sustenance. The rights of citizens were exercised mainly in the agora or forum, which became the focal point of democratic activity. One of the outstanding features of the city-state was the grandeur of the public buildings that stood in sharp contrast next to the crowded, jumbled dwellings of the teeming masses.

The bourgeois town, whose politics and productive activities were dominated by the merchant and craft guilds, was the last of the historic towns. It went through a large spectrum of development, and no one stage resembled another. The bourgeois town sprang up with the rise of the *bourgeoisie.* (See Figure 2.9.) During the early Middle Ages, there was little production and a high mortality rate for the towns in existence. Most towns could not even afford a city wall. During the late Middle Ages, however, wealth began to accumulate in the towns, and with the growth of wealth began the struggle between feudalism and capitalism. Although many burgher citizens lost the fight, a few of the cities in northern Italy, Belgium, Holland, and a few other cities in other lands succeeded in overthrowing the power of the feudal lords.

The discovery of the Americas and the ensuing commercial activities generated a demand for more and more markets and thus, for greater production. As a result of the demand for expanded production, there came a change in the economic structure. With the development of the industrial age came the beginnings of a new system of economic organization —capitalism. Capitalism, in turn, generated a need for more and more working places and for housing for the increasing number of workers concentrating in larger and larger numbers. Builders refortified and expanded the cities of the Renaissance, and the expansion of the cities brought in its wake widespread slum areas, whose eradication by scientific application became the foundation of modern town planning.

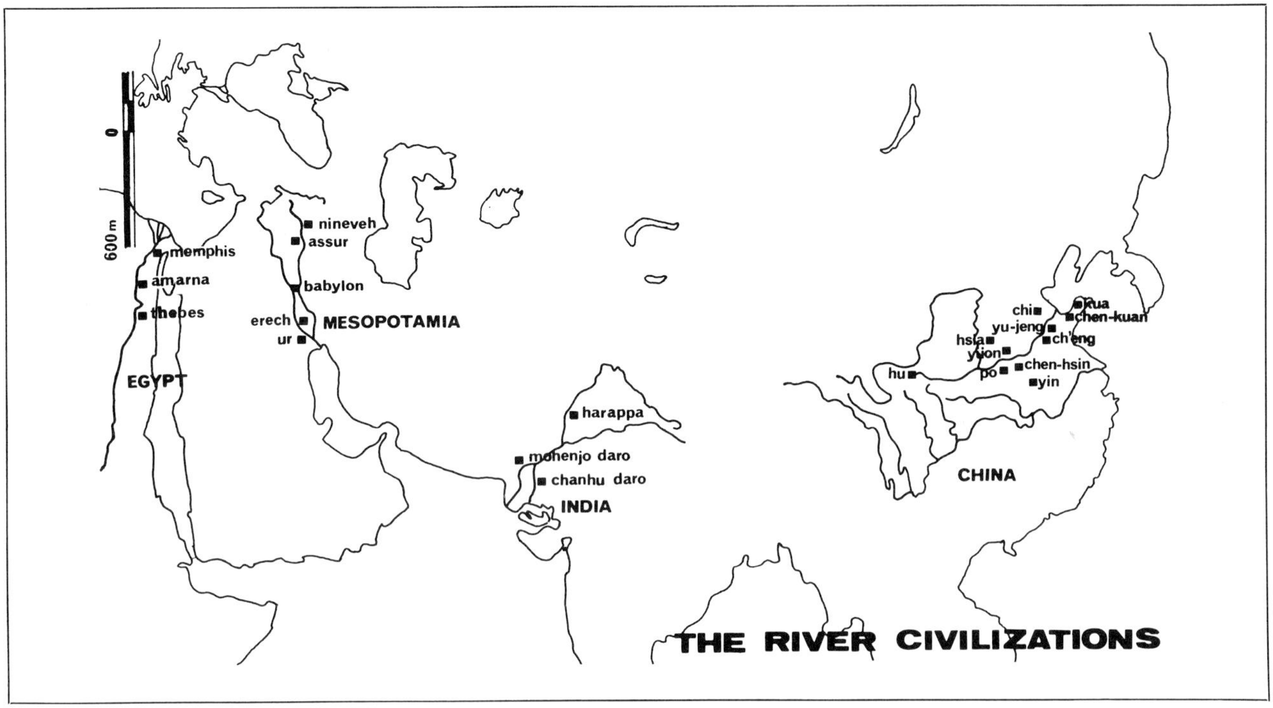

FIGURE 2.8

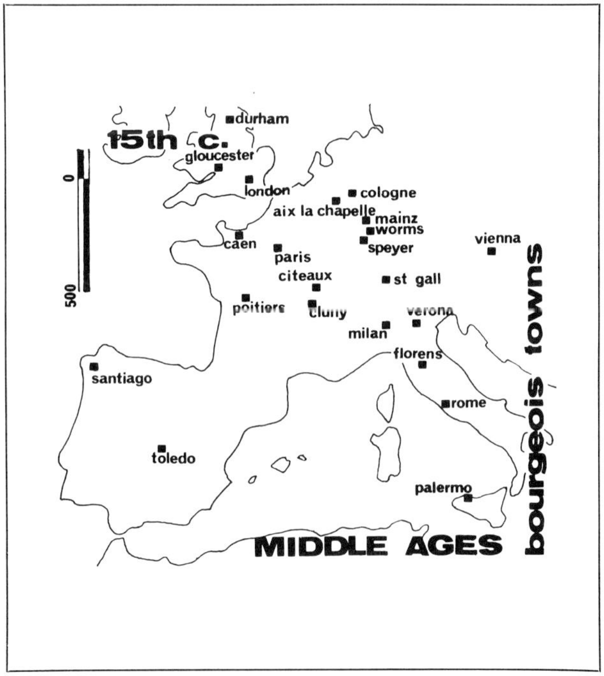

FIGURE 2.9

Those towns have reached their acme in the cities of today. Modern cities, with their skylines broken by numerous multistoried buildings and their mergence with other cities and surrounding areas, form almost a single urban complex—the megapolis. Monopolies and trusts, the aggrandizement of technological wonders, government support of production and nonproduction, the ease of obtaining foods from most other countries and the cross-pollination of cultures are all facets of most cities today.

In order to reveal the building and planning progress made during the ages, we will examine the architectural characteristics of each major cultural era. A survey of the aspects of the planning of the period and examination of the types of cities and of the society's activities in those cities will aid in making a general classification of the different types of cultures. By examining closely the various cultures and their progress in planning, the reader will grasp the role of planning in the past and its effects on the planning of today.

PRIMITIVE BEGINNINGS IN PLANNING

In their planning and building activities, primitive peoples drew on the remains of the building and planning arts of earlier peoples to improve their environment. Although there are numerous examples of early urban growth, no one period in time is fully represented. Remains classified as "primitive" may date back a millennium or may extend to the near past. Early civilizations achieved degrees of advancement at varying rates of speed, but they went through essentially the same stages, such as described by Paul Lampl.

> Initially there [were] open spaces around the irregularly located housing units which [were] generally oriented toward the prevailing breeze, and tracks rather than roads [followed] the established patterns of trails, trodden by flocks, donkeys and men to the fields and neighboring communities. [See Figure 2.10.] With the growth of the population behind a fortified enclosure, the open spaces [disappeared], the irregular interstices between the single houses [were] filled by an agglomeration of other buildings, the thoroughfares [were] reduced to a minimum, and only the narrow lanes and dead end alleys [were] left to provide access to most houses. Rounded corners often [eased] the confined flow of traffic. Nowhere [was] any room left for gardens or green areas.[23]

Use of the physical environment reflects both the culture of the people and their natural environment. In primitive societies, the design of the physical environment generally expressed the need for protection from physical elements and from attack. Man first used his physical environment by moving into caves for shelter and protection. Later, when he became more stationary, he learned to build his own shelters and to take advantage of natural features such as swamps, mountains, and rivers to secure his defense.

As man progressed, he began to recognize the fact that he must combine with other men to escape the dangers of isolation as well as the fact that many things can be done together that can be done alone. Thus there came into being permanent settlements that eventually evolved into cities. Mumford gives us a point in time when major features of the city were prefigured.

[23]Paul Lampl, *Cities and Planning in the Ancient Near East* (New York: Braziller, 1968), p. 21.

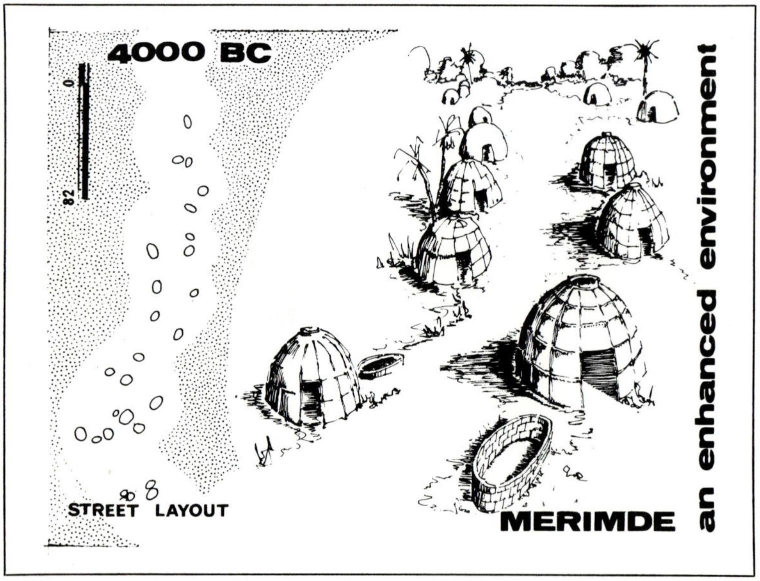

FIGURE 2.10

FIGURE 2.11

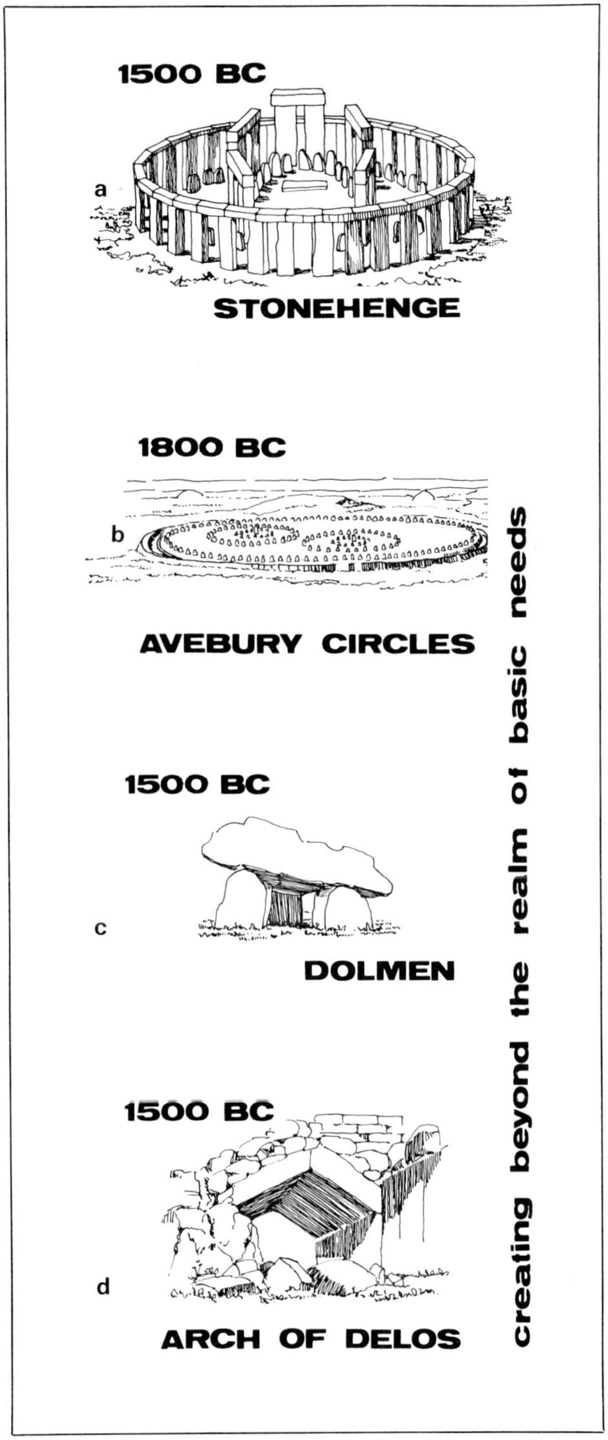

> By 2500 B.C. all essential features of the city had taken form and had found a place for themselves in the citadel, if not in the whole urban community. The walled enclosure, the street, the house-block, the market, the temple precinct with its inner courts, the administrative precinct, the workshop precinct—all these existed in at least rudimentary form; and the city itself, as a complex and powerful esthetic symbol, magnifying and enriching human potentiality, was visible. The desirability of these institutions and forms is almost as striking as the wide range of variations to which they have lent themselves.[24]

Man, in addition to his quest for self-protection and security, turned his interest and energy to different forms of ceremonial worship. Sometimes even before the fulfillment of his rudimentary desires, man's attention was directed to the establishment of monuments and tombs. The paleolithic drawings in the limestone caves of the Dordogne in France testify to such an early interest. Other such achievements, like Stonehenge (c. 1500 B.C.), Avebury Circles (c. 1800 B.C.), the Arch of Delos, and dolmen (c. 1500 B.C.), illustrate man's inherent drive to create beyond the realm of his basic needs. (See Figure 2.11.) These monuments follow the tendency of the late third or early second millennium, when religious structures were earthen mounds containing upright and lintel stones and forming chambers for burial of a varying number of persons. The oldest remains of towns have been uncovered in the Levant district of Palestine and on the Anatolian Peninsula of Turkey. One of the earliest urban settlements, Jericho, dates back to 8000 B.C. (See Figure 2.12.) The town ". . . developed over a mound of occupational debris covering an area of not less than four hectares. . . . It was fortified by a strong stone wall. Traces of curvi-linear houses of the period have been found."[25]

The ancient cities of the Levant district are also known for their remarkable engineering feats of supplying water to the hill cities. Arad, during the Bronze Age, and Lachish, during the Iron Age, collected runoff from a mountain in a catch basin, and

[24]Mumford, p. 90.
[25]Lampl, p. 34.

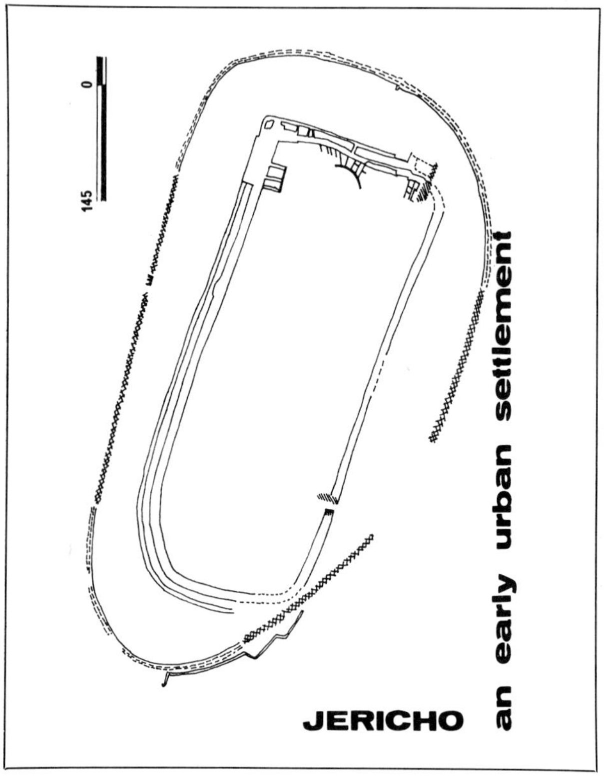

FIGURE 2.12

other cities dug wells deep enough to reach the water level. Many cities cut tunnels through rock to form protected access to the water supply.

In short it may be stated that the ancient cities of the Levant district grew out of earlier settlements in relatively defensible locations, where a reliable source of water was available, in a rather haphazard and uncontrolled manner. Planning initially was limited to the ramparts, the water supply, the temple and the palace. More comprehensive town planning schemes date in Syria mainly from the late Bronze Age and in Palestine from the Solomonic period.[26]

The peoples of the Anatolian Peninsula were as concerned with defense as were those in Palestine. (See Figure 2.13.) The Hittite city builders planned and built unparalleled stone masonry fortifications.

[26]Ibid., p. 41.

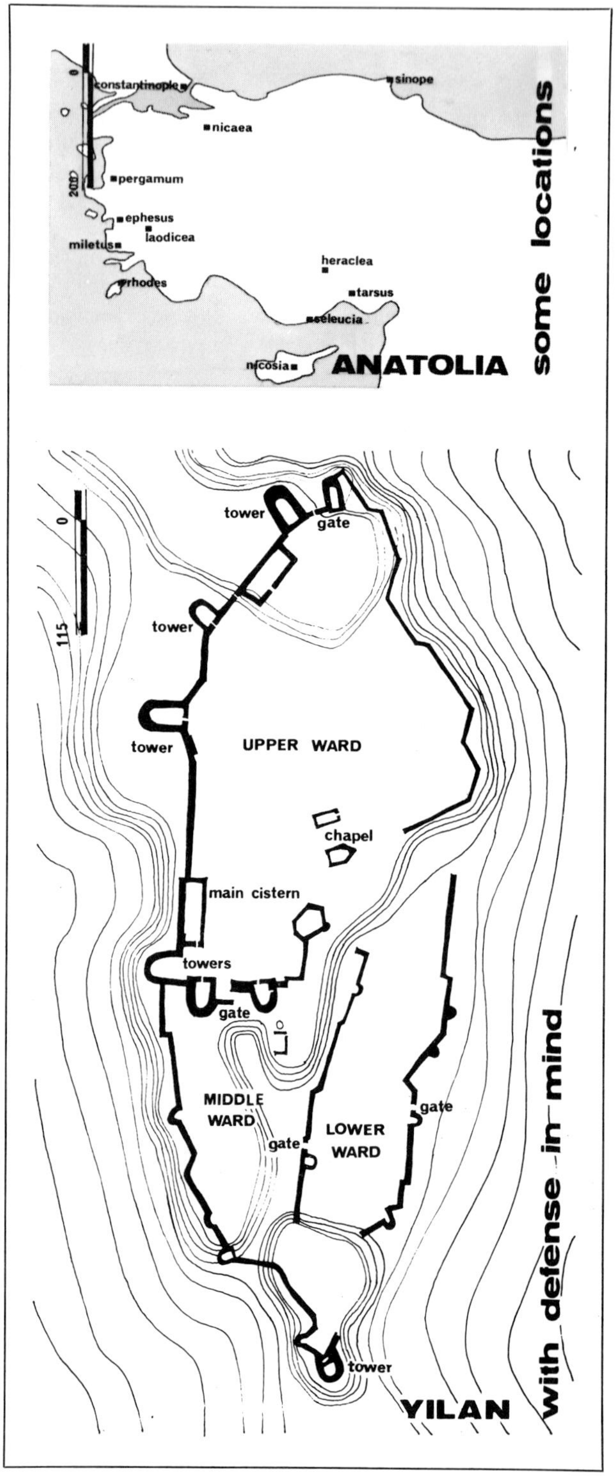

FIGURE 2.13

FIGURE 2.14
Map of ancient cities

Their skill, technical knowledge and engineering ingenuity aided in the construction of the walls, posterns and gates that remain a major feat of that era.

Anatolian cities seem to have been planned primarily with their defense in mind. They were built in strategic locations, with a minimal, oval or polygonal defense perimeter and skillful utilization of the natural topographical features. Their residential quarters grew mainly uncontrolled by organic agglomeration.[27]

Such agglomeration was basically a union of Neolithic culture and the more archaic Paleolithic culture. As a result of this union, widespread intermixture took place. New rigorous, efficient, and even harsh ways characterized the toilers' and task-masters' new activities. These, in turn were expressed by the straight lines in place of the former curved ones, by rectangles instead of circles, by bounded geometric plans rather than the open-ended circular forms and, finally, by the birth of abstractions, such as alphabets and mathematics.[28]

From the vestiges of the primitive ages developed the more highly civilized cultures, such as Egyptian and Near Eastern. Each step in progress was built on another, and from each step came a more solid foundation of planning.

The topography, the climate, and the material resources of these early civilizations were different, but they had one factor in common—the river, the first efficient means of mass transport. The river served to equalize surpluses, to make it possible to get to distant places and to help cities to increase in size and scope and productivity. (See Figure 2.14.) It also gave city rulers command over men and resources. Above all, the river made possible new activities; in fact, it brought into being a new institution—the market—whose urban form was clearly visible by 2000 B.C.[29]

Centered in the temple precinct, the economic dynamics of bartering, trading, procuring, storing and distributing gave rise to a wider scale of human intercourse—and, hence, to the planning of more and larger cities along the rivers of the Nile, The Tigris-Euphrates, the Indus and the Hwang Ho. Two such developments of urban life along the Nile and the Tigris-Euphrates will be examined for their efforts in mutal aid, long-term planning and patient application to the common task of building cities.

EGYPTIAN CITY PLANNING

The remains of the culture and activities of the early Egyptian civilization represent the Egyptians' concept of their gods, their godlike rulers and their subsequent relationship to the basics of existence. (See Figure 2.15.) The elaborate tombs and the massive temples, essentially all that is left of the Egyptian dynasties,

[27]Ibid., p. 46.
[28]Mumford, p. 27.

[29]Ibid., p. 70.

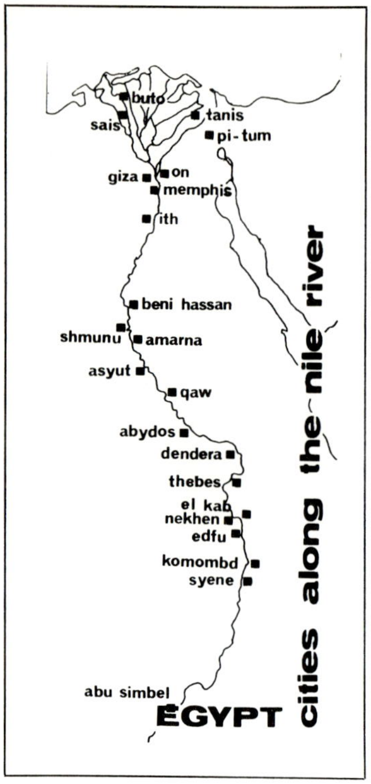

FIGURE 2.15

Map of Upper and Lower Egypt

are partly explained by the heavy emphasis that was placed on the religion of the society. The afterlife was all-important and everlasting whereas the temporary stay on earth was a mere burden to be borne.

Such views were expressed by the fact that the royal funerary monuments were built to withstand the ages (see Figure 2.16), and life on earth for the many was spent in a hut of sun-dried mudbrick, which disintegrated during the annual inundations. The powerful priesthood also influenced the buildings in Egypt. The power the priesthood wielded can still be seen in the splendor of the royal palaces and magnificent temples.

The clockwork regularity of the annual inundation of the Nile, the fertility of the soil and the materials in the soil equally prevailed on the Egyptian life style and productivity. The annual flooding not only provided a new layer of fertile soil to support the agricultural economy, but also left the laborer with time to spend on the construction of the monuments to the god-kings. Because of its composition, the soil provided the materials used in building the monuments. Having been instilled with a sense of security by the regular recurrence of the Nile inundation and the protective watchfulness of the gods, the Egyptian continued in his unquestioning faith in the omnipotent gods.

FIGURE 2.16

Left: Richly carved surfaces at the Temple of Ammon in Karnak, Egypt; right: Sphinx and Pyramid of Cheops

FIGURE 2.17

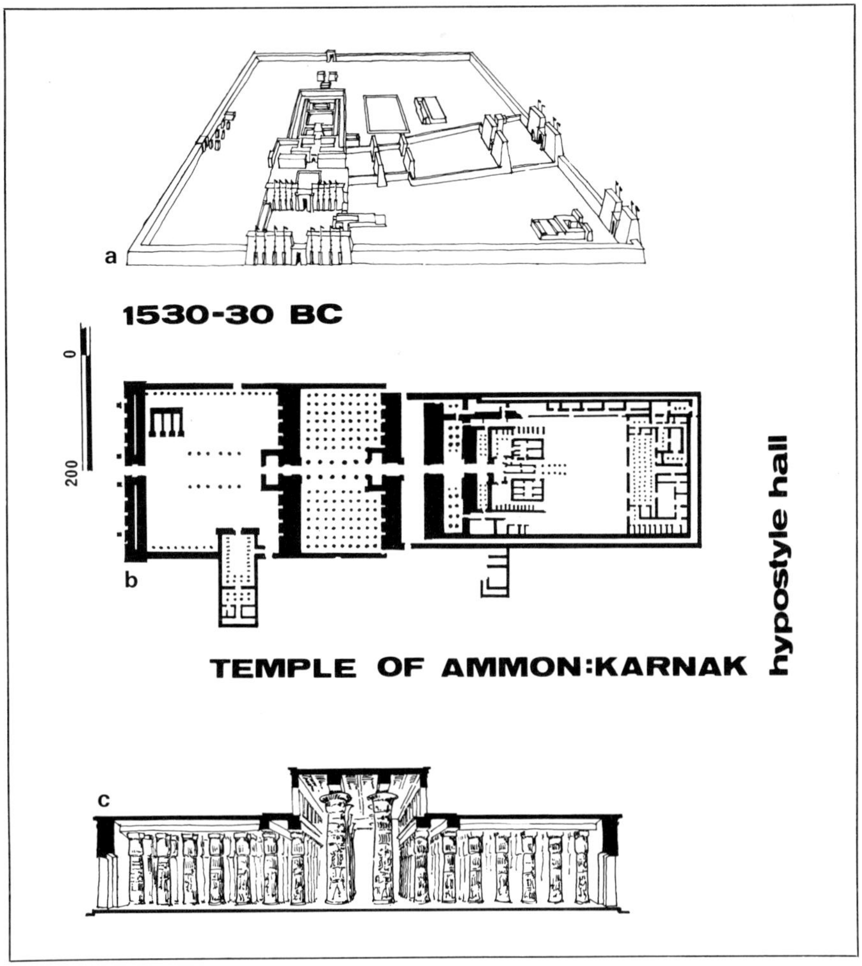

The annual inundations of the river caused by the melting of snows and heavy spring rains in the Abyssinian Highlands were predictable and reliable: they not only established a firm rhythm of seasonal occupations for the population, but also led to the concept of an established cosmic order that safe-guarded eternal renewal and promised permanence of life after death—ideas which found ultimate expression in the monumental mortuary art and architecture of Ancient Egypt.[30]

Religion brought into existence vast and splendid mortuary monuments. The pit graves dating from before 3200 B.C. gave way to brick-lined tombs with flat roofs at the beginning of the first dynasty. During the first and second dynasties, the mortuary structure progressed to the use of sun-dried bricks and then stone masonry. These tombs evolved into the mastaba, and eventually the earliest pyramid, the Saqqara, was constructed during Dynasty III (2778 B.C.).

[30]Lampl, p. 34.

The great achievements in Egyptian planning were the result of a strong central power with immense resources, which could call upon the most gifted architects and planners to strive for perfection in their tasks. Side by side with this purposeful high level planning in cases where special interests demanded it, a *laissez-faire* attitude prevailed in the absence of such interests.

FIGURE 2.18
One of six pylons at the Temple of Ammon in Karnak

The vast funerary monuments, temples and palaces, the pyramid cities and . . . towns were the types of construction to which the kings of Ancient Egypt paid their main attention and which bear the imprint of directed and controlled planning according to established rules. The great mortuary temple of Ramses III at Medinet Habu is representative of this planning in which all these types are combined in one building complex.[31]

The Egyptian style may be illustrated by the pyramids, the temple at Karnak and the Temple of Horus at Edfu. The form is basically triangular or rectangular, probably deriving from the Egyptian preoccupation with geometry and, in particular, from the method of triangulation that was developed to survey the land required by the changing bed of the Nile River. (See Figure 2.17.)

Using a heavy form (see Figure 2.18), the structures tend to be large and pretentious, with massive walls, sturdy and closely spaced columns, stone lentils and flat roofs. The early building does not deviate from the basic geometrical concept, as illustrated

[31]Ibid., p. 32.

FIGURE 2.19

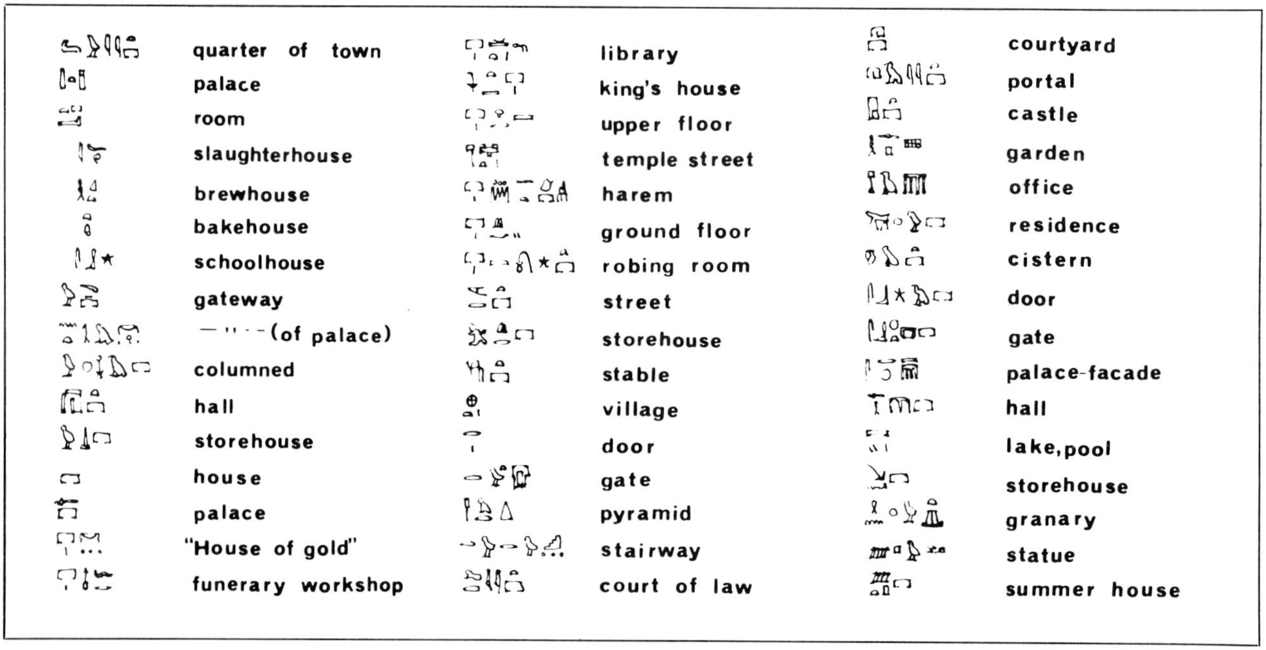

by the "Workman's Village" at the tomb of Ammakka.

Imhotep's great funerary complex for King Zoser (c. 2700 B.C.) at Saqqara demonstrates planning on the grandest scale.

Here the Egyptian genius for playing off heavy masses of masonry against vast open spaces, for the articulation of building elements, for balance or symmetry of solids and voids, and for the sophisticated use of straight and broken axes, has found full expression. While building programs and styles may vary, the principles of design and planning at Saqqara at the beginning of the III Dynasty for monumental tomb complexes hardly changed during the rest of Egyptian history.[32]

The design of an Egyptian temple typically included a forecourt followed by a long hall that led to a high-ceilinged nave. A sequence of small apartments and halls led from the nave to the sanctuary. Later temples, however, were centered on a main axis that became a walled open court with a columned vestibule and sanctuary. The functional programs

. . . and indeed the elements of composition could be of a different nature, but the philosophy of planning is the same. There is a consistent predilection for axial balance and symmetry, for crystal-clear decomposition of components and for a climactic or anti-climactic sequence of building masses or voids.[33]

The typical Egyptian building complex or system consisted of a combination of courtyards, courts, chambers, corridors and galleys, all enclosed by walls. See Figure 2.19 for a hieroglyphic version of this system. The temples were structured for splendor; the pyramids symbolized strength and massiveness. The monumental Egyptian structure was essentially oriented toward the gods. The stable conditions prevailing in Egypt permitted the royal city to develop much earlier than in other civilizations.

When a king ascended the throne of Egypt, he erected a new palace and a new pyramid, his future tomb. He founded also a new city for his court and administration. Behind this custom and practice was probably a magic concept, expressed in ancient rituals derived from Animism, which causes primitive man to shun all the belongings of a dead man. When a king, who was considered godlike, died, it was only natural that his palace-city should be abandoned and left to decay. Those royal cities of Egypt have entirely disappeared. Only their pyramids, the tombs of the dead kings, have survived. The long row of Pyramids south of the Great Pyramid at Kahfil are the only remains of once royal cities. The Nile's yearly floods have borne away the rest. The royal cities of Egypt are an expression of absolutism. It is not surprising that, when absolutism appeared again in Europe, the royal-city type was reborn.[34]

[32]Ibid., p. 29.
[33]Ibid., pp. 29–30.

MESOPOTAMIAN CITY PLANNING AND EDUCATION

Concurrent with, but distinctive from, the Egyptian civilization was the civilization that arose in Mesopotamia between the Tigris and Euphrates rivers. (See Figure 2.20.) A difference in environment, religion and society caused substantial diversity between the two cultures, as indicated by Mumford.

. . . one larger fact nevertheless begins to emerge : two contrasting archetypal patterns of urban life seem to have been formed in the great river valleys of the Near East. One expressed calmness and confidence, the other tempestuous uncertainty ; one, beset with danger and anxiety, piled up the symbols of power and fortified itself with heavy walls to keep

[34]Hilberseimer, p. 23.

FIGURE 2.20

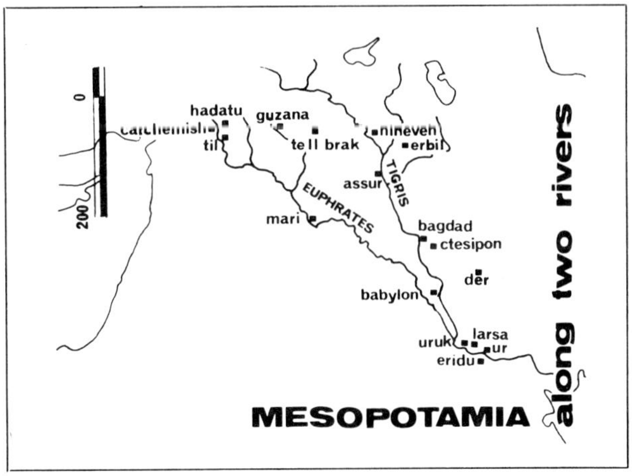

off those who "were planning evil," the other, trusting in the beneficence of the sun and Father Nile, knowing that one year would be like the next, imposed order in the name of justice and enthroned death in the gay garments of life. In one, the citadel formed the hard kernel of power that by its very explosion, destroyed itself as well as its object: in the other, the organic ritual of the village tempered and humanized all the new forces that were at the disposal of civilization: in that city, the Eloquent Peasant would still be heard. These polar contrasts, under new masks, are still in existence.[35]

Although the harsh topography was antagonistic to cities, the growth of the cities increased during the Mesopotamian civilization.

Within the relatively small area between the Euphrates and the Tigris where these rivers came close together, great and prosperous cities arose during the millenniums. One after another they rose and fell. As early as the Sumeric times, city states were fighting to subdue each other. Later, as larger states developed, they too fought each other with the same aim. Babylon, twice founded, succeeded itself and was succeeded by Seleucia. Seleucia was succeeded by Ctesiphon, Ctesiphon by Bagdad. The use of each new city meant the decline of the old one. People of the deposed city were sometimes killed or sold into slavery. More often they were transplanted to a new city. The oldest city always provided the building material for the new. The bricks made for Babylon were used to build Seleucia, Ctesiphon and finally Bagdad.[36]

Flood conditions, storms and fire were constant hazards to the lives of people within the city. The inhabitants also had to struggle with invasions and epidemics. Despite these hazards, cities flourished in Mesopotamia, adding yet another branch to ancient Near Eastern architecture and planning amidst the fluctuations between chaos and order.

Insecurity and intimidation were written all over the Mesopotamian record: even the school maintained a functionary with a lash to keep order. These practices left the impression on every part of life, in repeated acts of cruelty and violence, which reached a certain climax of wanton ferocity in the Assyrian monarch, Assurbanipal.... Under such conditions, the necessary co-operation of urban living [required] the constant application of police power, and the city [became] a kind of prison whose inhabitants [were] under constant surveillance: a state not merely symbolized but effectively perpetuated by the town wall and its barred gates.[37]

FIGURE 2.21

The walled fortress was essentially the city, as far as the Mesopotamian citizen was concerned. The artificial mound, known as the *ziggurat,* became the characteristic of Mesopotamian architecture. The White Temple of Erech and the Temple of Marduk both are built around a ziggurat. The agricultural society was superstitious and much concerned with symbolism. The ziggurat represented a holy mountain whose shrine at the apex provided an approach to the gods. (See Figure 2.21.) This form and design are clearly illustrated in Ishtar Ziggurat at Erech. Probably the best known of the Mesopotamian ziggurats is the Tower of Babel.

The rapid growth and the haphazard conglomeration of buildings in the large cities brought urban problems such as those known today.

It becomes again evident that the Mesopotamian architect or builder was not concerned with an overall composition or with comprehensive preplanning but only with individual edifices. The latter were placed according to their importance, functions or convenience where there was desirable open ground. Additional buildings, always planned from the inside out, were then juxtaposed and fell into the available space, leaving necessary thoroughfares and access lanes free for traffic.[38]

35 Mumford, p. 89.
36 Hilberseimer, p. 30.
37 Mumford, p. 83.
38 Lampl, p. 22.

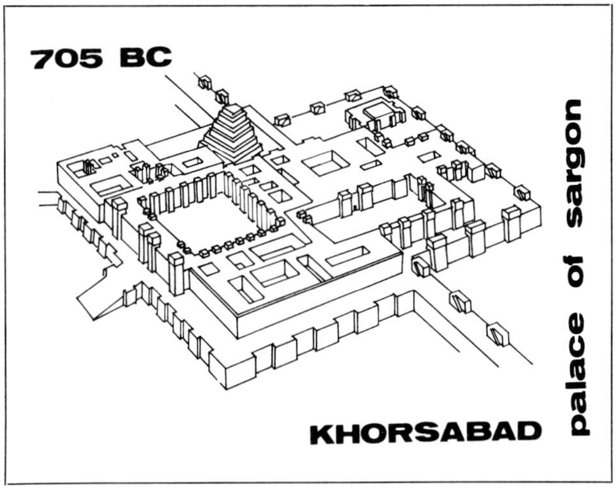

FIGURE 2.22

Despite this type of growth, city development and the importance of the temple fostered organizational planning to a degree unknown before. Plans extended beyond the mere construction of physical facilities and incorporated organizational work, division of labor and other aspects that characterize modern community development. Yet the Mesopotamian planners remained ignorant of the value of planning for a total city and concentrated instead on the symmetry, axes and balance of individual buildings, with a disregard for overall composition. The Mesopotamians were the first to perceive the need of planning, but restricted its application.

ASSYRIAN CITY PLANNING

The Assyrian culture grew out of Assyria's surrounding environment. To the south of Assyria's capital, Assur on the upper Tigris, stretched a vast treeless plain, to the west lay a widespread tract of arid land, to the north and northeast were mountain ranges and high plateaus—all of which made Assyria easy to attack and difficult to defend. Forced to maintain a hard military life by its lack of natural frontiers, Assyria became a nation of vigorous, harsh, and warlike people.

This harshness, a trait that was inherent in the nature of the Assyrians—a nomadic tribe from northern Mesopotamia—is illustrated in the palace of Sargon. This characteristic, however, did not prevent them from varying the architectural form of their ziggurat temples. Nor did it prevent them from introducing the arch into their buildings. Following the ziggurat tradition, they built many of their structures on high mounds to symbolize far-reaching power and political domination. Because of the Assyrians' life of war and conquest, ornate palaces are more frequently found than temples, such as the Palace of Sargon II in the City of Khorsabad. (See Figure 2.22.) It was built in 772–705 B.C. on the basis of a square plan for defensive reasons. The palace with its grand court, temples, service quarters, offices and residential areas constituted its own city, which was protected from attack by thick walls decorated with polychrome ornamental glazed bricks.

BABYLONIAN CITY PLANNING

The city of Babylon shows similarity of style, form and design of planning and architecture to those of other Near Eastern cultures, such as the Assyrian and the Egyptian cultures. The Babylonians were nomadic as were the Assyrians and, therefore, were exposed to the different ideas of adjacent peoples. Such exposure helped the Babylonians to build aesthetics into their physical facilities by the use of ornamental bricks whose construction and design were borrowed from the Assyrians, who in turn had learned from the Egyptians how to face the bricks with stone.

The original city of Babylon was rebuilt by Nebuchadnezzar and was noted for the grandeur and splendor of its buildings. Surrounded by a massive double wall, it was laid out along the banks of the Euphrates River and was connected by a permanent bridge spanning the entire river. Within the city was located the palace of Nebuchadnezzar. The palace roof was crowned by the tremendous Hanging Gardens, labeled by the Greeks as one of the Seven Wonders of the World. The city of Babylon, as rebuilt by Nebuchadnezzar, is almost a classic model of plan-

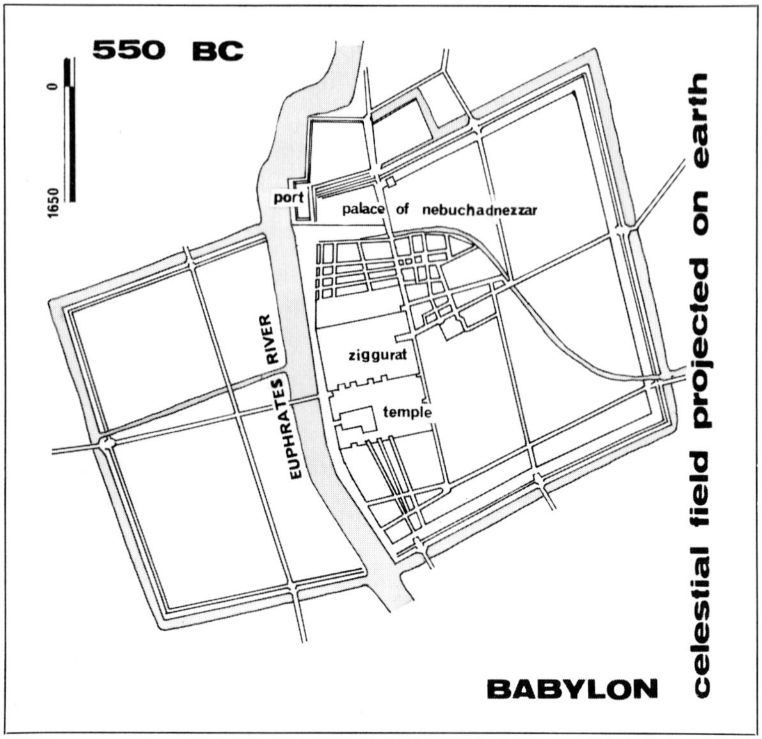

FIGURE 2.23

ning. It capitalized on the architectural and building technology of the day by combining appropriate aesthetics and embellishments that served the needs of the people.

Herodotus describes Babylon's shape as a square. [See Figure 2.23.] . . . Its shape was probably a reflection of a religious, astronomical belief. There is a square constellation of stars which the Babylonians called "the field" and which they imagined to be the agricultural land of the gods. The city of Babylon was supposed to be the projection upon earth of that celestial field.[39]

Babylon could not have remained a square for very long, even if it had been planned that way. The natural growth of the city, the topography and the geographic region precluded a continuation of such a plan. "But even at the time of Herodotus, Babylon was rectangular rather than a true square. It had been extended across the river to the west and its parts were connected by a bridge, the first passenger bridge of which we have any record."[40]

PERSIAN CITY PLANNING

The power and domination by different leaders were brought to bear on the cities, and their capture gave rise to empires. An excellent example of this was the Persian Empire. The Persians in quick succession from 549 B.C. to 525 B.C. defeated the Medes, captured Lydia and Babylon, which included Mesopotamia and Syria, and then conquered Egypt. During this short period of time, the Persians ruled the entire area of early civilized culture. They continued to build eclectically onto the ancient cultures. Their planning and building are illustrated by the Palace of Persepolis, which was the residence of Persian kings and represented a new city type. (See Figure 2.24.)

[39]Hilberseimer, p. 25.

[40]Ibid.

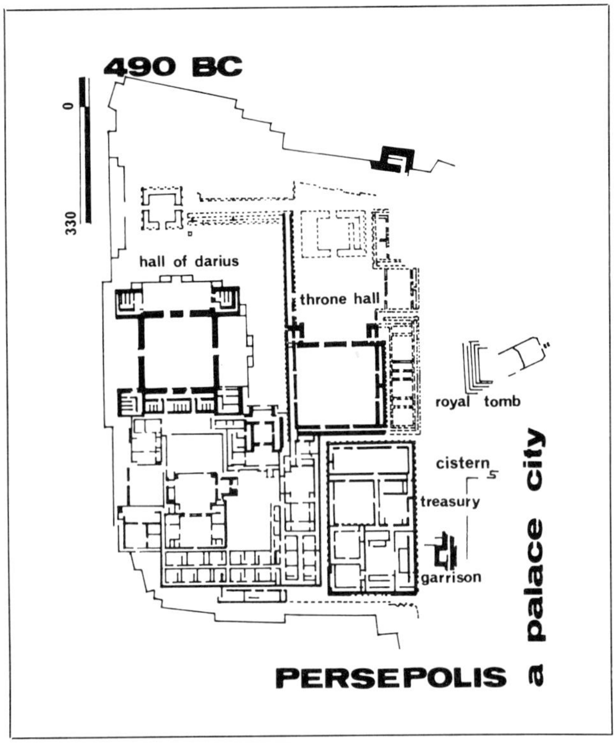

FIGURE 2.24

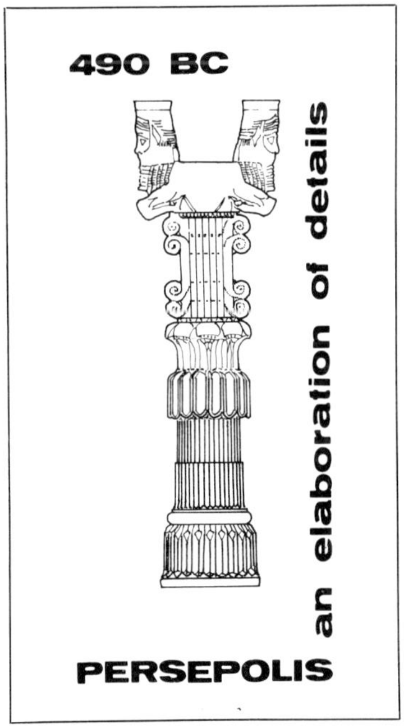

FIGURE 2.25

It was a palace-city with no fortification. Each palace, built by a different king, was on large artificial terraces. This city was a city for the king, his court, his nobles and his administration. The people to serve them were settled below the terrace.[41]

The Persians copied the Babylonians by building on high platforms of stone and emphasized massive flights of steps. They also stressed the use of columns in their constructions. Continuing the trend of the Assyrians and the Babylonians, they graced their buildings with sculpture. During the time of the Persian Empire, architecture consolidated the style, form and design of the numerous influences of Egypt, Syria and Babylonia. Such consolidations represent an extension of the early cultures and civilizations, and the Persians' contribution was primarily an elaboration of the details of earlier architecture. (See Figure 2.25.)

AEGEAN CONTRIBUTIONS TO PLANNING AND EDUCATION

Western civilization developed on the islands of the Aegean Sea, at a time parallel to the civilizations of Egypt and the Near East. Minos, a Cretan leader, founded the sea kingdom on the system of feudalism and communal exploitation.

To strengthen his kingdom and secure his trade, Minos established outposts, selecting their sites for the strategic possibilities, but also with due regard for the fertility of the soil on which they must depend for support. These fortress-castles towered over fruitful plains. [See Figure 2.26.] Most

[41]Ibid., p. 32.

FIGURE 2.26

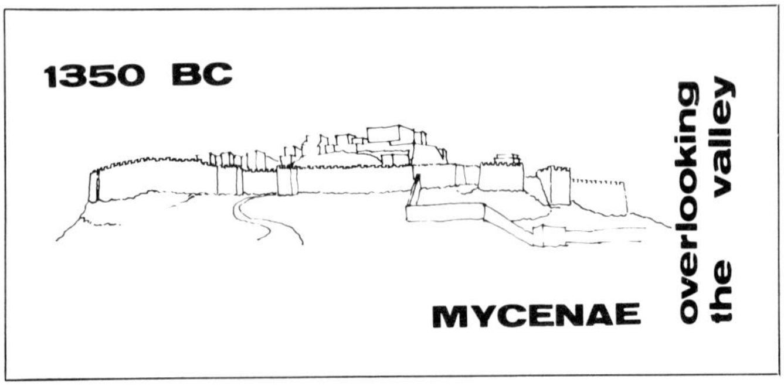

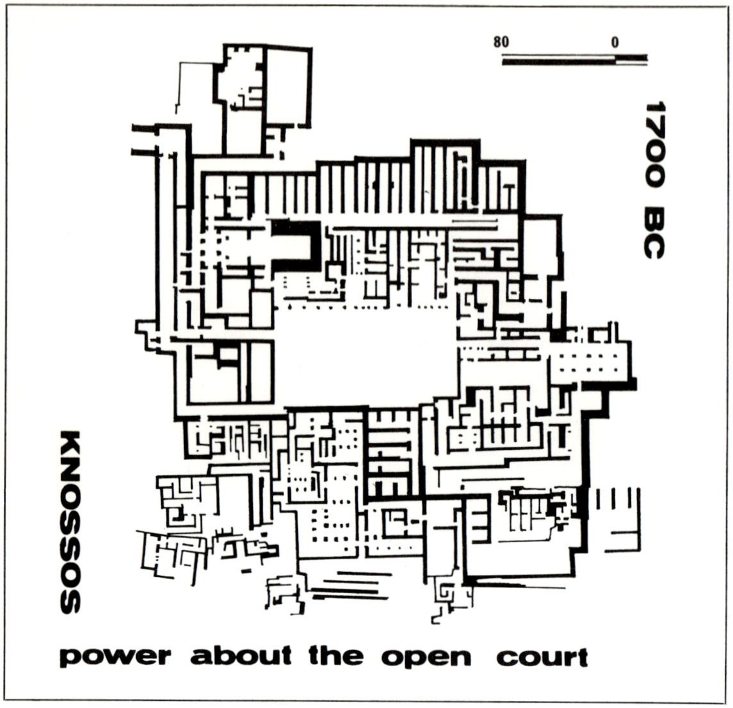

FIGURE 2.27

famous are those of the Argive Plain. Here the castles of Mycenae, Tiryns, and Midea were so located as to cover the passes leading to the plain, while Tarisa, on top of a free standing hill, dominated the whole area.[42]

Common to all settlements of Minos were the dominating positions of the castles or palaces. Next to these walls of protection were villages in which the subject people "... often reduced to serfdom, lived to till the fields for their masters and to mingle with the people of the castles only when danger loomed and they were summoned to help defend the stronghold. Such settlements were economically dependent on agriculture ...,"[43] wheras others depended on trade. None of these settlements constituted cities *per se*; they were never more than a saprophytic extension of the city, with no unified political or economic life nor any aims of their own. Urban concentrations, however, took on a somewhat unique form. Excavation at Gournia has revealed houses with stone foundations grouped close together around a palace. At Knossos, larger houses were discovered, built no doubt for nobles who lived close to the court. The palaces themselves differ widely in size, but were all built around a rectangular court. (See Figure 2.27.) "All show the tendency to relate the enclosed space to the open space of the landscape."[44]

As people began to travel and intermingle, they became less satisfied with their self-sufficient agricultural society and discovered the many benefits of a commercial economy.

Organized trade required harbor facilities, wharves, and shipyards, warehouses and houses for the people working there and for the sailors between voyages. When the Aegean civilizations advanced to the point where they could produce goods wanted everywhere, shops and settlement for workers and craftsmen must have been established.[45]

Historically, the significance of the Greeks in terms of planning dates from the time that the Dorians

[42]Ibid., p. 35.
[43]Ibid., p. 36.

[44]Ibid., p. 3.
[45]Ibid., p. 37.

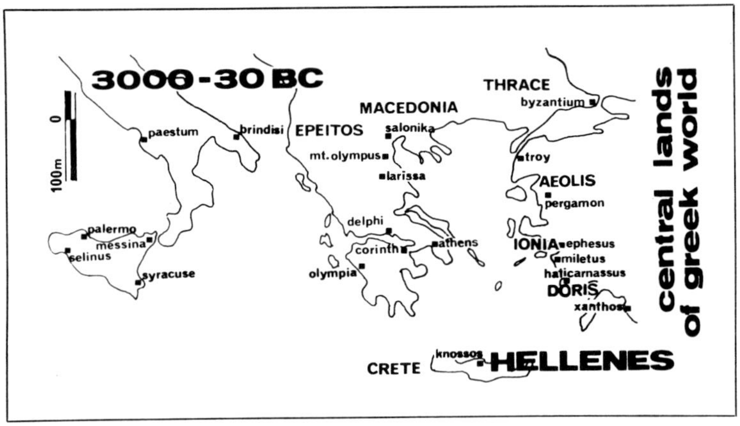

FIGURE 2.28

and the Ionians polarized. As important dialect groups, the Dorians occupied most of the southern islands in the southwest corner of Asia Minor, whereas the Ionians settled in the central Aegean region. (See Figure 2.28.) Because the nature of Greek topography was not conducive to the unity of the Greek peoples, the two formed quite distinct cultural groups.

Calling themselves Hellenes, the early Greek civilizations, which included both the Dorian and Ionian states, became known as the Hellenic civilization. The Hellenes had definite ideas about their city-states and maintained a ". . . clear sense of direction as they worked to make them the embodiment of their ideals. They thought clearly, too, about the relations of the city to its territory, about its living space and the ways in which the citizen could provide for his livelihood."[46] The Greeks in their civilization had a clear conception of a city and its area of sustenance. The location of the city, the activities of its citizens, its accessibility and defensibility were all considered during the planning stage.

The topography of the islands provided each city-state with seashores, plains and mountains. This mixture afforded magnificent views through an atmosphere of remarkable clearness. A land of incomparable beauty and character evoked in the Greek citizen a pride in and an intense love for his land. Extreme patriotism and major jealousies among the various city-states reinforced an inordinate spirit of the individualism and exclusiveness of the polis and of its citizenry.

The extent of planning at this period is exemplified by the city of Pergamum.

. . . a city state in Ionia, besides its notable industry of making books and parchment, possessed a code of building laws which regulated party-walls, dangerous structures, and such matters as the penetration of dampness from one property to another adjacent to it at a lower level.[47]

Pergamum itself was one of the greatest illustrations of planning in the ancient world. Although it was built on the ridge of a steep mountain and offered limited space, the buildings of the acropolis and the agora maximized their aesthetic and utilitarian aspects. The main hill housed the acropolis, the theater, the temple, and the agora, and there most of the activity of the polis took place.

The market played a major role in the Greek towns. The town of Miletus in Ionia was reconstructed in 480 B.C., having been destroyed by the Persians in 494 B.C. (See Figure 2.29.)

The town covered 222 acres, of which 52 were parks and gardens. It [was] planned on a chess-board system without any consideration for the deep coves and bays which penetrate the peninsula. The great market precinct between the bays [divided] the town into two parts. The smaller market near the

[46]Ibid., p. 40.

[47]Francis Swales, "Ancient Precedents for Modern City Planning," *Pencil Paints*, no. 11, **12**:813 (November 1931).

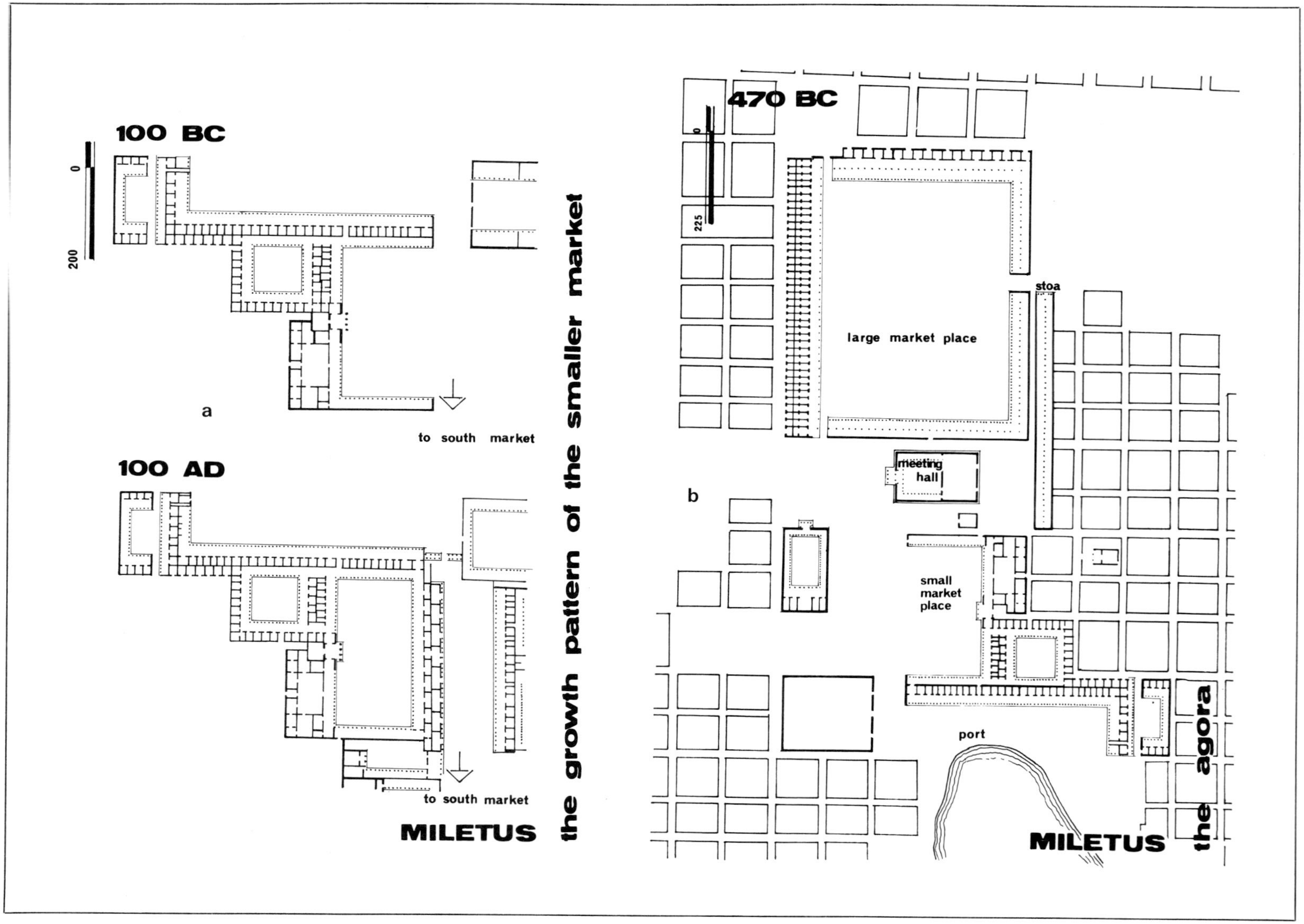

100 BC
0
200
a
to south market
100 AD
to south market
MILETUS
the growth pattern of the smaller market
470 BC
0
225
stoa
large market place
meeting hall
b
small market place
port
MILETUS
the agora

FIGURE 2.29

harbour [formed], together with the colonnaded south market and the processional way, the center of the city.[48]

The Greek city-states multiplied and prospered. (See Figure 2.30.)

Greek success in colonization was based on their thorough knowledge of their world and the people who lived in it. It was based also on their unique sense of social organization. They had the ability to make laws and the discipline to obey them. They were at once daring and conservative, proud of their habits and customs, regarding themselves as distinct from and superior to all others. Micias, the Athenian general, addressing his defeated army at Syracuse, spoke in this spirit: "... you are yourselves at once a city, whenever you sit down ... men make the city and not walls and ships without men in them ..."[49]

To sustain this spirit of individualism within the context of increased trading, every free-born citizen, whether rich or poor, shared equally. This opened up fresh chances for the ambitious citizen, a condition demanding a new kind of education. The old education was inept in accommodating change, as illustrated by Aristophanes, who in 423 B.C. wrote the following:

In the first place, boys were not allowed to utter a word. All those from the same quarter of the city were obliged to march together in good order through the streets to the music school, in the scantiest clothing, even if it snowed as thick as meal. There they were taught to memorize a song, without crossing their legs ... shouting out vigorously the melody handed down by our fathers.[50]

Such regimentation and restrictive learning no longer satisfied the need for special training to prepare the citizen for public life. To meet this need, schools of higher learning with definite courses of lectures and routine methods of criticism and discussion were established.

The ability to discuss and criticize was emphasized by Aristotle in his book *Politics*.

A city can be virtuous only when the citizens who have a share in the government are virtuous; and in our state all the citizens share in the government. Let us then inquire how a man becomes virtuous.[51]

The polis played a decisive role in the life of its people; each inhabitant took an active part in the maintenance and other ever-present obligations of citizenry.

The polis was more than a city. It was regarded as something higher than life itself, something to which life had to be

[48]Korn, p. 28.
[49]Hilberseimer, p. 51.

[50]William Boyd, *The History of Western Education* (New York: Barnes & Noble, 1969), p. 22.
[51]Ibid., p. 37.

FIGURE 2.30

subordinated. Not to be a citizen of a polis was considered a grave misfortune. To be deprived of citizenship was punishment second only to death. The polis was conscious of its power over the lives of its citizens: the citizens accepted this power freely and proudly.[52]

The Greek city-states were based on slavery, "but they provided for their citizens an opportunity for a rich and vigorous individual life."[53]

The communication among the city-states was minimal. The land was rough and mountainous and deeply indented by the sea. For this reason, the important industry was fishing, with agriculture and cattle raising in the valleys adjacent to the city. On the mountain slopes grew pine and fir, while on the plains grew figs, olives, oranges, lemons and grapes.[54] The roughness of the terrain plus the agricultural orientation made the city-states relatively self-sufficient. The smallness of the cities and their relative isolation made them even more self-sufficient.

Greece developed no large cities. Its ever-varying landscape, by its very formation, fostered the creation and maintenance of small states, conceived on the human scale in which the rich potentialities of the Greek spirit might unfold in utmost variety. The great cultural achievements of Greece may be due in part to the physical smallness of her cities. The smallness of the scale had political implications, too. It made it possible for each citizen to take his active part in the life of the city.[55]

Forces other than necessity to fulfill basic human needs, however, may have been at work—forces of an aesthetic and spiritual quality. The development of the Greek city-states could easily have been an expression of Greek creative ability and comprehensive sense of harmony. An urge to create a new way of life may have sprung from spiritual impulses that spurred the Greeks to transcend mere material needs.

"The demos may have gained consciousness and manifested itself with the creation of the agora, the center of political life."[56] The agora was not a marketplace alone, as some believe, but a political meeting place for the discussion of public affairs and a gathering place for the free men of the city. Aristotle remarked, "all trades should be excluded and no mechanic, husbandman or any such person allowed to enter unless he is summoned by the magistrate."[57] The agora also housed government offices, the gymnasia, the theater and the fountain. "People might still be allowed to live in their old villages, but their rights and obligations now had to be exercised in the polis."[58]

As the polis developed, so did rules and regulations. Greeks speculated on the ideal size of an urban concentration. Hippodamus of Miletus, philosopher and city planner, considered ten thousand citizens the ideal state.[59] On the other hand, Aristotle felt that the size should not be numerically set, but that it should be that which would ". . . enable the inhabitants to live at once temperately and liberally in enjoyment of leisure. It should be a territory which is all-producing, for to have all things and want nothing is sufficiency.[60]

Regarding location, Aristotle wrote:

. . . if we could have what we wish, it should be well situated in regard both to sea and land. It should be a convenient place for the production of the whole country. It should be difficult of access to the enemy and easy of egress to the inhabitants.[61]

For reasons of health, Aristotle decided that wind and water were the most important factors in ensuring civic well-being. Cities that lie toward the east are blown upon by the warmer east winds and as a result should be the healthiest because the city would enjoy milder winters. Concerning water, Aristotle felt that

There should be a natural abundance of springs and fountains in the towns, or, if there is a deficiency of them, great reservoirs may be established for the collection of rain water, such as will not fail when the inhabitants are cut off from the country by war.[62]

[52]Hilberseimer, p. 42.
[53]Ibid., p. 39.
[54]Ellwood P. Cubberley, *The History of Education* (Boston: Houghton Mifflin, 1920), p. 16.
[55]Hilberseimer, p. 39.
[56]Ibid., p. 42.
[57]Ibid., p. 43.
[58]Ibid., p. 42.
[59]Ibid., p. 40.
[60]Ibid., p. 41.
[61]Ibid.
[62]Ibid.

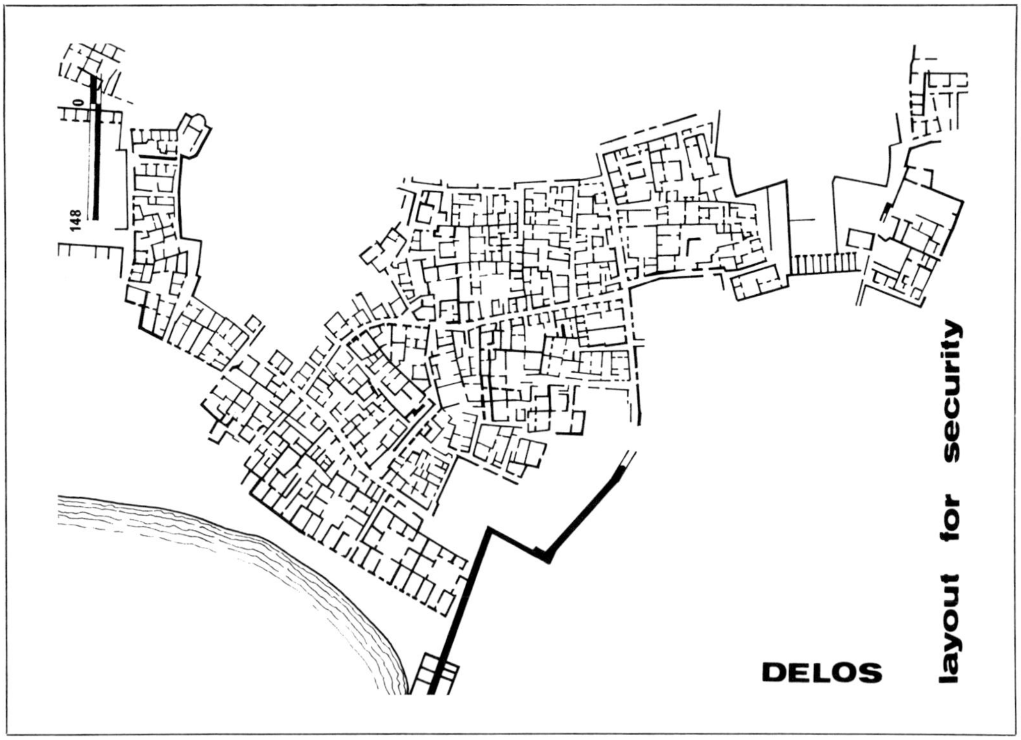

FIGURE 2.31

Agreeing with Hippodamus that cities should be planned with streets regularly laid out, Aristotle added,

For security in war the antiquated mode of building, which made it difficult for strangers to get out of a town and for assailants to find their way in is preferable. The whole town should not be laid out in straight lines, but only certain quarters and regions; thus security and beauty will be combined.[63] [See Figure 2.31.]

Hippodamus, the Ionian, was the first town planner to plan towns with broad, straight streets crossing at right angles and to make provisions for the grouping of residences. The city of Miletus was founded before the time of Hippodamus, but illustrates much of his thinking. Although Miletus was characterized by rectangular streets and a block system, rectangularity did not necessarily force an axiogeometrical pattern on the city. "Miletus is developed with great freedom. The free arrangement of its colonnaded halls and public buildings made possible any desired change without impairing the architectural harmony of the squares."[64] Hippodamus apparently was responsible for much of the emphasis on the rectangular town. "The planner Hippodamus is said to have consolidated the theory of the regular town—the gridiron plan. It is nowadays assumed that he was the first to systematize an idea which already existed a generation before him."[65]

Of all the city-states developed by the Hellenic Greeks, Athens (Ionian) (see Figure 2.32) and Sparta (Dorian) were the two most important. The Dorians and the Ionians differed markedly in character, which, of course, was reflected in their life styles.

The Dorian branches of the Greek family were in general practicable, forceful, but wholly unimaginative people. The

[63]Ibid.

[64]Ibid.

[65]Korn, p. 20.

FIGURE 2.32

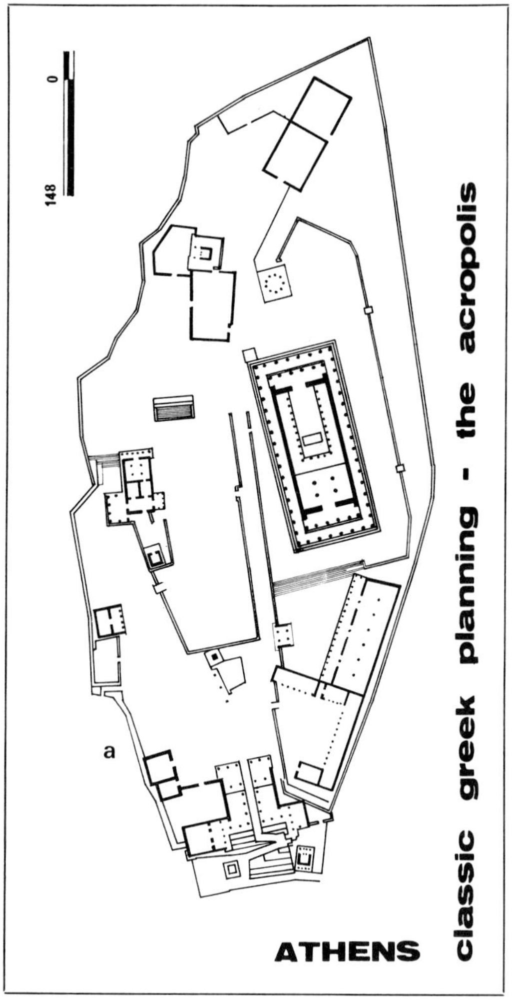

FIGURE 2.33

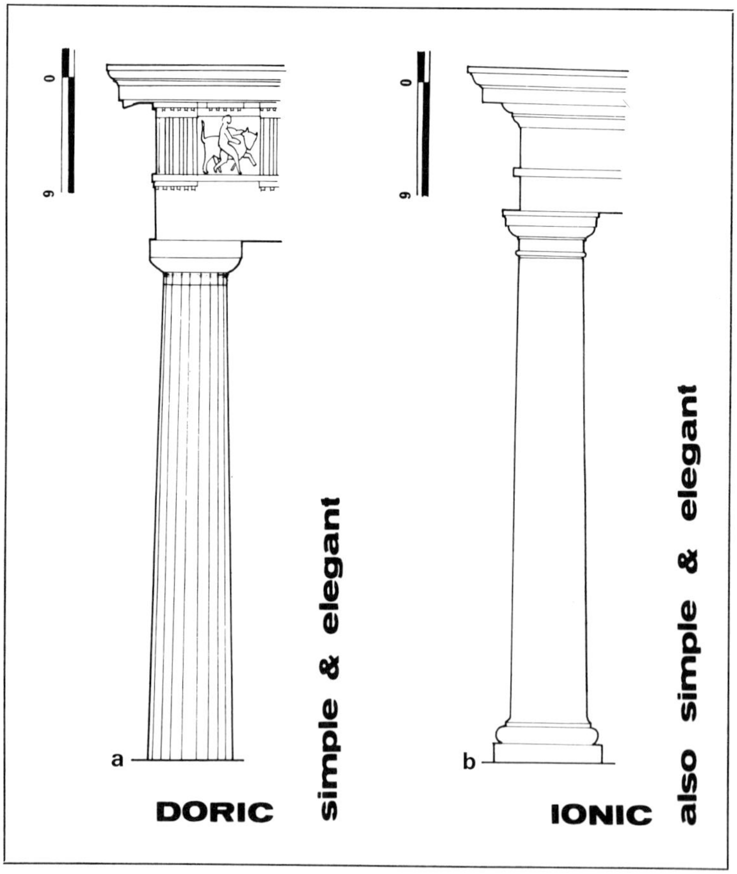

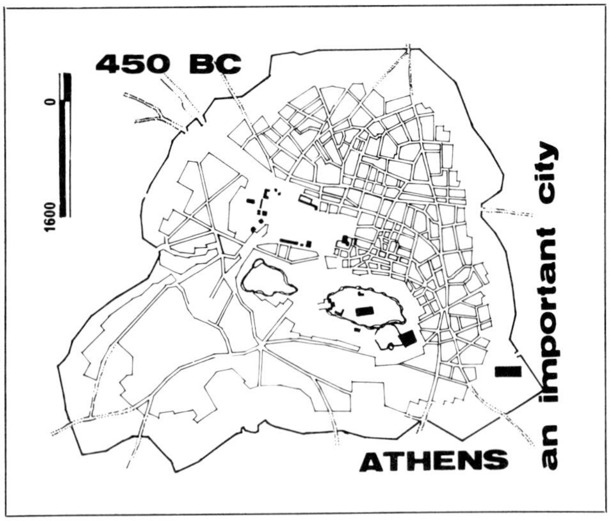

FIGURE 2.34

Ionic Greeks, on the other hand, were a many-sided, highly imaginative people who absorbed other races, which in part accounted for greater intellectual ability and versatility. Their abilities to adapt, to sense keenly the value of beauty in nature and art which helped to develop within them a wonderful sense of proportion and a capacity for moderation in most things accounted in part for their achievement in art, philosophy, literature and science.[66]

With its roots in the eastern Mediterranean civilizations, Greek temple architecture followed the monumental architectural styles of Egypt and Asia Minor in developing the primary style for the public and monumental buildings of Greece. By the sixth century B.C., both the Doric, from the mainland of Greece, and the Ionic, from the eastern shore of the Aegean Sea, were well-developed styles of architecture. The simplicity and elegance that are so highly characteristic of Greek planning are illustrated in the columns of the Doric and Ionic orders. (See Figure 2.33.) The classic Greek architecture is illustrated in the Parthenon and the Temple of Zeus.

The cities of the Hellenic period, however, were not well planned. The streets were narrow and crooked, and the cities grew in a haphazard fashion. Yet, there were beautiful cities constructed in early Greece.

Selinus, the farthest west of the Greek colonies on Sicily, had a layout remarkable for its simplicity. Standing on a precipice above the sea, its main street is crossed at right angles by side streets, the size of the blocks being determined by the plans of the houses which in their simplicity, contrasted with the splendid community buildings and temples.[67]

On the other hand, Dicaearchus observed,

The road to Athens is a pleasant one, running between cultivated fields the whole way. The city is dry and ill-supplied with water. The streets are nothing but miserable old lanes, the houses mean, with a few better ones among them. On his first arrival, a stranger would hardly believe that this is the Athens of which he has heard so much.[68] [See Figure 2.34.]

These types of contrasting views abounded in early Greece. Regardless of the lack of some aesthetic qualities in Athens, its great contribution to the world is well established. (See Figure 2.35.) The famous works of art and architecture, as well as its schools, drew visitors and students from all parts of the then-known civilized world. Athenian education was distinctive in that it was based on the heuristic methods of Socrates for discovering fundamental ideas relating man to his world.

This educational principle helped to establish Athens firmly as a center of intellectual activity. Regardless of whether the training was directed at fitting youths for taking part in public life or at following the old tradition of early Greek thought—which was learning for its own sake—the purpose of the training was the formation of social order. As such, the institutions of the state and their housing were in themselves highly educative. Some of them were as follows:

1 The Assembly, where the laws were proposed, debated and made.
2 The Juries, on which citizens sat and where the laws were applied.
3 The Theatre, where the great masterpieces of Greek literature were performed.

[66]Cubberley, p. 19.

[67]Hilberseimer, p. 61.
[68]Mumford, p. 163.

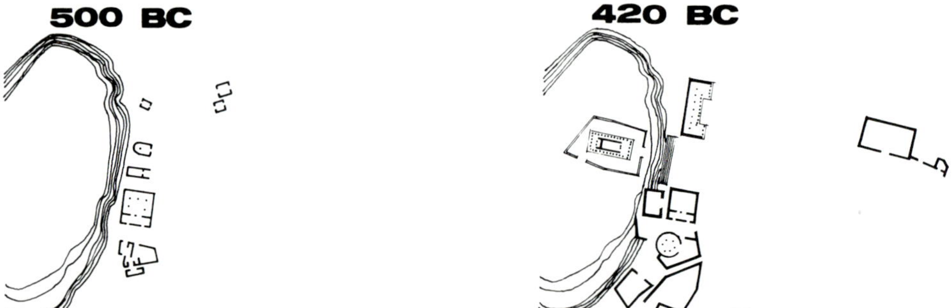

ATHENS AGORA

the values of athen's contribution were re-appraised

4 The Olympian and other Games, which were great religious ceremonies of a literary as well as athletic and artistic character, and to which Greeks from all over Hellas came.[69]

The games were one expression of the human spirit. "Under the impetus from these games," wrote Mumford, ". . . a new institution entered the Hellenic City . . ."[70] the palaestra or wrestling ground. Later it developed into an enclosed sports-ground for all manner of athletic contests and poetic exhibitions. For the mind was not left idle, despite the immense attention devoted to physical exercise.

With an emphasis on learning by doing, the city became the focus of learning to prepare the students ". . . to fear the gods, to respect their neighbors and themselves and to reverence the wisdom of their race."[71]

In summary, the Greek citizen learned the Delphic maxim: Know thyself.

In Athens in 350 B.C.,

[69]Cubberley, p. 36.
[70]Mumford, p. 138.

[71]Ibid.

FIGURE 2.35

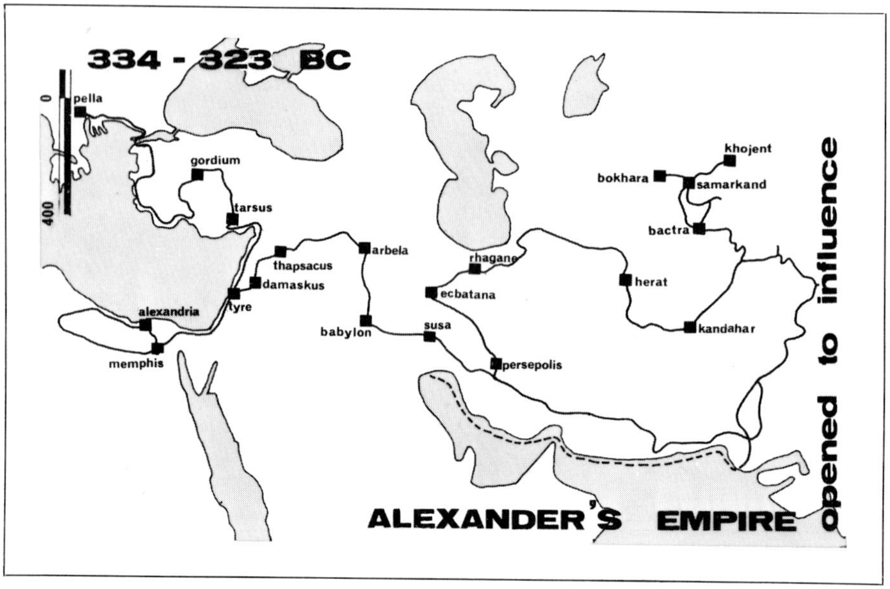

FIGURE 2.36

. . . a set of by-laws was issued. They included matters relating to the police, scavenging and the maintenance of order in markets and streets. These laws, forerunners of later town planning laws, show a growing interest in city administration.[72]

Near the dawning of the Hellenistic Age (in 336 B.C.), Alexander in 335 B.C. began his campaigns against Darius III, King of Persia, whose overthrow and eventual murder in 330 B.C. helped to open the entire Near East to Greek influence.[73]

As Alexander advanced eastward during his occupation of Persia (see Figure 2.36), he founded Greek colonies in order to avenge Xerxes' invasion of Greece in 480 A.D.[74] In this way, the Greek language and civilization were spread throughout the Near East. Alexander set in motion forces that would make his empire a melting pot, in which Greeks and Easterners alike would become one people. Some authorities believe that Alexander planned an integration of the peoples in his vast empire. Other authorities, however, ". . . insist that Alexander merely intended to Hellenize the East."[75]

As the Greeks spread the Hellenic culture throughout the Near East, they in turn were greatly influenced by the culture of the Near East. The result was a fusion of the two cultures, known as the Hellenistic culture.

Then as now, however, long continued political and cultural domination by an alien minority was impossible, and in the long run Alexander's conquests led to the creation of a new culture to which both East and West contributed a share and in which distinctions of race were of less importance than ever before.[76]

The possession of conquered territories, and the need to administer them as a single entity, required the construction of many new cities. This need for establishing cities gave architects a unique opportunity to explore, to develop and to build in novel ways.

Learning, during this period, flourished. The philosophical schools of Plato and Aristotle continued to exist, but declined somewhat in the shadow of the new Epicurean and Stoic schools of philosophy.

[72]Korn, p. 28.

[73]Joseph Ward Swain, *The World Empires: Alexander and the Romans after 334 b.c.*, Vol. II of *The Ancient World*, Harper Historical Series (New York: Harper & Bros., 1950), p. 16.

[74]Ibid., p. 24.

[75]Ibid., p. 29.

[76]Ibid., p. 31.

Epicureans stressed the problems of ethics and human conduct. They believed that life came from no plan and that the gods were indifferent to man. Stoics studied human conduct relative to logic and to the questions of what man can know and how he can be sure of what he knows. In contrast to the Epicureans, they believed that the world came from the universal law of nature, or God. Men were essentially alike; equal in their common humanity. "Stoic philosophers were for several centuries the leading teachers of world unity, and it was they who popularized the famous phrase, 'the Fatherhood of God and the Brotherhood of man.'"[77]

In other parts of the Hellenistic world, old ideas were being supplanted by new ideas. Under the ruler, Philadelphus, or Ptolemy II (reigned 285–246 B.C.), the highest development of domestic culture occurred as he encouraged, financed and built the city Alexandria, his capital.[78] Alexandria became the cultural center of the Hellenistic world. Its great library, some say, contained a million volumes, with a commensurate reading public. As a result, authorship became a recognized profession.[79] In addition, a museum for scientific study was established. Distinguished scholars and scientists were invited by the Ptolemies to conduct research. The Ptolemies also subsidized literary men and artists at their courts.

Often, however, the men who received these subsidies were forced to sacrifice their intellectual freedom. They made and said things to which no important person could possibly take exception, and sometimes their speculations were rather far removed from the pressing problems of the political and social world about them.[80]

However, collecting, copying, and preserving texts became the major activities, and they influenced the course of planning in many areas for the next one hundred years.[81]

The lodging and catering to students who came from all parts of the world became a considerable business for the Alexandrian. . . . Housing was an economic problem during the Greek domination of Alexandria, and its museum and library were as much in the nature of a modern publishing plant as they were in that of educational institutions. The marked racial differences of the three largest elements of the population—native Egyptians, Hellenic Greeks, and Jews—tended to instinctive classification of residential districts into three parts.[82]

With an increase in travel and the consequently wider communication, Greek people rapidly changed. "They became members of a larger entity brought about not by encirclement and enclosure, but by a vivid attraction. At the point of a meeting, they overcame the particularism and parochialism of their native city, engaged on a wider horizon."[83]

The development of the arts and greater communication had a profound influence on the political structure of the Greeks.

Potentially these practices had within themselves a basis for a new kind of urban policy, based on a confederated organization operated over wider areas not by a centralized command but through voluntary transactions and mutual services. If these efforts had been more thoroughly understood and more consciously appraised by the political thinkers of Greece, even as late as the fourth century, they might still have left their mark on the city.[84]

The change from Hellenic polis to Hellenistic metropolis was not sudden. In the Hellenic period, the community determined for its own good to remain small, for Aristotle taught the lesson of controlled growth to allow the citizens a chance to know one another. As a result, no provisions were made for the increasing complexities of an open society. This failure to understand the dynamics of human development as a key to urban form was glossed over for two hundred years by ever-increasing and one-sided reliance on the existing systems. To cope with this, planning was highly organized and ordered in sumptuously beautiful architecture that eventually overwhelmed the Hellenic citizen's capacity for creation. ". . . collection and classification became

[77]Ibid., p. 80.
[78]Ibid., p. 43.
[79]Ibid., p. 63.
[80]Ibid., p. 61.
[81]Cubberley, p. 49.
[82]Swales, p. 815.
[83]Mumford, p. 142.
[84]Ibid., p. 143.

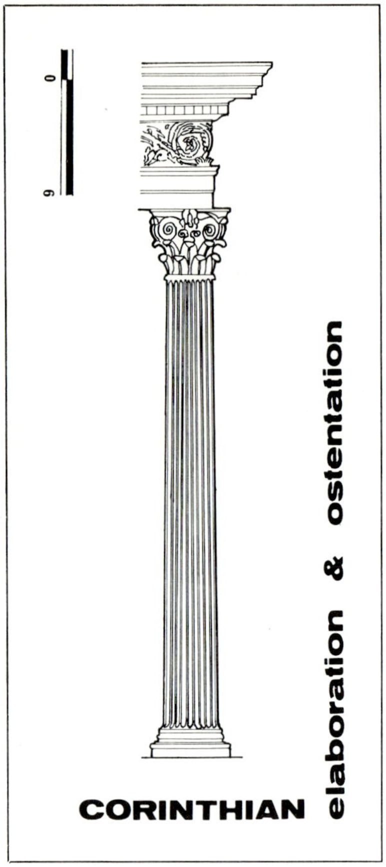

FIGURE 2.37

the chief avenues of intellectual activity."[85] Knowledge was substituted for responsible action. Yet, there remained an inability to cope mechanically with large quantities, political oppressions, class divisions and the ever-increasing discontent between the Greeks and the Orientals.

Despite these failures, the sophistication of Greek planning, fitting Greek activities (the content) to Greek architecture (the form), can be found in the ground plans of the Palace of Terrence and in the ground plan of the Parthenon, as well as in the plan for the Acropolis of Athens. These temples and the palace received great attention architecturally, but later, attention was also given to the buildings of the public sector. Size became important, and the harmony and simplicity of the Hellenic architecture gave way to the elaboration and ostentation of the Hellenistic architecture. For example, the Ionic was replaced by the ornate Corinthian capital. (See Figure 2.37.) Eventually, these endeavors could no longer be supported by the declining economy. Bureaucracies became corrupt, incompetent and oppressive.[86] Wars wrought terrific damage, with even greater damage being committed by native rebellions. Soon the Hellenistic world was torn with strife until Rome intervened and again established peace.

PLANNING AND EDUCATION BY THE ROMANS

The Roman character differed markedly from that of the Greek. Preoccupied with philosophy and aesthetics, sculpture and poetry, mental and physical development, the Greeks, in their architecture, reflected the simple elegance of their personality. The Romans, on the other hand, were more aggressive and politically inspired. Their energies were gregarious and unrestrained. Other characteristics are shown in Table 2.1, a comparative chart illustrating the differences between the Greek and the Roman characters, as well as their societies, which had profound effects on their planning and building of cities and on their educational practices.

The Romans were builders. Much of their planning and development was based on pressing and immediate practical needs. For governmental controls of subjugated peoples, they built bridges, sewers and viaducts. (See Figure 2.38.) They rapidly developed city plans that were constantly revised and used again.

> The greatest achievement in Roman civilization was the creation of cities. They arose everywhere in the vast empire, serving as administrative and market centers, as outposts of Roman civilization, and as forces drawing into unity a widely scattered Roman world. [See Figure 2.39.]

[85]Mumford, p. 189.

[86]Swain, p. 81.

FIGURE 2.38

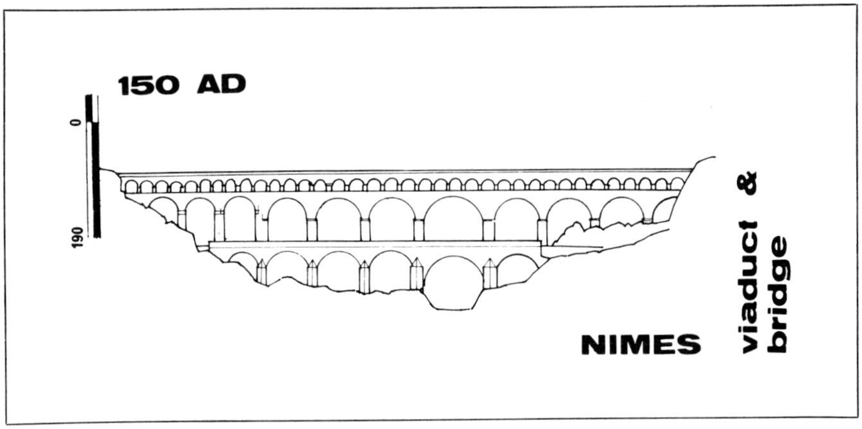

Table 2.1 Greek and Roman architecture

Greek	Roman
1 Imaginative, subjective, artistic and idealistic.	**1** Unimaginative, concrete, practical and constructive.
2 Contributed to the advancement of civilization in literature, philosophy and art.	**2** Contributed to law, order and government.
3 Lived a life of aesthetic enjoyment built upon the beauty of nature and art.	**3** The aesthetic and beautiful had little appeal.
4 The worth of a thing was intellectual and artistic.	**4** The basis of worth was the utilitarian character of the thing.
5 Worshipped the beautiful and good and tried to live life rationally and nobly.	**5** Worshipped force and effectiveness and tried to live by rule and authority.
6 Thought of government in personal terms.	**6** Thought of government in terms of law and duty.
7 Gave intellectual and aesthetic ideals to philosophy, literature and art.	**7** Gave governmental form, legal codes, commercial processes and engineering undertakings.

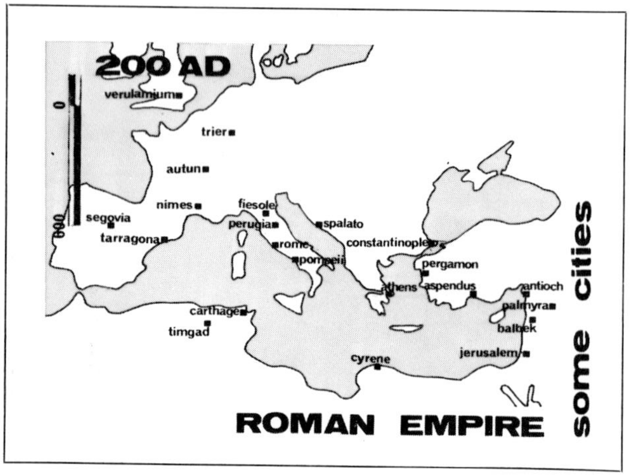

FIGURE 2.39

The new provincial cities were inhabited by Roman landlords and army veterans, who directed the predominantly agricultural economy. The landlords were responsible for taxes, measured by the amount of land they owned. They were, in effect, parasites upon the people living on the land. They oppressed the native population, reduced its members to serfdom. And yet, these cities propagated seeds of freedom, glimpsed the ideal of the self-governing community.[87]

The buildings, towns and architecture reflected the grandeur of the Roman Empire. The emperors regarded buildings as political tools and used them to impress their glory on the people and to establish for themselves eternal fame.[88] Rome became a world city and was inhabited by men from all over the civilized world. However, underneath the glory and grandeur (see Figure 2.40) festered all the human miseries inevitable in so vast an accumulation of people. These people for the most part lived in dismal, overcrowded apartments, whose

[87]Hilberseimer, p. 77.
[88]Ibid., p. 69.

FIGURE 2.40

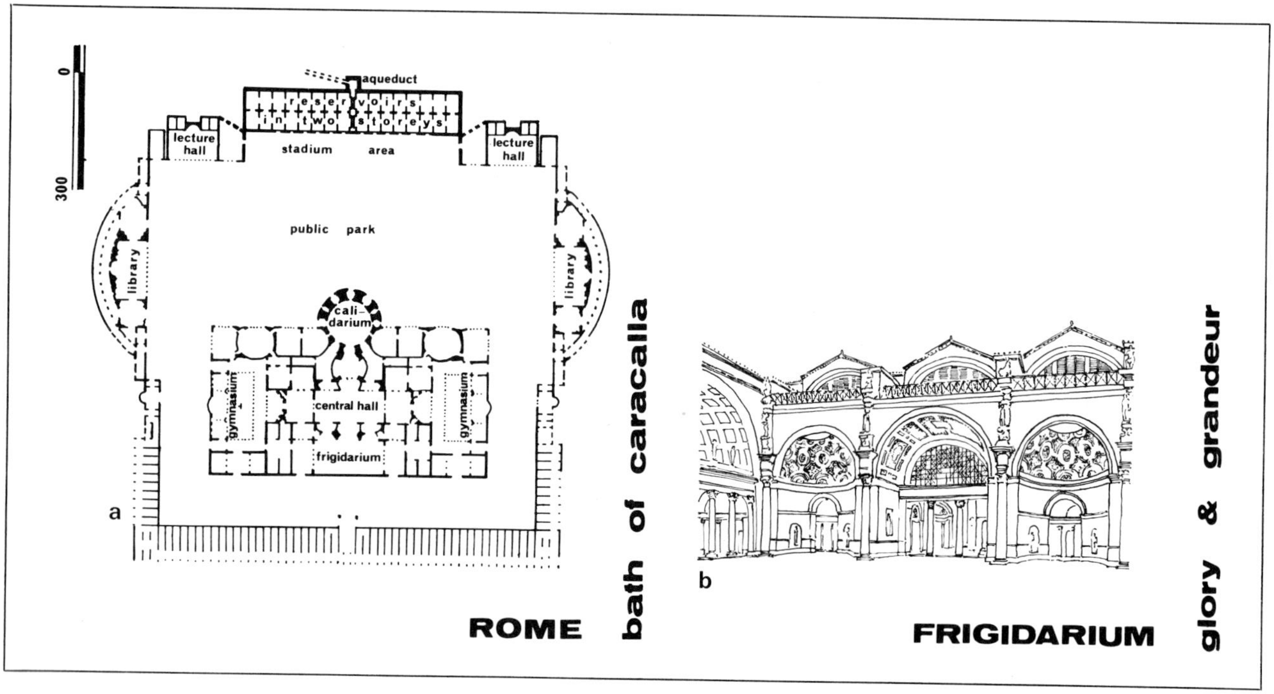

... development was brought about by lack of living space in those areas where such space was most needed. The aristocracy settled on the Caelian and Aventine Hills and had room to breathe. [See Figure 2.41.] The lesser people, crowded into the old city area, were jammed together in ever-increasing congestion. Apartment houses rose six or eight floors to provide "relief" from overcrowding. The size of individual apartments decreased. Streets were narrowed to make space for yet more building. Land speculation aggravated the situation; rents became unbearably high.[89]

To a lesser degree, the situations mentioned above existed in every large city within the Roman Empire. Also constant in its uniformity was Roman education, even under diverse conditions. For approximately four hundred years, slight differences in education were made. A fortunate free man could attend the primus magister to learn to read, write and count. Later, he could attend a grammar school to broaden his literary background. If successful in his grammar school studies, the free man might either attend a more specialized school or enter the study of a private tutor.

Beginning with Julius Caesar, who conferred the privilege of franchise on all foreign teachers, most of the emperors were patrons of learning. Augustus established the first public libraries in Rome, Vespasian (reigned 69–79) organized and supported schools by bringing teachers into the service of the state, and Quintilian, Nerva and Trojan lent large sums of money to farmers. These farmers paid interest, to finance a scheme of yearly allowances to aid boys and girls to the age of eighteen and fourteen, respectively, in obtaining an education.[90]

Antoninus Pius (reigned 138–161) terminated the method of occasional assistance by establishing the imperial system of education. He placed the obligation of paying salaries and giving privileges to special teachers on the municipalities in all Roman provinces. Capital cities had to maintain five grammarians; large cities maintained four grammarians and small cities maintained three grammarians. This responsibility made the city the harbor of education and its municipal council the harbinger of policies affecting the citizen's education.[91] As a result, the education of most great men took place in the city, for the city also served as the best classroom of experience. Such was the case of Augustine. Not until he went to the grammar school in the town of Madaura at the age of twelve (366) did he acquire a real love of studying. This feeling remained and served him in good stead when, at the age of fifteen, Augustine was sent to higher studies at Carthage. Involving himself in its many commercial, seaport and festive activities provided him enough experiences to enable him to take first place in the study of forensic rhetoric.

For Romans, in general, heavy emphasis was placed on architectural art in their daily lives. Thus the aesthetic as well as the utilitarian aspects of their architecture were stressed.

The change in Rome's political structure from Republic to Empire was reflected in its architecture. The informality of the buildings on the Forum Romanum had been an expression of

[89]Ibid., p. 70.
[90]Boyd, pp. 78–79.

[91]Ibid., p. 80.

FIGURE 2.41

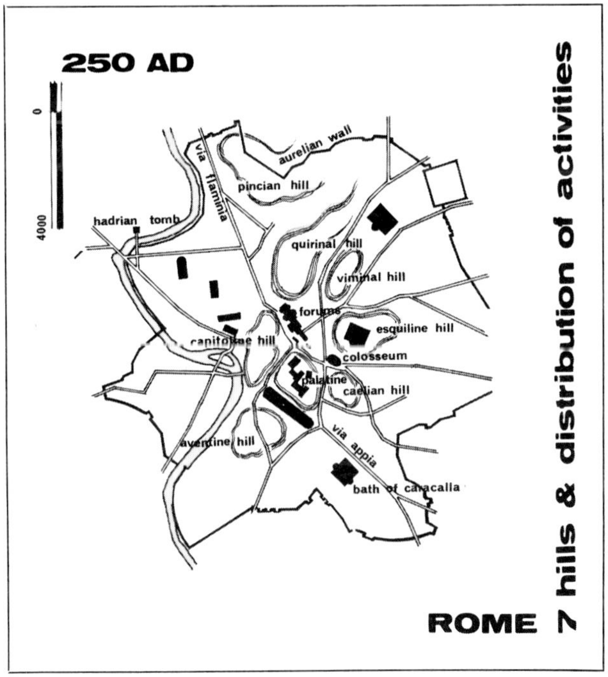

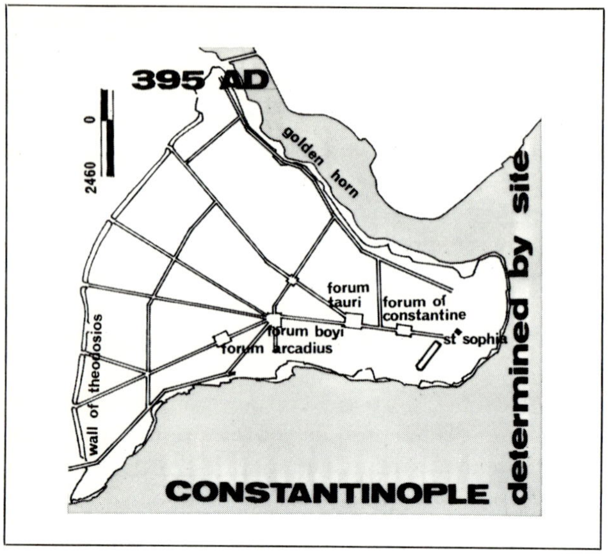

FIGURE 2.42

equality. These buildings varied in size, according to their functions, but not one tended to dominate the others. The Forum of Caesar's day was only a homogeneous temple site. The Temple of Augustus dominated his Forum, expressing dramatically the new spirit of government which elevated one person far above all others, subordinating aristocracy and people alike to the domination of one.[92] [See Figure 2.7].

Roman planning, building and architecture continued to go through transitional stages concurrently with the evolution of the Empire. As the Empire progressed, the architectural style became more ornate, and the grandeur of planning increased.

The shift in focal point of the Roman Empire from Rome to Constantinople also reflected the influence of the Empire throughout the civilized world.

The architectural character of Constantinople is determined by the topography of its site. [See Figure 2.42.] The city was irregular on its hilly north side, more regularly laid out on the south. But nowhere were axiality and symmetry dominating factors. The arrangement of the squares, with their imperial and public buildings, is free, more like Greek cities than Roman. The north side, in spite of its hills, was the more densely settled area. The south side was more open, its houses interspersed with gardens which, increasing in area toward the city wall, gave the city the look of the countryside. Around the busy harbor to the north, the Golden Horn, were the necessary harbor installations, warehouses, stores, factories, workshops and also the dwellings of craftsmen and traders. This concentration accounts for the greater density of this part of the city. The hills were recognized always as natural sites for significant buildings. The Greeks had once built their temples there. Now they became sites for Christian Churches. Later the Moslem would crown them with mosques. These mosques, all architectural variations of St. Sophia, dominate the city with domes and semi-domes, which contrast effectively with the horizonality of the houses on the hills as these follow the elevation and are like terraces attached to it.[93]

The development of Rome and Constantinople was quite different in terms of planning. Rome's history was long, whereas Constantinople's was short. Rome was an expression of many years of changes from small Latin villages to a great imperial capital, whereas Constantinople was built all at once.

Throughout the Roman sphere of influence, cities had developed substantial cultural and social activities, as well as performed remarkable engineering feats. Libanios' eulogy of his native city, Antioch, indicates the high level civilization reached in such Roman cities.

The water supply of our city is unsurpassed. Others may equal us in some respects, but they are all inferior to the abundance and excellency of our water. In the public baths, and in some private baths, each stream is the size of a river, and the rest are not much smaller. He who has the means to build a new bath need not fear that it will be dry when completed. Every part of the city sees to the elegance of its public baths. . . . The abundance of the flowing water can be measured by the number of dwellings; for there are as many flowing waters as there are dwellings. . . . Therefore, we do not quarrel at public wells as to who comes first to draw water; an evil true of so many reputable cities, where large crowds wrangle around the wells over broken jugs. As everybody has water within the house, we have fountains as an adornment of our city. . . . The sunlight is rivaled by other lights, lights which surpass those of the illuminations of Egyptian festivals. In our city, nights differ from days only by the variance in illumination; busy hands notice no difference and continue to forge, and whoever wishes sings and dances so that here Hephaestus and Aphrodite share the night.[94]

[92]Hilberseimer, p. 69.

[93]Ibid., pp. 76–77.
[94]Ibid., pp. 71–72.

Although Libanios was speaking only of Antioch, his obvious feeling of delight with that city was shared by many others for their own cities. The utility of the architecture of the Romans is reflected in their bridges and streets, in their villas and public buildings and in their theaters and amphitheaters. The forums and baths of Rome testified to the grandeur of Roman planning and architecture for housing large-scale activities. This scale was carried over to individual buildings, such as the Colosseum, built between A.D. 70 and 82, and the Pantheon, erected in A.D. 124. Their placement within the city fabric was purposefully planned so that they acted as magnets within the city's movement system. The grandeur, variety and functional utility of Roman planning and building have remained the standard for planning and building, even up to the present.

BYZANTINE INFLUENCE ON PLANNING AND EDUCATION

Byzantine architecture became influential in the West after the fourth century and especially flourished in the time of the Roman Emperor Justinian (reigned 527–565). Justinian brought an end to pagan schools by confiscating their resources. (See Figure 2.43.) In place of paganism, actions by the political decision-makers were guided by the tenets of Christianity, and, as a result, Christian buildings became the new focal points of the city. Their style was borrowed chiefly from the building characteristics developed by the Greeks, the Romans and the Egyptians. The most distinguishing and the most common characteristics found in Byzantine buildings, however, are the stylized circular domes and interiors, heavily decorated with paintings, sculpture and mosaics that served as a medium for illustrating to a largely illiterate population biblical stories and the tenets of the Christian Church.

St. Sophia in Constantinople (see Figure 2.44) is a classic example of this endeavor to teach those who could not read the sacred texts the traditions of Christianity. Much of its architecture was planned to inspire with a love of the faith those who saw and worshiped within it. Its overwhelming size was the antithesis of the fragile and costly pagan schools, which in most parts of the Empire had collapsed during the fifth century. Secular learning had almost ceased to exist and the only schools remaining were mostly private in nature.

The obligation for again undertaking the work of education fell on the clergy of the Church's eastern branch. Two canons were established around A.D. 680: one permitted priests to send their nephews or other kinsmen to school, and the other instructed

FIGURE 2.43

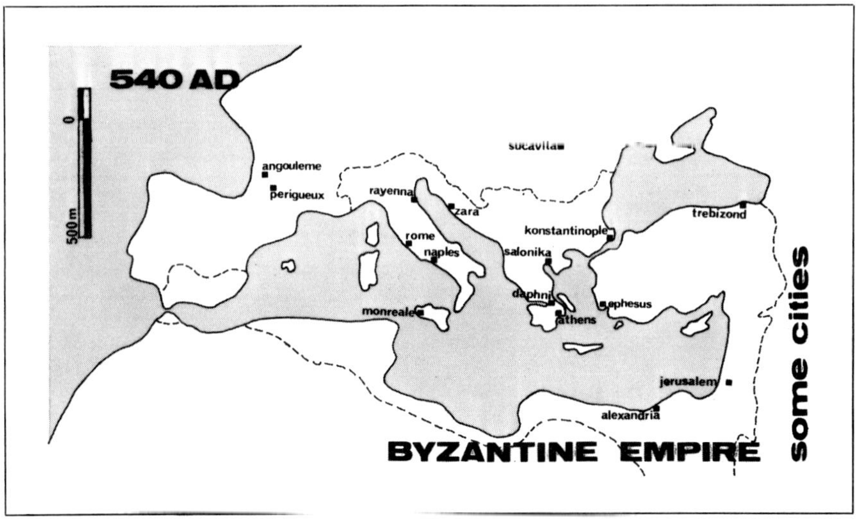

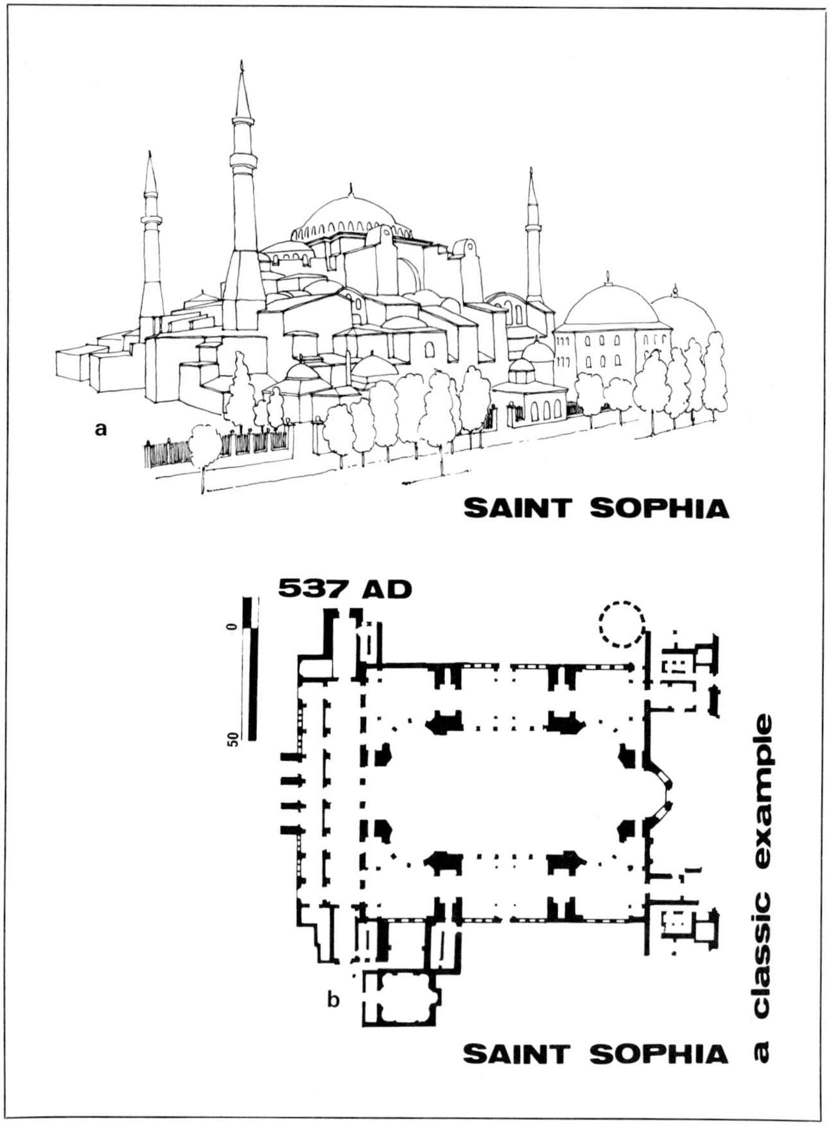

FIGURE 2.44

FIGURE 2.45

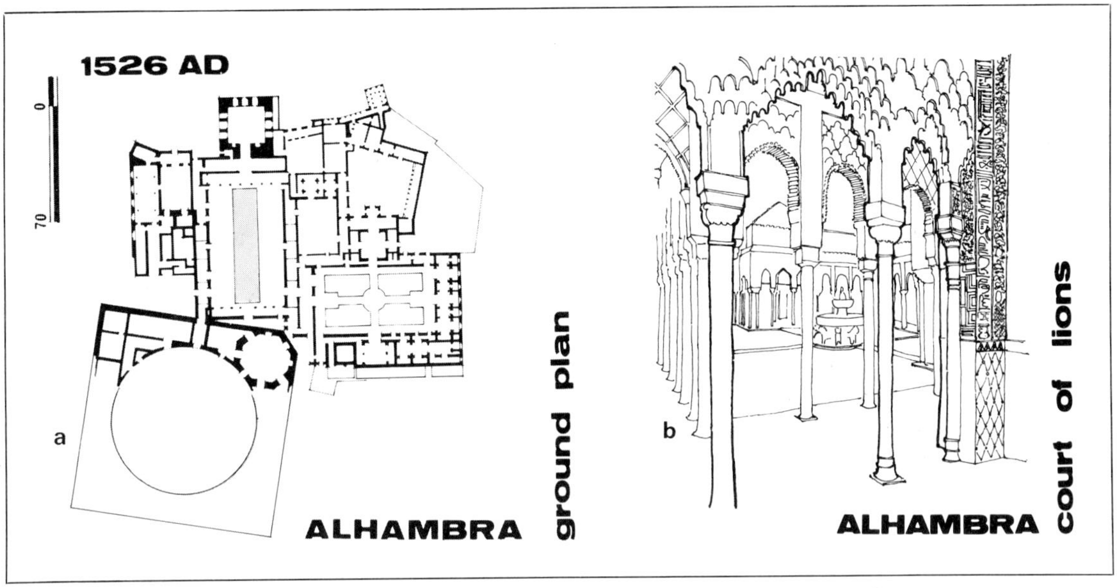

FIGURE 2.46

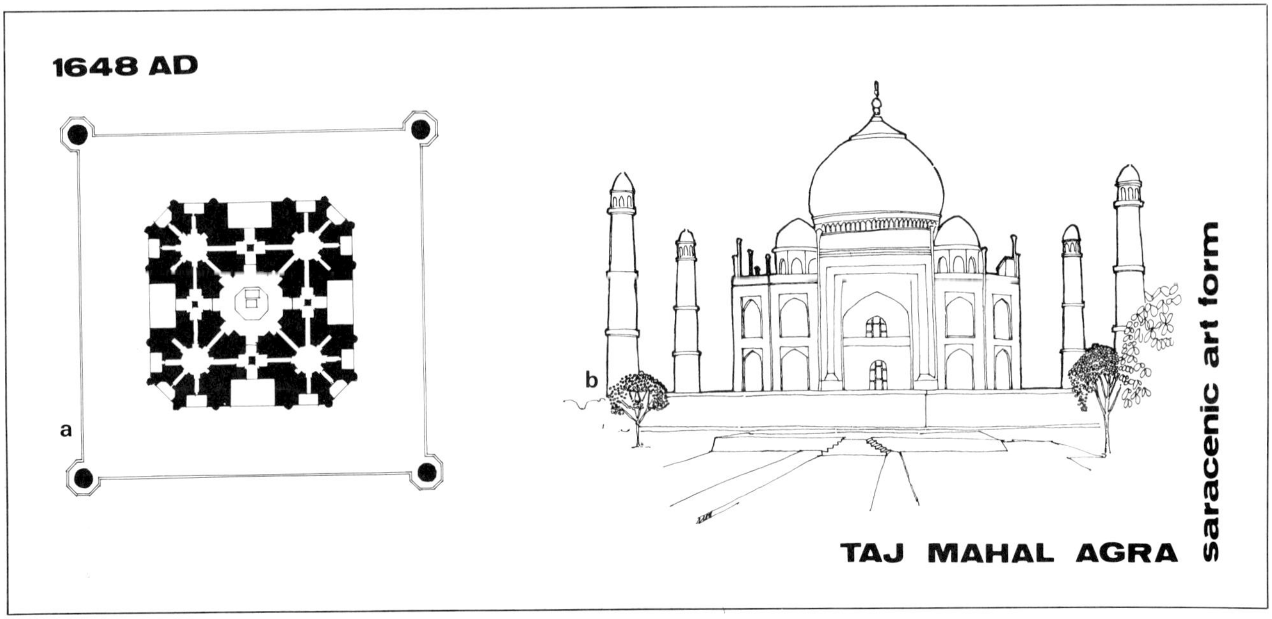

priests to teach grammar to the children of the faithful.

This movement for beginning schools again spread slowly throughout Europe during the ensuing two to three centuries. Similarly, the Byzantine architectural style also spread around the Mediterranean and up the Iberian Peninsula. Here, the fortress the Alhambra built near Granada illustrates Byzantine design in excellent fashion. (See Figure 2.45.) The ground plan of the Alhambra exemplifies the intricate design and the total planning system of a self-contained community. It included fountains, corridors, open courts and the numerous functional buildings required for housing the rulers and the courts that governed the western reaches of the Muslim Empire.

As Constantinople lost control of its empire to the Arabs, Byzantine architecture became dominated by the Saracen art forms, accounting for the somewhat Oriental flavor associated with the Byzantine. This style spread throughout the then-known civilized world and influenced the church architecture in such places as Moscow and Kiev, and other structures, such as the well-known Taj Mahal of India. (See Figure 2.46.)

ROMANESQUE INFLUENCE ON PLANNING AND EDUCATION

The Romanesque style is often thought to be based on Greco-Roman architecture. Although Romanesque buildings took on the character of a basilica, the form of the early Christian churches shows kinship to the Byzantine, Syrian and Persian forms of architecture. (See Figure 2.47.)

The consolidation of power in western Europe, and particularly the Carolingian Empire, brought about a rise in the stability of civilization and a greater amount of building than had been done previously. The feudal system accorded power to the landed gentry, and each of these holders of authority established his seat of power. The estates housed the nobility and their courts, the soldiers for protection, the serfs for production and the monastics for religious purposes. The estate, then, was the site of fortresses, castles, palaces, farming, monasteries and churches.

Bern and Nuremberg grew up under the protection of castles. At Carcassonne, the castle itself was incorporated into the city. At Rothenburg, the castle stands outside the city on a hill. St. Gael developed in connection with a cloister; Essen, in

FIGURE 2.47

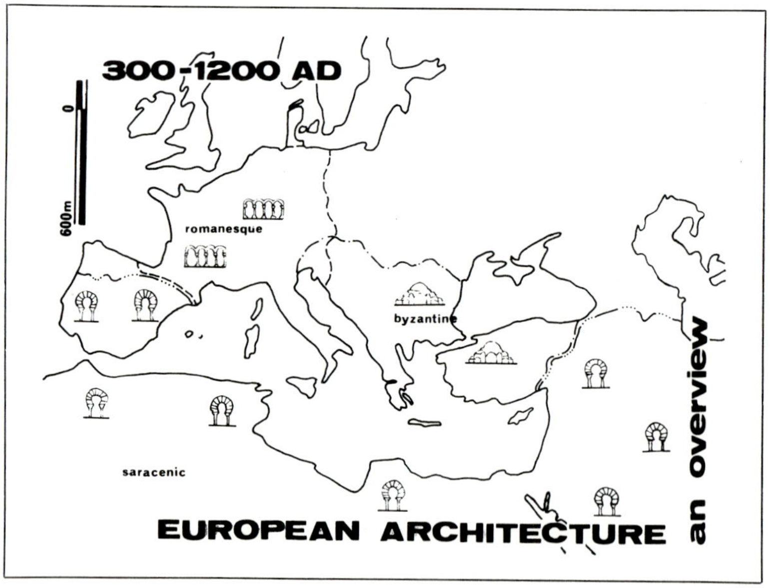

FIGURE 2.48

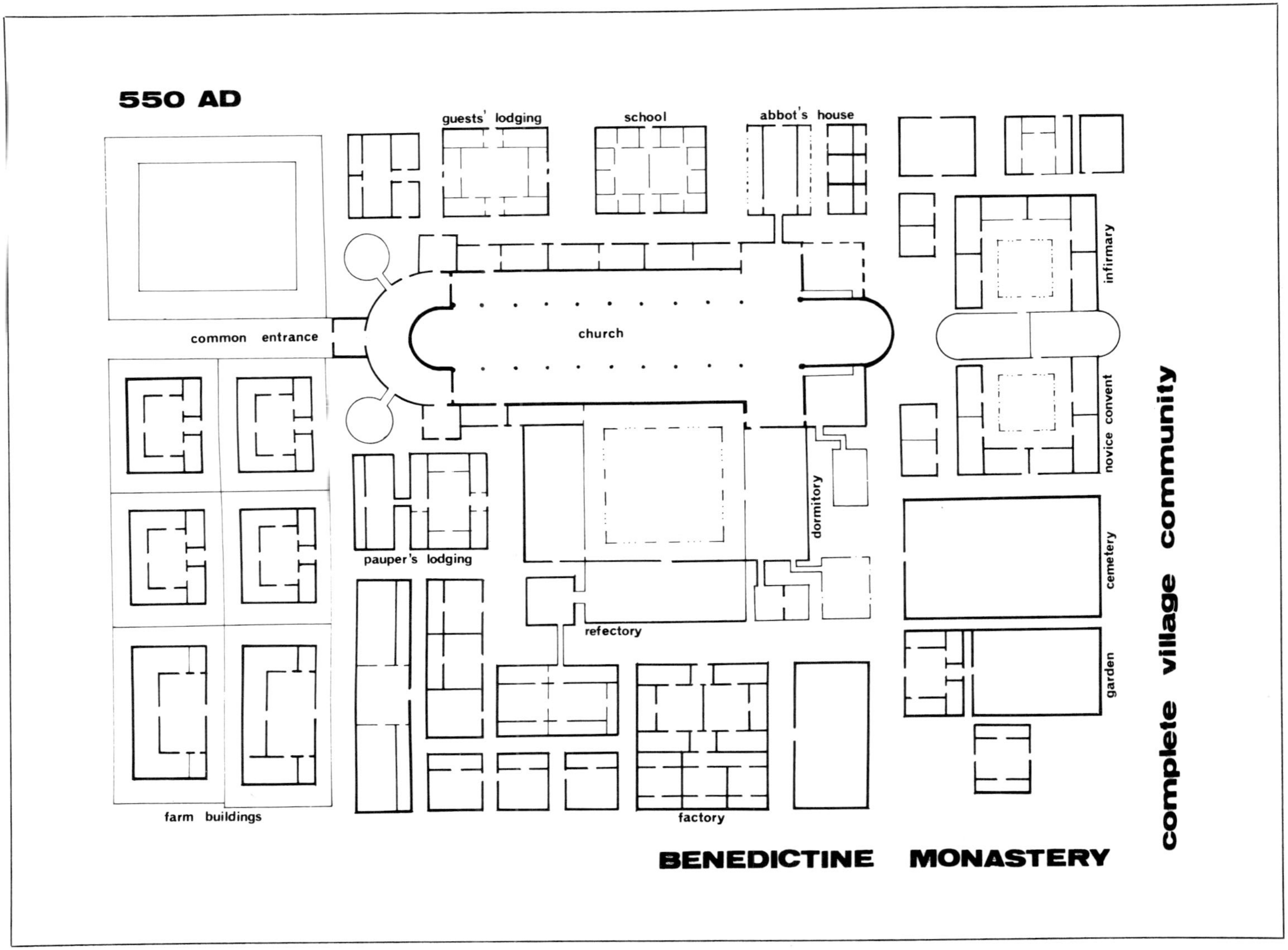

550 AD
guests' lodging
school
abbot's house
infirmary
novice convent
common entrance
church
dormitory
cemetery
garden
pauper's lodging
refectory
farm buildings
factory
BENEDICTINE MONASTERY
complete village community

connection with the seat of a bishop, Luebeck grew up between two older settlements. . . . Freiburg, Villinger, and Munich were all founded as market cities, to serve their regions.[95]

Favorable trade locations on old routes (Frankfurt, Strassbourg, and Cologne), natural resources (Lüneburg, Sheffield, Solingen, and Ghent), and power politics (Florence and Paris) all played their part in the growth and importance of cities.[96]

As trade, industry, and power increased, so did the population of the centers of the estates, and they soon became towns and cities. During the Middle Ages, distinct and well-differentiated groups existed within a population. The craftsmen, who were less concerned with making money, made possible the high standards of craftsmanship. The merchant was eager to make money and used the money as a source of power. The patricians administered the city, while the clergy made up the city's educated classes.[97]

Considerable progress had been made in general education, as a result of the joint efforts of Church and State. Educational reforms by Charlemagne brought a partial unity of purpose into education. Reinforced by the vigorous mentality of the barbarians from the north and the Moors, who kept alive a great deal of Greek science and philosophy in such cultural centers as Granada, the cities were again destined to be the birthplaces of learning.

With the rise in trade, the cities' decision-makers took greater interest in art, architecture and education. During the ninth, tenth and eleventh centuries, Romanesque architecture and education took on their forms. The churches were the most common buildings of the Romanesque period and represented, in greatness and remoteness, the rigid institution under which ordinary men had to live. Under such a system, individual enterprise was almost stifled. With the rise of cities, however, there arose a demand for education, and it was not long before towns of any significant size had their own schools. In appearance, these schools differed little from those of a monastery.

[95]Ibid., p. 88.
[96]Ibid., p. 92.
[97]Ibid., pp. 93–94.

Monasteries of the later period showed all the features of a complete village community. [See Figure 2.48.] Their buildings were grouped around several courtyards—a cloister court, inner court, common court and others. Besides the Cathedral, the Abbot's lodging and the Chapter House, the living quarters, dormitories and lavoratories for the monks, their library, scriptorium, refectory and kitchen, there were the guest house, hospital and school, the tribunal and prison, the workshops and servant's quarters, cellars and stables, the mill, bakery and brewery, and the gardens, orchards and fishponds. Outside the gate of the monastery, local trade developed at first, mostly in the form of barter. More trade, however, began to flourish outside the bishop's Cathedral which became the center of social life and was bound to grow into early towns.[98]

Toward the end of the Middle Ages, schools began to pass from Church control. The fact that townsmen took keen interest in their schools and shared in their maintenance made a great difference. As a result, schools became purely municipal institutions.

GOTHIC INFLUENCE ON PLANNING AND EDUCATION

Developing from the prevalent Romanesque architecture, the Gothic incorporated the spirit of the age into its artifacts. The first Gothic buildings originated in France and eventually spread to England, Austria, Germany, the Low Countries and northern Italy. (See Figure 2.49.) The thriving trading communities and the emerging power of the local governments inspired the architect to become more worldly, as he built to the skies.

Gothic architecture is known for its great heights, vertical lines, ribbed vaults, pointed arches, large stained-glass windows and flying buttresses. (See Figure 2.50.) The buildings were ornately decorated, not only with stained glass and mosaics, but also with numerous pieces of sculpture. This sculpture covered the exterior and interior of the buildings and communicated to all that individuality should be submerged for the good of all mankind and that reason should be subordinated to authority. Although the

[98]Korn, p. 38.

FIGURE 2.49

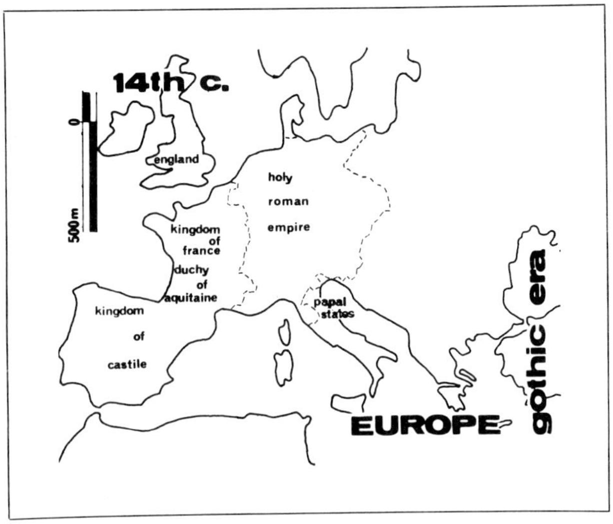

FIGURE 2.50

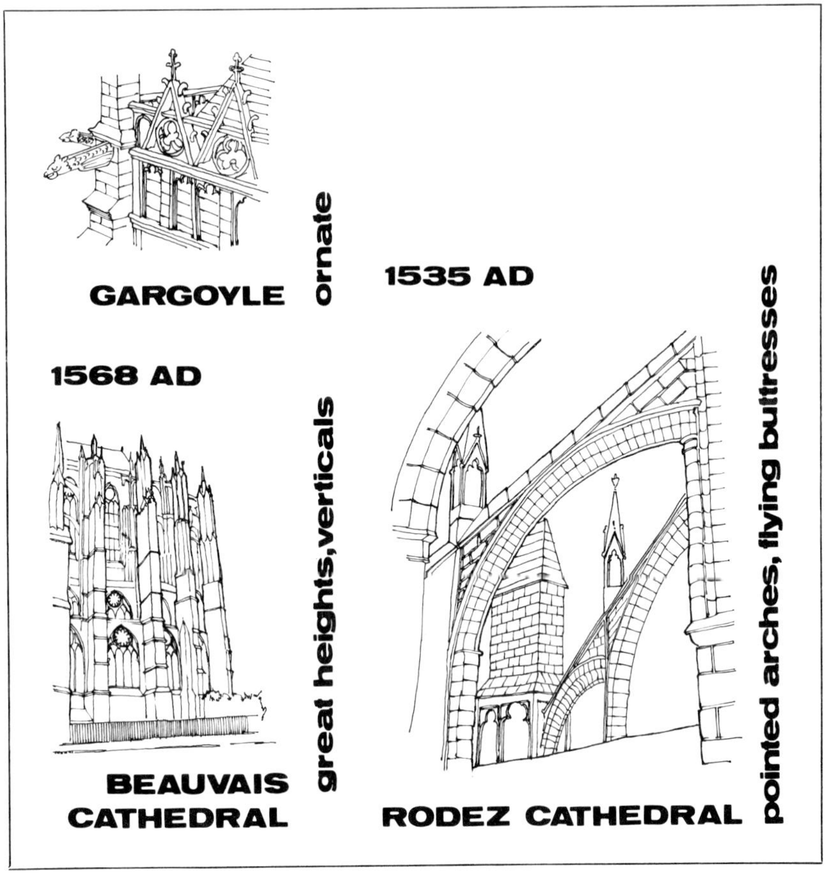

FIGURE 2.51

Gothic style in many ways seems to be more ornate than the Greek, Roman, Byzantine or Romanesque styles, it has certain likenesses and elegances that subdue the apparent ornateness. The Gothic style reflected the spirit of inquiry surging up everywhere in the towns, which were the centers of resistance to the barbarian invasions.

Notre Dame in Paris represents a combination of the Romanesque and the Gothic. (See Figure 2.51). It stands as the link between the two periods. It linked not only the two types of architecture, but also the two types of educational approaches that made Paris a center of learning. In the eleventh century, Notre Dame's educational reputation depended on its great teachers like William of Champeaux, who lectured "like an angel from heaven," and like Peter Abelard, who wrote, "Constant questioning is the first key to wisdom. For through doubt we are led to

FIGURE 2.52

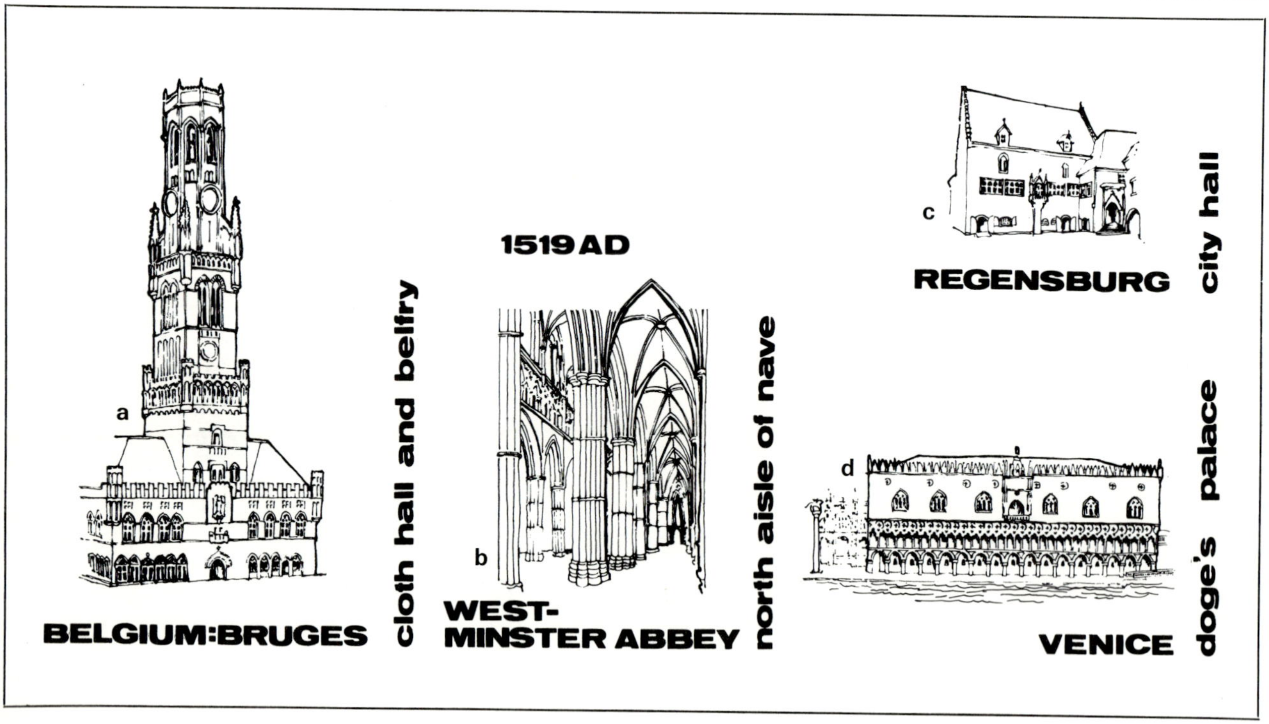

inquiry, and by inquiry we discern the truth."[99] Because of them and others, the tradition of learning became localized in enduring institutions, institutions that eventually became greater than their greatest teachers. The churches at Chartres, Reims, Milan, Westminster and Mont-Saint-Michel are familiar illustrations of Gothic architecture and school development. However, Gothicism in architecture should not be exclusively identified with cathedrals; in many European countries, architecture developed as a result of municipal patronage and set a pattern of organization in buildings whose vestiges still influence town halls and schools today. (See Figure 2.52.)

RENAISSANCE PLANNING AND EDUCATION

Cutting across several centuries in planning, architectural styles, and educational development, the Renaissance developed in various parts of Europe at different times. (See Figure 2.53.) The pace of the life, the new interest in man and prosperous economies led to the reawakening of the concept of man's individuality and innate worth. Great painters, sculptors, architects, planners, inventors and educators populated the cultural centers of the civilized world. The versatile Renaissance man became a standard, and all tried their hands at various disciplines. Michelangelo, Leonardo da Vinci, Pietro Vergerio, Vittorino da Feltre—the first modern schoolmaster—and others are only some of the many who produced the masterpieces that emerged from the Renaissance. (See Figure 2.54.)

The numerous planning contributions to Renaissance building include the straight street forming a vista, the chessboard pattern, the garden design, the "rond point" and new types of squares. The forecourt of St. Peter's piazza (see Figure 2.55), the monumental grouping on the Capitoline Hill in Rome (see Figure 2.56), the Nancy Market Place, the Roman Piazza del Popolo, and the Place des Vosges in Paris are some of the great squares that were laid out

[99]Boyd, p. 137.

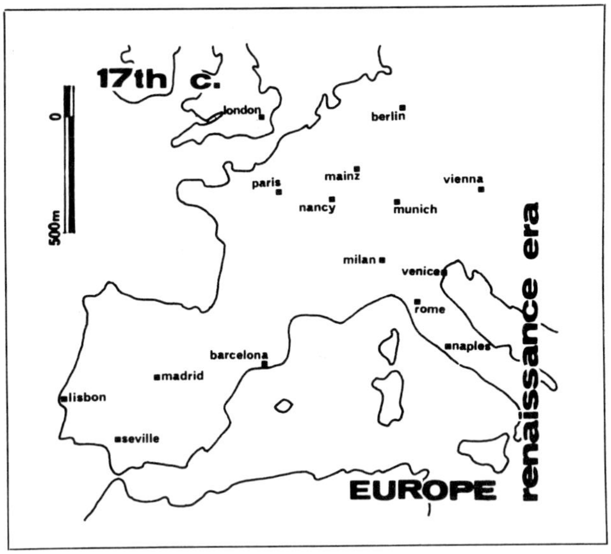

FIGURE 2.53

FIGURE 2.54

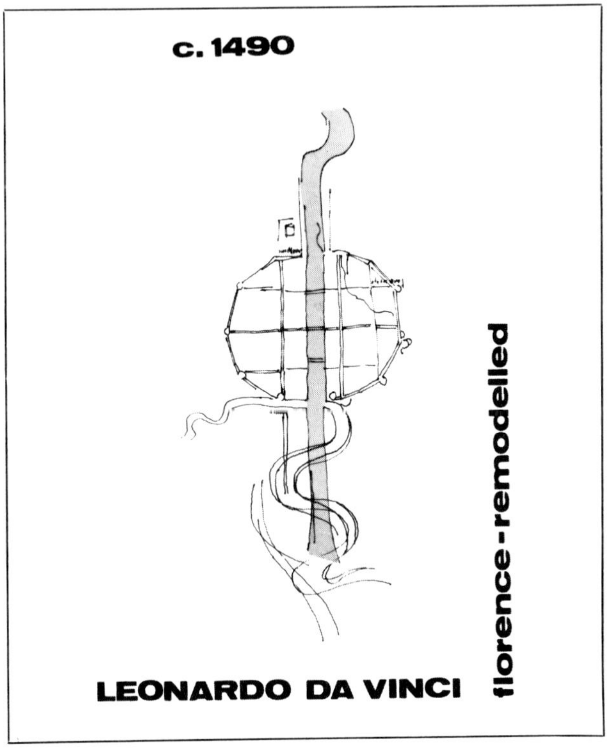

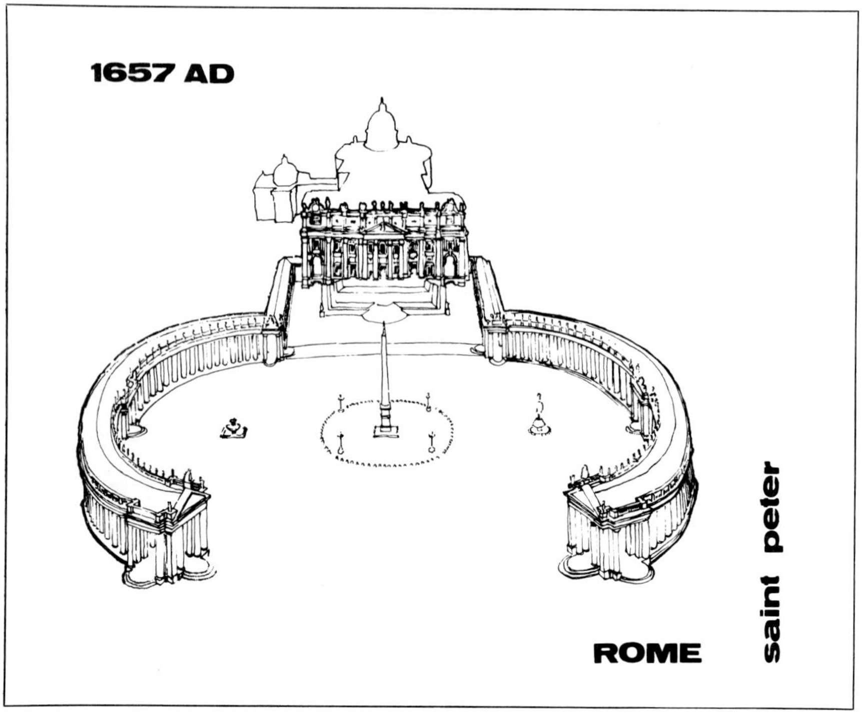

FIGURE 2.55

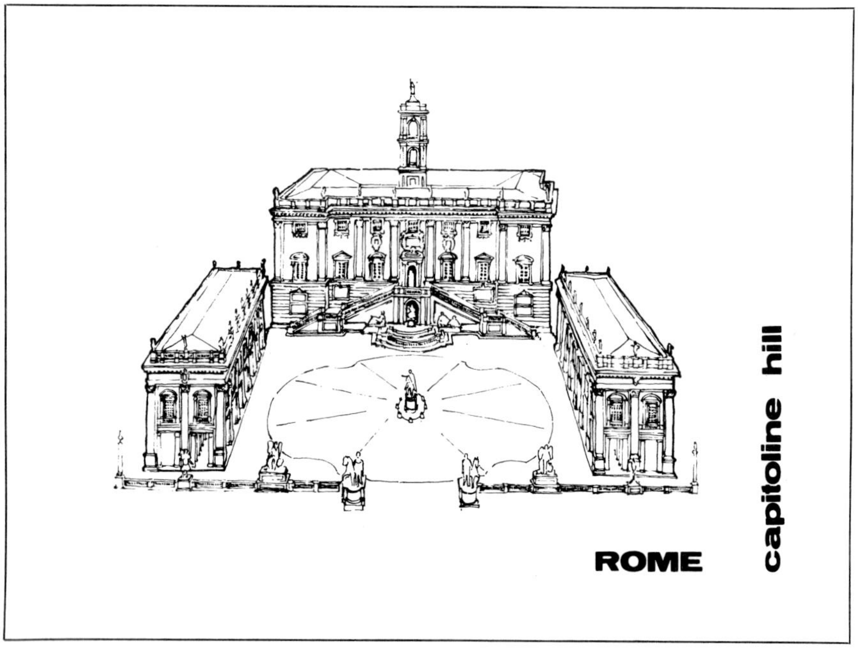

FIGURE 2.56

during the period and that became a distinguishing feature of European cities.

The numerous educational ideas of the Renaissance include the value of an all-round education for the man of affairs, the need to adapt subjects for learning to the individual and to the age of the pupil, the careful organization of schoolwork, the introduction of the humanities into the curriculum and the idea that education is as much a matter of social as of individual concern.

Because few new cities were started in the period, the Renaissance style in planning buildings and education was applied almost exclusively to town extensions and school reconstruction. "Scarcely any new towns were founded except as fortification."[100] This was not true during the Reformation, however, which brought about the creation of a system of schools for every section of the town and the transfer of authority in education from the Church to the State in most parts of western Europe.

This development was in concert with the emerging economic system known as mercantilism. Its theories were prevalent in most of Europe and were especially applied in the establishment of the colonies in the New World.

Mercantilism—sometimes called Colbertism, after its most ardent advocate Colbert (1619–1683), minister of Louis the XIV—is not a system so much as a number of theories about the role of the state and how to procure wealth and power. These aims are to be achieved through economic independence and a favorable trade balance. Consequently, it called for national shipping, a strong navy, protection of home agriculture and industry, and as great a stock of gold and silver as possible.[101]

These activities, along with the Reformation, threw the whole system of education into disorder. An urgent need existed for civic and political leaders plus education suited to the people at large. Schools of a new order were required. The time was past for schools where students spent twenty to thirty years in the study of Donatus, with no thought given to secular knowledge. Expanding political and economic needs called for a new type of education.

Martin Luther led in this movement. If only secular affairs were to be considered, there still was a need for good schools for both boys and girls, so that they might become men to govern the country well and women to manage their households efficiently. "The prosperity of a city . . . does not consist in great treasures, strong walls, and fine houses, but in clever, capable, wise, honorable, well-educated citizens who can acquire, hold, and utilize every treasure and possession."[102] Upon the community, therefore, as well as upon the parents, falls the obligation to educate the youth of the city.

Renaissance architecture was a "geometric clarification of the spirit,"[103] not a wholesale change, but a piecemeal modification of the historic city. The disorder and clutter of urban building that characterized the medieval city became intolerable. Crooked streets darkened by overhanging buildings became the abettors of crime, a growing danger to the citizens. To deal with this, the new planners tore down old buildings, eliminated the crooked streets and replaced them with straight streets and open rectangles—a program similar to that of today's urban renewal.

Such efforts took place in Rome, Florence, Sienna, Pisa, Venice, and so forth. In these cities, architects like Michelangelo, under political mandates, blended Roman, Gothic, and Byzantine features to design elaborate monuments that straddled the straightened streets and symmetrically dressed the new squares and piazzas. (See Figure 2.57.) This dressing was also applied to education. The concept of free personal development bound up in the ideals of social and political life was in most respects never realized. Each element—architecture and education—was used to impose order. Freedom for most individuals remained unfulfilled in civic and national life, and the grandeur of formal façades and higher education remained in the hands of a minority of people. In spite of this restriction, excellent examples of limited planning are seen at St. Peter's Basilica in Rome (see

[100]Korn, p. 58.
[101]Ibid., pp. 59–60.
[102]Boyd, p. 188–189.
[103]Mumford, p. 348.

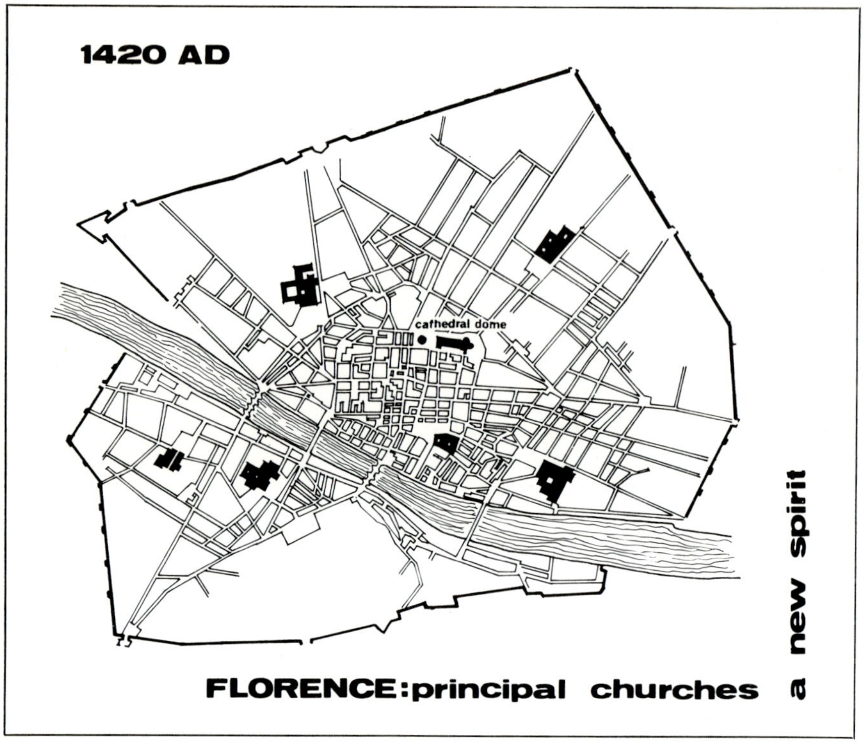

FIGURE 2.57

FIGURE 2.58

Figure 2.55), the Piazza San Marco in Venice (see Figure 2.3), Brunelleschi's Cathedral of Florence (see Figure 2.58), and at the universities of Heidelberg, Bologna, Paris and Prague.

Versailles illustrates, in an excellent way, some of the unique aspects of the Renaissance period. The royal community, designed mainly by Jules Hardouin Mansart, its gardens laid out by Le Notre, is an outstanding example of splendor and power.

> The gardens and grounds are a part of the architectural design, which is of great power and grandeur. The garden slowly falls to the lawns and to the Grand Canal, cruciform in shape, with a length of one mole, with near its western end a circle called the Étoile where eight routes meet. Beyond it the view fades into an endless countryside. The woods spreading out to the right and left are dotted with round clearings, and it is these circular areas with their radiating avenues which have had such a strong influence on eighteenth-century town planning.[104] [See Figure 2.59.]

[104]Korn, p. 61.

FIGURE 2.59

1746 AD

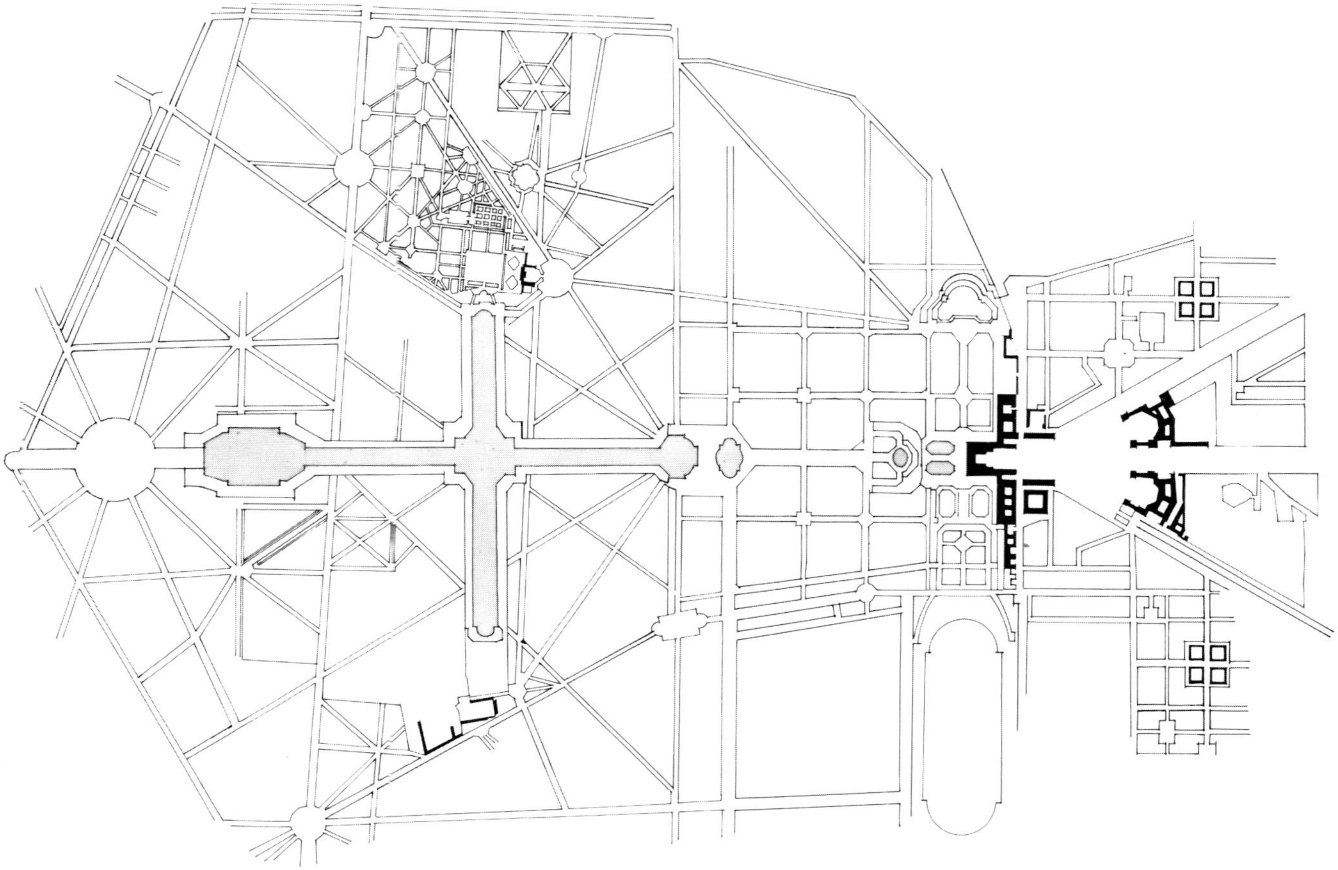

VERSAILLES

the gardens & grounds

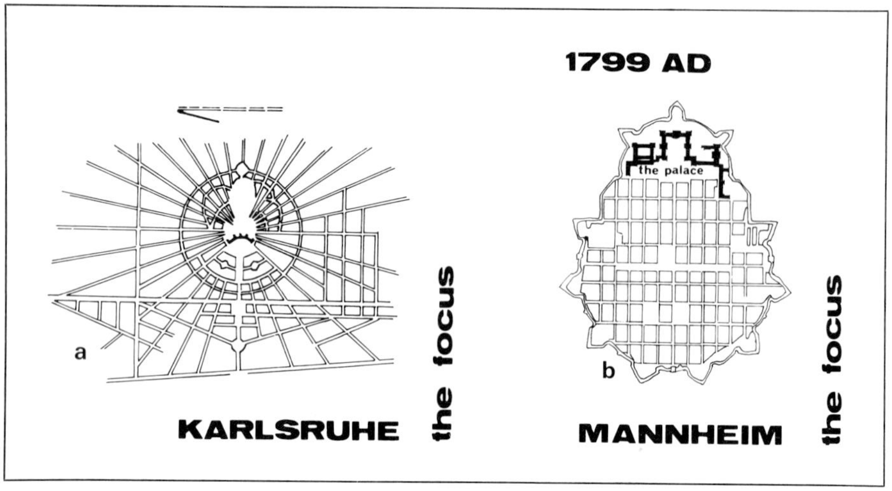

FIGURE 2.60

In addition to being the center of the French court, it was the center of special education. The court of Louis XIV set the social and intellectual fashions for all Europe. Here, highborn youths with their tutors acquired a knowledge of life and manners through personal contact with the French nobility.

The physical layout also became a model for later planning and building. Other cities imitated it, copying in detail from the original as much as economically possible.

Paris and Versailles became the models for the minor despots all over Europe: Pottsdam, Vienna, St. Petersburg and even the smaller sovereigns such as those of Karlsruhe and Mannheim tried to follow these examples. The town became the stage for imposing constructions, vistas, groups of courts, and piazzas, which had been first tried out in the design of the royal parks.[105] [See Figure 2.60.]

Experimentation in planning and education continued during the latter part of the Renaissance.

As the Reformation gave rise to the Counter-Reformation, the naturalism of the Renaissance was replaced with the supernaturalism of the Baroque. The static concept of the Renaissance changed into a dynamic one. This change is well illustrated by the successive alternations of the cathedral and Piazza of Saint Peter's in Rome.

[105]Ibid.

The centric structure, based on the Greek-cross, conceived by Bramante and maintained by Michelangelo, was nearing completion when the decision was made, under Pope Paul V, to substitute the Latin Cross plan suggested by Raphael. Carlo Moderne added the extension in front of the central edifice, following the pattern of Il Gesu, the church of the Jesuits.[106] [See Figure 2.61.]

In education, too, changes resulted from the religious conflicts. The difficulties were least felt in the southern countries of Europe, which remained predominantly Catholic, but were felt increasingly in the Protestant countries of northern Europe. Poorly equipped schools plus badly paid teachers led to educational stagnation over a considerable part of northern and western Europe by the end of the seventeenth century.

BAROQUE PLANNING AND EDUCATION

The baroque style represents an eclectic approach, drawing from various styles of architecture. During the time of Palladio's work, many of the artists were searching for innovative methods of design. They often disregarded established norms and developed innova-

[106]Hilberseimer, p. 179.

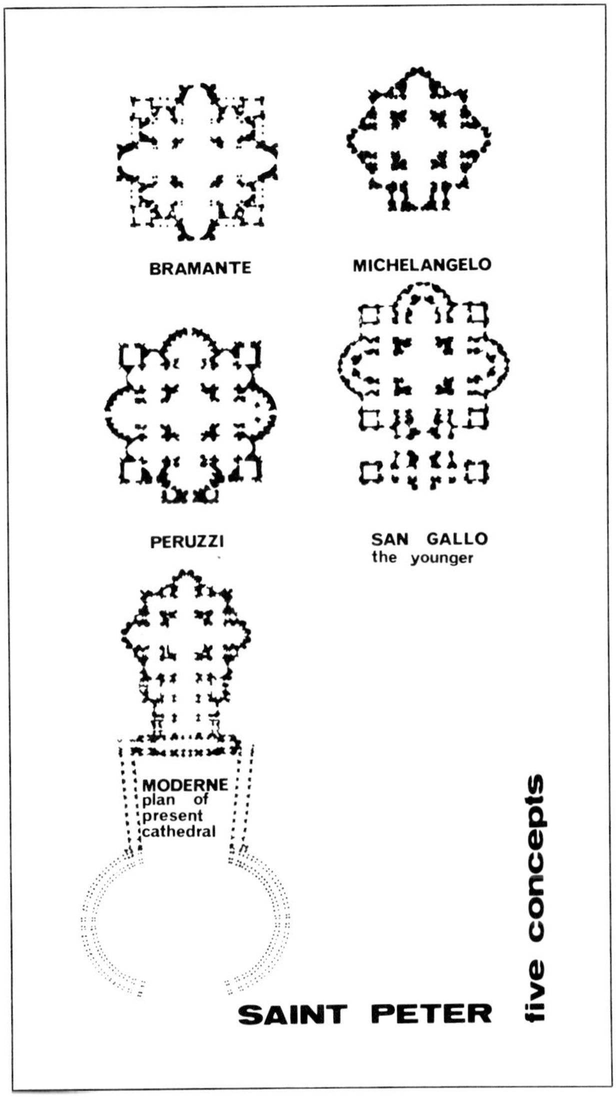

FIGURE 2.61

tive forms. The dominant characteristics of the baroque were its dynamic movement and gaudy display of unbalanced masses and lines. Although most of the buildings characteristically belonging to the period were erected during the seventeenth and eighteenth centuries, their origins can be found earlier in the Renaissance, in the sixteenth century.

Until now, the designers' energy had been applied to the interior form of the building. Having mastered these principles, the designer turned his extra energy to creating a setting for his structure. "Out of this grew the deliberate planning of a network of lines of design energy on a city-wide basis, providing channels for the transmission of the design energy of buildings already built and at the same time creating locations calling for a new design energy in buildings yet to come."[107]

New design energy in education also existed. De la Chalotais' *Essay* and Rousseau's *Émile* created widespread desire for educational reform. One such idea was the call for a comprehensive plan: national support for education, as education was really a matter of public concern. Features such as personalized instruction at the level of the child, greater stress on practical knowledge and emphasis on the mother tongue could be applied more easily in public than in Church-supported schools. The state alone should undertake the education of the future citizens. Remaining, however, was the problem of implementation. "Mirabeau, Talleyrand, Condorcet, Takanal, Lepelletier, Robespierre, Romme, Bauquier, all tried to solve the problem, and all failed."[108]

Reform in physical planning in some states, however, met partial success. One brilliant example was the work of Sixtus V, who became pope in 1585. His idea was to change Rome from a ". . . sprawling, disorderly city into a fitting capital of Christendom."[109] (See Figure 2.62.)

Extending from the Porta del Popolo in the northern wall of the city . . . in the foreground are three converging streets, the

[107]Edmund N. Bacon, *Design of Cities* (New York: Viking Press, 1967), p. 112.
[108]Boyd, p. 313.
[109]Bacon, p. 126.

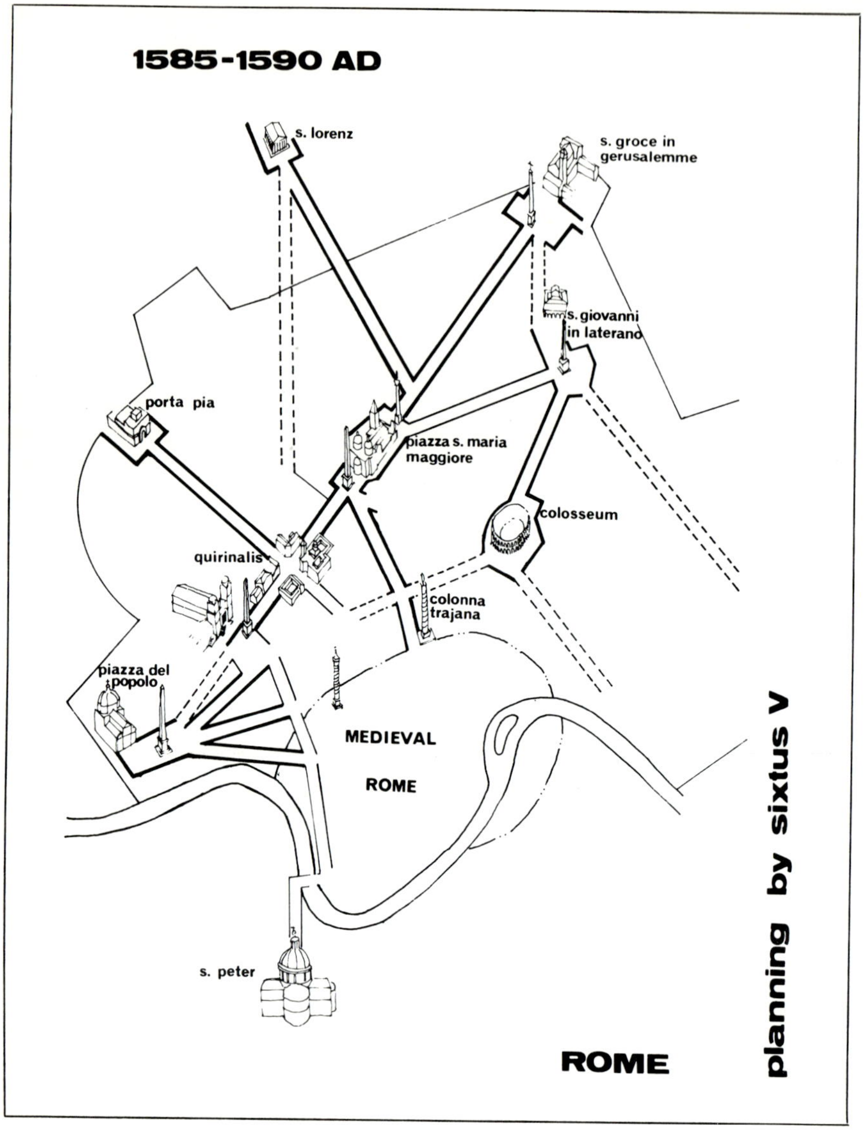

1585-1590 AD
s. lorenz
s. groce in gerusalemme
s. giovanni in laterano
porta pia
piazza s. maria maggiore
colosseum
quirinalis
colonna trajana
piazza del popolo
MEDIEVAL ROME
s. peter
ROME
planning by sixtus V

FIGURE 2.62

right hand one leading to Porto di Rippetta at the Taber River . . . to these streets Sixtus, in his mind's eye, added a fourth one extending directly to Santa Maria Maggiore. . . . Only the portion from San Trinita dei Monti . . . was built and . . . intersected by the old Strada Pia. . . . This connects with the Dioscuri . . . , clearly visible on the Quixinal Hill, and with Michelangelo's Porta Pia. . . .

From Santa Maria Maggiore one new road branches off to Santa Croce . . . and another one reached to San Giovanni in Taterano. From here another route led to the Colosseum.[110]

Sixtus' movement system was a "colossal intellectual feat" of changing a chaotic environment to one of order. His ideas remained strong and valid for over three centuries, as guides for other architects and planners.

By refusing to adhere to accepted standards and, yet, by basing their work on prior experiences, the artists created such works as the cathedral, the Charterhouse Sacristy in Granada, St. Paul's Cathedral in London (see Figure 2.63), the Villa Capra (see Figure 2.64), the Palazzo Iseppo dei Portii in Vicenza and St. Spirito in Florence. As these baroque monuments were built, the cities in turn became shaped by their style.

[110]Ibid., pp. 126–127.

FIGURE 2.63

FIGURE 2.64

The tendency toward openness is characteristic of Baroque cities. The discovery that the city may be open and connected with its landscape and even merge with it is an important one. The traditional concept had been that the city must be a closely built area, densely populated and wholly separated from nature. Now that concept could be abandoned; changes in the the structure of the state and in the methods of warfare aided this development. The great states beginning to emerge had to be defended at their borderlines. Only places of strategic importance needed to be fortified. Most cities could develop without the limitations of defense requirements. Older cities could expand beyond their walls. New cities could be built with no thought of fortifications. Kings and princes saw these new possibilities quickly and took advantage of them. Versailles and Karlsruhe demonstrated that the new princely cities could be closely related to and even interpreted by the landscape around them.[111]

In keeping with this new trend of openness in physical planning, education followed suit. Marquis de Condorcet gave three reasons. First, every citizen must be able to discharge his duties without dependency on others. Second, each citizen should make the fullest contribution possible to the well-being of his

[111]Hilberseimer, pp. 185–187.

society. Third, the perfectibility of mankind depends on education.

The term *baroque* is derived from the Portuguese word *barroco* denoting the irregular shape of a pearl. The acceptance of the baroque style was shown by the rapidity with which it spread throughout Europe in the seventeenth and eighteenth centuries. Its influence, as a model, spread widely, even to the designing and building of a new capitol, at Washington, D.C. As an educational model, the influence of the baroque style shaped the national programs of most of the nations of western Europe.

THE INDUSTRIAL AGE AND EDUCATION

The work of many centuries in planning architecture and education (PAE) seems to have been lost almost overnight. The Industrial Age arrived at a time when many modes of PAE were already present in the cities. Most of the aesthetic beauty existing in the various modes of PAE became lost in the maze of chaotic rubble. Yet, this industrial era had a profound effect on planning and education. Planners had many variables with which to work, including the change in scale, the unrestricted massing of populations, the concentration of industries and a conglomeration of quantity without quality. Robert Owen, a leading industrialist,

> realized that the self-made man postulated by economists and accepted by current opinion was a mere abstraction, since for the most part environmental conditions determined individual destinies. In order to improve the lot of the individual, the reformer had therefore to start with the environment which must be recreated in order to favor the individual before thought was given to any economic advantage, whether individual or collective.[112]

In organizing a factory community containing five hundred pauper children, Owen changed the whole character of the place by use of a variety of methods, including a free school for all children between the ages of five and ten. He, therefore, developed the thesis that the difference between good and bad men resolves itself into a difference of education. As a result, a community has its destiny in its own hands. (See Figure 2.65.)

With the mass movement to the cities and the vast amount of building came the dirtiness and ugliness so often depicted by such writers as Blake, Dickens and Goldsmith. The problems of the industrial city have

[112]Leonardo Benevolo, *The Origins of Modern Town Planning* (Cambridge, Mass.: M.I.T. Press, 1967), pp. 39–40.

FIGURE 2.65

been scrutinized, especially by two schools of varying thought.

One adhered to the view that planning must start again from scratch . . . ; the other that each problem must be dealt with, and each defect remedied, separately, without taking into account their inter-relationship and without having any overall vision of the town as a single organism. . . . The so-called Utopians—Owen, St. Simon, Fauvier, Cabet, Godin—belonged to the first group, though they did not merely write about their ideal cities, like More, Campanella or Bacon, but agitated for their realization in practical terms. The second group included the specialists and officials who introduced the new health regulations and services into the towns and who, because they had to find the technical and legalistic means to implement these improvements, laid the real foundations of modern town planning legislation.[113]

Although industrial growth and development affected the town substantially, town planning did produce considerable consequences for the prolifera-tion of urban communities. Among other effects, consideration was especially given to social problems.

Modern town planning is not merely an attempt to represent the process in visual terms by transposing its application to the problems of the use of space, but must also be regarded as a vital factor in the creation of a democratic society. Viewed in this way, town planning loses both the position which it had hitherto occupied in the shadow of absolute power, and its apparent ability to regulate the balance of the various forms of community ideally and definitely. It appears in a more humble guise as one of the techniques necessary to determine this balance and its aim is no longer the instant achievement of formal perfection, but a series of partial alterations, a reasonable compromise between the forces involved, a compromise which varies continually according to the changing relationships of these forces.[114]

The main elements of an industrial town were the factory, the railroad and the slum. (See Figure 2.66.) The development of the industrial society within a laissez-faire economic system occurred at its own rate. No particular segment of the industrial complex developed at the same time or at the same pace as any other segment. For quite some time, the factory was

[113]Ibid., p. xii.
[114]Ibid., p. 34.

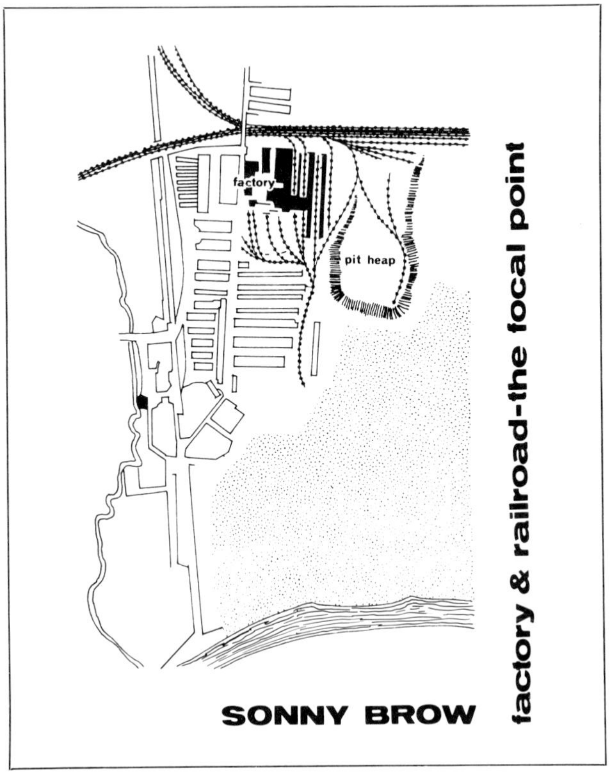

FIGURE 2.66

kept in the home. It was after the factory was central-ized for economy's sake that the great urban catas-trophe occurred. With so much growth and moving from the rural communities, the small towns were left desolate, and the factory towns were faced with an influx of people who were without housing. Thus came about the overcrowded and rundown slum areas fre-quently associated with industrial complexes.

Every other detail of life is subordinated to it. Even the utilities, such as the water supply, and the minimum of governmental offices that were necessary to a town's existence often, if they had not been built by an earlier generation, entered belatedly; an afterthought. It was not merely art and religion that were treated by the utilitarian as mere embellishments: intelligent political administration long remained in the same category. In the first scramble of exploitation, no provisions would be made for police and fire

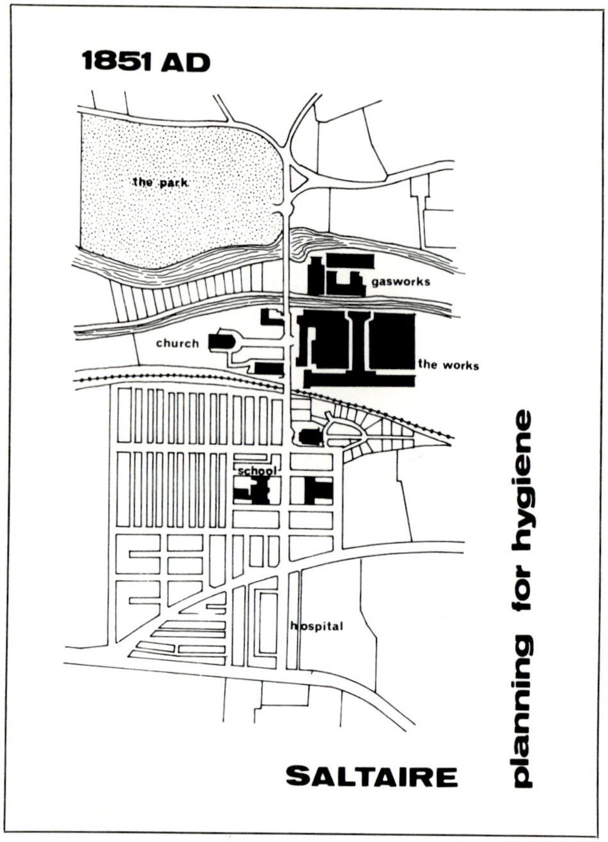

FIGURE 2.67

protection, water and food inspection, hospital care, or education.[115]

This rather dismal evaluation of the early industrial towns was further elaborated on by Wilhelm Heinrich Riehl who said, "No period was more impoverished than the eighteenth century in the development of a common community spirit; the medieval community was dissolved and the modern was not yet ready. . . ."[116]

All industrial development, however, was not bleak. A few enlightened industrialists, like Sir Titus Salt, built new communities such as his Saltaire to house workers. Salt believed in both religious and secular education as a means of improving the workingman's approach to life. He provided for both. On the main street above the factory in his town, he built schools that served both as recreational and educational facilities. (See Figure 2.67.)

The above represented the rare exception of planning and education. In most cases, the factory became the primary focal point. It usually claimed and used the best town sites. The early industrialist was typically unconcerned about the disruption of the natural topography or about ecology. The railroad carried into the heart of the city not only noise and soot, but also industrial plants. With these factories came more soot, dirt, filth, and horrendous living conditions. However, the factory worker was not the only one affected; pure disregard and the lack of technical knowledge ensured the ruin of the natural surroundings. The human became downtrodden and abused, and the rivers were polluted with chemical and physical wastes.

Every mistake in urban design that could be made was made by the new railroad engineers for whom the movement of trains was more important than human objects achieved by that movement. The wastage of space by railroad yards in the heart of the city only furthered its more rapid extension outward, and this in turn, since it produced more railroad traffic, gave the extra sanction of profits to the misdemeanors so committed.[117]

Birmingham, England, was described in the 1850's as follows:

. . . in no town in the world are the mechanical arts more noisy: hammerings incessantly on the anvil; there is an unending clang of engines; flame rustles, water hisses, steam roars, and from time to time hoarse and hollow, rises the thunder of the proofing house [where firearms are tested]. The people lived in an atmosphere vibrating with clamor; and it would seem as if their amusement had caught the general tone, and become noisy, like their inventions.[118]

The rapid growth of towns around the factories created health problems.

The new industrial environment was so glaringly lacking in the attributes of health that it is hardly any wonder that the counter-movement of hygiene provided the most positive

[115]Mumford, pp. 458–59.
[116]Ibid., p. 454.

[117]Ibid., p. 416.
[118]Ibid., p. 473.

contributions to town planning during the nineteenth century. The new ideals were provisionally embodied in a Utopia, called " Hygeia, or the City of Health " : brought forth by Dr. Benjamin Ward Richardson in 1875.[119]

Of course, the hygienic movement did not resolve the problems overnight. The industrial wastes, the air pollution, in addition to the toxic conditions associated with some factories, persisted. These problems exist today, and society, since the beginning of the century, is still demanding a solution of its planners.

To bring back fresh air, pure water, green open space and sunlight to the city became the first object of sound planning; the need was so pressing that despite his passion for urban beauty, Camillo Sitte insisted upon *hygienic* function of the urban park, as a *sanitary green*, to use his own expression....[120]

The problem of enforcement of sanitary conditions was of early interest. Sanitary legislation was the direct forerunner of modern town-planning legislation. The concern for sanitary conditions, however, was not new.

For the first time sanitary improvements, made originally in the Sumerian and Cretan palaces and extended to the patrician families of Rome at a later date, were now made available to the entire population of the city. This was a triumph of democratic principles that even dictatorial regimes could not inhibit: indeed, one of the greatest public benefits conferred by the overthrow of the Second French Republic, was in the redoubtable cleaning up of Paris under Baron Haussman, a service far more essential, indeed far more original than any of his more famous acts of town planning proper.[121] [See Figure 2.68.]

Side effects of the Industrial Revolution touched all aspects and activities of man. It transformed his whole relationship to all other men for all time to come. The fruits of the successful industrialist's industry were usually spent to better his own physical environment. His houses

... were the usual spacious, urban houses, with regular, often square, ground plans and high ceilinged rooms.... The principle of laissez faire was applied by the new urban

[119]Ibid., p. 478.
[120]Ibid., p. 475.
[121]Mumford, p. 477.

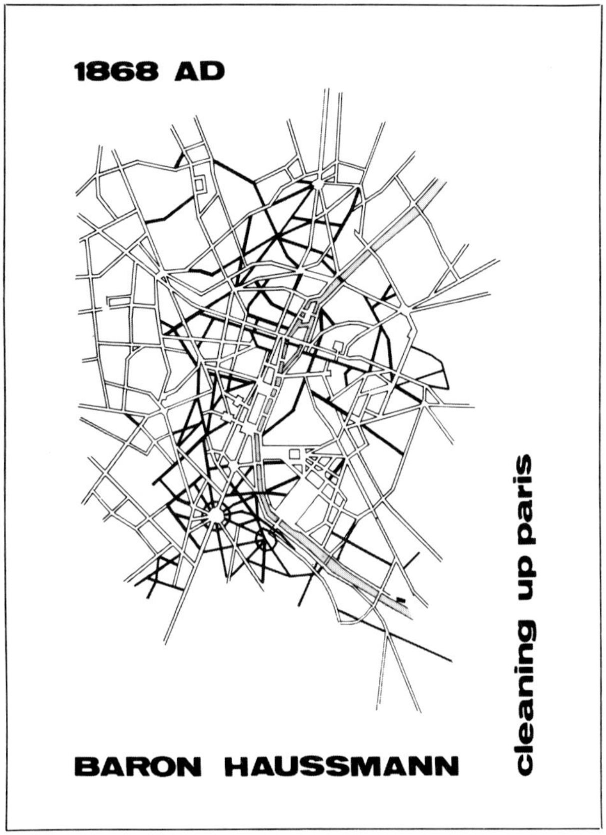

FIGURE 2.68

planners to both the environment and the buildings of man. The Romantic order was a revolt against order [see Figure 2.69] : a relief from the implacable necessities of a monotonous and often over-regimented daily routine. This exaggeration of playfulness and spontaneity with its rejection of traditional guidances and workmanlike disciplines, finally made its way into the education of the young.[122]

Success in industry was plainly attributable to efficient schools and technical training. Industrial prosperity, therefore, depended largely on mutually supporting endeavors. As a result, a parallel revolution also occurred in education. Education was seen as largely taking place in publicly supported schools, inseparable from public investment and legislation

[122]Ibid., p. 489.

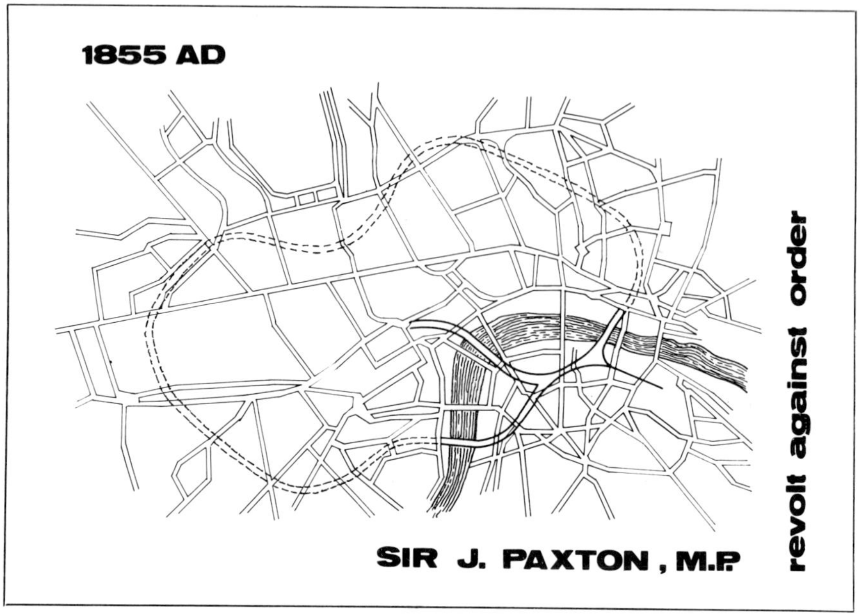

FIGURE 2.69

and intimately linked with electoral and economic prospects. Education was socially comprehensive. Education was positively linked with social and technological changes which were required if the Industrial Revolution was to continue reaching new levels of accomplishment.

In the late 1800's, some change began to take place in planning and education. For Camillo Sitte, city planning was an art of pure arrangement. (See Figure 2.70.) Fascinated with perspective, especially as provided by the baroque vistas, Sitte insisted that the city should be a work of architecture, to be conceived three-dimensionally. The character of the city lay in its public spaces with their rhythmic interrelationships. In summary, urban design to Sitte ". . . consisted in the arrangement of spaces in appealing and useful patterns and sequences, rather than the division of a site into building blocks separated by traffic arteries, as in a grid-system."[123]

The Austrian Engineers and Architects Association published an article on the lack of order in city planning in 1877 during the Ringstrasse project construction era. (See Figure 2.71.)

> The design of a city plan in its entirety, as well as in its detail, is an eminently artistic matter. City plans and city expansions are not accomplished with compass and ruler; needed are, as in all artistic tasks, ideas first of all and secondly a thorough understanding of the requirements of a metropolis and the demands of modern living—but also, and especially so, a sensitive feeling for space and an understanding of form.[124]

So we see emerging, by the end of the nineteenth century, a reaction against the ugliness of the industrial towns and an attempt once again to bring some symmetry and beauty into the overall planning and education.

THE GARDEN CITY CONCEPT

An important factor in the growth and development of urban planning was the concept of the Garden City. (See Figure 2.72.) In terms of form and design and aesthetic qualities, the Garden City added to the

[123]George R. Collins and Christine Craseman Collins, *Camillo Sitte and the Birth of Modern City Planning* (New York: Random House, 1965), p. 52.

[124]Ibid., p. 41.

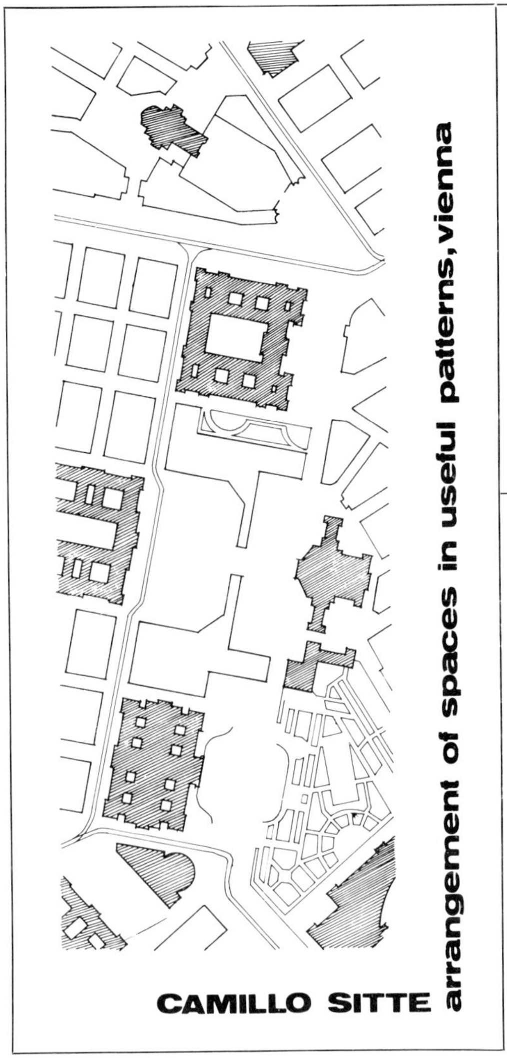

FIGURE 2.70

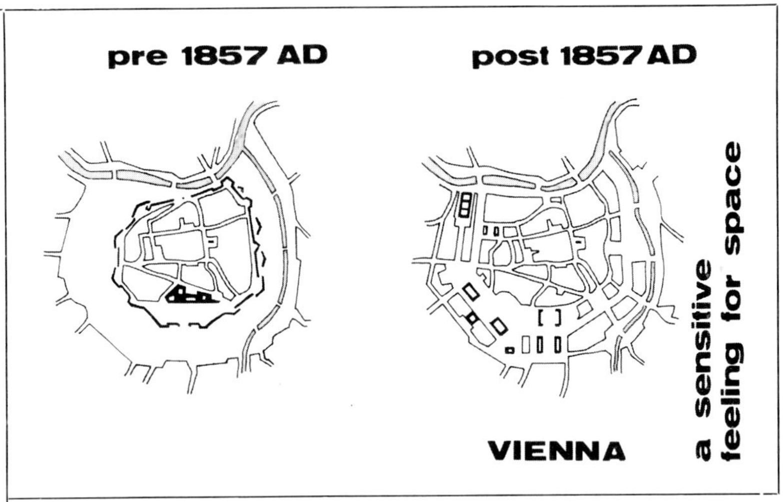

FIGURE 2.71

aesthetic appeal of the modern city. In 1919, the Garden Cities and Towns' Planning Association defined the Garden City as "a town designed for healthy living and industry; of a size that makes possible a full measure of social life, but no larger; surrounded by a rural belt; the whole of the land being in public ownership or held in trust for the community."[125]

[125]Ebenezer Howard, *Garden Cities of Tomorrow* (London: Faber and Faber, 1946), p. 26.

Sir Ebenezer Howard actually thought of the term *Garden City* as applying to a city in a garden, as well as a city of gardens. He was able to get a comprehensive view of the planning concept by exploring the whole problem of urban development. Howard also gave consideration to physical, social and economic functions, as well as to the integration of urban and rural patterns for the purpose of improving both urban life and rural life. Foreseeing the expansion of the municipalities, Howard was concerned about the potential

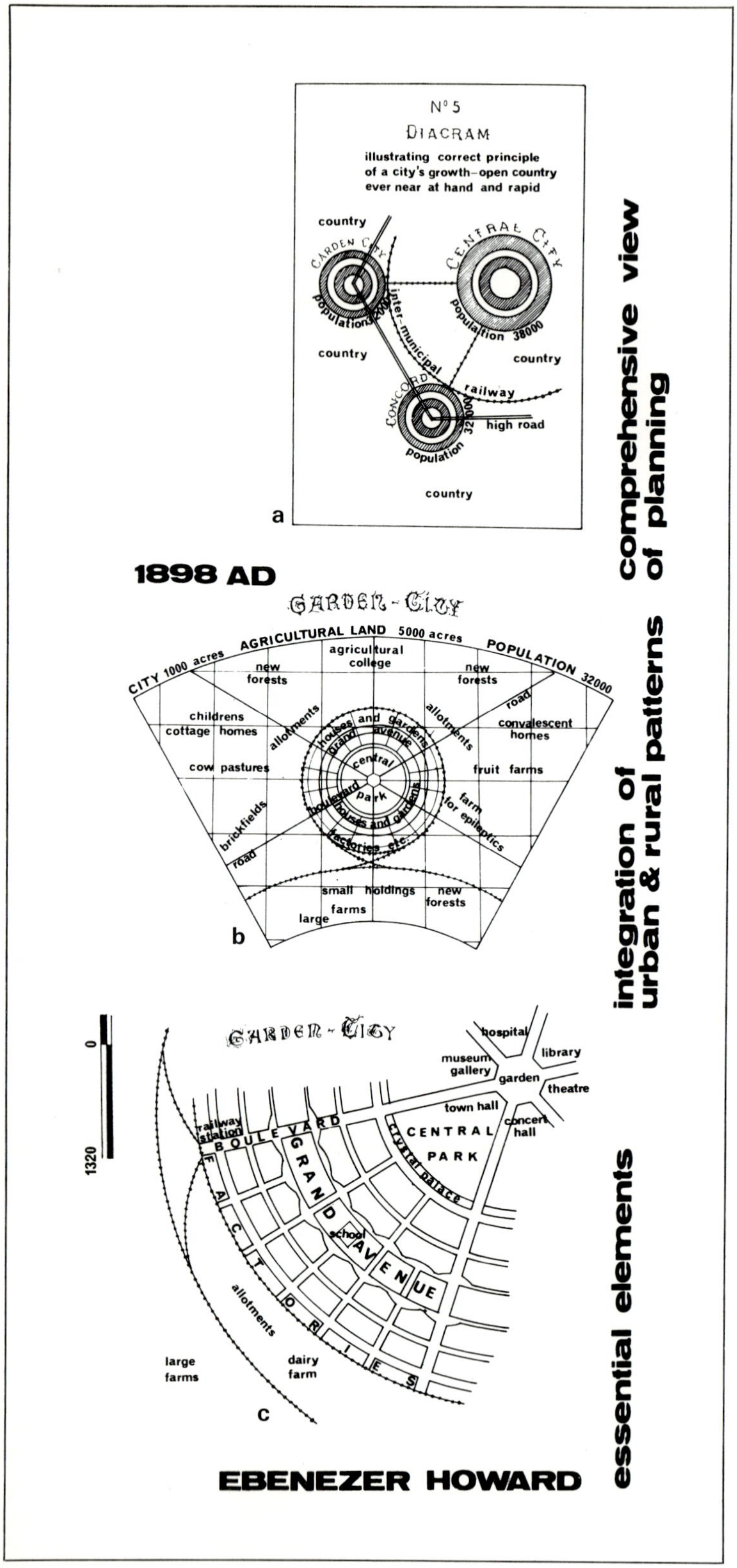

N° 5
DIAGRAM
illustrating correct principle of a city's growth—open country ever near at hand and rapid
country
GARDEN CITY
CENTRAL CITY
population 32000
population 38000
inter-municipal railway
country
country
CONCORD
population 32000
high road
country
a
1898 AD
GARDEN-CITY
CITY 1000 acres
AGRICULTURAL LAND 5000 acres
POPULATION 32000
agricultural college
new forests
new forests
childrens cottage homes
allotments
houses and gardens
grand avenue
central park
allotments
convalescent homes
road
cow pastures
fruit farms
brickfields
boulevard
houses and gardens
farm for epileptics
factories etc.
road
small holdings
new forests
large farms
b
0
1320
GARDEN-CITY
hospital
library
museum gallery
garden
theatre
town hall
concert hall
railway station
BOULEVARD
CENTRAL PARK
crystal palace
GRAND AVENUE
school
FACTORIES
allotments
large farms
dairy farm
c
EBENEZER HOWARD
comprehensive view of planning
integration of urban & rural patterns
essential elements

FIGURE 2.72

conflict of free enterprise and social control; his experimental concepts helped to integrate the two. "Howard's prime contribution was to outline the nature of the balanced community and to show what steps were necessary in an ill-organized and disoriented society to bring it into existence."[126]

Howard attempted solutions to the problems associated with overpopulated metropolitan areas: health, slums and inefficiency due to misplaced industries. He was concerned with the problem of continuity between urban and rural areas. He sought "... a marriage of town and country, of rustic health and sanity and activity and urban knowledge, urban technical facility, urban political co-operation."[127]

The essential elements of Howard's Garden City movement included:

1 Moderate-sized industrial and trading towns in close contact with a surrounding agricultural countryside, each a healthy, well-equipped and coherent community;
2 Zoning of areas within each town for ready access between home, workplaces, shops and cultural centers;
3 Limitation of density to safeguard light, gardens and

[126]Ibid., p. 33.

[127]Ibid., p. 34.

FIGURE 2.73

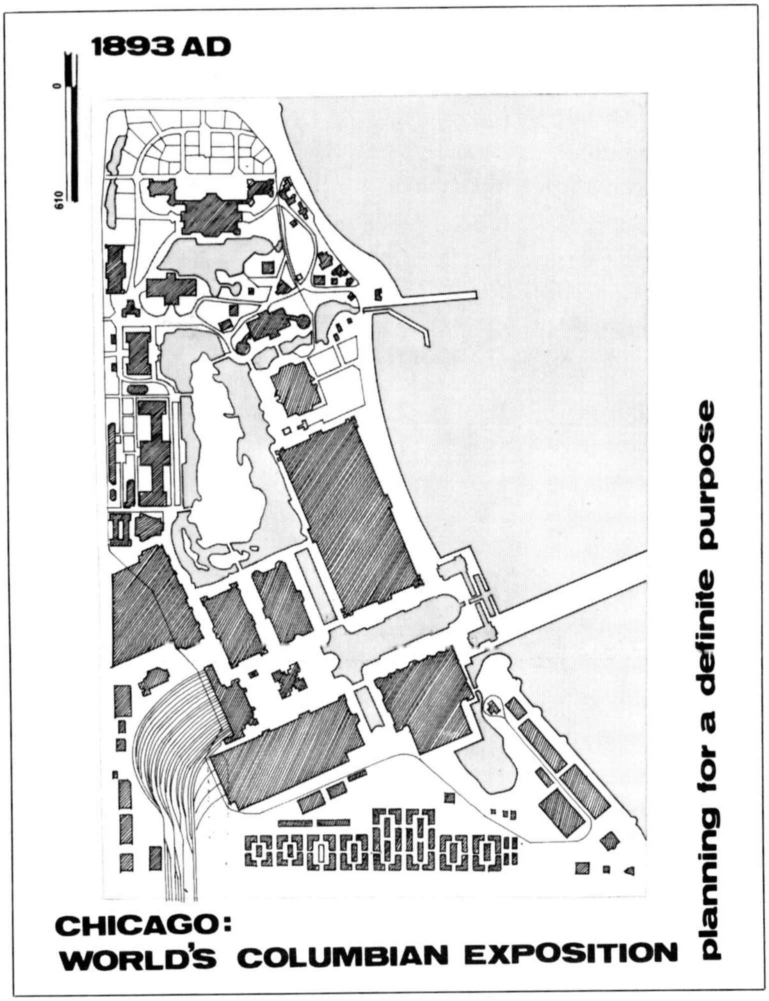

recreation space, but not exaggerated to the pitch of urban diffusion;
4 Civic design aiming at harmony rather than standardization;
5 Planned internal and external communications;
6 Unified site-ownership coupled with leaseholds, reconciling public interests with freedom of choice and enterprise.[128]

Another major contribution to the Garden City concept was the introduction of the theory of public ownership of land for town extensions, which assures both continuity and quality of design and urban form.

THE MEANING OF PLANNING AND EDUCATION TODAY

In tracing the historical development of planning and education, we have indicated their close relationship to the field of architecture and physical construction. Today's planning and educational efforts have substantially grown from the former, strictly piecemeal, or one-shot, efforts at solution to social problems.

[128]Ibid., p. 24.

FIGURE 2.74

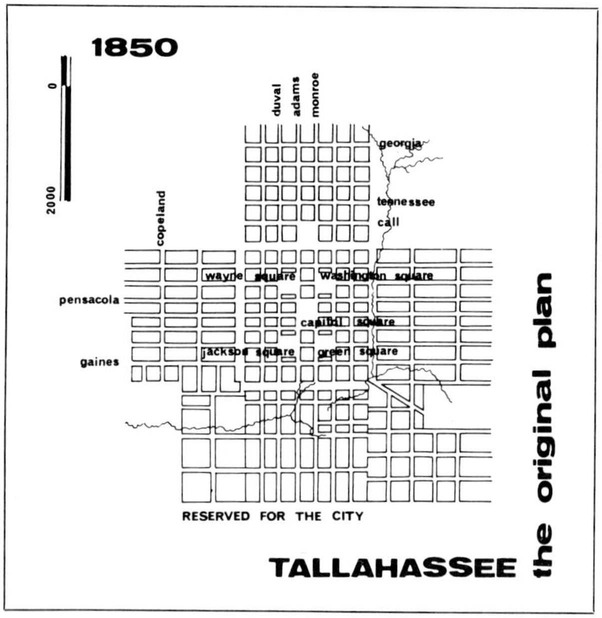

FIGURE 2.75

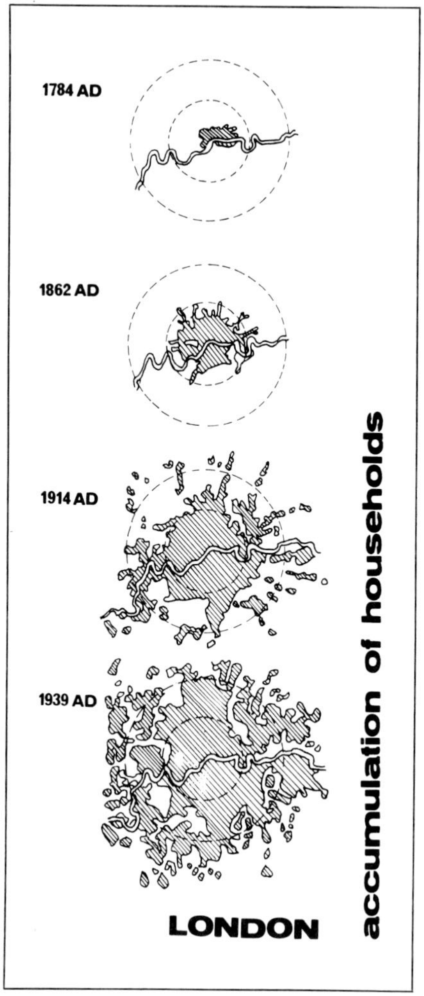

"Today it is properly taken to refer to 'any definite intention or undertaking', and as such it applies to almost everything people do."[129] (See Figure 2.73.) The meaning of the term *planning* has been substantially modified since its introduction about three hundred years ago.

The word "planning" derives from the Latin *planus*, meaning flat, and it first entered the English language in the 17th century. At that time it had a narrow and specific meaning,

[129]Brian W. Scott, *Long-Range Planning in American Industry* (New York: American Management Association, 1965), p. 18.

FIGURE 2.76

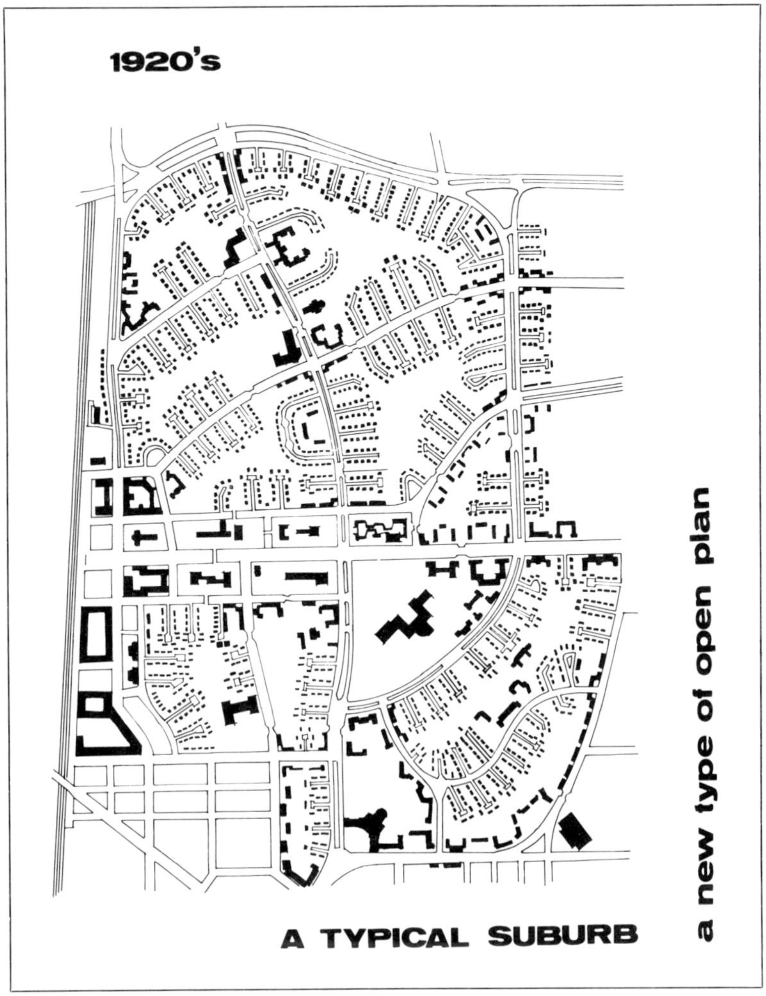

describing the act of drawing or sketching an object on a flat surface, such as the drawing of a blueprint.[130] [See Figure 2.74.]

In contrast, the term *education* has remained relatively true to its original meaning, which is "to lead forth," from the Latin *educere*. By combining *planus* with *educere*, a return to the basic concepts associated with planning and with educating—to lead forth with a proposed method of action—gives a new view of how to cope with the complex problems associated with transferring proliferating knowledge to an ever-growing heterogeneous population.

Recently, the terms *planning* and *education* have increasingly taken on connotations from the systems concept, in which the interaction of many variables are involved. The location of a given subsystem, such as a school within a community, necessitates analysis and planning that deals with land usage, transportation, curriculum offerings, community values and other tangible and intangible factors. Because planning and education have taken on a greater social orientation, the modern educational planner is also

[130]Ibid.

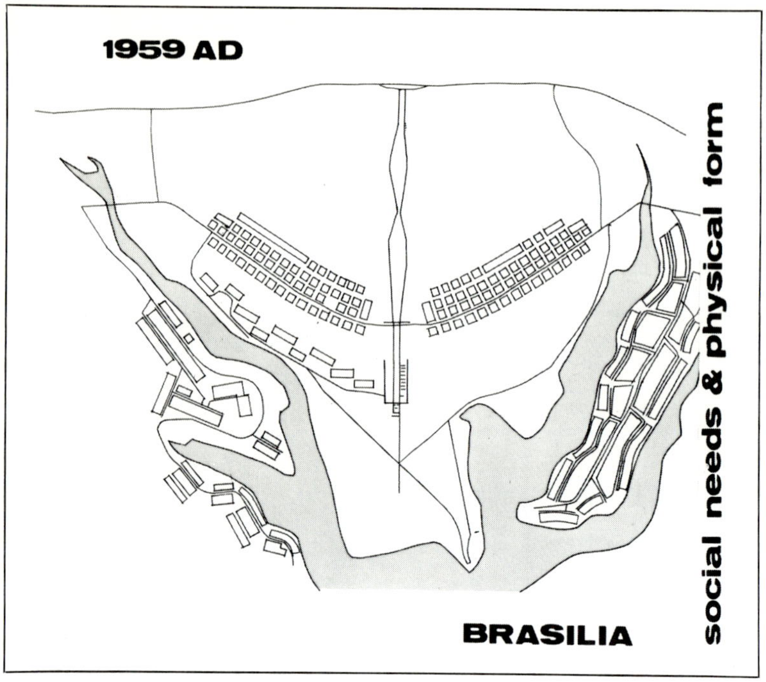

FIGURE 2.77

faced with problems associated with the socio-economic community, politics and the psychological characteristics of the people affected by educational planning. "At this point the facts call for a new confrontation of the respective programs of town planning and politics, to try and bridge the gulf that opened between them a hundred years ago. This is the task that faces us today."[131]

As we have seen in the historical development of planning and education, cities and education have undergone and are still undergoing perpetual change. (See Figure 2.75.)

> The City today is in the throes of another change, and it is enormously important that we should recognize what this change implies.... The main characteristics have been (1) *Protection*, (2) *Religious* or *Political*, (3) *Mercantile*, (4) *Manufacturing*. The fifth state which we are now entering is called *Servicing*, and it is a direct result of the accumulation of households that the earlier states encouraged.[132]

The ordinary schools have failed to keep up with the changes wrought in the structure of society by the Industrial Revolution. They have done little to make good the grave loss of educational opportunities to children that the spread of urban expansion has brought. This changing educational environment has yet to be met by a changing educational system.

Changes are clearly evident in the present expansion and development of our cities and education, particularly in the direction of suburban development. (See Figure 2.76.)

> Though the suburb lacked many of the attributes of the ancient city, it has served as an experimental field for the development of a new type of open plan and a new distribution of urban functions.
>
> Thus the suburb has prepared the way for a better order of planning, not yet fully expressed or achieved anywhere, in which both the static and dynamic functions, those of the container and the magnet, would find fresh expression. Though the suburb, as such, belongs to the past and has already been developed by the conurbation, some of the lessons that modern planners first mastered in the suburb must be incorporated into the new concept of the city.[133]

[131]Benevolo, p. 147.
[132]Tunnard, p. 19.

[133]Mumford, pp. 486–487.

While increasing in size, urban areas have also increased in complexity. The typical problems of most major urban areas are traffic congestion, depressed housing, the inadequacy and unequal distribution of open spaces and schools and the indiscriminately mixed development of incompatible urban activities. These characteristics are a function of rapid growth and the lack of appropriate planning.

The more constricted the old quarters of the city, the more closely packed its streets and houses, the greater was the visual relief of the suburb's openness: indeed part of the esthetic value of the suburb, its special psychological virtue, springs from the daily shuttling to and from the city, with its alternation of openness and enclosure, freedom and constriction, easy movement and clogged traffic, spaciousness and overcrowding. All the inherent esthetic values of the suburb are sharpened by these contrasts.[134]

The overt conflicts between planning and education have appeared in the actual buildings. In them, conflicts have arisen between social needs and what the architectural designers deemed necessary. (See Figure 2.77.) These conflicts have focused primarily on the inherent conflict between the cost of housing utilitarian requirements and personal aesthetic criteria. Utilitarian needs were emphasized following the Industrial Revolution.

... the ancient and vital art of architecture was threatened by powerful disintegrative forces. With respect to utilitarian needs, the traditional techniques of construction eventually fell hopelessly short of meeting the requirements and taking advantage of the opportunities presented by the new age of mechanized industrialization. Architectural revivalism struggled bravely with the social and technical forces of the age and frequently produced functionally successful and aesthetically valid works of building art, but as the century moved on revivalism grew increasingly out of touch with the realities of the time. [See Figure 2.78.] The ultimate artistic failure of architecture in the nineteenth century can be stated

[134]Ibid., p. 488.

FIGURE 2.78

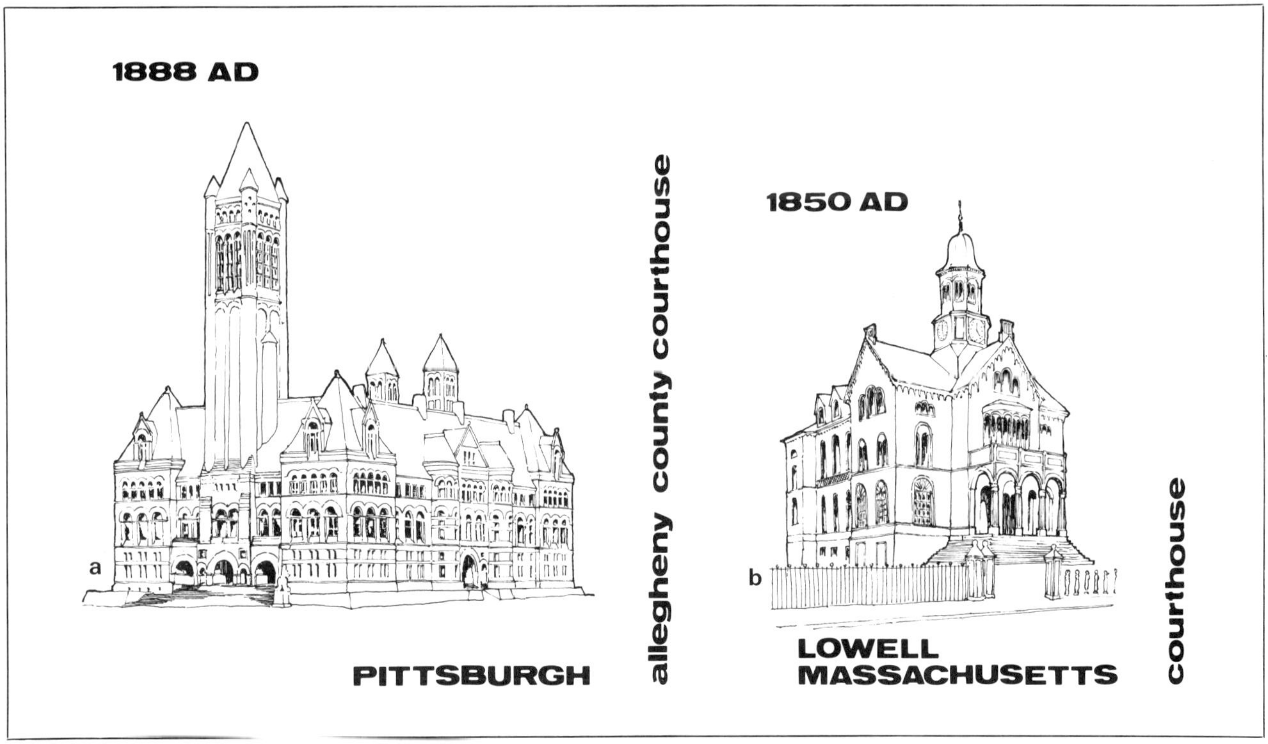

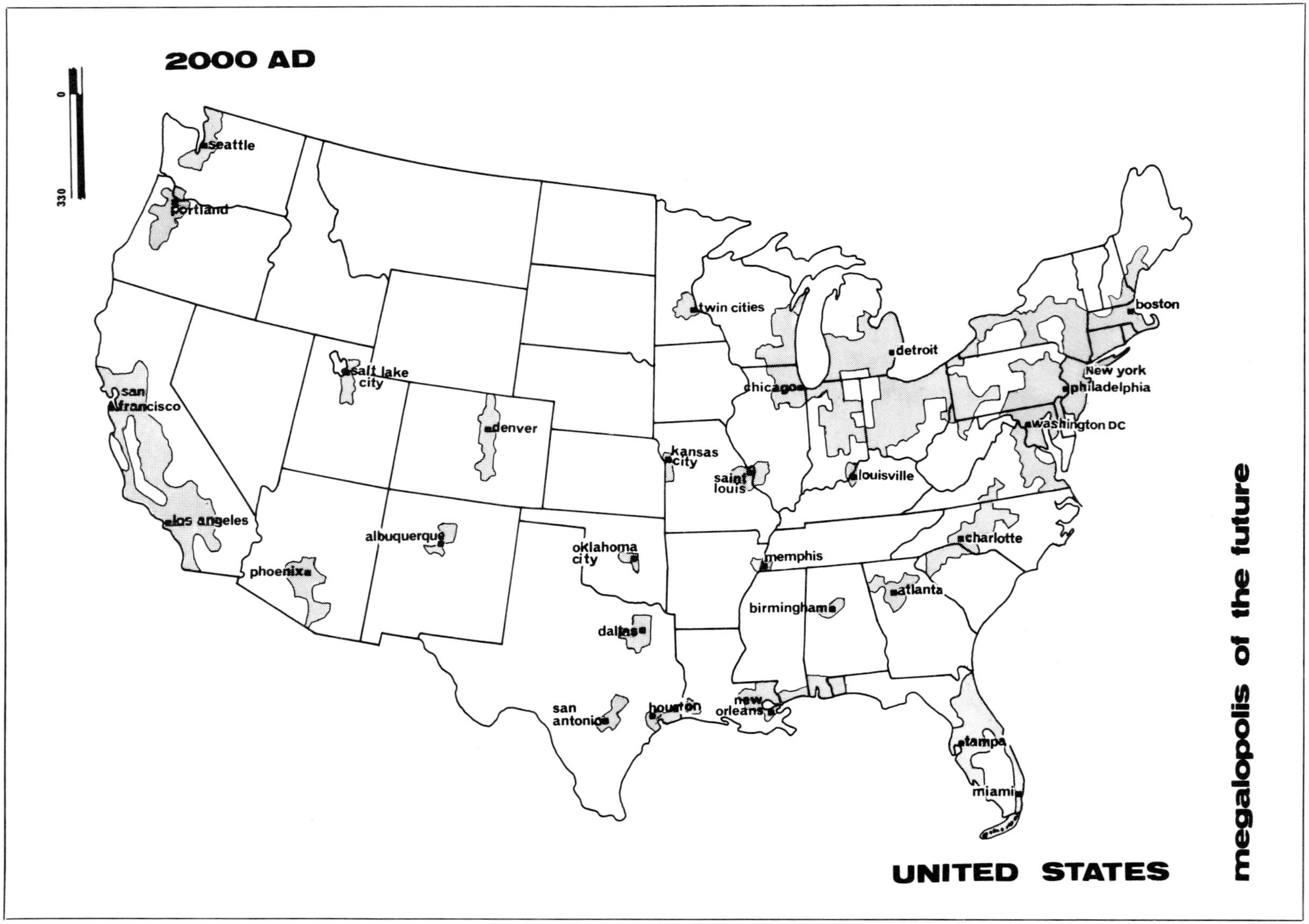
2000 AD
0
330
seattle
portland
san francisco
los angeles
phoenix
salt lake city
denver
albuquerque
oklahoma city
dallas
san antonio
houston
kansas city
saint louis
twin cities
chicago
detroit
louisville
memphis
birmingham
new orleans
atlanta
charlotte
tampa
miami
washington DC
philadelphia
New york
boston
UNITED STATES
megalopolis of the future

FIGURE 2.79

> very simply as the failure to form a consistent style. It was the failure to provide, in its own vocabulary, an aesthetic discipline that would combine the expression of science, technology, mechanized industry, and modern urban life with the deeper-lying emotional needs of the human spirit.[135]

This failure was also true of education. Educational and planning facilities were not necessarily the products of professional ignorance at the time the problem occurred. The complex and impressive challenges that planners and educators faced were so extreme that their talents were spent in finding ways in which known architectural and educational forms could be adapted to fit new exigencies. In most cases, solutions were developed after the fact and in most cases never really solved the problem.

Social commitment and technological know-how transcend the limitations imposed on past problems. Education, health, environment and technology have been shown to be inseparable. Education for the future cannot be simple schooling that extends only from the ages of seven to twenty-two. The pluralistic nature of modern society, the different levels of personal development, the increasing extension of personal and collective contacts and the acceleration of change make education now a total and lifetime activity.

No such thing as leaving education to chance can exist if our society is to avoid chaos. The growth of conurbations makes nonsense of any claim to complete community independence. (See Figure 2.79.) Suburban privileges, with pampered schools close to golf and country clubs and at an increasing intellectual distance from center-city schools, will produce yet another gap for allocating the public's limited resources. Some resources have already been applied to cities being built from scratch to become educative communities for learning-by-living. Their numbers and problems are still too scant to influence existing educational physical problems in established communities. In them, five main problems remain to be solved. First, what can be done to bring educational activities into closer relation to other urban activities, and what change will be required of the present physical facilities? Second, what can be done subject-wise that will have positive value and real significance with regard to personal participation within urban environments, and what kinds of physical housing will be required for them? Thirdly, how can instruction in the various subjects be more closely related to the student's own everyday experiences and occupations that take place in an urban environment? Fourthly, how can adequate attention be given to the individual pupil while the numbers continue to expand? Finally, what role can educational planning play with other community planning groups in solving these and other problems based on "what has been" and "what is" and "what should be?"

[135] Carl W. Condit, *The Chicago School of Architecture* (Chicago: University of Chicago Press, 1964), p. 2.

3 Determining "what is" versus "what should be"

"WHAT IS"

The population growth in the United States has created many other activities in both private and public sectors. Unfortunately, the prevailing pattern of public school organization in most cities remains true to its nineteenth-century roots. The assumptions were and are that schools must be independent of surrounding institutions; that suitable education will take place when students are divided equally among available teachers; and that school boards with lay members can direct school operations in accord with the public will. Today, educators, planners and the public at large are questioning the viability of these assumptions.

The conditions for educating are changing and with them the facts on which the planning for city schools was originally based. Shortcomings in the present school system are being considered and the following questions are being asked more frequently than before. How can educational opportunities be equalized? Why is change so difficult to bring about? What is education's role in urban renewal? How can parents take on a more effective role in school planning? What are the new roles of teachers in educational planning? What is the role of education in relation to other public and private agencies in influencing the development of the individual?

Today virtually every one of these problems has an

effect on every other problem found in a large city. City planning that does not include educational planning must be irresponsible even if it includes the routine approval of the size and location of new school sites. Any meaningful planning must also include questions of curriculum, attendance patterns, teacher supply, financial support, and all of the social, cultural, economic, and political interrelationships between the schools and the city.

Educational planners have the duty to discover the intentions of society, how they can be organized for planning, and once organized how can they be implemented. Without these steps planning might be wasteful.

One sure societal intention is societal involvement. In the future, learning will take place through students' active involvement. Their performance will be aided by the surrounding architecture and by their fellow students. Plays, music, sports—whatever the activity may be—will become part of a larger learning situation. The fact that masses of students will be present because of urban conglomerations makes it possible for subgroups to be assembled in smaller areas according to similar likes rather than by organizational fiat.

> Because of this, we are no longer sure of the direction in which our momentum is taking us. And the recognition of this fact leads to a general feeling of disquiet, reduced to the following question: "Is feasibility a good enough end in pursuit of which one can reach decisions and calculate the human risks and consequences of action in these perilous and uncertain times?"[1]

The educational planner must, therefore, proceed with the appropriate amount of caution in order to distinguish between the "can" and the "ought." He should proceed from the normative plan, which spells out the goals, through the strategic plan, which is based on policy, and the operational plan, which assumedly implements the appropriate policies. As the technological advances from an economic base continue, different perspectives will develop insofar as human behavior is concerned and a greater stress will be placed on leisure time as opposed to the traditional orientation toward work-production. In a very real sense all citizens in both the economic and leisure realm are reaching the stage where they are more free to participate in the various activities of society. For in both work and play the individual is becoming much more prominent and the individual's place in society is gaining new status. The changes now taking place in American society are profoundly different from the days when this country was founded.

> The result of ... farm-type Colonial-era thinking is to create the sort of problems that result when every one goes to work at the same time, eats at the same time, has recreation in the same time, gets up and goes to bed at the same time. The way we solve the problem is to build generating capacity in our power plants for peak hours; to build highways three times as big as they need to be, to take care of peak traffic to and from work, and to overload our parks, resorts, beaches and other recreational areas to the saturation point two days a week and leave them virtually deserted all the rest of the time. As population increases, and becomes more highly congested in urban areas, the problems compound, too, and we are forced into an insensate frenzy of designing and building to take care of urban problems created by rural thinking.[2]

In order to cope educationally with societal problems, recognition of the role of change, and indeed of the importance of change, is necessary.

> ... we seek to control the rate at which it [change] affects our lives. We create institutions which serve as instruments to preserve some change we feel is good and to slow down that rate at which it is changed by still other innovations. Our system of law is an instrument for preserving certain acceptable changes in the conduct of an individual or social environment; our formalized religions are institutions for preserving what were at one time great changes in the ethical and moral valuations of men; governments, devices for preserving past changes in the relationship between an individual and the society in which he lives.[3] [See Figure 3.1.]

We see then a philosophy of educational planning emerging that is both specific and general, that is humanistic yet technologically oriented, that seeks invariant principles in order to establish stability, yet

[1]F. S. Hopkins, "Technology vs. Ethics: Must 'Can' Imply 'Ought'?" *The Futurist,* no. 1, **3**:13 (1969).

[2]Don Fabun (ed.), *Dynamics of Change,* Part II (Englewood Cliffs, N.J.: Prentice-Hall, 1967), p. 21.

[3]Ibid., Part I, p. 9.

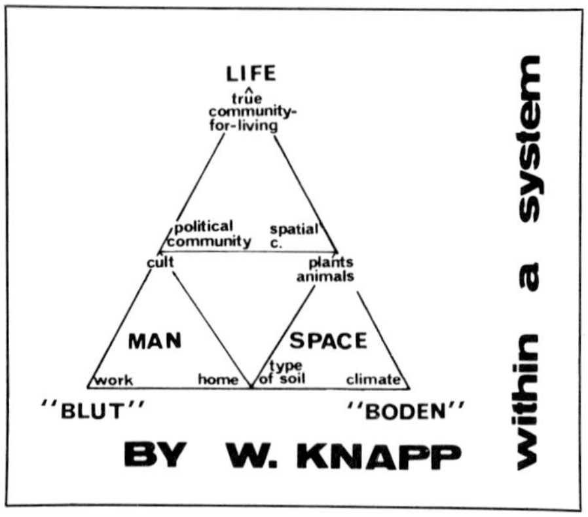

FIGURE 3.1

recognizes the profound changes that are going on in this country today. Educational planners and educational planning processes must somehow reconcile these diverse differences in an attempt to set up guidelines that will give some balance to the educational system and bring some order out of the randomness.

"WHAT SHOULD BE"

A philosophy of educational planning

Planning is systems oriented; that is, it is specific in the solution of a given educational problem, but it carefully considers all of the interacting components or subsystems involved. Planning's

> ... field of action ... is not narrowly specialized, but rather concerns itself with the relationship of things to each other, a profession that calls for a broad understanding of a number of related disciplines and for competence in their integration and coordination when applied to a geographical area. A planner brings method and balance to the process of exploiting land areas and natural resources for the benefit of an organized society. His tools are the ability to analyze and reconcile, the power and imagination to synthesize and give form, and the willingness to communicate and to persuade.[4]

Increasing the demand for systematic planning has encouraged the evolution of a philosophy of planning. Planning *per se* attempts to bridge such polarizations as unity and diversity, part and whole, small and large, simple and complex, order and chaos. (See Figure 3.2.) Any appropriate philosophy of planning must somehow consider these extremes and attempt a synthesis that is realistic and relevant.

The continuity of time carries forward random activities, as well as those activities that are purposefully planned and nurtured. Naturally involved in handling various segments of society, the educational planner must be constantly aware of the various societal values that manifest themselves, such as schooling. Planning involves creativity and leadership as well as functional blueprints for pragmatic affairs.

> Although planning in general answers very tangible functions, ultimately its object differs in no way fundamentally from that of any other creative activity; i.e., to express through men and for men the real essence of existence. The more tangible functions are only relevant in so far as they adjust man's environment more accurately to his elementary inclinations.[5]

The problem is to find the very essence of the need and to translate someone's ideas into accomplished facts. "What you should try to accomplish is built meaning. So, get close to the meaning and build!"[6] The educational planner does add something unique in his own right to the process and objective of the planning function. He is not a technician who follows directions. "Planning merely for essentials can never be other than barren."[7] Completely immersing himself in the project, the educational planner must comprehend the totality of social aims and of all their aspects. He must not be concerned with the narrow confines of a single building or a single subset of social aims.

> The wise planner will ask, "Why should I plan?" before he inquires, "What shall I plan?" He will survey his fields of operations to learn the nature of the material with which he has to deal. He will look at it from every angle and measure

[4]Pietro Belluschi, "The Education of Planners," *Training for Town and Country Planning: Housing, Building and Planning*, no. 11 (New York: United Nations, Department of Economic and Social Affairs, 1957), p. 25.

[5]Alison Smithson (ed.), *Team 10 Primer* (Collection of Assorted Articles about the Works of the Members of Team 10 Primer) 1968, Massachusetts Institute of Technology.

[6]Ibid.

[7]Robert S. Malkin, "The Place of Lesser Details in Urban Planning," *Synthesis* (Cambridge, Mass.: Harvard University, Graduate School of Design, April 1957), p. 91.

FIGURE 3.2

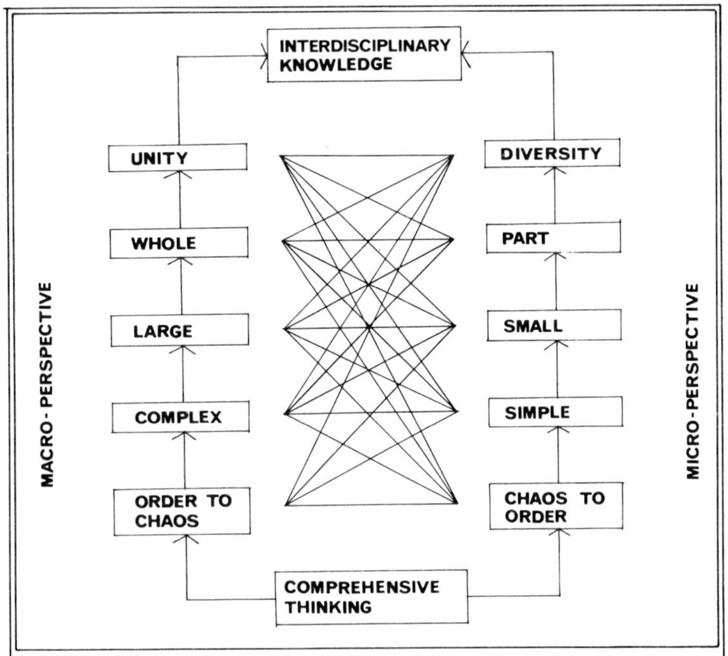

PLANNING BY SYNTHESIZING

with every available criterion until he has in his mind a complex of the whole field's content.[8]

Planning technology continues to stress the technical aspects of educational planning and the concomitant specificity of educational objectives: "... reliance on vague policies, objectives and guidelines should keep the supposed framework for individual decisions fluid, with every detail dependent upon every other, to the point of utter ultimate confusion."[9] The basic principles of educational planning are not greatly different from the principles of any systematic conduct; they include a fundamental truth, a settled rule of action, a governing rule of conduct, and a basic law or doctrine.[10] (See Figure 3.3.)

[8]"The Philosophy of Planning," *Town and Country Planning,* no. 17, **5**:2 (1936).

[9]George Raymond, "Notes on the Meaning of Physical Planning," *Pratt Planning Papers,* no. 1, **2**:3 (1963).

[10]Norman Pearson, "Towards Principles of Land Planning," *Planning Outlook,* no. 2, **4**:18 (1957).

The following considerations help to delineate the scope and area of planning:

1 The scope and extent of the problem.
2 The extent to which issues are involved in the planning solution.
3 The effect of an analysis of the problem and the acceptance of the solution.
4 General awareness of the existence of a solution.[11]

There are no necessities, but everywhere possibilities; and man, as master of the possibilities, is the judge of their use. This, by the reversal which it involves, puts man in the first place—man, and no longer the earth, nor the influence of climate, nor the determinant of localities.[12]

Many forces contribute to the direction which educational planning theory and philosophy are taking.

[11]E. Gordon Ericksen, *Urban Behavior* (New York: Macmillan, 1954), p. 426.

[12]Ibid., p. 415.

FIGURE 3.3

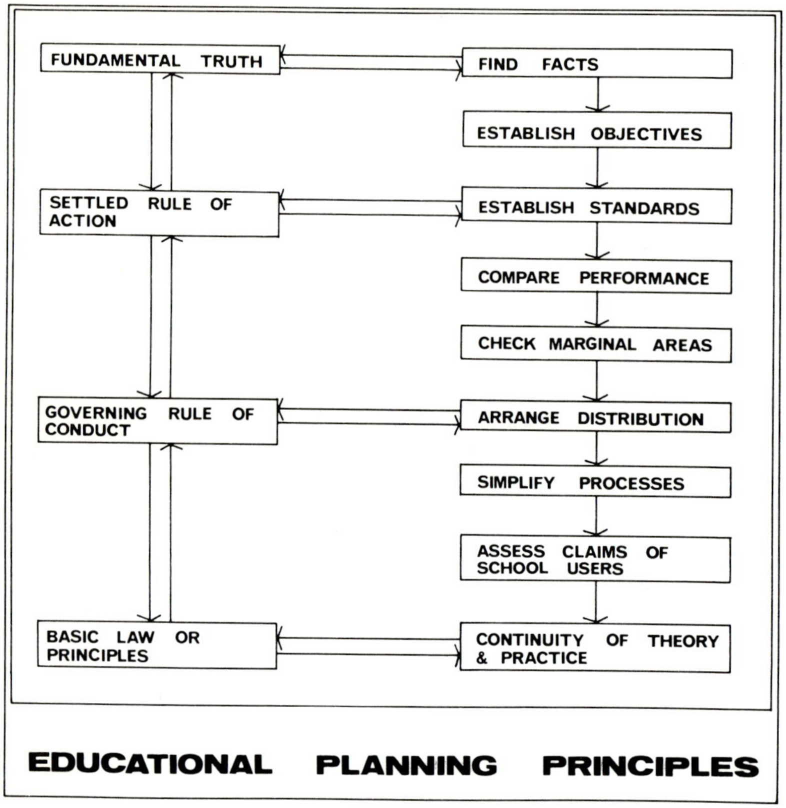

The planner's new role and his rising influence are partly the result of changes in the city and in city hall. The new problems in the city and the gradual replacement of the working class machine politician by the middle-class, college-educated politician-administrator, supported by professionally trained bureaucrats have made city governments much more responsive to expert advice, while the reduction of class differences between the planners and the new politicians has improved communications between them. In addition, downtown business and property interests have become more favorable to planning, partly because they, too, face new problems they cannot solve themselves and partly because the planners share other concerns of revitalization of the central business district. Moreover, planners are becoming more sympathetic to the city and are giving up their traditional antiurban ideology. As the suburbs threaten to engulf the city and to endanger the survival of the upper-middle-class culture and civic institutions that have traditionally been located in the city, the planner has become an advocate of urbanism, supporting schemes to bring the middle class back into the city.[13]

As trends change throughout the country, so do planning theories and philosophies. Ian Wilson has indicated eight such tendencies in a study conducted for General Electric:

1 Increasing affluence—per capita disposable income will increase by about 50 per cent and will have some far reaching consequences in terms of changing spending habits, markets and economic attitudes—discretionary income will be spent on such things as travel, leisure, cultural and " self-improvement " activities. Money will be much more taken for granted, much less of a motivator and relegated to the category of " means " rather than "ends."

[13]Herbert J. Gans, "City Planning in America: A Sociological Analysis," *People and Plans: Essays on Urban Problems and Solutions* (New York: Basic Books, 1968), p. 69.

2 Economic stabilization—further flattening of the business cycle due partly to government policies, computerized inventory control and long range program with large, fixed overhead costs, which place a premium on stable production.
3 Rising tide of education—the individual will have more self-respect, desire to be treated more as an individual, will be less tolerant of authoritarianism and organizational restraints; " will have different and higher expectations of what he wants to put into a job and what he wants to get out of it."
4 Changing attitudes toward work and leisure—the notion that hard work must be tolerated because it is unavoidable will be less accepted. There will be a lower frustration tolerance for hardship.
5 Growing interdependence of institutions—there will be an increasing mixture of the public and private sectors.
6 Emergence of the " post-industrial " society—this suggests greater service economy as opposed to production.
7 Pluralism and individualism—there will be a tendency toward greater individual importance within the structure of society, suggesting a deviation from centralization.
8 The Negro/Urban Problem—specific solution not predictable.[14]

As technology increases, the idea that leisure and work are both equally valid activities is being more generally accepted. That is, leisure is increasingly being considered as a right rather than a privilege. The old work-leisure division may become a three-way division: work, educational development, and leisure-relaxation: ". . . tomorrow's blue collar workers may adopt present day middle class work values, while the professional and scientific workers of the future may tend to be less driving and more avocational in their attitude toward work."[15] The new outlook toward leisure and its relation with work productivity is being profoundly influenced by technological developments that induce greater productivity and consequently less production time.

Productivity is such that our economy can produce all the " things " society needs with only a fraction of the total labor force. By 1975 no more than one-fourth of the labor force will be directly involved in manufacturing products, mining, growing crops, constructing buildings.[16]

Certainly these concepts affect the educational planning philosophy. Long-range plans must take into consideration the dominant attitudes that prevail.

In a technology-dominated age such as ours and as a result of forces and attitudes that have brought this dominance, " can," a conditional and neutral expression of feasibility begins to read as if it were written " ought," which is an ethical statement denoting an imperative. Thus feasibility, which is a strategic concept, is elevated into a normative concept, with the result that whatever technological reality indicates we can do is taken as implying that we must do it. The strategy dictates its own goal. The action defines its own telos. Aims no longer guide invention; inventions reveal aims.

Because of this, we are no longer sure of the direction in which our momentum is taking us. And the recognition of this fact leads to a general feeling of disquiet, reduced to the following question: " Is feasibility a good enough end in pursuit of which one can reach decisions and calculate the human risks and consequences of action in these perilous complex and uncertain times? "[17]

An enumerated set of procedures also has been relatively well established:

1 Use of the normal processes of research to find facts;
2 Use of facts as the basis for establishing policies, objectives, programs and procedures;
3 Establishing standards or controls on the basis of comparative case-studies;
4 Use of these controls or standards to compare the performance with the program or the agreed optimum;
5 Having established these conditions, to concentrate on the marginal areas, on adequacy and revision of standards, and in practice on deviations from the accepted standards;
6 Attempting to arrange functional distribution to generate the minimum of traffic and friction;
7 General attempt to simplify the processes involved;
8 Complete impartiality in assessing the claims of various land uses, or in studying problems; and
9 Maintaining continuity of theory and practice.[18]

[14]Ian H. Wilson, "Industry Study Foresees Educational Institutions Dominant in the U.S.," *The Futurist,* no. 1, **3**:17–19 (1969).
[15]Ibid., p. 18.
[16]Ibid.
[17]Hopkins, p. 130.
[18]Ibid., p. 23.

The structural and dynamic nature of planning was suggested by Adrian Berrington, who ". . . . called planning an activity which deals with the morphology, anatomy, physiology and biology of towns."[19]

Educational planning philosophy must remain cognizant of the centrality of man and his problems. As related to planning Frederick Polak observed ". . . the history of culture is the history of its image of the future. . . . Thinking about the future is not only the mightiest lever of progress but also the condition of survival."[20] Additionally, Bertaux claimed,

> The future of a culture can be predicted by the power of its thinking about the future. No culture can maintain itself for long without a positive and generally accepted image of the future. A culture which shuts itself up in the present or, what amounts to the same thing, in a shortsighted perspective of the future, has no future.[21]

Present forces interacting with the past give direction to future activities: "The future . . . is capable of becoming an element of determination in the causal chain. Through an image of the future, the time-to-come is already affecting the present."[22] Although a certain amount of determinism indeed exists, activities of the future are not completely predestined. In *Man Evolving* Dobzhansky wrote,

> By changing what he knows about the world, man changes the world he knows; and by changing the world in which he lives, man changes himself.
>
> In our context I would say: now that so much of the environment of man is man-made, by reshaping his environment, man is now—consciously or not—shaping the man of the future.[23]

Educational planning, a dynamic process affected by many types and intensities of outside forces, ". . . attempts to reconcile these myriad interests in terms of a development policy whose objective is the creation of the best possible physical environment. In these

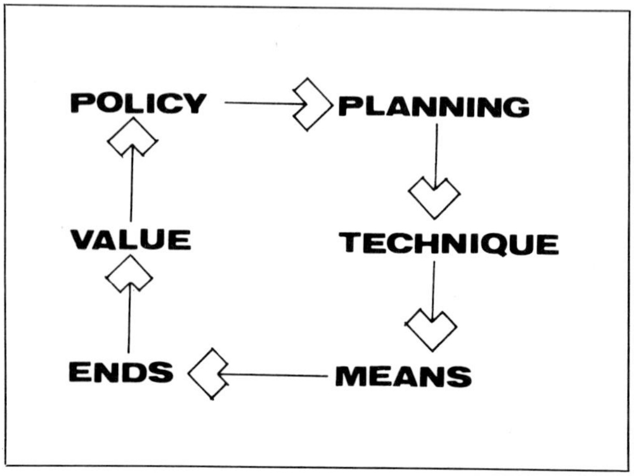

FIGURE 3.4

terms, it must be considered to be a political process rather than a technical one."[24] The plan, therefore, is a conglomerate of many subsystems of activities, many of which influence other subsystems; it

> . . . consists of the totality of arrangements decided upon in order to carry out a project.
>
> The idea of a plan is thus definable by two elements:
>
> 1 a project, that is, an end which one proposes to achieve; and
> 2 the arrangements decided upon in order that this end may be achieved, that is, the determination of the means.
>
> A determined end and means, equally determined, for the attainment of this end, constitutes the essence of every plan; and this is what in particular distinguishes a plan [see Figure 3.4] from a mere project.[25]

It is essential to consider planning from the point of view of well-laid-out principles but at the same time each plan should be so designed that it is flexible enough to adapt to changing circumstances. The problem then is to become specific without being rigid, and general without being chaotic.

Because all plans involve trade-off throughout their duration, flexibility and willingness to adapt are naturally assumed. Everything happens in the micro-

[19]Eric C. Embacker, *The Urban Evaluation Theory* (Rexdale, Ont.: CopiRite Reproductions Company, 1966), pp. 1–2.

[20]Pierre Bertaux, "The Future of Man," *Environment and Change*. Papers Commissioned by the American Institute of Planners and Presented at the Washington Conference, October 1967 (Bloomington, Ind.: Indiana University Press, 1968), p. 19.

[21]Ibid.

[22]Ibid., p. 20.

[23]Ibid., p. 18.

[24]E. A. Levin, "What Is a Planner?" *Plan* (Canada), no. 3, 2:48 (1961).

[25]Charles Bettelheim. *Studies in the Theory of Planning* (New York: Asia Publishing House, 1961), p. 3.

cosm and does so in the "... same relationship pattern of interaction as in the macrocosm. There is a problem of priority and predominance and the problem is resolved for us by the hierarchies of function."[26] In educational planning as in any other human activity, two opposing aspects are usually present: control and randomness.

> The more you go into a larger scale the more the order becomes obvious, its identification easier. The more you get into a smaller scale, the element of randomness becomes predominant. In terms of planning decisions, we cannot afford to include in large scale models random elements belonging to the small scale end of the spectrum.[27]

Planning procedures involve an almost unique arrangement and mixture of practice and theory: "Theory and practice are not separate. There is a ... constant interchange, a feedback system."[28] As planning is a mixture of theory and practice, the term *plan* relates to other concepts. *Plan design, program proposal,* and *scheme*

> ... refer to sets of ideas developed to accomplish a desired result. *Plan* is both the most informal and the most general. It can refer at one extreme to a tentative unverbalized cluster of notions, and at the other, to a detailed final draft stating the precise methods by which to proceed: a vague plan to go there sometime; plans for a merger that filled six filing cabinets. *Scheme* is also informal, but is restricted in meaning either to a vague, unverbalized notion or to surreptitious or unsavory ideas. Unworkability may be implied in the former case, conspiratoral plotting in the latter: coming up with scheme after scheme for getting rich quick; their carefully worked out scheme for assassinating the prime minister. *Design* relates to that side of plan that suggests a detailed final draft. It can suggest harmony and order as the salient feature of the plan; it can also suggest a symbolic rather than literal rendering of the work to be done....[29]

Just as the term *plan* is closely related to many other ideas, planning itself "... is very inclusive and comprehensive and ... it is an activity to be joined in by many variously talented people."[30] Planning is becoming more and more a catalyst for action in democratic societies. It does not impose equalitarian physical patterns on individuals; instead educational planning is a task of coordination and guidance. Educational planning must search for the best solution within the fiscal and social limits of a political unit and aim to fulfill the community's goals, whether expressed or not.

The role of values

One limit that the educational planner must recognize is associated with values and their role in shaping physical, economic, social, and political areas. For shaping and evaluating planning a free and open society is committed to a system of values to serve as criteria; otherwise, optimum educational development will not result. Research in education associated with urban management has made significant progress along some lines, but in other areas research has barely begun to shed light.

Values are imbedded in the mores of the people and in the cultural history of the community. Because they generally represent the desires of the people, the educational planner should include them with the other factors before projecting his plan.

> ... planning is not a pure science, devoted to the assembling of information for its own sake. However, it does not follow that the planner can best serve the public interest by avoiding "esoteric abstractions." On the contrary, research in planning and urban theory is essential to the development of the profession as a servant of the public.[31]

Certainly the basic needs of the citizens form the heart of the educational planning process. Conse-

[26] *Advanced Studies in Urban Environments, Toward an Urban Model,* A Study by the Master Class in Architecture, Serge Chermayeff, Professor in Architectural Design (New Haven: Yale University, 1967), p. 28.

[27] Ibid., p. 28.

[28] Ibid., p. 30.

[29] S. I. Hayakawa and Funk & Wagnalls Dictionary Staff, *Modern Guide to Synonyms and Words* (New York: Funk & Wagnalls, 1968), p. 447.

[30] Rexford Guy Tugwell, "Realism in Planning Practice and Planning Education," *Training for Town and Country Planning: Housing, Building, and Planning,* no. 11 (New York: United Nations, Department of Economic and Social Affairs, 1957), p. 29.

[31] Twin Cities Metropolitan Planning Commission, *Values and the Planning Process, The Joint Program, Design Section,* no. 9 (July 1963), p. 3.

quently it would be "dangerous to deny the importance of a knowledge of values to a profession concerned with the comprehensive development of human environment.[32]

There are several reasons for giving consideration to the role of values in the educational planning process:

1 Values, being " irreducible absolutes of quality " supply the impulse or motivation to define a goal and to seek policies as ways or methods of working toward the goal, and to find implementing devices (systems, institutions, or procedures) to give it socially recognized form. Values are, therefore, the monitor by which the process can be given positive direction. Without an explicit understanding of the underlying values, a consistency of direction cannot be assured.

[32]Ibid., p. 4.

2 As values are at the root of a social order, reference to them will avoid possible conflict between individual goals and their attendant policies and implementing devices. Conversely, they may also explain seeming goal contradictions as being different aspects of a value system.

3 Values, being so often implicit, may become blurred, or even forgotten in the process of time. By making them explicit, they can take their rightful place as the foundations of society, or be rejected as being anachronous, shallow or even destructive.

4 Through a knowledge of values, we may be in a better position to create an equitable balance between goals and expose false goals and to locate weaknesses and gaps in our goals-, policies-implementing devices system.

5 It is difficult to avoid personal bias in a field such as planning. There is, therefore, the danger of creating plans for planners rather than for the public in general. By beginning investigation at the values level, it should be

FIGURE 3.5

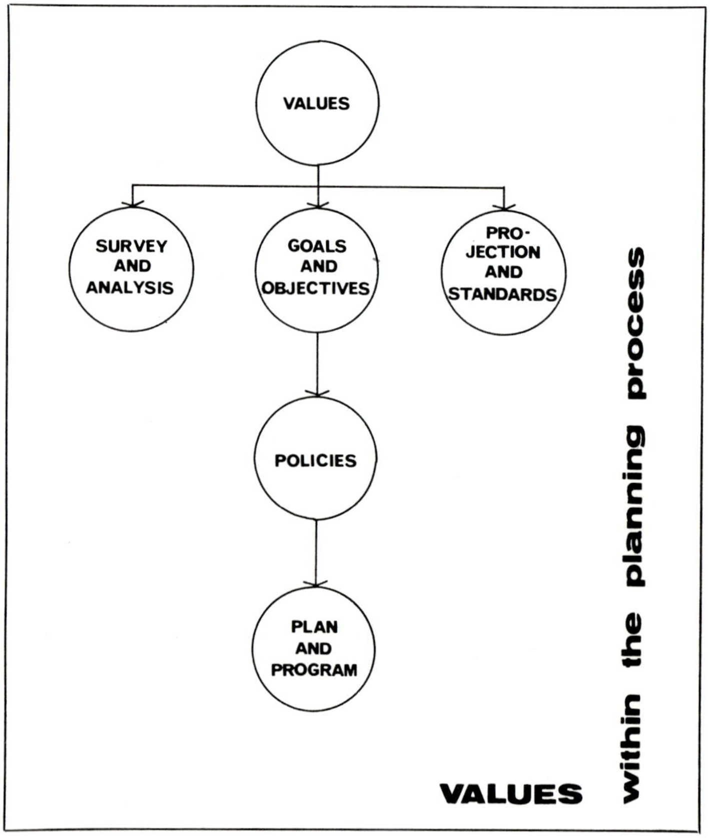

easier to avoid unintentional bias. Plans would, therefore, be more realistic and responsive to actual needs.

6 The planning process, especially at the metropolitan level, may seem esoteric to the layman. Planning decisions often appear arbitrary. If, however, policies and plans were appraised on the basis that they satisfied certain agreed values and goals, the decisions as to policy and plan can be recognized as means for furthering our deepest needs rather than appearing to be ends in themselves.[33]

These concepts illustrate the fact that "the values are given the planner by the culture itself."[34] In Figure 3.5 the structural relationship among values, goals, and the planning process is diagrammatically demonstrated. But the diagram does not depict or predict the social implications of long-range planning.

Some will find creative outlets in the arts, sports and the more traditional leisure-time activities. But, in addition, learning may become the major nonpaid occupation of large segments of the population. The signs are by now beginning to show in the expanding demand for adult educational programs, the rapid growth of educational television, the sales boom in books and magazines, and the growing interest in music, theatre, and the traditional fine arts.[35]

Because of changing societal structures and behavioral patterns, the educational planner must place greater emphasis on the role of values.

The role of educational planning

To solve many of our problems will require a change in our customary approaches to educational and community planning. New organizations for plan making, implementation, and finance will be needed. Large-scale and long-range community planning will be needed. It should be noted, however, that the gap between how educational planning is being carried out and how it ought to be carried out is so wide that it cannot be closed by small-scale tinkering with existing procedures.

What is required is a central planning body that includes educational planners along with other public and private agency's planners who share responsibility for projecting goals and setting timetables. Only in this manner can any hope of commensurate action surmount the constant need of meeting one educational crisis after another. What, then, are some roles for educational planning?

Educational planning must center its attention on community life and help its client plan on a broader basis. Educational planning must become the link between educational activities and larger urban activities. Educational planning must include plans that help prepare individuals to cope with the complexities of urban life; plans must include anyone, regardless of age or previous education. Educational planning must coordinate planning for desirable social, cultural, and recreational activities for the entire community. Educational planning must be for the individual's occupational and social development.

Educational planning must work more closely with other human service planning agencies. Relationships must be strengthened between the planning of programs for education and the planning of library programs, museum programs, and recreational programs, or the planning of programs with local communications media or even scientific groups.

Educational planning must be participatory planning that provides socially and racially integrated educational experiences. Such experiences will hopefully emphasize similarities rather than differences, reducing the mistrust now plaguing many of our cities.

Educational planning must produce programs that are student-centered rather than custodial-centered or administrator-centered, or even teacher-centered. The programs must be structured around experiences that are relevant to urban activities. The experiences must also reinforce the student's desire to assume responsibilities and develop strong self-concepts so that he can meaningfully participate in an urban society.

Educational planning must become increasingly specialized but at the same time be general enough to adapt, change, expand, or contract to accommodate

[33]Ibid.

[34]Ralph G. Crouch, "A Study of the Goal Formulation Process." Prepared for the Department of City Planning, Los Angeles, Calif., September 30, 1964, p. 60.

[35]Melvin Webber, "Planning in an Environment of Change, Part I: Beyond the Industrial Age, *Town Planning Review,* no. 3, **39**:186 (1968).

changing social needs. Educational planning must include short-range planning, middle-range planning, and long-range planning.

Educational planning must be accountable planning. Therefore, educators and citizens must maintain a continuing dialogue regarding the refinement of educational objectives and the explication of the steps required for their fulfillment.

Educational planning must also include decisions made at the community level and not just those at school district or state levels. Evidence exists that decisions made at the school board level are constrained by conflicting interests. Hence resolutions are frequently so general that special needs of the community are neglected.

Educational planning in concert with total community planning must include the use of any community resource appropriate for learning. This approach means making the entire community a positive educational force. Past performances have proved that schools make little difference unless their efforts are reinforced by parents, neighborhood businesses, churches, professional organizations, and community clubs. An example: a service station could become an extension of a school, giving the student practical experience and also modest pay.

How can coordination and cooperation be achieved between educational planning and other community planning programs? Some ways of doing so are by

1 Simultaneous planning of programs and facilities.
2 Providing for joint- or multi-occupancy of certain facilities.
3 Combining similar programs where duplication is likely, and planning steps to avoid duplication.
4 Maximizing the output of various funding sources.
5 Establishing and possibly pooling an information and data bank.
6 Establishing continuing communication between the various planning groups.

The interdependence of educational planning with other community planning must be recognized. Educational planning is not competent in the planning of special programs to solve problems that are not directly educational. The real challenge is to meld together an effective working coalition of various planning groups that have competence in specialized areas. This coalition then becomes a part of social planning, the aim of which is to obtain a richer set of experiences for more people. This requires, in addition, knowledge of the prevailing school/community philosophies, the values held, school/community potential resources, and their constraints.

4 Resources and constraints

IDENTIFYING POTENTIAL RESOURCES AND CONSTRAINTS

To what extent is planning possible? To what extent do the results of planning justify the necessary investment of resources and expenditure of energy to overcome constraints? The answers to these questions must be feasible and worthwhile as they apply to the results of planning, compared with the results of nonplanning. Achieving optimal solutions depends on utility, the availability of resources, and the nature of the constraints. The aim, therefore, in allocating resources among various educational activities is to ensure desirable results, which, as we have noted, are usually matters of value judgment.

Value judgments stem from value patterns that underlie the structure of any social system and specifically its educational system.[1] As an interdependent subsystem of society the educational system's basic orientation is toward the value pattern, which serves as a guide for all human endeavors.

Educational planning is no more than the judicious juxtaposition of ideas and the simultaneous implementation of those ideas toward common goals, requiring resources and at the same time overcoming the constraints associated with using them.

[1]Talcott Parsons, *Structure and Process in Modern Societies* (New York: Free Press, 1965), p. 20.

Individual resources and constraints

The purposes of education should be the physical and mental development of the individual as well as public requirements.

It is through an understanding of the individual and the nature of the changes occurring in him over a period of time that an educational planner can act. His planning must accommodate the individual, for the individual is the primary unit. His experiences are the guidelines to planning and his experiences are enhanced by his environment.

No individual can exist without an environment. No individual can exist in an environment of his exclusive creation. No individual can survive except as a nondisruptive member of an ecological community, and in today's terms this means for most individuals an urbanized community. (See Figure 4.1.) Consequently, every individual must adjust to the other individuals of the community and to the environment in order to survive. The individual is constrained by certain basic needs, needs being identified as differences that exist between "what is" and "what should be" relative to a defined behavior and relevant values. The principal needs are classified as life-maintaining, life-enhancing, and life-completing urges.

Tables 4.1, 4.2, and 4.3 illustrate how educational resources can supply the various needs and urges beginning with life maintaining, whose aim is "to keep alive" (Table 4.1).

Life-enhancing needs, whose objective is "to live well," can be supplied by the following educational resources (Table 4.2).

The life-completing needs and urges consist of feelings for nature, materials and forms and accompanying kinship with these various elements (Table 4.3).

The needs and educational resources shown in these tables are not meant to completely supply the individual with fulfillment. To complete himself as a

Table 4.1

Life-maintaining needs and urges	Educational resources
1 Hunger and thirst	School lunches
2 Shelter	School buildings
3 Rest and sleep	Dormitories
4 Acquisition urges	Lessons and learning
5 Contest and conflict	Athletics, speech debates, and so on
6 Holding, hoarding, defense	Tests
7 Fabrication, making of tools	Vocational and technical education
8 Making symbols	Art, music, sculpture, and so on
9 Curiosity, orientation drive, exploration drive	Field trips

Table 4.2

Life-enhancing needs and urges	Educational resources
Play	Physical educational programs
Sport	School's varsity programs
Companionship	Fellow students, teachers, principals, and administrators
Group pride and self-identity	Classroom unit, school, school district, and so on
Ritual, image	School song, school mascot, school leadership

Table 4.3

Life-completing needs and urges	Educational resources
Light	Window lighting, windowless lighting, and so on
Textures	School floor surfaces, wall surfaces, ceiling surfaces, grounds and playfields about the school, buildings, trees, and so on
Spaces	Classrooms, lofts, gyms, offices, and so on
Rhythms	Finger plan, egg-crate plan, campus plan, and so on
Sounds	Plays, audio equipment, teacher teaching, and so on
Smells	Lunch room, locker rooms, flowers, and so on

FIGURE 4.1

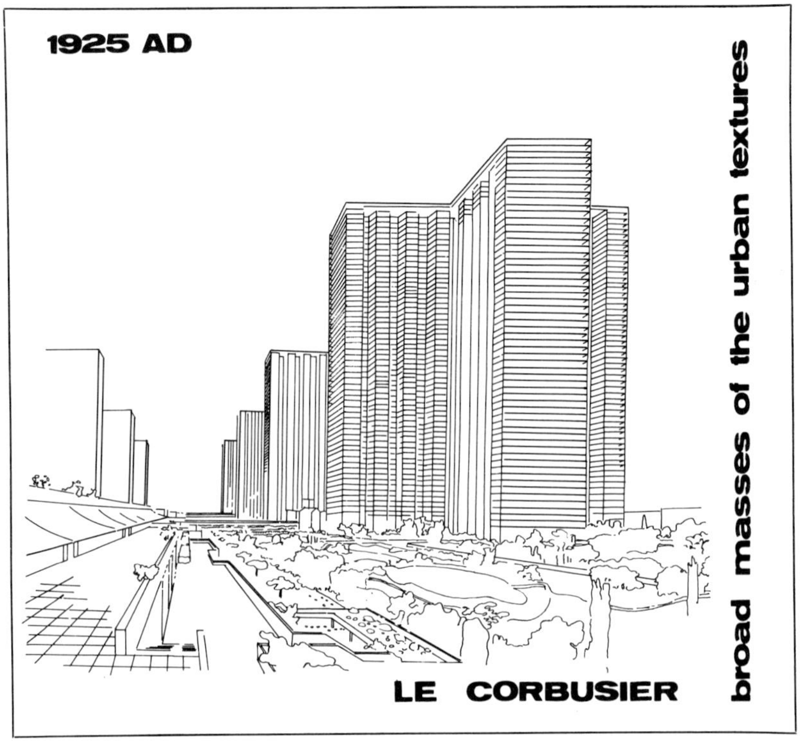

human being, the individual must have aesthetic satisfaction both in what he finds about himself and also in what he creates for himself. Supplying the resources for such experiences is the school's responsibility. Unfortunately, a survey of most schools, new and old, reveals a serious defect in the physical facilities and in the satisfaction of individual needs. Consequently, the limitations experienced by the individual often diminish his readiness to act in a positive way. This is most apparent today with such labels as "the urban crisis," "the ecological crisis," "the population bomb," "*God's Own Junkyard*," and so on.

Institutional resources and constraints

Many crises and environmental problems are due to institutions' inabilities to cope with change or to plan and implement programs for the corrective or creative use of social and physical resources.

A number of theories have been proposed to explain this phenomenon. One such set of theories developed by March and Simon categorized them as follows:

1 Theories of conflict—conflict between individuals, their role playing, or between their personalities;
2 Theories of motivation—the individual's needs, drives and motives; and
3 Theories of decision-making—the individual is characterized as a rational being but with certain limitations.[2]

In each case, the individual's conflict, motivation, and decision-making are characterized by the group of which he is a part.

Individuals generally act and react in groups. Their characteristics are defined in groups. Their

[2]Daniel E. Griffiths, "The Nature and Meaning of Theory," *Behavioral Science and Educational Administration*, Part II, ed. Daniel E. Griffiths and Herman G. Richey (Chicago: University of Chicago Press, 1964), p. 112.

characteristics are defined by the relatively stable relationships that individuals in various positions have with each other and with the group.

Such relationships are established and maintained in generalized patterns; some are organized as institutions.

An *institution,* in this book, is defined as a collection of individuals characterized by purposive action that is dependent on the voluntary cooperation of its members—and sometimes the involuntary cooperation of its members. The institution is, therefore, a system comprised of physical, biological, personal, and social components that by purposive action have systematic relationships. In summary, institutions are systems of the consciously coordinated activities of at least two individuals. As such, institutions, as organizations, have valid characteristics that can be effectively investigated and that have a profound influence on the distribution of public resources.

Institutions have the following characteristics:

1 Institutions have fixed jurisdictional areas that are ordered by rules, policies, regulations, and laws.
2 Institutions are hierarchically organized with levels of graded authority that ensure a system of super- and sub-ordinate individuals in which superordinated individuals supervise subordinated ones.
3 Institutions' purposes and means for accomplishing them are based on written documents.
4 Institutions' works are administered by full-time, trained individuals.

These institutional characteristics determine what resources are required and what constraints are to be applied in their distribution. Decisions affecting the investment of resources and the constraints required by and imposed on the system constitute the essence of educational planning. Planning, then, must help to ensure that the distribution of resources is optimal, that the levels and priorities of investment are so determined as to achieve the desired results in education, and that resources are used in educational projects for the highest social good. To achieve such aims, the planner must recognize the five following characteristics of institutions.

1 Institutions are place oriented. Very often in education comparisons of effectiveness or efficiency are made between two teachers, two schools, two school districts, or even between two state educational systems. Often these studies are not adequate because only similarities are measured instead of differences, which always exist at different locations. Educational work is always different when the location is different. Thus, if a large number of persons contribute to a complex organization (such as a school district) doing the same type of work (such as teaching), the educational planner's coordination of their efforts will involve a plan for geographical coordination.
2 An institution's work occurs in a given period of time. This is one of the most obvious bases of division of work in continuous-service enterprises such as education. The scheduling of work is among the most complex tasks of educational planning. Coordinating a time-schedule assignment of educational activities for individual learning needs with the available resources and the constraints tied to their use is possibly the most important single phase of educational planning.
3 An institution's work involves individual work: students with teachers, teachers with parents and principals, principals with school administrators, and so on. As a result, educational planners must also be social planners.
4 An institution's work consists of all of the things being done. In some cases it is expressed in terms of the resources to be used and in others in the services to be performed. The question, then, for educational planners is what point of view should be considered for planning. In most cases, the emphasis will be on the ends to be accomplished and the educational objectives to be achieved.
5 An institution requires a process by which work is done. Educational plans are also expressed in terms of processes. Such processes rest on the

natural adaptation of individuals, the increase in skill from experiences in planning, or the increase of knowledge obtained by the study of planning.

Institutions, such as educational institutions, are vehicles of cooperation that yield impressive results with planning. This function helps to correlate the efforts of individuals in such a way as to produce the optimal use of resources with minimal constraints.

In planning, the whole must be broken into parts. Analysis of the educational system as a system of parts allows for the coordination of the various parts. The nature of this process is of critical importance to the systems approach to planning.

5 Establishing educational planning parts and priorities

Educational planning consists of two major components—the planning process and the planning content. (See Figure 5.1.) In this book a seven-phase planning-process model has been constructed to include a series of interrelated steps capable of producing educational outputs with the social, economic, and physical details involved in an educational problem. These details constitute the content, the second major part of educational planning.

This technique helps to indicate the background needed for the practice of educational planning. It indicates desired educational outcomes and associates them with the various existing conditions. It suggests the extent to which these conditions can be controlled. It also helps to predict the conditions that have desirable or harmful side effects and which so far have been unknown.

Although comprehensive educational planning is far short of current demands, the field has developed enough to bring the parts together. One method for identifying, analyzing, designing, evaluating, and monitoring the parts is the *systems approach.*

THE SYSTEMS APPROACH

The term *systems approach* is difficult to define because it covers a variety of techniques, technologies, and approaches. It will be observed, however, that when various authors' formulations of definitions are ex-

FIGURE 5.1

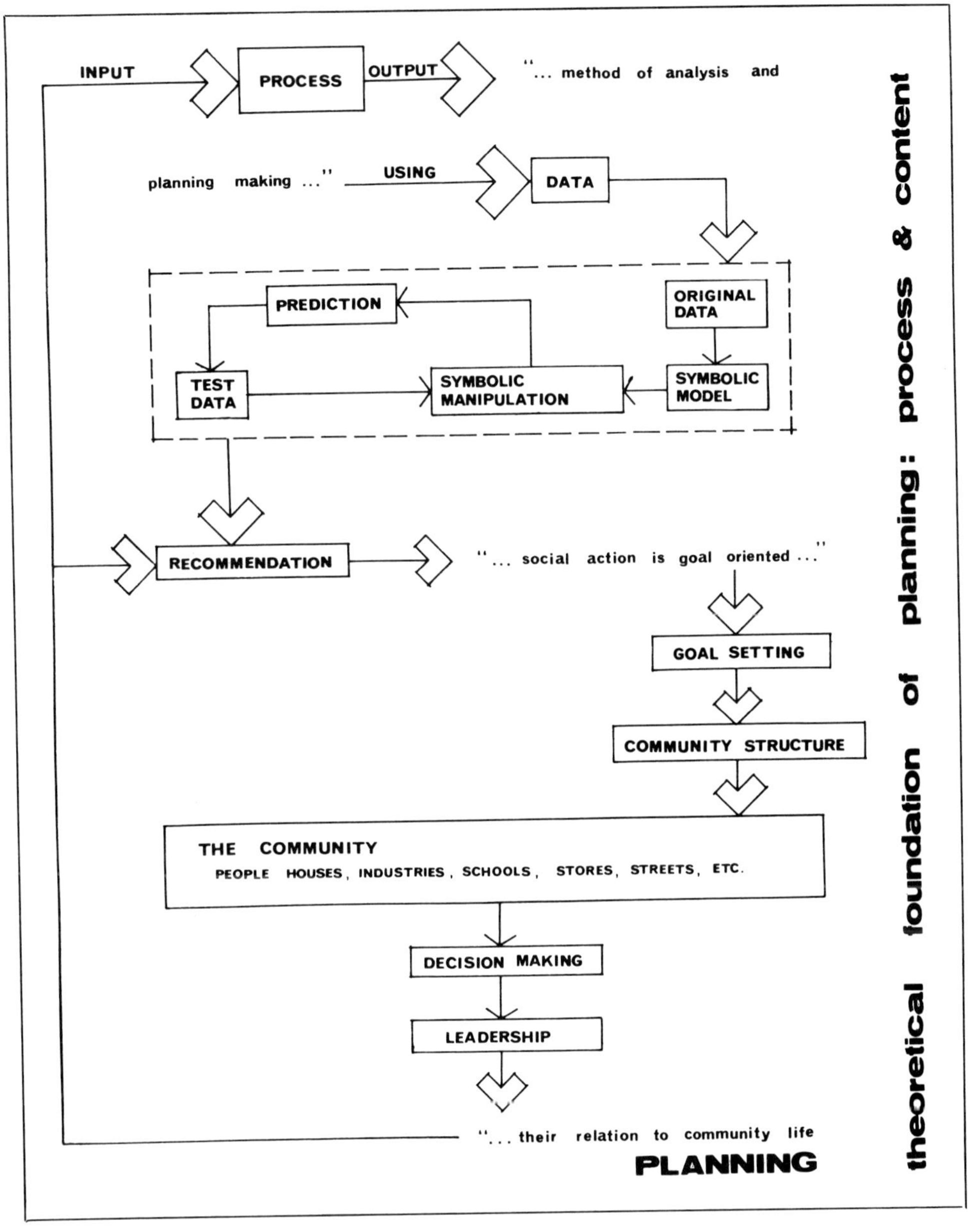

INPUT
PROCESS
OUTPUT
"... method of analysis and
planning making ..."
USING
DATA
PREDICTION
ORIGINAL DATA
TEST DATA
SYMBOLIC MANIPULATION
SYMBOLIC MODEL
RECOMMENDATION
"... social action is goal oriented ..."
GOAL SETTING
COMMUNITY STRUCTURE
THE COMMUNITY
PEOPLE HOUSES, INDUSTRIES, SCHOOLS, STORES, STREETS, ETC.
DECISION MAKING
LEADERSHIP
"... their relation to community life
PLANNING
theoretical foundation of planning: process & content

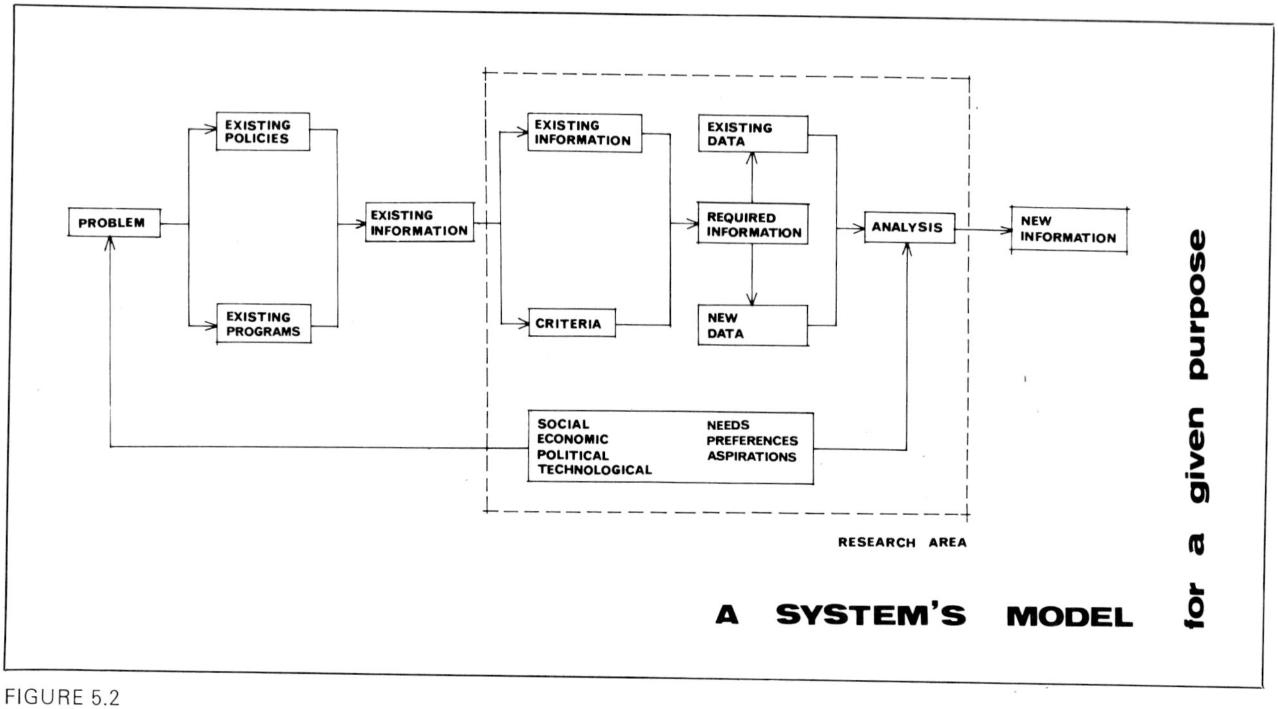

FIGURE 5.2

amined, several invariant characteristics emerge. Chorofas, for example, states

> In the course of evolution of human knowledge we have experienced a growth of new and promising disciplines. One of them is systems analysis; its foundations have been derived from studies of dynamic systems and their functioning components. A system is a group of interdependent elements acting together to accomplish a predetermined purpose. *Systems analysis* is an attempt to define the most feasible, suitable and acceptable means for accomplishing a given purpose.[1] [See Figure 5.2.]

A similar definition has been given by Flagle:

> To begin with the definition, a system is an integrated assembly of interacting elements designed to carry out cooperatively a predetermined function. The living organism, the animal, or above all, the human body with its central nervous system, is an example par excellence of a system.[2]

A definition presenting basically the same point of view with a systems engineering orientation has been given by Morton:

> The systems engineering method recognizes each system as an integrated whole even though composed of diverse specialized structures and subfunctions. It further recognizes that any system has a number of objectives and that the balance between them may differ widely from system to system. The methods seek to optimize the overall system functions according to the weighted objectives and to achieve maximum compatibility of its parts.[3]

It should be noted that the essential concepts expressed by Chorofas, Flagle, and Morton all contain the idea of an integrated assembly. Through its various components, this assembly is able to act as a unified whole. These definitions are similar to the *American College Dictionary* definition of a *system*, as "an assemblage or combination of things or parts forming a complex, or unitary whole." When an analytical approach is suggested, ambiguities sometimes arise from the reference to the system as being a whole.

[1]Dimitris Chorofas, *Systems and Simulation* (New York: Academic Press, 1965), pp. 2–3.

[2]Charles D. Flagle, William H. Huggins, and Robert H. Roy, *Operations Research in Systems Engineering* (Baltimore: Johns Hopkins Press, 1960), pp. 59–60.

[3]J. A. Morton, "Integration of Systems Engineering with Component Development," *Electrical Manufacturing,* **64:**85–92 (August 1959).

When one speaks of a system in an educational context, one is not necessarily referring to the entire educational system; rather, the system must be very carefully defined and specified, just as one specifies the population to be studied when doing statistical sampling.

One might, for example, be dealing with an educational transportation system, an educational food-service system, an educational building system, an educational management-information system, or an educational activity system. Careful specification of the boundaries of the system helps to define the problem and makes more probable the solution of the problem. The boundary concept has been noted by Chorofas:

> In mathematics when talking of systems we mostly have in mind a set of laws. In the physical sciences we use the word system to mean a portion of the universe around which we draw an imaginary boundary for the purpose of study of what is enclosed inside this boundary. In engineering the word system is mostly interpreted as meaning an organized working total, an assemblage of objects united by some form of regular interaction or interdependence. Systems may themselves be subsystems of other larger ensembles; hence, the idea of drawing an imaginary boundary holds true with every usage of the systems concept.[4] [See Figure 5.3.]

The boundaries of systems study, particularly in the field of education, cannot be too clearly defined. This fact has been noted by Wiener:

> We as human beings are not isolated systems. We take in food which generates energy from the outside and are as a result parts of that larger world which contains those sources of our vitality. But even more important is the fact that we can take in information through our sense organs and we act on information received.
>
> Now the physicist is already familiar with the significance of this statement as far as it concerns our relations with the environment. A brilliant expression of the role of the information in this respect is provided by Clerk Maxwell in the form of the so-called Maxwell Demon. . . .[5]

Two ways of creating a new kind of system have been recognized. "One way is by introducing new parts within an old arrangement while the other way is by rearranging in a new pattern the existing parts."[6] The basic need now in urban education is not the creation of new parts but a more effective rearrangement of the existing parts. Rather than minimize their force within the existing arrangement, one should, reorganize the parts that might conflict in a system whereby they complement each other.

Systems studies can become extremely sophisticated, but even with highly sophisticated technology and analysis, the final decision must still rest with a human decision-maker. The general systems concept has been carried over to the urban education operating system, ". . . characterized by land, buildings, people, jobs, amenities, costs and revenues with many decision-makers and controls . . ."[7] (See Figure 5.4.) The real contribution of a new management technology rests primarily in its furnishing the human decision-maker with more effective information. The systems approach, whether simple or complex, is basically a scientific, quantitative approach. It proceeds from a careful analysis of the content and of the planning process required for its implementation.

THE COMPONENT: EDUCATIONAL CONTENT

A functional approach to educational planning requires a clear delineation of the educational system. To be comprehensive, a necessary assumption for our educational planning process model, the educational system has to be considered all-inclusive. A second assumption of our educational planning process model is that the major focus of education is on meeting the specific educational needs of each student as well as society.

The systems approach to educational studies involves not only the various parts of the educational content but also the total content.

[4] Chorofas, p. 4.

[5] Norbert Wiener, *The Human Use of Human Beings* (Garden City, N.Y.: Doubleday, Doubleday Anchor Books, 1956), p. 28.

[6] *Advanced Studies in Urban Environments, Toward an Urban Model,* A Study by the Master Class in Architecture, Serge Chemayeff, Professor in Architectural Design (New Haven: Yale University, 1967).

[7] Cyril C. Herrmann, "Systems Approach to City Planning," *Harvard Business Review,* no. 5, **44**:73 (September/October 1966).

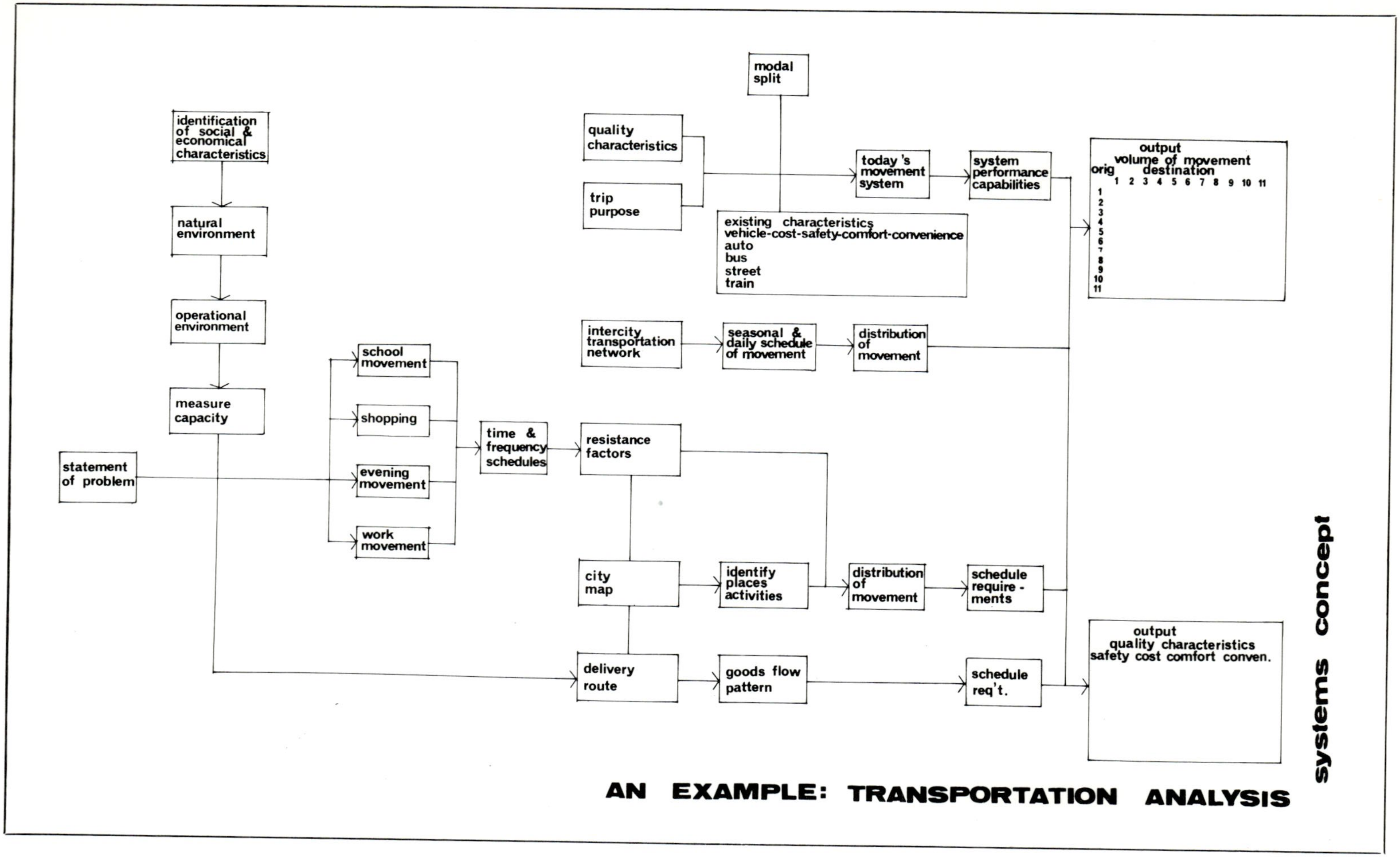
identification of social & economical characteristics
natural environment
operational environment
measure capacity
statement of problem
school movement
shopping
evening movement
work movement
time & frequency schedules
resistance factors
city map
delivery route
quality characteristics
trip purpose
modal split
today's movement system
system performance capabilities
existing characteristics
vehicle-cost-safety-comfort-convenience
auto
bus
street
train
intercity transportation network
seasonal & daily schedule of movement
distribution of movement
identify places activities
distribution of movement
schedule require - ments
goods flow pattern
schedule req't.
output
volume of movement
orig destination
1 2 3 4 5 6 7 8 9 10 11
1
2
3
4
5
6
7
8
9
10
11
output
quality characteristics
safety cost comfort conven.
AN EXAMPLE: TRANSPORTATION ANALYSIS
systems concept

FIGURE 5.3

FIGURE 5.4

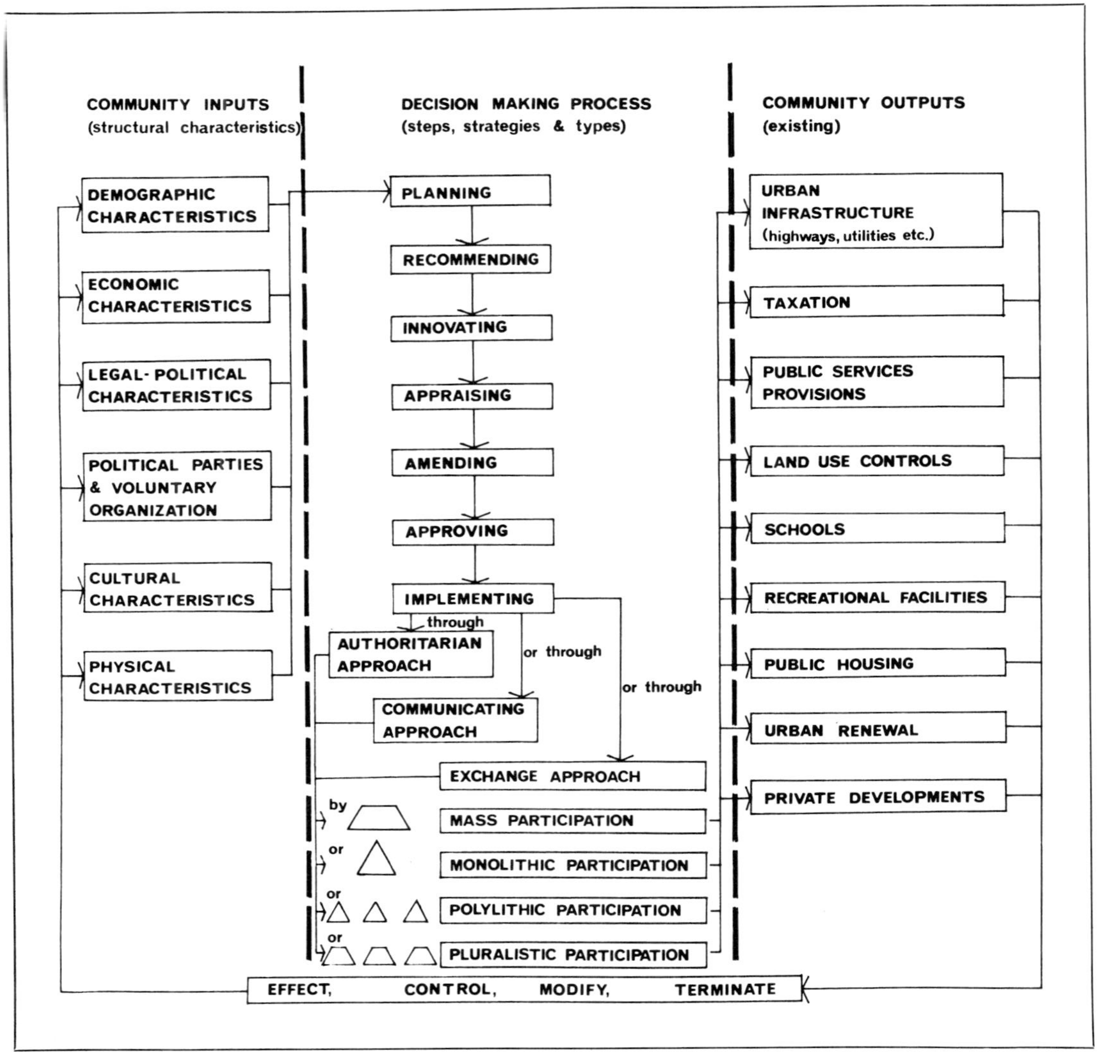
COMMUNITY INPUTS
(structural characteristics)
DEMOGRAPHIC CHARACTERISTICS
ECONOMIC CHARACTERISTICS
LEGAL-POLITICAL CHARACTERISTICS
POLITICAL PARTIES & VOLUNTARY ORGANIZATION
CULTURAL CHARACTERISTICS
PHYSICAL CHARACTERISTICS
DECISION MAKING PROCESS
(steps, strategies & types)
PLANNING
RECOMMENDING
INNOVATING
APPRAISING
AMENDING
APPROVING
IMPLEMENTING
through
AUTHORITARIAN APPROACH
or through
COMMUNICATING APPROACH
or through
EXCHANGE APPROACH
by
MASS PARTICIPATION
or
MONOLITHIC PARTICIPATION
or
POLYLITHIC PARTICIPATION
or
PLURALISTIC PARTICIPATION
COMMUNITY OUTPUTS
(existing)
URBAN INFRASTRUCTURE
(highways, utilities etc.)
TAXATION
PUBLIC SERVICES PROVISIONS
LAND USE CONTROLS
SCHOOLS
RECREATIONAL FACILITIES
PUBLIC HOUSING
URBAN RENEWAL
PRIVATE DEVELOPMENTS
EFFECT, CONTROL, MODIFY, TERMINATE

One example of the systems approach to content analysis is the following subsystem model. This model is not meant to be all-inclusive but indicates only one of the various approaches to a systematic treatment of the content.

I. An educational management information system

A. On students

1) Provides information on grades, test scores, medical examinations, attendance, and other student factors.
2) Provides information on student's out-of-school experiences that have significant effects on his learning process, for example, occupation and income of his parents, characteristics of his home and community, place of birth, and so on.
3) Provides information that compares student's achievement with that of other students in his community and school district, and so on.
4) Provides information on curricular, extracurricular, and supplementary education and community sponsored programs.
5) Provides an identification number that will follow the child's career when and if he moves from school to school and that will follow him as an adult in terms of employment, income, social participation, and so on.

B. On staff

1) Provides information on teacher skills, preference, and educational preparation.
2) Provides information for assigning and scheduling teachers.
3) Provides information on actual functions performed by teachers.
4) Provides information that compares effectiveness and performance of teachers, such as classroom style, experience, social and economic status, and so on.
5) Provides information that forecasts needs for various teaching skills required, their future availability, and the best means for in-service training.

C. On buildings

1) Provides information on location, type, size, capacity, structural systems, construction, cost, maintenance cost, and so on.
2) Provides information on school equipment, location, age, cost, and utilization.
3) Provides information on school environmental quality, possible community use, and so on.

D. On programs

1) Provides information on what was done for each student, how it was done, where it was done, by whom, how much it cost to do it in time and money, and what the intended effect was compared with the actual educational effect.
2) Provides information on available curricula, how each subject is taught, an evaluative procedure for testing each student's performance against established objectives, and so on.
3) Provides information on the effect of each project on teaching and learning.
4) Provides information that compares the cost and effectiveness of different projects.

E. On finances

1) Provides information on the dollars received and spent.
2) Provides information on what has been acquired through the expenditure of dollars and the educational effects of this consumption of resources.
3) Provides information for bookkeeping and routine reporting.
4) Provides information for cost projections.

II. An educational activity system

A. On "in-place" activities

1) Provides information on the precise nature of the activity, numbers involved, equipment required, and so on.

2) Provides information on space requirements for accommodating activities, establishes environmental quality requirements, e.g., foot candles required, decibels permitted, air changes required, and so on.
3) Provides information on appropriate facility locations and relational requirements with other activities.
4) Provides information on intensity of activities, students per square foot, schools per community, and so on; and on spatial configurations required.

B. On time schedule
1) Provides (information on school term types), length of term, and so on.
2) Provides information on frequency of service; monthly, weekly, daily, or as required.
3) Provides information on number of sessions per day, or modules available, length of modules per activity, number of modules per day per activity.

C. On curriculum and instructional programming

D. On community-related programs
1) Provides information on types, kinds, and quality of activities for evaluating cooperative educational programs.
2) Provides information on cost utility studies to reduce public expenditure on similar programs provided by different public agencies.
3) Provides information on activities appropriate for many types of interests possessed by members of community.

III. An educational communication system

A. On transportation
1) Provides information on students' movements from origin to destination: how many, when, and by what mode of travel.
2) Provides information on traffic volumes required, frequency of service, and intensity.
3) Provides information on routes available, capacity of existing routes and potential increase being planned, and routes' environmental quality.
4) Provides information on cost between various modes or routes in return for resulting quality.
5) Provides information on safety standards.

B. On information itself
1) Accepts and gives out data in a variety of forms, e.g., telephone messages, radio, television, computers, and so on.
2) Uses sensory impressions including sights, sounds, smells, and so on.

C. On energy
1) Operates lights, air-conditioning and heating units, ventilators, stoves, and so on.
2) Supports learning experiments, e.g., scientific experiments, auto-driving programs, vocational programs, and so on.

IV. On educational facilities systems

V. On educational operations systems

A. On management systems
B. On food-service systems
C. On maintenance and operations systems
D. On inventory-control systems

Such a systems approach, delineating the various parts of educational content, permits the educational planner to evaluate the effect of potential educational plans. He can assess the use of specific types of equipment or facilities in combination with certain kinds of teachers and certain kinds of teaching techniques, in certain programs, and with the student's own learning characteristics. The systems approach shortens planning time and makes possible relatively complex data analysis at an acceptable level of cost. The systems approach helps the educational planner to determine the best planning strategy for organizing staff, students, programs, and materials. Organizing them becomes the second component—the educational planning process—of the educational system.

THE COMPONENT: EDUCATIONAL PLANNING PROCESS

To understand any process requires an understanding of the problem, and in our case an educational problem. Realistic educational objectives can be established and used as aims for organizing the educational planning process. In addition it is necessary to identify the inputs and outputs of the process, along with specific characteristics and the relationships that link them together. Criteria are used to measure outputs in relation to the established educational objectives. A framework for the educational planning process, using the systems approach, is shown in Figure 5.5.

The inputs and objectives as determined by values are the stimuli that energize the educational system and provide it with the content of its operation. Outputs are the results of processes and are the objectives toward which processes are directed. Values, objectives, inputs, processes, outputs, and criteria define the course that the study of a particular educational problem takes. Each is subject to environmental circumstances that enhance or impose limitations on how the objectives are achieved. These constraints help to define a system's boundaries and the conditions under which the process operates. Once the outputs are obtained they are compared with the criteria. This comparison is used as feedback, which permits modification of the system. The inputs and outputs, their properties and relations, constraints and feedback along with values and objectives define the educational planning process. (See Figure 5.6.)

This generic model is process oriented and points not only to the ultimate result but also to the intermediate results. The model requires the division of complex educational problems into their component parts. The solution for the whole problem is thus made possible through the organization of serially related, manageable segments.

Within the framework, above, a model for the educational planning process can now be completed. To this framework is added the seven-phase model being used as the guideline for this book. The two models now become one model, as Figure 5.7 illustrates.

Within this framework, the educational planner can make decisions on the basis of a simplified model that captures the main features of a problem. It is necessary to make decisions that have a certain amount of flexibility built into them: the system (education) cannot be too rigid if it is to be practical. Educational practice must be flexible enough to absorb changes without the educational system's breaking down. The model, therefore, must be simple, changeable, and easily managed to be acceptable to the educational planners using it; otherwise, the model will become ineffectual. The utility must always be balanced against the cost in time, effort, and understanding.

SUMMARY

A functional approach to the problem of educational planning requires a clear delineation of the educational system. The educational planner must consider the whole spectrum of education, from the values held by the community to the student's use of the skills and knowledge obtained. At one end of the spectrum he must clarify the values and express them as objectives of the proposed educational system and the activities for which it is designed. At the other end of the spectrum he must consider educational activities in operation. He will, therefore, seek to incorporate content, processes, and other features into the model. In the middle of the spectrum, the educational planners must take into account the planning process and the use of technical tools such as simulation, linear programming, gaming theory, queuing theory, and other various techniques. Thus the planning process opens up new educational design possibilities, it ensures that the proposed educational program can be built, and it permits costs to be kept in line with the benefits received. Consequently, to be truly effective, the educational system has to be considered as an all-inclusive process.

FIGURE 5.5

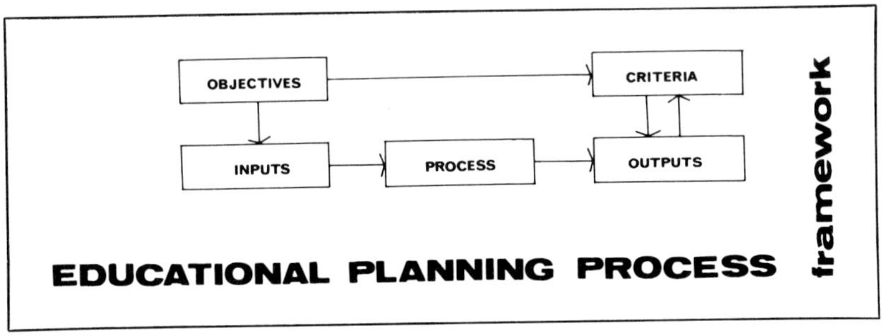

FIGURE 5.6

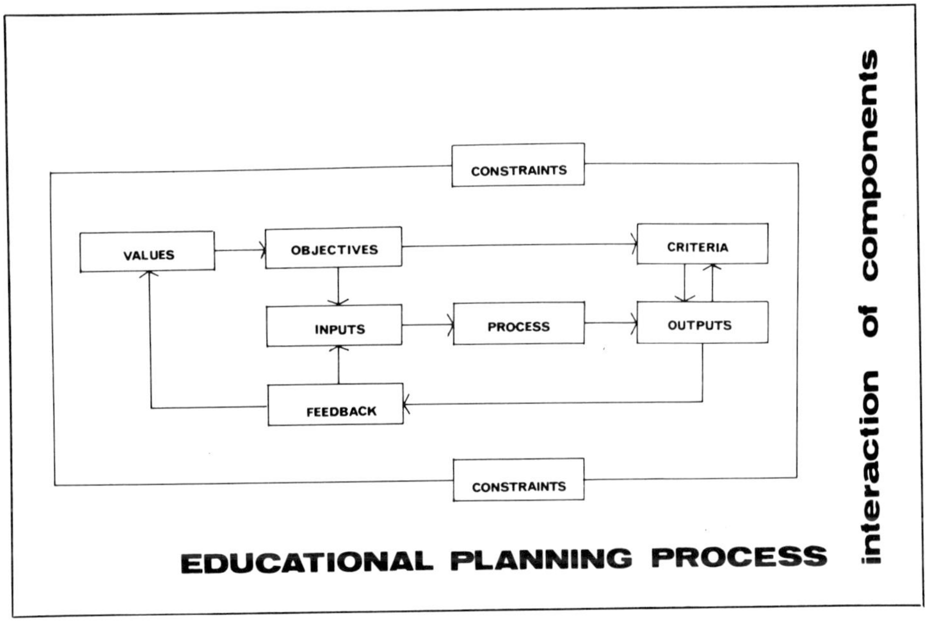

FIGURE 5.7

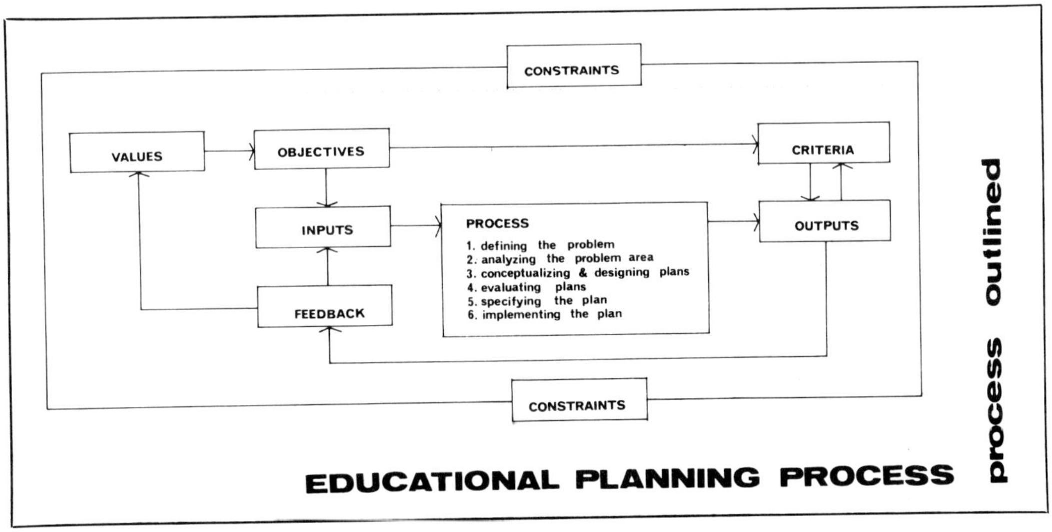

Part Two

Analyzing the planning problem area

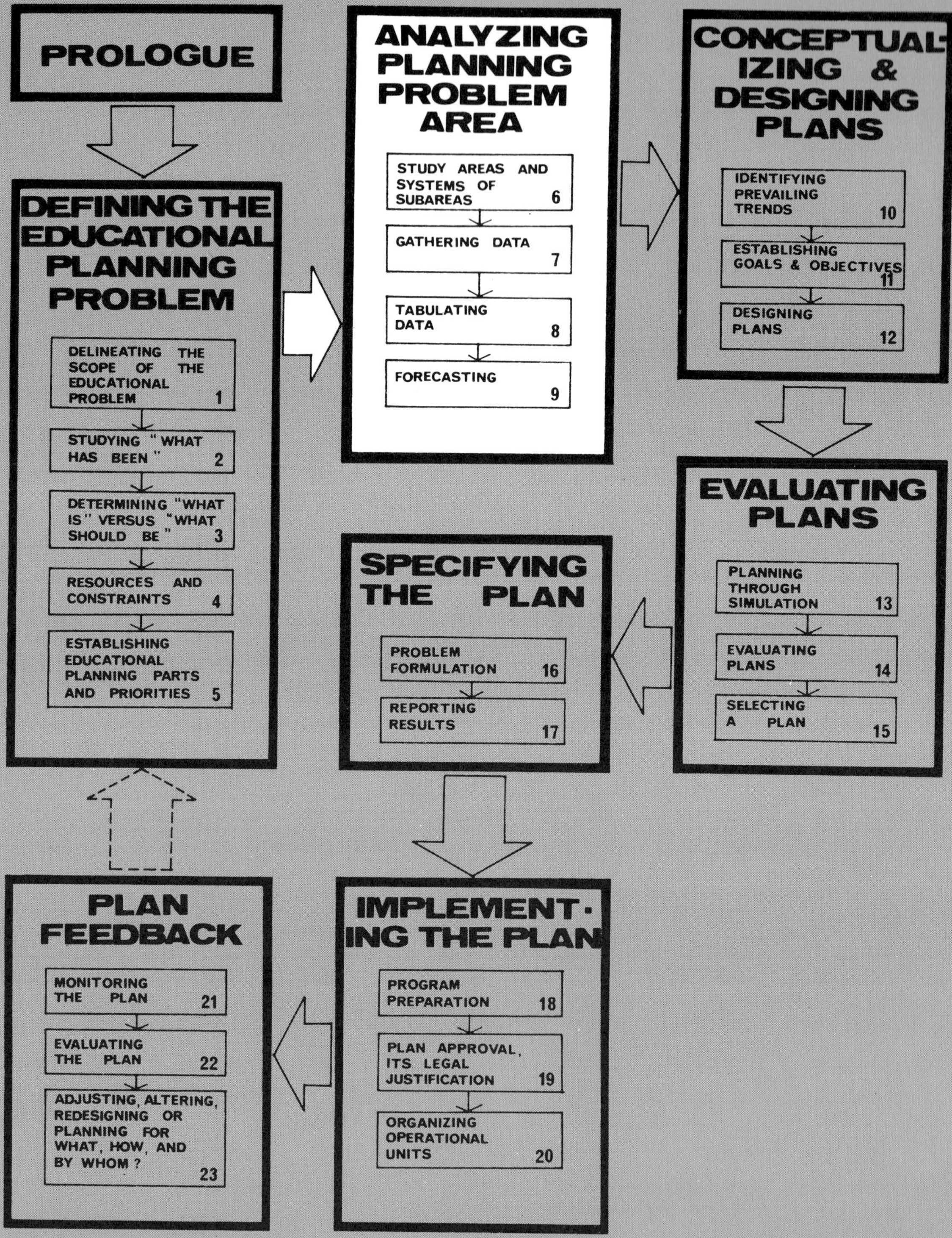
PROLOGUE
DEFINING THE EDUCATIONAL PLANNING PROBLEM
DELINEATING THE SCOPE OF THE EDUCATIONAL PROBLEM 1
STUDYING "WHAT HAS BEEN" 2
DETERMINING "WHAT IS" VERSUS "WHAT SHOULD BE" 3
RESOURCES AND CONSTRAINTS 4
ESTABLISHING EDUCATIONAL PLANNING PARTS AND PRIORITIES 5
ANALYZING PLANNING PROBLEM AREA
STUDY AREAS AND SYSTEMS OF SUBAREAS 6
GATHERING DATA 7
TABULATING DATA 8
FORECASTING 9
CONCEPTUALIZING & DESIGNING PLANS
IDENTIFYING PREVAILING TRENDS 10
ESTABLISHING GOALS & OBJECTIVES 11
DESIGNING PLANS 12
EVALUATING PLANS
PLANNING THROUGH SIMULATION 13
EVALUATING PLANS 14
SELECTING A PLAN 15
SPECIFYING THE PLAN
PROBLEM FORMULATION 16
REPORTING RESULTS 17
IMPLEMENTING THE PLAN
PROGRAM PREPARATION 18
PLAN APPROVAL, ITS LEGAL JUSTIFICATION 19
ORGANIZING OPERATIONAL UNITS 20
PLAN FEEDBACK
MONITORING THE PLAN 21
EVALUATING THE PLAN 22
ADJUSTING, ALTERING, REDESIGNING OR PLANNING FOR WHAT, HOW, AND BY WHOM? 23

Introduction

The work of the educational planner is tenuous and difficult. He must be aware of the many forces at work on educational institutions at present as well as those anticipated in the future. Although he is aware that there will be unpredictable influences on the institutions, his work requires that he design guidelines by which the institution can chart its way to some appointed time in the future.

There are, in addition, certain fundamental facts of social existence during the learning process of which the planner must be cognizant. He must know that men have their own individual space requirements and that at the same time they require many kinds of spaces to accommodate their gregariousness. He also knows that all men seek to measure and maintain an equilibrium between their psychological and sociological needs. Because there are finite approaches to the kinds and types of learning spaces and the distribution of learning tools and movements, the planner may rely on a finite number of well-established principles in designing an educational system for the future. In this design, the resource allocations, along with social, economic, and political consequences, play a major role in solving problems. Where people are concentrated there will be demands for flexibility and a transformation of the established educational structure. With these constraints in mind the educational planner seeks to formulate an educational design, whether it be physical, management, or curriculum oriented, that will fit the physical, political, economic, social, and psychological aspects of its urban environment.

Certain principles have been observed in urban educational planning:

1 *There is a possibility to have an objective system as a basis of [an urban educational] organization or a basis for any planning.*

2 *The archetype [urban educational] organization (pattern) is of a limited number.*

3 *Any transformation is but a shifting of one pattern into another.*

4 *There are some "ideal" infrastructures permitting this shifting with maximum efficiency.*

[The ideal infrastructure] . . . is an effort to fix and to organize the objective elements of [an urban education.] It assures static security (antigravitation), space organization, supply of energy, water and circulation. Now, such "objective" elements have to be organized in a neutral way, i.e., in a way that does not impose preconceived ideas for any individual occupation.

Electricity networks are neutral and objective; so should it be essentially, with "ideal" infrastructures. The basic effect of such a structure consists in separating, fixing and neutralizing the objective functional elements from the intuitive ones, as we saw above.

Obviously enough, these objective elements (the infrastructure) don't determine the character of [urban education]. The character of [urban education] should arise, intuitively formed by the inhabitants themselves (as in the historical past) or by their trustees.[1]

Recently, new approaches associated with the quantitative, scientific methods falling under the domain of systems analysis have been useful to the planner. There has been increased use of computers and operations research techniques applied to planning the physical environment. Increased attention is being given to the technology of computer graphics, which allows the designer more time for creating physical environments than did his former intuitive approach. Such tools and their concomitant technology should go far in providing designers, especially educational designers, a new liberation from the tedium of the drawing board, allowing them to spend their time on the more creative kinds of output related to actual educational needs. In summary, although the planner's methods are still basically eclectic, borrowed from the social and quantitative disciplines, it has become increasingly clear that there is a set of invariant tools that are extremely adaptable to the planner's unique areas of investigation and work. As these tools of sophisticated technology become more refined and new ones are introduced, a more systematic philosophy and a well-grounded theory of planning educational environments will emerge.

[1]Yona Friedman, "Towards a Coherent System of Planning," *Architectural Design*, **34**:372 (August 1964).

The steps for analyzing the planning problem areas include:

Step 6 Studying areas and systems of subareas
Step 7 Gathering data
Step 8 Tabulating data
Step 9 Forecasting

6 Study areas and systems of subareas

An analysis that answers overall educational systems problems should do the following:

1 Determine the potential effects of a variety of process decisions on the various components of the educational system.
2 Evaluate alternative methods of education with respect to a particular educational problem.
3 Pinpoint critical areas requiring substantial research and development.
4 Evaluate the relative cost benefits of various educational systems.
5 Conduct in-depth analysis of specific educational systems and their components.

To meet these five objectives, the program of analysis must be flexible, and the level of detail must be consistent with the nature of the educational problem being investigated.

ANALYSIS TO ESTABLISH EDUCATIONAL OBJECTIVES

In order to design a total educational environment one must begin with a comprehensive analysis of its present condition. This analysis can present a comprehensive view not only of the current situation but of the resources available for future utilization. A convenient system or method that might serve as a guide for the designer would involve two broad categories: (1) a careful survey of the educational area for visual or social design potentials and (2) a classification of education by a convenient category system. (See Figure 6.1.) The educational designer in his preliminary survey should look for the demands for education by various groups within the community, should study the specific educational system's characteristics, should look for constraints on the educational system, should analyze the required educational system's specifications and should delineate the systems of values held by the community.

The educational planner

> . . . can do this systematically by searching for three kinds of elements with aesthetic potential. These are things that are noticed because of their surface qualities; things which are interesting because they are significant forms or combinations of forms; and, thirdly, fixed expression of society. The latter contain or symbolize meanings or experiences —the overt, built-in poetry of the culture.[1]

A systematic study of the educational environment might go through three phases. A superficial examination of a panoramic view of the educational environment could occupy the first stage. Secondly, the educational environment can be investigated in depth. After the elements are identified in terms of the educational systems that they cover and their purpose for being, then the educational planner may study the more sophisticated problems dealing with the interrelationships among the various elements. There are several questions that should be posed at various stages in the analyzing process concerning the compatibility or noncompatibility between the individual learner and the learning environment. What are the effects of compatibility or noncompatibility (1) On other educational aspects—such as location and costs, for instance? (2) On sociological goals (e.g., center-city educational programs versus suburban educational programs)? On producing alienation? (3) On reducing or enhancing the individual's freedom of choice and his ability to assert his uniqueness? (4) On causing disorientation? (5) On leading to

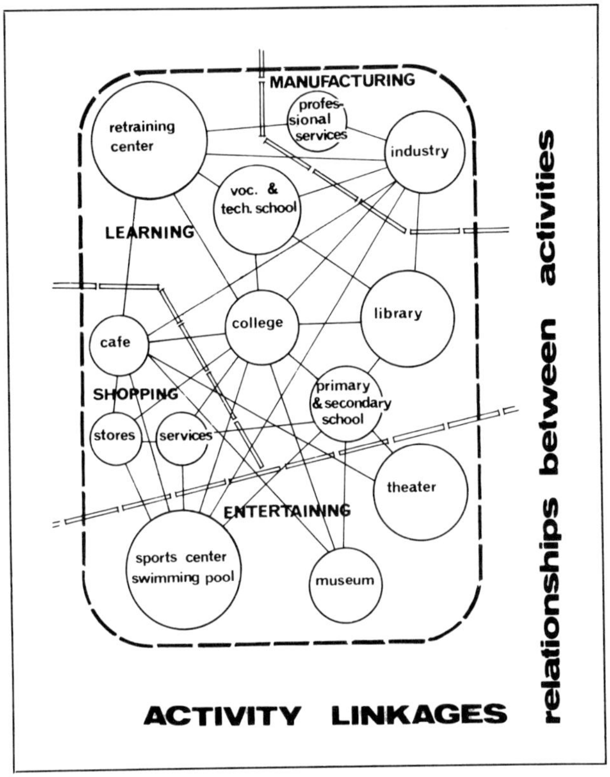

FIGURE 6.1

such rapid and fluid change as to prove socially unacceptable within the community?

It is extremely difficult to transplant historical examples of education to a new urban environment, whether or not they have been successful in other urban contexts. This direction negates a fundamental tenet of education: the need to be compatible with all the elements involved—student, teacher, space program, and so on. The planner must constantly realize that his planning does not take place in a vacuum: the planning process that he creates must be an expression of the needs of the client, whether that client is an individual, a group, or an urban community. Again, the planner's problem is to create a visual presentation of an idea or a set of ideas. The success of his plan will depend, to a great degree, on how much the form reflects the educational requirements of the client.

[1]Stephen W. Jacobs, "Design Resources of the City," *Planning for Urban Aesthetics.* A Report to the Fifth Annual Conference of the Organization of Cornell Planners, October 27–28, 1961 (Ithaca, N.Y.: The Conference, 1961), p. 8.

Historically, the educational planner has been more concerned with bits and pieces of education rather than with the overall educational system. In more recent years, however, the educational planner has become more interested in the overall problems of educational planning rather than the more narrowly defined problems of curriculum, or building, or transportation. This trend is reflected in the following dimensions of the new education: (1) increased scale, (2) comprehensive educational planning, (3) feasible alternatives, (4) urban educational design, (5) educational systems engineering, and (6) decision-making processes.

Education, then, is much more than mere knowledge. It is an expression of the physical, emotional and financial aspects of the user. Education must reflect some real program and gauge its success by its service to the user's needs. It has become increasingly clear that the user's needs interrelate with many other needs within the urban environment; therefore, a given structure cannot exist solely for one person's requirements but must also recognize the greater needs of society. In this respect, aesthetic and functional qualities become equally important. The field of education has broadened its scope considerably. Good education should deal with life itself, which implies knowledge of biological, social, psychological and economic problems.

The educational planner must develop a profound insight into the development of the environment and must acquire an understanding of the various associations among the components of or the activity systems within the environment. This is true at all levels of design including educational: "The process of designing a great city or a simple chair differs only in degree, not in principle. It embraces the whole orbit of manmade, visible surrounding."[2]

An individual reacts to his total environment. Frequently reacting to trivial things, the interplay of various environmental influences continuously determines the individual's actions and reactions to those environmental influences. The educational planner needs a knowledge of the psychological makeup of the individual in order to create an appropriate educational design. The positive influences of the environment might be considered in the light of the individual's interaction with an environment.

The idea that environmental factors influence an individual has implications for a learning environment. The planner of an educational environment must have a keen sense of the psychological factors influencing the student and must in many subtle ways weave these factors into the educational environment.

ANALYSIS OF THE VARIOUS EDUCATIONAL SYSTEMS

Many systems comprise the educational environment. They can be identified readily if education is defined as the equipping of individuals for acting in and creating usable environments. Four subsystems are implied: educational activities, educational communication, educational facilities and educational operations. Because a system consists of processes, the educational system may be depicted as follows:

Activity processes
Communication processes
Facility processes → The education system
Operation processes

The concern of the comprehensive educational planner is with the total educational process. He cannot divorce himself from the problems of the student, the teacher, or the administrator. What the educational planner does affects the total system. In turn he is affected by the educational requirements arising out of the various processes. Because of these relationships, the educational planner must analyze carefully the way in which the subsystems are related to one another. Clearly, some sort of cyclical relationship exists. The communication processes affect the way the facility performs and in turn are affected by operations. The form of the relationship is shown in Figures 6.2 and 6.3.

[2] Walter Gropius, *Scope of Total Architecture* (New York: Harper & Row, 1955), p. 20.

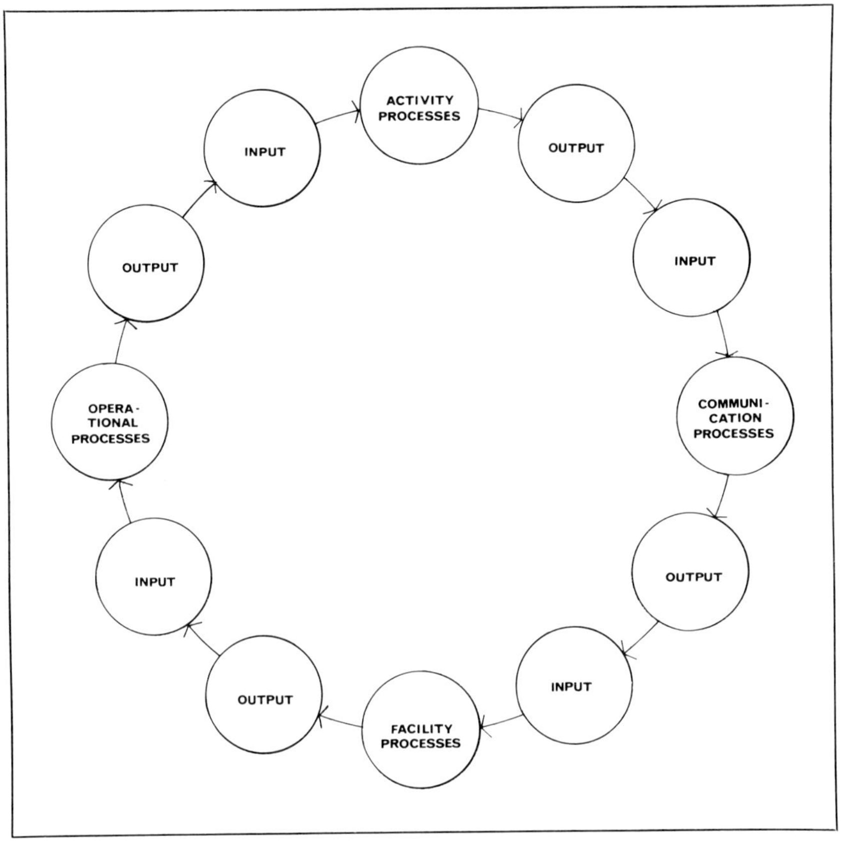

FIGURE 6.2

FIGURE 6.3

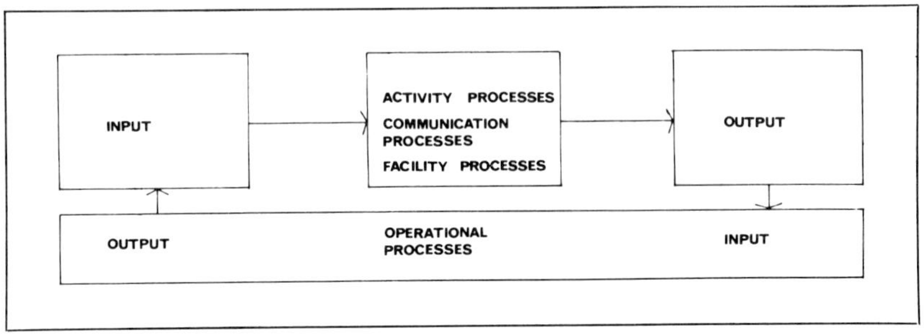

Together, these educational subsystems characterize human behavior:

(*input*)		(*process*)		(*output*)
Student	→	Educational processes	→	Student behavior

Each process as a system is described in the sections that follow.

Educational activity systems

The learning processes form the foundation for educational planning. Educational activities include all activities, curricular and otherwise, performed directly for students, as well as those activities carried out as auxiliary to the learning process. The educational activity system includes such activities as the following:

Curriculum planning
Resource planning
Instructional strategies and programming
Community/school interprogramming
In-service teacher training
Evaluation

Curriculum planning is perhaps the oldest form of educational planning and also the most basic kind of systematic educational planning. Curriculum planning is involved directly with educational objectives, for it deals with such activities as what to teach, how to teach it, to whom, and with what resources. Curriculum planning requires basic decisions on how educational resources, student and teacher time, space, and equipment are allocated. Unfortunately, curriculum planners must work with "givens," for they do not usually decide how many and what kind of spaces are required, how many teachers to hire and with what qualifications, what equipment is to be bought, or how many students are to take part in the activities.

At the other end of the relatively isolated planning in curriculum is the community/school interprogramming of activities. One such example is the "High School with No Walls" in Philadelphia, known as the Parkway school system. In this system, instructional activities take place at more than three-hundred sites, such as churches, automobile garages, and skyscraper office buildings.[3] Home-room activities are scattered about the city, making the city itself the classroom and the activities of the city their curriculum. The effectiveness of these activities is illustrated by the dropout rate and the fact that many students linger long after the scheduled activities are over and often volunteer to participate in various weekend activities.

These two opposite approaches to educational activities hint at the widening attention being paid to educational activities systems. These two approaches directly involve the student's behavior, and the behavior patterns lie at the very heart of the educational planner's concern. Such activities give rise to the problems that the educational planner is called upon to solve. He must manipulate those patterns, whether on a school scale, a community scale, or even a city scale.

The survey of educational activity systems has a central place in the information needs of educational planning. It deals with the actual workings of students, teachers, and so on. It integrates and illuminates neatly all other forms of information, e.g., population, programs, facilities, equipment, and so on. By focusing on one particular activity at a time (e.g., on the space that it occupies) and by studying the auxiliary services that interact with it, the educational activity system survey performs an integrating function.

The survey requires the following:

1 Establishment of the precise nature of the activity(ies) carried on by a unit of students and teachers or students or one student.
2 Description of the nature of the space it occupies —its location, size of floor area, services required, and so on.
3 Outline of a social profile of those participating in the activity.
4 Record of the frequency, form, and volume of all forms of services engaged in the activity.

[3]Henry S. Resnik, "High School with No Walls," *Pennsylvania Education,* no. 3, 2:6 (May/June 1970).

Such an outline is broad enough to help the educational planner devise his own educational activity system surveys suitable for use in particular circumstances.

Educational communication systems

The educational system represents a complicated communications system in which interactions through direct and indirect confrontations are continuous. The various levels of these confrontations have great relevance for the educational planner.

The dynamics of the educational system might be considered in terms of continuous movements or flows of activities from one node that is an "in-place" activity to another. Such activities involve four basic kinds of communication such as, students, teachers, etc., movements; equipment, supplies, etc., movements; information transfer; and energy transmission. Integrating these various subsystems into an operation system is the responsibility of the educational planner. This integration is accomplished through appropriate arrangement in time, space, and scale.

Educational movement systems

Educational movement systems become the primary motivators for assigning locations to various educational activities and permit the movement of students and others within the various sections of the educational area. Planning in the movement field affects other planning areas and should consider its far-reaching effects. Educational goals and educational needs should be the primary factors in determining the form, structure, and operation of movement systems.

Movement systems for people and goods Serving several functions, movement forms the basic structure of the school and links its various activity systems, as do the transportation systems of the city. Movement affects the school economy because it influences the amount of time between nodes of activities. The movement system takes on consumer characteristics in the sense that it is purchased as are other consumer goods; that is, by some trade-off process.

The movement problem has three aspects—assignment, routing, and minimal path requirement between the points of origin and destination. The following example illustrates the three aspects. In a population area containing three schools, each area has a different capability in terms of programs. There may be reasons to assign students throughout this population area to any one of the three schools in order to provide the most efficient education for all. Therefore, the first solution of the movement problem would be to assign students to the most appropriate school. Second, the route should be the shortest distance by bus. This is a purely mathematical problem, merely computing the distances a bus must travel to pick up all the students and transport them to the schools. The third aspect of the problem involves getting the bus from the overnight parking position to the first pickup point at a minimal distance. Work is progressing rapidly on this problem, and it should be solved soon. The problem is of interest here because, as for so many educational problems, the school system must assume responsibility. It has been solved on relatively intuitive bases for years and yet lends itself well to the new technology now available to education.

Movement analysis takes on various aspects and must be concerned with policy problems within the system and with alternative approaches, problem solving, and evaluation in terms of cost-utility analysis. The approaches, solution and evaluation can be studied in terms of the effects of a variety of policy and regulatory decisions on the various elements, the evaluation of alternative modes of transportation with respect to particular requirements, the identification of critical areas requiring substantial research and development, the evaluation of the relative cost benefits of ad hoc transportation systems, and the conduct of engineering analyses of specific systems and their components.

The analysis should be centered on the basic aspects of the movement or transportation system, such as movement demands, constraints, engineering specifications, cost, safety, convenience, and the particular characteristics of a system. (See Figure 6.4.) The key aspects of the transportation system analysis

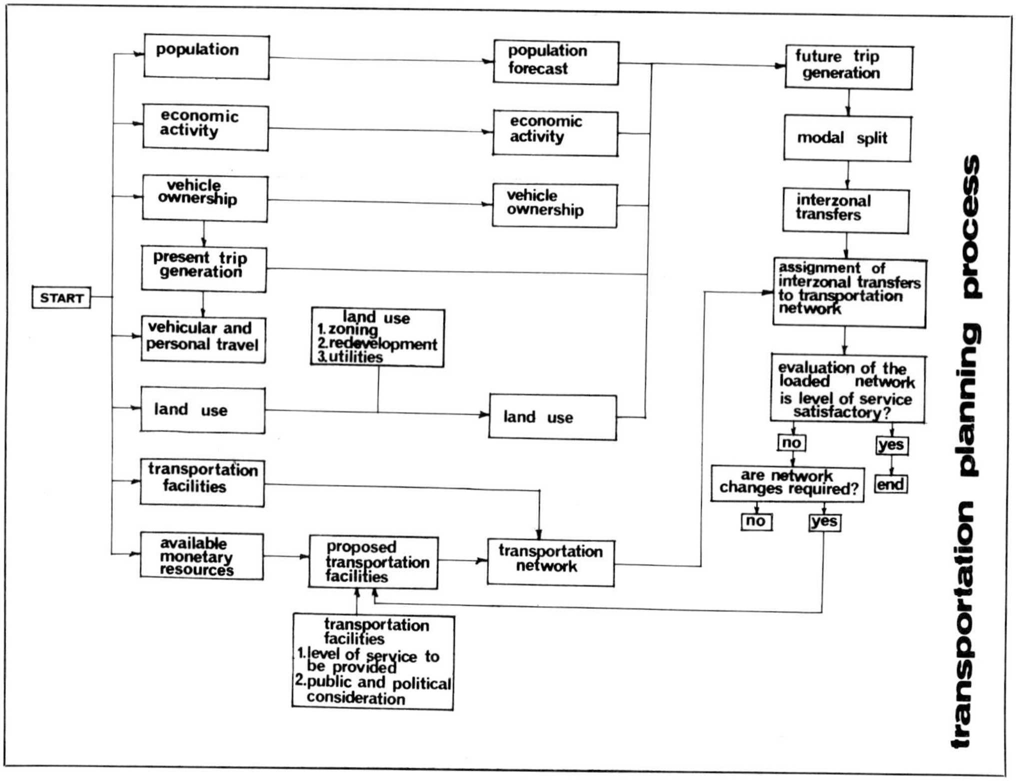

FIGURE 6.4

Analyzing transportation for potential educational use

are cost, comfort, convenience, safety, and demand. Data are gathered from objective measurements of comfort and safety and are represented by cost and utility ratios. The cost might be a simple dollar amount, but the utility may be a composite number. The impact of the transportation design on the overall educational urban design is quite extensive; the transportation system analysis should be an inherent part of the overall analysis of the educational urban design. In addition, the design should be based on long-range total planning rather than on a mere modification of the present system: the educational planner, working with the transportation planner, must be flexible in his outlook and understand not only the technical aspects of transportation planning but he also must have an overall idea of the many interacting subsystems.

When one studies transportation through the eyes of a systems analyst, he must pay attention to overall traffic movements and patterns, which combine the transit traffic, pedestrian traffic and auto and bus passengers. The growing interest in the city as a classroom necessitates the integration of educational traffic patterns into the overall traffic pattern. After all, the destination of the student may not be where the auto would be parked; instead considerable movement might take place after the individual has left the automobile and moves about on foot. Transportation analysis involves a combination of quantitative and qualitative approaches:

. . . to insure that no consequences are overlooked and that none are either under- nor over-valued, and it is to provide the planner every opportunity of dealing properly with the uncertain future, with conflicts, with system interactions and with pecuniary and non-pecuniary objectives . . . and to guarantee as much as possible that objective rather than subjective values and decisions will be forthcoming . . . to utilize human resources more effectively.[4]

This combination of quantitative and qualitative testing requires various statistical applications in transportation analysis.

In multiple testing, computers make traffic assignments to alternative plans in rapid order. State of the art computer programs have four prime characteristics. First, they deal with more than one mode of travel. Second, they must have fast inputs so a variety of plans can be tested. Third, they must have visual outputs, as flow diagrams, and fourth, they must have what I call an economic output, which is a summation of the cost, the time, the accidents and the other characteristics of the plan itself.[5]

Appropriate distribution forecasts enable the planner ". . . (a) successfully to simulate past growth, (b) to take changes in accessibility into account, (c) to display the results for visual inspection as well as to maintain the necessary accounting totals, and (d) to take into account zoning, planning acquisitions of public lands and other exogenous factors."[6]

[4]Martin Wohl, "Transportation System Concepts and Issues," *1966 National Transportation Symposium* (New York: American Society of Mechanical Engineers, 1966), p. 73.

[5]Roger T. Creighton and John R. Hamburg, "State of the Art in the Urban Transportation Planning Process: 1966," *1966 National Transportation Symposium* (New York: American Society of Mechanical Engineers, 1966), p. 106.

[6]Ibid., p. 105.

With this in mind educational planners in concert with transportation planners analyze trip purposes as well as the frequency of use, population density, nodes and lengths of the links. Of course, emphasis should also be placed on *future* development of the movement system. Thus, any analysis should be oriented toward future uses instead of current usage. By surveying various users, needed information can be gathered and applied to ensure optimum space usage in terms of growth, current usage and anticipated demands. Such an analysis must include residential, business, industrial, recreational, and other land uses in concert with educational requirements in designing a movement system. In light of these considerations it is anticipated that greater emphasis will be placed on human behavior within the transportation area in addition to the basic economic factors. It is possible with current technologies to simulate various configurations of space usage of fixed facilities and human behavior within an area serviced by a movement system. The computer simulations are invaluable to the planner; they clearly designate in graphic form the data that are essential to a pertinent examination of the system.

Many transportation systems, both school and urban, have developed in a haphazard fashion. Because the system, by definition, is a set of interconnecting terminals, it behooves the planner to design a system that will ensure an optimal operation and one that will be consistent with all other aspects of the community and school in long-range developments. Figure 6.5 illustrates the interconnecting aspects of a transportation system.

It is absolutely essential that various planners, including the educational planner, cooperate with the transportation expert because movement of any kind is an inherent part of other activity systems within the urban educational area.

It is important to point out that the bulk of the population increase is occurring and will continue to occur in the outlying portions of the metropolitan area. . . .

This fact, combined with the growing capacity of residential, commercial and industrial developers to lay out whole new communities in one fell swoop offers unparalleled opportunities to coordinate transit and highway systems with these land-use developments to create new suburban

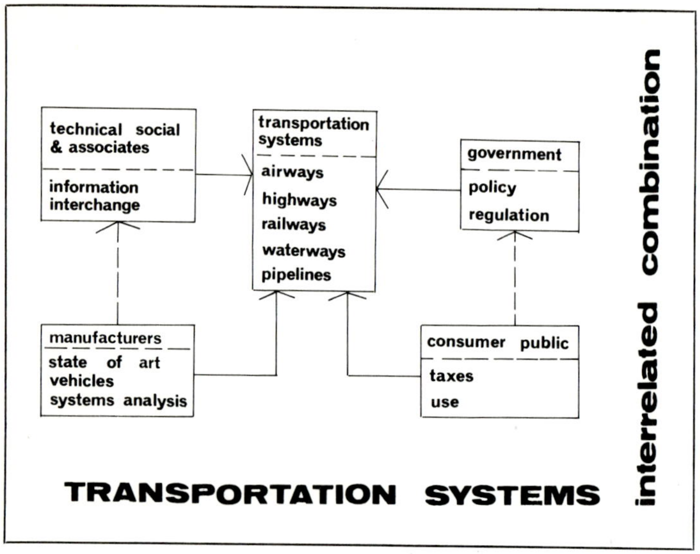

FIGURE 6.5

environments with a vastly higher level of diversity, variety, comfort, efficiency, productivity, and attractiveness than we have ever been able to achieve before.

This is why highways should not be the sole concern of the highway engineers and why transit should not be the sole concern of the transit operator.[7]

Educational information systems

A second component of the educational communication system is the educational information system. Its analysis must proceed from an understanding of the manner in which information is to be used. Because of planning's particular nature, differences in requirements exist for information systems oriented toward planning and information systems oriented toward day-to-day learning operations.

Day-to-day learning operations data include information transmitted between individuals, telephone messages, and television programs, as well as those sensory impressions obtained from the environment. The urban and educational spaces contain distinct and recognizable qualities that affect an individual's perceptual satisfaction with his learning environment. Size, density, grain, shape and interval patterns of school and urban spaces are learning dimensions that can be observed. These consciously or subconsciously influence the experiences in the individual's daily activities. The appropriate placement of schools and key activity areas, the appropriate design of the transportation facilities throughout, the climate and cultural attitudes are essential data that feed sensory impressions.

The mission of the educational planner is, in general terms, to determine requirements and formulate plans for educational growth and development. For a given area these missions should fulfill community goals. The educational planner's mission is also to effect the optimal allocation of limited resources consistent with educational requirements and plans. An information system for the educational agency must be able to support those missions.

The educational planner is interested in the past and the present only to the extent that the past and present affect the shape of the future. (See Figure 6.6.) Generally, his technique is to obtain an actual cross section of information for several points in time, past through present, to project the trend for the future. As a result, his work is less clearly defined and his focus is on aggregate rather than individual entities. He is also concerned with relationships among data

[7]Smerk, p. 74.

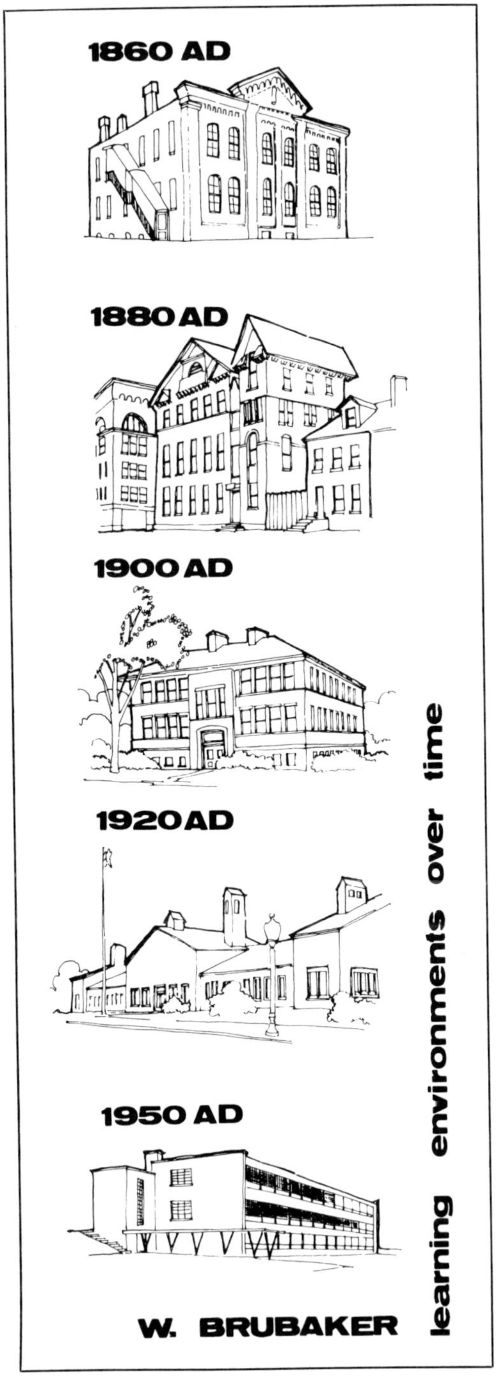

FIGURE 6.6

and is dependent in large measure on data outputs from various sources. To support the educational planner's efforts, the information system must be open-ended and flexible, must permit him to employ a wide variety of data-handling capabilities and must permit him to apply advanced methods of analysis.

The most effective method for determining user requirements is a heuristic one. The planner must begin to acquire the data that seem most consistent with present planning objectives and procedures. They permit a data base to evolve as new needs arise or as new data sources become apparent. In following this approach, the educational planner should consider the categories of data common to most educational activities, existing checklists of educational planning data and data elements, and present organizations of data bases.

Comprehensive educational planning requires many data elements, ranging from the individual student to facilities, to fire protection, to student population projections. However, it is neither possible nor desirable to attempt to specify in advance a set of data items that represents an ideal data base for all comprehensive educational planning activities. The major emphasis has been on an integrated student file. Planning, however, must be based on a broader range of data than that encompassed by a student file.

A viable educational information system should have clearly stated system objectives, provide effective system management, provide procedures for data-base management, and possess a capable data-processing system.

System objectives should be clearly stated and include such elements as the following:

1 The data collected should be capable of supporting a multiple-mission-oriented educational program.
2 Data should be collected on a continuing basis with procedures for systems maintenance and data upgrading.

Systems management includes a plan to provide appropriate software and hardware designed to meet the systems' needs. Evidence of effective management also includes assurances of the availability of resources

—personnel, data-processing systems, and so on—to meet educational requirements. This includes a means of controlling and evaluating the effectiveness and efficiency of performance.

Data-base management that supports multiple-mission-oriented educational programs includes procedures for data-base documentation, data compatibility, data-access control, and provision for continuing data acquisition.

Consideration must also be given the possession of a capable data processing system. This system consists of computer hardware and software. In education, an information system for planning is required to possess a very broad range of capabilities in the data processing system. These capabilities must include the following activities:

1 A system that can accept and put out data in a variety of forms.
2 A system capable of handling large volumes of data.
3 A system that can operate on individual values in a data set.
4 A system capable of manipulating and altering data-set structures.
5 A system that can display data.
6 A system that can provide for fact retrieval and statistical analysis.
7 A system that can provide data-base reference service and documentation.

At the present time no adequate general-purpose software is available, so that educational planning agencies must use existing software or develop their own. The common procedure of hiring a few programmers to begin to develop an educational information system without first thoroughly analyzing the requirements, cost, and time can be wasteful. The educational planner should first give consideration to the anticipated needs of the users and his interaction with the data base. In addition, the educational planners must consider the processing flexibility that will be required to support educational planning activities before launching any programming efforts. Such an approach results in an information system that is easy to modify and expand.

Educational energy systems

The educational communication system involves also energy and its transmission. This system is based on the assumption that energy is an ever-changing product that results from the sociopsychological needs of an individual, which his ethnic, social, economic, and political environments have dictated. Another assumption based on the requirements of the individual's well-being at any given time dictates the amount of energy to be supplied. This assumption is that the individual is a nonstationary, open system undergoing continuous interchanges with his environment. The level of energy required is subject to the educational activities taking place; to the number of individuals taking part; to the length of time of those educational activities; to the facilities themselves, their material, composition, arrangement, and sizes; and to adjacent environments and all their properties. The objective is to provide a physical environment with specified characteristics. These characteristics include temperature ranges achievable by heating and cooling systems; light intensities, qualities, and the variations possible with the artificial and natural lighting devices appropriate for the activity in progress; and the degree of sound absorption and reflection required.

Thermally related environments of extremes can create substantial physiological stresses that can affect mental task performance and learning. Conditions that are not extremes, on the other hand, can produce adverse effects of a minor nature, which in some cases can be overcome by some type of incentive, such as an exceptional teacher or an individual motivated to perform his best in the activity.

The factors of a thermally related environment affected by energy are as follows:

1 The air dry bulb temperature.
2 The relative humidity.
3 The individual's skin temperature.
4 The mean radiant temperature of surrounding surfaces.
5 The velocity of air movements.

6 The amount and type of clothing worn by the individual.
7 The amount of physical exertion.
8 The degree of acclimatization to prevalent atmospheric conditions.

To attempt even a cursory analysis of light energy in a book of this type would be out of place. To obtain a summary of various arrays of light sources, their brightness characteristics, and the various processes for evaluating the inner reflections in spaces can be largely obtained in publications of the Illumination Engineering Society.

This organization has established standards of quality and quantity for interior illumination. Their reports pertain to such matters as brightness and brightness ratios in the visual field, brightness levels, visibility levels, foot-candle specifications for various tasks, reflective values, glare, quantity of illumination, and systems of illumination. When these elements have all been considered, energy can be specified that should result in the desired environment. Of importance, these elements should be so coordinated as to permit the freedom of choice necessary in educational planning.

Concerning sonic environments and their effect on the learning process, no satisfactory answers yet exist. However, a sizable amount of specific knowledge of the engineering applications of acoustics and the manipulation of sound for desired effects has accumulated. Various books and numerous technical and trade journal articles are available on these subjects.*

In analyzing a sonic environment, the educational planner should note and measure sound with respect to the following conditions:

1 Sound must be intense enough for all individuals to hear.
2 Sound should be uniformly distributed about the space.
3 The reverberation time within the space must fall within a certain range depending on the volume and intended use of the space.
4 The background or interfering noise must not be too intense.

No single fixed environment can be designed to fully satisfy all conditions of educational activities. One possibility is to group individual activities according to acoustical preferences for some educational activities and to provide adjustable sonic conditions for other particular learning activities. Extreme quiet would not seem to be an appropriate sonic environment for many learning activities. Possibly background noise of low frequencies would serve some educational activities, as now exists in many of the new schools. Despite this trend, scientific analysis is still too limited to apply such concepts as "annoyance," "bothersome," and "distraction" to the learning process.

Educational facilities systems

Closely allied with the energy subsystems of light, air, and sound is the environmental performance of spaces and spatial arrangements. The objective of the educational facility system is to provide physical environments that aid individuals. The visual aspects of the environment are also included in the analysis.

Analytical work involves the individual school facility and its relationship to the total urban physical form. The first approach includes site analysis, topographical studies, climate studies, utility surveys, environmental quality and needs assessment, and utilization studies.

Analysis also includes built-in as well as moveable equipment, its location, capacity, age, cost, and utilization. This information along with the facility information given above can be used to project and appraise the location or relocation, selection and acquisition of the entire physical apparatus. To be complete, however, these individual facilities must be related to the entire facilities of the city possibly adaptable for educational activities.

The second approach involves a survey of the total urban physical form. Several survey methods have been developed. One method is the Williams Visual Survey Model, which consists of two parts:

*See References for Chapter 6 at the end of this book.

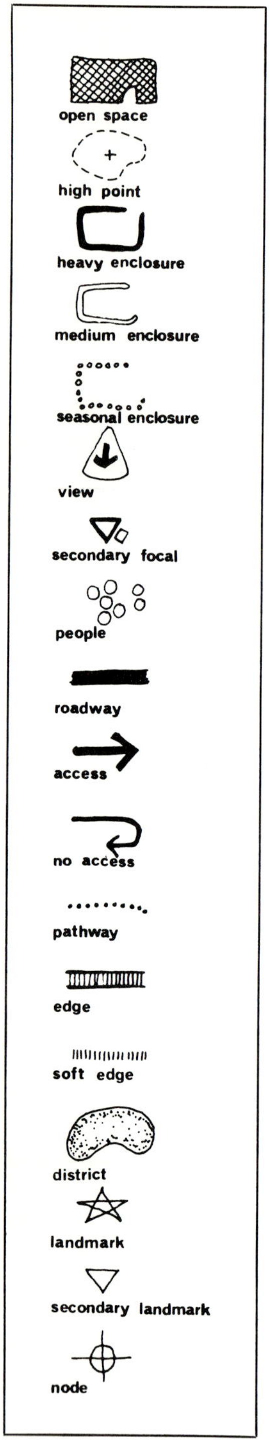

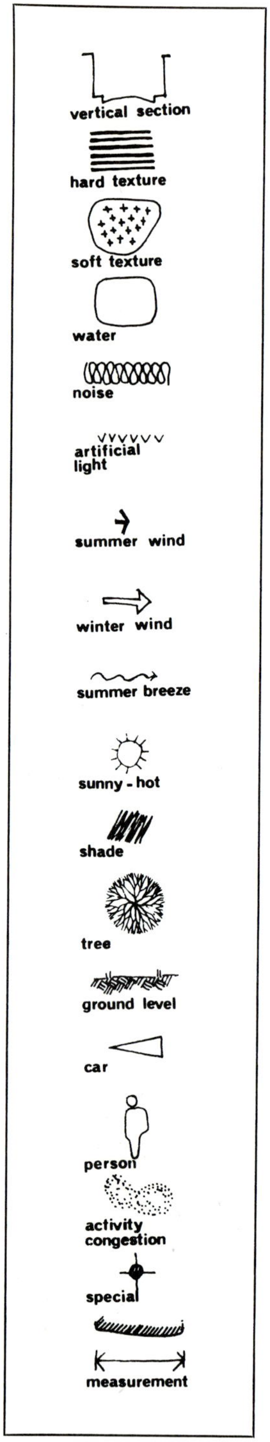

FIGURES 6.7 and 6.8

(1) identification of the three-dimensional characteristics of the city's site and man-made features and (2) the significant paths and vantage points for perceiving the city. The city's site contains six basic ground forms:

(1) level of gently sloping or rolling site, (2) sloping sites, backed by hills or steeper slopes, (3) valley or gorge sites, (4) amphitheatrical or fan-shaped sites, (5) bowl-shaped sites, and (6) ridged or hilltop sites.[8]

The man-made features are classified according to:

(1) urban textures, (2) green areas, (3) circulation facilities, (4) paved open spaces, and (5) individually significant architectural masses, including vertical slab-like, massive and horizontal forms.[9]

The second part directly records the panorama, the skyline, the vista, the urban open space, and the experience of the individual in motion. These perceptions are sketched directly on maps, in sketchbooks, or in photograph albums to display visually the aesthetics of the environment. (See Figures 6.7 and 6.8)

Another method is the Lynch Visual Survey Model, which consists of a two-part investigative technique containing a field survey for recording key perceptual features, such as edges, district, path, nodes, and landmarks, and population interviews to evaluate sensitivity to these various urban parts. In Jacobs and Jones' Visual Survey Model attention is given to "(1) sensory material, that is, color, texture, pattern, shape, and rhythm; (2) noteworthy forms of both an isolated kind and as an interrelated series of forms; and (3) expressions of historical or symbolic significance."[10]

The basic approach involves a comprehensive analysis of city resources that can be used for educational activities. (See Figure 6.9.) The impact of such an approach may appear to be radical but

[8]F. Stuart Chapin, Jr., *Urban Land Use Planning* (Urbana, Ill.: University of Illinois Press, 1965), p. 334.
[9]Ibid.
[10]Ibid., p. 336.

FIGURE 6.9

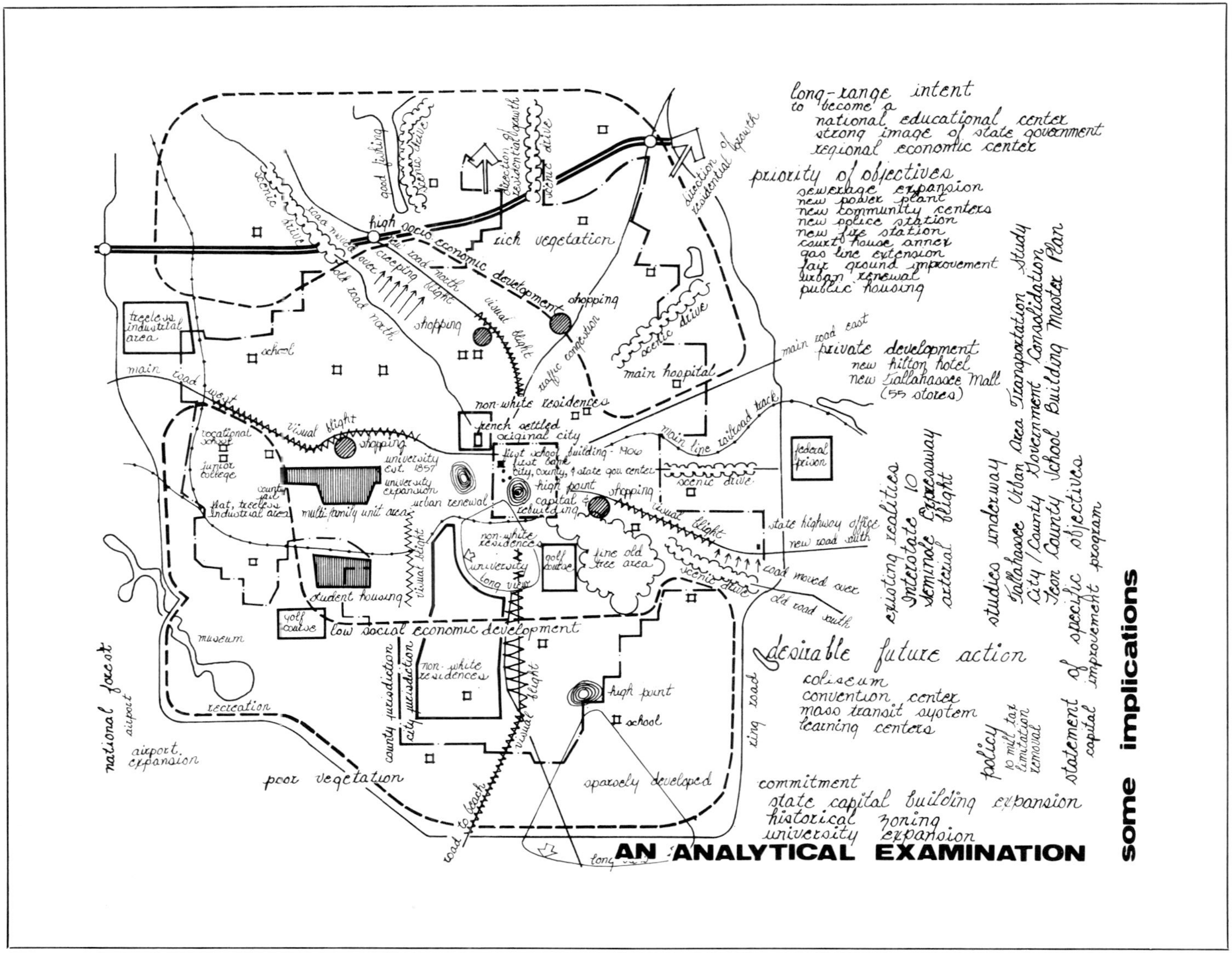
AN ANALYTICAL EXAMINATION
some implications
long-range intent
to become a
national educational center
strong image of state government
regional economic center
priority of objectives
sewerage expansion
new power plant
new community centers
new police station
new fire station
court house annex
gas line extension
fair ground improvement
urban renewal
public housing
private development
new Hilton hotel
new Tallahassee Mall
(55 stores)
existing realities
Interstate 10
Seminole Expressway
arterial blight
studies underway
Tallahassee Urban Area Transportation Study
City / County Government Consolidation
Leon County School Building Master Plan
statement of specific objectives
capital improvement program
desirable future action
coliseum
convention center
mass transit system
learning centers
policy
10 mill tax limitation removal
commitment
state capital building expansion
historical zoning
university expansion
high socio economic development
low social economic development
rich vegetation
poor vegetation
scenic drive
good fishing
direction of residential growth
shopping
visual blight
creeping blight
traffic congestion
main hospital
main road east
main road west
new road north
old road north
old road south
new road south
road to beach
king road
main line railroad track
federal prison
state highway office
non-white residences
french settled original city
first school building - 1906
first bank
city, county, & state gov center
high point
capital & rebuilding
university est. 1857
university expansion
urban renewal
multi-family unit area
student housing
golf course
fine old tree area
university long view
treeless industrial area
vocational school
junior college
county fair
flat, treeless industrial area
school
museum
recreation
national forest
airport
airport expansion
county jurisdiction
city jurisdiction
sparsely developed

learning doesn't occur just during period 2 in Room 141 in PS 26. Learning activities can be subtle occurrences. As Stephen C. Pepper wrote, of urban aesthetics,

> We do not get completely used to most of them. They do not . . . sink out of all consciousness. Our perceptions have merely become very much dulled to them. They take a slow grinding toll on our nerves, and . . . a beautiful city . . . still caresses our nerves and soothes us with its scarcely perceived delights.[11]

This assemblage of data provides the educational planner with information about facilities relevant to availability, location, equipment, environmental quality and appropriate educational activities for specified groups of students and teachers.

The analysis will help to discover what facilities will be needed, decide how best to schedule the use of existing facilities, and determine future sites for learning activities. The system will also provide reports on the construction of new facilities and the acquisition of new equipment. Furthermore, such an analysis will provide the basis for a complete evaluation of the educational effectiveness of various types of educational facilities and noneducational facilities.

Educational operation systems

Operational systems include those that are not directly involved with the learning process but rather aid and support the learning activities. They include the following:

- Library service systems
- Audiovisual service systems
- Systems provisions for textbooks
- Personal-guidance and counseling systems
- Health-service systems
- Social-work services
- Food-service systems
- Instructional supervision services for staff
- In-service education
- Research and statistical services
- School/community recreational programming
- Library services to public
- Civic activities (exhibitions, concerts, lectures, musicals, and so on)
- Facilities for community use
- School/community planning
- Employment-placement services
- Past school-performance services
- Administrative and management systems
- Facilities-maintenance and operation systems
- Financing and budgeting systems
- Inventory-control systems
- Purchasing systems
- Legal-service systems

Such an extensive list of systems does not permit a definitive analysis of educational operation systems. Instead, the planner, must search his own local sources, his state educational library, the publications of the U.S. Office of Education, or journals and books of private educational organizations and individuals.

SUMMARY

Study areas can be delineated by the use of the *systems approach* and consideration of the problem as embedded in the total education system. The four natural systems are as follows:

1 The educational activity systems.
2 The educational communication systems.
3 The educational facilities systems.
4 The educational operation systems.

Because of the variety of needs for each system it is possible to delineate only in most general terms the data required by the educational planner.

[11]Sidney H. Williams, "Urban Aesthetics," *Town Planning Review,* **25**:95 (July 1954).

7 Gathering data

APPROACHING A DATA-GATHERING PLAN

A data-gathering plan must include procedures for acquiring, organizing, and updating data, rather than simply listing desired data items. These activities must be so executed that the data are available at the time and place of decision-making. The problem then becomes one of finding ". . . measurements that will show not only the difference between more or less, but how much more or less."[1]

This statement applies to the present and future conditions of students, staff, facilities, programs, and finances. In the past, most data collected were required by an educational agency without much regard to the other data needs of the community.

Recently, however, the data base has been expanded to include events common to both education and various city agencies. This chapter will present various aspects of data gathering to help an educational planner select, organize, and utilize data suitable for his own needs. Five major phases of any data system should be followed. First, data are collected and entered into the system. Second, data are filed or placed in storage. Third, data are mani-

[1]Ayers Brinser, "Standards and Techniques of Evaluating Economic Choices in Environmental Resource Development," ed. F. Fraser Darling and John P. Milton, *Future Environments of North America* (Garden City, N.Y.: Natural History Press, 1966), p. 243.

pulated according to preestablished rules. Fourth, data are presented in usable form. Fifth, data are moved from one point in the system to another.

Attention for gathering data is focused on those applications of data processing peculiar to education. Attention, however, is directed not at the data required for day-to-day operation but only at the data required for educational planning, including short-, middle-, and long-range planning. It also includes the data required for general decision-making; for research such as studying relationships, making projections, furnishing social and physical profiles, and monitoring the various educational activities; and for simulation operations.

DESCRIBING INFORMATION AND DATA

A distinction is made between information and data. Information refers to knowledge acquired by, derived from, or inculcated by observation, by reading, or in conversations. It is untreated and may or may not be a given fact whose validity remains to be proved. Data, on the other hand, are facts; something known that forms the basis for conclusions. Data are documented, purged or subjective treatment, and ready to support the plan in an objective manner. Both information and data are used by the educational planner.

Educational planners use several types of information. One type is nominal, which is used to identify or name objects or elements. Another is directive information for suggesting or interpreting. Designative information individualizes objects or elements, whereas conceptual information relates defined entities. Representational types convey concepts, and procedural information instructs action. Empirical information portrays experience of action, whereas evaluative information helps to measure experience. An example of each type can be given by an educational planner's list of activities, as follows:

Educational planning	Nominal
Programming	Directive
Planning elements	Designative
Preliminary designing	Conceptual
Planning graphs and charts	Representational
Organizational planning	Procedural
Curriculum planning	Empirical
Planning implemented	Evaluative

The various types of information together form an information system. It includes people, procedures, computer hardware and software, and a data base. This base theoretically includes all data required for educational planning. A data element is a student, an activity, a place, an object, or even a piece of information. The combining of several elements forms a set, e.g., all thirty-student classes in all schools of the school district. This information is given by the attributes or properties of the set. Each attribute, in turn, is described by means of a data item and each data item has a data value. For one element in the set (e.g., schools) the data item (name of school) has a data value.

An entity identifier is a data item with a unique data value for each member of the entity set. The data item, 370311, is an entity identifier for the entity "school." Identifiers can be of two kinds. Ordinal identifiers, which, in addition to uniquely identifying the entities, also provide information about relationships. The second kind of identifiers, called nominal, are used solely for purposes of identification. An example of a nominal identifier is the social security number of a student.

Data base is defined simply as a collection of data values. Their physical representation may be in such forms as marks on paper, holes in cards, or magnetic spots on tape. The form needed depends on the individual educational planning program, the type of equipment available, and the user's requirements.

SOME METHODS FOR GATHERING DATA

The most obvious and frequently used collecting procedure in arriving at a data base is to ask the user what data he would like. Unfortunately, educators are prone to overstate their requirements and the educational planner many times has an excess of useless data. Obviously, a carefully integrated plan must be established that includes data availability, acquisition costs, data usage, and optimum data-base content before definitive requirements are set.

The least costly method of collecting data is the mailed questionnaire. In many cases, however, this technique is insufficient for determining the user's requirements. Another method is interviews. Some investigators discount this as possibly too subjective. The most productive is collection from an existing operational information system combined with a heuristic one. This approach builds on an established base line and permits the data base to evolve as new needs arise or as new data sources become apparent.

Some sources of data are the various departments of local and state governments, such as their planning agencies, tax assessors's office, and building and zoning offices. Other community sources are the newspaper companies and utility companies, such as the electric, water, and telephone. Data from administrative files, however, should not be integrated into a planning data-base without careful examination of their applicability and utility. Many files will be useful in updating permanent point-in-time files, but care should be taken to process them only if there is a foreseeable method of integrating these files into a well-defined data base oriented to support educational planning.

Data sharing is another approach. Many educational functions interrelate, and different educational departments often have common data requirements. Also, individual departments may be both users and suppliers of data required by other departments.

FIGURE 7.1

CENSUS	OF	AGRICULTURE
CENSUS	OF	CONSTRUCTION INDUSTRIES
CENSUS	OF	BUSINESS
CENSUS	OF	BUSINESS, MANUFACTURES & MINERAL INDUSTRIES
CENSUS	OF	GOVERNMENT
CENSUS	OF	MANUFACTURES
CENSUS	OF	MANUFACTURES & MINERAL INDUSTRIES
CENSUS	OF	TRANSPORTATION

This situation is giving rise to an increased development of integrated data files and results in a good data source.

A considerable amount of useful data is available from local metropolitan transportation studies. They have engaged in many data-collecting activities that have included field surveys, aerial photography, and mailed questionnaires. Again, their activities are concerned with measurement of the transportation behavior connected with trip generation, trip distribution, modal split, facility utilization, and network loading, which would require pruning and reformulation to fit educational behavior.

A fundamental source of educational planning data is the Decennial Census. (See Figure 7.1.) The 1970 Census has both an increased amount of data to be produced and more emphasis on small-area data, especially useful for educational planners. Plans are under way to prepare maps and address guides for cities with populations of fifty thousand and more as well as for central cities in urbanized areas.

KINDS OF REQUIRED DATA

Data related to people

Population size, composition, and distribution furnish the educational planner with excellent indicators of space requirements. Distribution provides data relevant to the location of various land uses and facilities along with educational ones within the urban form. A census of population composition would

> . . . assist in estimating residential space requirements for various dwelling types consistent with existing and anticipated family sizes, income levels, and the needs of each segment of the life cycle. They assist in determining the amount of space needed for recreation areas, schools, and other community facilities for all segments of the population.[2]

Population size is a major element to be considered in planning educational land usage because ". . . size

[2]F. Stuart Chapin, Jr., *Urban Land Use Planning* (Urbana, Ill.: University of Illinois Press, 1965), p. 181.

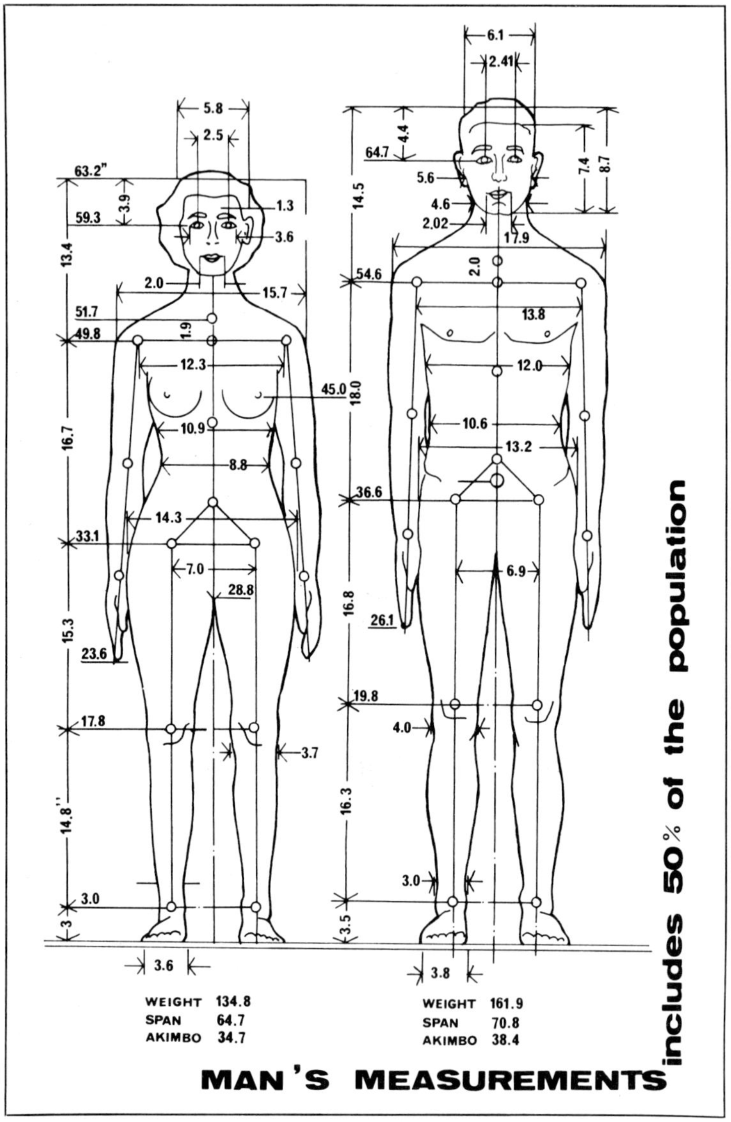

FIGURE 7.2

Space needs on an individual scale

FIGURE 7.3

Space needs on an urban scale

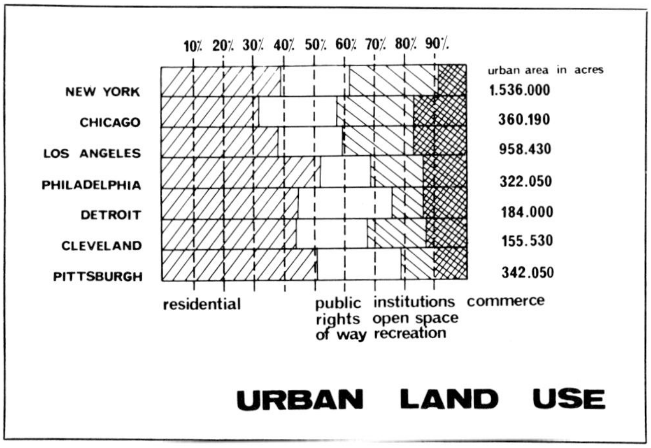

FIGURE 7.4

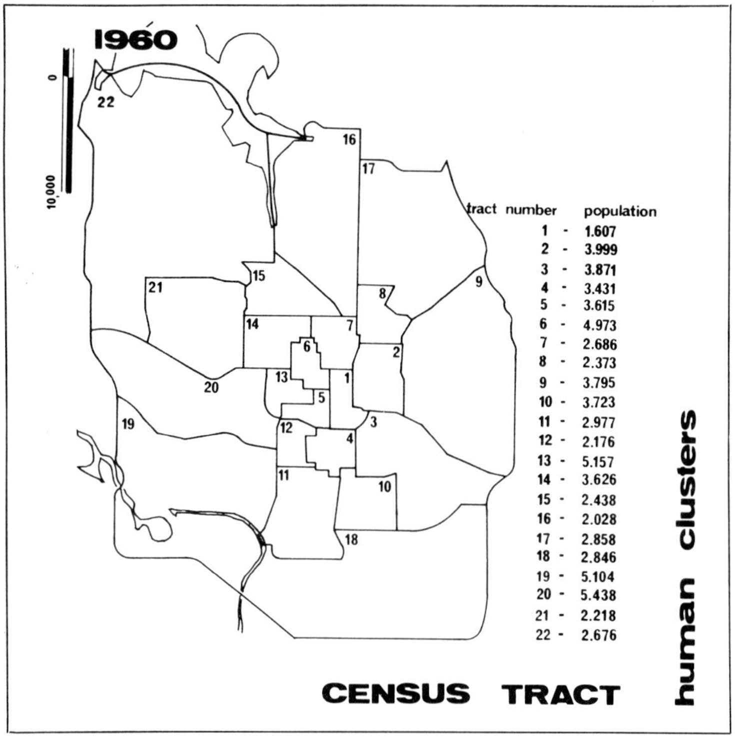

gives an indication of the overall dimensions of the physical environment and supplies a basic yardstick for the estimation of space needs for various catagories of land use."[3] (See Figures 7.2 and 7.3.)

"Population" is a label that applies to clusters of humans, meaning

> . . . the total number of persons in a given area at a given time.
>
> As demography has developed, so has the need for more adequately defined areas, i.e. areas defined in ways that comprise the natural socio-economic clusterings or groupings.[4]

The social and human clusters have been further delineated by the U.S. Bureau of the Census, which used census tracts (see Figure 7.4), urbanized areas, and standard metropolitan statistical areas to break down groups for their data gathering. Basically these are references to mere counts of people rather than references to any particular political or administrative unit. They are designed to provide information about populations that belong together on the basis of various social, economic, or cultural characteristics. Categorization or characterization of socio-economic groups generally follows clearly defined and identifiable traits such as sex, age, race, color, place of residence, place of birth, parentage, school enrollment, years of school completed, marital status, relationship to the head of the household and the number of children. Economic characteristics like employment status, period of employment, occupation, industry worked in, class of worker, place of work, and income are included with the other statistics.

[3]Ibid.

[4]Warren S. Thompson and Daniel T. Lewis, *Population Problems* (New York: McGraw-Hill, 1965), p. 57.

Data related to place

Complicated land-use statistics cover a variety of interacting kinds of activities in which relationships

FIGURE 7.5

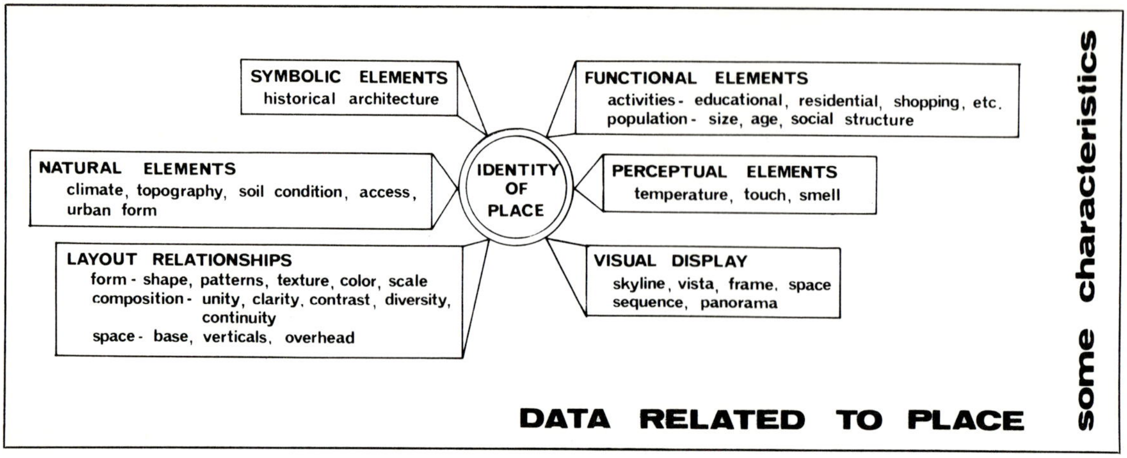

are not always clearly defined. (See Figure 7.5.) "No single index can afford comparisons of all relevant aspects of a distribution. No single statistical measurement exists which represents an entire land use configuration."[5]

Consideration of land use statistics involves background information that extends beyond mere numbers. (See Figure 7.6.)

The analysis of land use may be extended to distinguish between land covered with buildings and essential areas for storage, parking and circulation as distinct from land use for gardens, open spaces, and for traffic needs. At a density of fourteen dwellings to the acre, about a fifth of the land is covered by buildings, the rest being largely for outside storage, parking and access. The area of land for educational purposes covered by school buildings is probably about one-tenth. For transport and public utility purposes for the commercial areas and for most other town purposes about one-fifth or one-sixth of the land is probably covered by buildings, most of the balance being essential outside space.[6]

We now turn to some basic numerical data associated with statistical compilations.

The urbanized population of the U.S. as a whole used about 44% more land per person and twice as much land as a whole in 1960, as was used by the urbanized population in 1950. . . . (About .205 acre per person in 1960 census .152 acre per person in 1950. The total land use came to 25,544 square miles for 95.8 million people in 1960 versus 12,804 square miles for 69.3 million people in urbanized areas in 1950.) . . . a growth of 38% in the urbanized population was accompanied by the growth of 100% in land use.[7]

Land-use patterns, of course, are not linear, and the increase in the intensity of land use is the results of decisions being made by thousands of individuals in a relatively short period of time. (See Figure 7.7 for some early concepts on land use patterns.) Although change in land usage is also a function of the locational patterns of the American population, the transportation systems affect the amount of space required per person. As the country moves toward a more urbanized citizenry, the proportion of the amount of land required per person decreases. Over two thirds of all Americans now live in urban areas; approximately one third of the population is clustered in metropolitan areas of more than fifty-thousand people. One of the most pronounced influences on land requirements is the tendency in the United States for people to seek apartment or multifamily dwellings instead of the once well-established single-family dwelling. The tendency toward multifamily units may not always be the most desirable, but American interest and

[5]Louis K. Lowenstein, "The Location of Urban Land Uses: A Rejoinder," *Land Economics,* **43**:239 (May 1967).

[6]P. A. Stone, "The Impact of Urban Development on the Use of Land and Other Resources," *Journal of the Town Planning Institute,* **47**:129 (May 1961).

[7]Robinson Newcomb, "Urban Land Use Shifts to Low Gear," *The Appraisal Journal,* no. 3, **32**:376 (July 1964).

economic considerations have caused the multifamily units to become increasingly popular.

There are several paradoxical aspects to the statistics of land usage (See Table 7.1.) For example, although urban use of land grew roughly four times as much as did the actual population, again there are many factors involved in land use beyond merely housing. Changing urban-rural mix, changing living habits and patterns, changing requirements of various kinds have all contributed to the land-use pattern. (See Figure 7.8.) Tables 7.2 and 7.3 from Newcomb illustrate various urban-nonurban population patterns in terms of the historical past and the projected future.

FIGURE 7.6

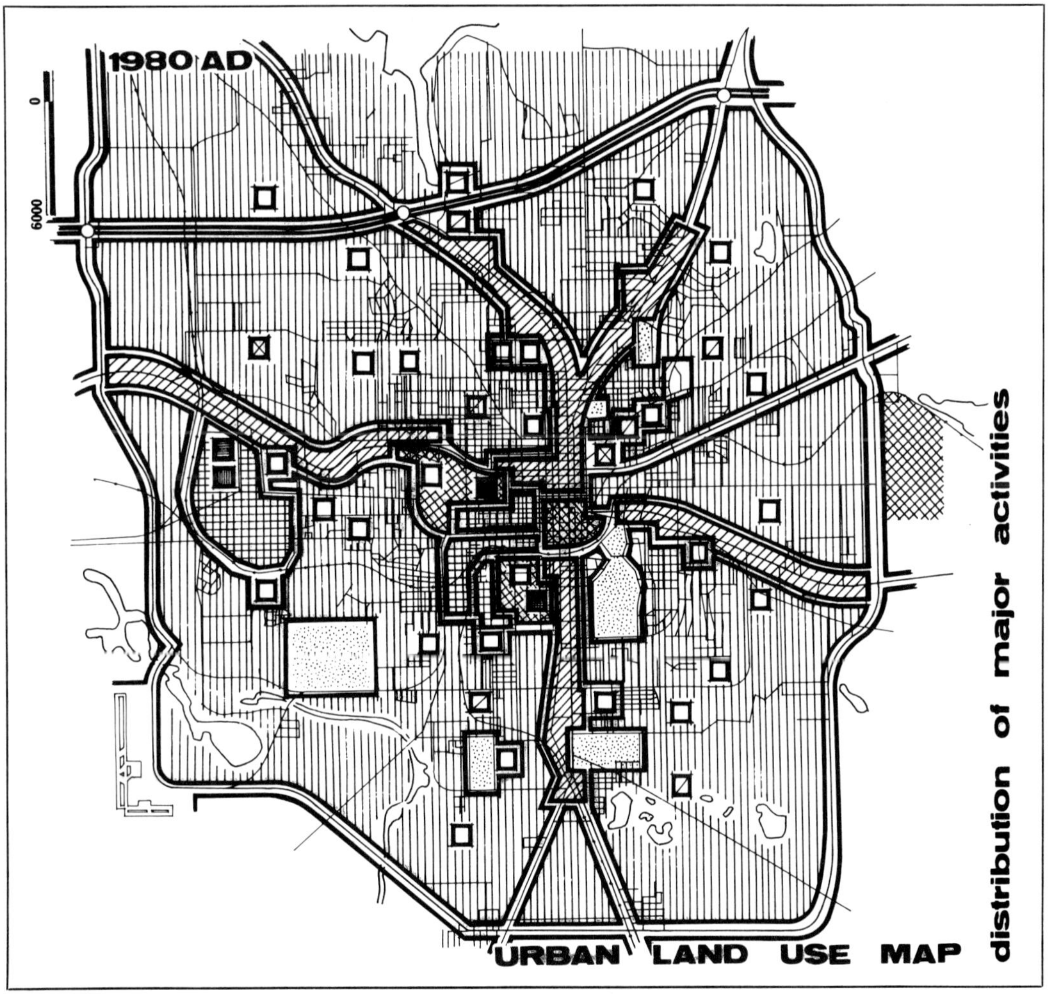

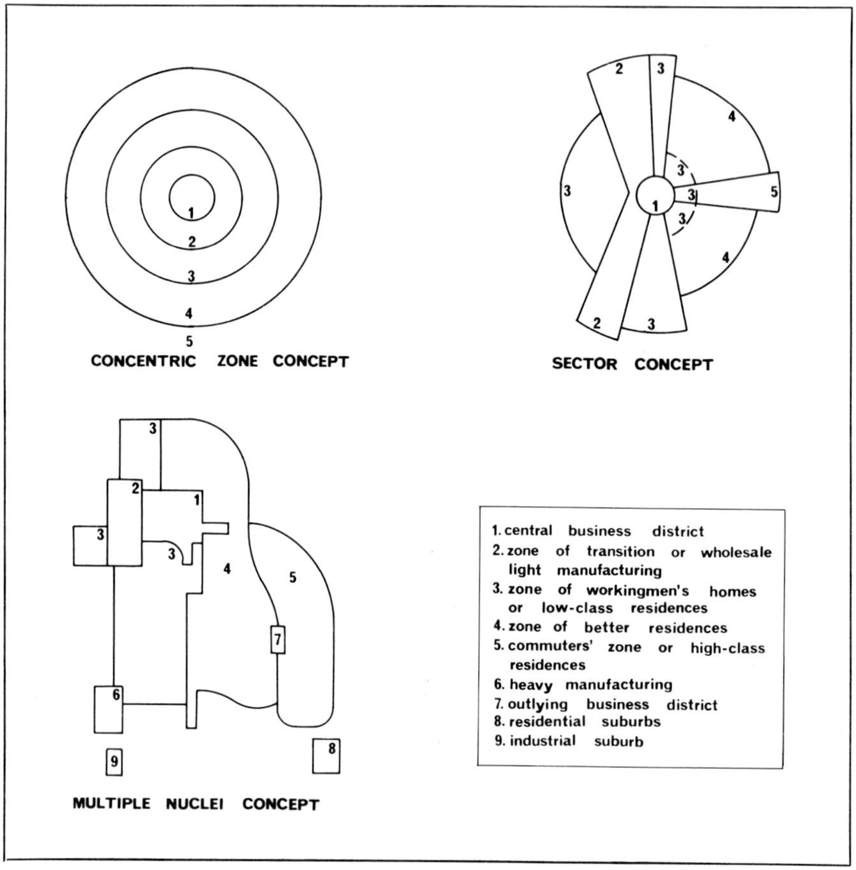

FIGURE 7.7
Some early concepts of land use patterns

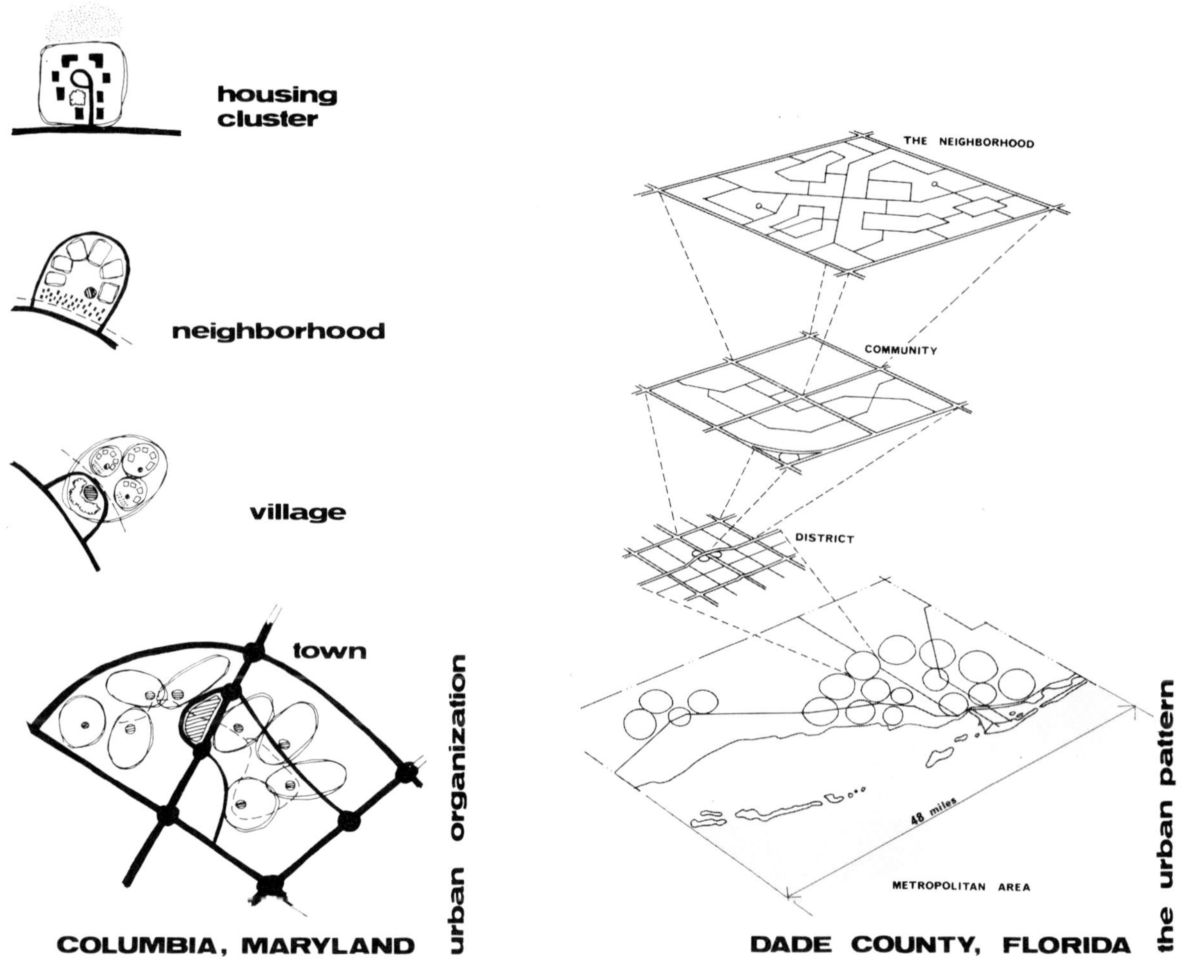
housing cluster
neighborhood
village
town
COLUMBIA, MARYLAND
urban organization
THE NEIGHBORHOOD
COMMUNITY
DISTRICT
48 miles
METROPOLITAN AREA
DADE COUNTY, FLORIDA
the urban pattern

FIGURE 7.8

Table 7.1 Tallahassee

Subject	Quantity
Total population	**48,174**
Nativity and parentage	
Native	47,512
Native parentage	46,004
White	30,257
Nonwhite	15,747
Foreign or mixed parentage	1,508
White	1,420
Nonwhite	88
Foreign born	662
White	566
Nonwhite	96
State of birth	
Total native population	47,512
Born in state of residence	25,517
Born in different state	18,971
Born in U.S. outlying area, at sea, etc.	168
State of birth not reported	856
Residence in 1955	
Population five years old and over, 1960	42,945
Same house as in 1960	16,217
Different house in U.S.	25,249
Same county	9,983
Different county	15,266
Same state	8,078
Different state	7,188
Abroad	694
Not reported	785
Year moved into present house	
Total	48,174
1959 to 1960	18,634
1958	5,299
1957	3,348
1954 to 1956	6,894
1950 to 1953	5,361
1940 to 1949	4,537
1939 or earlier	1,676
Always lived in this house	2,425

Table 7.2 Various urban–non-urban population patterns in terms of the historical past and the projected future

Year	Resident population (in millions)		Area in square miles		Population per square mile	
	Total	Increase in decade	Total	Increase in decade	Total	Increase in decade
All urban areas						
1980	199.0	41.5	73,350	17,700	2,640	3%
1970	157.5	32.2	57,650	17,450	2,730	12%
1960	125.3	28.5	40,200	17,200	3,115	26%
1950	96.8	—	23,000	—	4,210	—
Urbanized areas only						
1980	169.0	41.0	60,350	17,700	2,800	7%
1970	128.0	32.2	42,650	17,150	3,000	25%
1960	95.8	26.5	25,500	12,700	3,572	31%
1950	69.3	—	12,800	—	5,408	—
Outside urbanized areas						
1980	30.0	0	15,000	0	2,000	0%
1970	30.0	.6	15,000	300	2,000	0%
1960	29.4	1.8	14,700	4,500	2,000	23%
1950	27.6	—	10,200	—	2,600	—

SOURCE: Ibid., p. 329.

Table 7.3 Allocation of increases in land use

	1950–60	Per cent	1960–70	Per cent	1970–80	Per cent
All urban areas						
Total increase in square miles due to density	17,000	100.0	17,450	100.0	17,700	100.0
Decrease due to population increase	10,438	60.7	7,090	40.6	2,460	13.9
Growth in area in decade	6,762	39.3	10,360	59.4	15,240	86.1
		74.8		43.4		30.7
Urbanized areas only						
Total increase in square miles due to density	12,700	100.0	17,150	100.0	17,700	100.0
Decrease due to population increase	12,700	61.3	8,535	49.8	4,020	27.1
Growth in area in decade	44,910	38.7	8,615	50.2	13,680	72.1
		99.2		67.3		41.5
Outside urbanized areas						
Total increase in square miles due to density	4,500	100.0	300	100.0	0	0
Decrease due to population increase	1,110	24.4	0	0	0	0
Growth in area in decade	3,390	75.6	300	100.0	0	0
		44.1		2.0		0

SOURCE: Ibid., p. 380.

Data related to movement

A better understanding of the alternatives for transportation is given in the following tables. Table 7.4 presents a matrix of the different modes of transportation (foot, bus, rail, taxi, or car) according to variable, fixed, and total expense and percentage of an average $8,000 income. This table is based on a typical Chicago family with a yearly income of $8,000 and shows the various ways in which money can be spent on transportation. Another way of looking at the problem of transportation cost is illustrated in Table 7.5, which is a matrix showing income levels ranging from $6,000 to $20,000 per year and the different means of transportation. The annual commuting expenses are given in dollars reflected as a percentage of income. In Table 7.6 the family's cost of transportation is added to the price of their residence. The table is set up in matrix form giving house prices from $15,000 to $35,000 on one axis and the daily transportation expense on the other axis. (See Figure 7.9.)

It becomes apparent from these three tables that the location of the house must be considered when a home is purchased. The tables also illustrate the cost of transportation as a functional mode of transportation:

> ... 11 cents of every dollar spent by consumers for goods and services is spent for transportation and 10 cents of those 11 cents go for the automobile. We spend more for auto transportation than we spend on doctors, religion, charities, telephones, radio, television, furniture, electricity, gas, books, magazines, and newspapers put together.[8]

Much of the transportation by private automobile is due to the necessity of travel to work. (See Figure 7.10.) "According to the 1960 Census of Population about 64 per cent of all work trips in U.S. urban areas were made by auto. Only about 20 per cent of all urban area work trips were made by public transit; . . . indeed, almost half as many people walk to work as use public transit in urban areas."[9] The

Table 7.4 Yearly transportation costs by various means of a typical Chicago family with income of $8,000, to work

Means transportation	Variable expense	Fixed expense	Total expense	% of $8,000 income
By foot	$ 20	$80	$100	1.3
By bus	125	80	205	2.6
By rail	240	80	320	4.0
By taxi	375	80	455	5.7
By car	438	80	518	6.5

SOURCE: George M. Smerk (ed.), *Readings in Urban Transportation* (Bloomington: Indiana University Press, 1968), p. 84.

Table 7.5 Percentages for several different annual incomes and for several different means of movement

Income ($)	By foot ($100)	By bus ($205)	By train ($320)	By taxi ($455)	By car ($518)
6,000	1.67	3.42	5.33	7.50	8.63
8,000	1.25	2.56	4.00	5.67	6.48
10,000	1.00	2.05	3.20	4.55	5.18
12,000	.83	1.71	2.67	3.79	4.32
14,000	.71	1.46	2.29	3.25	3.70
16,000	.63	1.28	2.00	2.84	3.24
18,000	.56	1.14	1.78	2.53	2.88
20,000	.50	1.03	1.60	2.28	2.59

SOURCE: Ibid., p. 85.

[8] Ibid., p. 87.

[9] John R. Meyer, "Urban Transportation," *The Metropolitan Enigma/Inquiries into the Nature and Dimensions of America's Urban Crisis,* ed. James Q. Wilson (Cambridge, Mass.: Harvard University Press, 1968), p. 43.

FIGURE 7.9

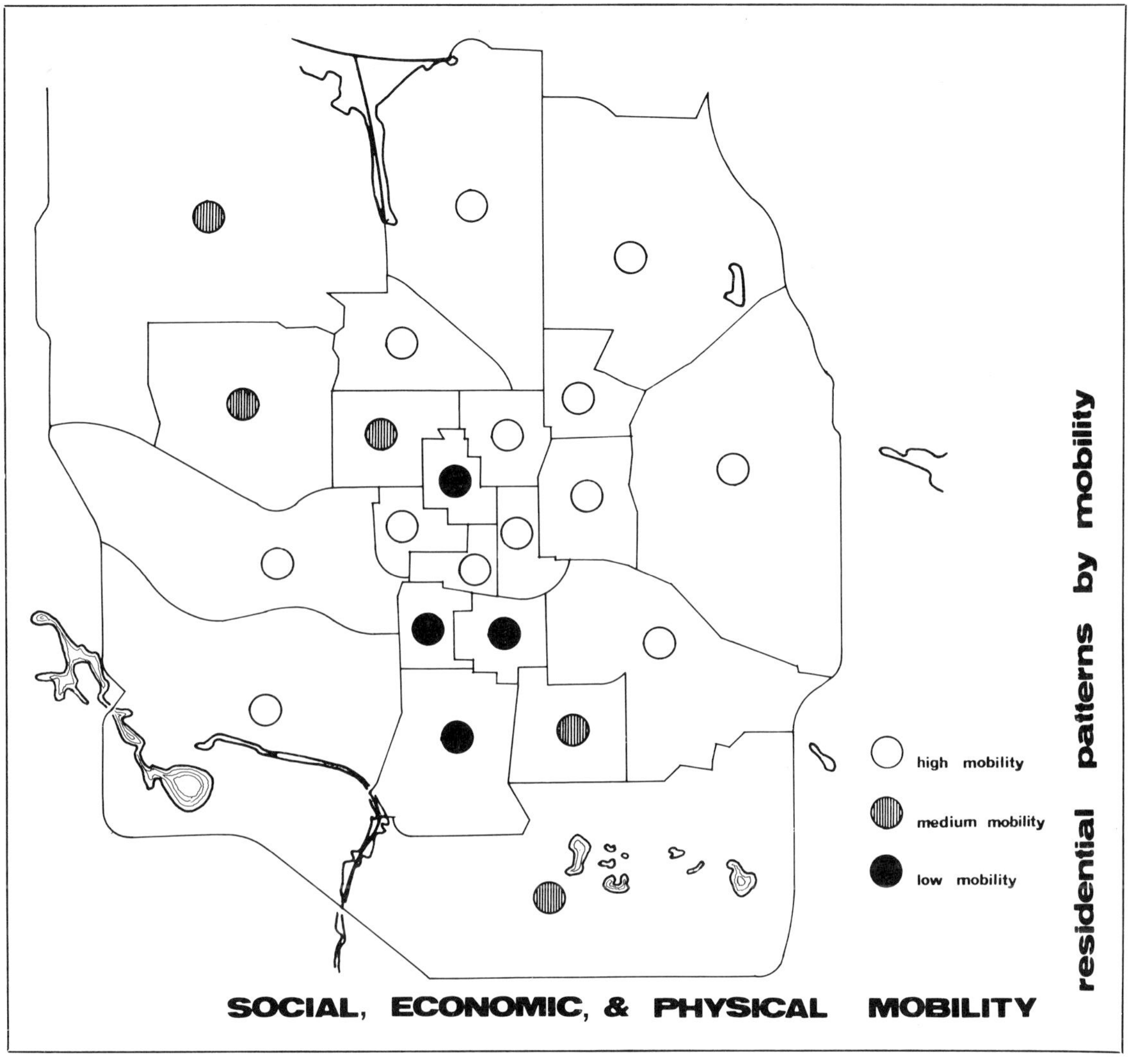

Table 7.6 Cost of commuting added to the price of house

Daily transportation expense	$ .40	$ .80	$1.20	$1.60	$2.00
A $15,000 house represents an investment of	$17,000	$19,000	$21,000	$23,000	$25,000
A $20,000 house represents an investment of	22,000	24,000	26,000	28,000	30,000
A $25,000 house represents an investment of	27,000	29,000	31,000	33,000	35,000
A $30,000 house represents an investment of	32,000	34,000	36,000	38,000	40,000
A $35,000 house represents an investment of	37,000	39,000	41,000	43,000	45,000

SOURCE: Ibid., p. 86.

location and purpose of a trip is a local matter when public transportation is concerned. Seventy per cent of all public transit work trips in the United States are made entirely on local streets or highways.[10]

The magnitude of automobile use in the United States is illustrated by the fact that there are almost one hundred million vehicles on U.S. roads. California alone has over 11 million automobiles, whereas New York has over 6 million.

Table 7.7 shows that there are approximately 2½ million people who are directly employed in transportation. The population growth, family-income growth, and highway vehicular growth are illustrated in this table. The distribution of the various modes of transportation is indicated in Table 7.8.

Data related to economics

The various operational problems combined with the changing trends in consumer demands further complicate the problems for the urban and educational planner. Of major concern to the area of urban economics is the decline of the central city in the United States. (See Figure 7.11.) Several reasons have been cited for this decline:

1) Developments in transportation and communication have made different parcels of land increasingly interchangeable for most manufacturing, retailing, wholesaling, residential and other uses. 2) Many activities once willing to pay the higher costs of central locations no longer find it to their advantage to do so. 3) Firms previously restricted to a fairly limited number of central locations by the need to be near ports, freight, and passenger terminals, rail lines and the like now depend to an ever increasing extent on trucks. 4) . . . rapid increases in automobile ownership have relieved many firms from their need to be located conveniently to mass transit facilities in order to attract labor force. 5) . . . with abundant free parking firms in outlying areas often find they have an easier time of attracting a larger force than they once did at their central city locations. 6) The transportation and communications savings [that caused] many firms to choose central locations have become smaller or disappeared entirely.[11]

[10]Ibid., pp. 43–44.

[11]John F. Kain, "A Short Course in Urban Economics Program on Regional and Urban Economics. Discussion Paper No. 29," *Harvard Joint Center for Urban Studies,* Harvard University and M.I.T., March 1968, p. 3.

Table 7.7 People directly employed in transportation

Mode	Number of people
Railways	750,000
Local/inter-urban	250,000
Airways	225,000
Highways	1,000,000
Pipelines/waterways	275,000
Total	2,500,000

SOURCE: Ibid., p. 4.

Table 7.8 People directly employed in transportation

Mode	Percentage
Private auto	89.8
Airways	5.1
Buses	2.6
Railway	2.2
Waterways	0.3

SOURCE: Winfield H. Arata, Jr., "Transportation and Technology Trends," *1966 National Transportation Symposium* (New York: American Society of Mechanical Engineers, 1966), p. 5.

Probably a major aspect of the decline of the city has been the influence of the cultural characteristics of Americans, who prefer open spaces with their residential dwellings. The more affluent have been able to move to suburbs because they can afford the houses in the suburbs and the transportation to and from work. The less affluent have remained in the central city to be near their place of employment and have occupied housing units primarily owned by absentee owners. Such an arrangement causes general deterioration of the property because the tenents are usually unconcerned about the upkeep and the absentee owners prefer not to invest appropriate maintenance monies. People have also attempted to relate the decline of the central city to the redistribution of employment following World War II and the removal of home-building and war-time controls. The changing status of the distribution and movement of jobs in industry is illustrated in Table 7.9, which compares the central city and the ring around the central city in 1950.

FIGURE 7.10

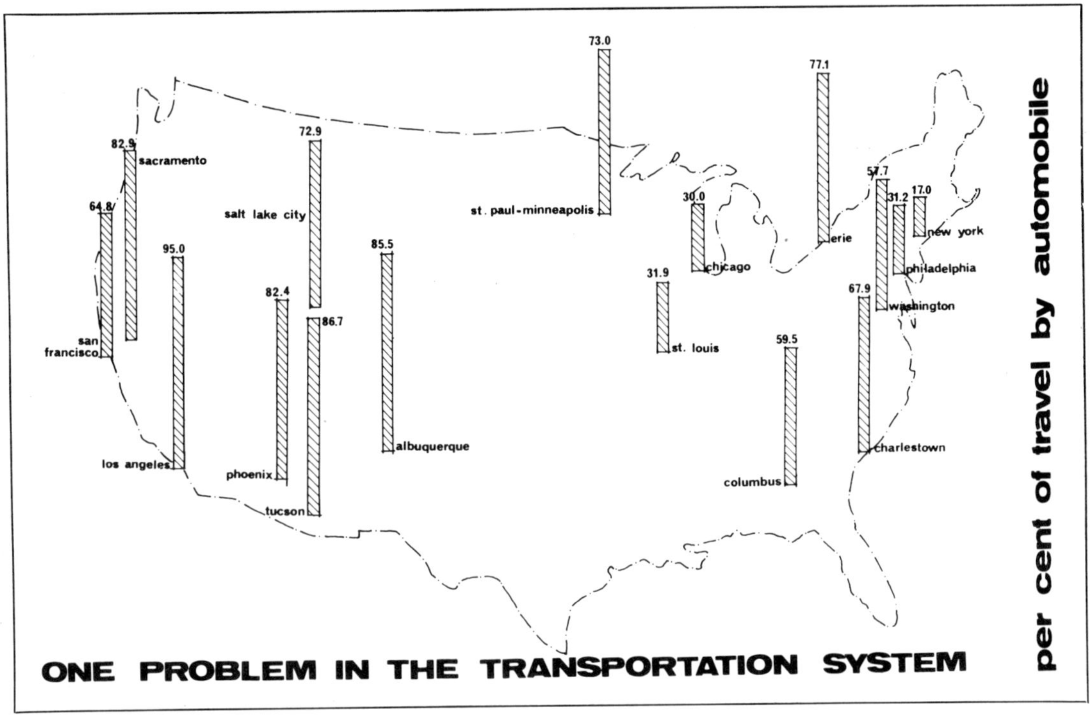

The role of manufacturing is critical in the formulation of the metropolitan spatial structure. (See Figure 7.11.) Ordinarily, manufacturing facilities help to create the residential structure. Seldom does the residential structure create the role of the manufacturing company in the urban form. As the analytical technology of the urban planner becomes more efficient, more precise information will be gleaned from the urban environment and consequently more precise measurements and results of planning can take place.

The first step toward meeting the public problems of an area is a detailed knowledge of its economic base. Knowledge about the economic base is essential to mold public decisions in the form of master plans, zoning ordinances, transportation plans, renewal programs and other public improvement plans. Public policy towards taxation, distribution of municipal costs and municipal borrowing should take such information into account. Private investment plans call for a knowledge of the market prospects in the region.[12]

[12]Charles M. Tiebout, *The Community Economic Base Study.* Supplementary Paper No. 16 (Committee for Economic Development, 1962), p. 7.

Throughout economic planning appropriate cognizance must be taken of the consumer's behavior. Consumer behavior is considered to be adaptive and does not follow a rigid Pavlovian type of reflex; it considers behavior or human response as a function of both the individual and his environment. The individual is a part of the social milieu and honed by the education he receives. One's aspirations are considered dynamic characteristics,

. . . social learning, that is the acquisition of new opinions and attitudes by very many people, is slow and gradual except under the influence of major events which call for a reorganization of the cognitive map in which they occur rarely. Group belonging influences salients of information received as well as the learning process (social facilitation). Satisfaction and success serve as reinforcing factors and promote learning. Specific rewards seen as attainable constitute the strongest stimulus to effect.[13]

One of the most influential characteristics insofar as

[13]George Katona, "Consumer Behavior: Theory and Findings on Expectations and Aspirations," *American Economic Review,* no. 2, **58**:21–22 (May 1968).

FIGURE 7.11

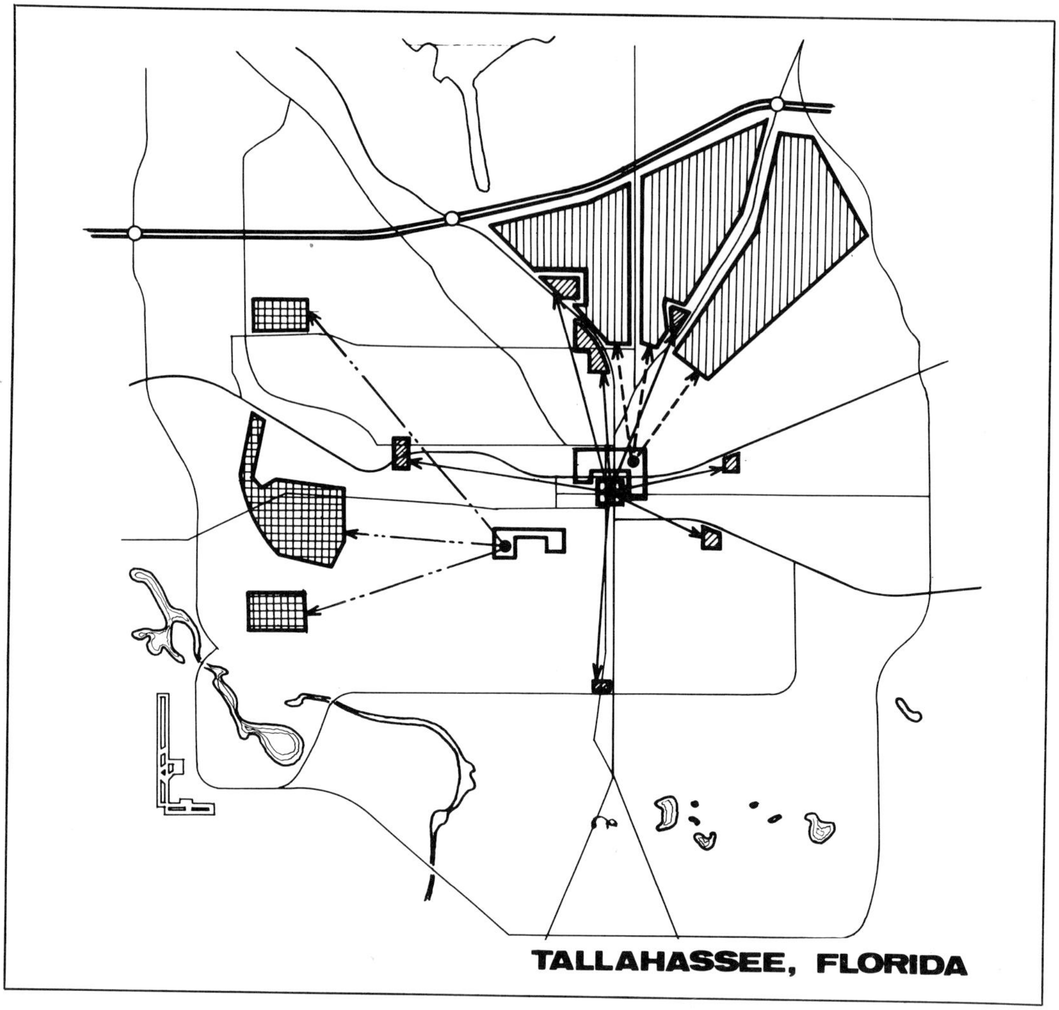

urban economics is concerned is that of rapid economic growth, which is highly relevant to the overall problems of urban planning. "The rate of economic growth is in my view the most important parameter to city planning."[14] It seems increasingly clear that the two factors, urban planning and urban economics, go hand in hand. Because urban economics is so closely related to the physical form and structure o the urban environment, it seems unreasonable to proceed with either urban economics or urban planning without incorporating the other. Both are concerned with the problems of people and their physical environment. The field of urban economics is merely a little less inclusive than that of urban planning.

Local urban economics is concerned primarily with those functions occurring within a given metropolitan area. Although the growth of cities depends to

[14]Gunnar Myrdal, "National Planning for Healthy Cities: Two Challenges to Affluence," *Planning for a Nation of Cities,* ed. Sam Bass Warner, Jr. (Cambridge, Mass.: M.I.T. Press, 1966), p. 17.

a great extent on the income derived from ouside the metropolitan area, this section concerns *local* urban economic factors. There are many definitions of a local urban economic area: one is the primary trade area; another is dependent on census data; another is a study of interacting factors that depend primarily on other factors within the local area. On the other hand, the distance factor involves regional concepts as opposed to local ones.

Various variables have been used as the basis for measurement of urban economics. A market survey is one of the normal studies by which the economic base may be classified. Other such commonplace things as employment, payroll, value added, value of production, physical production, dollar income, and expenditure accounts may also be used statistically to classify the economy of a community. Employment is probably the most commonly used of these measurements. (See Figure 7.12.)

Employment records do furnish a reasonably clear picture of the urban economic base because employment reflects the various kinds of economic activity involved in the locale. (See Table 7.9.) When employment is used as a measurement, it is usually expressed as a ratio of the number of workers in a given area to all workers in the basic line. Information can be gathered from the employment base by the use of either economic surveys or some type of statistical sampling technique that gives an appoximation of the employment picture based on the data available from manufacturers, the population, and various economic baseline activities. The basic employment picture is usually related to such high-employment areas as manufacturing, wholesale-retail trade, finance, transportation, government, and the professional fields, as well as skilled labor. Ratios may be expressed in terms of the cities' total number of workers in each line of activity (as the denominator

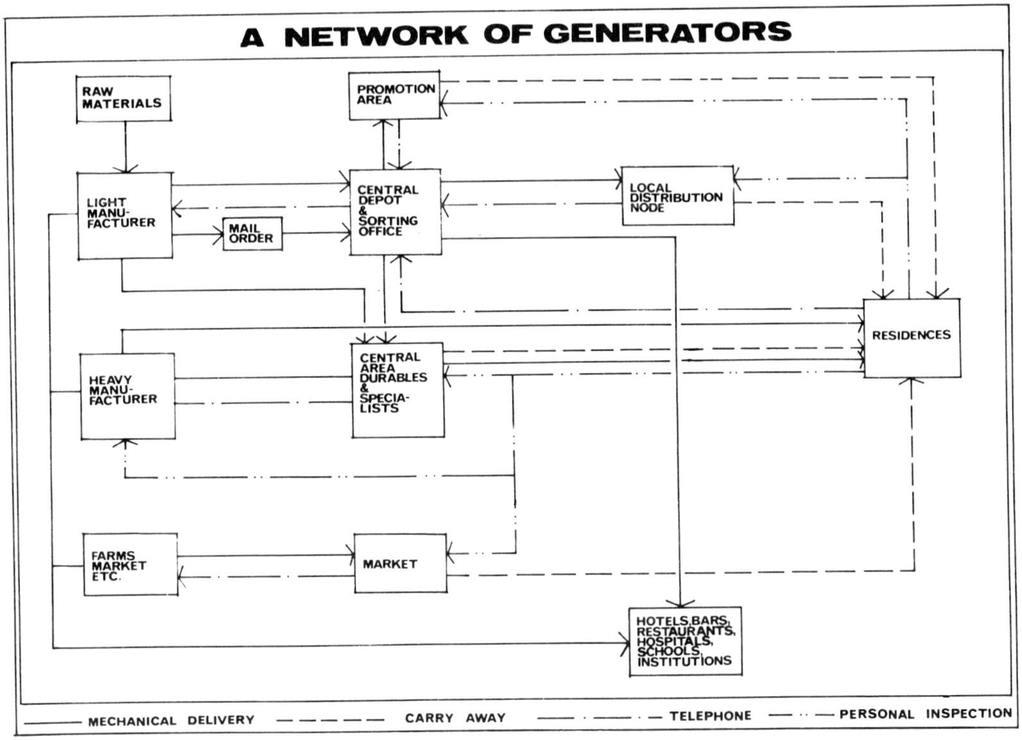

FIGURE 7.12
Economic generators for an urban community

Table 7.9

Subject: Industry Group of Employed
Place: Tallahassee, Florida
Time: 1960

	Numbers	Employed
Primary activities		
Agriculture	122	
Forestry and fisheries	56	
Mining	25	(203)
Secondary activities		
Furniture, lumber, and wood products	466	
Primary metal industries	4	
Fabricated metal industries	4	
Machinery	36	
Electrical machinery, equipment, and supplies	12	
Motor vehicles and equipment	9	
Transportation equipment	34	
Other durable goods	101	
Food and kindred products	229	
Textile mill products	—	
Apparel and other fabricated textile products	13	
Printing, publishing, and allied products	282	
Chemical and allied products	29	
Other nondurable goods	53	(1,272)
Service activities		
Construction	1,379	
Railroad and railway express service	88	
Trucking service and warehousing	74	
Other transportation	200	
Communications	299	
Utilities and sanitary service	161	
Wholesale trade	549	
Food and dairy products stores	349	
Eating and drinking places	691	
Other retail trade	1,938	
Finance, insurance, and real estate	802	
Business services	163	
Repair services	143	
Private households	1,420	
Other personal services	880	
Entertainment and recreation services	172	
Hospitals	512	
Educational services		
Government	4,071	
Private	237	
Welfare, religious, and nonprofit organizations	256	
Other professional and related services	487	
Public administration	2,585	
Industry not reported	567	(18,023)

Table 7.10 Relative population increases and decreases in the U.S. through history

Item	Central City			Ring		
	1948–1954	1954–1958	1958–1963	1948–1954	1954–1958	1958–1963
Employment						
Manufacturing	15	30	28	6	9	11
Wholesaling	16	18	21	4	0	1
Retailing	27	17	37	4	0	0
Services	7	4	15	2	1	0
Population (legal boundaries)	17	16	18	1	2	0
Population (1950 central city boundaries)	21	22	24	1	1	0

SOURCE: Ibid., p. 19.

in the fraction) and the number of workers in a specific area (as the numerator). Such ratios furnish figures that are relevant when one city is compared with another.

The picture of metropolitan growth by now is relatively clear. Since World War II it has been extremely rapid, but the growth has been distributed haphazardly. While the outlying areas of metropolitan locations have grown quite rapidly, the central city has hardly grown and consequently has declined in relative proportions. Population shifts have taken place where more affluent members of the area have fled to the suburbs and the less affluent have migrated to the inner city. Table 7.10 indicates the proportionate increases and decreases in the urban population in the United States. At the start of the Industrial Revolution the rural areas lost much of their population to the metropolitan areas, and since World War II the city has declined while the suburbs have exploded.

The fourteen areas of the lowest growth rate lost on the average 117,000 people, 66,705 manufacturing jobs, 14,350 retailing jobs, and 6,493 wholesaling jobs, and gained 4,123 selected service jobs.[15] The data presented so far do not cover such important central business district (CBD) employment activities as central office employment, banking, finance, and business services.

[15]Kain, p. 26.

The evidence regarding CBD employment levels is far from clearcut. Even so it suggests that CBD declines are somewhat smaller than in the immediately surrounding areas. This is consistent with the views of those who emphasize the importance of increased employment in the central city office employment. In an increasing number of central cities the most rapid declines appear to be taking place in the core areas that surround the central business districts.[16]

Recently, a like tendency for industry to shift to the suburbs has been observed around large metropolitan areas such as St. Louis, Boston, and Seattle. The electronics industry, which requires highly skilled people, tends to locate in the more attractive suburbs rather than taking over old buildings in the central business district. Table 7.11 indicates the growth of this suburban ring over the past several years.

Population shifts and the shifts of industrial organizations toward the suburbs have played a role in determining the future form of the urban setting. It is becoming increasingly obvious that the most central parts of the metropolitan areas are losing employment to the outlying areas and that this process is accelerating. It is reasonably commonplace now for central-city employment rates to be declining. The metropolitan spatial structures are also undergoing rapid change as population shifts and employ-

[16]Ibid., p. 26.

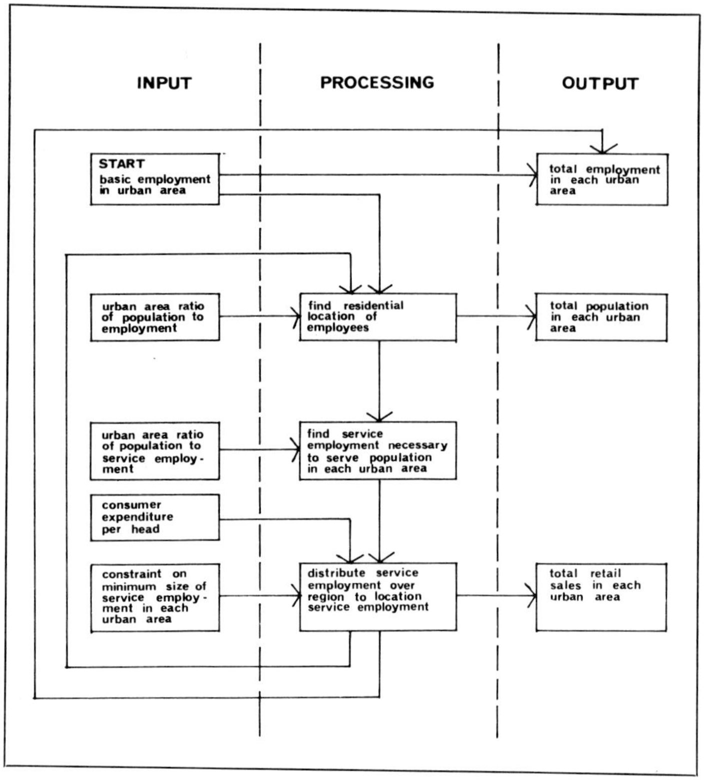

FIGURE 7.13
Employment breakdown

ment opportunities become dispersed throughout the metropolitan region. Manufacturing generally determines housing locations and patterns. The basic structure of the local economy is dependent on both the industry and the business sectors, whether the sector is a complex of production institutions or their markets.

Data related to education

Data related to population, place, movement, and economics directly and indirectly affect data related to education. If education is indeed concerned with the obtaining, researching, and dispensing of knowledge, then whatever activity occurs must be preceded by and fed back into education. The significance of this fact reflects the particular responsibilities of the educational agency and hence also the nature of an educational agency and the nature of an educational data-classification scheme. When the requirements for data are analyzed, it becomes apparent that they always describe characteristics of population, place, movement, economics and interrelated activities. Therefore planning activities should be concerned

Table 7.11 Suburban ring share of SMSA's employment and population by selected year

Item	1948	1954	1958	1963
Employment				
Manufacturing	33.1%	38.6%	42.0%	51.8%
Wholesaling	8.2	14.5	20.7	28.6
Retailing	24.7	30.6	37.2	45.4
Services	15.2	21.6	26.1	31.3
Population	36.0	43.5	48.2	54.3

SOURCE: Ibid., p. 27.

with structures and functions rather than with one or the other alone. Instead of finding out the number of rooms available for educational activities, the planner should find out the nature of the activities, for whom and for what they are planned, and cost information.

Data related to people fall into two broad groups. One group consists of personal identification (name, age, sex, race, ethnic origin, and so on). The second describes the status of specific persons with respect to certain educational functions (grade standing, probation, employability, and so on). Place data include locational information (street address, room number, school district, and so on), land and structural characteristics (age, color, size, condition, and so on), and possibly cultural characteristics (rural, suburban, urban, racial breakdown, ethnic characteristics, prevailing economic profile, and so on). Movement data include origins and destinations (from Room 210 to Room 450, from school to city museum, from school to home, and so on), channel capacity (1 school bus/5 minutes/lane, 54 students/3 minutes/door, 5 students served food/1 minute, and so on), and structural and possibly occupant characteristics. Economic data include two phases—the input (revenue received and applied) and the output (benefits or utilities obtained). Each phase is applicable to operating (teacher's salary, food purchased, cleaning buildings, and so on); to capital outlay (new school construction, site purchased, and so on); and debt servicing (bond obligations, contracts awarded to other agencies, and so on). Activity data combine certain people, places, and economic data with instructional programming (general educational program, occupational program, special education program, and so on); servicing (teacher preparation, library, food program, community-related activities, and so on); and time (units, frequencies, and length).

SUMMARY OF CONSIDERATIONS

Gathering data differs widely among educational planners. The differences reflect the different events impinging on the educational organization and its environment. Gathering data, therefore, serves as the sensory organ of the educational organization.

An educational organization of even modest size generates an enormous volume of data. Obviously, not all events are recorded. Many data are totally irrelevant, whereas some have considerable potential value but the cost of gathering them does not justify the effort. As improvements in data-gathering techniques are made, data formerly ignored will be added to the data base.

Reducing the volume of the data gathered helps eliminate errors. Often data gathering represents the most significant cost in operating an educational information system. One way of reducing the amount of data is to monitor the environment less closely. By gathering fewer entities, the educational planner may reduce the volume of data gathered without decreasing the data volume. Another way is to avoid gathering the same information more than once. Still another way of reducing the volume of data gathered is to predict rather than gather the data. Often, predicted data is better than new data gathered after the events have occurred.

The volume of data generally gathered is so enormous that it must be reduced if the educational planner is not to be overwhelmed with trivial information. One reducing method is to filter out insignificant information. Identifying exceptions requires a complete formalization of the educational planning process in order to know which plans require what. In this manner the plan helps to establish a set of tolerance standards to use for screening out the insignificant. Obviously, the educational planner faces the possibility of eliminating significant data as insignificant, but as the decision and planning processes become better understood it is possible by experience to reduce errors.

Another reducing method is to aggregate data. The usefulness of this process rests on the assumption that the eliminated data are not needed for the purpose at hand. For example, student grades might be aggregated along the lines of similar courses and the teachers of those courses, leaving the data classified in terms of time period. Thus, all entities included within a data cell are homogeneous with respect to the classification criteria and are considered identical events as far as the classification scheme is concerned. If data values are incompatible, they must be converted to a common unit of measure by a weighing factor associated with one of the values.

The gathered data constitute the building blocks of educational planning or any planning. As a result, planning agencies are heavily dependent on data exchange with each other and this exchange requires data compatibility.

8 Tabulating data

Tabulation permits educational planners to deal with families of data for various kinds of analyses. It helps to simplify problems of communication among members of the profession. It assists in determining the transfer value of analytical methods between one planning group and another. It gives opportunities for comparative studies. Tabulating also offers more systematic research into educational trends. To the above advantages, however, must be added the danger of inflexibility and delay as a result of the mechanics required to keep tabulations up to date.

When the purposes of the data users are known tabulation may be quite profitable. For example, the definition of a data value affects the nature of analysis. If, as an illustration, the objective of an educational study is the evaluation of the impact on an area from movements, the inclusion of walk trips as a separate category in the definition of movement is certainly significant. In one case, there may be many walk trips occurring because of the high density of a neighborhood. In other cases, fewer walk trips may occur because of other environmental factors, even though the density is similar. If data tabulated by the educational study does not include walk trips it may be useless for analyzing walk purposes.

Other examples of the need for tabulation arise when data from two sources are combined, or when data connecting two different sets of entities are compared, or when analyses are made on data from the same set of entities but at two points in time. Such

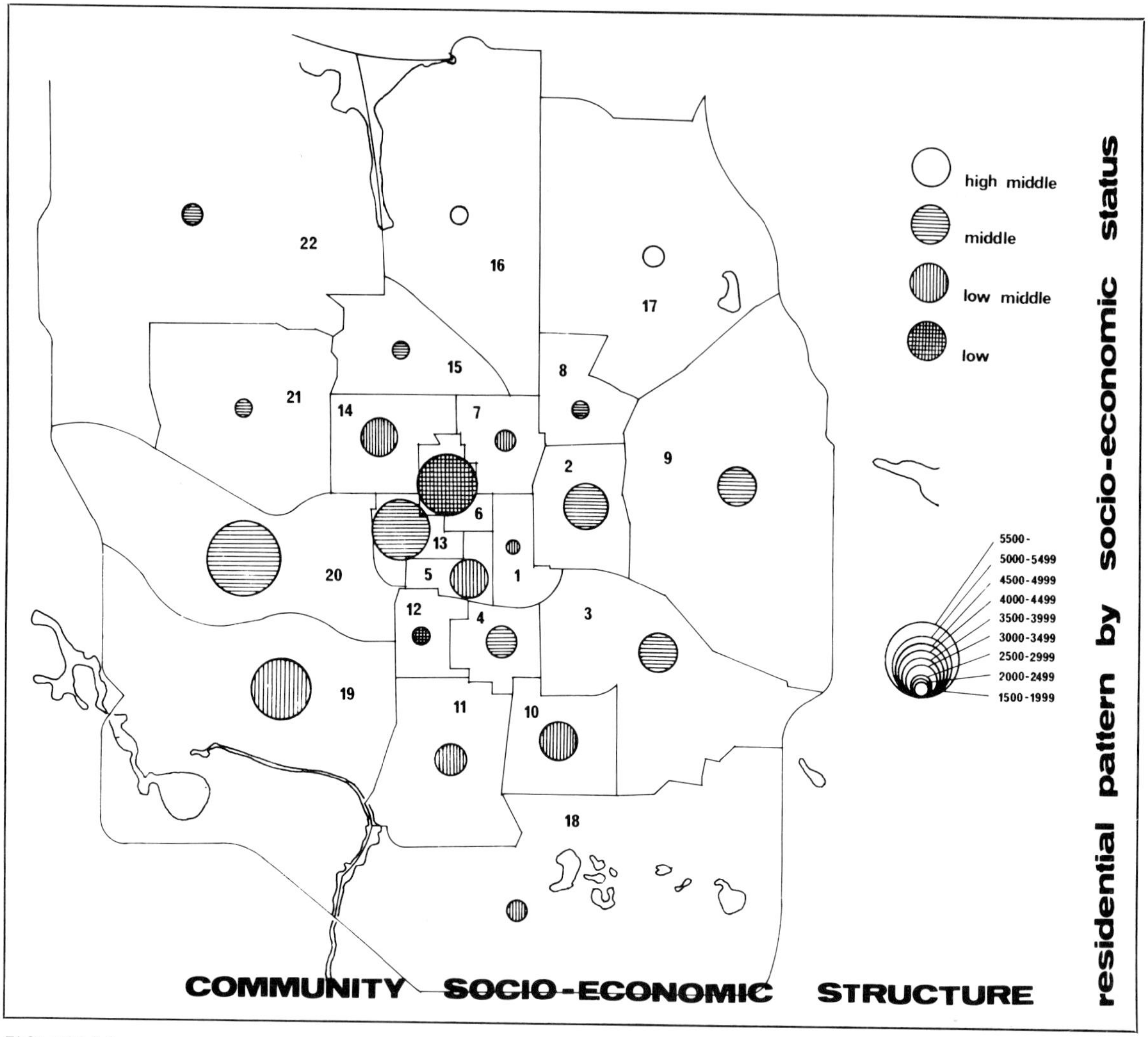

FIGURE 8.1

values are assigned to data as number of students, number of movements, number of school types on the assumption that all those assigning the values are using the same data definition.

Many different ways of tabulating are now possible. The problems arising from lack of tabulation have been widely recognized. In this book, these problems are discussed in terms of people, places, movements, economics, and activities—the same classifications used to discuss data gathering.

TABULATING PRACTICES USED FOR PEOPLE

There are various reasons why the characteristics of people must be tabulated. Social scientists and government officials need comparative data of geographical regions. (See Figure 8.1.) An inventory of human resources reveals birth, death, migration, and growth. Also, population data can be used by the planner to formulate physical and social structures. Census data are used by government agencies primarily as inventory items. Because of the complex nature of society, census-type data are essential tools for comprehensive and detailed analysis of the characteristics of a population. The data ascertain the complexity of society by listing the different roles that the members of that aggregation fill. Meaningful planning can take place when statistical data reveal a detailed knowledge of the various social, economic, and political characteristics that are found within a population; detailed information on the relative proportions of the population within a class further elaborates demographic composition. (See Figure 8.2.)

Some demographers have preferred to use only such basic information as age and sex in order to differentiate populations; others have included groupings according to race. Although age, sex, and race are biological aspects of life, the social scientist considers them primarily social factors. The United States Census defines race as simply the categorization of white and nonwhite. "The nonwhite category

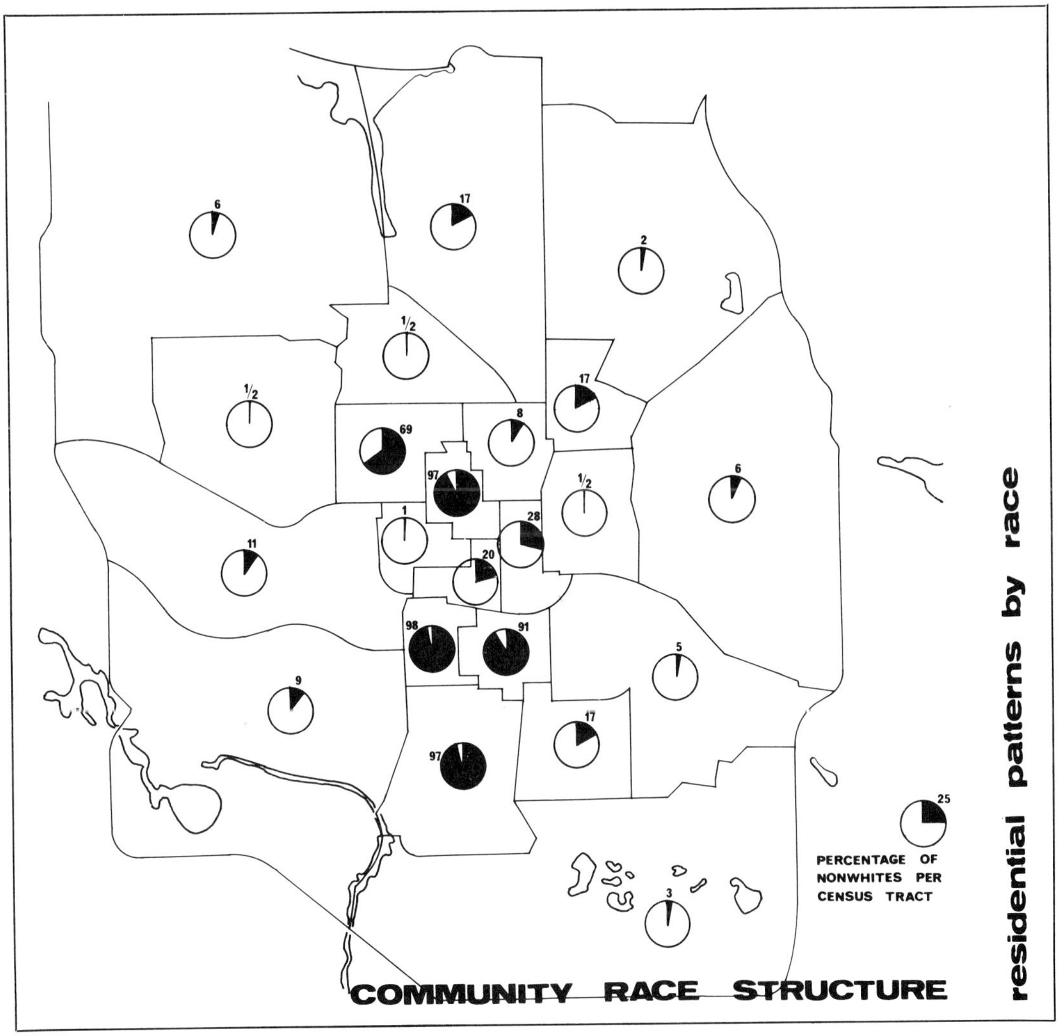

FIGURE 8.2

is subdivided into Negro and other races. Other races include Indian, Japanese, Chinese, Filipino, and a residual category called all other."[1] Racial differences along with age and sex are frequently used

> . . . for establishing the degree of an individual's eligibility to occupy various social, economic, and political statuses. In many societies a person's racial status determines where he can live, what occupations he can enter, and how much political power he can exercise.[2]

Frequently census data on smaller scales will circumscribe ethnic groups within a certain community. The Irish, Poles, and Italians in the American community are people

> . . . who are identified on the basis of a common culture and who therefore have a sense of collective identity. These groups may also share a common language and religion, and occupy a given piece of territory. An ethnic population may or may not be a nationality in the sense of having a political as well as a cultural identity. Some national and ethnic groups think of themselves as having a common biological ancestry. The term ethnic correctly applies to such populations as Poles, Hungarians, Gypsies, Jews, Amish, French Canadians, Mexicans, Italians, Slovaks and Afrikaners. . . . An ethnic or national population may be made up only of members of a particular race, or it may cut across several racial categories. An individual's membership in an ethnic category is nearly always a matter of birth rather than of choice or achievement; in this respect ethnicity is similar to age, sex, and race. The characteristics used to identify ethnic or national groups are cultural characteristics such as language, manner of dress, food habits, and religious observances. These traits are learned; they are socially, not biologically, transmitted from generation to generation.[3]

In the measurement of sex composition the common ratio is the number of males per one hundred females of the male population divided by the females and multiplied by one hundred. The value of such a relative figure becomes apparent when one is comparing the sex compositions of all population groups regardless of other statistical boundaries. The relative worth of this ratio can be observed by an examination of the figures in Table 8.1.

For the analysis of age composition, statistical manipulations become more complicated because of the diverse possibilities in grouping ages. The median age is generally employed to determine the age distribution of a population. The median is the number that falls where equal amounts fall above and below it. One of the great advantages of the median age is that it is not influenced by extreme values. Because specific changes in birth and death rates frequently cause extreme fluctuations in the statistics, the figure that is unaffected by such variations is the most useful. Typical age tables are found in Table 8.2.

The dependency ratio is used with some frequency to distinguish age composition. The dependency ratio describes a population by categorizing people according to their positions as producers or consumers. One expression is the consumer-producer index. But despite its being a numerical expression it is not necessarily applicable to every situation. The youth-dependency ratio, another dependency ratio, is a numerical index of the number of people under fifteen years of age divided by the population group between fifteen and fifty-nine inclusively. Another expression of the age-dependency ratio uses persons over fifty-nine and divides that number by the number in the middle age group. Some dependency ratios in various regions in the United States are given in Table 8.2.

There are several ways to present the age and sex compositions of diverse populations. The characteristics of a group may be graphically plotted to form a pyramid. (See Figure 8.3.) If the younger age groups are located at the bottom, the base of the pyramid is established and the increasingly older age groups are plotted to form the apex of the pyramid. Either absolute numbers or proportions may be used in the calculations that structure the distributions in the pyramid. A proportion pyramid, which is a graphic representation of age-group data, is given in Table 8.2.

The interpretation of the population pyramid relies heavily on the background information supplied by the demographer. Pyramids can take on

[1]Warren S. Thompson and David T. Lewis, *Population Problems* (New York: McGraw-Hill, 1965), p. 68.
[2]Ibid.
[3]Ibid., pp. 68–69.

FIGURE 8.3

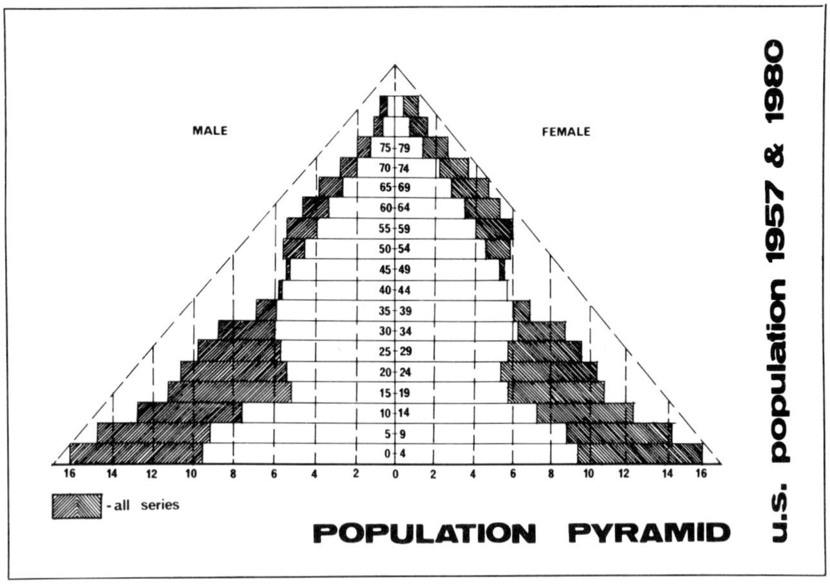

varying shapes from a triangle with either concave or convex sides to an L-shaped figure. These pyramids reveal more information when the same populations are compared at different times. Such a comparison discloses the relative proportion of the population and graphically determines its rate of rise or decline.

Because the American population has been becoming increasingly urbanized it has been necessary to look at the population composition in terms of this urbanization. As early as 1910 the U.S. Bureau of the Census defined urban population,

> . . . saying simply that all people living in incorporated places of 2500 or more . . . were classified as urban.
>
> [The definition had two primary virtues:]
>
> (1) It fitted the facts of settlement; because 2500 was the lower limit for urban places, urban communities were clearly separated from the more scattered farm and village communities; and (2) the definition was simple and could be easily applied to the first census thereby providing data which have made possible comparisons of the urban-rural composition of the population from 1790 to 1950.[4]

By 1950 a new definition of urban population had been formulated. The U.S. Census Bureau developed a new concept of urbanized areas by considering an urbanized area in terms of a physical city rather than a legal one. Caused by the urbanization of American society, the new definition distinguished the urban area around the outer limits of the central city from the central city. The 1950 Census separated incorporated places of 2,500 or more people from the central city, and suburban areas from the adjoining rural areas. In the 1960 definition the U.S. Census Bureau categorized urban areas as those areas, whether incorporated or unincorporated where 2,500 or more people resided. (See Figure 8.4.) Although certain states have special definitions of urban areas, the general definition included persons concentrated in groups of 2,500 or more regardless of the legal structure of the area. No particular definition of rural populations has been established; it has been assumed that anyone not in an urban area is in a rural area. Table 8.3 furnishes a comparison of the increase in the urban population of the United States as a result of the definition change from 1950 to 1960. The 1960 Census distinguished between farm and nonfarm population on the basis of people's living on places of ten or more acres with sales of $50 or more in 1959, or less than ten acres but sales of $250 or more in 1959.

[4]Ibid., p. 129.

Table 8.1 Sex ratios

1 Sex ratio of the population of the U.S. by region and division and time e.g. from 1900 to 1960 (U.S. is divided into 4 regions—Northeast, North Central, South and West and 9 divisions—New England, Middle Atlantic, East North Central, West North Central, South Atlantic, East South Central, West South Central, Mountain and Pacific)

Geographic region and division	Year 1960	1950	1940	1930	1920	1910	1900
Northeast	94.7	96.1	98.6	100.0	100.6	102.3	100.0
New England	95.0	95.7	97.0	97.2	98.5	99.3	97.7
M. Atlantic	94.5	96.2	99.1	100.9	101.4	103.3	100.9
etc.							

2 Sex ratio of the population and sex ratio at birth. Selected countries and territories : latest date available

Region and country or territory	Total population		At birth	
	Date	Sex ratio	Date	Sex ratio
Africa				
Algeria (Muslim)	1954	102.9	1956†	109.0
Mozambique	1950	91.7	1957†	105.3

† Data are of unknown completeness

3 Sex ratio of the population of the U.S. by size of place, 1960 and 1950

Year	U.S.	Urban					Rural		
		Total	Urbanized area		Other 1,000 and over	Urban 2,500 to 10,000	Total	Places 1,000 to 2,500	Other rural
			Cent'l urban cities	fringe					
1960	97.1	94.1	92.9	96.2	94.1	93.5	104.3	94.1	105.8
1950	98.7	94.7	93.5	95.1	93.3	93.1	104.9	94.3	106.4

4 Sex ratio of the population of the U.S. by urban rural residence, 1910–1960

Year	Urban	Rural	
		Nonfarm	Farm
1960	94.0	103.3	107.2
1950	94.6	103.6	110.1
etc.			

5 Sex ratio of the population of U.S. by color and race, 1860–1960

Year	All class	White	Nonwhite							
			Total	Negro	Other races					
					Total	Indian	Japanese	Chinese	Filipino	Others
1960	97.0	97.3	94.3	93.3	111.5	101.1	91.6	139.4	172.4	131.1
1940	100.7	101.2	96.7	95.0	140.5	105.5	130.9	285.3	680.2	249.3
1900	104.4	104.9	101.0	98.6	185.2	101.5	2369.6	1887.2		
1860	104.7	105.3	101.2	99.6	260.8	119.0		1858.1		

6 Sex ratio of the white population of the U.S. by nativity, 1850–1960

Nativity of population	1960	1950	1940	1930	1920	1910	1900	1890	1880	1870	1860	1850
Total white	97.3	99.0	101.2	102.9	104.4	106.6	104.9	105.4	104.0	102.8	105.3	105.2
Native	97.5	98.6	100.1	101.7	102.7	102.8	102.9	102.1	102.1	100.6	103.7	103.1
Foreign-born	94.2	103.8	111.1	115.8	121.7	129.2	117.4	118.7	115.9	115.3	115.1	123.8

SOURCE: Ibid., pp. 75, 76, 80, 83.

Table 8.2 Effects of death rates and birth rates on the median age of a population

1 Median age of the population of the U.S. by regions, 1820–1960

Year	Total	Northeast	North Central	South	West
1960	29.5	32.4	29.7	27.3	28.8
1940	29.0	31.2	30.3	25.5	31.0
1890	22.1	25.3	22.2	18.8	25.2
1820	17.0	17.7	15.6	16.4	—

2 Median age of the population of the U.S. by color and nativity, 1880–1960

Year	Total	Native white	Foreign-born white	Nonwhite
1960	29.5	28.5	57.7	23.5
1940	29.0	26.9	51.0	25.2
1900	22.9	20.3	38.5	19.9
1890	22.0	19.5	37.1	18.5
1880	20.9	18.4	38.3	18.0

3 Median age and dependency ratio of the population of the U.S. by regions, urban-rural residence, nativity, and color, 1960

Median age and dependency ratio	All classes	Regions				Residence group				Nativity and color			
		North-east	North Central	South	West	SMSA	Urban	Rural		White			Non-white
								Nonfarm	Farm	Total	Native	Foreign-born	
Median age	29.5	32.4	29.7	27.3	28.8	30.1	30.3	26.8	29.6	30.3	28.5	57.7	23.5
Dependency ratio													
Total	90.7	83.1	93.8	96.5	90.3	85.4	85.7	102.8	105.4	88.9	90.3	68.3	106.3
Youth (0–19)	73.5	64.7	74.7	80.1	74.0	69.3	68.9	84.5	86.2	71.1	75.2	11.9	93.7
Aged (65 and over)	17.2	18.4	19.1	16.4	16.3	16.1	16.8	18.0	19.2	17.8	15.1	56.4	12.6

SOURCE: Ibid., pp. 86, and 97.

People who were not grouped with the farm population but lived in rural areas comprised the remainder of the rural population. According to the 1960 Census, a geographical area was considered to be metropolitan if it held a concentration of at least fifty-thousand people whether or not the area was a legal entity. Although there were pragmatic exceptions to the 1969 Census definition, the metropolitan area was generally characterized by a commonality of work and housing of a nonagricultural nature.

Data may be retrieved from census tracts according to various population characteristics (see Figure 8.5) and numerous combinations have been used to demonstrate the diverse types of population compositions. The following enumeration of available population characteristics with their census years illustrates what data can be found; however, the list is not definitive: (1) labor-force participation rate by sex, U.S.: 1940–1960; (2) intercensal rates of increase of the population, 14 years of age and over, and labor force by sex, U.S.: 1940–1960; (3) percentage of the population in the labor force, by age, male, and female, U.S.: 1940–1960; (4) percentage of population 14 years of age and over in the labor force by color and sex, U.S.: 1940–1960; (5) employment status and selected labor force characteristics by color and sex, U.S., urban and rural: 1960; (6) percentage of economically active by sex, and nonworker to worker ratio for selected countries: around 1950; (7) industry group of employed persons, U.S.: 1940–1960;

FIGURE 8.4

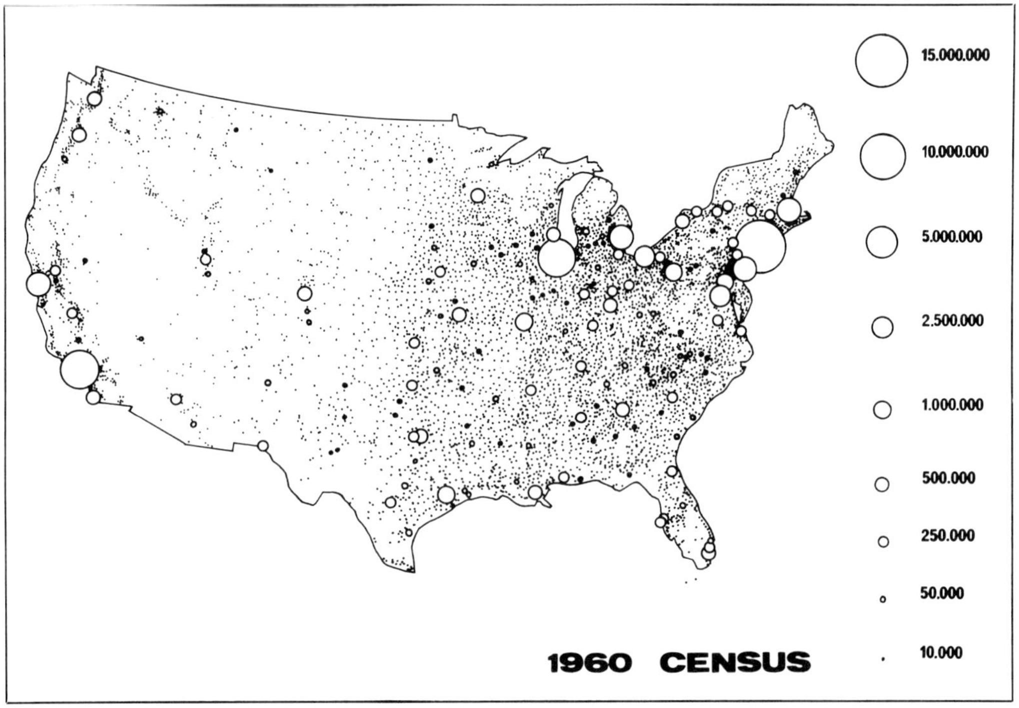

Table 8.3 Composition of the increase in the urban population of the U.S. resulting from the change in definition of "*urban*," 1950 and 1960

Composition	1950	1960
Total urban under 1950 and 1960 definitions	96,467,686	125,268,750
Total urban under 1940 definition	88,927,464	113,056,353
Net increase in number urban	7,540,222	12,212,397
Net increase in percentage urban	8.5	10.8
Increase in urban under new definition	7,877,819	12,720,334
Within urbanized areas	6,203,596	10,733,350
Outside urbanized areas	1,674,223	1,986,984
Loss from urban under new definition for urban under 1940 rules	−337,597	−507,937

SOURCE: Ibid., p. 133.

(8) industry group of employed persons for selected places: 1960; (9) occupational composition of experienced labor force, U.S.: 1900–1960; (10) percentage of change in occupation groups of employed persons by decade, U.S.: 1900–1960; (11) occupational composition of employed labor force by color, U.S.: 1940–1960; (12) occupation groups of employed persons by color and sex, U.S.: 1940–1960; (13) median years of schooling (1962), median income (males, 1959), by occupation group, U.S.; (14) employment by occupation groups, U.S.: 1960 and projected 1970; (15) median income in U.S. by sex, color, and size of place of residence: 1959; (16) income of husband, wife, families, head wage-earner, two children under 18, by color, U.S. total population and U.S. urban: 1959; (17) median income of families, by color, U.S.: 1947–1962; (18) percentage of persons 25 years old and over completing specified years of school, U.S.: 1940, 1950, and 1960; (19) years of school completed by persons 25 years old and over, by color and sex, U.S.: 1960; (20) median school years completed, by sex, color, and residence, U.S.:

FIGURE 8.5

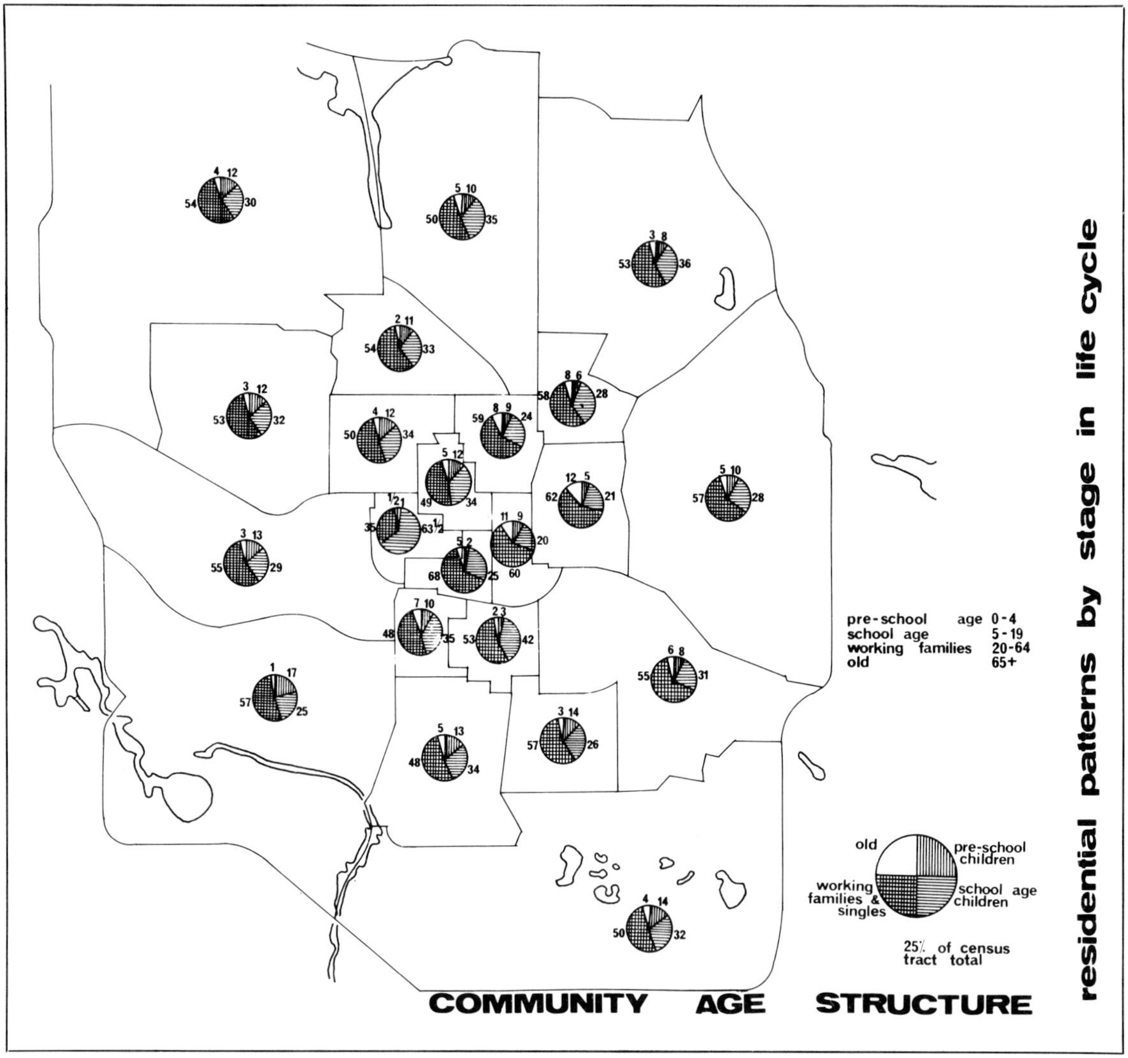

1940–1960; (21) percentage of persons of specified ages enrolled in school in census years, U.S.: 1910–1960; (22) school enrollment for civilian, noninstitutional population 7 to 34 years old (total number enrolled and proportion in different levels of schools, by age and sex), U.S.: 1960; (23) school enrollment by level of school, U.S.: estimated 1950–1960, and projected to 1980; (24) population by race, in number and percentage, U.S.: 1790–1960; (25) number and percentage distribution by race and color, U.S.: 1930–1960; (26) number and percentage of distribution of "other races," U.S.: 1860–1960; (27) intercensal increase by race and color, U.S.: 1930–1960; (28) number and percentage of distribution and difference of white, Negro, and other races, U.S. (50 states) and continental U.S. (48 states): 1960; (29) number and percentage of distribution of Negro population, U.S. by regions: 1860–1960; (30) number and percentage of foreign-born in white population, U.S.: 1900–1960; (31) country of origin of foreign stock,

U.S.: 1960; (32) percentage of distribution of foreign-born, 1960, and foreign-born white, 1910, by mother tongue, U.S.; (33) nativity and parentage of population, U.S., for regions and selected states: 1960; (34) number and percentage of foreign-born white and foreign-born nonwhite, living in different types of communities, U.S.: 1960; (35) percentage of white foreign-born constituting the total population in the ten largest cities, U.S.: 1950 and 1960; (36) percentage of distribution of population by broad religious groups, selected countries: latest year available; (37) number of churches and of members, by religious group, U.S.: 1963, (38) church membership as percentage of population, U.S.: 1850–1962; (39) percentage of distribution of population 14 years old and over, by sex and marital status, U.S.: 1940–1960; and (40) percentage of distribution of population 15 years of age and over by sex and marital status, selected foreign countries: latest available year.

Before 1970, the Census Bureau was concerned with production problems—enumeration and processing. Today, however, the Bureau's concern has changed, to include the service capabilities of satisfying user demands. User demands usually encompass current information for planning; e.g. information peculiar to special geographic areas, different breakdowns of categories and cross-tabulations, and information in machine-readable form. A data base will be available ". . . from which a variety of data tabulations and special services can be extracted in a variety of media. . . ."[5] The 1970 Census purposes were as follows:

More data. There will be a few new subjects on the 1970 census questionnaire. More importantly, as part of the regular publication program, there will be more items of information (representing primarily more cross-tabulations), particularly for small geographic areas. Summary tapes will contain even more items.

Data available sooner. The first final tabulations on summary tapes will be available within months after census day.

Greater areal detail and flexibility. Small-geographic areas

[5] *1970 Census User Guide,* Draft No. 2., April 1969, U.S. Department of Commerce, Bureau of the Census, p. 13.

Table 8.4 1970 census data—population item

Population items	Complete-count or sample percentage 1960	1970
Relationship to head of household	100	100
Color or race	100	100
Age (month and year of birth)	100	100
Sex	100	100
Marital status	100	100
State or country of birth	25	20
Years of school completed	25	20
Number of children ever born	25	20
Activity five years ago	—	20
Employment status	25	20
Hours worked last week	25	20
Weeks worked last year	25	20
Last year in which worked	25	20
Occupation, industry, and class of worker	25	20
Income last year:		
Wage and salary income	25	20
Self-employment income	25	20†
Other income	25	20‡
Country of birth of parents	25	15
Mother tongue	25	15
Year moved into this house	25	15
Place of residence five years ago	25	15§
School or college enrollment (public or private)	25	15
Veteran status	25	15
Place of work	25	15‖
Means of transportation to work	25	15
Occupation-industry five years ago	—	5
Citizenship	—	5
Year of immigration	—	5
Marital history	25	5¶
Vocational training completed	—	5
Presence and duration of disability	—	5

SOURCE: Ibid., p. 22.
† Single item in 1960; two-way separation in 1970 by farm and nonfarm income.
‡ Single item in 1960; three-way separation in 1970 by social security, public welfare, and all other receipts.
§ This item is also in the 5-percent sample but limited to state of residence 5 years ago.
‖ Item will be expanded to include street address where the appropriations for the 1970 censuses make this possible.
¶ In 1960, whether married more than once and date of first marriage; in 1970 also includes whether first marriage ended by death of spouse

such as census tracts and city blocks will be identified in more parts of the country as part of the regular tabulation program. The Bureau will also have the capability in many areas to produce special tabulations for user-defined areas.

Regular or general tabulations available in several media. Tabulations available on the printed page will also be available on tape and microfilm copy created from tape.

Special services. These include special tabulations, a variety of public use samples, computer-produced analytic reports, matching studies, computer graphics. Their development depends on successful coordinated efforts between the Bureau and the user.[6]

Specifically the 1970 Census included the items listed in Table 8.4.

The general tabulations of these items are available to users at low cost in the following media: printed reports, summary tapes, and microfilm.

The printed reports include the following volumes.

1970 Census of Population

Volume I *Characteristics of the Population*

Volume I, *Characteristics of the Population,* [is] the basic printed publication of population census results. Volume I consisted of separate parts for the United States, the 50 States, the District of Columbia, American Samoa, Canal Zone, Guam, Puerto Rico, and the Virgin Islands. Each part of four Chapters, A, B, C, and D.[7]

Chapter A *Number of Inhabitants*

Chapter A, *Number of Inhabitants,* [presents] final population counts for States (or outlying areas) and counties and their urban and rural parts, SMSA's [Standard Metropolitan Statistical Area] urbanized areas, incorporated places, unincorporated places of 1,000 inhabitants or more, and minor civil divisions.[8]

Chapter B *General Characteristics of the Population*

Chapter B, *General Characteristics of the Population,* [includes] data on age, sex, marital status, color or race, and relationship to head of household (i.e., 100-percent or complete-count items) for States, counties, urban and rural parts, SMSA's, urbanized areas, [and] places of 1,000 or more. . . .[9]

[6]Ibid., pp. 13, 14.
[7]Ibid., p. 50.
[8]Ibid.
[9]Ibid.

Chapter C *General Social and Economic Characteristics*

Chapter C, *General Social and Economic Characteristics,* [presents] sample data on nativity, parentage, State of birth, country of origin, mother tongue, place of residence in [1965], year moved into present house, school enrollment by level and type, years of school completed, families and their composition, fertility, veteran status, employment status, weeks worked in [1969], year last worked, occupation group, industry group, class of worker, place of work, means of transportation to work, and income of persons and families. Each subject [is] shown for States, counties, urban, rural nonfarm and rural farm parts, SMSA's urbanized areas, and urban places of 10,000 or more.[10]

Chapter D *Detailed Characteristics*

Chapter D, *Detailed Characteristics,* [includes] most of the subjects covered in Chapter C, cross-classified by age, color, and other characteristics. Additional information on families, household relationship, the institutional population, single years of age, detailed occupation and industry, and hours worked was also presented. Each subject [is] shown for States, urban, rural nonfarm and rural farm parts, large counties, cities, and SMSA's.[11]

Volume II *Subject Reports*

As of this writing no planning on this volume had begun.

Volume III *Selected Area Reports*

As of this writing no planning on this volume had begun.

1970 Census of Housing

Volume I *State and Small Areas*

Two chapters have been developed, one for complete-count data and one for sample.

Volume I [includes] occupancy characteristics of housing units, vacancy status, crowding, structural characteristics, condition and plumbing facilities, heating and household equipment, fuels, and financial characteristics. Some of all of these subjects [are] for States, urbanized areas, SMSA's by counties, urban places of 50,000 or more, the urban balance of the SMSA, and the rural portion of the SMSA, places of 25,000 to 50,000, 10,000–25,000, 2,500–10,000,

[10]Ibid., pp. 50, 51.
[11]Ibid., p. 51.

Table 8.5 1970 census data—housing item

Housing items	Complete-count or sample percentage 1960	1970	Housing items	Complete-count or sample percentage 1960	1970
Number of units at this address	—	100†	Number of units in structure	20	20
Telephone	25	100‡	Whether a trailer	25	20
Access to unit	100	100	Farm residence	25¶	20
Kitchen or cooking facilities	100	100	(acreage and sales of farm products)		
Complete kitchen facilities	—	100	Land used for farming	25**	—
Condition of housing unit	100	—			
Rooms	100	100	Source of water	20¶	15
Water supply	100	100	Sewage disposal	20¶	15
Flush toilet	100	100	Bathrooms	20	15
Bathtub or shower	100	100	Air conditioning	5	15
Basement	20	100	Automobiles	20††	15
Tenure	100	100	Stories, elevator in structure	20‡‡	5
Commercial establishment on property	100§	100	Fuel-heating, cooking, water heating	5	5
Value	100§	100	Bedrooms	5	5
Contract rent	100§	100	Second home	—	5
Vacancy status	100	100	Clothes-washing machine	5	5
Months vacant	25	100	Clothes dryer	5	5
			Dishwasher	—	5
Components of gross rent	25	20	Home food freezer	5	5
Heating equipment	25	20	Television	5	5
Year structure built	25	20	Radio	5	5

SOURCE: Ibid., p. 23.

† To be collected only for coverage check purposes; will not be tabulated.

‡ Required on 100-percent basis for field follow-up purposes in mail areas.

§ 100-percent in places of 40,000 or more inhabitants, 25-percent elsewhere.

¶ Omitted in places of 50,000 or more inhabitants.

** For renter-occupied and vacant-for-rent units outside places of 50,000 or more inhabitants.

†† 20-percent in places of 50,000 or more inhabitants, 5 percent elsewhere.

‡‡ Collected only in places of 50,000 or more inhabitants.

1,000–2,500, counties not in SMSA's and rural portions of counties.[12]

Volume II *Metropolitan Housing*

Volume II, *Metropolitan Housing*, [consists] of housing characteristics data for the United States, each division, and each SMSA of 100,000 or more.[13]

Volume III *City Blocks*

Volume III, *City Blocks*, [presents] a limited set of complete data for occupied housing units in individual city blocks. Characteristics included tenure, condition, plumbing, average number of rooms, crowding, units occupied by nonwhites, and total block population.[14]

[12]Ibid., p. 51.
[13]Ibid., p. 52.
[14]Ibid., p. 52.

Volume IV *Components of Inventory Change*

As of this writing no planning on this volume had begun.

Volume V *Residential Finance*

As of this writing no planning on this volume had begun.

Volume VI *Rural Housing*

This volume has not been published.

Volume VII *Housing of Senior Citizens*

Volume VII, *Housing of Senior Citizens*, [presents] housing and household characteristics for units occupied by persons 60 years old and over, for the U.S., 50 States and D.C., and selected SMSA's.[15]

[15]Ibid., p. 52.

1970 Population and Housing Censuses

Census Tract Reports presents complete-count data in separate tables from sample data.

The tape reports, the second medium available for public and private users, are issued in the format described below:

First Count Summary Tapes [were] the first tapes available. These tapes [contained] 450 items of final complete-count population and housing data, summarized for enumeration districts (in non-mail census areas) or blockgroups (in mail census areas within census tracts in file (a), and for States, counties, congressional districts, places, and minor civil divisions in file (b).

The subjects tabulated include age, sex, color, marital status relationship to head of household, crowding, tenure of occupied housing units, vacancy status, units in structure, rooms, plumbing facilities, basement, telephone, value or rent, and heating equipment. Many tabulations are cross-classified by color. First Count file (a) will be contained on about 160 reels of tape for the Nation; file (b) on about 36 reels. The files [are] issued by States, the reel(s) for the first State processed [became] available July 1970 and the last State by the end of 1970.[16]

This production schedule represents a considerable improvement over 1960, when Advance Reports containing selected final complete-count population and housing figures were not all issued until April 1961. Moreover, the First Count Summary Tapes contained substantially more data than printed or available on tape in 1960 or to be printed in 1970. *No* data summaries for enumeration districts, and blockgroups, or minor civil divisions will be printed. They will be available only on tape. Summaries for other areas will be more extensive on tape than in the printed reports.

Second Count Summary Tapes, organized into three files, [were] the next tape product from the 1970 census. Second Count file (a-1) [contained] 1750 cells of complete-count population data, summarized for States, SMSA's, urbanized areas, counties, places and minor civil divisions; file (a-2) 1750 items of complete-count housing data, summarized for the same areas; file (b) 3500 items of complete-count population and housing data (the same as in the two previous files), summarized for States, counties, and census tracts with place or MCD components.

[16]Ibid., p. 56.

Second Count tapes contain the same subjects as the First Count tapes but in much greater detail. Each Second Count file . . . contained . . . about 105 reels for the Nation. The tapes [were] issued by States from November 1970 to February 1971.

Block Summary Tapes, containing 250 items of complete-count population and housing data for city blocks (in urbanized areas of cities of 50,000 or more population and other areas which contract for block statistics), [became] available [in mid] 1971. The delay in issuing block tapes [was] due to the necessity [of checking] block geographic codes very carefully. Block group totals derived from the block tapes may not equal totals on the First Count tapes. The latter are issued as soon as possible and are not subject to such precise geographic verification. The Block tape file [is] contained on about 300 reels for the Nation. Note that these tapes contain fewer data items than carried on the tapes for larger areas, but considerably more, particularly population characteristics, than available in 1960 or to be printed in 1970.

Sample Summary Tapes containing sample population and housing characteristics [became] available after July 1971. The subject content of these tapes [was] not determined, [as of this writing] but [plans have been made for] considerably more data than [were] available in 1960. . . . Sample data summaries [are] not available for areas smaller than census tracts.[17]

Microfilm, yet another medium for dispensing general tabulated data, includes printed volumes of the content of the Census and the Census summary tape. The Census summary data, however, are not organized into tables but rather are presented in matrix form with the addition of column and row-heading identifications.

A number of geographic tools for users are available. Metropolitan maps, a base map (scale of 1″ = 800′) and a stock map (scale 1″ = 1,600′) of all SMSA (Standard Metropolitan Statistical Areas) areas, aid those users needing small-area census tabulations. The MRF (Master Reference File), another tool, contains numerical codes and associated place names for every area recognized in Census tabulations. A third tool, the *1970 Geographic Code*

[17]Ibid., p. 57.

Scheme book, contains Census tracts, block group codes, and population and housing counts. The *Address Coding Guide* (ACG) tool specifies blockface codes for summarizing the records of individual blockfaces, which otherwise are not available because of their confidential restrictions. The *Dual Independent Map Encoding* (DIME) is a procedure to ". . . [allow] computer display of data on maps, calculate areas of blocks, tracts, etc., calculate the distance between any two points, [access] retrieval data for areas specified as lying within a given distance of a particular point and accomplish other analyses."[18]

Last, under general tabulations and services, the Census provides the public-use samples, with additional data on the individual's community or neighborhood with such variables as the percentage of the population with income below the poverty level, the percentage of institutional population, the percentage of owner-occupied housing units, and so on.

A second major area of the Bureau's work is the special tabulations and services requested by a user and paid for by him. These services involve retabulation of basic record tapes to obtain data summaries for geographic areas not recognized in the general tabulations. Also, the user may request different subject content not available in general tabulations. An example of such a request is the Office of Education's programming to develop and provide for school districts a special tabulation package of census tract type. Other special services are matching studies, e.g., matching 1970 Census questionnaires to hospital admissions records. Still other services are computer-produced analytic reports, computer graphics, and software packages for census-data analysis.

In addition to the population and housing censuses, other censuses provided by the Bureau are as follows:

Governments—Taken every five years in years ending with 2 and 7. (First census in 1850.) Government concepts definitions apply to the 1962 and 1967 censuses.

Business—Formerly taken every five years in years ending with 3 and 8. (First census in 1930.) Beginning in 1967 taken every five years in years ending with 2 and 7. Business concepts definitions apply to the 1963 and 1967 censuses.

[18]Ibid., p. 68.

Manufacturers—Same comments apply. (First census in 1870.)

Mineral Industries—Same comments apply. (First census in 1840.)

Transportation—Same comments apply. (First census in 1963.)

Construction—Taken every five years in years ending with 2 and 7. (First census in 1967.) Construction concepts definitions apply to the 1967 census.

The above five censuses are known collectively as the Economic Censuses.[19]

Agriculture—Taken every five years in years ending with 4 and 9. (First census in 1840.) Agriculture concepts definitions apply to the 1964 and 1969 censuses.[20]

These new data allow appropriate plans for facilities for Civil Defense, transportation, parking, central business districts, industrial areas, and especially education. To accomplish these plans, completely automated information derived from studies of the origin and destination surveys of transportation planning might be entered on mark-sense cards or analytical record sheets. From them studies are made of the differences and similarities by relationships and comparisons. Such tabulations approximate the events and provide a general picture of the people, places, movements, and activities being considered for planning. The Bureau of the Census, as an example, devised a technique for Civil Defense agencies to use in studying potential disaster areas from air attacks. Based on the total daytime population located in certain areas during work and school hours, the technique uses distribution data for residential areas and integrates this information into various other population density poles throughout a time span. Even though this information is all fed into Census tracts to be used for Civil Defense purposes, it can be extricated and applied to long-range planning and especially to emergency projects.

Another technique analyzes populations by comparing the ratios of different population areas like the central city and the suburbs. After graphic plotting,

[19]*Census User Dictionary*, 2nd Draft, 1969, U.S. Dept. of Commerce, Bureau of the Census, Washington, D.C., p. 1.
[20]Ibid., p. 2.

these ratios are matched with the capacities of the shelter areas. Yet another technique is the zonal method, which uses Census tract data and focuses on the central business district rather than on the residential or central city and the peripheral city. It, too, matches population densities with the capacity of various buildings and considers the vacancy rates, and so on. Basically, the technique is constructed around concentric areas emanating from the central business district.

Several techniques are currently used. Some of the more popular are 1) the migration and natural increase method; 2) the proration method; 3) the censal ratio method; 4) the vital rates method; 5) the dwelling unit method; and 6) the composite method. The selection of any particular method to be used ". . . will depend upon the use to be made of the estimate, the level of accuracy required, and the time and staff experience available."[21] The U.S. Bureau of the Budget has used two primary approaches. The first was developed in 1947 and led to the development of the second, which was refined in 1956 and 1957. Both approaches are based on the following formula:

The civilian population of an area at the close of a period is equal to its population at the start of the period plus natural increase (the excess of births over deaths) during the period, plus the net migration during the period, minus the net loss of population to the armed forces. The total population is equal to the civilian population plus the number of persons in the armed forces stationed in the area.[22]

Educational departments, transportation departments, health services, and various other agencies and administrative units are interested in census data. These agencies use figures from the U.S. Bureau of the Census and compile further data that will complement their studies. They gather such data as:

1) Civilian population at the time of the last census,
2) Natural increase from last census to current date,
3) Estimated net civilian migration for the same period,
4) Net loss to the armed forces during the same period,
5) Estimated current civilian population (sum of Items 1, 2, and 3, minus Item 4),
6) Military personnel stationed in the area,
7) Estimated current total population (sum of Items 5 and 6).[23]

A later procedure of the Census Bureau ensures that it ". . . develops an estimate of the hypothetical enrollment based on natural increase along with the difference between the hypothetical and actual enrollment being used as the determinant of net migration."[24]

The migration and natural increase method is illustrated in Table 8.6. The appropriate use of this method requires that both migration and natural increase be considered simultaneously. The procedure begins with inserting the current population estimate and adjusting it according to migration and the natural increase rates, and the survival factor. The various procedural methods apply in the total population figures rather than in sex groups and age brackets. Regular graphics-plotting is applicable for interpretative purposes. The graphics data revealed in the trend lines may be extrapolated to yield the desired information. The natural increase component can be derived from recorded birth and death rates. This approach like other census projections depends heavily on extrapolation and consequently suffers from the same source of error.

The proration technique is relatively straightforward. The demographer obtains current data from a geographical entity, and, assuming that the relative proportion of this distribution has remained static from the last count, he estimates current population figures. The censal-ratio method is related to some base-line indicators, such as voter registration or utility connections. An extrapolation of the equations derived from past growth factors provides the estimated population. The censal-ratio method is advantageous because it is a direct step down from the Census tract data. Observed trends in vital statistics,

[21]F. Stuart Chapin, Jr., *Urban Land Use Planning* (Urbana, Ill.: University of Illinois Press, 1965), p. 184.

[22]"Illustrative Example of a Method of Estimating the Current Population of Subdivisions of the United States," *Current Population Reports,* No. 133 (Washington, D.C.: Bureau of the Census, Department of Commerce, March 16, 1956), p. 1.

[23]Chapin, p. 185.

[24]Ibid., p. 187.

Table 8.6 Migration and natural increase method

Year	Population*	Net migration		Population after adjustment for net migration ±	Natural increase		Population after adjustment for natural increase
		Rate ±	Amount ±		Rate	Amount	Next year's population
1965							
1966							
1967							
1968							
1969							
⋮							
1985							

SOURCE: p. 206.

school enrollment, listings in city directories, electric meters, water meters, telephone installations, and other data have been found to indicate population changes clearly.

In order to employ these statistics, it is essential that the recording be done regularly and at reasonably short time intervals.

The logical steps involved in the estimation of net civilian migration according to component Method II are as follows: (1) Net migration rates for children 7 1/2 to 15 1/2 years old (i.e., between exact age 7.50 years and exact age 15.50 years at each estimate date) are developed on the basis of data from the 1950 Census and statistics on school enrollment in the elementary grades 2 to 8. (2) These rates are multiplied by a factor (varying for each estimate period but the same for all States to which the method was applied) to obtain the estimated migration rates for the total population. These factors are based on several kinds of evidence concerning the age structure of interstate migration. (3) The resulting rates are applied to the civilian population of all ages in each State in 1950 (and to children born since 1950) to obtain tentative estimates of net civilian migration for the period since 1950. (4) These tentative estimates of net civilian migration are adjusted proportionately to add algebraically to the national estimate of net immigration for this period. This general procedure has been illustrated in Current Population Reports, Series P-25, No. 133, by a step-by-step application to a particular area.[25]

[25] *Current Population Reports,* Series P–25, no. 165 (Washington, D.C.: Bureau of the Census, November 4, 1957), p. 2.

The vital-statistics rate-method uses crude birth and death rates and expresses them as ratios in terms of specified populations. That is, the birth rate is calculated by the ratios of births or deaths per thousand population. By the simple multiplying of the ratio times the population under consideration, trends can be anticipated. The step-by-step procedure for doing this is explained in the various sources dealing with population statistics.

The regression method for estimating populations is based on a statistical sampling procedure, usually a least squares procedure, where progression lines, linear or otherwise, are formulated and projections are made from the derived regression equations.

Another variation of the application of proportion or ratio procedures is the use of previously prepared forecasts for some larger geographic area. After determining the relative proportion of the population under consideration in that larger portion, one multiplies the given population by the ratio. If a group with certain common characteristics composes 10 per cent of the population of the United States and if the metropolitan areas of one million or more are considered and are representative of the nation's population, then 10 per cent of the cities' populations would possess that characteristic. These diverse prorations and other ratio procedures are variants of the proportionate technique. In the estimating of employment opportunities, if 5 per cent of the people in a new area were employed in a given industry and if there were 50,000 people in the metropolitan area, then approximately 2,500 positions would exist for employment in that metropolitan area for that particular industry.

Arithmetic and geometric proportions, trend extrapolation from least squares and estimates based on logistics curves are appropriate for estimating on a short-term basis. All estimating techniques assume that a trend will continue in the future as it has during the past.

Some specific figures for establishing various rates include the following: crude birth rate, which is the number of births over the total population; age-specific death or birth rates, which indicate the number of persons of a given age who were born or died; age-standardized birth rates, which are based on age-specific death rates and supplies for different populations. Life tables, designed primarily by insurance actuaries, compile statistical data regarding life expectancy. These tables can be found in various insurance documents.

Cohort population studies offer yet another technique: observe a group born in a given year over a period of time while taking measurements on a desired population characteristic. Because population studies must abide by sound statistical sampling procedures, it is essential to employ control factors for possible differences among divergent populations. Some basic theories assume that

> . . . the form of government, in the political, economic and social organization and institutions, of the United States will remain substantially unchanged. No all-out war, internal revolution, nation-wide devastation, epidemic, or other disaster will occur. No large scale epidemic, destruction by military action, fire, earthquake or other disaster will occur in the area or within the geographical or economic region to which the area is closely related.[26]

In addition there are some special assumptions:

> 1) No major recession and continued full employment: 2) a down swing in the business cycle, with unemployment leveling off at "X" per cent of the civilian labor force; 3) if a military base exists in the area, assumptions must be made concerning international conditions and size of the armed forces; 4) if an extractive industry exists in the area, assumptions must be made concerning exploitation policy; and 5) assumptions must be made concerning the structure and vitality of the economy.[27]

Continual analyses of populations provide the statisticians with experience and allow their formulas to be tested. The accurate estimations are essential to the educational planner and to the success of his work. With successive analyses becoming more accurate, the problems caused by fluctuating populations can be alleviated.

TABULATING PRACTICES USED FOR PLACES

There are numerous approaches to studying land use and facilities. Some of the common types include the land-use survey that develops a classification scheme to record the use of space. (See Table 8.7.) Another approach surveys the structures and the environment and analyzes the status of the structures and the physical condition of the area and the facilities. Because it attempts to record and classify according to the category and the condition of all land improvements within the area, this survey is especially suitable in cases of urban renewal or studies preceding urban renewal. A cost analysis, another study method of land use, attempts to determine the various policies associated with the cost of land usage. (See Figure 8.6.) The resultant data provide information relative to land and structural values. Yet another approach maps the various physiographic characteristics of the region. (See Figure 8.7.) The maps are designed to show both the natural and the man-made characteristics of urban environment (see Figure 8.8), and they indicate not only the various alterations that have been made, but also the street layouts, lots, and other divisions imposed by regulations. (See Figure 8.9.) A further study-approach pattern is the attitudinal survey,

[26] *Current Population Reports,* Series P–25, no. 165 (Washington, D.C.: Bureau of the Census, November 4, 1957), p. 201.

[27] Ibid.

Table 8.7 Summary of land uses

Class of use	Total planning area			Inside city limits			Outside city limits		
	Acres	Per cent of total land	Per cent of developed land	Acres	Per cent of total land	Per cent of developed land	Acres	Per cent of total land	Per cent of developed land
All educational									
Primary									
Junior high									
Senior high									
Junior/senior high									
Junior college									
All residential									
One-family									
Two-family									
Multifamily									
Retail business									
Wholesale and other									
Industrial									
Transportation and utilities									
Streets and railroad									
Rights-of-way									
All public									
Public									
Military									
Institutional									
Water areas									
Vacant and nonurban									
Total									

which reveals public attitudes and feelings regarding land use. Land-use surveys classify and record space in use based on the type of activity. Vacant-land surveys, another approach, classify and record the use capabilities of vacant parcels and open spaces. Hydrological studies examine drainage systems and potential flood areas. Structural and environmental quality studies reveal the physical condition of structures, their quality, and other factors, for example, social, health, economic, and physical, associated with blight and obsolescence. Cost-revenue studies examine public policies and practices in supplying services and facilities for various activities and their effect on public financing. Land-value studies provide information about how land is priced and what is the most economic use of that land. Aesthetic studies identify vistas, focuses and axes, natural features with special development potential, special building groups with symbolic significance, and so on. These studies usually precede any reasonably significant change that is proposed for the urban area.

Traditionally the land-use survey has been concerned with the use of ground space. The surveys have been of industrial use, commercial use, public use, and residential use; each survey includes numerous subparts. However, the planner now is interested in

FIGURE 8.6

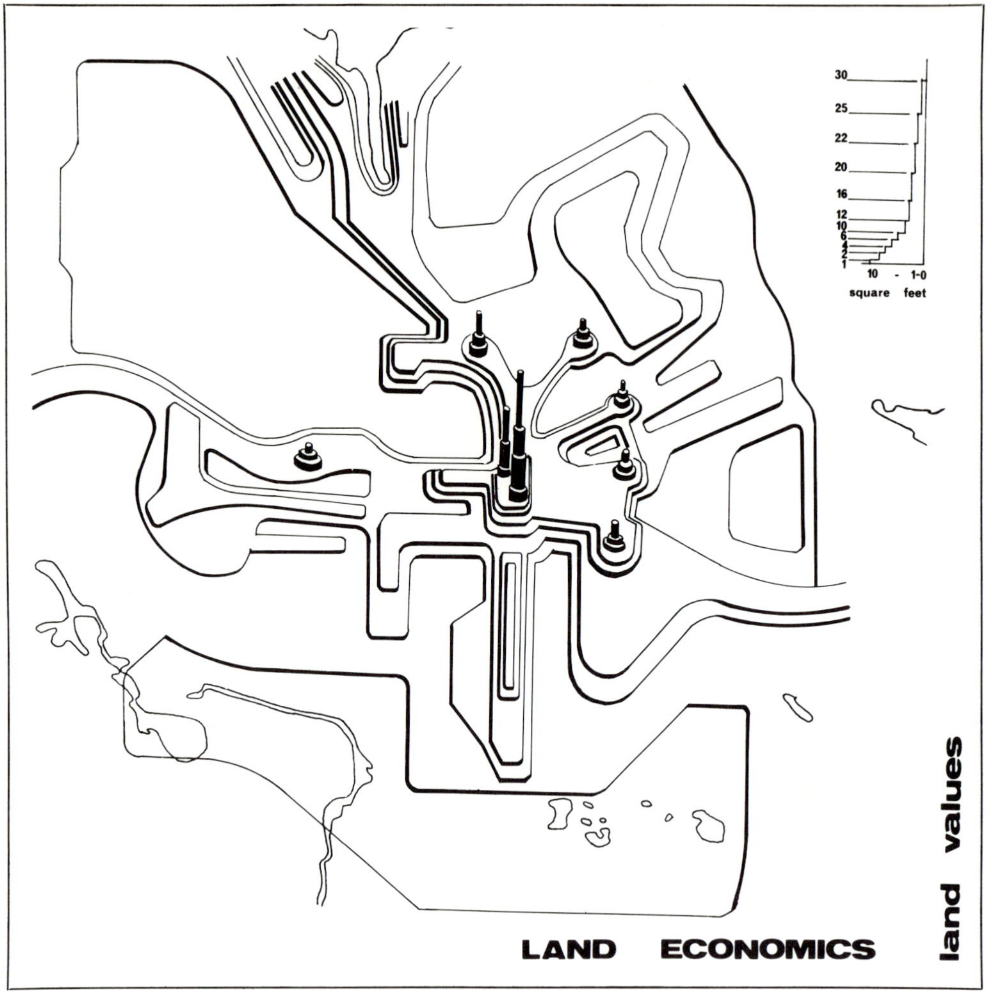

the use of space both inside and around the buildings. His interest in space uses as they reflect specific clusters of human activities extends to actions that tie into both local and nonlocal activities and communications systems.

Land-use data may be presented by the land development diagram, which shows the distribution of land and its urban use without distinguishing between classes of uses or the intensity of land development. The machine method of analysis divides land areas into cells of uniform size and records the gradations from a white to a black pattern, indicating the compactness of urban development according to intensity of use. Black indicates that all land in the grid cell is taken up by urban use, whereas the various other tones (gray to white) signify decreasing urban use in the grid cell. Residential, business, and industrial ground-use statistics are the data used in graphic representations. Conventional land-use maps show the various land-use patterns and relationships among land uses for large metropolitan areas. These areas are generally represented by colors as follows:

Residence	
low density	yellow
medium density	orange
high density	brown
Retail business	red
Transportation, utilities, communications	ultramarine
Industry and related uses	indigo blue
Wholesale and related uses	purple
Public buildings and open spaces	green
Institutional buildings and areas	gray
Vacant	uncolored

Although maps are composed by the human hand, machine methods of data handling can be used. In the CBD overlay, uses occurring at each level can be pictured in various levels of intensity. These diagrams may be composed by the computer.

Numerous applications of land-use surveys exist. They frequently involve the preparation of preliminary land-use plans, comprehensive plans, transportation studies, utility-service area-analyses, thoroughfare, parking, mass transportation, transit, trucking, railroad, airport and residential neighborhood studies, CBD analyses, the organization of industrial districts,

FIGURE 8.7

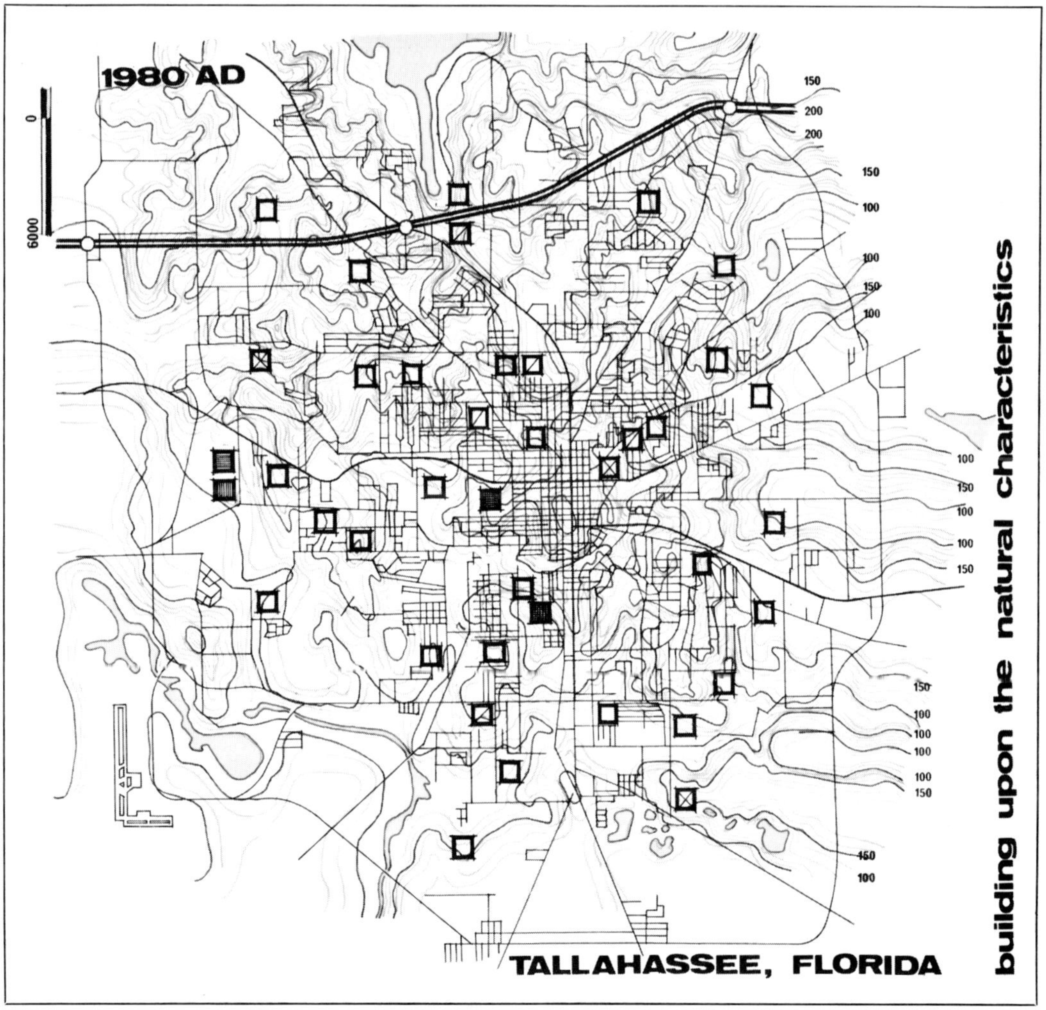

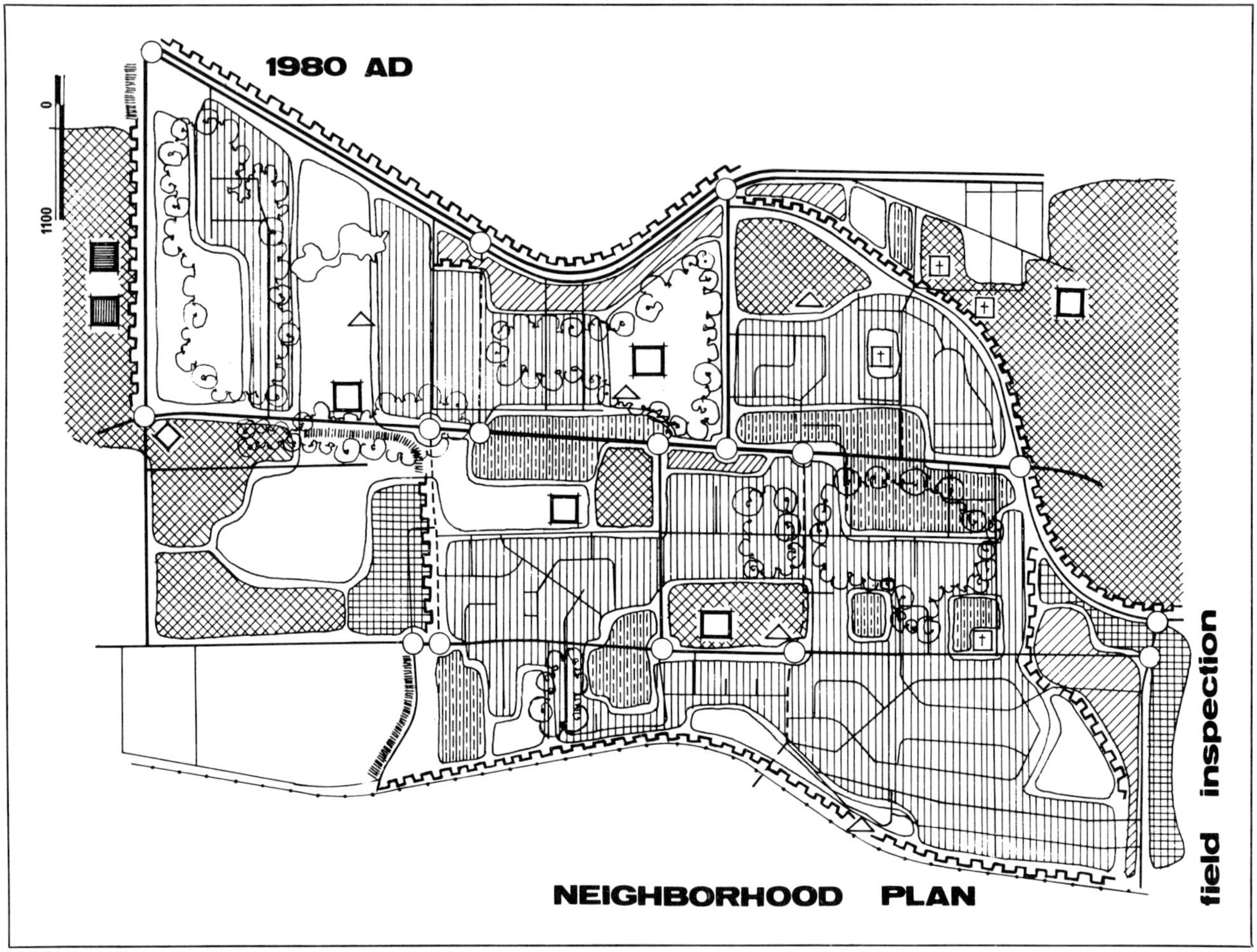

FIGURE 8.8

school districting, and basic references for redevelopment and rehabilitation plans. The surveys are also a primary source of information for site-planning work on recreation areas, school sites, housing developments and shopping centers. The surveys furnish the baseline data to be used by planners and citizens who are preparing for the growth and development of the urban area.

Two primary types of surveys associated with land-use studies are the inspection type and a combination of inspection and interview. The inspection survey involves either a field recording system, which notes land usage directly on maps, or a coding system that is keyed to a reference map. Frequently associated with real property studies, the inspection-interview analysis may be quite elaborate and involve a full-scale automated data system. It is often combined with studies done by various agencies within the urban community that are concerned about land use. The two major methods of reporting land-use data are maps and statistical tables. Maps are graphic representations of actual land use. Statistical presentations usually involve frequency tables that tabulate various categories of land usage. (See Table 8.8.) The tables might be simply a summary of current land use, presenting various sections of the area along one axis and the types of classifications of land use along the other.

Although the commercial applications of the survey techniques are somewhat specialized, no highly sophisticated methods have yet been devised to analyze the quality of retail areas. Statisticians have used vacancy rates, declining rental rates per square foot of floor area, measures of the building, structural conditions, parking and loading facilities, and transportation to quantify areas. In a St. Louis study an approach using the inspection interview included such things as building features (access and egress, type of construction, age, story and ceiling heights, floor characteristics, and column spacing); building appurtenances (fire escapes, fire protection systems, heating systems, characteristics, and utilities); building conditions (structural condition, plumbing, heating, wiring, and infestation); building occupancy (design use, nuisances, and convertibility); site features (shape, topography, rail facilities, and loading and parking facilities); and code violations (various kinds). Environmental quality factors, such as traffic arteries, mass transportation, utilities, adjoining street conditions, block size, mixtures of land uses, expansion opportunities, desirability of location, and vacancy history, are paramount to the planner's work.

As a brief final word on the studies approach to urban land-use, the problem of classification is considered. Classification or coding schemes usually involve parcel characteristics; structural characteristics refer to location areas and ownership. The structural characteristics include the types of buildings, the total floor area, and the ground-floor area, whereas the land-use traits are classified into residential, manufacturing, retail, professional, and municipal. A standard classification scheme is advantageous because it expedites communication, assists in the legal problems of transferring land, aids in continuous studies of land, and helps to maintain understandable records of land use. The primary objective of classifying vacant land is to determine its suitability for future development and to identify its potentials. These classifications will usually correspond to already-established developed land. Topographically, land may be categorized as prime, marginal or unusable.

FIGURE 8.9

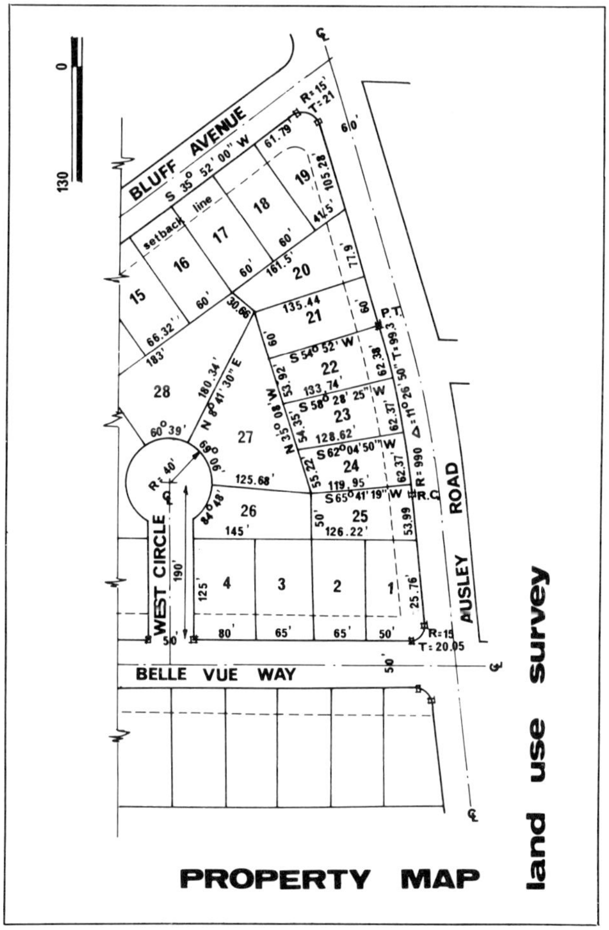

Table 8.8 Population density per land use

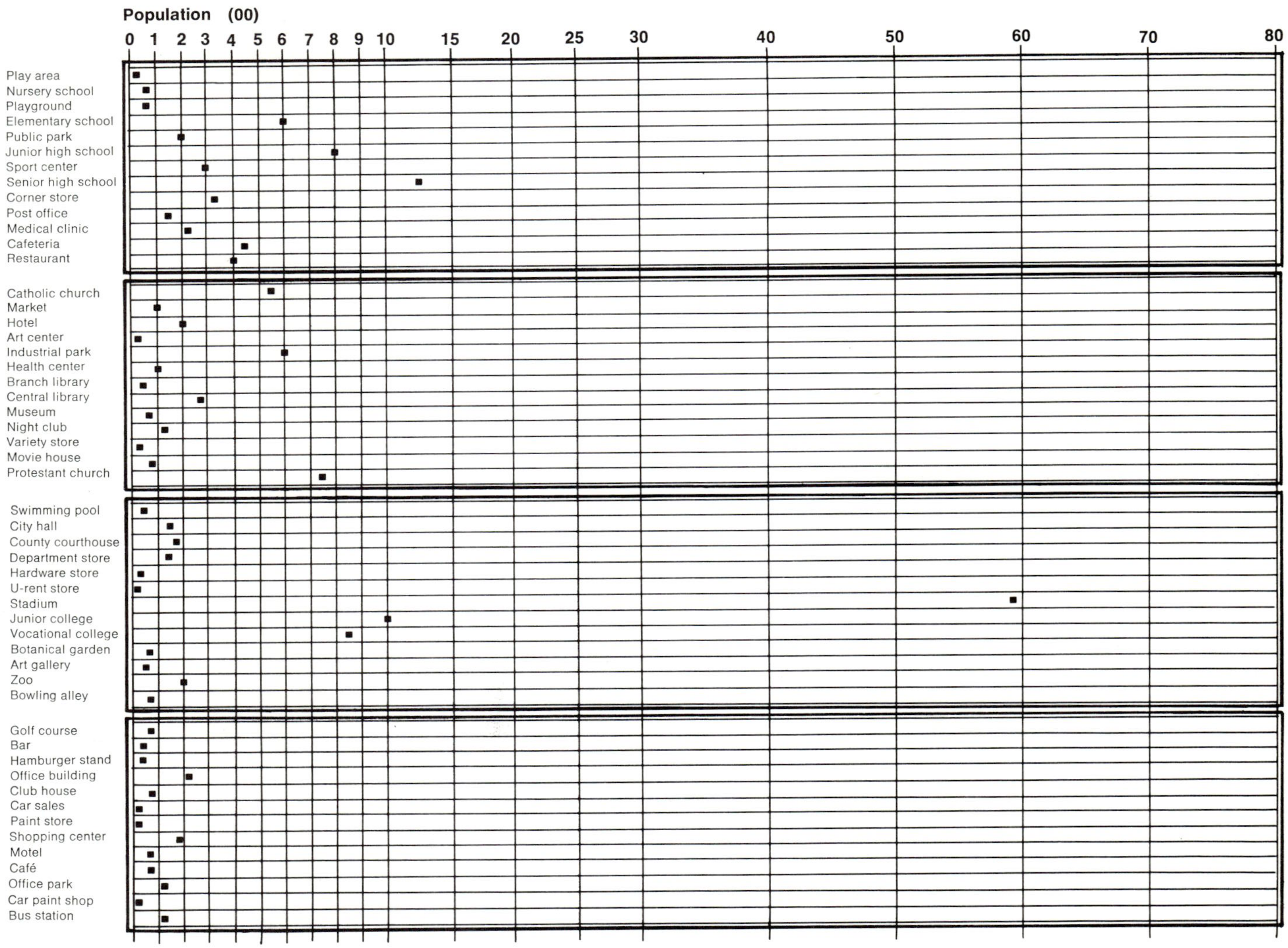

Prime land is suitable for building in its present state; marginal land can be developed after extensive preparation or modification; unusable land is not economically feasible for use. There are various other characteristics associated with the classification of land: improvements already available; needed improvements, such as water, sewers, and power; and extensive improvements, like drainage or removal of physical obstacles. No clear-cut guidelines have been established for classifying land as prime, marginal, or unusable. There are, however, rule-of-thumb procedures that are applicable to most land. Nearness to railroads, minimal slope, appropriate drainage, and nearness to sewer and water lines are desirable features in most cases and they can help in the reclassification of land. However, the specific use to which the land is to be put has a major bearing on the necessity for these features.

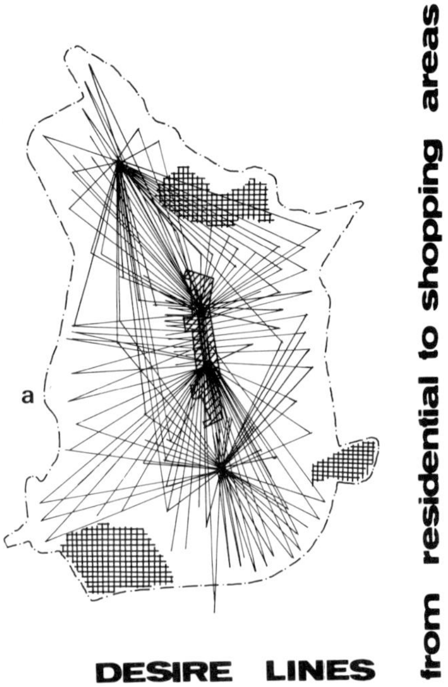

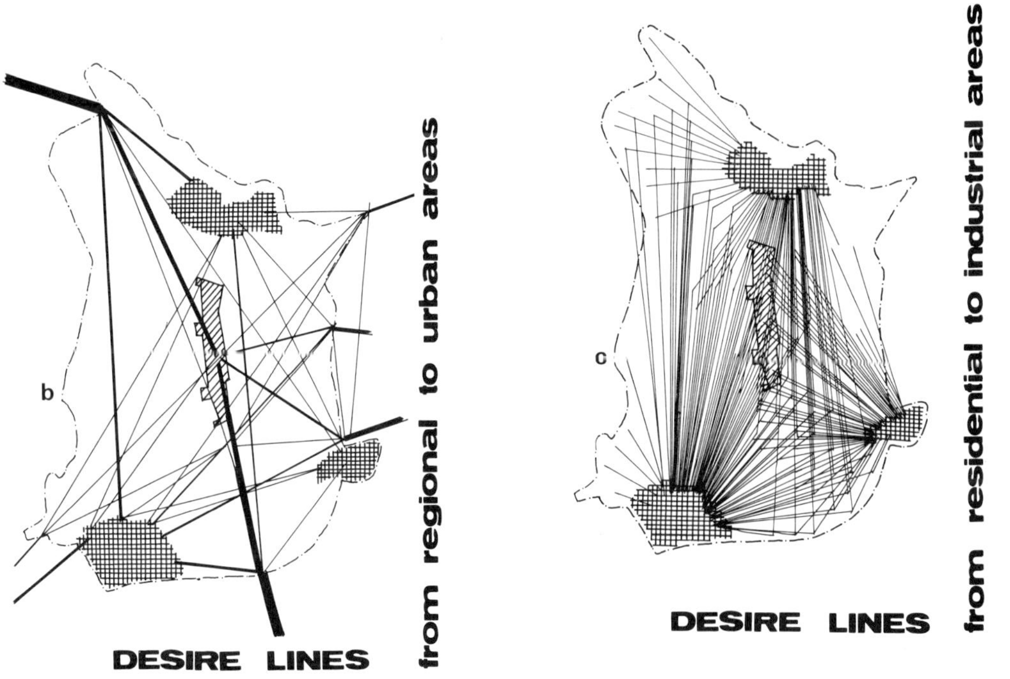

FIGURE 8.10

TABULATING PRACTICES USED FOR MOVEMENT

Movement applies to people, goods, services, and energy. Studying movements involves certain basic components common to all. One component is the object: its size, quality, shape, frequency, and intensity of movement. Another component is the object's modes of movement, its size, its comfort and safety in motion, its form of power, its length of usefulness, and so on.

Because movement is essentially between located or "in-place" activities, activities can be described in part by their location and destination. (See Figure 8.10.) These spatial separations take many forms: the child brought to school by bus or walking from bus to homeroom; the book, from publisher to wholesaler to retailer to school-district distribution center to school bookroom to homeroom for child to read; message from principal to child; television signal from studio to television set to child, and so on. Note should also be taken of movements involving sensory data. Such data from the environment impinge on the human senses, creating in the child impressions of many hues, especially in schools. Sociological analyses have shown that the child's educational behavioral growth is strongly affected by his environment.

Modes of transmission, or conveyors, include cars, buses, pipelines, electric wires, electromagnetic radiation, and human senses. Particular concern is with movement that tends to be regular and persistent. Little importance is assigned to trips that occur only once or twice as opposed to daily or weekly trips.

The *channel* is defined as the means of all movement for accommodating the conveyors. The planner's interest is in specially adapted channels devised for frequent, patterned, and regular use: sidewalks, pathways, tracks, roads, pipelines, conduits, cables, hallways, corridors, and so on. In fact, any means of movement falls within this area. (See Figure 8.11.)

The geometry of channels is a most important characteristic. Many kinds of networks exist, such as grid, circular, linear, and radial. (See Figure 8.12.) Maps of channels provide a rich store of information: map displays, shape, texture, interchanges, and the positional importance of channels and nodes.

The types of data required for analyzing and planning movement require, first of all, volume studies: travel-time studies and studies of capacity. Parking and traffic control-device studies in addition to the listed studies give the planner a base on which to assort data concerning routes and their area of coverage, services required; passenger riding habits, running times to meet service demands, speed of conveyor, and other general operating data.

Various types of models assign loads of movement to channels. The most common model used in transportation planning is the gravity model. This was developed originally from an economic concept designed by William Reilly. The most common form of the gravity model in use today is the following equation:

movement from area or zone $_i$ to area or zone $_j$ ($_i$ represents one zone, $_j$ another zone and $_k$ represents all zones in the study)

$$M_i = P_i \frac{A_j F_{ij} K_{ij}}{\sum A_k F_{ik} K_{ik}}$$

where

M = number of trips
P = production at the zone
A = attraction of zone or zones
F = a friction from zone $_i$ to zone $_j$ (e.g., travel-time factor)
K = socio-economic adjustment factor

The assumptions of this model are (a) that distance or travel time is the criterion of travel, (b) that travel-time factors are constant over time, and (c) that the K factor can be predicted even on a zonal basis.

An example of how the gravity model works is shown in Figure 8.13.

This example shows only one trip purpose. Most studies, however, include additional purposes such as the ones below:

FIGURE 8.11A

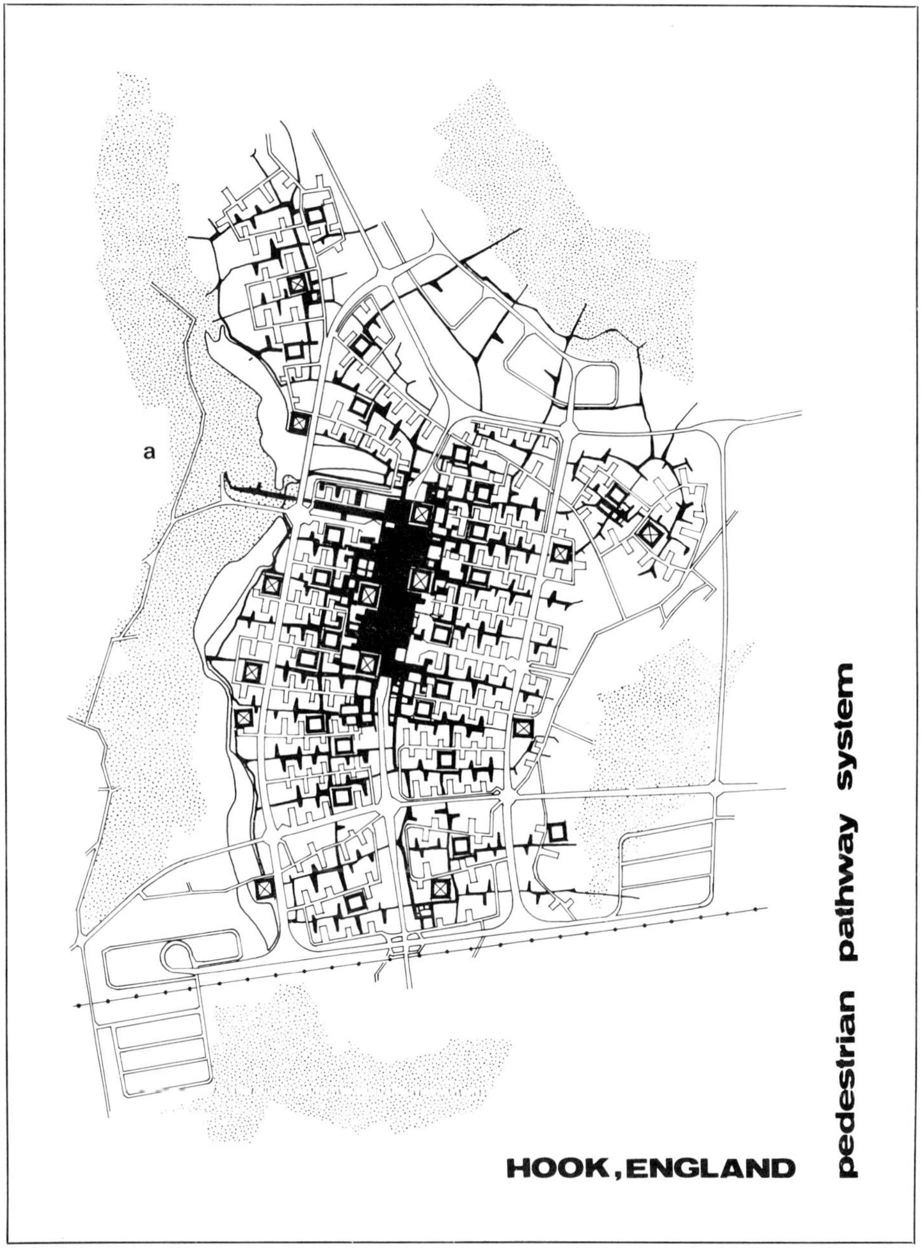

FIGURE 8.11B

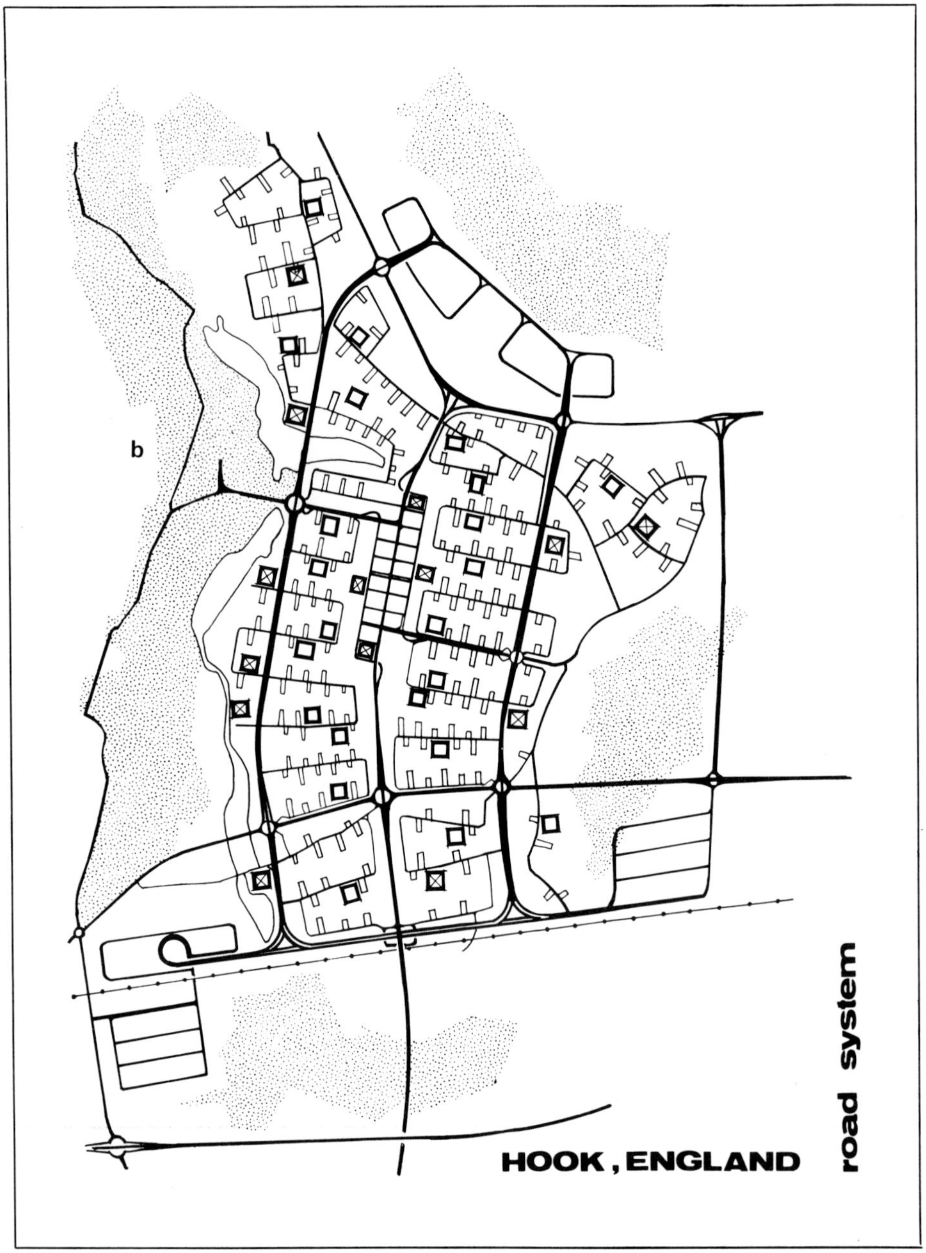

FIGURE 8.11C

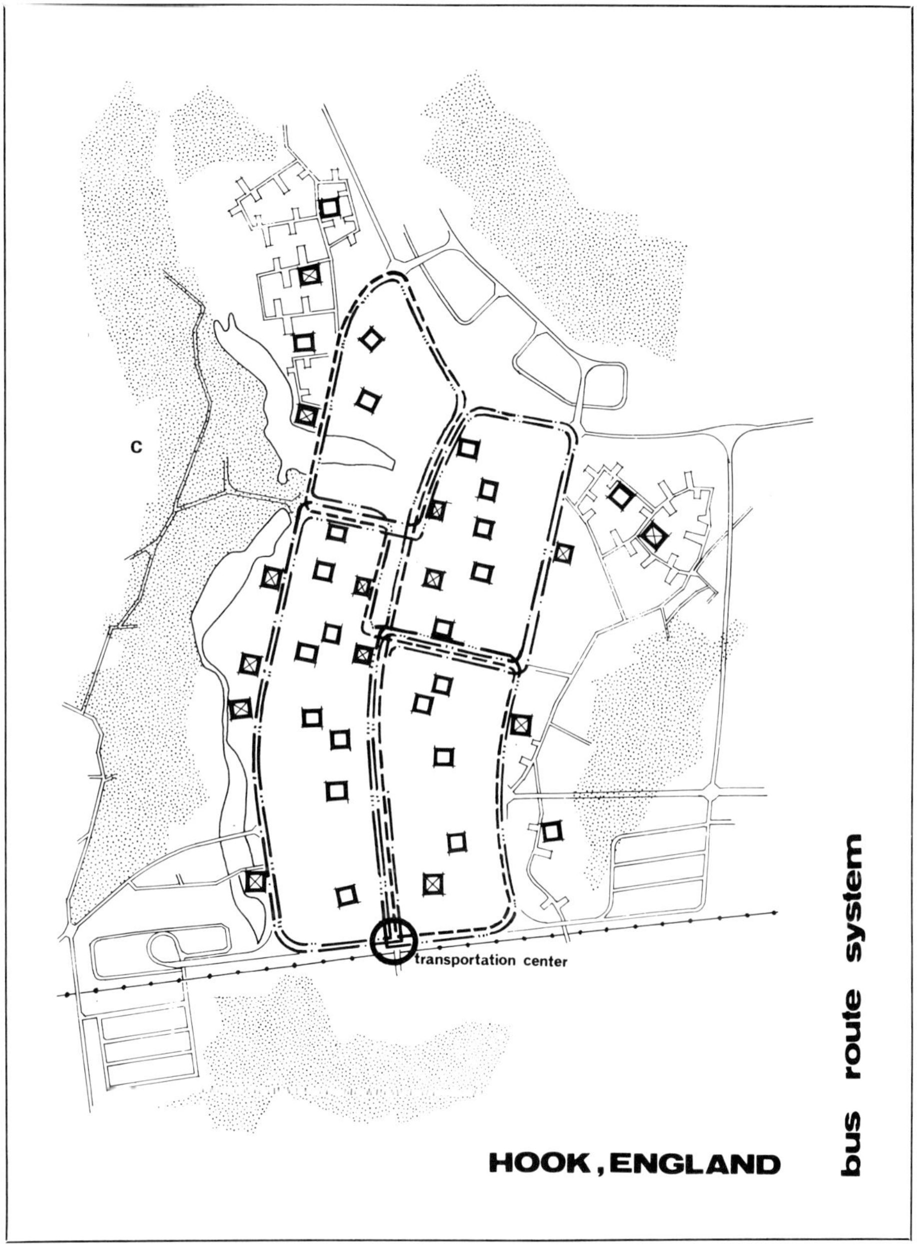

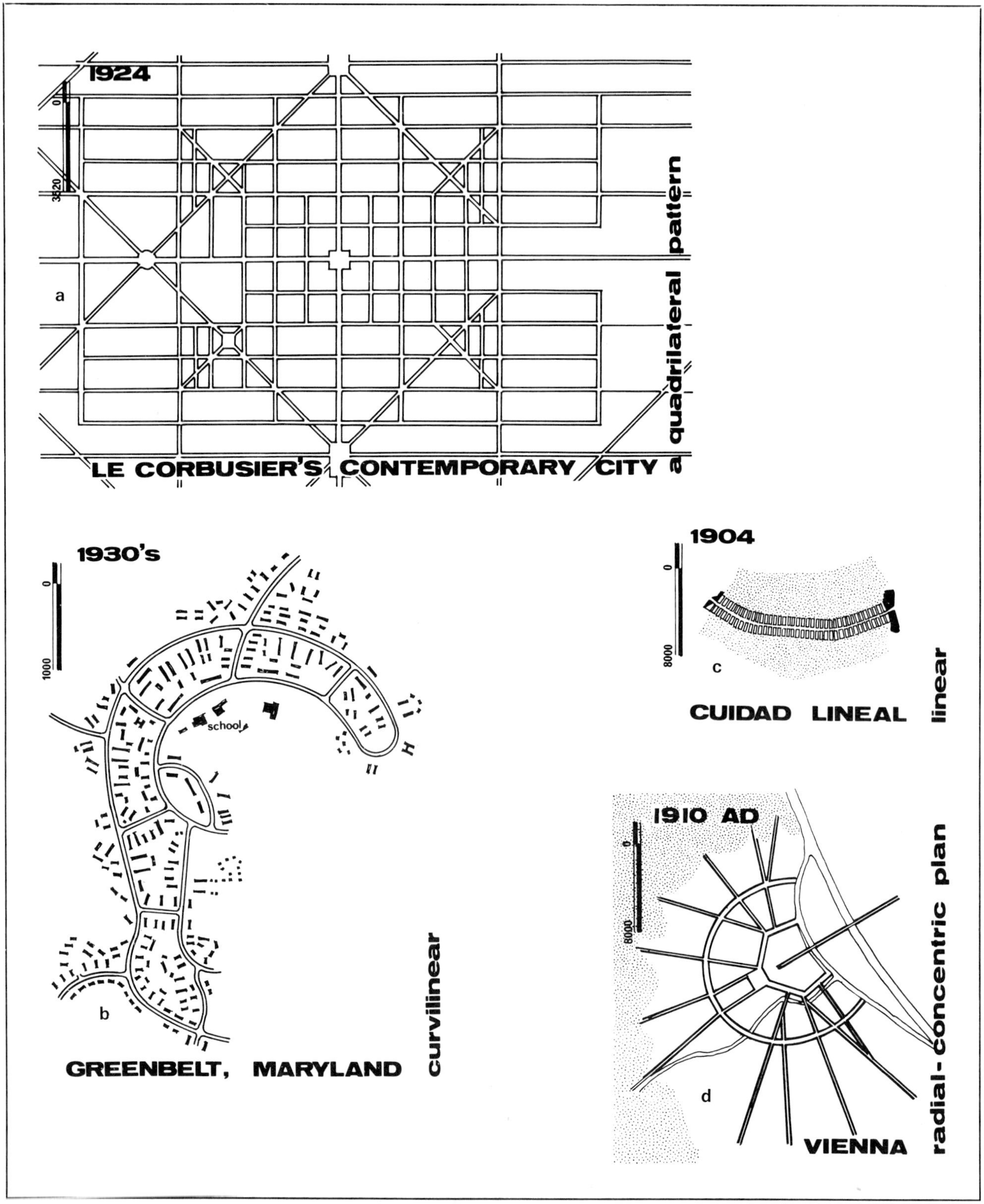
1924
0
3520
a
LE CORBUSIER'S CONTEMPORARY CITY
a quadrilateral pattern
1930's
0
1000
school
b
GREENBELT, MARYLAND
curvilinear
1904
0
8000
c
CUIDAD LINEAL
linear
1910 AD
0
8000
d
VIENNA
radial-concentric plan

1 Home-based to work
2 Home-based to shopping
3 Home-based to school
4 Home-based to social activities
5 Home-based to miscellaneous

} 80% of all urban trips (items 1–5)

6 Non-home-based } 20%

As no growth factors are included, the gravity score must be calibrated for each purpose. From Figure 8.14, a poor fit between the origin- and destination-obtained data and the data resulting from the gravity model requircs another F_{ij} or new travel-time factor. The new

$$F_{ij} \text{ (new travel-time factor)} = \text{old } F_{ij} \times \frac{O \,\&\, D\%}{G\,M\%}$$

With the new F_{ij} a recalculation for trip assignments to all zones is made until one iteration achieves a good fit among the origin and destination and gravity model curves. When good fit occurs the trips assigned to each channel will provide a network of channels

FIGURE 8.13

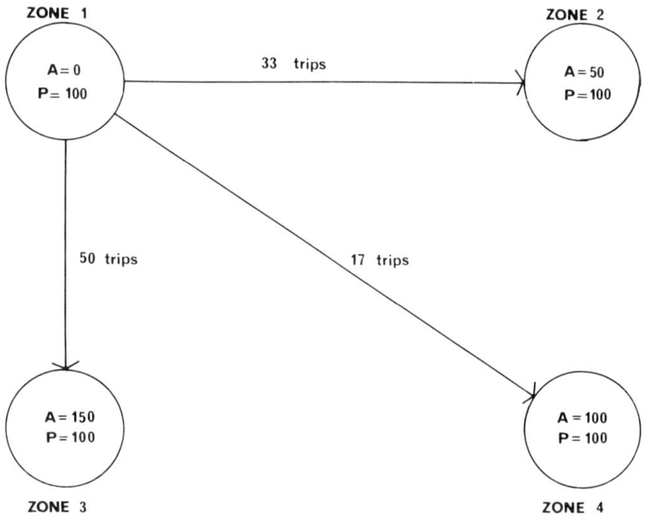

ZONE	A_j (attraction)	F_{ij} (friction)	$A_j F_{ij}$	$\frac{A_j F_{ij}}{\Sigma A_j F_{ij}}$	P_i (production)	M_{ij}
1	0	∞	0	$\frac{0}{30} = 0$	100	0
2	50	.2	10	$\frac{10}{30} = .33$	100	33 trips
3	150	.1	15	$\frac{15}{30} = .50$	100	50 trips
4	100	.05	5	$\frac{5}{30} = .17$	100	17 trips
				$\Sigma = 1$		

must be 1 for model to complete assignment to all zones

GRAVITY MODEL calculations

FIGURE 8.12 (opposite)

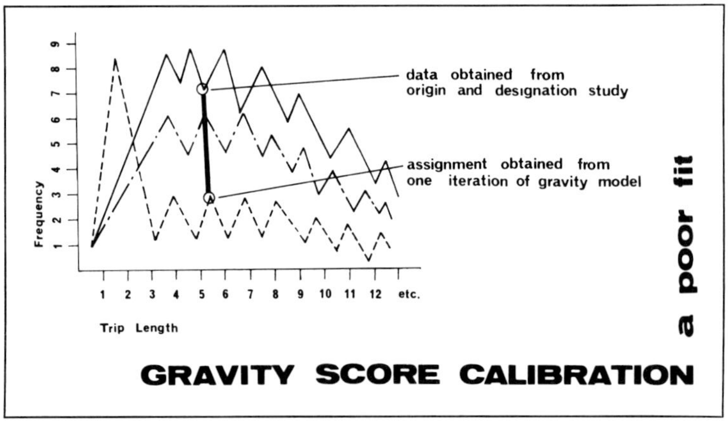

FIGURE 8.14

capable of accommodating the movements. The basic gain of such a model is that it allows the educational planner to estimate the capacity of many kinds of channels, from hallways to roads on an educational campus.

Other models are growth models, the intervening models developed by the Chicago transportation study, and the equal-opportunity model, whose gigantic data requirements helped to terminate the famous Penn Jersey transportation study.

Germane to all studies is the need for various types of data. One such study is of the origin and destination data that show where movements want to go. Another is an inventory of facilities that determines what exists. Yet a third set of data is travel times between various zones or nodes of activities. Accident data constitute a fourth set that shows points of friction or designs not capable of withstanding the flow. The last set of data includes volume studies recording the number, frequency, and intensity of moves.

A common tabulation of movement is illustrated in Table 8.9, showing movements to a school.

TABULATING PRACTICES USED FOR ECONOMICS

Land-use cost is often the determining factor in choosing a site, for example, a school site. Land values are influenced by two factors: one is basic economics; the

Table 8.9 Movements to a school

From	To	Object moved	Means	Frequency	Time	Note
415 Fairway Drive	Pineview School	Student	Bus	5/week	7:40–8:00 a.m.	
705 Pine Street	,,	Student	Bus	5/week	7:45–8:00 a.m.	
⋮						
874 Circle Street	,,	Teacher	Car	3/week	7:30–8:00 a.m.	MWF
1511 14th Street	,,	Teacher	Car	5/week	8:30–9:00 a.m.	
⋮						
School District Warehouse	,,	Groceries	Truck	1/week	Irregular	
P & T Plumbing Co.	,,	Plumber	Truck	4/month	Irregular	
School District Office	,,	50 letters and packets	Truck	2/day	8:30 a.m. 2:15 p.m.	1/2 volume in July and August mostly before 12
Hartsfield School	,,	Conversation	Telephone	3/week	Irregular	

other is purchaser satisfaction. The straightforward economic approach is a development of land values based on the payment of a reasonable price. Such a price is established over a period of years and is primarily based on comparable land within the urban area. The question of purchaser satisfaction, however, is a more abstract one. It is difficult to determine why a firm or an individual may feel that a piece of land possesses prestigious qualities and why one is willing to pay a bonus for it. Purchaser satisfaction will not only vary from individual to individual but will also fluctuate at different times for the same individual.

The two measures used to determine land costs are the acreage and the frontage by foot. Land more remote from the central city is likely to be sold by the acre or a fraction thereof. However, business land in highly dense areas is usually sold according to the linear foot frontage, i.e., the linear feet facing a thoroughfare. The size of the property also causes the price of land to vary, depending on its distance from the central business district. These considerations account partially for the desirability of land that borders an urban area to be used for residential purposes, because the amount of land may be increased while the cost remains constant. Although distance from the central city is important in itself, distance is also consequential in the specific location of land, suggesting the importance of the value of adjacent property or the environment in which the land is located. The quality of the location is characterized by density, improvements in the property itself, and in adjacent properties and zoning. Ordinarily, it is necessary to separate the cost of the land *per se* from the improvements on the land because the prospective use of the land may make the improvements unimportant. Unrequired improvements are usually removed to allow the purchaser to develop the land for his own needs.

Often units of measurement are selected because of their relation to the study and because of the availability of data. Such units might include: 1) sales, which record the total transaction; 2) added value, sales less the cost purchased from other sources; 3) potential income increase: rent, future sale, and so on; and 4) satisfaction or utility derived.

Indirect measures of the community's economic base

There are several methods that may be used to determine indirectly the economic base of an urban community, an indicator of the degree of willingness to support education financially. The assumption method arbitrarily determines the classification of export, import, and local. This applies to employment as well as production, marketing, and services.

The location quotient method uses the following formula to calculate potential employment in a given industry, such as education for a self-sustaining population:

$$\frac{X}{\text{total local school employment}} = \frac{\text{national employment in education}}{\text{total national employment}}$$ [28]

However, the assumption of uniform demand, the calculated productivity index, and the philosophy of product mix are not given full consideration by the ratio, and, thus, many scholars have felt that the formula is not valid.

The minimum-requirements technique calculates the percentage of the total labor force employed in each industry in several communities. Then the percentages may be ranked in descending order.

> Thus, for example, 4.2% of the total employment in community 43 might be the highest for the [education] industry. The next highest per cent in [education] may be community 83 with 4.1%. And, finally, community 14 has the smallest per cent, only .7% employed in [education]. The presumption is that .7% is the minimum required by any community [of similar sizes] to satisfy its own needs. All employment in other communities above this amount is considered as export employment [or above what is required].[29]

[28]Charles M. Tiebout, *The Community Economic Base Study*. Supplementary Paper No. 16 (Committee for Economic Development, 1962), p. 47.

[29]Ibid., p. 49.

Direct measures of the community's economic base

The economic status of various population sectors may be established by a direct measurement of their economic activities. Commodity flows can be counted by use of the ICC's Waybill data or by the sampling of freight-car, airplane, barge, truck, and pipe-line movements, or income earned as a result of a certain level of educational attainment. An analysis of money flows is another register of economic activities. Surveys of the local economy can be accomplished through interviews and mail questionnaires. The structural interrelationships in the local economy are also measures that can be applied to analyze the economic situation. A short-run analysis of community residents' income is directly or indirectly dependent on the three sectors dealing with exports, local investment, and local consumption. Other factors are the income generated by the investment sectors, whether exported or local, and the income generated from local consumption.

Measurement and projection devices for long- or short-range planning generally employ local investments as a variable factor. Local investment figures, such as of investments made in education rely heavily on exports, imports, federal grants, local business investment, local housing investment, local government investment, and the current expenditure and total income of the industries that have regional or national markets. As can be seen in this list, no area can be considered in isolation. When regional or national business fluctuates, so too will economic factors within the local economy. This constant interaction of various economic factors suggests the hazards of looking strictly at local urban economy; any type of estimating procedure must consider the fact that the various urban economic factors are directly related to regional and national variations. And, naturally, the validity of the estimate will vary according to the information available regarding the nature of this interaction. Estimates in the past have depended on "best judgments" made by persons familiar with the basic economy. This procedure is beginning to change, and new base studies are becoming available. Although the base studies are more specific in pinpointing the problem areas, the traditional "expert judgment" attempts may be more accurate in the base-study forecast. However, regardless of the value of "expert judgment," there is a tendency where technology is available to expand the use of such technology. A mixture of personal knowledge and experience and technological data is usually the most effective.

One technique for tabulation is the input/output method. (See Table 8.10.) It is based on the postulate that any given line of economic activity bears a measurable relationship to every other industry in the economy. These relationships are set forth in a series of equations that are readily made by computers.

Another tabulation technique is the social-account system. It is essentially double-entry bookkeeping. It sets up accounts on the basis of asset changes without tracing interchanges, as input/output tabulation does. The areas of tabulation are consumption accounts, investment accounts, and savings accounts.

Ratio techniques or approximation analyses involve a series of interlocking ratios of manufacture, wholesales, retail sales, and receipts from services among the local area, the subregion, the region, and the national areas. The table formed by tabulation shows in a gross manner the relative position of the local area within a framework of a whole system of study areas.

The mentioned techniques, for example, the input/output model, can be applied to educational management. The main inputs of a school are entering students, teachers, building, materials, money, and demands from parents, employers, and legislatures for certain courses and standards. The outputs are graduates, drop-outs, custody of individuals during certain hours, some extracurricular programs of service and entertainment, and jobs.

One of the important uses of input/output tabulations to control the many educational elements is to ensure consistency. Are there enough inputs to produce planned outputs? Other controlling features of the input/output tabulations are the elimination of unemployment among graduates and of the failure of certain courses because qualified teachers, appropriate materials, or properly prepared students are not avail-

Table 8.10 Input-output analysis

Industry producing	Urban area												
	Education 1	Agriculture 2	Mining 3	Heavy manufacturing 4	Light manufacturing 5	Power and communication 6	Transportation 7	Trade 8	Insurance and rental 9	Business 10	Personal service 11	Construction 12	Households 13
1 Education													
2 Agriculture													
3 Mining													
4 Heavy manufacturing													
5 Light manufacturing													
6 Power and communication													
7 Transportation													
8 Trade													
9 Insurance and rental													
10 Business													
11 Personal service													
12 Construction													
13 Households													

able. In fact, studies in this area have led to the development of a new discipline called *economics of education*.

Economics of education

The economics of education has become quite an extensive field in its own right, and only a cursory treatment can be given it at this time. In general, economists have approached the problem of the economics of education essentially as one of investment in human resources. Certainly, any consideration of the economic development of a region or locality should examine the development of human resources. Unfortunately, most of the work done in education as an investment has been so restricted that it looks on changes in income as the primary variable in education's value. But the benefits of the individual and the direct benefits to society must also be acknowledged. It is inconceivable that a society could develop into a highly technological state without a sound educational system. Therefore, viewing an investment in education as strictly an income level is much too restrictive. Recent developments in this country indicate that the expectations and returns on education extend beyond mere economics.

> The use of education as a means for adjusting to social change brought about by economic development is certainly necessary, but education may also be employed as a directive agent, pointing the younger members particularly to niches in an overall social structure of a type that is believed to be most desirable by contemporary social philosophers.[30]

Recent developments certainly have implications for educational planners. The complexity of the situation is becoming increasingly apparent to those reforming the curriculum to make education more meaningful and relevant to present-day students.

> Planners are obliged to assess from estimates and measurements made within the society those approaches which seem to be the most suitable for solving the problems of the immediate and foreseeable future. When funds are scarce (a condition that exists almost universally), planners must search for criteria that determine which educational programs deserve increased allocations. These criteria will, for the most part, be provided by educators themselves, but they are expected to coincide to an important extent with judgments derived from such reference systems as the human's resources analysis and the principles of lifelong education. . . . Planning for education must rest as far as possible upon an expert appraisal of the situation, and the decisions must be arrived at by the established democratic processes. In addition, the implementation of decisions must be administratively simple and effective.[31]

Educational planners and decision-makers at all levels must no longer look on education as a portion of welfare but consider it in terms of the development of potential human resources. The technological developments in this country and the basic economy of technological service focuses on education as the primary method of developing the required manpower. For many technically oriented industries, like the software field of the computer industry, human resources are the only resource; technically trained people comprise the heart of such industries. Therefore, education has become a fertile force that is producing technically trained people who are becoming the primary economic asset of many companies.

> . . . "Brains" (human or otherwise) are employed to manipulate symbols. A sequence or network of such symbol manipulations uses up a minute amount of energy to eventually release, triggerlike, large amounts of energy through the more brutal medium of generators, muscles, and machine tools. In a modern assembly or disassembly plant, a growing majority of people, wearing white collars, or blue denims as well, do the brain work of inspecting, deciding, reporting-shunting, pushing buttons—and not the muscular work of shaping or carrying material masses; and a growing proportion of machines, called controlled mechanisms, are [sic] also busy with inspecting, reporting, deciding, and not transforming or transporting matter and energy.[32]

This change in modern society toward more skilled personnel demands that human resources be viewed in a different light. The techniques of tabulation mentioned earlier allow the educational planner

[30]Richard L. Meier, *Developmental Planning* (New York: McGraw-Hill, 1965), p. 267.

[31]Ibid., p. 270.

[32]Jacob Marshack, "Economics of Inquiring, Communicating, Deciding," *The American Economics Review. Papers and Proceedings of the Annual Meeting of the American Economic Association*, Washington, D.C., December 28–30, 1967, **58:**2 (May 1968).

to gear educational activities in concert with the requirements of society. For example, to train an individual to become a draftsman and at the moment of employability to learn that computers now do the work is inappropriate. To minimize such results the application of input/output analysis, the social account systems, and the approximation analyses provides workable analytical tools for determining society's skilled personnel demands and the educational equipment necessary to meet those future demands.

TABULATING PRACTICES USED FOR ACTIVITIES

Tabulating activity analyses are done in many different ways. To list summaries of tabulation would serve little purpose. Instead, listing possible tabulations will illustrate the usefulness of analyzing activities as a foundation for educational planning. (See Figure 8.15.)

The first consideration generally is people. Specifically, the educational planner is interested in the number and proportion of individuals involved in a given learning activity. Table 8.11, therefore, shows the quantity of individuals and their distribution percentage-wise according to activity by sex and time of day.

From this tabulation many other relationships between individual, activity, and time can be formed. A few are listed below.

1 Percentage distribution of time among different activities.

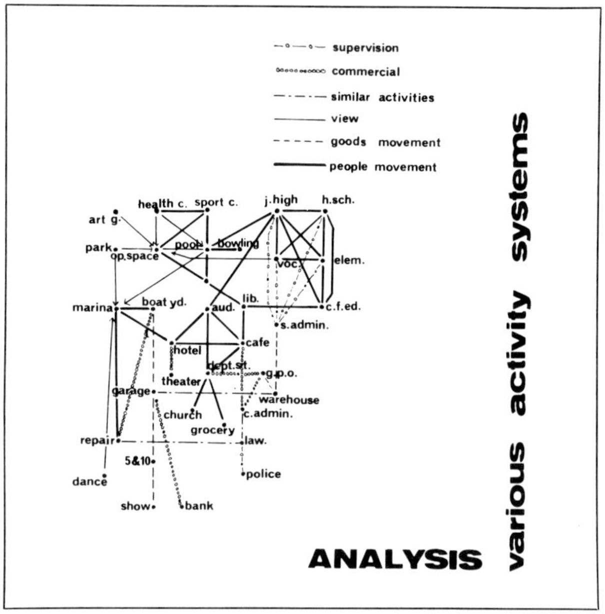

FIGURE 8.15

2 Percentage distribution of time among different activities for one day, or for certain periods of time.
3 Percentage distribution of individuals by activities.
4 Percentage of individuals in one activity against all other activities.

Table 8.12 is the percentage of time spent in an activity by various classes, or by various teacher groups, or by various mixtures of groups.

A second major consideration is the location analysis of activity systems as shown in Table 8.13.

Table 8.11 Distribution of activity by sex and time

Type of activity	Male							Female							Total						
	8	9	10	11	12	1	2	8	9	10	11	12	1	2	8	9	10	11	12	1	2

Table 8.12 Distribution of activity by class or by teacher groups or by other mixtures of groups

Type of activity	Grade 1	Grade 2	Grade 3	Grade 4	Grade 5	Grade 6	Grade 7

Table 8.13 Distribution of activities by location

Location	Male							Female							Total						
	8	9	10	11	12	1	2	8	9	10	11	12	1	2	8	9	10	11	12	1	2

One such tabulation is the percentage of individuals distributed according to location, time of day, and sex.

Another tabulation is of the percentage of time spent by sex and location as shown in Figure 8.16.

Percentage distribution of time spent in different locations by day and by individual is yet another tabulation, as indicated in Table 8.14.

A variation of the tabulation in Table 8.14 is the percentage distribution of occupied location by time and by the number of individuals, as in Table 8.15.

Table 8.14 Distribution of time and location by individuals

Location	Day								Name of individual
	Time								
	8	9	10	11	12	1	2	Total	

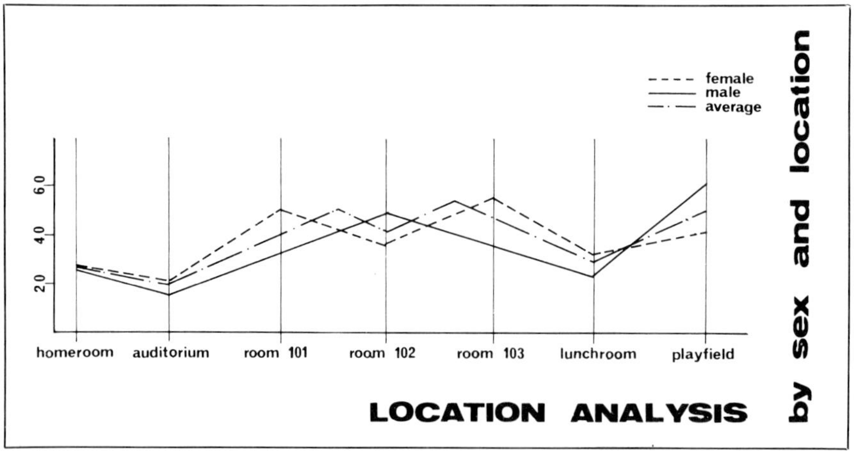

FIGURE 8.16

Table 8.15 Distribution of location by time and number of individuals

Location	Time occupied							Total
	8	9	10	11	12	1	2	

To the tabulation in Table 8.15 can be added the percentage of individuals per teacher per location by time periods based on an established instructional unit, e.g., twenty-five students per teacher. (See Figure 8.17.)

The tabulation shown in Figure 8.17 can be summed for each room to give yet another tabulation showing its percentage of use by day and these summed to give a tabulation of room use by week or by month or by year, if necessary. (See Figure 8.18.)

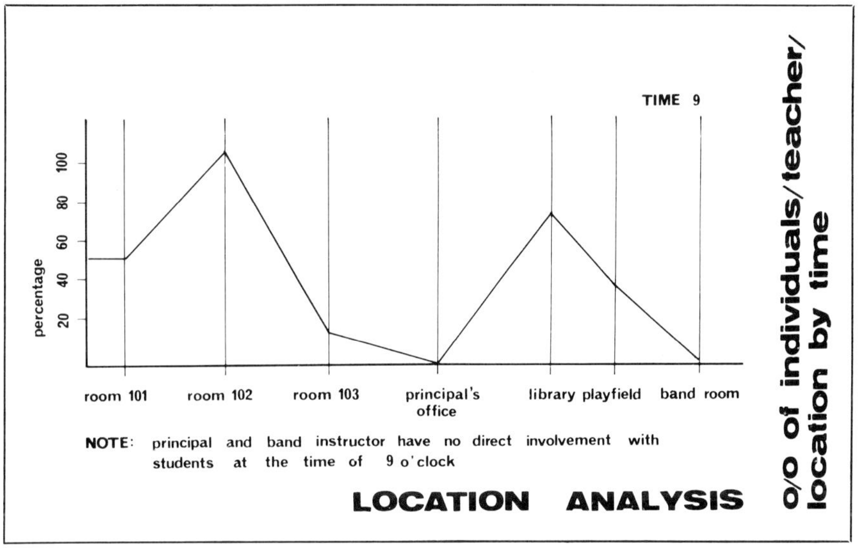

FIGURE 8.17

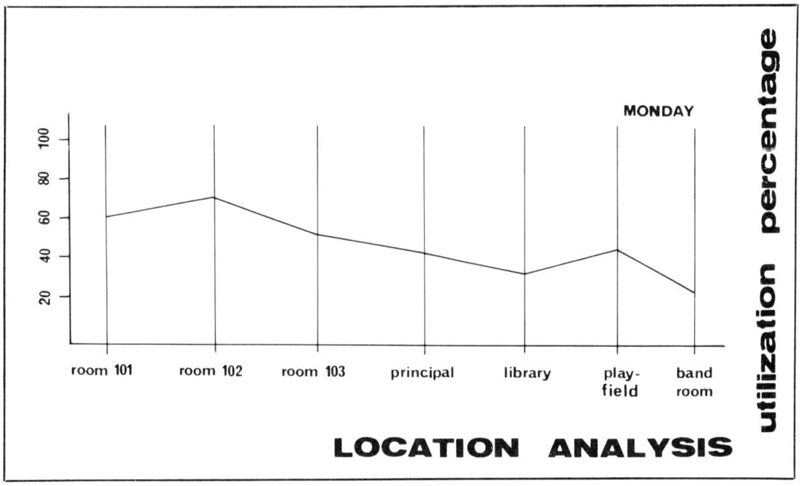

FIGURE 8.18

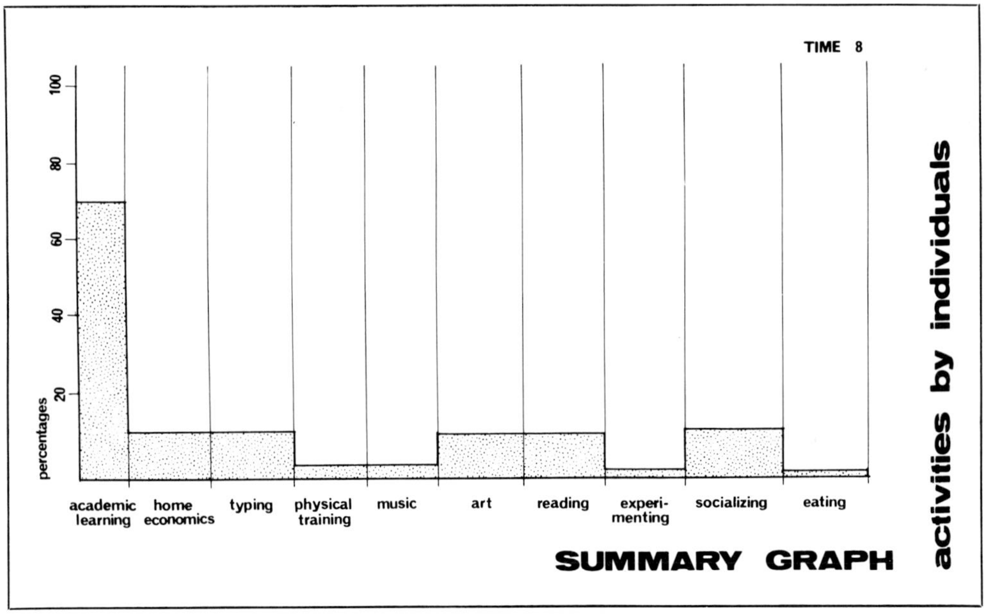

FIGURE 8.19

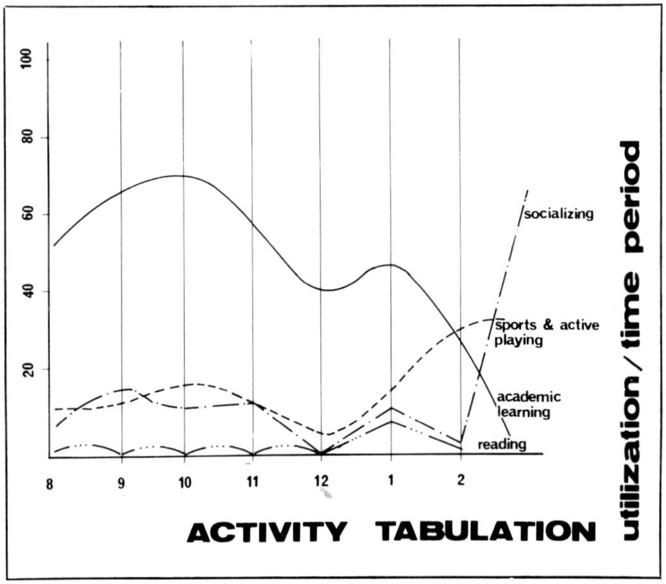

FIGURE 8.20

A percentage summary of activities by individuals with relation to total school enrollment is also possible in a tabulation by time. (See Figure 8.19.)

The tabulation in Figure 8.19 can be summed to give the proportion of total time devoted to essential, highly committed, and leisure activities within a school (see Figure 8.20). An example follows:

A = Academic learning
B = Sports and active playing
C = Reading
D = Socializing

As a final example of activity tabulation, a graph showing individuals by activities at specified times can be displayed on a two-dimensional spatial chart of the school's total site to show how, in some cases, some educational resources are exceedingly underused. (See Figure 8.21.)

These examples of activity tabulation indicate various ways that an educational planner—by use of charts, tables, and graphs—can increase the use of educational resources. It helps him to understand the relative significance of the many factors that he must consider in the decision-making process.

FIGURE 8.21

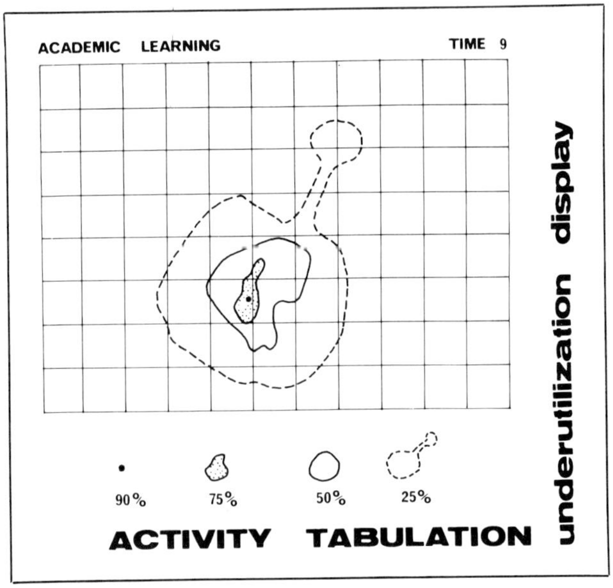

SUMMARY

Perhaps the single most important tabulation concerns population. Certainly current population estimates and studies of the present composition and distribution of population are essential as a point of beginning in educational planning analyses. They also serve an important function in day-to-day decisions. Frequently, however, the initial comprehensive educational plan can be scheduled only around a decennial census period to take advantage of the detailed and accurate data available only at that time. But no amount of scheduling obliterates the necessity for studying future population prospects. Perhaps the single most important population study is the population forecast. No educational planning activity is fulfilling its proper function unless plans are developed for foreseeable future activities.

9 Forecasting

Civilized men have long been occupied with the problems of projection. P. E. Rosove has identified the following twenty-two methods for forecasting:

1 Brainstorming (the authors).
2 Delphi technique.
3 Expert opinion (the many contributors to this book).
4 Literary fiction.
5 Scenarios (Chapter 1).
6 Historical analogy (Chapter 2).
7 Historical sequences (Chapter 2).
8 Content analysis (the whole book).
9 Social accounting (Chapter 9).
10 Primary determinant.
11 Time series (Chapter 9).
12 Extrapolation (Chapter 9).
13 Contextual mapping.
14 Morphological analysis (the comprehensive educational planning model of this book).
15 Relevance trees.
16 Decision matrices (Chapter 9).
17 Deterministic models.
18 Probabilistic models.
19 Gaming.
20 Operational simulation.
21 Cost-benefit analysis.
22 Input/output tables (Chapter 9).[1]

[1]P. E. Rosove, *A Provisional Survey and Evaluation of the Current Forecasting of the Art for Possible Contributions to Long-Range Educational Policy Making* (Santa Monica: Systems Development Corp., 1967), pp. 12–16.

At once we see the problem of forecasting as being intimately bound up with scientific methods and theory building. Many methods and theories are available but answers to certain basic questions are necessary to a forecasting technique.

How far should the forecast be carried? Are different periods recommended for different activities, e.g., projecting population, capital improvements, budgeting, and so on? How are the steps for which the forecasts are made determined? Will the way the plan will be implemented affect the forecast?

To answer these questions, the following sections include the various considerations required for forecasting, some methods for forecasting for various aspects (people, plans, movement, economics, and activities) of educational systems, and a projection of the educational system as a whole.

CONSIDERATIONS REQUIRED FOR FORECASTING

Forecasting involves assumptions about likely conditions. To determine the assumptions, two categories—basic and special assumptions—can be established. Basic assumptions are about such factors as the number of births to occur, deaths, rate of population migration, the form of government, and political, economic, and social organizations.

Special assumptions center on essentially local conditions. Will there be a major recession or not? Will full employment be a reality? Will business continue in an up-down cycle? Will public policy permit exploitation of the local environment? What changes planned for will become a reality? Based on these variables and others, the problem then becomes one of selecting those assumptions to be used for educational planning purposes.

Other considerations are related to observed data and their cause-and-effect relationships. Three levels exist: first, a deterministic causality in which if one event occurs another occurs also; second is the probabilistic causality in which if an event occurs, a probability (p) exists that another event will also happen; third, there is a correlation in which an event occurs in association with another event but no observable cause-and-effect relationship exists between them.

Consideration must also be given to how far forecasts should be carried. Sometimes a twenty-five- to thirty-year plan (long-range planning) is demanded; or a ten- to fifteen-year plan (middle-range planning) is required; or a more detailed plan (short-range planning) is needed. These three types of plans depend on what is needed. In the past, short-range planning has been the dominant plan method with almost complete exclusion of the other two types. Therefore no paths were available for the educational system to follow. As a result, educational programming was nearsighted in providing for the immediate needs of individuals. Comprehensive educational planning involves a selected path to be followed. The path will be precise for the early stages and increasingly fuzzy as the time period extends into the future.

The way the plan is implemented constitutes another consideration. As mentioned above, a plan is a charted path or a trajectory of changes that requires certain controls for it to be implemented. If deviations occur, they must be noted in time for corrective actions to be applied. Also, if there are unforeseen conditions detrimental to the individual's environment, controls should be such that remedial action can take place. Consequently, planned paths of action must be measurable at suitable time intervals. The best milestones occur in census-taking years but conditions in the future may force shorter counting intervals.

Projections of various aspects (people, employment needs, educational needs, and so on) must be made simultaneously. The time intervals of these projections must be the same to allow comparisons in the actual state of affairs. A common practice is to set n, $n + 5$, $n + 10$, $n + 15$, $n + 20$, and so on, to fit the decennial count.

SOME FORECASTING METHODS

The most common forecast in use by educational planners is the population projection. Its use indicates

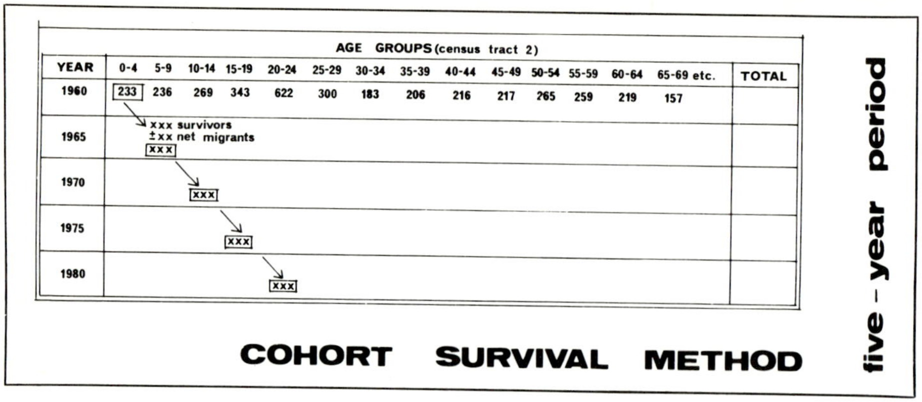

FIGURE 9.1

the overriding priority already established for determining future educational resources. It forms a framework for a great deal of subsequent work in devising, testing, evaluating, and implementing an educational plan. Most of the important decisions about educational services are derived from population forecasts.

One method for forecasting populations used by many educational planning agencies is the cohort-survival method. (See Figure 9.1.)

Age groups are extracted from the latest census. The first step requires the educational planner to take the appropriate age group and take from it the number of deaths appropriate for that group available from an abridged-life table. The next step estimates the number of net in-and-out migrations by age groups for the same interval of time; the results are entered as the second adjustment. The sum of survivors and the in-and-out migrants from the original age group furnishes the estimate for the next higher age group at the beginning of the next five-year period.

The emptied slot of the previous age group for the same year is filled also from the previous age group of the previous year. The original slot, now empty, is filled by the application of the approximate fertility ratio to the number of females of child-bearing age (usually fifteen to forty-four) at the beginning of the last period. Computer programs are available for quick processing.

The migration and natural-increase method is similar in many respects to the one just described. Two components rather than three, as in the cohort-survival method, are used. As a result only total populations are capable of being forecast. Current estimates of population are taken and adjusted for migration

Table 9.1 Migration and natural method

Year	Population	Net migrants		Population after adjustment for net migration (±)	Natural increase		Population after adjustment for natural increase next year's population
		Rate (±)	Amount (±)		Rate	Amount	
1965							
1966							
1967							
1968							
⋮							
1985							

and natural increases on a year-by-year basis until the forecast date is reached. Past net-migration rates are determined by past relationships between the direction and volume of net migration for both slow and rapid economic expansions. These figures are then projected to fit the economic outlook. Other approaches for determining net migration rates are used, such as employment forecasts or educational forecasts. Other resulting ratios based on total population are then extended by mathematical or graphical extrapolation. Natural increases are generally based on subjective extensions of past minimum and maximum rates. These may be computed from recorded birth and death statistics. Caution should be used in projecting these figures, as past records are based on depression and wartime fluctuations in births. Table 9.1 illustrates the forecast procedure.

The mathematical and graphic methods referred to are trend extrapolations by the least-squares method and by logistic curves. The assumption is made that some forces that operated in the past will also operate in the future. The arithmetic approach results in a straight-line projection and assumes the same numerical change for similar periods of time. The geometric projection is also a straight line but on semilogarithmic graph paper, signifying similar rates of change over similar periods of time. The least-squares method for fitting a straight line is commonly used for representing total population data derived from points representing births, deaths, and net migration overtime. This approach is most useful for short-term forecasting. (See Figure 9.2.) The ratio and apportionment methods are applicable to successively wider geographical areas, e.g., from county to subregion to state to regional to national levels. The requirements include a time series of population for the county level and a forecast for the national level. In a ratio method using county and national levels the population data for the national level are noted. Next plotted are the population data over the same time period for the county level compared with the national level and the ratio derived are plotted. A curve is fitted to the data and by least squares or graphic methods extrapolated to intersect the projected value for the national level at the given forecast

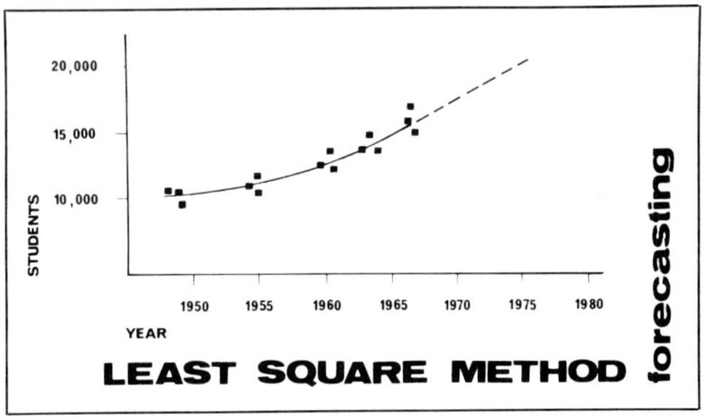

FIGURE 9.2

date. The apportionment method is broadly similar. Instead of one level of difference, a series of ratios representing each level are developed and plotted, also in a time series. Curves are fitted and these are then projected to the forecast date.

The matrix method, one of the latest and potentially the most fruitful method, uses matrix algebra. The initial age and sex distribution is represented as a column vector. The differences between births and deaths are handled by a "survivorship matrix," which operates on the original vector to project the population through successive time periods.

Table 9.2 (matrix method) illustrates the point; in this table b_2, b_3, b_4, $b_5 \ldots b_n$ are the age-specific birth rates and S_1, S_2, S_3, $S_4 \ldots S_n$ are the probabilities of surviving from n to $n + 5$, if a five-year interval

Table 9.2 Matrix method

Age group vector	Survivorship matrix							
	0	b_2	b_3	b_4	b_5	b_6	b_7	$\cdots b_n$
0–4	S_1	0	0	0	0	0	0	0
5–9	0	S_2	0	0	0	0	0	0
10–14	0	0	S_3	0	0	0	0	0
15–19	0	0	0	S_4	0	0	0	0
20–24	0	0	0	0	S_5	0	0	0
25–29	0	0	0	0	0	S_6	0	0
30–35	0	0	0	0	0	0	S_7	0
⋮								
100	0	0	0	0	0	0	0	S_n

is being used. Using a set of matrices makes possible a variety of forecasting procedures.

Economic forecasting methods fall into two groups—the analytical and the short-cut methods. One analytical method is input/output analysis. After the use of estimates for the various economic goods and services listed in the known input/output tabulation, and an adjustment for dollar value and anticipated changes in the economy, the refined coefficients are then applied industry by industry to obtain the output for the forecast date. These data give total economic outputs. Estimates of forecast data on labor productivity are obtained by a projection of the dollar output per worker for all listed industries in the initial year of the study. The actual employment estimates are obtained by the dividing of values for estimated future output by the appropriate values for output per worker. Obviously, this method depends on the availability of data and on technical know-how, but, if these problems are solved, educational planners can readily plan educational programs that are more appropriate for increasing efficiency in the economic development of education.

Other economic forecast tools are methods that use income statistics. The basic requirements of these methods are trend analysis of past production and past worker outputs and suitable national forecasts of both production and output per workers. These data are utilized by the ratio and apportionment and matrix methods but with minor modifications to fit the problem.

Some short-cut forecasting methods for economics are the apportionment technique and the direct and indirect ratio procedures. The apportionment technique is superior to the ratio procedures as it accounts for employment trends in related areas that share in overall trends. Another method for economic forecasting is the social accounts methods. Even though its development is in the initial stages, its potential value to the educational planners' understanding of the economic environment warrants mention. The method is similar to the input/output analysis but it uses money rather than production and employment as the measure of the interrelations within the economic system. It includes capital formation, investment, trade, and production. The matrix for income and expenditure relationships among all sectors is used to obtain projections of income for each sector. Estimates of productivity by projected income per worker at the levels of employment are forecast.

Population and economic projections have a wide range of applications. The number of potentially new or rehabilitated spaces that will be required is indicated. This, in turn, influences activities, such as education. This process can be refined, for instance, one can compare the demand for social activities with the supply of students derived from population projections. The degree of sophistication for projecting place and activity needs will be controlled by the form of the population forecast. If a simple total population is used then a crude activity rate will result; if males and females are projected then separate male and female activity rates will result; if cohort-survival is used then activities can be projected in terms of age and sex groupings. If one knows the projected activities, the projected population, and the projected economic environment, then the number of projected places or spaces can be determined by a technique such as the matrix-method.

Projecting spaces must be done so that the activity and the space are related to the same areal unit. Second, the time intervals between the steps in projection should be the same. Third, it is the place or space characteristics that are being projected, e.g., cost values, adaptations, physical appearances, sensory qualities, and so on. The object of projecting is to have the best possible data throughout the planning stages. This need is poignantly demonstrated by the approximately 50 per cent of the schools now in operation that are incapable of housing new educational programs.

In summary, all of the relevant aspects of a place require projecting and at some trial interval such as a five-year interval. The objective is to show potential places that are capable of accommodating educational activities at future times. A combination of various factors—people, economic, cultural, and others are involved.

Last, the projection of movement is primarily concerned with the patterns and volumes of future interactions. Patterns of movement are generally associated with a particular activity. This being so, the projected activities described by their characteristics—for example, number of students at a certain school, their parents' per capita income, car ownership, and so on—make projecting patterns of movement possible. In this case the number of projected movements becomes the dependent variable X, and the characteristics by activity of the independent variables Y_1, Y_2, T_3, and so on. Using multiple regression analysis with the following form

$$X = A + B_1 Y_1 + B_2 Y_2 + B_3 Y_3 \ldots \ldots B_m Y_m$$

with A's and B's coefficients derived in the course of statistical analysis, the number of movements of each kind of projected activity by frequency, by purpose, and by mode of movement is possible. Clearly movement forecasting is not a simple matter. Careful analysis, therefore, requires that projections of people, places, economics, and activities must be done in order to derive relationships among them.

PROJECTING THE EDUCATIONAL SYSTEM AS A WHOLE

Projecting certain parts of an eductional system without considering the other parts impinging on the whole educational system is unrealistic. Our concern in comprehensive educational planning involves guiding and controlling the educational patterning of people, places, movements, economics, and so on. It follows then that in projecting educational systems as a whole one must include all the parts. Given such-and-such an educational policy with such-and-such assumptions about people's behavior (a, b, c, and so on), what changes in places (p, g, r, and so on) and movements (x, y, z, and so on) can be expected at times t_2, t_3, and t_4? A model, as Lowry wrote "... consists of names, variables embedded in mathematical formulae ..., numerical constants ... and a computational method ... the pattern generated is typically a set of values of interest to the planner or decision-maker, each value tagged by geographical location and/or calendar date of occurrence."[2]

Projecting a whole system must include an understanding of educational patterns and changes in the past and the projection of these into the future. The assumption is that future relationships and coefficients can be derived. In our case the system as a whole is best modeled in a way that simulates changes in the five central features (people, place, movement, economics, and activity) as they occur through time and that simulates the reaction of each to changes in the other.

A recursive model is the most promising for handling these conditions. It simulates the evaluation of the educational system in a series of steps by taking the output of one time-stage as the input of the next. This then becomes a trajectory showing the way the system is expected to evolve through time.

Data describing the educational system are in many cases capable of being reduced to matrix and map forms. The matrices show the number of people in various places, or activities in various places, or a cost matrix of places, and so on. A typical forecast might consist of a set of matrices and maps (people, places, movements, costs, activities) for each of the years 1972, 1977, 1982, 1987, and so on.

[2]Ira S. Lowry, "A Short Course in Modern Design," *Journal of the American Institute of Planners*, no. 2, **31**:158–166 (May 1965).

Part Three

Conceiving and designing plans

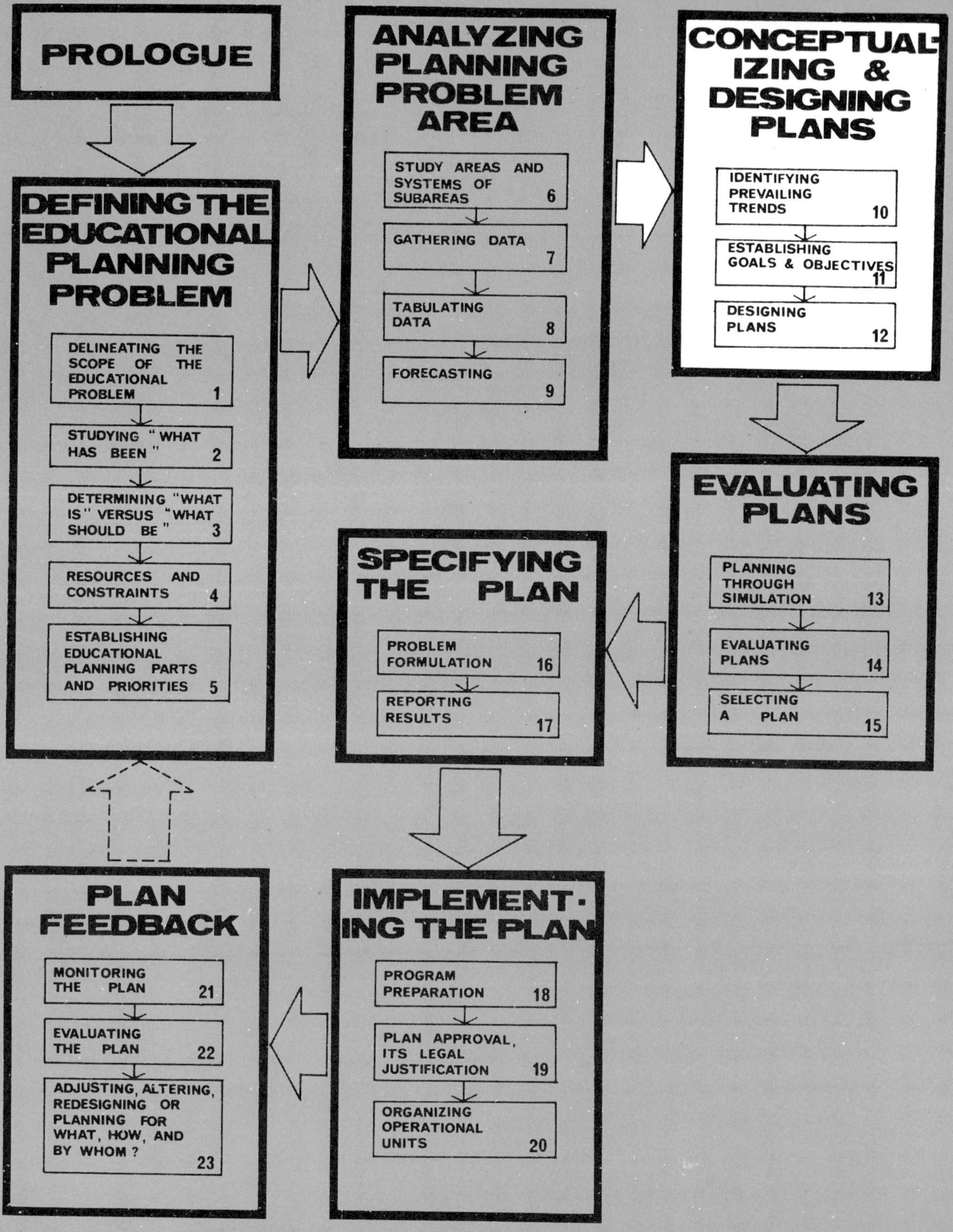
PROLOGUE
DEFINING THE EDUCATIONAL PLANNING PROBLEM
DELINEATING THE SCOPE OF THE EDUCATIONAL PROBLEM 1
STUDYING "WHAT HAS BEEN" 2
DETERMINING "WHAT IS" VERSUS "WHAT SHOULD BE" 3
RESOURCES AND CONSTRAINTS 4
ESTABLISHING EDUCATIONAL PLANNING PARTS AND PRIORITIES 5
ANALYZING PLANNING PROBLEM AREA
STUDY AREAS AND SYSTEMS OF SUBAREAS 6
GATHERING DATA 7
TABULATING DATA 8
FORECASTING 9
CONCEPTUALIZING & DESIGNING PLANS
IDENTIFYING PREVAILING TRENDS 10
ESTABLISHING GOALS & OBJECTIVES 11
DESIGNING PLANS 12
EVALUATING PLANS
PLANNING THROUGH SIMULATION 13
EVALUATING PLANS 14
SELECTING A PLAN 15
SPECIFYING THE PLAN
PROBLEM FORMULATION 16
REPORTING RESULTS 17
IMPLEMENTING THE PLAN
PROGRAM PREPARATION 18
PLAN APPROVAL, ITS LEGAL JUSTIFICATION 19
ORGANIZING OPERATIONAL UNITS 20
PLAN FEEDBACK
MONITORING THE PLAN 21
EVALUATING THE PLAN 22
ADJUSTING, ALTERING, REDESIGNING OR PLANNING FOR WHAT, HOW, AND BY WHOM? 23

Introduction

The third phase of any planning exercise is conceiving and designing plans to satisfy the problem defined in phase one and specified in phase two. What are the social, economic, and political trends that will affect the concept? How should the aims to overcome or use these trends most effectively be established? Once the aims are established how are plans designed for achieving them? The answers to these and other questions comprise the purpose of Part Three.

One technique for conceiving plans is the following three-step process:

Step 10 Identifying prevailing trends
Step 11 Establishing goals and objectives
Step 12 Designing plans

These three steps are discussed in Chapters 10 through 12.

10 Identifying prevailing trends

ESTABLISHING A BACKGROUND

In a discussion of the trends of educational planning, past and current tendencies must be observed within the boundaries of their environment, and the educational planner must study the prevailing patterns and trends among people, places, movements, economics, and activities. (See Figure 10.1.)

When one is considering the planning environment, attention must be directed toward the people and their functions within that environment. Planning involves guiding and controlling the use and development of human and physical resources for maximum social and economic benefits.

In the United States the major planning activity has been directed at the physical environment and has been carried out by city planners. They, in general, have considered the city as a depository of human activities where people have established networks of communications. The planners have tried to balance the effective regulation of the functions of the city against a maximum amount of freedom for the residents. The planner accomplishes this by an understanding of the dynamics of a given city, including the movements of people and the various subsystems, such as education, that are a part of the city. (See Figure 10.2.) Of course, many subtle influences act as regulators in any city. Even though social units may appear to be acting within a black

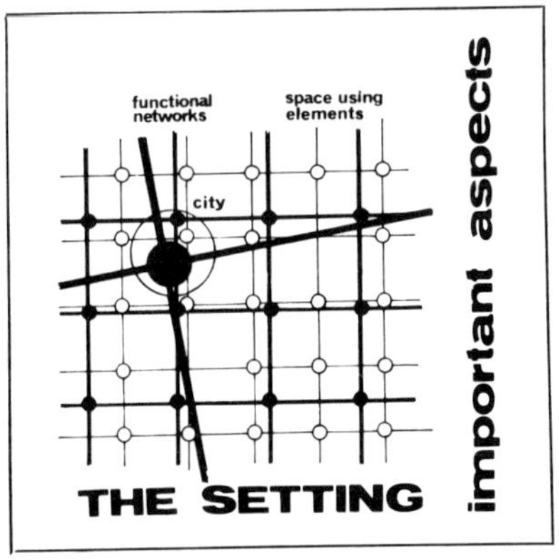

FIGURE 10.1

box, principles have been developed for predicting human activities. In addition, scientific facts are being uncovered showing the influence of physical environments on the behavior of people within various kinds of unique physical environments. This balanced interplay of formal and informal rules and regulations has been noted by others.

This distinction between " visible " and " invisible " parts, related to the hardware city, could be expressed thus : visible parts will be called the elements directly utilized by the inhabitants during their activities (furniture, sanitary and electric equipment, partitions, shelters, vehicles, etc.) ; the

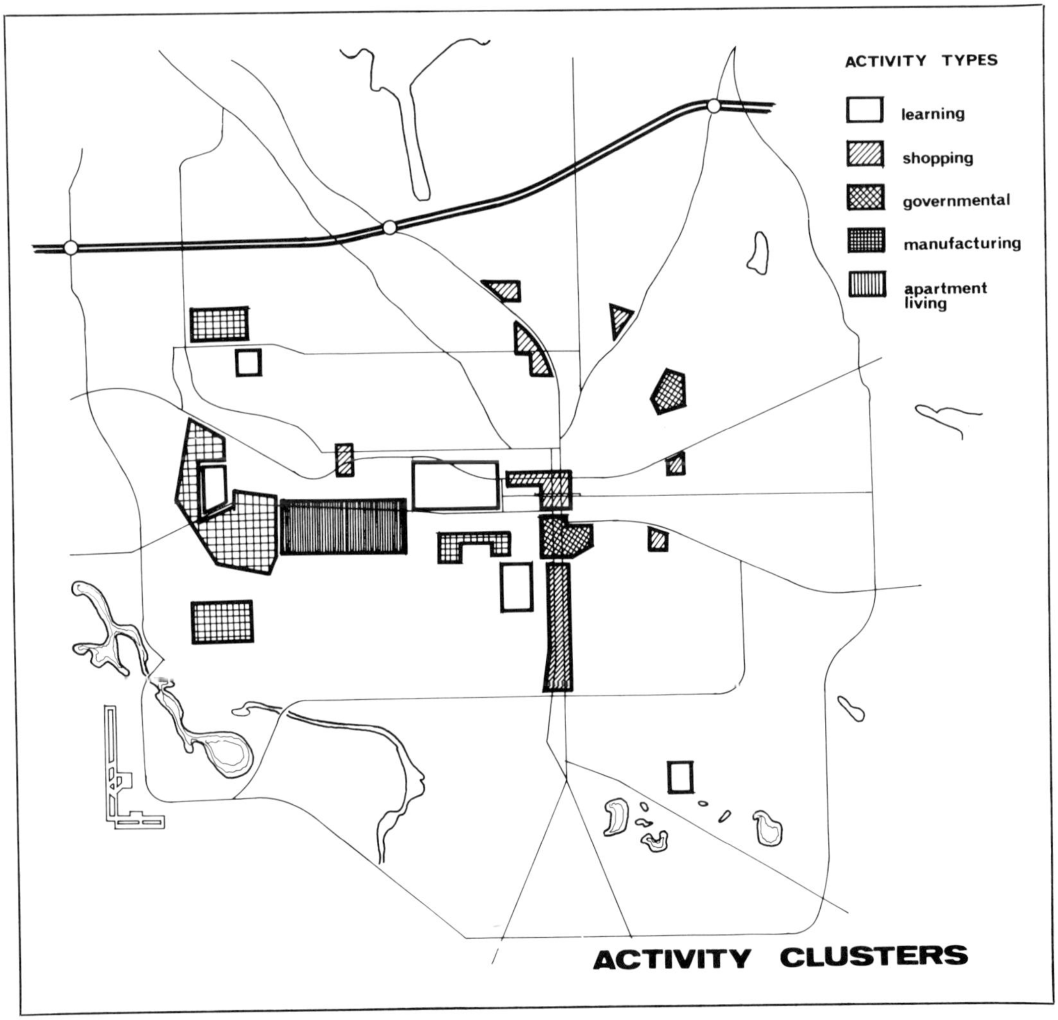

FIGURE 10.2

invisible parts will be, on the other hand, the indirectly used elements (water networks, sewers, electricity networks, etc.). These indirectly used elements (networks) we shall call "infrastructure," and the directly used elements will be named "fillings in the infrastructure." Our program will first consist of determining the infrastructure as a fixed network and considering the "fillings" as mobile fittings within the infrastructure.[1]

Further elaboration of the infrastructure seems to be required: just what is the nature and purpose of the infrastructure as superimposed over the city concept?

The infrastructure can be conceived as three possible arrangements: (1) Linear infrastructure: it forms a "tree" conducting commodity supplies (water, electricity, traffic, etc.). The fillings are arranged along this tree. (2) Planar infrastructure: it is a closed network in one plane, conducting commodity supplies. The fillings are arranged in the mesh of this network. (3) Spatial infrastructure: it conducts commodity supplies along a three-dimensional closed network. Fillings are arranged in the "hollows" of this network. [See Figure 10.3.]

On considering the number of possible variations of arrangements of fillings in each infrastructure, the most variations making the most use of the infrastructure should be considered.[2]

As a general rule for planning, the linear infrastructure allows less variation than the other two. The planar infrastructure allows fewer variations than the spatial infrastructure, which allows the most variations because it is less vulnerable to accidental breakdowns and has the maximum possible variations of patterns.

In some ways the city may be considered as an elaborate and dynamic combination of linear, planar, and spatial infrastructures.

The city, as a mechanism, could be described as a labyrinthine configuration of departure points and target points, separated by obstacles.

The mechanism can be studied by observing the frequency of the movements of the inhabitants between departure or target points. The result of this observation will indicate the behavior pattern of the inhabitants.

Here, we arrive at a very important conclusion: the sum of the movements in the labyrinth belongs to a dimension, which does not depend upon the configuration of the labyrinth, but upon the frequencies of visits to certain "addresses" (targets) in this labyrinth.[3]

FIGURE 10.3

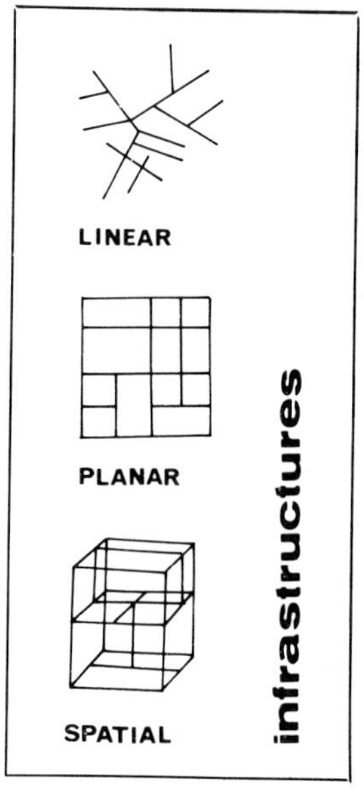

The concept of a dynamic, changing system found within the city calls attention to the growth and development of its form. What specifically is urban form?

It is the total physical environment required by modern society, comprising all types of settlement and their related landward areas which on average should not be less than eight times the size of urban development areas. In other words, in a continuously developed region the areas of towns, in round figures, should not exceed ten per cent of the area of the region.[4]

It is, however, questionable whether such rules of thumb have any meaning as metropolitan areas continue to develop as they have in the past. This, too, is recognized by Childs: ". . . fundamentally, urban

[1] Yona Friedman, "A Research Programme for a Scientific Method of Planning," *Architectural Design*, **37**:379 (August 1967).

[2] Ibid.

[3] Ibid., pp. 380–381.

[4] Derek Rigby Childs, "Trend, Countertrend of Counter-drift," *Architects' Journal*, no. 3, **139**:121 (1964).

form is a virtually continuous form, which is not so much mysterious as highly complex in structure. It is a form which can be understood only if its component parts are always considered in context and never in isolation."[5]

The complexity of urban form and structure does have profound implications for planning cities as well as school systems.

The five basic principles of physical planning are: (1) according to its context, there is a limit to which any form of development can be carried. Beyond this there will be either loss of efficiency or character or both; (2) the larger the size of area subject to urban development the lower the overall density should be. Conversely, the smaller the area the higher can be the density. (Density here refers to population density which relates distribution of population to living standards.) (3) The higher the general standard of living prevailing in an area, the lower the overall density should also be. (4) Again, the higher the general standard of living, the greater the interdependence of activities between different areas. (5) Broadly speaking, the above four principles apply to all scales of urban form from the smallest to the largest.

The five principles are, in themselves, simple but in the interactions become extremely complex. Their value is that their application in conjunction opens the way in planning to opportunities for much greater use of imagination and of individual solutions than has commonly been supposed possible.[6]

The concept of density should not be rigidly interpreted. (See Figure 10.4.) In the United States planners have traditionally been impressed with the expansiveness of the country and, therefore, have emphasized openness in planning. In many of the older cities of Europe and elsewhere in the world where population density is extremely high, the objective of planning is to make the best use of available space in a highly populated area. As urban areas become more complicated (see Figure 10.5), a greater flexibility in planning will be required in order to integrate the people with places, movements, cost, and activities. Particular consideration must be given to communications and the concept of movement. The sense of balance between necessary regulation and control and the inhabitants' independence must be maintained.

[5]Ibid.
[6]Ibid., p. 122.

FIGURE 10.4

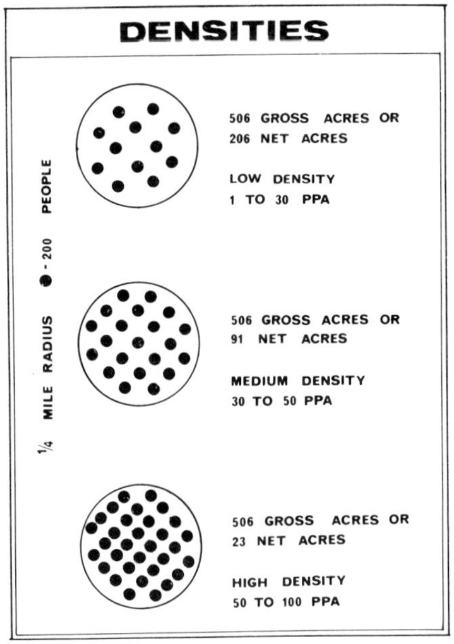

The educational planner will contribute much only if he can appraise the effectiveness of the various programs in which he has a hand. Buildings and other spaces express in part a complex social system. Each aspect lies in a causal relationship to all others, so that each is defined by, and has meaning only with respect to its relation to the others. Planning the physical aspects of educational facilities must agree with all other plans of government and nongovernment agencies. Each should trace out the probable consequences of its plan in the community.[7] (See Figure 10.6.)

Such activity involves many people from many segments of society.

There are thus (relating to the extensive contribution of engineers, architects, and others and their research on school and college buildings) extensive sources both directly and

[7]Melvin M. Webber, "Comprehensive Planning and Social Responsibility: Toward an AIP Consensus on the Profession's Role and Purpose," *Journal of the American Institute of Planners*, no. 9, **29**:232–241 (1963).

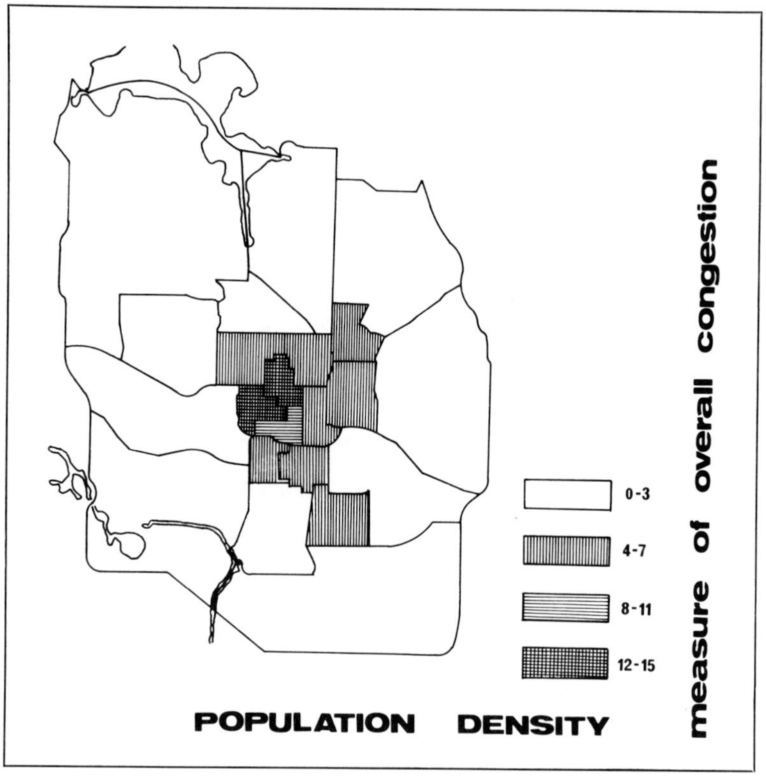

FIGURE 10.5

indirectly related to the subject which are not strictly educational research. Since, however, some such sources are a part of the prevailing technology in this field divergence into various interdisciplinary areas is common to specialists in school and college facilities, their planning, their design and their construction.[8]

The principles of planning, particularly in the physical environment, are all relevant to planning educational environments. Four areas of concern to planners are (1) the wide range of human activities encompassed by the various kinds of educational institutions, (2) human requirements for physical facilities, (3) the planning of physical facilities in terms of processes and techniques, and (4) the administration of the school plant and equipment.[9]

[8]Chester W. Harris (ed.), *Encyclopedia of Educational Research,* 3rd ed. (New York: Macmillan, 1960), p. 1008.
[9]Ibid., p. 1009.

Because education is an activity system within the total environment, planning for educational systems should be integrated directly into other municipal activities. Because the educational system is not a closed system, it interacts continuously with other parts of the urban mechanism. Certain principles are the same for the city and the school system. The plan for learning reflects an analysis of the learning-activity systems and a careful projection of future learning requirements for expansion and renewal. Future development in learning areas can be predicted to ensure the best possible physical environment for learning. This in turn ensures the economical use of a cost-revenue point of view.

The prevailing patterns and trends as they affect people, places, movements, economics, and activities blend together into a meaningful picture that impinges upon the educational processes.

FIGURE 10.6
Tracing some consequences

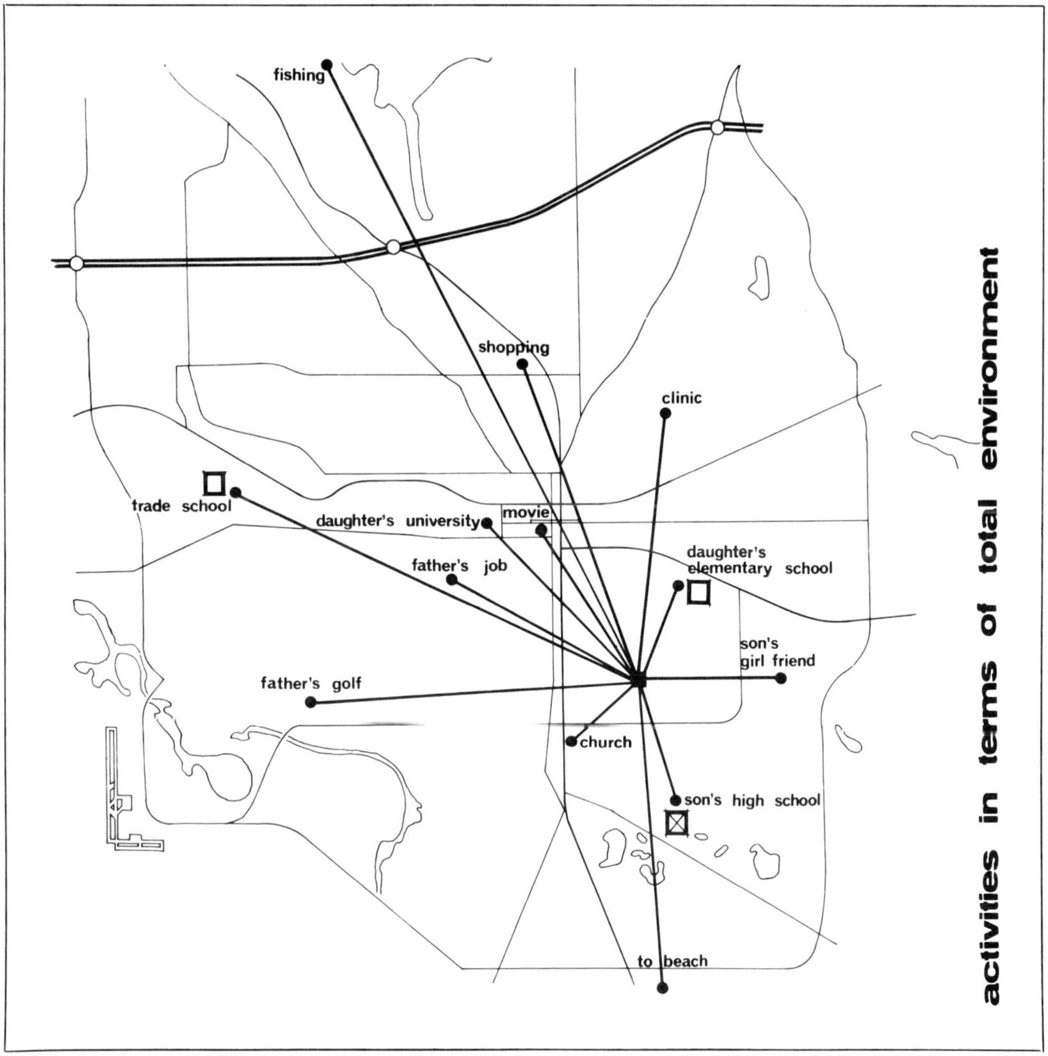

PREVAILING PATTERNS AND TRENDS AMONG PEOPLE

First, the educational planner

With the great demands for successful environments the educational planner must be suited to his work. He should be a skillful analyst, an effective evaluator, and a proficient designer. The planner is a professional who by experience and/or education is capable of conceiving the guidelines to carry a task through to its completion. As an analyst and a synthesizer, he understands the whole, the contributions of the components of an educational system, and the interaction of those components with each other to produce an efficiently operating whole. A knowledge of the community, form and structure, land uses, regulatory procedures, transportation, demography, social interaction, and school systems is a necessary part of his background. In addition to being a pragmatist, he might be a quasi romantic. However, the planner is not the architect. The planning function is much broader than the design of a building. Designing a school system within an urban framework involves a greater amount of knowledge and skill than does the visualizing of one school building.

The design for the physical environment, like the design for the building, reflects the activities that will take place within its space. It is imperative that the educational designer realize that he is not producing only a work of art, a consideration missing from most deliberations on schools, but also a functional learning environment within which the educational activities do indeed operate.

> Everything that an architect does is first of all answerable to an institution of man before it becomes a building. You don't know what the building really is, unless you have a belief behind the building, a belief in its identity in the way of life of man. . . . It isn't you that you're making. It isn't just a question of believing something yourself, because the reality you believe isn't your belief, it's the belief of everyone: you are simply the radar of this belief.[10]

[10]Ibid., p. 48.

The specific direction of planning and planners is by no means clear. Subject to the many political, social, and economic forces attendant on every project, the planner is compelled by necessity to be highly flexible. However, the planning discipline appears to be breaking off into two major directions.

> One is toward methodical rigor: toward the evolving of concepts and theories of method—planning method or design method—and the use of systems analysis, mathematics, and the computer, to make the complexity manageable. The other direction is toward the partial and incomplete: toward philosophies of the circumstantial and incremental notions of how to live with complexity and contradiction.[11]

It is the problem of the architect to make the best use of space, whereas the planner must construct a system in which the interacting components can function effectively. The concept of flexibility has become more and more prominent in the architectural design of buildings as well as in the designing of physical environments. Two concepts stand out quite clearly: one, changes in teaching-learning activities, and two, involvement of supporting communitywide activities that contribute to the development of a learning system.

> Who has the energy to initiate or even arbitrate over the whole design process? Nobody. Centralized design control does not work.
>
> Change made by any one generation to the general scene in terms of building and engineering works is relatively small, and no matter how large the area of development may be, it cannot stand alone, and its effectiveness must also be measured in its interactions with what exists and with what it calls into being, both socially and plastically. . . . Buildings should be thought of in the beginning as fragments; containing within themselves a capacity to act with other buildings; be themselves links in systems of access and servicing.[12]

The functions of an educational planner are many and varied. He is a constructor and implementer of plans, guidelines, or goal achievement. He constantly monitors and evaluates plans and acts as a political buffer to assure completion of the plans. According

[11]Ibid., p. 43.
[12]Ibid., p. 44.

to Dollard and Parker, the basic roles of the planner may be summarized under four headings. As an institutional leader, the planner supervises the needs of his agency; he hires, develops, and maintains the staff and directs their work. Occupying the role of the professional planner, he becomes involved with analysis and design; hence, plans are created and implemented. The political atmosphere of the community is constantly monitored by the planner. He identifies and uses various strategies to persuade political thinking toward the desired goals. The skillful use of communications assures the political acceptance of the plan. Observation of the community reaction allows the necessary modifications of the plan. His final role as promoter is to keep the public informed. Work with various power groups and special interest groups allows them to be informed of progress and needs with a clear presentation of the educational objectives of the overall plan.

The trends in educational planning, therefore, seem to be greater flexibility in training educational planners and, consequently, a greater flexibility in the designing of the physical environment for learning. The rapid changes in a technological society demand that the physical environment for learning be equally flexible in order to ensure that the learner can continue to cope with future social, political, cultural, and physical changes.[13]

The work of an educational planner requires succinct interpretations of societal needs and ways of planning to satisfy them. The plan, therefore, must be comprehensive if it is to include the physical plan, the social plan, the economic plan, the transportation plan, and the educational plan. They must all be balanced between what is desirable and what is possible. "Designing man-made environments requires a broad spectrum of design, one to match the growing complexity of human ecology in a man-made environment."[14] (See Figure 10.7.)

[13]R. T. Doland and J. A. Parker, "Roles of the Planner: A Problem of Identification," *Urban Growth Dynamics*, ed. F. Stuart Chapin, Jr. and Shirley F. Weiss (New York: John Wiley, 1962), pp. 188–198.

[14]Advanced Studies in Urban Environments Toward an Urban Model," A Study by the Master Class in Architecture, Serge Chermayeff, Professor in Architectural Design (New Haven: Yale University, 1967), p. 9.

Second, man and his environment

Professional interest in the relationship between man and his environment is not new. Psychologists have investigated and debated the nature-nurture controversy for decades. The concept is relatively simple; an individual is born with a potential for developing behavioral patterns, and the environment is a major determinant of those behavioral patterns. Interest in the environment's impact on the individual dates from the early Greeks.

From early times there have been two types of environmental theory, one based on physiology and one on geographical position; both are in the Hippocratic Corpus. In general, the environmental theories based on physiology have evolved from the notion of health and disease as indicating a balance or imbalance respectively of the humors, and from empirical observations such as the advantages of certain town or house sites, situation with relation to attitude . . . or nearness to water, and to prevailing winds. Since Greek times, these theories have shown the effects of their origin; to very recent times they have been based on a psycho-physiological theory (the mental and physical stimulation of invigorating climate) or a geographical position, the latter types often being associated with the literature of political and economic theory.[15]

It would be naïve to assume that environmental influences are restricted to such static and mechanical forces as physical and geographic factors. Modern psychologists have studied other profound environmental subtleties associated with personality development and, consequently, with family, cultural, and situational behavior patterns. Recent studies of ghetto living demonstrate the extent to which environment shapes behavior. Although the low quality of the physical environment may traumatize the individual personality, the overall cultural milieu is considered as important or even more so than the physical quality. The sociocultural mores were emphasized by the development of religious philosophy, which stresses man's relationship with God as opposed to his physical environment. These theories insist on the individual's ability to rise above his physical environment and determine his own behavioral patterns and individual destiny.

[15]Clarence J. Glacker, *Traces on the Rhodian Shores* (Berkeley: University of California Press, 1967), pp. 80–81.

FIGURE 10.7

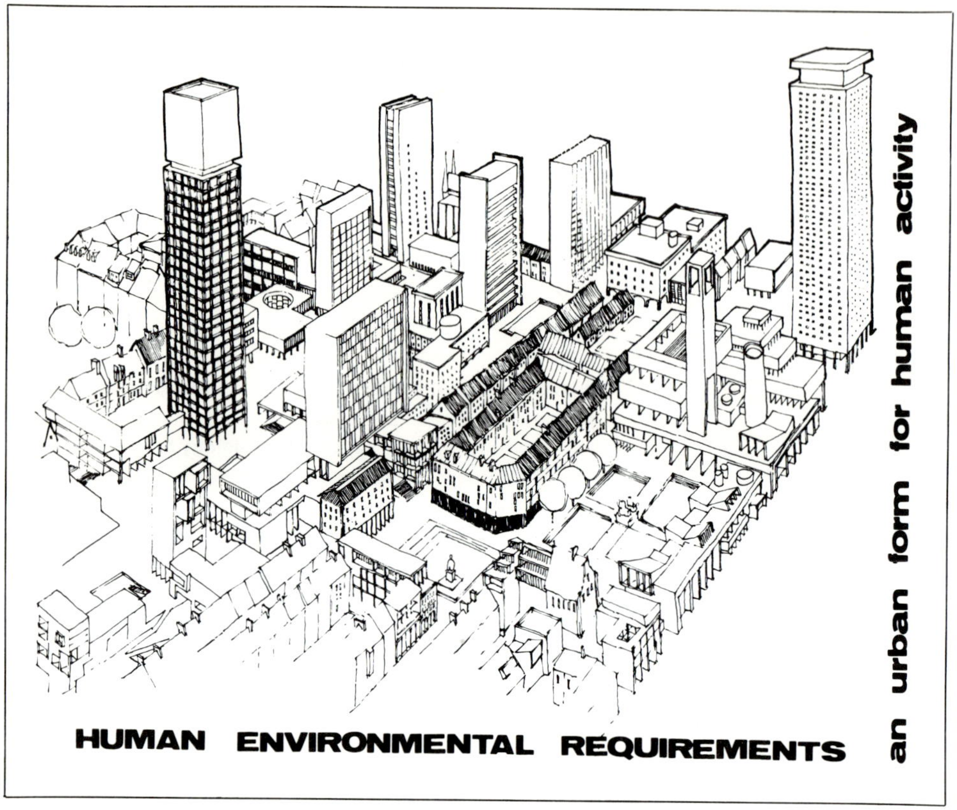

Man's adaptability is probably his most distinguishing social characteristic. His great ability to adapt to varying social and physical environments, his inventiveness, and his capability to profit from past experiences and modify his environment have been his most amazing attributes. Therefore, man is the epitome of the cybernetic or feedback model—while he is being influenced by the environment, the information returned to him from his environment permits him to influence the environment. This process of social and technological evolution has not only solved many of man's environmental problems but has created new ones, e.g., the destruction of natural resources, pollution, and the disruption of natural ecological systems. The religious, evolutionary, and ecological theories that attempt to explain man's relationships to his environment all encompass the holistic concept of nature. The three theories rationalize man as a component operating within the general environment, and interacting with the environment, and as an essential part of the overall system. Scholars at different times have placed varying degrees of emphasis on the relative influence of the environment and of the individual. The religious thinkers have placed greater stress on the individual's freedom of thought, whereas the Darwinian evolutionist has emphasized the molding of the individual by the environment. Modern ecology looks on the dynamics of the entire system in holistic fashion with the various components continuously interacting as essential parts of the system. Ecology emphasizes the concept of the individual reacting inside a system as opposed to the individual acting outside one.

Although there is not yet a comprehensive theory of the nature of man's interactions with his environment, substantial progress has been made toward a better understanding of those interactions. Generally, such studies are approached from such points of view as "... the physical environment as it affects and is affected by man's behavior, the perception and evaluation of the physical environment and the interrelations which exist between the social and physical environments. Each of these aspects of environmental research is interrelated with the other."[16] Different disciplines approach the study of the man/environment problem from other points of view.

> For economics, environment is traditionally viewed as land. A member of the trinity of productive inputs. . . . In anthropology, environment is . . . important especially as a setting for primitive cultures. But more often than not it proclaims the triumph of culture over a single physical setting. Sociology . . . sees the physical city as the dependent entity, a function of social organizations and change. For many psychologists, the environment is but neutral stuff that must wait patiently for form and meaning obtained only through the mind and senses. Even in geography, . . . the study of environment calls for apologetics.[17]

In addition to the perspectives of different disciplines, there is a natural tendency for appraisals of the environment to be colored by the individual's own perceptual background. Probably no completely objective perception of the environment exists. ". . . Only degrees of distortion which are minimized in rigorous scientific description, what is perceived as reality may differ from person to person and it seems likely that in such elementary ways as viewing abstract designs people vary in the spatial styles in their preference, e.g. of vertical as against horizontal lines."[18]

Current interest in the interaction of organisms and their environment has given rise to a relatively new discipline called ecology. This is related to the term *ecosystem*, which was introduced by the botanist A. G. Consley approximately a quarter of a century ago. "The ecosystem . . . may be defined as the interacting environment and biotic system . . . a natural unit . . . in which the exchange of materials between the living and non-living parts follows similar paths."[19]

Like the term *systems* as it is used in a general scientific sense, ecosystems are defined according to specified boundaries and can be small or large. What may be a complete system in one sense may be a subsystem in another sense. The essential aspect of ecosystems is interaction. "Ecologists use the term ecosystem to refer to a community together with its habitat. An ecosystem, then, is an aggregation of associated species of plants and animals, together with the physical features of their habitat. Ecosystems . . . can be of any size or ecologic rank . . . at the extreme, the whole earth and all its plant and animal inhabitants together constitute a world ecosystem."[20]

Considerable literature now exists on various ecological systems. Definitions that clarify the concept of ecosystem are beginning to emerge.

> An ecosystem is a functioning, interacting system composed of one or more organisms and their effective environment, both physical and biological. All ecosystems are open systems. Ecosystems may be stable or unstable. The stable system is in a steady state. The entropy in an unstable system is more likely to increase than decrease. There is a tendency towards diversity in natural ecosystems. There is a tendency towards uniformity in artificial ecosystems or those strongly influenced by man.[21]

The basic hereditary mechanisms, the genetic characteristics, and the basic instinctual mechanisms as well as a neurological system that allows rapid flexibility in learning are all factors that contribute

[16] Gary H. Winkel, "Editor's Introduction and Preface," *Environment and Behavior*, no. 1, **1**:5 (June 1969).

[17] Robert W. Kates and Joachim F. Wohlwill, "Man's Response to the Physical Environment," *Journal of Social Issues*, no. 4, **22**:22 (October 1966).

[18] George F. White, "Formation and Role of Public Attitudes," *Environmental Quality in a Growing Economy*, ed. Henry Jarrett (Baltimore: Johns Hopkins Press, 1966), p. 111.

[19] Otis Dudley Duncan, "The Ecosystem Concept and the Problem of Air Pollution," *Environment and Cultural Behavior*, ed. Andrew P. Voyda (Garden City, N.Y.: Natural History Press, 1969), p. 459.

[20] Richard M. Sax, "The Planning Process for Social and Physical Planning and the Need for an Environmental Design," *Contra Costa Council of Community Service* (Walnut Creek, Calif: By the Council, November 1965), p. 459.

[21] Ian T. McHarg, "The Place of Nature in the City of Man," *The Annals of the American Academy of Political and Social Sciences*, **352**:4–5 (March 1964).

to the effectiveness of the organism's adaptation to its environment. In man, of course, strong psychological factors require the fulfillment of such needs as sexual satisfaction, aggressiveness, security, recognition from one's peers, and love. The field of education must recognize the work being done by ecologists and environmental planners. As C. G. Jung pointed out,

. . . as man is influenced by his education, he is just as surely influenced by the planned form of his surroundings. . . . Technical abstract work leaves the workers unsatisfied. Unsatisfaction leads to the search for substitutes, . . . we need psychic nourishment. We do not find it in the apartment house from which no green lawn, no tree in blossom can be seen . . . we need to be able to project ourselves into things. . . . Everything which surrounds me belongs to me and it is precisely here that the tenement or apartment house is fatal in that it provides so few opportunities for creating forms.[22]

The ecologists and the psychologists see the environment as consisting of many diverse conditions and forces that tend to act together in influencing the individual. The individual, on the other hand, develops unique perceptual abilities. The educational planner interprets the environment and adapts it to man's needs.

Perceptual development

The concept of the environment's impinging on the perceptual development of the learner has profound potentials for education. Educational planners should capitalize on the environment in order to enhance the stimulus-seeking nature of the learner. The essential condition to improved learning is an environment in which the learner finds himself relatively secure yet one that stimulates him to further exploration and intellectual development. The educational process should be based on the individual's physical participation in the environment, thereby allowing him to derive a better understanding of the environment and a better understanding of what is to be transmitted in the education process.

The concept of relevance under this theory is given high priority. It assumes, for example, that the resources throughout the community can be used in the educational process. There are many cultural, recreational, and athletic resources within many communities that are not used by the educational system. If one considers the educational system as an inherent part of the total ecology of the urban system, then full use of the resources of the larger urban system is in order. A good deal can be learned on how to integrate the resources from studies of primitive cultures and particularly the cultures of human settlements as shown in Part One of this study. Another approach to investigating communities recently developed is that of ekistics.

Ekistics is the science of human settlements. The term derives from the Greek work " OIKO," meaning settling down, and denotes the existence of an overall science of human settlements conditioned by man and influenced by economic, social, political, administrative and technical sciences as well as the disciplines related to the arts . . . ekistics is a science whose task is to examine the human settlements from every point of view in order to develop solutions of the problem involved.[23]

Ekistics involves an integration of various disciplines. The approach is essentially integrative in the sense that it looks on the community as a composite of various interacting variables. (See Table 10.1.)

Ekistics studies human settlements by the classification of problems and solutions based on the scale of ekistics units from the smallest one—the room—to the largest one—the universal city—covering the entire earth. It also studies the same phenomena by nature and intent of the related disciplines. We can thus classify the human settlements on a three dimensional grid selecting several types of two dimensional projections forming grids where we can inscribe and study all the related phenomena . . . we see that ekistics is in the center of five circles representing the basic fields of knowledge, economic social, political and administrative, technical and cultural disciplines. If we now combine these disciplines with the scale of ekistic units we have an ekistic grid on which we can study the importance and impact of everyone on the corresponding ekistic units. On the basis of such grids we can also study all other types of ekistic phenomena. The methods which ekistics uses correspond to those used by the disciplines contributing to it, as well as

[22]Hans Carol, "C. G. Jung and the Need for Roots," *Landscape,* no. 3, **14**:2 (Spring 1965).

[23]C. A. Doxiadis, "Ekistus," *Ekistus,* **34**:131 (August 1967).

Table 10.1 The ekistic scale

Community Scale	i	ii	iii	I	II	III	IV	V	VI	VII	VIII	IX	X	XI	XII
	1	2	3	4	5	6	7	8	9	10	11	12	13	14	15
Ekistic Units	Man	Room	Dwelling	Dwelling Group	Small Neighborhood	Neighborhood	Small Town	Town	Large City	Metropolis	Conurbation	Megalopolis	Urban Region	Urbanized Continent	Ecumeno-polis
Elements: Nature															
Man															
Society															
Shells															
Networks															
Synthesis															
Population ^{t} (thousands) ^{m} (millions)	1	2	4	40	250	1.5^t	7^t	50^t	300^t	2^m	14^m	100^m	700^m	5.000^m	30.000^m

to all their combinations. Why this is indispensable can be understood if we consider the five elements forming human settlements: nature, on which the settlements are created; man, for whom they are created; society, which forms, but also takes shape within the networks (roads, water, power, etc.) forming their circulation system; and finally the shells (houses, buildings, etc.) which house all their functions. Proper approach to every type of problem of human settlements requires a method for broadening the frame of our study. For example, a city does not exist as such, but only as the heart of a wider rural area which may contain many villages as well as many other cities and functions. The same holds true of any part of a city. To be guided in broadening the frame of our observations, we should remember that any part of an urban settlement is only just one part of a larger network.[24]

Ekistics offers, then, an integrated study approach that uses the various sociopolitical and economic procedures that continuously interact within a community. Not only are these facets important in themselves but the total understanding of the various interactions among the many subsystems can substantially contribute to our better understanding of the urban processes and in particular the conditions under which the educational activity systems must operate.

As we have explored the development of the theoretical framework of man-environment relations, we have seen the continuous development of technology and sophistication of approaches to a better understanding of the man-environment problem. Beginning with a general theoretical framework associated with religion and based primarily on an interpretive relationship to God, we have progressed through the Darwinian concepts of evolution, in which the principles of interaction of man with his environment have become clearer. Finally, with new disciplines such as ecology, which applies the methods of science and mathematics to the study of man-environment problems, we have begun to develop a basic theory that accounts for the development and maintenance of human behavior operating within various types of complex environmental systems.

Interrelationships

The designer may be helped by the work of the ecologists, who are essentially systems oriented;

[24] Ibid., p. 132.

they look on the total operating system as being an interaction of many component parts, man being one part. As technology has reached higher levels of sophistication, the interrelatedness of the many operating components has become more complex. Technologically increased efficiency of one part of the system may be of short-term benefit if other parts of the system are irreparably impaired. The educational planner must be able to recognize imbalance in the relationships within a system and avoid these situations. If this is accomplished, many of the problems facing society may be alleviated.

Modern society is also becoming aware of the checks and balances associated with social relations. The individual cannot function effectively completely by himself, neither can he function completely on the basis of collectivism. There has to be a balance between the rights of the individual and the rights of the group. Any cursory evaluation of metropolitan areas confirms the interrelationships among various behavioral groups with their unique social attitudes and among individuals with their unique personalities and needs. The balance that must be maintained among their various social, cultural, and economic parts becomes evident. Man and his environment "... form a complex, interacting system involving man's perception of that environment. It is becoming increasingly clear that the relation of man and his physical environment is complex, multifaceted, and multilayered; that the linking of single variables or stimuli with specific responses will hardly work."[25]

The change of life from a simple rural environment to a complex urban milieu has rapidly taken place in the United States over the past several decades. (See Figure 10.8.) Educational and urban planners must recognize this changing environmental scene and plan accordingly. At the same time, it must not be forgotten that man is essentially individualistic even though he operates within a social and urban context. Preparation for planning educational environments, therefore, should include

FIGURE 10.8 A and B (opposite)

> ... enough biology so that the ... [planner] ... would emerge with some understanding about [how] biological systems work. Enough engineering to give a sense of man's power to alter the physical environment in both adaptive and non-adaptive ways, and enough of the humanities and social sciences to give a feeling for what men think they want, what they really want, and how human institutions work to forward or frustrate human desires ... anything less is inadequate to the purpose.[26]

The educational planner must be aware that although he is dealing with a complex, interacting system, he is still concerned primarily with man who is "... a complex psychological organism responding simultaneously to internal and external forces which can be differentiated into basic drives, adjustment mechanisms, and value orientations. Human nature is pliable and human development must be viewed dynamically."[27]

Man-environment interactions can be thoroughly understood only when examined from a comprehensive point of view; i.e., the study should focus on man operating within a complex system that is comprised of many nonhuman components. Political, social, physical, climatic, economic, and many other forces are all impinging on the behavioral patterns of the learner who operates within the environmental context. It is necessary that activities be organized into patterns that will have a goodness of fit within the complex interrelationships operating within the environment. Modern urbanology is therefore a study of man operating individually and aggregately within subsystems, many of which man himself has created. These man-made institutions, of course, become essential components operating within the larger ecological system. "Ecological thinking cannot become effective in society unless its growth is matched by the growth of institutions embodying and implementing ecological concepts. If man's future domin-

[25]Amos Rapoport, "Some Aspects of the Organization of Urban Space," *Response to the Environment,* ed. Gary J. Coates and Kenneth M. Moffett (Raleigh: North Carolina State University, 1969), p. 123.

[26]Robert S. Morrison, "Education for Environmental Concerns," *Daedalus,* **96**:1219 (Fall 1967).

[27]Eli Ginzberg, *The Development of Human Resources* (New York: McGraw-Hill, 1966), p. 4.

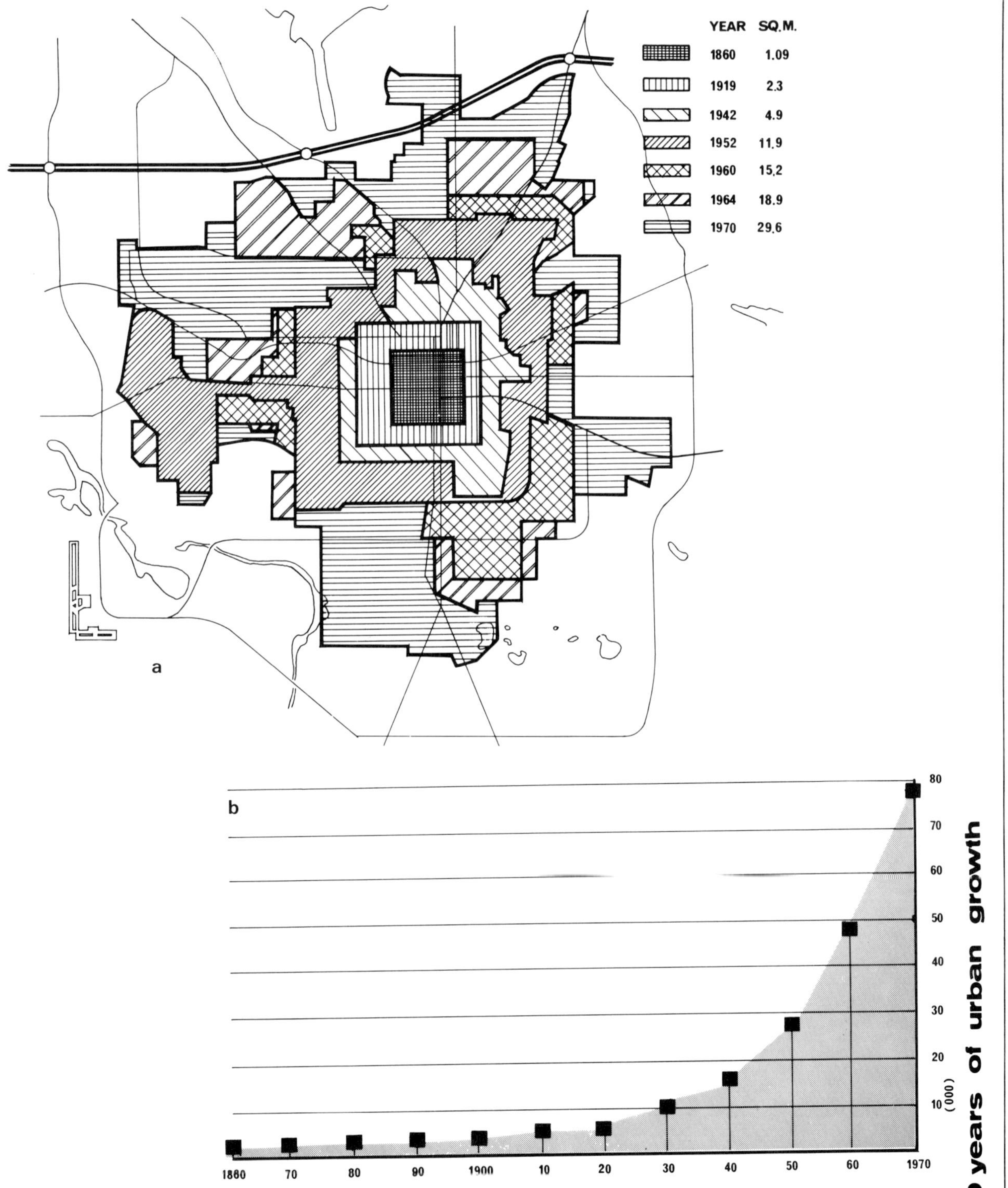

TALLAHASSEE

110 years of urban growth

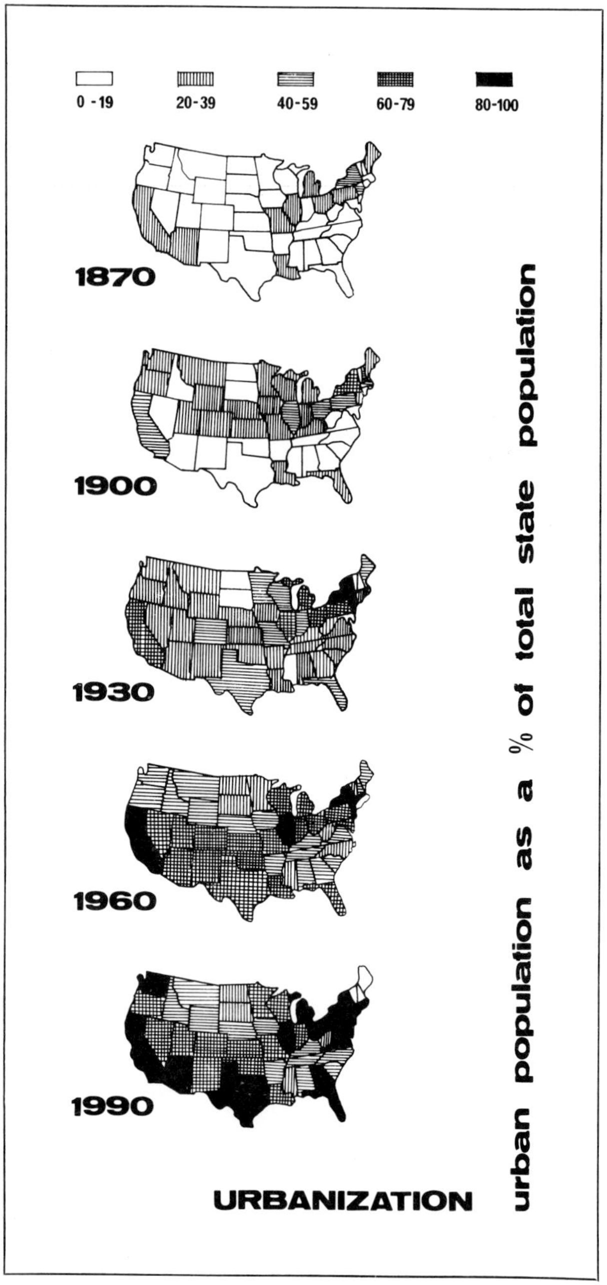

FIGURE 10.8C

ion over his environment is to be other than ephemeral, some major changes in his institutions for environmental management will have to be made."[28]

Certainly one institution in which such major changes can be made is the school. At the present time, no demonstrably good models of schoolhouses encompassing the comprehensive environmental approach have been organized. Techniques are now available for systematically analyzing the educational environment and determining those aspects of the environment that are conducive to good educational behavioral outputs and eliminating those that are not conducive. As indicated earlier, certain behavioral outcomes are predictable from known behavioral patterns when these behavioral patterns are manifested in certain environments. It would seem clear that some classification scheme, such as the input/output model, might be able to outline reasonably clear-cut expectations from the creation of certain environmental inputs. This assumes, however, that the environments would be flexible enough to assure the adaptability that human beings will require. This adaptability would be predicated on the assumption that the individual reacts to his environment but also actively modifies it. If this assumption is true, then any educational environment that forces common behaviors on all students is doomed to extensive failure.

PREVAILING PATTERNS AND TRENDS AMONG PLACES

From the beginning of civilization, the physical environment has influenced man's social development. It was not a coincidence that early civilizations began along the Nile and Euphrates rivers; man used those natural elements which were beneficial in fulfilling his social goals. Today, some physical

[28]Lynton Keith Caldwell, "Public Policy Implications of Environmental Control," *Social Influences and the Environment: Conference on the Present and Potential Contribution of the Social Sciences to Research and Policy Formulation in the Quality of the Physical Environment*, ed. Morris E. Garnsey and James R. Hibbs (Boulder: University of Colorado Press, 1967), pp. 83–84.

designers are offering man a renewed contact with the natural elements: sunlight, fresh air, open spaces, and natural vegetation. If this is not possible, the designers abstract these listed elements from their natural surroundings and bring them to man in artificial urban centers.

Another important concern of physical designers is the creation of urban forms that reveal man's environment as part of an organic natural order and again, if this is not possible, the designer considering man as a species with certain fine characteristics strives to make him be at home in a created environment.[29] (See Figure 10.9.) This he does by creating focal points of interaction in order to enhance choice in activities and associations for buildings. Because an individual needs a certain amount of interaction with the natural environment, it is only appropriate that designers attempt to capitalize on the natural environment when designing the architectural form. This helps satisfy the emotional as well as the material needs of the individual. Influences from the environment are not merely physical. The physical stimuli

[29]Carol Leggitt, *Social Values and Urban Form* (New Brunswick, N.J.: Urban Studies Center at Rutgers University, 1964).

FIGURE 10.9

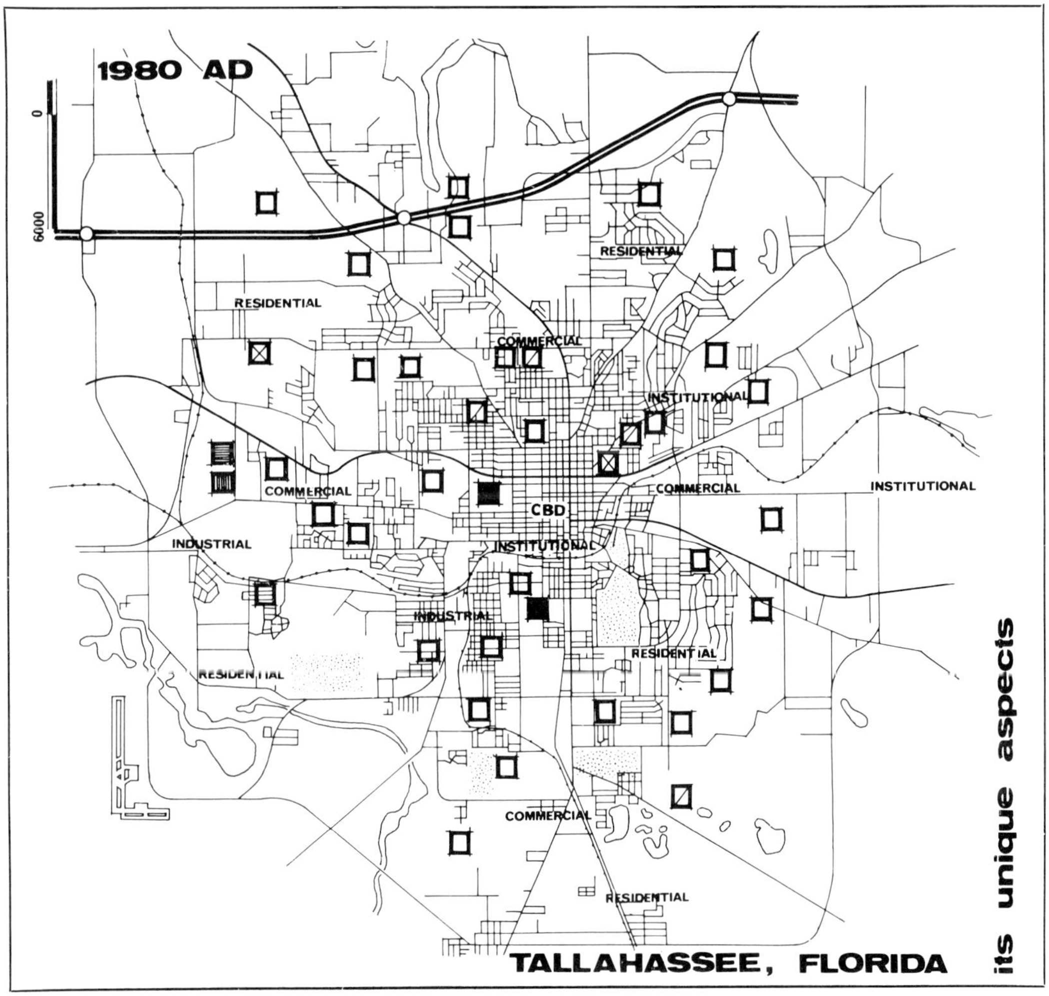

combined with man's perceptual facilities and the merger of these two create an aura within which the individual operates. The environment does not always directly impinge on the individual to modify his behavior; it also influences his behavior by being a source of nourishment, food, shelter, and aesthetic qualities.

> Neighborhood surroundings, both the social and the physical environment, are extremely important—possibly more so than the living quarters. In recognition of the importance of the neighborhood, efforts to improve slum conditions have given increasing attention to providing better community facilities—schools, parks, clinics—and to improving public services . . . improvements in housing must be accompanied by related community development if they are to have significant impact on the lives of people who are now in inadequate housing.[30]

In other words, the learner operates within a total ecology. He does not merely live in a school building but in subsystems of physical and social influences that form his entire community. Indeed, the learner's life style tends continuously to expand his sphere of influence through interaction until some external limitations are placed on that expansion. This barrier is always being tested, however, for there is a natural tendency for the learner to want to influence his environment, to expand, and to play a maximum role in giving to, as well as receiving from, the total environment.

> People are alienated from their physical environment if they are unable to leave their personal imprints on their immediate surroundings. Relegating human beings to the role of passive spectators of their environment threatens their mental equilibrium, and robs them of the opportunity to assert their authority to develop mastery over their places of habitat.[31]

One measure of the influence of the environment is the degree to which it is responsive to the individual learner. A suitable environment can effectively influence the individual's behavior and help to exploit the development of his basic potential. Sociologists have demonstrated that a suitable lifetime environment elicits the good qualities and habits of man and that it induces the shaping of his cultural profile and boosts his feeling of identity with society. A high-quality environment for life entails positive, though indirect, consequences in the productivity of labor and the economic use of leisure time and contributes toward the good state of health and population.[32]

A balance, however, must be maintained between the influences of the environment and the influence of the learner on the environment. Imbalance has produced unfortunate side effects that have begun to affect the learner's life style.

> The quality of the physical environment is being deteriorated by human actions; that to check the processes of deterioration and, hopefully, to reverse them will require new knowledge and policies to guide human actions; . . . furthermore there is the question whether ecology can somehow weld together the physical, biological and social sciences to help define and achieve an environment of a quality satisfactory to human well-being and aspirations.[33]

Unfortunately, the powerful vested interests that would be affected by such corrective processes impede most progress in this area. The elimination of smoking, for example, would affect the tobacco industry. Controlling automobile exhaust involves both the petroleum and the automobile-manufacturing industry. Sadly enough, many of the attempts to involve industry in costly social projects have been unsuccessful. The vested interests, when they become involved, focus on the selection of a piece of the problem rather than looking at the overall system and studying all the ramifications and the interactions of various components of the system.

When the whole system is examined, corrective

[30]Bernard J. Frieden, "Housing and National Urban Goals: Old Policies and New Realities," *The Metropolitan Enigma/Inquiries into the Nature and Dimensions of America's Urban Crisis,* ed. James Q. Wilson, (Cambridge, Mass.: Harvard University Press, 1968), p. 162.

[31]Karl Linn, "Neighborhood Commons," *Architectural Design,* **38**:379 (August 1968).

[32]Vladimir Matousek, "The Development of an Environment for Life in the Towns and Villages of Czechoslovakia," *Ekistics,* **25**:352 (May 1968).

[33]Stanley A. Cain, "Can Ecology Provide the Basis for Synthesis Among the Social Sciences," *Social Sciences and the Environment: Conference on the Present and Potential Contribution of the Social Sciences to Research and Policy Formulation in the Quality of the Physical Environment,* ed. Morris C. Garnsey and James R. Hibbs (Boulder: University of Colorado Press, 1967), p. 35.

action can be taken for some components of the system, so that the overall system will operate most effectively. The analogy is quite clear in the field of educational planning where one particular area of interest might grow disproportionately as a result of passing interests. But the overall development of the complete system must be enhanced. In educational planning this overall systems approach applies to the physical facilities as well as to the academic programs. The physical environment should be capable of supporting the learners in their set of activities. An appropriate setting emphasizes the student as an individual and produces a more positive self-concept because it clearly depicts the individual's role in the educational system.

Some physical influences

To maintain an ideal environmental condition at all times is not possible. As the environment departs from the expectations and needs of the learner, it is assumed that the environment will have a less positive effect on him and he will more readily seek changes, in some cases to the detriment of others who are learning. The educational planner must produce a long-term design that prevents eventual detriment to the learner. Cases exist in which long-range planning could have effectively eliminated deterioration, e.g., ghetto schools, "blackboard jungles," and juvenile delinquency, to cite a few examples. The balance of environmental actions on the learner is a combination of his sensory inputs from and perceptual interpretations of the environment. His perceptual interpretations are colored by his experiences and behavioral patterns, which have been established throughout his lifetime. In a highly urbanized area, the types of experiences that learners acquire differ substantially from those in less urbanized areas because of the dissimilarity of natural environments. The more highly developed the urbanized area, the greater is the tendency to shut out the natural environment, causing the individual to learn to perceive his environment in terms of man-made items. This tendency forces the educational planner to program into the educational form some of the characteristics found in nature. Many artificial forms, if carefully and sensitively done, can be substituted for natural forms. Because there is a human need for stimulation from a natural environment, planners have begun to compensate for the loss of those sensory inputs by developing artificial inputs that are appropriate substitutes for the natural terrain. Environmental influences come about from several dimensions: the extent of view; the nature of the foreground, the middle ground and the background; discontinuities; the direction and quality of lighting; the degree of enclosure; the presence of isolated forms; surface shapes; and the ephemeral features.[34]

Some of the stimuli develop from both natural and man-made things; daily lunar and seasonal periodicities, bioclimatology, the organic world of pathogens and disease, the geophysical hazards, earthquakes, hurricanes, tornadoes, rising noise levels, compacting urban space, and sensory deprivation form an environment that is too artificial.[35] (See Figure 10.10) There seems to be little question that the environment does indeed play a major role in the shaping of behavioral patterns.

> Current research suggests that crowding, inadequate plumbing and ventilation, and insufficient wiring and lighting clearly contribute to the spread of respiratory and digestive diseases and to home accidents. Morbidity and mortality rates are sensitive to housing conditions. . . . Lack of space and of privacy appears to interfere with children's study and with parental control. There is evidence that housing is an important factor in self-perception. Houses that convey an obvious image of neglect and inferior status have been found to influence the self-evaluation and motivation of people who live there, leading to feelings of pessimism and passivity.[36]

The task of the educational designer, in terms of

[34]Kenneth Craik, "Human Responsiveness to Landscape: An Environmental Psychological Perspective," *Response to Environment,* ed. Gary J. Coates and Kenneth M. Moffet (Raleigh: North Carolina State University, 1969), p. 173.

[35]Robert W. Kates and Joachim F. Wahlwill, "Man's Response to the Physical Environment," *Journal of Social Issues,* no. 4, **17:**24 (October 1966).

[36]Bernard J. Frieden, "Housing and National Urban Goals: Old Policies and New Realities," *The Metropolitan Enigma/ Inquiries into the Nature and Dimensions of America's Urban Crisis,* ed. James Q. Wilson (Cambridge, Mass.: Harvard University Press, 1968), p. 161.

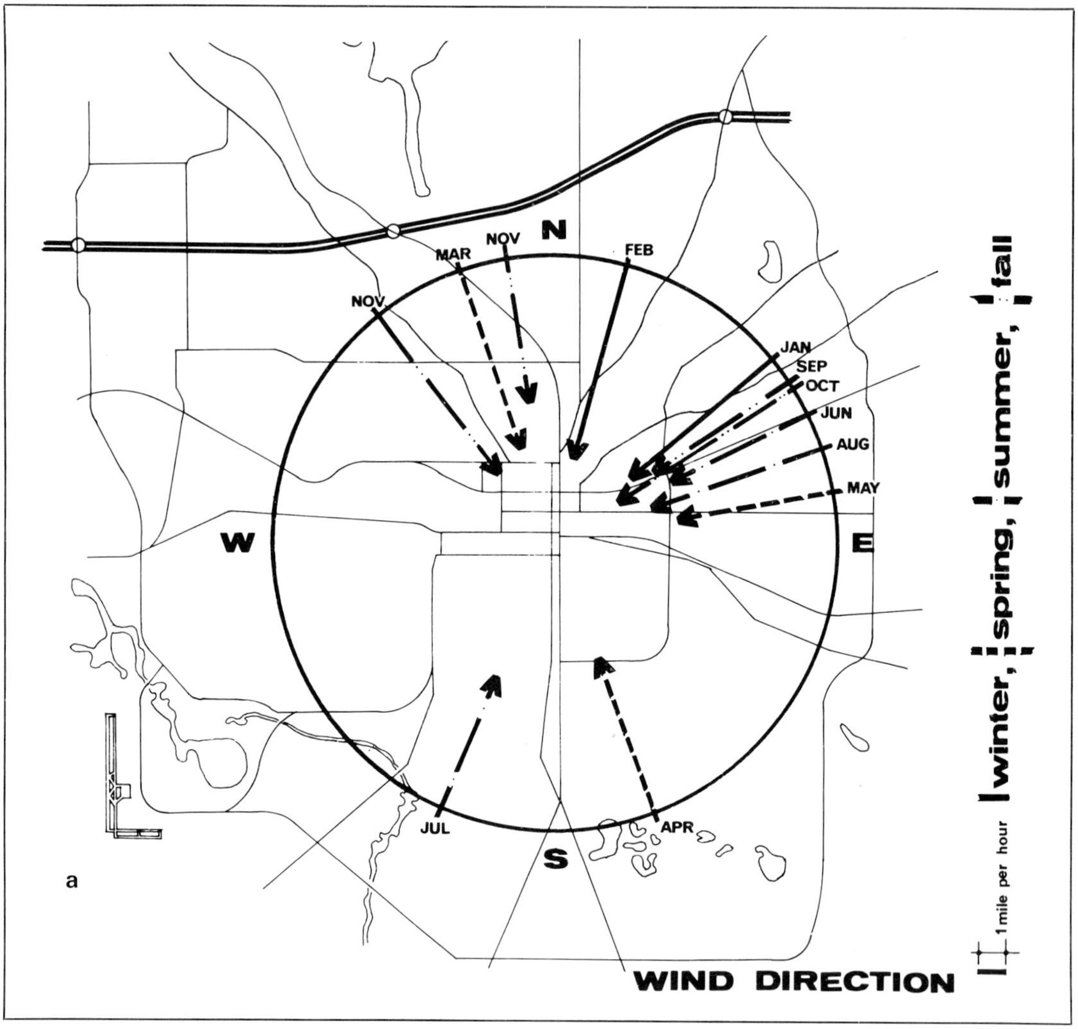

FIGURE 10.10 A, B, C
1969 Tallahassee climate

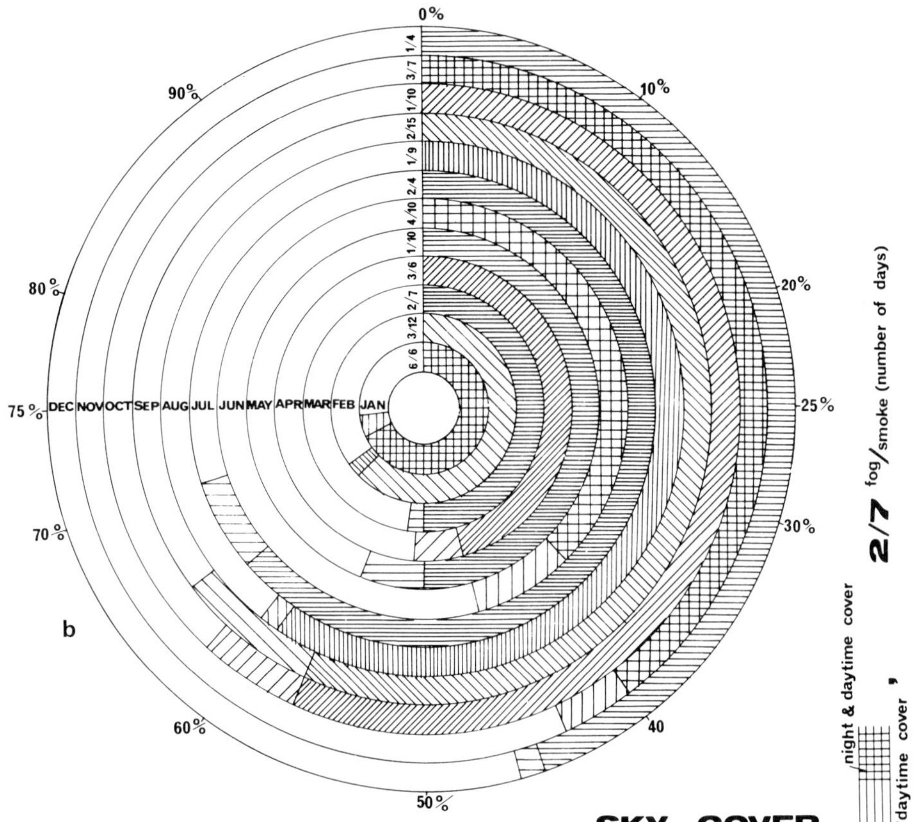
0%
10%
20%
25%
30%
40
50%
60%
70%
75%
80%
90%
JAN
FEB
MAR
APR
MAY
JUN
JUL
AUG
SEP
OCT
NOV
DEC
1/4
3/7
1/10
2/15
1/9
2/4
4/10
1/10
3/6
2/7
3/12
6/6
2/7 fog/smoke (number of days)
night & daytime cover
daytime cover

b

SKY COVER

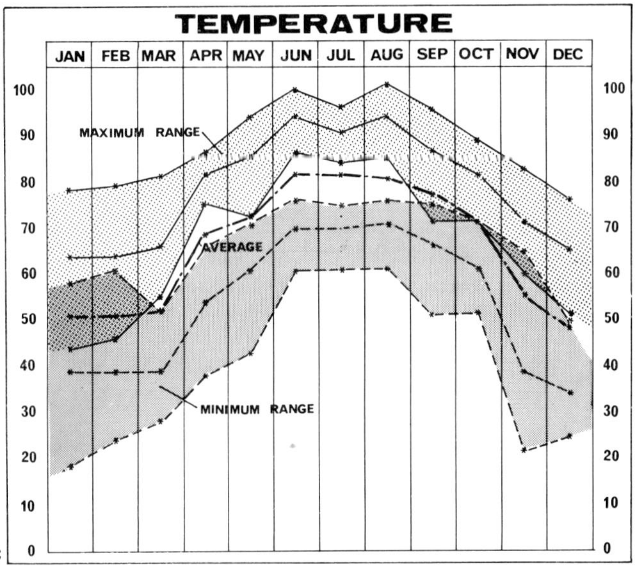
TEMPERATURE
JAN
FEB
MAR
APR
MAY
JUN
JUL
AUG
SEP
OCT
NOV
DEC
100
90
80
70
60
50
40
30
20
10
0
MAXIMUM RANGE
AVERAGE
MINIMUM RANGE

c

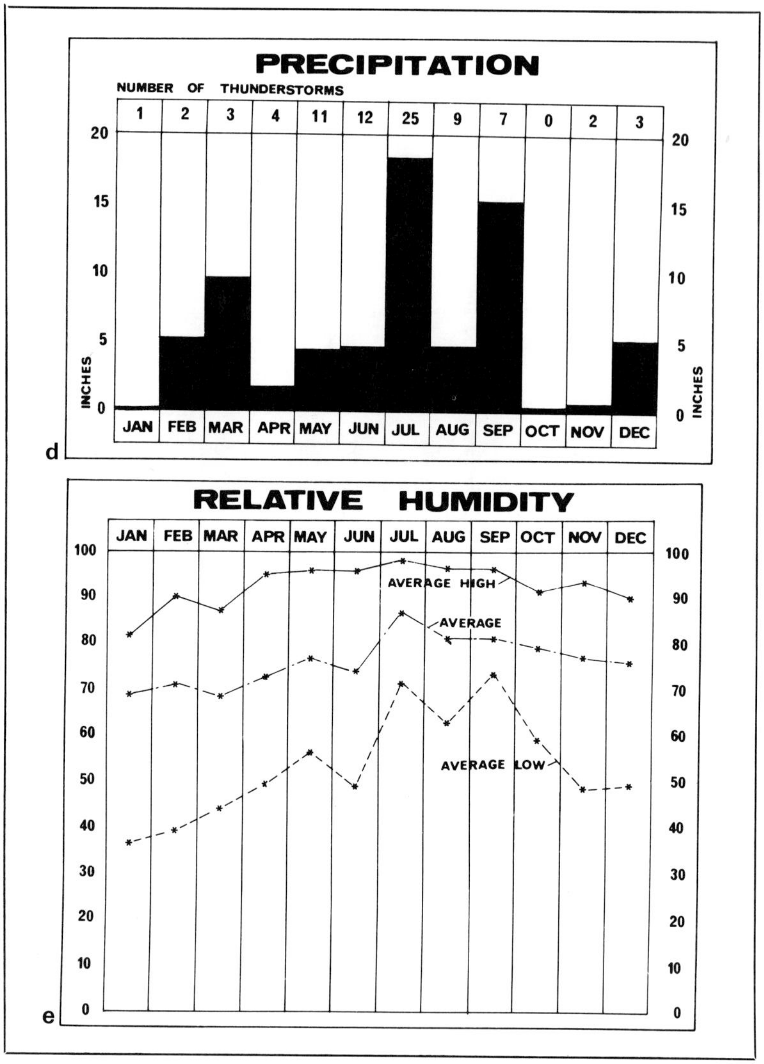

FIGURE 10.10 D and E

the physical environment, then, is a complex one. The designer's primary responsibility is to create an educational form that will produce situations that endow the learner with effective influences for positive behavior. The educational environment, therefore, must be considered as one manifestation existing within the boundaries of the urban activity systems. (See Figure 10.11.)

. . . Each person in a culture lives his life by moving from situation to situation, he builds his life up as a kind of necklace by stringing together those situations which are available to him in his culture. In a successful culture, the set of situations which is available to him is sufficient to allow all the inner forces which develop in him, free play. In order to criticize a culture, we must find in the lives of its members recurrent situations which expose the members to conflicts which they cannot resolve within the framework of the cultural institutions and situations that the culture normally makes available to them.[37]

[37]Christopher Alexander, "Major Changes in Environment Form Required by Social and Psychological Demands," *Ekistics*, **28**:79 (August 1969).

FIGURE 10.11

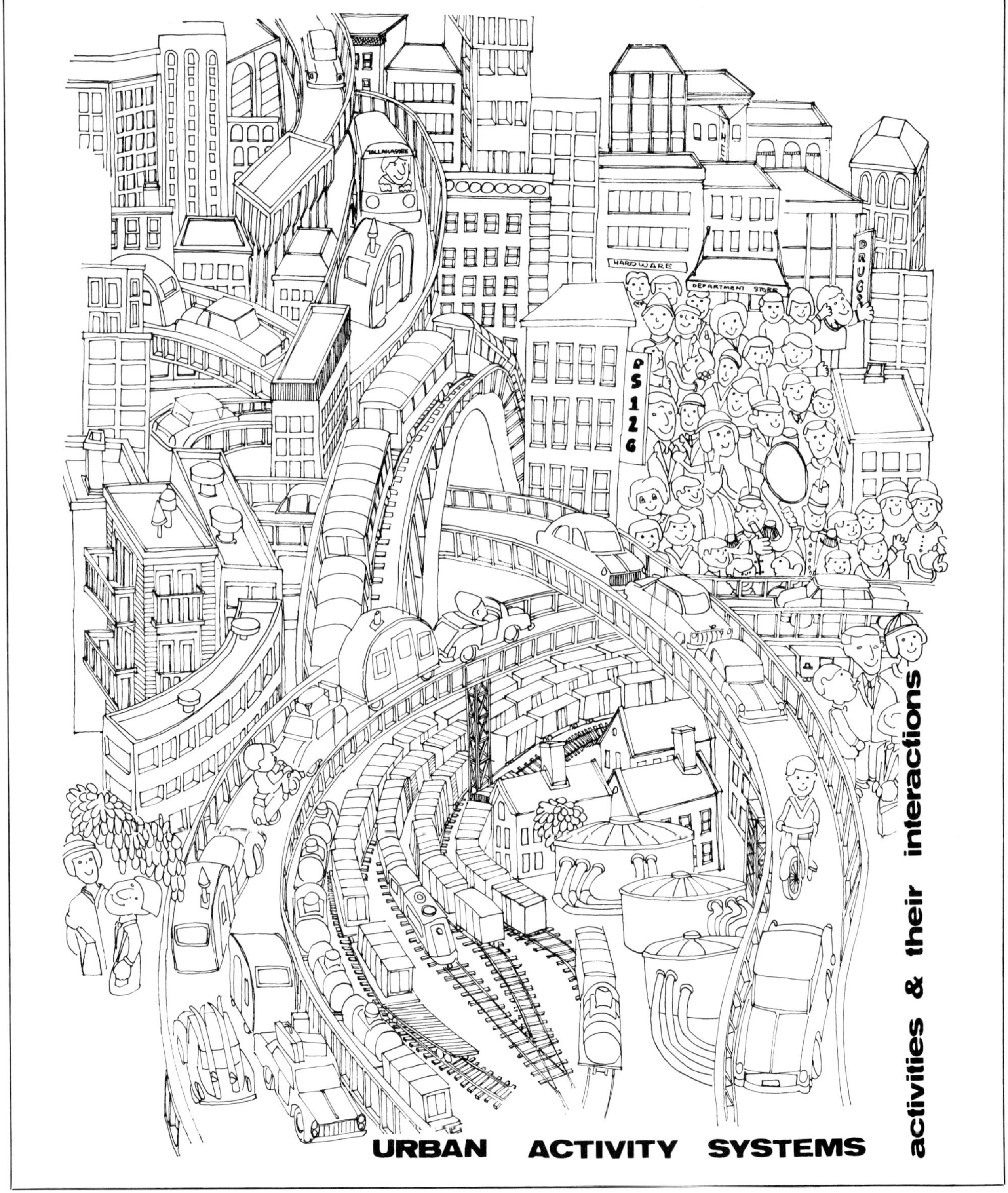
TALLAHASSEE
HARDWARE
DEPARTMENT STORE
DRUG
PS 126
URBAN ACTIVITY SYSTEMS
activities & their interactions

To determine which factors are effective and which ineffective, the educational planner must thoroughly analyze the total urban environment in which learning is to take place and use those physical components that aid the learning process. Planners and architects, in general, seek out standards and criteria of human stress as well as measures of human tolerance. (See Tables 10.2 and 10.3.) What is needed is a set of indices to measure exposure levels, to establish priorities, and to evaluate existing situations as various environmental factors change and influence the learners.[38] Only through subjective evaluation of the qualities of a given environment will the designer be able to design effectively an optimally functioning system. Such a system will allow educational activities to take place in harmony with other urban activities as learners move from one learning node to another node within the overall system.

Territoriality of place

In moving about, the learner is always a part of his environment. He is dependent on the environment for his basic biological needs; he is also dependent on the environment for his psychological and sociological cues. It is essential that he be considered a part of the environmental system. This has some profound implications for the educational environment, in which the learner is neither passive nor entirely active. The environment is not pouring information into him, nor is the learner completely active at all times in acquiring information. The continuous interaction between the individual and his environment is what constitutes an effective learning environment. Because identifying with the learning environment is critical to the student's effectiveness, the design of the educational environment should continuously affect the learner and also be affected by him. A dynamic learning environment is essential because familiarity causes the individual to accept cues automatically and be less perceptive of the environment. If the environment constantly changes, it will be more stimulating and challenging to the user.

[38]Richard A. Prindle, "The Health Aspects of the Urban Environment," *Ekistics,* **25**:430 (June 1968).

Within the larger scheme of things each individual tends to migrate toward his own little niche. "For every species of living organisms there is a particular pattern of environmental dimensions, corresponding to what is usually referred to as an ecological niche which represents its naturally selected match between circumstances and species schema."[39] (See Figure 10.12.) A niche might simply be the physical space required by a specific biological type, and might serve only the function of satisfying the organism's biological needs. On the other hand, the niche could refer to a place of aggregation where one individual functions within one system and where interactions among various groups and species also occur. Another view might be the specific behavioral patterns the individual develops and the territoriality required to permit those behavioral patterns to function effectively.

> Observations on territoriality and dominance . . . have thrown useful light on the physiological and behavioral effects that are likely to result from excessive crowding in human societies. In brief, there is much reason to believe that laying claim to a territory and maintaining a certain distance from one's fellow constitute biological needs that are probably as essential for man as they are for animals. However, the expressions of these needs are culturally conditioned. The distance considered proper between persons in a group varies from culture to culture. People reared in cultures where close contacts are good manners appear "pushy" to those belonging to social groups in which propriety demands greater physical separation. In contrast, the latter will appear to the former as behaving in a cold, aloof, withdrawn and standoffish manner.[40]

The suggestion of interpreting cultural cues related to territoriality emphasizes the general interaction of the individual in a social, psychological, and physiological system. Each group separately limits cues; the individual can differentiate the cues and does not receive input from the general environment. The educational profession, for example, is concerned primarily with the symbolic and formal cue systems associated with the cultural environment. The inter-

[39]S. B. Sills, "An Interactionist Looks at the Environment," *American Psychologist,* no. 11, **18**:701 (November 1963).

[40]René Dubos, "Promises and Hazards of Man's Adaptability," *Environmental Quality in a Growing Economy,* ed. Henry Jarrett (Baltimore: Johns Hopkins Press, 1966), p. 28.

Table 10.2 Human comfort zone

Environmental elements	Lower limit	Upper limit
Light	20 FC	100 FC
Atomic radiation	0 REM/year	0.2 REM/year
Noise	0 DB	85 DB
Mechanical vibration	0 CPS	1 CPS
	0 in	.005 in
Ventilation	13 cu. ft./min.	20 cu. ft./min.
Oxygen	15%	60%
Temperature } interrelated	65°F	75° F
Humidity } interrelated	30%	70%
Heat loss	330 BTU (rest)	1450 BTU (active)

Table 10.3

Feet	0	1	2	3	4	5	6	7	8	10	12	14	16	18	20	22	30
Vision Detailed vision (vis < of fove. A1°)	Vision blurred	Enlarged details-eyeballs, pores		Normal facial details-eyelashes	Hair seen			Lip movement visible			Face visible		Head bobbing visible		Distant vision		
Clear vision (vis < at macula 12°hor, 3°vert)		25″x3″ on eye nostrils or mouth	3.75″ x.94″ upper or lower face	6.25″ x1.60″ upper or lower face	10″x2.5″ upper or lower face or shoulders			20″x5′ 1 or 2 faces			31″x7′5″ faces of 2 people			4′2″x1′6″ torsos of 4 people			6′3″x1′7″ torsos of 4 or 5 people
60° Scanning		1/3 of face distorted	Face undistorted	Can't count fingers	Gestures seen			Whole body visible					Postural communication begins to be important				
Peripheral vision		Head against background	Head and shoulders	Finger movements seen	Whole body			Other people seen if present					Other people become important in peripheral vision				
Oral-aural		Whisper		Conventional voice							Loud voice			Full public			
Olfaction Breath Body odor Foot odor																	
Thermal Conduction Radiation																	
Kinesthesia Elbow room Elbow room Touching distance		1 Person	2 Persons	Outside													
Feet	0	1	2	3	4	5	6	7	8	10	12	14	16	18	20	22	30

SOURCE: Modified from "Chart showing interplay of the distant and immediate receptors in proxemic perception," in Edward T. Hall, *Hidden Dimension* (Garden City, New York: Doubleday & Company, Inc., 1966), pp. 119–120.

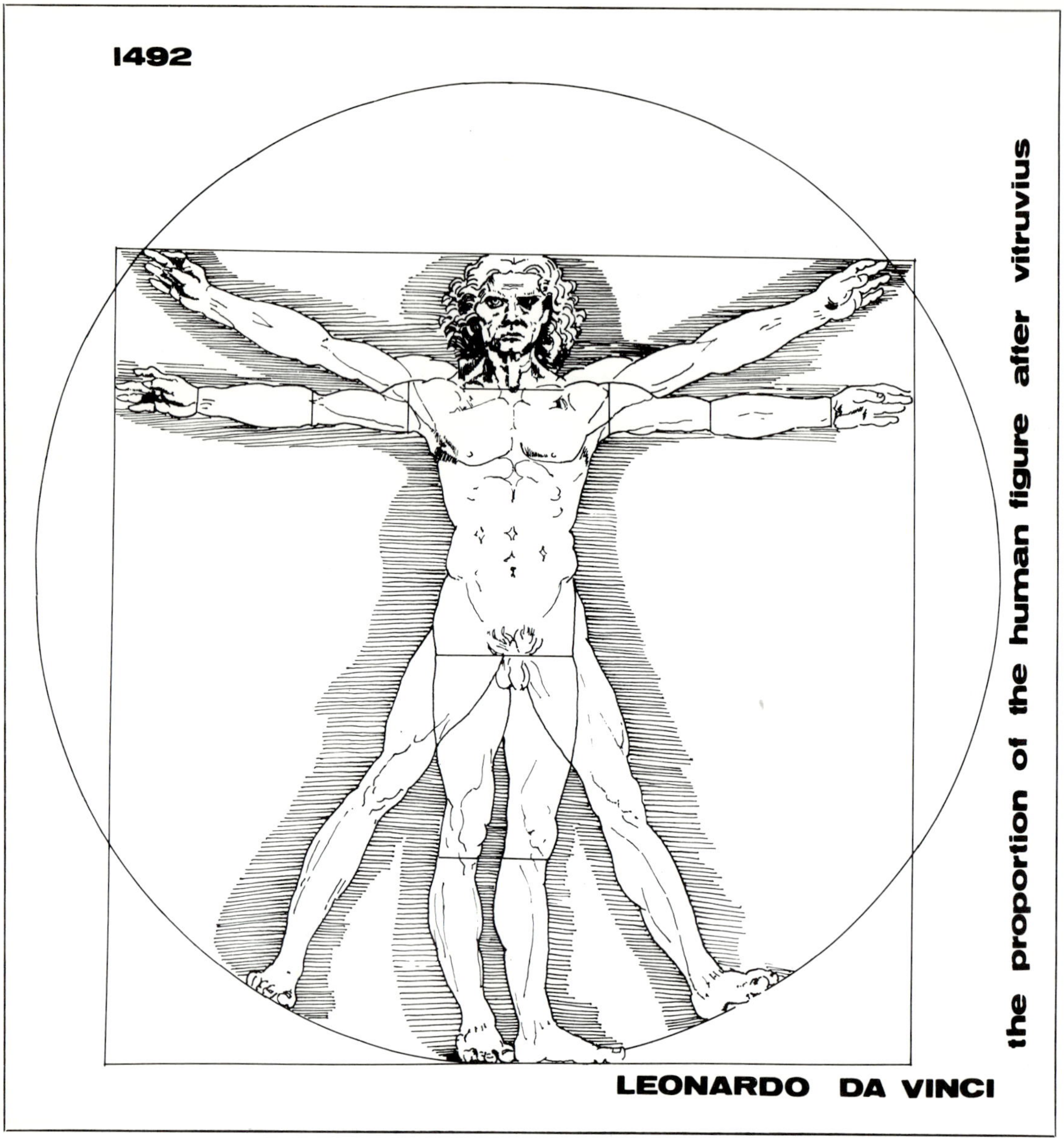
1492
the proportion of the human figure after vitruvius
LEONARDO DA VINCI

FIGURE 10.12

Table 10.4 Distance in man

Distance	Phase	
	Close	Far
Intimate	Physical contact	6″ to 18″
Personal	$1\frac{1}{2}$′ to $2\frac{1}{2}$′	$2\frac{1}{2}$′ to 4′
Social	4′ to 7′	7′ to 12′
Public	12′ to 25′	25′ or more

acting cultural, social, psychological, physical, and environmental factors complicate the concept of cues about one's territoriality. (See Table 10.4.) Emotional attachments and other determinants color one's interpretation of the cues limited by the environment. However, it is generally assumed that the individual develops a somewhat emotional detachment from his environment. He could not remain psychologically functional if he reacted to every cue on an emotional basis. An appropriate balance is desirable between emotional detachment to and detachment from the environment. The complexity of large urban areas with innumerable cues, where emotional detachment becomes excessive, creates an impersonal type of behavior that is also unfunctional. A desirable solution to excessive impersonalness is an interesting, changing environment that continuously captures the attention of interest of the learner yet does not permit over-emotional attachments to single long-term parts of the environment. Such an environment permits the expression of the strong territorial attachment without the overly emotional attachment to an unchanging, overly familiar set of cues.

The concept of territoriality denotes a basic drive to own or dominate a specific territory. This characteristic is quite common in all animals. Bird watchers have long observed the dominant behavior among birds who have staked out a specific territory. They show aggressive behavior as well as dominance and protectiveness.

Confinement studies of humans disclose many dominance phenomena. Examining the records of all aggressive acts between mental patients, Esser was able to discern a relatively stable dominance hierarchy. Replacements of patients as well as staff temporarily increase the number of aggressive acts and dominance displays. Changes in medication as well as clinical symptoms will move a patient up or down within the hierarchy. Altman and Haythorn studied pairs of sailors in confinement where the individuals gradually withdrew from one another or "cocooned" so that each person rigorously respected the zone of personal space around his neighbor. Pairs that were incompatible in terms of dominance, both sailors either very high or very low so that no easy accommodation was possible, adhered more rigorously to preferences for a particular bed, table or chair. If we accept the authors' operational definition of territoriality (the consistent use of particular beds, chairs, and table areas), there is an interesting parallel to the animal studies which show that both territoriality and dominance behavior are always maintaining a social order, and when one system cannot function, the other takes over.[41]

Much of the territoriality behavior is associated with a particular role that the individual assumes within that area. There is a tendency for people to test their roles continuously and move up the hierarchical dominance ladder whenever possible. These territoriality relationships are evident in fields where administrative positions are given high priorities. The level of administrative position may be completely unrelated to competence or contribution within the organization, yet positions and facilities are assigned according to a hierarchical structure. Education is particularly liable to this practice; administrators do not directly influence the academic program but they are given substantial preferential treatment over teachers, who do contribute to the system. To overcome this deficiency, educational planners must design learning territories that express the basic objective of the educational enterprise, that is, to locate and distribute learners', teachers', and administrators' territories in such a manner that appropriate educational experiences will naturally occur.

It has been observed by many investigators that people form emotional attachments to their homes and their neighborhoods. Urban planners and renewal experts have noticed that tearing down an old, established neighborhood and erecting new facilities often provoke a strong psychological trauma within the

[41]Robert Sommer, *Personal Space, The Behavioral Basis of Design* (Englewood Cliffs, N.J.: Prentice-Hall, 1969), p. 13.

residents of the area. It is difficult for most planners to understand the inhabitants' resistance to moving from shoddy surroundings into a newly developed area. This same phenomenon has been observed by educators and child psychologists, who have noted the difference between children's behavior when they are at home and away from home. Studies suggest that the high degree of mobility currently prevalent in American society may substantially annul or increase territorial identification.

The concept of territoriality has had a strong influence in Western society and its effects can be observed in many activities. Trespassing, or invading the property of the owner against his wishes, is punishable by law. The basic concept of territoriality is prevalent in the way we handle a specific piece of real estate, for example, the assurance which a title to property gives to the owner that this is his territory. This assurance to the possessor also extends into his psychological strivings for various roles as well as strivings for dominance within the social scheme. In a legal sense one need not necessarily own the property to assert his territorial rights but must merely be in possession of it. This requires specific definition because people may occupy the property and not be in possession of it; they may own it and not be in possession of it; they may be in possession of it and not own it. These possibilities indicate the necessity of distinguishing between the legal and the psychological concepts of territoriality.

The role of perception

Man views his environment in terms of his perceptual background. The forms, shapes, and masses have no particular meaning in themselves but become expressive only in the light of man's perceptual experiences. The environment *per se* has little significance to the learner until he is actively involved and interacting with that environment. As a learner involves himself with the environment, he interprets his own perceptual background and responds to continuous cues from the environment. Environmental interest depends on its relevance to him and the variety of experiences that it affords him. Every interaction with the environment is a complex event that involves psychological, physiological, biological, and social stimuli. "When people speak of a high quality of an environment vista, they often mean that the stimulus which it offers has led to a perception and accompanying response by the viewer which they regard as good for the viewee. The proper test is not the landscape itself but the response of whoever is stimulated by it."[42]

The role of environmental stimuli has been of interest to the psychology profession since its inception. However, even though an entire theory of psychology was based on the stimulus-response paradigm, psychologists have focused little attention on the role of the physical environment in behavior. Most psychologists theorize that behavior is conditioned by reward and punishments that are not given or affected by the environment. The fact that psychologists have been concerned primarily with the artificially imposed stimulus-response paradigm does not negate the very strong influence that environmental factors have on behavior. Studies that indicate the stimulus-response aspects of behavioral patterns can be found in the professional literature. Psychologists also acknowledge that man is an active learner who constantly seeks new stimuli and will look for situations that furnish stimulation to fill his own perceptual needs. Newness, complexity, intensity, and continuous variation are stimuli that fulfill man's need for change. Although man is a continuously adapting animal, it is paradoxical that at the same time he seeks out environmental stimuli that will subject his system to disequilibrium. Long-term adaptation results in boredom, whereas disassociation with the environment and continuous deprivation of environmental stimuli produce serious psychological trauma.

Man's responses to his environment and, specifically, to his perception of his environment, have been demonstrated in studies of sensory deprivation and

[42]Robert M. White, "Program Decisions in the Environmental Sciences," *Social Sciences and the Environment: Conference on the Present and Potential Contribution of the Social Sciences to Research and Policy Formulation in the Quality of the Physical Environment*, ed. Morris C. Garnsey and James R. Hibbs (Boulder: University of Colorado Press, January 31, February 1–2, 1967), p. 111.

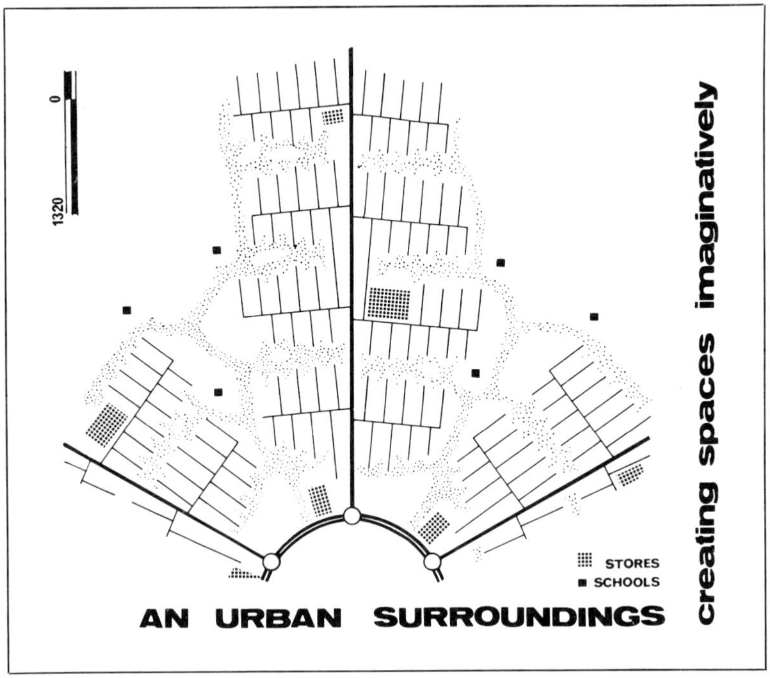

FIGURE 10.13

more casual studies involving visitors at exhibits who tend to move a little faster or slower depending on the decreasing or increasing visual inventory. Behavior, of course, is a complex phenomenon and depends on various experiences as well as one's psychological makeup. "A competent inquiry into the problems of mind and milieu can . . . not be limited to the study of mental performance and physical behavior. It must also try to penetrate the domain of our emotions."[43] (See Figure 10.13.)

PREVAILING PATTERNS AND TRENDS IN MOVEMENTS

Movements in general

One of the first steps toward a scientific trend in studying motion began with Galileo's study of falling bodies. Since that time the study of motion has produced mathematical tools, such as the calculus, that have been decisive in shaping our present environments. Today, people, objects, messages, and energy are cast in an orbiting web of activities moving from node to node.

These mobile configurations are no more revealing than those movements in an urban environment. (See Figure 10.14.) Traffic grows and disintegrates, traffic changes shapes and sizes, and traffic's position relative to itself never is the same. (See Figure 10.15.) However, the individual still attempts to perceive his environment as constant and stable.

Movements saturate the individual's urban experiences. Each day, students begin their learning experiences with motion by merely having to travel to a center of learning. Yet these experiences are never made a part of the educational program, formally or informally. As a result many individuals are not aware of clutter, congestion, and hazards.

Congestion, however, is really not a modern problem; it has existed in urban areas for a considerable period of time. "Ancient Rome had such serious

[43]A. E. Parr, "Psychological Aspects of Urbanology," *Journal of Social Issues,* no. 4, **22**:44 (October 1966).

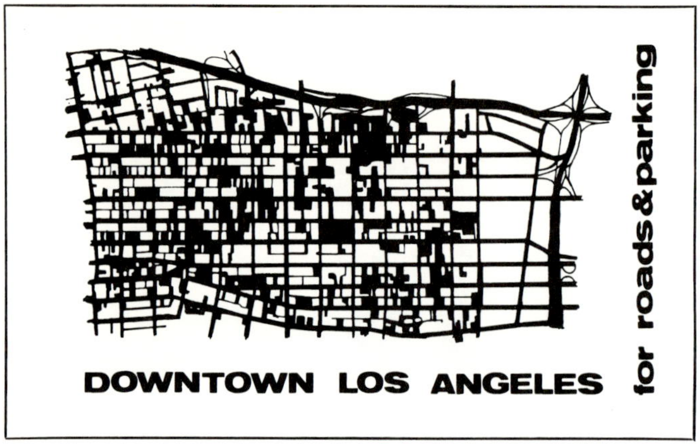

FIGURE 10.14

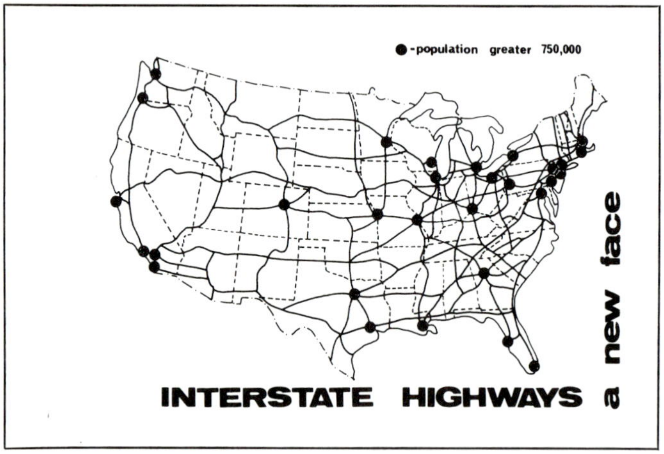

FIGURE 10.15

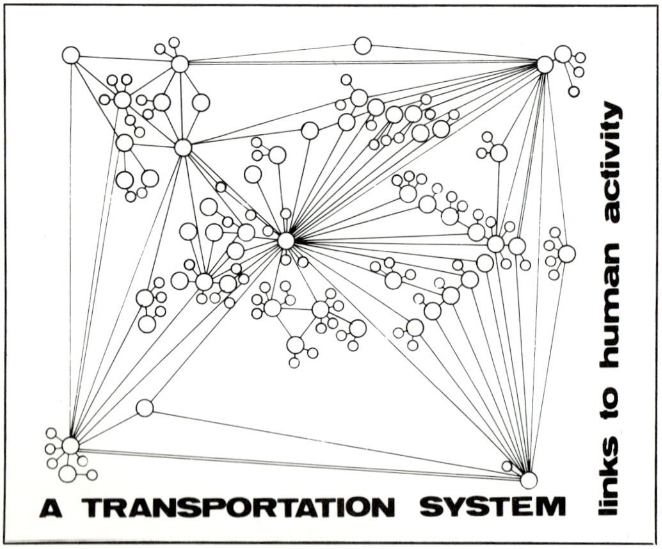

FIGURE 10.16

traffic jams that all except public vehicles were banned from the downtown streets during daylight hours."[44] Even in the Victorian period the air

> . . . was blue from the exchange of vituperation between drivers contending for the limited space and was rendered pungent by the universal use of the horse as a source of power. Blue and pungent air is now supplied by exhaust vapor, but the competition for space continues—albeit with more sophisticated conveyances than in times gone by.[45]

Today these conditions are more prevalent than ever, yet too many school programs have not solved the problem of movement.

The study of motion has been largely neglected. (See Figure 10.16). As a result, planners have by and large ignored the study of movements except for a few transportation planners and a few educational planners who have been concerned with school bus routes. Yet, no thought is given to the educational values of motion, lessons such as the awareness, the understanding, and the mastery of elements in motion. The learner, or any individual, selects and organizes his perceptual environment through his physical senses. He does so for purposes of orientation, or for more effective use of the signs of his environments for the purpose of increasing his margin of safety while moving. He does this through his visual, kinesthetic, tactile, and auditory senses. He applies them to such measures as velocity, direction, and distance. The more correlation there is among these sensory cues and measures the more efficient his motion becomes and the more effectively he sees, hears, and touches while dawdling, strolling, walking, stepping, hopping, running, climbing, or driving.

Motion clarifies the environment. It leaves telltale signs. Ruts in the road, trees bent by the wind, the school bus's arriving, the laughter of approaching students, or the sounds of a marching band leave cues for mastering the environment.

Today, many movements are regulated: students walking down corridors at 8:55, 9:55, 10:55, 11:55 and so on; school buses five days a week, morning and afternoon, stopping and starting at the same spots almost at the same times are a few of many expected patterns. These added to other movements of the urban complex have created confusion, delays, temper flare-ups, and increased costs.

Trends, nevertheless, are developing toward bringing a small measure of order to movements. Knitting together the different movement systems (walking, slow speed, high speed, private, public, and special) is being tried in such new towns as Cumbernault, Scotland. These towns are proving that forethought and understanding can eliminate cost. The present isolation of school bus systems from urban transit systems, the lack of pedestrian ways to and from schools and other community centers, the noisy expressways adjacent to the school, and the screeching jets overhead are major disrupters of the learning process. These situations are forcing the educational planner whether he wishes to or not to join with other planners to help find answers for the problems of urban movements.

The rigid barriers that once separated educational planners from discussion about urban affairs are disappearing. The improvement of education and the improvement of movement are not isolated phenomena but are integrally tied at many points. The educational planner will be required to know what transportation technology is offering (Starcar, Hovercraft, Carrell Mobile, and so on) in terms of urban travel patterns, model choice, terminal problems, trip generation models, trip distribution models, and traffic assignment. (See Figure 10.17.)

Some principles related to movement

To help the educational planner understand movement patterns and trends some basic principles of transportation planning developed by Marvin Mannheim follow:

Principle 1

"The basic components of a transportation system are (a) the persons and things being transported; (b) the vehicles in which they are conveyed; and (c) the

[44] George M. Smerk (ed.), "Urban Mass Transport at the Ebb," *Readings in Urban Transportation*, George M. Smerk (ed.) (Bloomington: Indiana University Press, 1968), p. 3.

[45] Ibid.

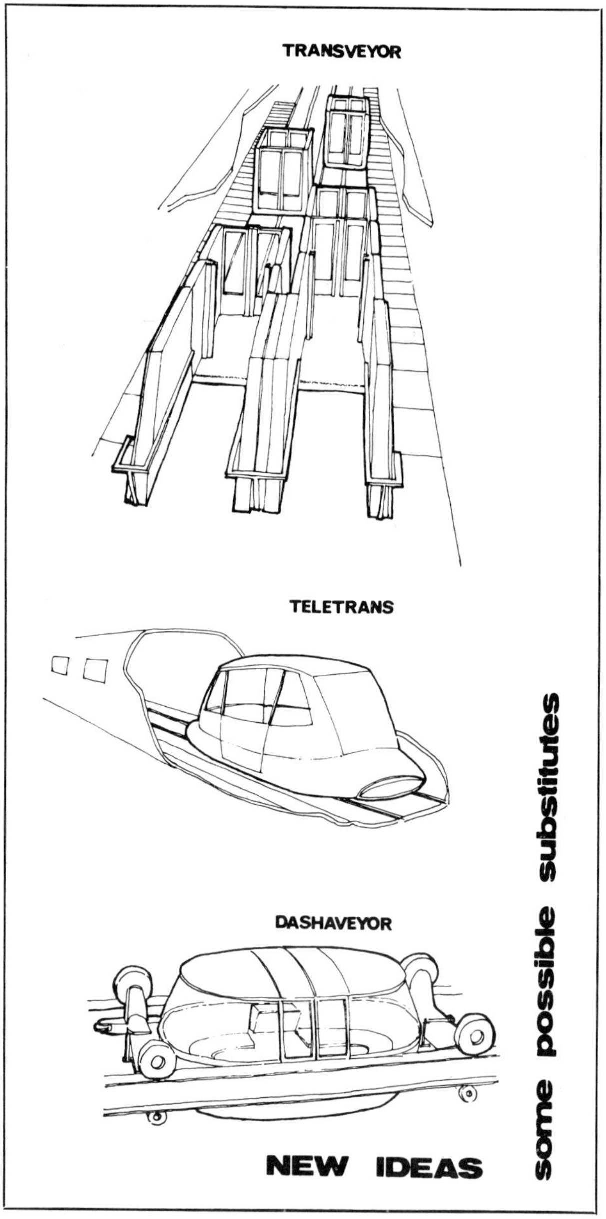

FIGURE 10.17

networks through which the vehicles move." This principle describes the transportation systems as a set of vehicles that are responsible for moving people or items between two nodes through a fixed network. The network is a set of various nodes, which are fixed facilities, and links, which are the connectors between the fixed facilities. The links may be rail lines or airways or sidewalks. This principle is helpful in transportation analysis because it describes transportation as an integrated system and gives the planner a basis for his study.

Principle 2

"All movements through the transportation system must be considered." The transportation system will indeed include a number of different types of persons and things and, therefore, the purposes of the movements will vary substantially. Any consideration of the transit system must carefully analyze the components of the system according to the use to which the system is to be put.

Principle 3

"Movements must be considered from their initial origin to their final destination." A transportation system is an integrated system encompassing diverse components. Rather than concentration on a subset of the system, all the transportation facilities must be efficient. This principle becomes increasingly important when various modes of travel are linked into one system.

Principle 4

"All modes of transportation must be considered." This is an extension of the prior principle.

Principle 5

A transportation system is a particular form of market in which supply and demand reach equilibrium within the constraining channels of the transportation network. Specifically: (a) a number of levels of service variables are necessary to define the interaction between supply and demand; (b) the volume, composition, and time dependency of the demand for transportation depend upon the level of service at which transportation is supplied; (c) the level of service supplied by a transportation system depends for given resource inputs upon the volume, composition, and time variation of demand; and (d) determining the level of service at which supply and demand are in equilibrium in a particular context is usually computationally difficult because of the complexity of the transportation network and of the transportation demand.

This principle calls attention to the primary variables of a transportation system: the time, safety, comfort, and convenience of and the cost to the traveler.

Principle 6

The spectrum of transportation options potentially available include (a) routing and time schedule for a particular trip or shipment; (b) systems operations, including routing and scheduling of vehicles, pricing, and types of services offered; (c) changes in non-fixed resources such as vehicle characteristics and availabilities, and procurement of new equipment; (d) changes in fixed facilities, such as link and node characteristics, and network structure; and (e) introduction of basically new transportation technologies including vehicles, fixed facilities and operating policies.

Here attention is called to the various options open to the decision makers when considering a metropolitan transportation system.

Principle 7

"Transportation is not an end in itself." Illustrations of broader objectives for transportation might include stimulating economic growth, channeling the population into a specific region, or serving a market objective.

Principle 8

"There are a variety of transportation-related options available; particularly important are those which can influence directly or indirectly the demand for transportation." Transportation planning must be a component integrated into overall urban planning. Because transportation is not an end in itself, it must be integrated into the overall urban system.

Principle 9

"There is a spectrum of direct and indirect impacts of transportation [systems] relevant to the choice among alternative systems and policies." The choice of a transportation system might influence such factors as dollar costs associated with capital investments, vehicles purchased within an area, the economic growth of the sector and residential spread or relocation. The planner must acknowledge the impact of a system on a population and must also choose the one that will best benefit the area.[46]

PREVAILING PATTERNS AND TRENDS IN ECONOMICS

Basic urban economic issues are tremendously important for the educational planner; they are wide-ranging, complex, and lacking in baseline data. Because the decision-making apparatus for handling these problems has not been effectively developed, the organizational problems that contribute to inefficiency are manifold.

The economic problem of organization is that of allocating numerous kinds of tasks, symbol manipulating as well as physical, to numerous transformers arranged in a complex yet efficient network (such as in an urban community). And further complications, of a different kind, arise when a single organizer is replaced by several. Their beliefs and utilities are not the same. They engage in a non-constant sum game. The economist's problem is then shifted from the search for optimality to the search for stability: he tries to explain, as does the biologist or anthropologist, why certain arrangements, certain allocations of tasks and incentives (rewards) have a greater chance to survive over a given period than other arrangements, and under what conditions.

The criterion of survival, viability, stability guides the social scientist who describes, and tries to explain, the existing institutions. Yet not everything that is stable is desirable. Some wicked dictatorships have been quite stable. Along with the stability criterion the economist uses a weak collective optimality criterion, a modest common denominator on which people might agree in spite of their divergent utilities and beliefs: an arrangement of tasks and incentives is optimal in this modest sense if there is no feasible

[46]Marvin L. Mannheim, "Principles of Transport System Analysis," *Highway Research Record No. 180,* National Research Council Publication 1511 (Washington, D.C.: Highway Research Board, 1967), pp. 12–17.

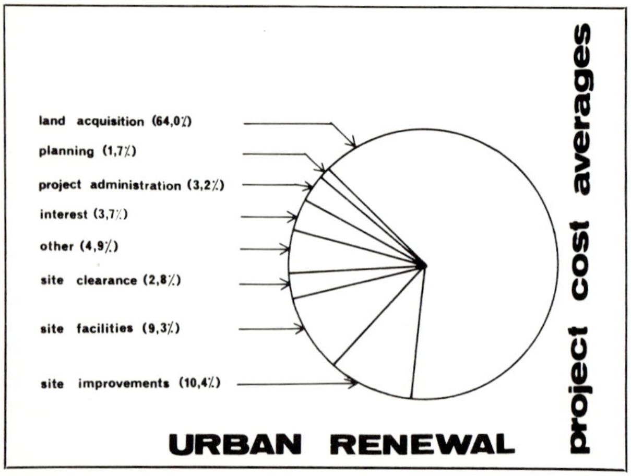

FIGURE 10.18

arrangement that would be better or at least not worse for all members of the organization (such as members of an urban community).

What then if we consider the whole society as an organization? How should incentives and tasks be allocated in a way that is stable or is collectively optimal, or if possible both. Further, some of us cannot help but smuggle in our own values, in particular a high valuation of liberty and equity. I suppose "public policy," "public good" in our tradition, means somehow to reconcile the criteria of stability and of collective optimality with those of liberty and equity. Though the economic theorist prefers to hide behind the technical term "welfare economics," he means not just—the Department of Health, Education and Welfare but much more, the whole public policy. Nor is our special concern only education, even if taken in the broad sense of the communication of what my chart calls "data," to the whole or some parts of the public. For research, inquiry has been also our concern here. Public policy problems in the field of symbol manipulation are crudely exemplified by questions such as "When, if at all, should the government subsidize or protect research and teaching and the dissemination of news?"[47]

The educational planner along with his fellow planners must be able to coordinate the diverse activities in the urban setting and to guide various kinds of activities for the best possible results. Economic order is described

... as a circumset of an institution. Examples of such institutions are private enterprises, public enterprises, markets, social insurance schemes, tax systems, monetary systems and the hierarchies of public authorities. Institutions in turn are characterized by certain rules of conduct or as instruments of the society's economic policy. Examples are tax rates and social insurance benefits. Apart from the static concept of an optimal order there is a continual process of striving for or managing the optimal order which we usually call economic policy.[48]

The role of urban renewal

One set of important economic policies that has become a continuing process is urban renewal. (See Figure 10.18.) It generally is a traumatic experience for a community because it normally occurs under involuntary circumstances. When an area requires urban renewal, the society was either unable or unwilling to maintain or renovate the area: the renewal process is thrust on both owner and tenant. Renewal also involves public and private interests, and both must be considered in such areas as zoning codes, clearance problems, and the relocation of people. (See Figure 10.19.) Because urban renewal projects influence people's lives for years in the future, appropriate studies should be made to ensure that the project will be effective. Many public meetings should be held for all those with vested interests of any kind so that compromise may be made among the conflicting interests. Because urban renewal is made necessary by problems that have not been effectively resolved, planners have an opportunity to capitalize on the past mistakes of a region and to avoid them in the future.

Essentially, the urban renewal problem is one of appropriate land use that reconciles conflicting public and private interests. Urban renewal affords the planner an opportunity to design comprehensive schemes involving various activity systems and to do this through advance planning instead of allowing

[47]Jacob Marschak, "Economics of Inquiring, Communicating, Deciding," *American Economic Review. Papers and Proceedings of the 80th Annual Meeting of the American Economic Association,* Washington, D.C., December 28–30, 1967, **58**:16–17 (May 1968).

[48]J. Tinbergen, "Planning Economic Western Europe," *International Encyclopedia of the Social Sciences,* **12**:103 (1968).

FIGURE 10.19

(a) Reclaimed land, (b) Historical preservation,
(c) New housing required, (d) New community center

haphazard growth. By forcing planners to act as general designers rather than building designers, renewal projects are focusing planners' attention in new directions. They must look at the physical setting and the present physical structures and must reuse and revitalize some structures, such as historical buildings, that must be integrated into the new fabric of a planned community. The physical settings in American cities is somewhat different from those in Europe, where areas heading toward decay may contain *many* historical monuments and structures that must be retained. In the United States the slum area is usually deteriorating tenement housing and in many cases the area can be completely redesigned from the ground up, especially by the construction of schools, cultural centers, housing, and business and industrial facilities.

The generation of new tax money has contributed greatly to the revitalization of the central cities. For years, residents have been fleeing to the suburbs, leaving the central city with low income residents and major tax problems. Successful urban renewal, e.g., Baltimore's Charles Center and Pittsburgh's Golden Triangle, has contributed substantially to the solution of renewing. It should be remembered by both planners and city officials that the ultimate objective of urban renewal is to create a better environment for the citizens of the area. The motives of persons responsible for urban renewal are not always clear. Because the objective of urban renewal is the welfare of the people, the rewards for assisting the decision-making apparatus are not always as clear-cut as the profit-making motives of a business enterprise. The magnitude of vested interests also complicates the decision-making process; urban renewal projects may be bogged down for years in political bickering by various interest groups. Fortunately, however, as urban renewal projects become more common, appropriate procedures are beginning to take form, and the tragic mistakes of the early urban renewal projects are not being repeated.

As time has gone by there has been a greater emphasis on the local direction of urban renewal projects. Federal funds have become more plentiful and the idea of matching funds more liberally interpreted. In 1965 a further expansion of urban development by the federal government was initiated by the Public Works and Economic Development Act. The act was designed to be more comprehensive than previous legislation and to integrate the various levels of activity of a given community in the formulation of long-range plans. In addition to providing direct grants, the act also included manpower-training assistance as well as incentives for business and industry to locate in central-city areas. Throughout the development of federal participation in these projects, however, the type of participation has remained the same: the federal government has furnished technical assistance to aid local communities in planning their urban development projects. This aid has taken four basic forms:

> . . . (1) capital grants for the execution of renewal plans and for research in renewal; (2) loans to assist in the planning and execution of renewal projects; (3) insurance and purchase of mortgages on property in renewal areas and on property necessary for relocation of persons displaced by renewal; and (4) provision of technical assistance.[49]

Income, employment, and culture

Frequently considerable stress is placed on income and employment in determining or defining distressed areas. But a more sophisticated yardstick of unemployment rates is needed to qualify an area for redevelopment.

> The concept of differentials may be retained to measure relative distress, but the basis of comparison should be changed from a national to a metropolitan regional yardstick. Furthermore, the focus of the differentials should be broadened to include gaps in living standards and in other measures of economic and social progress. Designation should be primarily based on an examination of historic patterns, including differences in quantifiable indices like wage rates, incomes, housing, school achievement rates and unemployment rates. It should also take into account the intangible and unquantifiable elements which tend to be responsible for measurable symptoms of distress.[50]

[49]Wilton S. Sogg and Warren Wertheimer, "Legal and Governmental Issues in Urban Renewal," *Urban Renewal: The Record and the Controversy,* ed. James Q. Wilson (Cambridge, Mass.: M.I.T. Press, 1967), p. 129.

[50]Melvin R. Levin, "New Criteria for Redevelopment Areas," *Land Economics,* **49**:25 (February 1968).

The problems of areas being considered for redevelopment are usually so profound that popular statistics indicate vast cultural, economic, and social-psychological problems within the depressed area. Therefore,

> . . . the tasks confronting the redevelopment areas involve priority efforts to attack the lingering problems of hard core unemployment and sub-employment. But equally important, it must be recognized that it is vital to achieve a profound transformation of redevelopment area physical and cultural patterns. Unless this is done, the distressed area problem will remain a permanent affliction.[51]

The predicaments of a resident within a redevelopment area are myriad. For example, such a person

> . . . often suffers from a self-reinforcing pattern of substandard education, substandard wages and substandard physical environment. There is a danger that persistent economic, social and cultural disparities will create a self-reinforcing, two societies pattern with one type of area enjoying the full benefits of technological and cultural progress while the disadvantaged area lumbers along in the rear, only very slowly reducing the gulf which separates it from its neighbors.[52]

Unhappily, the gap that separates the culturally deprived person from the other end of society's spectrum is not being closed, and the disparity is becoming greater. Planners must be aware of this disparity and take deliberate actions that will benefit those people who are divorced from the cultural offerings of American society.

The problems associated with urban renewal are basically the problems associated with new employment patterns and a consequent improvement in educational offerings. There is a need for a more comprehensive systems approach to the problem of urban renewal. It must consider the many interacting and interrelated activity systems associated with a given area. A community renewal program

> . . . requires that the entire city be analyzed in all its functioning aspects . . . the community renewal program must concern itself with commercial and industrial facilities and with their potential growth or decline, with public improvements which will be necessary to preserve the downtown commercial core, with ways to raise the earning capacity of low-income groups, and with those amenities which are best calculated to regain a high percentage of middle-income families.[53]

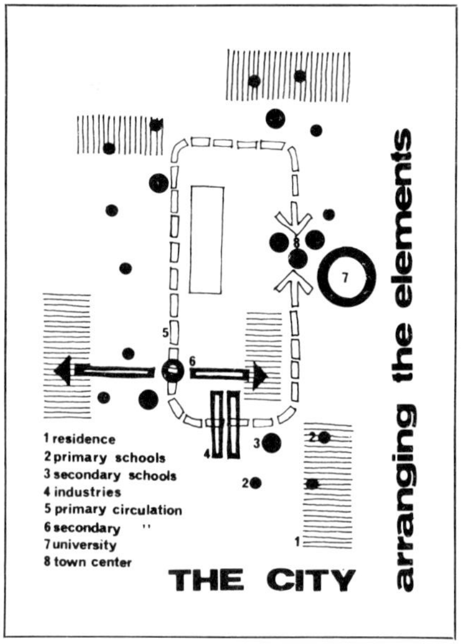

FIGURE 10.20

Some problems are associated with urban design. All aspects of the community must be subjected to appropriate analysis to provide a better understanding of the activities involved in the community and an appropriate solution. (See Figure 10.20.)

> Emphatically, public leadership provides the indispensable ingredient in achieving good urban design. . . . No fact comes through more clearly from visiting with hundreds of renewal and governmental officials, and walking through scores of projects, than the central importance of a deep personal commitment to good design.
>
> Good design costs more than mediocre and bad designs. Perhaps not in terms of increased construction costs, but certainly good design costs much more in terms of the time, energy, concern and commitment of designers.[54]

The design being referred to here is not restricted to the design of specific structures; the entire region of

[51]Ibid., p. 34.

[52]Ibid.

[53]Cyril C. Herrmann, "Systems Approach to City Planning." *Harvard Business Review*, no. 5, **44:**72–73 (September/October 1966).

[54]Roger Montgomery, "Aesthetics in Urban Renewal." *Journal of Housing*, no. 11, **22:**602 (December 1964).

development is part of the design—the social as well as the physical aspects of the buildings and the integration of the two. The design plans are

> . . . active instruments of public policy that unify responsibility and guide actions by the various agencies and individuals associated with redevelopment and rehabilitation. Design plans show through verbal statements, drawings, diagrams, models and similar means, the design objectives for a project or an area. They should exhibit built-in flexibility. The degree of detail must vary with the situation in which they are used.
>
> . . . design provides the structure on which all else depends. It forms an armature at once place-setting and pervasive. Public works design sets a standard for private action. It forms a network that can knit together the parts of an area into an articulate and handsome whole.[55]

The role of policy

Policy stems from many decisions made at all levels of planning and executing urban renewal. The ultimate solution of all internal conflicts determines policy. Policies associated with buildings and their condition and with property values and property, and policies that affect the available municipal services must be explicit enough to allow proper decision making.

Policy should certainly give careful consideration to the people who are to live in the area. Their willingness and ability to pay the taxes on and to live in the redeveloped area must be ascertained; if the policy associated with the renewal actually meets the needs of the area, it must also meet the general requirements of the larger urban area of which it is a part. Zoning influences policy because zoning laws can profoundly affect the future development of the urban renewal area. Sometimes areas can be rezoned to fit project plans, but often it is necessary to modify the plans to fit existing zoning. Zoning policy is usually relevant to urban renewal areas and to the adjacent territory. If the zoning ordinances are to be waived or changed, the effects on the adjacent and surrounding areas must be examined. In the last analysis it is necessary to follow the principles laid down by the common law; good common sense and reasonable decisions must be used to determine effective and efficient policies.

A certain amount of social engineering has been employed in urban renewal projects, primarily by the redistribution of the resources. If profitable development programs are accomplished through private enterprise, there is very little need for federal government subsidies. However, where local facilities are not adequate, the federal government is justified in assisting by reallocating resources in either business or housing. The redistribution of resources can be direct or indirect; it can subject some people to heavier taxes in order to redistribute their income among poor people. Another kind of redistribution is the financing of public housing, which assures the person in need of better housing.

Several arguments have been put forth for the allocation of funds for urban renewal, such as "market-measured gains exceed market-measured costs, but market imperfections prevent private action."[56] Inertia, ignorance, uncertainty, and dealing in small parcels are common causes of real-estate-market imperfections.

> The values of most properties are greatly influenced by their surroundings. Unless the latter are also changed, the highest re-use value potential cannot be realized and private renewal will not take place. If the whole area is renewed, however, new land uses can be attracted which will result in an entirely new set of environmental linkages and re-use values.[57]

There are ways for a community to overcome natural inertia. One way for the public to acquire property is through eminent domain. This should be a last resort, but if no other way is found to accomplish the renewal, then eminent domain is justifiable. This concept is also applicable to public assistance; if the good of the community outweighs the problems involved in acquiring the land, then public action is justified. Renewal does, however, affect the private sector because renewal will enhance the adjacent land.

Several possibilities exist regarding the impact of

[55]Ibid., p. 603.

[56]R. H. Schaaf, "Public Policies in Urban Renewal: An Economic Analysis of Justifications and Effects," *Land Economics*, **40:**69 (February 1964).

[57]Ibid.

renewal on the allocation of resources. Among them are the following:

> . . . the private profitability conditions for renewal are satisfied. This means that the postrenewal occupants are willing to outbid the prerenewal occupants for the use of the site by enough to absorb the entire depreciation replacement cost of the prerenewal improvements. The improvement in land use more than offsets the wastes of clearance and net resource allocation has been improved at least by the yardstick of private market criteria.
>
> . . . The past renewal users are willing to outbid the prerenewal users for the cleared site, but only after it has been cleared. Renewal improves the allocation of land resources but not by an amount equal to the depreciated replacement cost of the renewal improvements. If the prerenewal improvements are socially unacceptable, however, their destruction does not represent a social waste of resources and the improvement in land uses could justify clearance.
>
> . . . The prerenewal users would, in theory, outbid all others for the use of the site following clearance. The difficulties of reproducing the old buildings and the many complexities and controls that attend the resale process normally mean that new uses will take over the renewal areas following clearance. Under the conditions in this third situation, however, the prerenewal occupants are the most efficient users of the site and renewal has resulted in a misallocation of land resources.[58]

Frequently urban renewal has unanticipated effects beyond the immediate use of the changed environment. It may create a new *esprit de corps* within the urban area that will hasten other improvements and developments. The side benefits frequently far exceed expectations—increased efficiency in movement, increased aesthetic appeal of the environment, and increased elimination of areas of tension resulting from slum clearance. These characteristics are difficult to measure, but the effects are observable. The changing market conditions that result from renewal projects frequently stimulate additional business, which causes greater expenditures and further economic benefits.

Frequently disadvantages accrue as part of renewal projects. When substantial shelters are removed, additional burdens are added to the building industry and prices may rise. Thus another economic factor that was not considered in the original planning must be considered. However, because the renewal process merely speeds up the natural decaying operation, the buildings are removed at a more appropriate time and urban renewal expedites a process already under way.

Under most circumstances, there are several prime motives for initiating an urban renewal project. Some of the obvious benefits to be derived include: building or rebuilding a section of the city that has degenerated, affording better land use and improving revenue sources. The magnitude of urban renewal in such large metropolitan areas as Boston is impressive. In the past seven years over one-half billion dollars in new construction has been completed, is under construction, or is on the drawing board in Boston. Greater stress has been placed on the commercial than on the housing aspects in many areas of our cities. Pressures are increasing in the political, economic, social, and technological spheres to enhance urban renewal and restoration. An increasing amount of activity is involving both public and private sectors, and much of the emphasis today is coming from the demands of slum residents, who for years have had no interest in their environment and who are only now becoming sensitive to the opportunities and responsibilities of the neighborhood in which they live.

General considerations

The availability of services to be used on the land influences land cost in terms of both basic economics and purchaser satisfaction. In considering environmental influences undesirable and unsatisfying activities, services, and improvements should be scrutinized; a school should not be located near an airline flight pattern or other source of loud noise that would constantly irritate or disrupt learning activities. Expressways and other structures that divide a school's site should be analyzed, and thought should be given to the possibility and cost of going either over or under the dividing structure to give integrity to the site. Inconvenience and convenience are also important and are related to the problem of economics. It has

[58] Ibid., pp. 70–71.

been indicated that the greater the distance from the central city the lower the land values; this decrease in land values is a curve that follows a negative exponential form. One variable shows the interdependence of satisfaction and economics: the greater the distance the more expensive the transportation. But transportation is a nuisance factor as well as a cost and convenience factor, illustrating negative effects on both satisfaction and costs.

There are other factors besides basic economics and satisfaction, of course, that influence land values. For example, the public good might require that a certain piece of land undergo condemnation proceedings and the right of eminent domain may prevail over the desires of a landowner. Landowners, knowing that a schoolboard has become interested in a tract of land for a new school, have placed exorbitant prices on the land, forcing the schoolboard to go to the courts to condemn the land for acquisition. The same situation often arises in the acquiring of land for highways when government officials have projected the location of a thoroughfare. Owners, disagreeing with the evaluation of the price of the land, have been taken to court and the property has been condemned and purchased at a fair market price. The more common way to establish land prices is free, open bidding on the open market. The seller attempts to get the maximum price for his land and the purchaser tries to pay a minimum. The assumption is that the buyer and the seller have complete information about the land in the area and bid accordingly. This, in effect, is a form of auction, the land going to the highest bidder.

Another economic concept, discussed by Bettelheim, is the concept of economic conjunctives, a form of forecasting, which relates in advance the future economic situation. It is based on present objective data from which the future development is projected. However, it only forecasts; it does not influence economic factors.[59] Although both planning and conjunctives imply a preliminary operation of forecasting, conjunctive analysis considers economic activity as developing spontaneously. In fact, economy evolves in accordance with its own laws ". . . by virtue of an inner determinism, a necessity. . . ."[60] Planning, on the other hand, assumes that the economy may be influenced by the action of men. But economic planning by no means interferes with free economy and personal freedom. Public planning should be as much a part of the urban environment as individual corporate planning. Because a corporate enterprise would never proceed without relatively clear-cut goals and objectives, haphazard development in urban areas is an even greater folly.

PREVAILING PATTERNS AND TRENDS IN ACTIVITIES

The study of educational activity systems should logically follow a study of the activities of learners, their spatial distribution within the urban environment, and their relationship with other urban systems, such as

> . . . the physical systems of various interrelated land uses and transportation; economic and social systems; communication and political systems. These systems, both tangible and intangible, interact with each other and are in a constant state of flux. A major change in any one of these systems may have direct and eventually indirect repercussions on the others.[61]

The separate consideration of each of the systems mentioned by McConnell leaves the total resources required essentially fragmented. To overcome this fragmentation a new systematic approach—the activity system—has been developed to provide links among the diverse resources, for example, among people, their activities, and their places. Integrating these with the social structure has helped to make regular and routine these activities as well as provide a factual basis around which physical features can be built. The keys to such an approach are interactions, communications, and linkages.

> Linkages between parts of a system change in response to economic determinants; and increasingly the physical

[59]Charles Bettelheim, *Studies in the Theory of Planning,* reprinted (New York: Asia Publishing House, 1961), p. 3.

[60]Ibid., p. 5.

[61]Shean McConnell, "Urban Systems," *Official Architecture and Planning,* no. 11, **32**:1376 (November 1969). Architecture and Planning Publications, London.

planner must understand the economic systems that affect the activity systems he is seeking to influence. The physical planner can no longer ignore the workings of the market and the pursuit of profit, since these activities impinge only too obviously on all the activity systems. . . . Furthermore, the economic factors that affect so many personal, institutional and commercial decisions tend to be influenced by the efficient or inefficient operation of the publicly controlled communications systems. . . . This line of reasoning leads quickly to the political need for decision-making and illustrates the close interaction of planning and political theories; and incidentally takes us from spatial interaction to political interaction.[62]

The educational planner of the past has been unable to assess the extent of the basic changes in urban educational needs and ". . . to anticipate the space-related kinds of activities and persons and institutions which are likely to be dominant . . . in the future."[63] But with the study of activity patterns, which are constantly changing in scale, organization, linkages, and groupings, better theories may ultimately result in improved facilities for urban education.

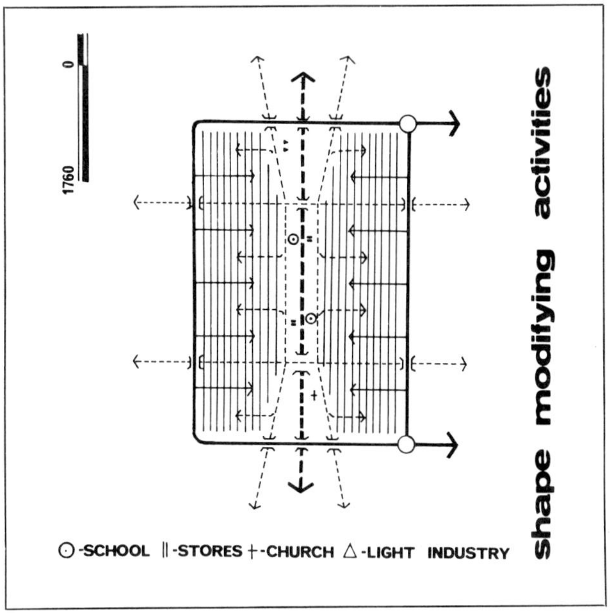

FIGURE 10.21

The concept of educational activity systems

An educational activity system may be thought of as an organized pattern of behavior involving a set of people who are bound together by a common goal. The activity system might focus on cultural, economic, social, or recreational events. It is a subset of a larger pattern of activity systems. (See Figure 10.21.)

Activity, stripped of all paraphernalia, is essentially a learner's means to an end, or ends. Seldom, however, does he attempt to come face to face with why he is engaged in that activity. In many cases he has no tools for such a task.

Consideration of a system of interrelated activities, involves attention being applied to each aspect of the activity. A person writing, for example,

> . . . requires a pencil, paper, desk, floor, chair, light, proper clothing, weather protection, relative quiet, tolerable temperature, freedom from annoying odors. These elements basically form the . . . [activity of] writing.
>
> All of the items and conditions mentioned, and in some instances many more, contribute to the act of writing. The failure of any one of these could cause a discontinuance of the task. Yet, the potential of failure is often high because many of the items are not designed, then the writing task may proceed efficiently and enjoyably.[64]

In the analysis of simple activities such as writing, basic principles can be gleaned for use in the analyzing of more complex systems of learning activities. First, we must define what we mean by *activity*. To date the term has not been defined satisfactorily because of lack of knowledge and because of the lack of technological tools.

Some definitions

Activity systems have been defined as the behavior patterns of individuals acting as individuals or as members of a group (including families, institutions, and firms) that affect the urban, physical, and spatial pattern. This point of view stresses the reasons people choose to act as they do. However, it is not realistic

[62]Ibid., pp. 1376, 1379.
[63]Ibid., p. 1376.

[64]Niels Diffrient, "Form and Circumstance," *Landscape*, no. 1, **18:**16 (Winter 1969).

to assume that human behavior is constant. Human behavior is continually changing in response to social, technological, financial, and political systems. As a result attitudinal studies are essential to any project in which behavior is a factor. Although activity systems are essentially means by which an individual seeks some goal, he seldom consciously defines his ultimate objectives. Activity systems are usually made up of various interacting subsystems, each of which contributes to the system outcome in proportion to its utility for the individual. The system may be either open or closed. If it is open, it interacts with other subsystems within the larger environment, whereas a closed system operates without interactions with other systems or with minimal effect from the other systems. The activity system need not necessarily be in equilibrium. It might be in imbalance, and it might produce the necessary energy to accomplish the goal and disappear when the goal is accomplished.

In order to understand activity systems more clearly it would be helpful to have precise definitions of specific situations. Although planners have not been able to agree on the common definition of different situations, one might define the situation of a person involved in a given task. The success or failure of a given task depends on the individual's perceptions of the situation and the physical objects required to accomplish the task. It has been suggested that a better understanding of activity systems might be derived by a partitioning process that would categorize and clarify the components of related activity systems. The following benefits have been suggested as possible results of partitioning:

> (1) Categorization is the means by which the objects of the world about are identified. (2) Categories permit the ordering and relating of classes of events into super-ordinate systems. (3) Categories provide direction for instrumental activities in advance of it [sic]. (4) The establishment of categories based on a set of defining attributes reduces the necessity of constant learning by establishing data for future use.[65]

[65]Charles H. Bevnette, "A Linguistic Structure for Architectonic Communication," *Response to Environment,* ed. Gary J. Coates and Kenneth M. Moffett, Student Publications of the School of Design (Raleigh: North Carolina State University Press, 1969), pp. 113–114.

The systems approach to problem solving follows essentially a partitioning process as it divides the overall problem into such parts as problem definition, analysis and synthesis, solution formulation, and modification through monitoring. The architectural process has been partitioned into client-contract-program elements, preliminary design, presentation, working drawings, construction, supervision, and follow-through.[66] The engineer might partition his activity systems into interpretive directions, structural elements, structural organization, building form, building technique, functional use, and consequent evaluation.[67]

The study of engineering sciences aids the understanding of activity systems. Whenever possible, engineers have reduced the basic principles of transportation, exchange, transfer, communications, and distribution to analytical rigor wherein the variables are controlled and dealt with separately.

> The processes of change and control which appear in engineering systems also appear in biological systems, social systems, political systems and in other relationships between men. A basic question arises: Are the processes of interaction but physical entities so different from the processes of interaction between non-physical entities that one cannot expect to apply the same principle? If we believe in the basic unity of nature, and in the ultimate goal of scientific generalization, we should hold some hope for the possibility that the advances in the sciences of change, which we call the engineering sciences, can be extended to non-engineering areas of study.[68]

Much of the work in the area of systems procedures has been derived from the hard sciences and in engineering: . . . "The nature of systems is employed by the scientist in his day-to-day work. Conceptions of interdependent variation of cause and effect, or even of mere patterning of sequence, derived from the idea that nature . . . manifests itself in collections of elements with more than nominal properties of

[66]Ibid., p. 116.
[67]Ibid., pp. 116–117.
[68]George J. Maslach, "The Reorganization of Educational Resources," *Daedalus,* **90:**1205 (Fall 1967).

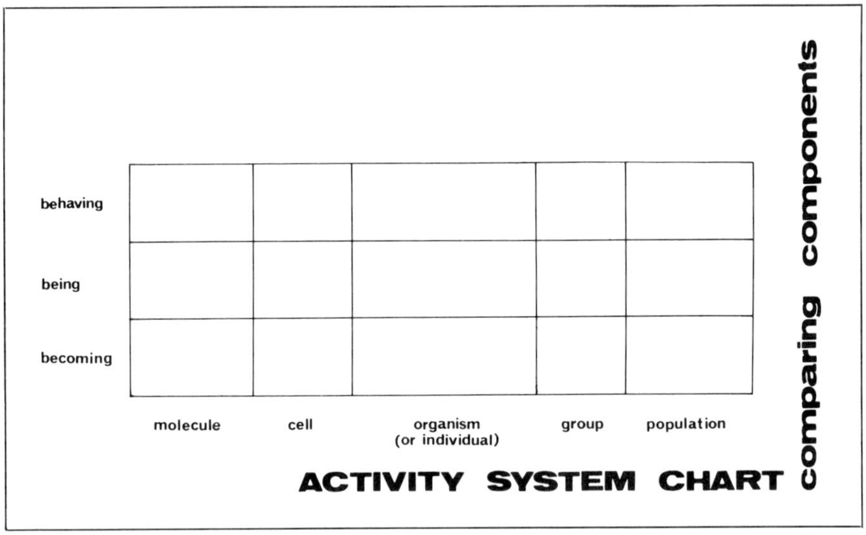

FIGURE 10.22

unity."[69] There are various behavioral systems, including social, physical, engineering, biological, and even psychological. Such a concept is useful to the planner because it helps him to perceive the problem in its entirety and to look for a solution to the *total* problem. When the planner considers activity systems, he also considers them in terms of their interactions with the total environment rather than the mission of a specific activity system.

Activity systems can be approached from various points of view. For example, one can consider the components, the structure, or the functions of the system, or the distribution of subactivities as they change over time or space. The relationships of the system to the various aspects of the environment and the general taxonomy or classification of various systems can be compared with the use of a breakdown such as that shown in Figure 10.22. This chart might be helpful in the comparison of the various levels of different activity systems. Table 10.5 is a classification scheme for urban activity systems.

As an aid in understanding the activity systems one might also go through a process of subdividing. Starting with the major categories, divide each major category into its first subcategories, then divide each first subcategory into second and third categories until the smallest unit for analysis is found. All activity systems are linked together by some invariant nodes. The dynamics of the activity system evolve from the functional interrelationships among the various nodes that link activity focal points. F. Stuart Chapin has spoken of the properties of activity systems as linkages—interaction—centralized or decentralized characteristics of the systems, human behavior, and culture.

> The concept of activity systems as used here is concerned not only with the identification of spatial patterns of these systems, as they exist, but also why they take the form they do and how activity patterns are likely to change in the future. The concept recognizes that different agents—firms, institutions, and families and individuals—call for differing types of activity investigations. The concept further views behavior patterns of these entities as they may be manifest in particular spatial forms as having important value-based areas of investigation.
>
> This . . . involves the study of attitudes and motivations as they relate to activity patterns of spatial significance.[70]

[69]Otis Dudley Duncan, "The Ecosystem Concept and the Problem of Air Pollution," *Environment and Cultural Behavior,* ed. Andrew P. Vayda (Garden City, N.Y.: Natural History Press, 1969), p. 457.

[70]F. Stuart Chapin, Jr., *Urban Land Use Planning* (Urbana: University of Illinois Press, 1965), pp. 229–230.

Table 10.5 Classification scheme for urban activity systems

Activity agents	Activity types	Activity systems
Firms	Productive activities	Goods-producing activities (extraction, processing, communications, distribution) service activities.
Institutions	General welfare activities	Human development activities (education, religious, recreation, basic community service activities, police, fire, water, waste, etc.) Activities for welfare of special groups (labor, social, etc.).
Individual	Residential activities	Income-producing activities, Child-raising and family activities, education and intellectual development activities, Spiritual development activities, social activities, recreation and relaxation, club activities, community service activities, political activities, shopping activities, health-related activities, etc.

SOURCE: Ibid., p. 226.

The effectiveness of activity systems in their accomplishment of specified goals will depend on the difficulties encountered within the environment, the effectiveness of the organizational effort, the internal efficiency of the organization, and the motivation or usefulness of each participant.

The basis of activity systems

There are five primary characteristics that furnish the basis of an activity system:

1 The place where the activity is done.
2 The time at which the activity is done.
3 The person or persons doing the activity.
4 The physical objects required for doing the activity.
5 The method or process by which the activity is done.

It is impossible to avoid geographical specialization because an activity occurs in a particular area. Activities denote a system of individual efforts at a physical location. Often such a system is so obvious that the significance of differences in the location of the activity is overlooked. Teaching a second-grade class of children from middle-class families in one part of town may require the same kind of teaching used in a second-grade class in another part of town, but the teacher realizes that, as a system of concrete activities, it may be radically different and moreover that effective and efficient work may depend on a specialized knowledge of the neighborhood from which the pupils come.

The relation between seasons and between night and day is an obvious basis of activities. Illustrative of the time factor are the limitations of human endurance. The specification of activities with respect to time is one of the most obvious reasons for the division of activities in a continuous and sequential pattern. Scheduling such activities is a complex aspect in the coordination process. Although scheduling has been neglected in the general consideration of specialization, the capacity or the disposition to adhere to time-schedule assignments may dictate the selection of the people who participate in an activity. The participants and their acquired experience and the organization of the activities are all important aspects of the activity system. Formal and informal groupings and their communications influence the coordination within the activity system. The tangible or intangible loyalty, the prestige, the pride, the monetary or other material inducements, the responsibility, and the differences in personalities of the participants in any system must all be considered.

Obviously, the most important aspect of any activity is the delineation of its objectives. In many cases these can be expressed in terms of materials, but in others, where services are performed, the objectives must express specifics. After the objectives and means have been determined, the method or process of the activity must be selected. The choice rests on the superior method or process—a selective process precedes the working process—or on one's increasing skill from repetitive experience or on increased knowledge by study and experience.

The ecological aspects of educational activity systems

Ecology is the study of the interaction of organisms with their environment. Human ecology, therefore, is a study of the interaction of humans with their surroundings. Unfortunately, people are often thought of as operating within isolated environments. Educational planners must look on the individual as interacting with the environment and as participating in various activity systems that involve a larger activity system. The ecological system is a dynamic one. The physical environment and the individual interact and influence each other. Man is not a closed system; he is physically and socially involved with his environs. The internal mechanisms of his body, which seem to be automatic, are actually reacting and responding to the external environment. The true ecological environment, however, includes activities associated with social, political, economic, psychological, and physical factors. As the individual interacts with his environment, so too do various subsections of the environment interact among each other.

Current technological innovations in transportation and communications have made the environment expand exponentially. News from remote areas of the world is announced instantaneously and modifies the behavior of national officials in countries throughout the world. Cities have always been the focal point of human activities. They have become increasingly so as societies have become urbanized through the development of technology.

It is essential that the educational planner understand the true nature of ecology. Too frequently planners are concerned about some subsystem rather than the total system. They focus their attention on points of immediate concern without thoroughly understanding and investigating the implications for the total system. A thorough analysis of the whole system is required and any design program for an urban area must investigate the patterns of traffic, demography, population density, and land uses. Usually it is better to do one's planning by clusters. "There is one principle of arrangement that is universally applicable . . . the principle of clustering from a social point of view. . . . Two activities placed side by side are much better than one isolated from the other. This is primarily because of people's love of the sight of activity."[71]

Clustering activities could be thought of as formulating activity systems that focus on people. (See Figure 10.23.) People have a natural propensity to group together in both formal and informal groups.

> . . . one art form of the mass culture of the future is the fair, where the audience is in the spectacle and the spectacle is, in a sense, created by the fact of their involvement. The performance is in the architecture, in the crowds of people on foot or seated together in vehicles; the plays, music, dance, painting and sculpture which reveal themselves in that context become part of a larger situation. The sheer mass of people present in one general area makes it possible for subaudiences to assemble themselves in smaller areas, when otherwise no one would assemble in such large numbers were the whole spectacle not there to begin with. Like a good circus, there is a lot going on which cannot be absorbed all at once. But the circus exists only because there is an audience which wants to have a lot going on.[72]

But man does not respond only to the actual stimulus of his environment, he also relates to space. The spatial components of the environment have a subtle effect on the individual as he spends his time within them. (See Figure 10.24.) He is not consciously influenced by the spatial environment as he is by activity systems such as a social situation or a fair. But even under subtle circumstances, he interprets his own role and its relation to the environment in which he finds himself and responds accordingly. Freud's work on the subconscious reaction to bells, when their sound depressed a patient because of associations with an unhappy event, demonstrates the effect of subtle physical

[71]Elizabeth Wood, "The Physical Plan and Planning with People," *Ekistus*, **24**:406 (November 1967).

[72]Harold Taylor, "The Arts in Modern Society," *Environment and Change, The Next Fifty Years.* Papers commissioned by the American Institute of Planners (Bloomington: Indiana University Press, 1968), p. 33.

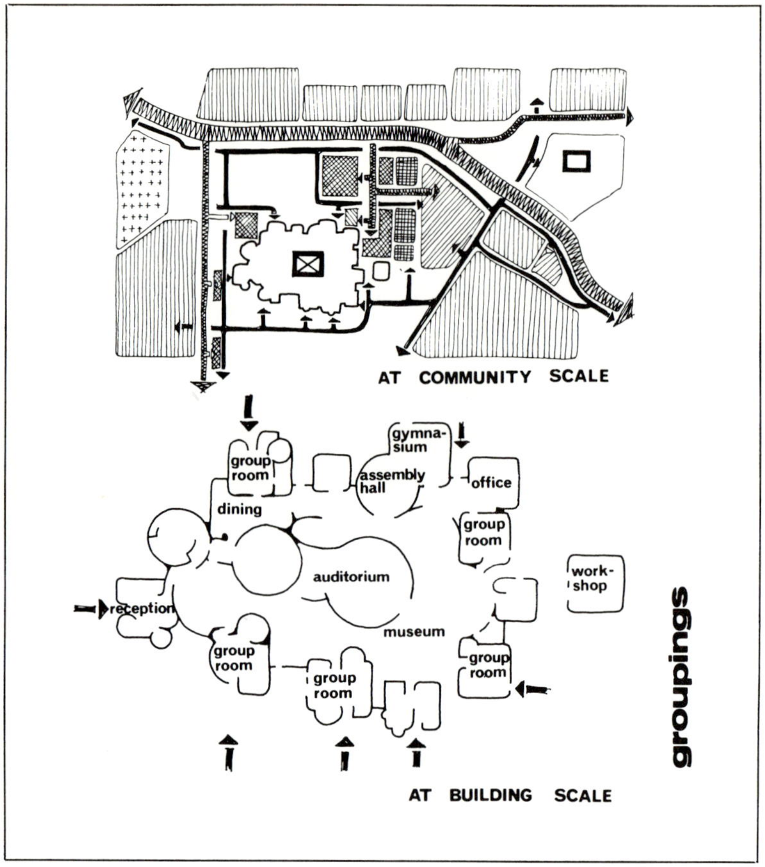

FIGURE 10.23

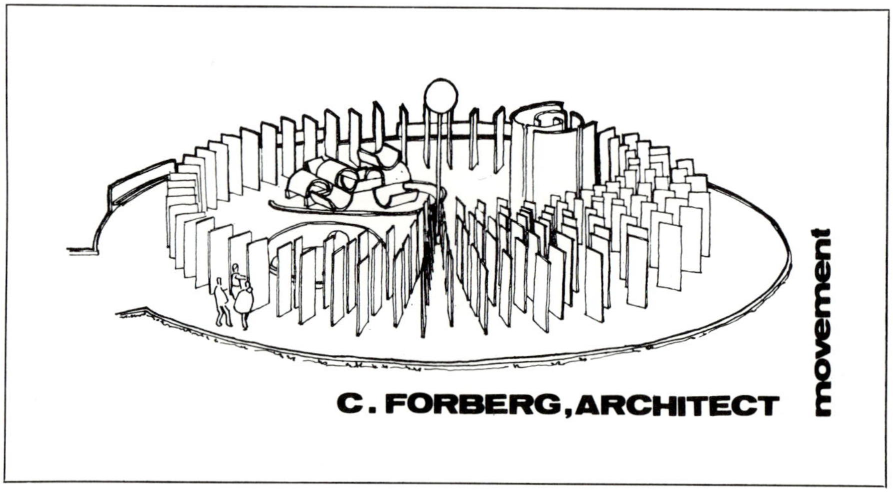

FIGURE 10.24

surroundings on the inhabitants. This combination of conscious and unconscious interaction with the environment is a true subject of human ecology. Looking at the individual and his environment as an ecological system accentuates the relationship between function and form. This is particularly true when the building housing an activity must express a philosophy relevant to the activity. In fact, without such relevant expression the building does little to enhance the environment and often detracts from it. "Planning should be seen as a manifestation of the ever-growing tendency consciously to organize human activities. In this process there is a continuous search for efficiency in the broadest sense."[73] The integration of ideas, activities, and the environment is the true function of the planner.

The utility of analyzing educational activity systems

An individual's degree of participation in an activity system is related to the value to be derived by the individual or from the activity's use to him. Most people need to participate in some kind of activity system. Action, as a primary instinct or propensity in man, has long been psychologically recognized. "It is an observable fact that men are usually active, that they seek objects of activity."[74] Gregariousness is one of man's primary instincts. It causes the individual to involve himself in various social activities and creates interactions between the individual and his social environment. Modern communications technology has greatly enhanced the individual's ability to interact with his environment, in both the immediate and the more distant settings. This notion of interaction is central to the concept of the activity system, and its study

> . . . should provide a basis for understanding and discovering an essential order to the way concentrations of human beings come about. It is argued here that the key to understanding this order and its evolution is to be found in the study of activity patterns of urban residents and how human satisfactions and dissatisfactions affect choice in activities. Further, it is argued that activity patterns, particularly those that relate to the way in which people use city space and community facilities, affect their choice of residence. In short, if the needs of human interaction hold the key to the spatial organization of cities, it is argued that the framework must be developed from a study of the origins of these needs and how they are satisfied.[75]

Understanding the interactions within these activity systems, therefore, seems to be the key to comprehending large urban-scale activities. There are probably three essential ingredients in this conceptual scheme: "(1) a value system component that operates and (2) the choice mechanism, which in turn produces (3) an activity component. Essentially it utilizes choice theory to convert human motivations (input) into human activity in the city (output) with the social system mediating man's choices."[76]

The key word in the study of activity systems and man's participation in the various activity systems seems to be *utility*. *Utility*, defined as subjective preference, dictates man's involvement in activity systems; ultimately, it motivates the degree to which man will participate in these activity systems and, therefore, it determines the influence that the individual and the environment have on each other. The model design provides continuous feedback from the environment to the individual. Feedback of this sort allows the individual to modify the environment, which in turn creates new environmental qualities that affect the individual again in the form of feedback. This constant interaction between the individual and the environment has, as its primary integrator, the utility factor because the individual will participate in the system only if it is of some use to him. One must understand that man will congregate in settlements primarily because of the fulfillment of needs and satisfactions gained from interaction in the community. These needs take on various forms, such as social achievements, personal gain, or physical victory over

[73] J. Tinbergen, "Planning, Economic: Western Europe," *International Encyclopedia of the Social Sciences*, ed. David T. Sills, vol. 12 (New York: Macmillan and Free Press, 1968), p. 103.

[74] Chester Barnard, *Functions of the Executive* (Cambridge, Mass.: Harvard University Press, 1968), p. 118.

[75] F. Stuart Chapin, Jr., "Activity Systems and Urban Structure: A Working Schema," *Journal of the American Institute of Planners*, no. 1, **34**:12 (January 1968).

[76] Ibid.

the environment. Whatever the motivation, it is useful to the individual because it gives him an identity whereby he can monitor his own behavior and determine how useful the system is to him. One's participation in activity systems is constantly colored by his subjective interpretation of his own role in the system and the benefits he might reap. External objective factors and their influence on the individual are important but the individual's subjective preferences must not be overlooked. Major disagreements among people in the same environment usually arise because their perceptions of that environment differ. For the designer this has profound implications. A man's value system is really the standard by which the designer must measure his solution to the design problem: "Every society has some inconsistency between its different norms and values. In some cases, different values cherished in the same society may be quite contradictory. This inconsistency creates dilemma for the individual and interrupts the orderly patterned behavior of the group."[77] The individual's value system influences his role in a psychological, physical, and sociological context. In other words, a value system determines the environment in which the individual lives and the one that he wishes to create. Table 10.6 summarizes the basic human needs.

[77]Twin Cities Metropolitan Planning Commission, *Values and the Planning Process*, The Joint Program, Design Section, Paper No. 8 (Minneapolis: By the Commission, July 1963), p. 4.

Table 10.6 Basic human needs

Need	Negative counterpart
1 Life-maintaining needs	
Hunger, thirst, shelter	Excess
Rest and sleep	Sloth
Motion and repose	Frenzy and drunkenness
And other psychological needs	
Hunting and acquisition urges	Exploitation
Contest and conflict drives	Destruction
Holding, hoarding, defense	Miserliness
Sex drives	Sadism, masochism
Nesting, nurturing	Tyranny
Fabrication, making of tools, making of finalities	Image breaking
Herding urge	Hermitism, alienation
Speech drive, making of symbols	
Curiosity, orientation drive	Know-nothingism
Exploration drive	Parochialism
2 Life-enhancing needs	
(The objective here is not "to keep alive" but to live well!)	
Play	Destructive play
Sport	Destructive competition
Companionship	Obsessive companionship
Group pride	
Compassion for the group	Hate
Self-identity as involved in the group	Self-destruction
Ritual, myth, image	Disdain of ritual and myth

Need	Negative counterpart
3 Life-completing urges	
(Feeling for nature: kinship with the earth, with water, fire, and air. Feeling for aesthetic materials and aesthetic forms)	
Light	Darkness
Textures	
Spaces	
Rhythms	
Sounds	Silences
Smells	
Feels	
4 Horizon feelings	
The urge to know—science, philosophy	
The urge to connect with the past—love of history, love of past places, past people	
Hope—the urge to connect with the future	
Mortality—sense of terminus	
5 Beyond the horizon feelings	
Immortality in the sense of living on in one's children	
Immortality in the sense of living on in one's group, one's nation, one's own creations	
Sense of cosmic identification (Plato, Stoics)	
Religious immortality (e.g., Christian)	

SOURCE: Edward F. Sekler (ed.), *Historic Urban Spaces*, Reports and Discussions from the Seminar U.D. 1–5b (Cambridge, Mass.: By the Harvard University Graduate School of Design, 1966), pp. 1–3, 1–4.

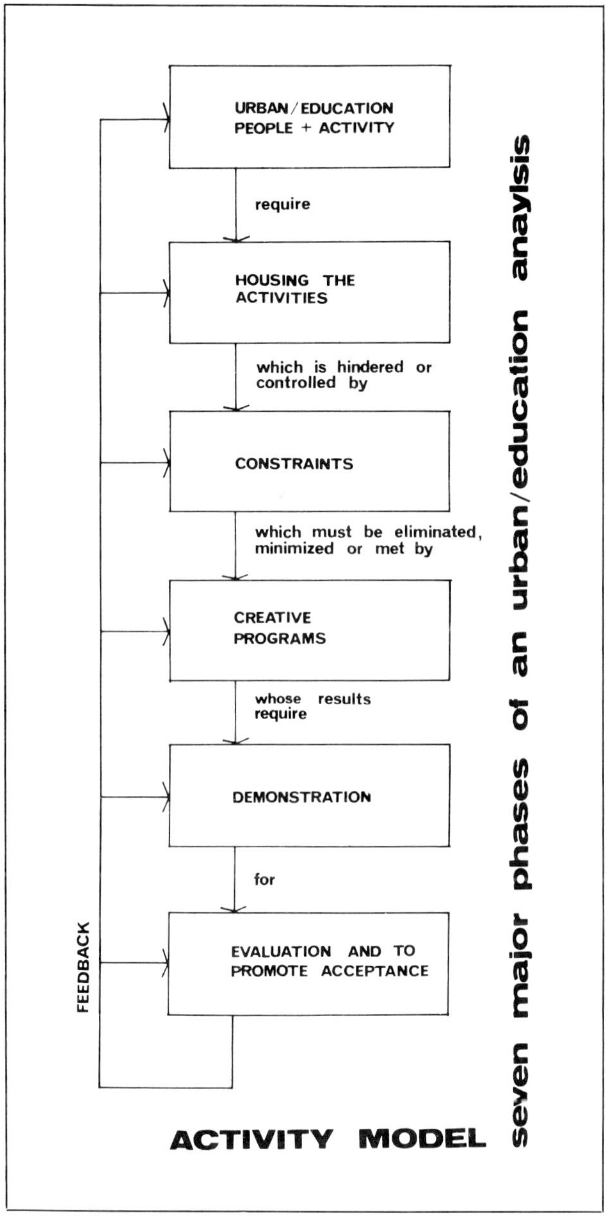

FIGURE 10.25

Table 10.6 reflects the overall continuum of basic human needs. However, it is important to make a distinction between actual and preferred needs and the activities associated with those needs. Many of these actual and preferred needs will be modified by the group within which the individual functions. The educational planner today recognizes not only basic psychological and sociological needs but also the current vast changes in those needs. Illustrative of these changes are the new attitudes toward work and leisure.

An educational activity systems model

There are seven major phases in the analytical investigation of urban educational activities as set forth by Figure 10.25.

The dynamic nature of the model permits

1 The establishment of empirical goals until research reveals the real goals.
2 The identification of activity constraints and of permitted tolerance levels within the creative program until the real significance of constraints is measured.
3 The initiation of several demonstrations based on judgment to hasten information feedback.
4 The establishment of criteria for evaluation, with continuous and continuing measurement of activity achievement.
5 The establishment of a cost-effectiveness program ". . . to determine priorities for creative and demonstration projects, first using empirical data, then real information."[78]
6 The continuous adjustment, modification, and replacement of programs of activities as information becomes available.[79]

To set priorities among the various activities, a cost-effectiveness program must be established and continually updated:

Step 1

In dollars, establish the net potential gain from each constraint removed or minimized, e.g.:

[78]Ibid., p. 4.
[79]Ibid.

1 The reduction of the cost of housing and/or the servicing of the activity.
2 The increase in the number of participants in an activity.
3 The increase in the number of activities with the same amount of housing.
4 The decrease in the amount of juvenile delinquency, public property destruction, police patrol, and so on.
5 Total dollars saved.

Step 2

In dollars, determine the cost of the program to minimize or remove constraints.

Step 3

Steps 1 and 2

$$= \$ \frac{\text{saved}}{\text{spent}} = \text{potential ultimate cost effectiveness}$$

Step 4

In dollars, determine the cost of implementation.

Step 5

In dollars, figure the dollars saved by the potential influence of the implementation or the removal or minimization of the activity.

Step 6

Steps 4 and 5

$$= \$ \frac{\text{saved}}{\text{spent}} = \text{potential immediate cost effectiveness}$$

Step 7

Steps 5 and 6

$$= \frac{\text{potential immediate cost effectiveness}}{\text{potential ultimate cost effectiveness}} = \text{leverage.}$$[80]

With the leverage stated numerically, setting priorities among various activities becomes more objective than the subjective selection of a few individuals.

The following questions and descriptions characterize each phase of the educational activity systems model.

PHASE 1 *Urban education = people + activity*

a) People
How many?
How old are they?
What skills do they possess?
What are their other activities?
What role or roles do they play in these other activities?
What do they know?
What do they need?
What are their problems?
What are their values?
Where do they go?
What do they do with the experiences gained from the activity?
What would they like to do in the activity?
Where would they like to do the activity?
What would they like to have?
What are their aspirations?
What are their capabilities?

b) Activity or Activities
What is available?
What is required?
What is wanted?
How should it be provided?
Where should it be?
What is its significance?
What does it cost?
What time period does it require?
What are its benefits?

c) Relationship of People and Activity to Space
What is the present relationship?
What is required?
What is wanted?
How should it be provided?
What are the benefits?[81]

[80]Ibid., p. 6.

[81]Ibid., p. 8.

PHASE 2 *Housing the activities*

What are the structures required?
How many structures are needed to satisfy the demand?
To what standards must they be built?
What are their performance requirements in terms of the following factors:
- quality
- livability
- rehabilitation
- function
- adaptability
- convertibility
- maintainability
- efficiency

How do the learning structures fit the community's overall plan?
What do they cost:
- new?
- if they require replacement?
- if they require rehabilitation?
- to maintain and operate?

What are the costs of the supporting utilities?
Who owns the housing structures?
Who manages them?
Under what taxation, zoning, and other administrative regulations are they operated?
How are the structures financed?
What has been the cost of their past upkeep related to the activities that took place there?
How are the structures amortized?
What systems and techniques have been used in their construction?
What are the tax implications of their changing from private to public use?[82]

PHASE 3 *Constraints affecting activities*

a) Political and Legal Constraints
What are the taxation policies of the local, state, and federal governments that would affect the activities?
What are the zoning restrictions?
What are the building-code requirements?
What are the local customs of the community?
What are the political ramifications related to the activity or activities?
What are the formal and informal decision-making channels supporting or inhibiting the activity or activities?

b) Safety Constraints
What are the fire-prevention procedures?
Does structural integrity exist?
What are the security measures against crime?
Are adequate resources available for carrying out the activities?

c) Health Constraints
Is overcrowding prevalent or possible?
What process is available for waste disposal?
Does the activity produce pollution—noise, air, waste, and so on?
Are temperature, humidity, and air flow adequate?
Are there adequate utilities?

d) Physical Constraints
Is the space adequate?
Is congestion possible?
Is the transportation adequate?
Are materials and services available in the right amount and can they meet changing needs?

e) Economic Constraints
What are the economic risks involved?
What are the land costs?
What are the construction costs?
What are the operating costs?
What are the financing capabilities?
What are the financing practices?
What are the social costs?

f) Technological Constraints
What are the probabilities of taking advantage of existing technology?
What are the opportunities for taking advantage of new technology?
What human skills and abilities are required?
What is the nature of the activity?
What portions of the activity are better adapted to machine operation as opposed to human intervention?

[82]Ibid., p. 9.

g) Social Constraints
What are the personal preferences?
What changes are required in personal behavior?
What influence does population growth and mobility have?
What are the educational gaps?
What social hindrances exist in the communication system?
What are the social taboos?
What cultural constraints impose restrictions?

Phase 4 *Creative program*

a) Components of the Activity Systems Creative Program
  (1) The demand component—". . . the total time that people would choose to spend on a particular [learning] activity, having regard to personal commitments, income, etc., if the appropriate facility together with a defined range of other facilities were available."[83]
  (2) The social component. Choice of activity is constrained by the following factors:
    (a) commitment to various levels of activities—essential, optional, and leisure—and the level of commitment dependent on the individual, his age, sex, and other characteristics;
    (b) cost
      [1] private cost—percentage of individual's income spent on learning activities, and
      [2] public cost-percentage of community's expenditure spent on learning activities; (see Step 1 through Step 7 above)
    (c) social exclusiveness
      [1] racial segregation,
      [2] socio-economic differences,
      [3] entry rules applicable, and to each activity;
    (d) energy expenditure
      [1] health status,
      [2] nutritional deficiencies,
      [3] age-amount of energy a person is willing to expend,
      [4] sex, and
      [5] personal choice within the limits of free choice, i.e.,
        (a) enjoyment,
        (b) skills and abilities, and
        (c) challenge and competition; and
    (e) availability
      [1] what community resources are required for the activity to take place, and
      [2] what other activities must proceed before the activity under consideration can take place.[84]
  (3) The linkage component—
"Linkage factors . . . are: (1) awareness . . . the level of knowledge about the availability and characteristics of [an activity] . . . (2) accessibility . . . the amount of time people are prepared to spend travelling . . . in proportion to the available time and activity time. (3) attraction/detraction . . . [certain activities] grouped in close proximity to one another will mutually attract or detract. [The level of participation in an activity may be increased by the attraction of other activities as a result of reducing travel time and increasing awareness levels, e.g., the sidewalk schools.]"[85]
  (4) The environmental component
    (a) climate
    (b) energy sources
    (c) waste disposal
    (d) utility distribution
    (e) protection against intrusion
    (f) movement of people and objects
    (g) communication systems
    (h) physical facilities—type, capacity, quality, location, and so on

[83]Ray Maw, "Construction of a Leisure Model—Part Two—The Model," *Official Architecture and Planning*, no. 8, **32**:928, (August 1969), Architecture and Planning Publications, London.

[84]Ibid., pp. 924–925.
[85]Ibid., p. 928.

(5) The time component
In this analysis the following terms are used:
(a) Total Time—total amount of time within a specified period
(b) Essential Time—period of time fully committed to essential activities
(c) Optional Time—period of time not fully committed to essential activities
(d) Leisure Time—period of time relatively free of commitment. . . .
(e) . . . Block of Time—period of time of a specified duration
(f) Time-Tie—committed point in time. . . .
(g) . . . Available Time—block of time within two time-ties
(h) Travel Time—period of time spent in traveling
(i) Preparation Time—period of time necessary to prepare for an activity
(j) Activity Time—period of time spent on an activity. . . .[86]

(6) Aims of the activity systems creative program
(a) optimal use of the space in the community
(b) increase in public participation for the individual as well as for social gains
(c) increase in the participation of private enterprise and use of their research and development competence
(d) creation of flexibility and versatility in the use of building spaces
(e) making standard those aspects of the activity to free the participant for the creative aspect associated with the activity
(f) nailing down the advantages associated with doing an activity for the community's decision-makers
(g) initiating new activities for buildings designed for other activities
(h) predicting the activities for a particular facility over a number of years.[87]

[86]Ibid., p. 925.
[87]*Research and Experimental Strategy for Community and Urban Excellence*, Building Research Advisory Board, Division of Engineering, National Research Council, National Academy of Sciences, Washington, D.C., April 1967, pp. 11–12.

PHASE 5 *Demonstration*

A possible initial demonstration follows.

1. Determine the number and nature of the learning activities required to act as incentives for public and private enterprises to overcome such problems as the following:

> The complete pattern of life imposed upon citizens of the . . . [Tampa Model City Area] . . . is such that the education they receive is making, at best, a neutral contribution, and in most cases, a negative contribution to the development of those individuals. Life chances of the residents of the target area are not enhanced through education. . . . The problem of education . . . is to convert the region from one that is educationally repulsive to one that is a magnet of high quality education for a lifetime through the injection of revolutionary plans and principles.[88]

2. Work with all pertinent segments of people involved in an activity ". . . to evolve plans for equitable solution to problems that may evolve from innovation in building and provide a demonstration project to illustrate effectiveness of plan."[89]

3. Design an activity/facility throughout a geographical pattern. Demonstrate the economics of the new patterns of distributing the costs of space by increasing the social utility and improving the quality of activity performance. Show the advantages of flexible distribution as opposed to the rigidity imposed by the combining and centralizing of learning activities.

4. ". . . optimize design of each type of housing with available technology; establish performance specifications; work with private enterprise in conduct of demonstrations in situations where constraints are purposely minimized or eliminated; . . . "[90] and evaluate participant acceptance of innovations.

5. Select several teams—teachers, architects, contractors, curriculum supervisors, educational administrators, manufacturers, and interested citizens—and establish a paid competition for the best economically possible design in combination with item 4.

[88]*Tampa Model Cities Program*, Part I, "Interim Report," City Demonstration Agency (no date given), pp. 4–10, 4–11.
[89]*Research and Experimental Strategy*, p. 13.
[90]Ibid.

6. Demonstrate the practicability of the concept.

PHASE 6 *Evaluation and acceptance*

Evaluation and acceptance—evaluate new learning activities systematically in terms of the following:

Performance
Cost
Standard of living
Impact on sound economics
Physical and intellectual resources
Participant satisfaction
Social and market opportunities
Others[91]

Each of these phases has to be measured for a given activity. These measurements, in turn, can be grouped under three headings.

1 Those that can be determined from available sources.
2 Those that require special surveys.
3 Those that cannot be determined by normal survey methods.[92]

The reliability of the model, therefore, depends directly on its ability to quantify the various aspects of the activity. The general criterion, however,

> . . . is that the total [activity system] should operate in an optimal fashion. This means that many suboptimizations and their relations to the total functioning system must be taken into consideration. Frequently, it is discovered that subsystems must function in less than optimal fashion in order that the total [activity] system may operate optimally.[93]

PHASE 7 *Feedback*

Continuous adjustments, modifications, and establishment of supplementary activities can take place almost simultaneously as the information evolves.

[91]Ibid., p. 15.
[92]Maw, p. 929.
[93]Frank W. Banghart, *Educational Systems Analysis* (London: Macmillan & Co., 1969), p. 42.

SOME POSSIBLE EDUCATIONAL PLANNING TRENDS

Educational planners will become members of the general advisory staff to advise key politicians concerning all city activities and resource uses. As a result, educational planners will become more involved than before with purely political questions, thus increasing the power of planners and involving them in political conflicts. They will help to coordinate operating programs of other city departments with school programs and hence they will become more effective members of community activity groups.

Educational planners will increasingly emphasize quantitative planning. Educational planners will have specialties in several areas. Some will be primarily economists; others sociologists, administrators, systems analysts, political scientists, or architects.

Educational planners will make extensive use of data-coordinating and data-processing systems for quantifying the information. Educational planners through interaction with other groups will produce educational plans more and more in concert with general urban plans. Planning for a single educational plan will be replaced by a continuous planning process. This process will include specification of goals and objectives, developing strategies to obtain them, producing educational plans within the broader framework, and adjusting feedback from the community.

Educational planners will increasingly work outside the purview of the red-brick schoolhouse. As more and more of the community becomes the classroom, e.g., the Castle Rock High School in Tacoma, Washington, and the Parkway Program in Philadelphia, educational planners will interact more and more with urban planners. They will be concerned with fitting the activities into patterns of individualized learning. Conceivably, houses of varying numbers of students will be scattered about the city as opposed to the impersonal concentration of thousands of students in one building. Teachers will become managers of the educational program and the learning process, seeking out and organizing learning experiences that can occur anywhere in the community.

11 Establishing goals and objectives

A variety of social, economic, and public interests affect educational decision-making. This variety of factors demands allowances for alternatives. To select one alternative, or a set of alternatives, from another requires a logical structure within which choices can be made.

To choose among sets of consequences requires criteria relevant to overall socio-economic effectiveness. To establish these criteria does not mean, however, that the educational planner must wait until a comprehensive urban plan is developed or that the community must be of one mind with respect to education. It does mean that many factors exist to facilitate or to hamper the design of an educational plan.

In this chapter, goals will be discussed in terms of their meaning, nature, functions, and characteristics.

GOALS, THEIR ROLE IN EDUCATIONAL PLANNING

Goals, according to the accepted definition, are ends for which a design is made. The design, therefore, must provide the participants in a plan with a direction, in the sense that goals are ideals. These ideals are statements; in this case, they are statements of the educational purpose, concerning a desirable state of affairs and covering a wide range of priorities.

Selecting and ordering them on the scale demanded require comprehensive planning.

The reason for this approach is that planning's goals and objectives embrace

> ... the civilized life of man in all its major aspects: the destiny of the land, the forests, the water, the cities, and the countryside; the knowledge of man through biology, sociology and psychology; law, government and economics, art, architecture and engineering. As all are interdependent, we cannot consider them separately in compartments. Their connectedness directed toward a cultural entity is undoubtedly of greater importance for success in planning and housing than finding ever so perfect practical solutions for limited objectives.[1]

Goals ignite action that determines the entire course that planning takes. This course, however, is beset with troubles, for no goal can ever be perfectly achieved, and no goal can be perfectly formulated. Goals change with time, which modifies the given goal. Also, goals are subject to changing cultural values, to changing technological know-how and to the changing whims of the people involved. Their values, therefore, serve as means for goal setting. (See Figure 11.1.)

Goals furnish a rule of choice among possibilities. Some typical goals follow:

1 Goals are optimizing in form, e.g., the lowest cost for the highest educational excellence.
2 Goals are satisfying, e.g., equal opportunity for all.
3 Goals are incremental in form, e.g., increase classroom supply.
4 Goals are positive or negative in form, e.g., provide more space for learning.

Regardless of aim, goals must be relevant, must be realizable, possess clarity of purpose and be operational. Yet the goals should also be general, community oriented and long-range. Goals should ask the following questions:

Choice of what?
For whom?
To what degree?

[1]Walter Gropius, *Scope of Total Architecture* (New York: Harper & Row, 1955), p. 73.

FIGURE 11.1

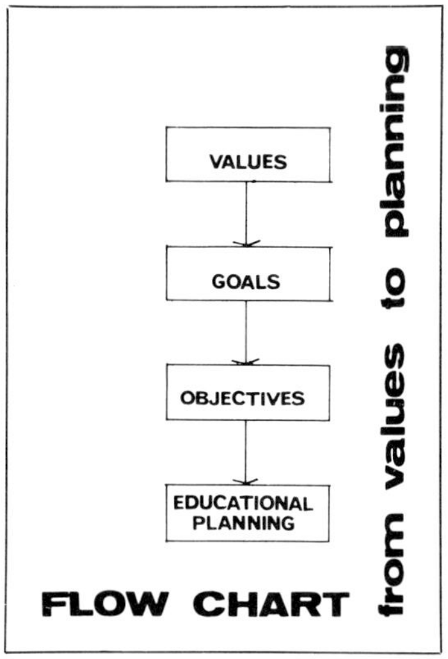

At what rate?
Under what conditions?
In what priority?
How will the goal be recognized when reached?

According to R. C. Young, there are five steps in the process of establishing specific goals:

1 Defining the limits of contingency establishes the boundaries of the plan and those portions that the planner's decisions will affect. For example, he can predict the way in which the establishment of an educational park will affect employment, taxes, the economic base of society and the distribution of the school-age population.
2 From the boundaries established, the planner further reduces the extent of his alternatives by eliminating those that do not seem useful and profitable. None of the alternatives should increase the obligations of the existing tax base; it should increase employment potentials or should enhance the educational community or should fulfill educational requirements or should provide ample space in all of its facilities.
3 By comparing the merits of the alternatives, the planner can determine the beneficial and detrimental effects of various combinations of goals and subgoals and can thus choose the best ones.

FIGURE 11.2

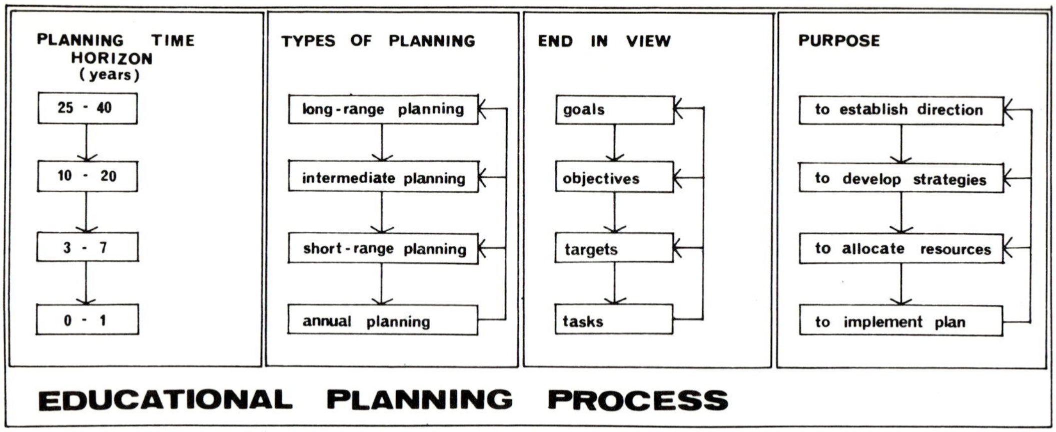

4 The planner next evaluates the relative worth of the goals by comparing the environmental factors with the goals and objectives. Goals should be concerned with the conditions from which they arise.
5 When the final decisions have been made and the goals and objectives have been settled then a statement of policy should be made. The policy then acts as the guidelines, e.g., should the implemented policy provide the maximum number of educational stations regardless of location or should the implemented policy establish the educational park in a prestige area?[2]

This five-step procedure suggests the following format for developing goals:

1 Conduct an overview of the problem on (a) the general purpose of the study, (b) the problems anticipated, (c) the methodologies to be used, (d) the relation of the old studies to the new, and (e) discussion of scale relationships, e.g., on a school, a district or a statewide level.
2 Analyze the historical background of the problem by studying the historical development of the forces that brought about the existing situation, and learn the reasons why they developed.
3 Work from an outline that provides a new starting point based on the planning process and that serves the focus by providing target dates and constant feedback.

In establishing goals, some conflicts will naturally arise. There will be disagreement on questions concerning the role of goals as the ends or means of a project, the ends of the intermediate goals and the values of the educational goals. There will also be disagreement on the time frames for the achievement of the goal. The goal itself will influence the level of agreement and the desirability of a specific time frame. Short-term goals are usually set for five- to ten-year periods, whereas intermediate goals require planning for ten to fifteen years, and long-range planning spans fifteen to twenty-five years. (See Figure 11.2.)

Goals emerge from a thorough analysis that reveals the various needs and potentialities of the educational program and the possibility of its attainment. The analytical examination usually includes:

1 Nature, composition, and dynamics of education.
2 Historical facts and trends descriptive of its past, and indicative of its future.
3 Socio-economic, institutional, technological, cultural and other internal and external limitations and potentialities.
4 Human and material resources available for directed change.

[2]R. C. Young, "Goals and Goal-Setting," *Journal of the American Institute of Planners,* no. 2, **32**:76–85 (March 1966).

5 Existing realities, either desirable for retention or impractical to change within the planning period.
6 Commitments for the future, established by prior actions and events, available resources, and existing realities.
7 Tentative priority of goals: specific and general; near-term and long-range.
8 Projection of probable consequences of the application of available resources to different sets of goals.
9 Examination of, selection among, or amalgamation of several most desirable and feasible courses of future action and intent.
10 Derivation of a current statement of strategy, policy, specific objectives, and accomplishment for the planning period.
11 Programmes of priority action and progressive implementation.
12 Periodic and emergency re-analysis; review, modification, or revision of intent, objectives, and comprehensive plan.[3]

The following is a list of suggestions of the kinds of broad goals possible for educational planning:

1 Education should help solve the social, physical and financial problems that currently prevent minority groups from actively participating in community affairs.
2 Education should foster individuality, by providing the individual with the capacity to make his own decisions.
3 Education should provide a vast arena of understanding and respect for people of different occupations, color, class or creed.
4 Education should involve the individual in relating to all aspects of community life.
5 Education should prepare the individual for the world of employment.

OBJECTIVES—THE CRITERIA OF EDUCATIONAL PLANNING

The realization of goals becomes possible through objectives. (See Figure 11.3.) Objectives are statements that are capable of both measurement and attainment. As a result, objectives cannot be changed continuously, because a minimum amount of stability is essential to the educational plan. For these reasons, among others, preparing a set of objectives becomes a crucial step in the educational planning process. (See Figure 11.4.)

There are various types of objectives: "established objectives, which are designed to maintain essential services; alternative objectives, which are designed to improve this facility, possible objectives, which include a combination of various events not now existing and unlikely for sometime in the future."[4]

Any type of objective must be operational or measurable, as just stated. This requirement is necessary to the measuring of educational outputs against the achievements established in the objectives. Achievements, however, require definitions and specifications of how they are observed and measured. This measurability, in turn, shows the degree of success obtained and demonstrates that the planned educational activities did have the effects attributed to them.

In the systems approach, objectives are not fully specified at the start of the educational planning

[3]Melville C. Branch and Ira M. Robinson, "Goals and Objectives in Civic Comprehensive Planning," *Town Planning Review,* no. 4, **38**:263 (January 1968).

[4]William Ewald, Jr., "Introduction," *Environment and Change, The Next Fifty Years.* Papers Commissioned by the American Institute of Planners and presented at the Washington Conference, October 1967 (Bloomington: Indiana University Press, 1968), p. 4.

FIGURE 11.3

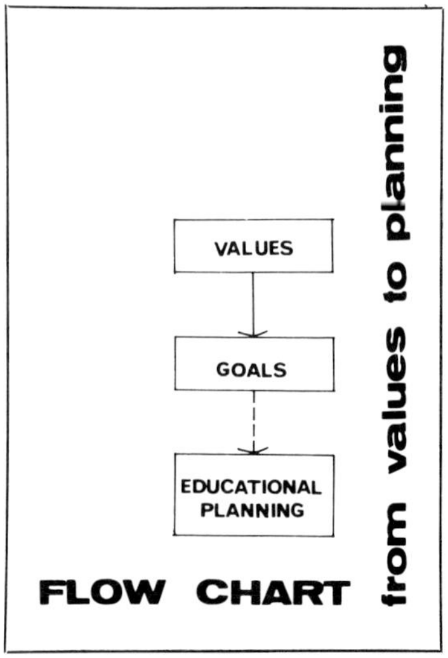

FIGURE 11.4
Steps towards objectives

exercise. In some cases, the objectives become modified or new objectives are generated from the analyses applied during the definition of the planning problem. Such activities generally reveal new objectives never before exposed or utilized. Additionally, the set of actions originally contemplated by the educational planner to achieve predesigned objectives sometimes fails. Thus, the objectives that are specified originally are marginal, until serious scanning of the possible impact of the planned-for activities takes place.

The factors influencing the setting of objectives are the available educational resources, the existing commitments, the internal operating requirements, external trends and events, the numerous needs, and the many interconnections of all of these factors. The difficulty is that, as yet, no analytical technique exists that permits complete quantitative comparisons among the many different elements of the planning process. Until such techniques are developed, partial quantitative-statistical subsystems analysis, logical reasoning, confirmed experience, structured judgment and continuous observations must be used.

One attempt is illustrated by Morris Hill.

The objectives are defined operationally rather than in abstract terms. The consequences of each alternative course of action are determined for each objective. The incidence of the benefits and costs of each course of action measured in terms of the achievement of the goal is established for each [objective]. The relative weight to be attached to each group is also established.

[In the following table] the conceptual product of the analysis is given. . . . In the table, a, B, Y . . . are the descriptions of the [objectives]. Each [objective] has a weight 1, 2, 3 . . . as previously determined. Various groups a, b, c, d, e . . . are identified as affected by the course of action. These groups may be combined in any meaningful manner in order to indicate the differential incidence of costs and benefits. A relative weight is determined for each group, either for each [objective] individually or all [objectives] together.

The letters A, B . . . are the costs and benefits which may be defined in monetary or nonmonetary units or in terms of qualitative states.

Costs and benefits are recorded for each objective according to the parties that are affected. A dash (—) in a cell implies that no cost or benefit that is related to that objective would accrue to that party if that plan were effectuated. A particular party may suffer both costs and benefits with respect to a particular objective. Thus, the reduction of noise may be a relevant objective of a plan for improved transportation facilities. A particular location may simultaneously experience a decrease of noise from one source, e.g. as a result of the proposed diversion of heavy automobile traffic from that location, and an increase of noise from another source, e.g. from a new transit route proposed for that area.

For certain of the [objectives], Σ indicates that summation of the costs and benefits is meaningful and useful. The total cost and benefits with respect to the [objectives] can then be compared. This will be the case when all the costs and benefits are expressed in quantitative units. When this is not the case, i.e., for the intangibles, the costs and benefits and their incidence are best stated as explicitly as possible and then left to the judgment of the decision-makers. It is most unlikely that all the costs and benefits of all the [objectives] can be expressed in the same units. In this rare case—which may occur when only one or two [objectives] are valued by the community—it may be possible to arrive at a grand cost-benefits summation. However, this is highly unlikely.

For each plan, the product of the analysis is a table similar to [the one following]. . . . As was mentioned earlier in the face of uncertainty, a range of costs and benefits is preferable to the prediction of unique outcome. Thus the letters A, B . . . should not be considered as a single value but rather as a range of values.[5]

[5]Morris Hill, "A Method for the Evaluation of Transportation Plans," Highway Research Record, Number 180, Highway Research Board Division of Engineering, National Research Council, National Academy of Sciences, National Academy of Engineering, Washington, D.C., 1967, pp. 24–25.

Table 11.1. Costs and benefits in the objective-achievement matrix

Conceptual product of analysis									
Objective description		a		B		Y		8	
Relative value		2		3		5		4	
Incidence		Costs	Benefits	Costs	Benefits	Costs	Benefits	Costs	Benefits
Group affected	Relative weight								
Group a	1	A	D	E	—		N	Q	R
Group b	3	H		—	R		—	S	T
Group c	1	L	J	—	S	M	—	V	W
Group d	2	—		T	—		—	—	—
Group e	1	—	K		U		P	—	—
		Σ	Σ			Σ	Σ		

SOURCE: Ibid., p. 25.

This is one way of analyzing the objective-achievement matrix model. The concept is based on a hierarchy of objectives, beginning with goals derived as ideals. "An ideal is like a horizon allowing for indefinite progression in its direction but always receding. Ideals are characteristically of intrinsic value and are prized in themselves."[6]

A point requiring emphasis from the matrix in Table 11.1 is the probabilistic nature of, or uncertainty between, the educational inputs and the educational outputs. Even though the prevailing tendency is to establish objectives of a deterministic nature, a good program might also be computed on a probability distribution.

In setting objectives, a frequent approach is either to maximize an objective using a fixed input or to minimize the amount of an input necessary to satisfy a fixed objective. Education not only has several inputs (people, places, movements, costs and activities), but also several outputs (objectives). Unfortunately, no common scale for measuring the values attached to outputs exists in education and, hence, education exists in an argumentative environment, a state that has both beneficial and harmful effects.

Objectives also differ in the probable time required for their attainment. (See Figure 11.2.) An example for short-range educational planning (five to ten years) is that of constructing two elementary schools or establishing an educational planning section with one general planner, two physical planners, one social planner, one economic planner, one specification writer and one secretary. An objective for middle-range educational planning (ten to fifteen years) could be acquiring six sites for new educational facilities of completing a feasibility study for establishing an educational planning section. For long-range educational planning (fifteen to twenty-five years), a possible objective might be to make extensive changes in the science curriculum program or replace old facilities with six school centers strategically placed within areas of high population densities.

To these three ranges of planning activities can be added objectives related to people, places, movements, economics and activities. Regardless of subject setting, measurements in the form of standards for each must be carefully determined; such procedures have recently been criticized as inflexible and, in many cases, inaccurate. One alternative to establishing standards is to set appropriate ratios as objectives to allow for adaptability or interaction among any of our five major variables.

[6]Ibid., p. 22.

Objectives can be clarified through dialogues between the educational planner and the public or its representative, the school board. The first step for the educational planner to undertake is a thorough study of relevant press, radio and television material; public statements of representative groups; and an understanding of the prevailing patterns and trends. From these sources, a great deal of information can be obtained. Another source is the educational planner's ability to sense latent aspirations. Finally, a good source is a direct dialogue with those involved in the educational process.

Following these investigations, the educational planner must prepare the goals and objectives. For each goal and objective, the expected effect must be spelled out, not only for the whole educational system, but for significant sections, such as people, places, movements, economics and activities. Each goal and objective should be worked out in specific terms or, rather, a range of alternatives. The assumptions on which each objective rests must be clearly expressed and inconsistencies spelled out. Brevity and clarity should act as hallmarks for communicating the objectives. Two aids for getting the message across are graphs and maps. With these and other tools, the objectives are ready for presentation and for reactions. The precise way in which the presentation is carried out depends on the particular circumstances, the personality of the people involved and the underlying goals of the various public groups. After the dialogue, a reformulation of the objectives may be necessary and, again, a re-presentation of newly formed objectives. After several interactions-presentations, discussions, reactions and reformulations, an agreement on a package of goals and objectives may be reached, to form the basis for designing the final plans.

12 Designing plans

The concept of designing plans should be considered in terms of "what, why and how" and the philosophy, objectives and processes existing in the urban educational scheme. These subjects cannot be approached effectively, without an understanding of the nature of design itself. A comprehensive definition of design would be most useful. However, what is known of design is broad and extremely subjective. Therefore, the following definitions of design, formulated by leaders in the planning field, are set forth to establish the boundaries of the subject. Once the varying nature of the subject has been observed, the philosophy, objectives, and processes of design can be studied to indicate future implications.

SOME THOUGHTS ON DESIGNING

Burnham Kelly:

. . . One tends to suspect that the real value of the term (and it can be a very great value indeed) is that it offers a good rallying device for an interest on the part of all these men (architects, landscape architects, city planners), and others, who have in the past been occupied with smaller and simpler matters and have tended to neglect important aspects of their professional responsibilities.[1]

[1]Jacqueline Tyrwhitt, "Definitions of Urban Design," *Synthesis* (Cambridge, Mass.: Harvard University Graduate School of Design, April 1957), p. 28.

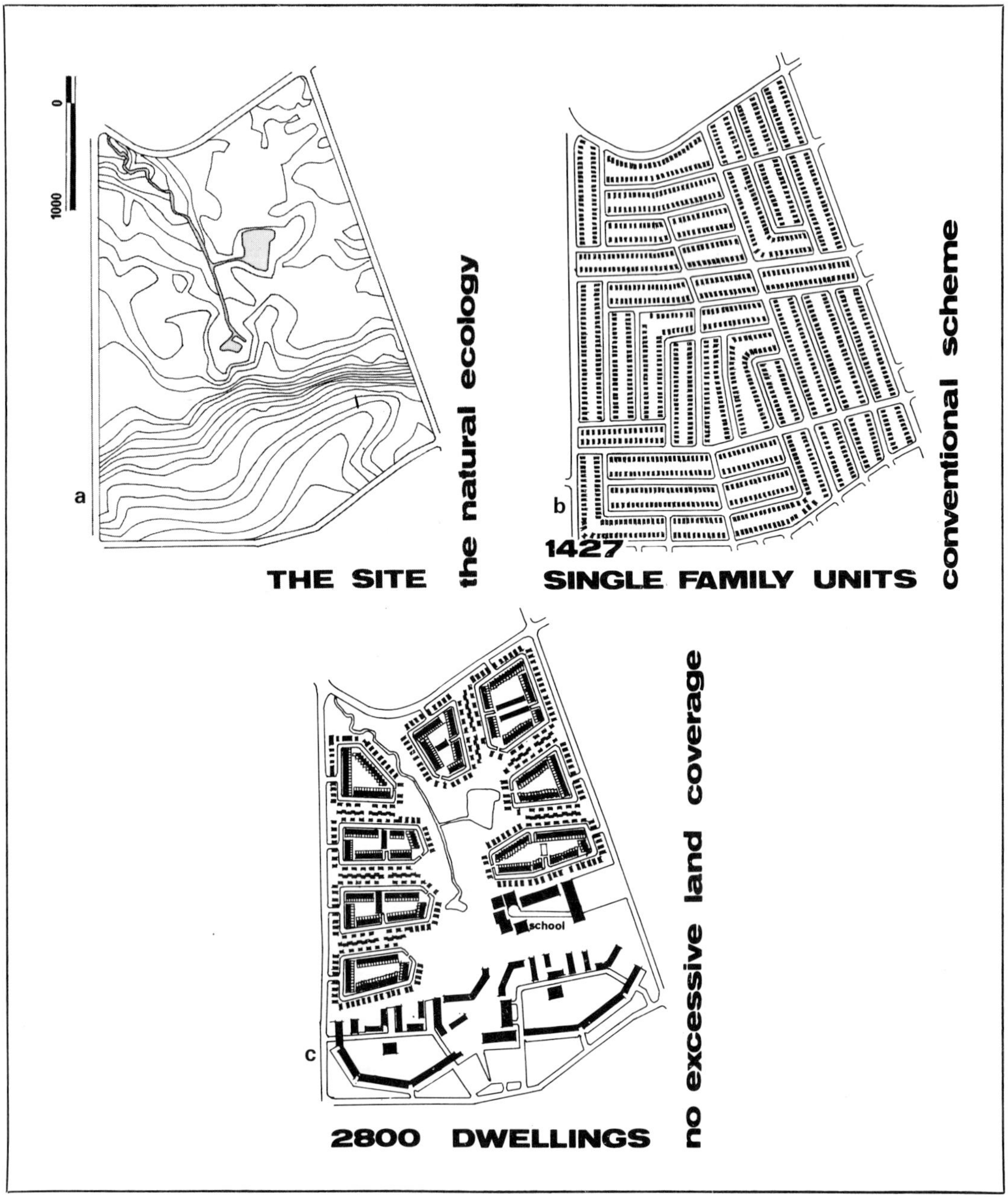
0
1000
a
THE SITE
the natural ecology
b
1427
SINGLE FAMILY UNITS
conventional scheme
school
c
2800 DWELLINGS
no excessive land coverage

FIGURE 12.1

Le Corbusier:

Urbanism is the most vital expression of a society. The task of urbanism is to organize the use of the land to suit the works of man, which fall into these three categories: (1) the unit of agricultural production; (2) the linear industrial city; (3) the radio-concentric city of exchange (ideas, government, commerce). Urbanism is a science with three dimensions. Height is as important to it as the horizontal expanse.[2]

Richard J. Neutra: "Giving shape to a community and moulding its activities is urban design. [See Figure 12.1.] It deals with the dynamic features not only in space, but in time as well."[3]

Walter Gropius:

Good urban design represents the consistent effort to create imaginatively the living spaces of our urban surroundings. [See Figure 12.2.] In order to supercede today's soul-destroying robotization, the modern urban designer's exciting task is to satisfy all emotional and practical human needs by coordinating the dictates of nature, technique and economy into a beautiful habitat.[4]

S. Giedion: "Urban design has to give visual clues to the relationship between You and Me."[5] (See Figure 12.3.)

Thomas H. Creighton: "Urban design is, to me, the three-dimensional expression of the social factors that induce people to gather together in cities . . ."[6] (See Figure 12.4.)

Lloyd Rodwin:

. . . I suggest the civic design is the part of the theory and art of city planning concerned with organizing the major components of the physical environment so that the parts form and reflect a satisfying aesthetic unit; and in which the theme of the synthesis finds rich and varied means of expression in the details of the urban development . . .[7]

Orlindo Grossi:

Isn't urban design that art which formulates dense human environment—people, buildings, space, services—into meaningful, vital, aesthetic experience, and doesn't this design use tools—sociological data, engineering services,

[2]Ibid.
[3]Ibid.
[4]Ibid.
[5]Ibid.
[6]Ibid.
[7]Ibid.

FIGURE 12.2
(a) Designed shapes all round
(b) Vista from a seat

FIGURE 12.2, *cont.*

(c) Sky street
(d) Skyline and harbor from an apartment
(e) Working with nature
(f) Creating a free environment for students

FIGURE 12.3

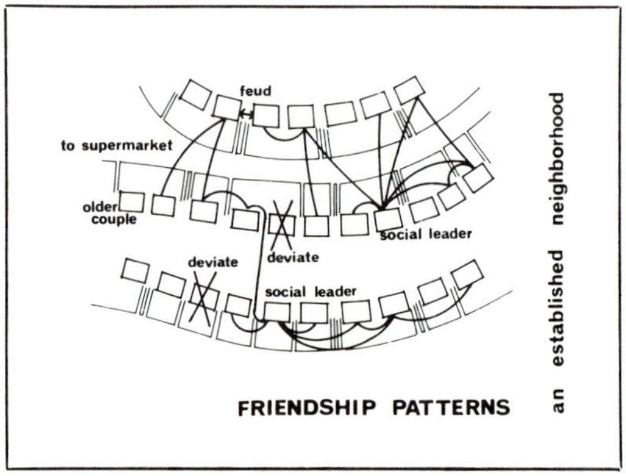

FIGURE 12.4

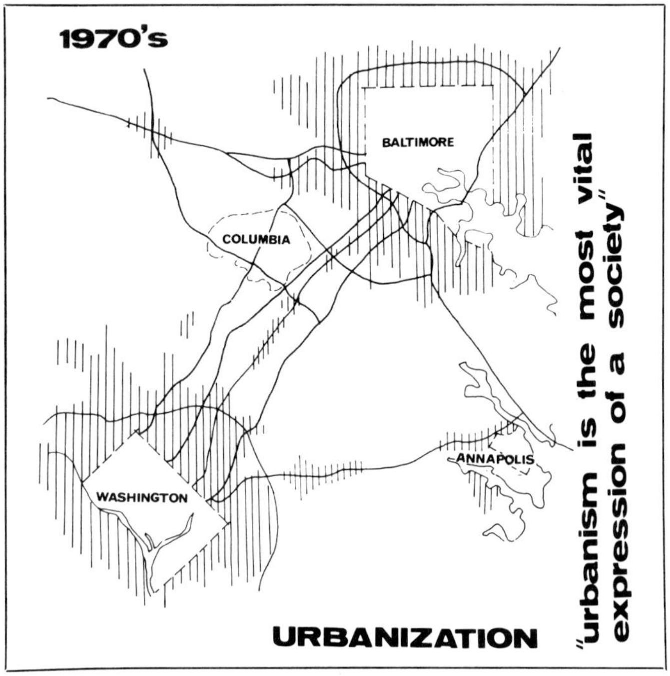

technological advances, economic values, among others—to develop essentially a better art of living?[8] [See Figure 12.5.]

Christopher Tunnard: "The city is, or could be, man's supreme creation. All its monuments from triumphal arches to man-hole covers—bear testimony to this fanciful suggestion through their design."[9]

Sidney L. Katz: "The field of urban design deals with integrated concrete solutions to the specialized social needs and interrelationships of individuals, families, neighborhoods, communities, cities, regions, states, nations, and the world."[10]

William Zeckendorf: "The city is one of man's greatest creations. Its form should be a natural expression of its varied functions harmoniously organized by artifice. The man who searches for a better city pattern should take the analyses of economists as a basis from which to work. Imagination must create the edifice."[11]

[8]Ibid.
[9]Ibid.
[10]Ibid.
[11]Ibid.

Richard G. Stein:

. . . Our schemes must be comprehensive and bold and must originate in the social and cultural refinements of the people who will use them, and yet they must be sufficiently humble to recognize that an individual is about six feet tall, walks only three miles per hour and can only recognize another individual if he is within 200 feet.[12]

L. Hilberseimer: "Planning deals in general with the search for harmonious relationships between man, techniques and nature and specifically, with the development of the city's different parts, each according to its function and its efficient relationship to other parts and to the whole . . ."[13]

William N. Bryger: "Urban Design: the art and science of resolving the chaos of our cities . . ."[14]

Pietro Belluschi: "Our present efforts in city planning are directed towards goals beyond mere creation of forms. [See Figure 12.6.] Whether we like them or not they reflect the ideals of our American

[12]Ibid.
[13]Ibid.
[14]Ibid.

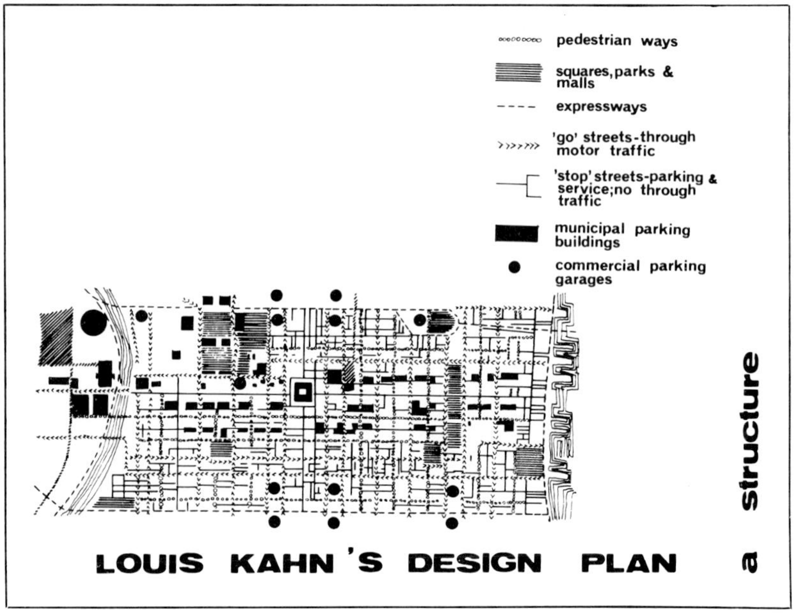

FIGURE 12.5

way of life and as such are the substance of our culture."[15]

Charles Abrams:

Urban design in a democratic society is more than houses, factories and public works on a blueprint. It is one of the many technical aspects of a process involved with people, their needs, wants, desires, their foibles and idiosyncrasies, their laws and their institutions. It must detect all these, guide them in part, but be guided by them in the main as a single facet of a great complex that includes the human being, every human being in himself, and as part of the greater community.[16]

Catherine Bauer: "Urban design is the organization of the physical environment for the urban life to meet human needs. In this sense 'design' is the step in the planning process where objectives are translated into concrete, spatial terms."[17] (See Figure 12.7.)

A. C. Shire: "Urban design is the arrangement of spatial elements and physical plant of a community of people engaged in non-agricultural pursuits so that these may be enjoyed according to the criteria of the age . . ."[18]

John M. Gaus:

Urban design is the arrangement of the land, water and other physical structures of a city. This arrangement may be the product of human design based on deliberate effort to reflect public needs and resources, made by the authorized public officials, and also of the decisions of individuals and groups reflecting their own objectives and modified by external influence of market, law and knowledge.[19]

Charles M. Haar:

I do not believe it's possible to define "urban design" in the abstract, for until one knows for what purpose a definition is being made (a statute, a hortatory epistle for architects, or a general communication to the layman), and in what context (individual, or group buildings, facilities or other appurtenances) the definitional problem becomes a painful and fruitless dispute. To show how poetic (and to some extent empty) even courts can become when dealing with the subject, consider this extract from a judicial opinion: "the accommodations, through unity in construction, of the variant

[15]Ibid.
[16]Ibid.
[17]Ibid.

[18]Ibid.
[19]Ibid.

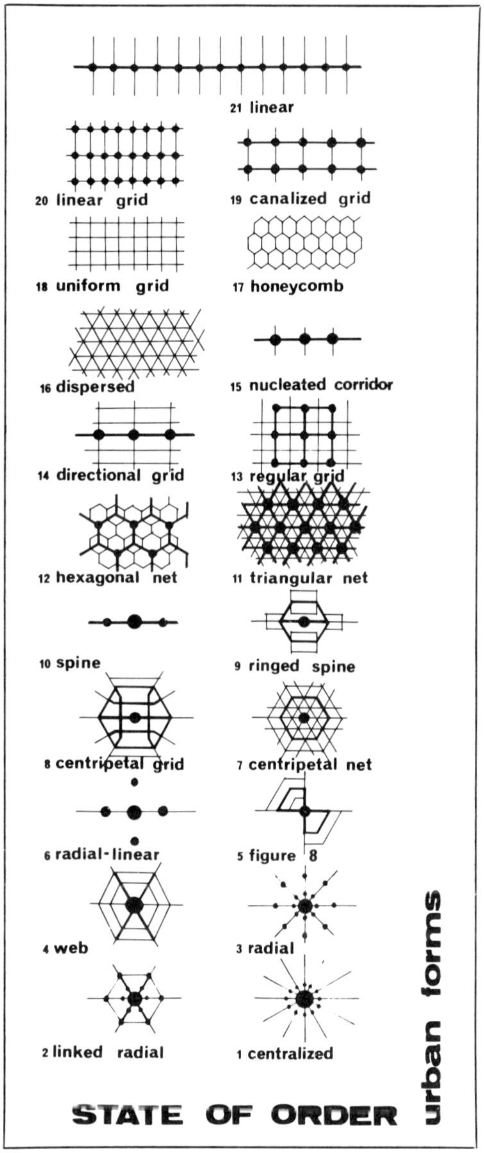

FIGURE 12.6

FIGURE 12.7

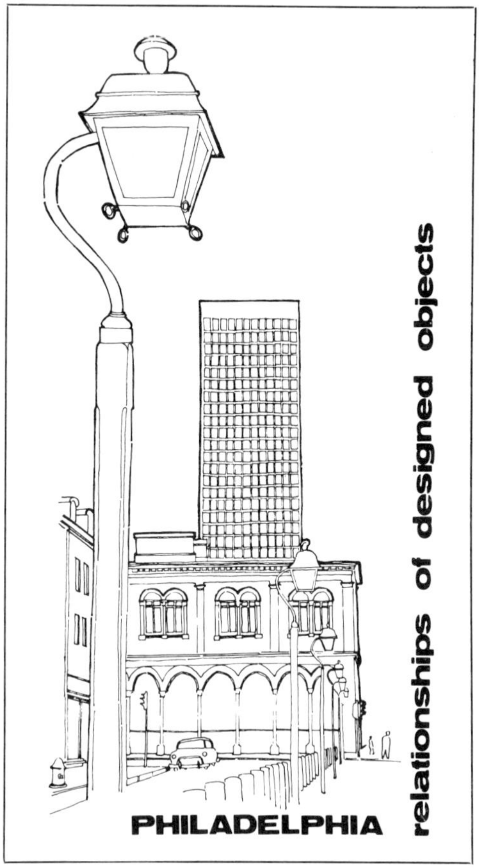

interests seeking expression in the local physical life to the interest of the community as a social unit."[20] [See Figure 12.8.]

Lonberg-Holm:

Design is but one aspect of a development process which spans six phases. For the development of any new form or activity pattern can be analyzed as a process comprising six characteristics and interacting phases: (1) research (analysis), (2) design (synthesis), (3) production (formation), (4) distribution (dispersion), (5) utilization (performance), (6) elimination (termination). To achieve a rhythmic and balanced continuity in development there must be a progressive elimination of the old along with the emergence of the new. The two most important phases of this development process are research and elimination—research for the continuous exploration of new human needs,

[20]Ibid.

FIGURE 12.8

FIGURE 12.9

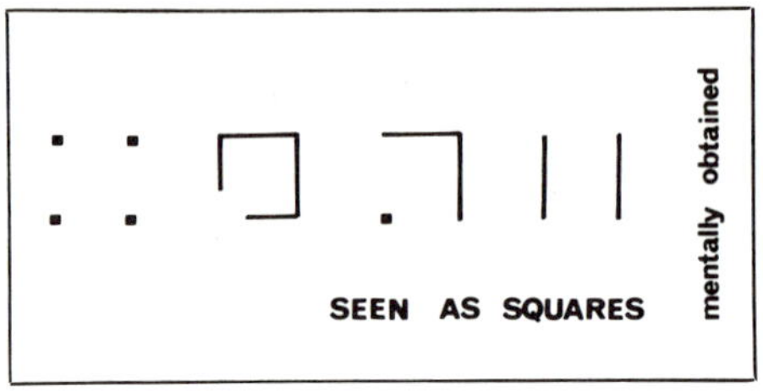

elimination for the continuous rejection of obsolete structures. This involves the concept of "time zoning" to control the life span of structures of all kinds.[21]

THE CONCEPT OF DESIGNING PLANS

Design involves three essential ingredients: material, form, and the dynamic interrelationships of the components within the whole. Material is a basic building block that is derived from the physical environment, and it is the basic medium with which the designer works. Form represents the arrangement of material—the shaping of the physical materials into an appropriate outline for housing the activity systems. (See Figure 12.9.) The final aspect of the design problem is the dynamic arrangement of the various movements into an integrated whole. Such a concept of design emphasizes the influence of the artist on the design process, much like the sculptor's influence on the statue or the painter's influence on his composition. It is obvious that, of the creative ideas put into a design, the ultimate design bears the stamp of the designer and is truly unique. A design is made by creative technicians who combine their technical capability for expressing ideas with a creative and ingenious imagination that reassembles and rearranges the order of things. Much of the creativity stems from the symmetry, integrity, beauty, and function of the natural environment. New designs not only derive their inspiration from old forms and natural structures, but they also represent subsystems of larger systems. It must be remembered that although a design may possess a great deal of autonomy, it is still considerably dependent on its interactions with the larger environment. The designer must constantly remember that, although the basic design process involves the arrangement and recomposition of material, he must design a dynamic system that reflects the movements and activities of people. Thus, the designer must not only be technically competent in the physical design and materials and have an artistic and imaginative talent, but must also be thoroughly grounded in human behavior and the needs of society. Grillo has devised a triangular concept of designing, shown in Figure 12.10. The multiple components of the design process point out two basic needs: (1) an effective

[21]Ibid.

procedure for locating human activities (whether or not one is concerned with one or many different land uses) and (2) a strengthened understanding of land uses, before designing a physical environment.

The emphasis on movement in the design process accentuates the fact that the design itself must be constructed to permit appropriate activities to function within the physical environment. This emphasis on movement in the design process also stresses the fact that design itself is a dynamic and active process rather than a mechanical reproduction of a physical representation. A design cannot be static either in the process or in the final form. The design is a catalyst and has the power to give formal meaning to the urban environment and to give its citizens a sense of urban personality. The design environment is defined as "... that set of physical elements in the environment which is under the control of the environmental designer."[22] By its very nature, the creative act of designing the finished product reflects much of the personality of the designer. (See Figure 12.11.)

> The vicarious attributes of designer experience, conventional wisdom and intuitive guessing, all have a role in the design process; but alone they are not good enough. The move toward more refined understanding of man-environment relations as they impinge on the design process is as irreversible as it is necessary.[23]

The designer must have a broad, mature philosophy of society and the technical skills for necessary analysis, in order to evolve an appropriate plan.

> Urban design is an attempt to replace specialization ... specialization such as traffic engineering, industrial exploitation of land, housing development, etc.... by a comprehension that is achieved through combining a few studies in depth with an increased awareness of many related areas which contribute to a more correct total picture even when they cannot be studied in detail.[24]

[22]Raymond G. Studer, "Some Aspects of the Man Designed Environmental Interface," *Response to Environment,* ed. Gary J. Coates and Kenneth M. Moffett, Student Publication of the School of Design (Raleigh: North Carolina State University, 1969), p. 78.

[23]Ibid.

[24]Edward F. Sekler (ed.), *Historic Urban Spaces,* Reports and Discussions from the Seminar U.D. 1–5b (Cambridge, Mass.: Harvard University Graduate School of Design, 1966), p. 1.

FIGURE 12.10

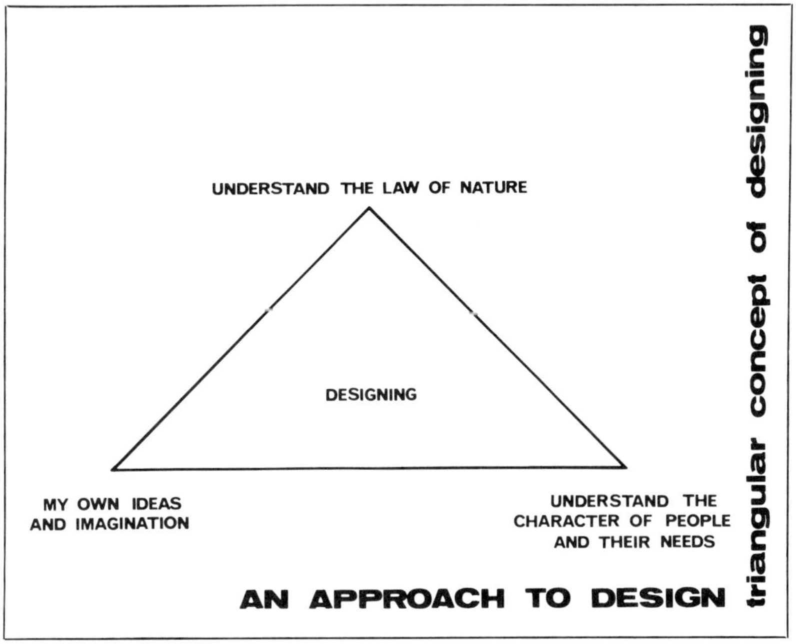

FIGURE 12.11

The designer can usefully employ the discipline of systems analysts. Technical competence and a general orientation provide an approach to the total picture and completion of the design. Much stress in design is placed on the optimization of functional relationships. Designing plans, in effect, is the design of the relation between facilities and their interconnected arrangement in space and time. The essential components of the design deal with the interactions or interrelations among the various activity systems within the design area.

Urban design is the rational process of giving physical form to the city. It implies the logical interrelation of functional, aesthetic and social needs into a physical framework. It attempts to achieve a coherent, yet varied, order in which individual parts can be identified and related to the over-all form.[25]

[25]*Background,* Preliminary Report No. 1 (San Francisco: San Francisco Department of City Planning, 1969), p. 25.

In a more poetic sense, Gropius has stated that ". . . design is neither an intellectual not a material affair, but simply an integral part of the stuff of life, necessary for everyone in a civilized society."[26] (See Figure 12.12.)

There seems to be general agreement that the essence of the definition of design involves the interaction of the various activity systems that will exist within the design area.

INFLUENCES ON DESIGNING PLANS

The design problem is a complex one and is influenced by many factors, including such things as cultural and political influences along with natural and man-made environments. Other factors that

[26]Walter Gropius, *Scope of Total Architecture* (New York: Harper & Row, 1955), p. 7.

influence plans include climate, psychological and technological factors and social and cultural interchanges. These cultural interchanges have become increasingly important and are influencing technologists in the structuring of our environment and its communication power. The plan, when translated into physical form, is essentially an open system that has many activity systems constantly interacting.

Other considerations involved in designing plans include the use of time, the comprehensive planning and development of the urban area, social interactions, economic development, and the way in which educational planning influences them. Such an approach assumes the use of the most modern technology for both analysis and planning. Only when these considerations have been studied in terms of their interactions will the comprehensive educational plan approach the optimum. The successful design must be a composition in which all elements seem to come in their natural order without giving the impression that the elements have been forced into place or that they have resulted from a compromise. To arrive at such a solution is particularly difficult when conflicting forces are present. (See Figure 12.13.)

FIGURE 12.12

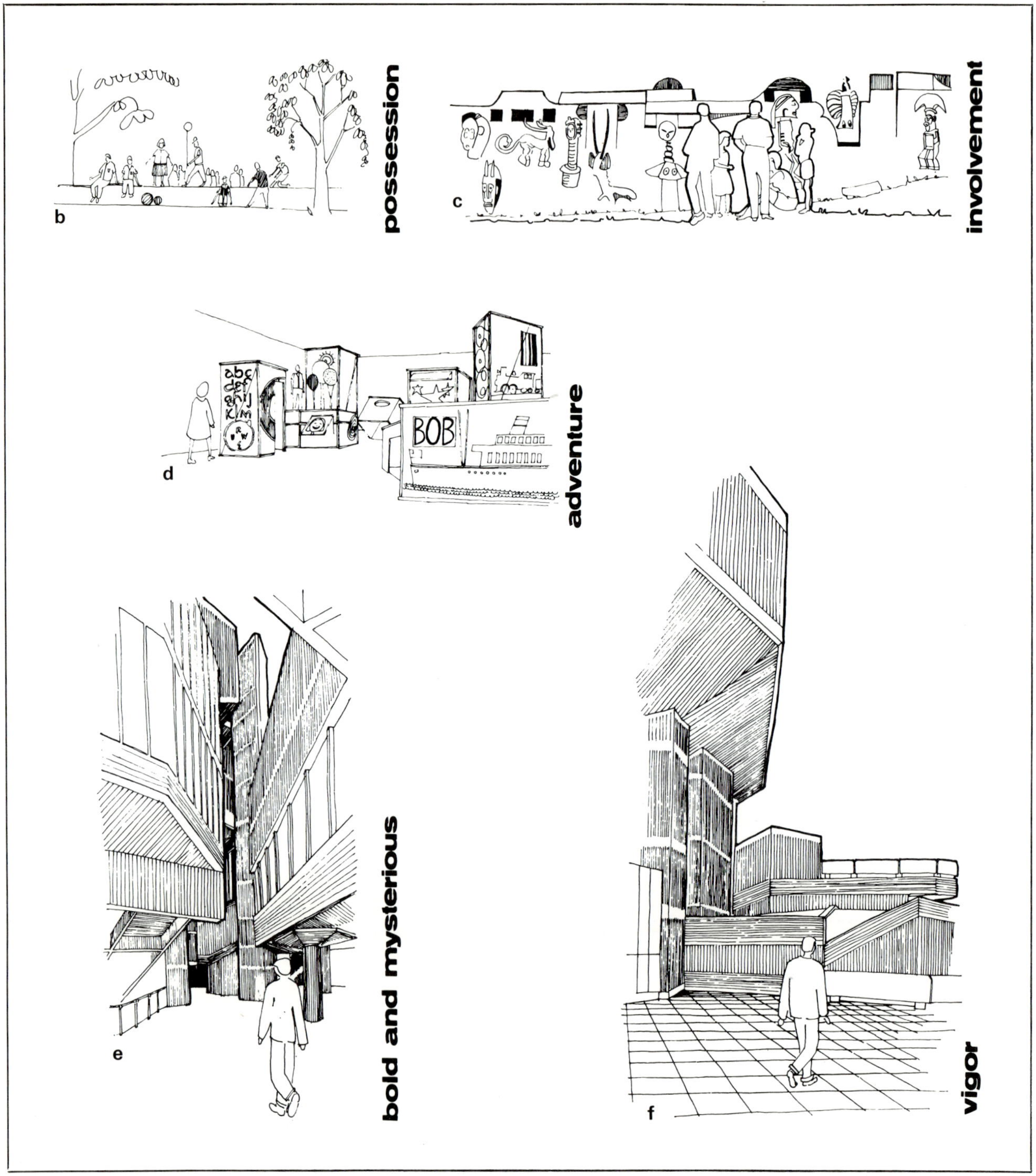

FIGURE 12.12, *cont.*

FIGURE 12.13

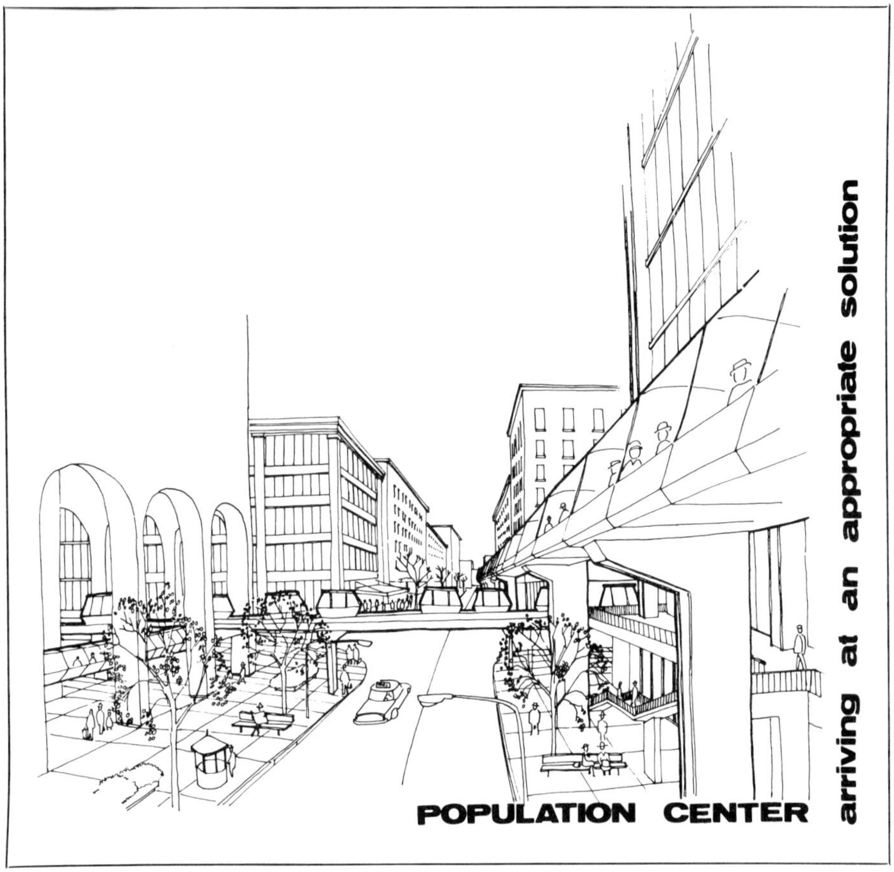

The ultimate solution to the design problem is based on the assumption that each case will be unique and each solution must reflect that unique problem. (See Figure 12.14.) Specific programs for each project, therefore, need details about the essential ideas and data that reflect and represent the design of that problem.

THE DESIGN PROCESS

As a pragmatic process the design activities begin with a reconnaissance of the design environment and a preliminary period of research during which appropriate data about the design solution are derived and some type of graphic documentation is composed.

> The series of operations leading from the definition of the design problem usually posed in terms of abstract needs and concepts to the preparation of physical design plan. The design process includes a broad scope of activities ranging from field surveys and the definition of the specific objectives and alternative solutions for achieving them to the articulation and integration of the initial concept and physical proposals [See Figure 12.15]. The task of designing an open space system, [begins] with the consideration of needs of the people that will use the space, the land available for development to design criteria and principles applicable to the site and [culminates] in actual play system.[27]

The process of designing plans proceeds through the original definition, the collection of data, the preliminary trial solutions, the modification of the

[27] *Background,* p. 26.

FIGURE 12.14

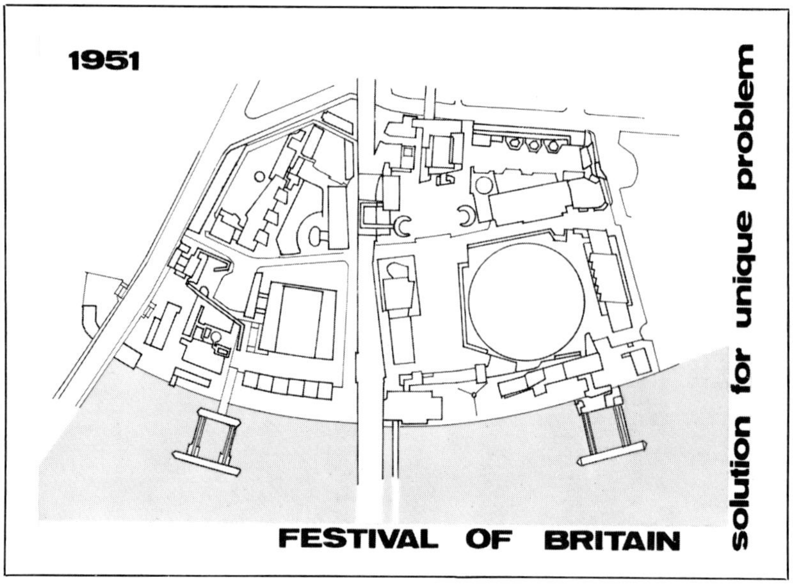

FIGURE 12.15

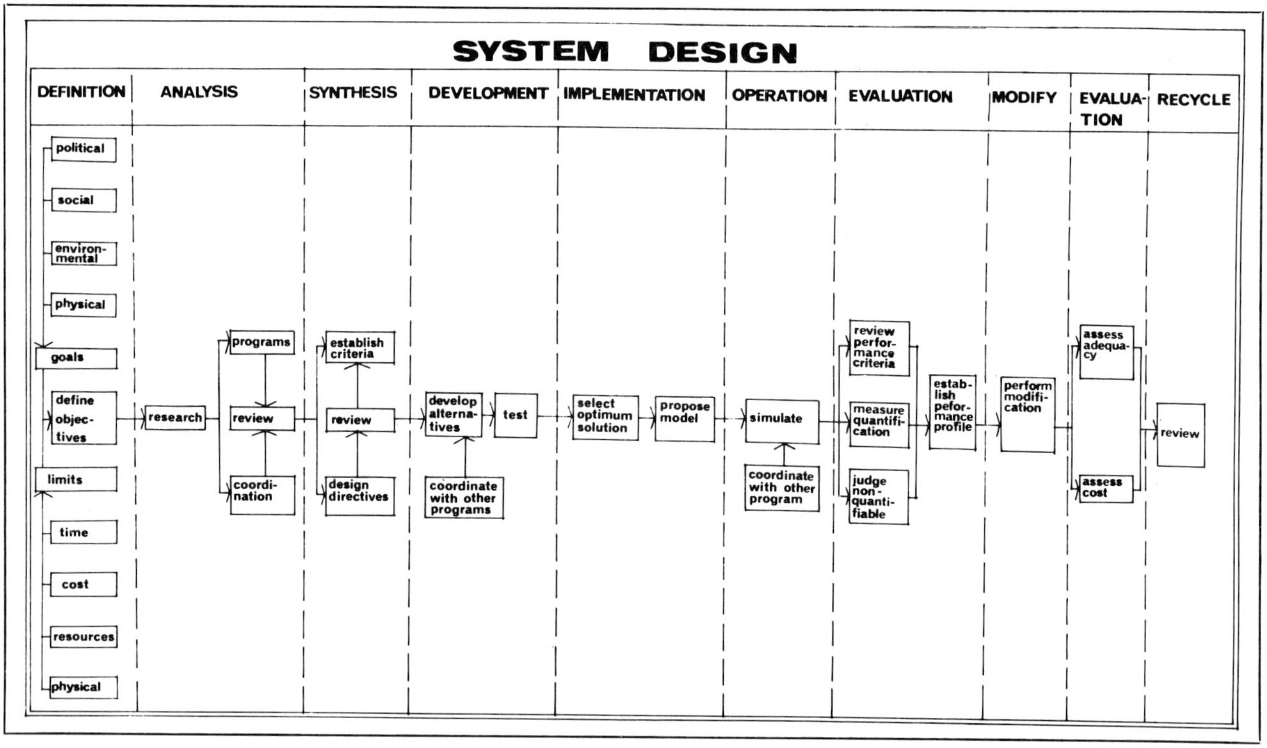

tentative solutions and a final plan. Throughout this period, the planner tries to interpret societal needs and fulfill them with a physical form. The planner is required, therefore, to develop some kind of methodology that will express the basic wishes of his client, proceed through some type of analytical procedure and translate the wishes of the client into a design. (See Figure 12.16.) It has become increasingly apparent that the planner must be aware of the changing nature of the physical form and its relation to human endeavors. Therefore, he must design with the greatest degree of flexibility, while interpreting the present needs of the client; his plan should include contingency factors that will allow planners to cope with future changes.

A designer would profit more from training in the techniques of systematic observation than in the empty rituals included under the category of an experimental design. It is extremely difficult, if not impossible, to execute a rigorous experiment that deals with important relationships under natural conditions. Experiments in the field are replete with unanticipated variables and past *ad hoc* explanation. . . . The field investigator must be extremely sensitive to the structure of the environment, the important processes that are taking place, the people with whom he works, the administrative procedures that must be followed.[28]

Plans must be flexible; they must never be static or superimposed on the environment. They must, indeed, be a translation of the environment. (See Figure 12.17.) The question is essentially one of utility, where *utility* is defined as "personal preferences." Needless to say, it is almost impossible to plan an environment that will completely benefit each person. However, there is a flexibility about human beings that allow them to adjust their environment to their own psychological makeup, rather than passively adjust themselves to the environment. The environment does influence an individual, but human nature resists Pavlovian stereotyping from an environment. The central focus for the planner is on

[28]Robert Sommer, *Personal Space, The Behavioral Basis of Design* (Englewood Cliffs, N.J.: Prentice-Hall, 1969), p. 166.

FIGURE 12.16

human activity systems, which are dynamic interacting components of the larger system. Design under these circumstances is a process of interpreting human needs, rather than furnishing a physical environment that merely reflects the designer's ideas. The design process, therefore, is participatory planning in the true sense of the phrase. Although the designer must constantly interact with those people whose desires are to be fulfilled, his creative aspirations must not be negated. The ultimate plan should furnish form to the client's needs and, at the same time, should display uniqueness and creativity. (See Figure 12.18.)

Designing plans requires a series of steps or procedures, including visual observation; the analysis of social and economic data; the establishment of a concrete plan; architectural tests in terms of acceptability; determination of scale and of the influence on the city fabric; the preparation of a design brief; and the development of techniques for systematic, visual and topographical surveys and analysis. Significant characteristics should be appropriately recorded and a planning language developed that includes both the old and the new urban fabric. New urban relationships between buildings and landscape form need identification. The specific requirements, a three-dimensional framework for the site and the proper placement of the necessary elements should be worked out. Density problems (see Figure 12.19) demand

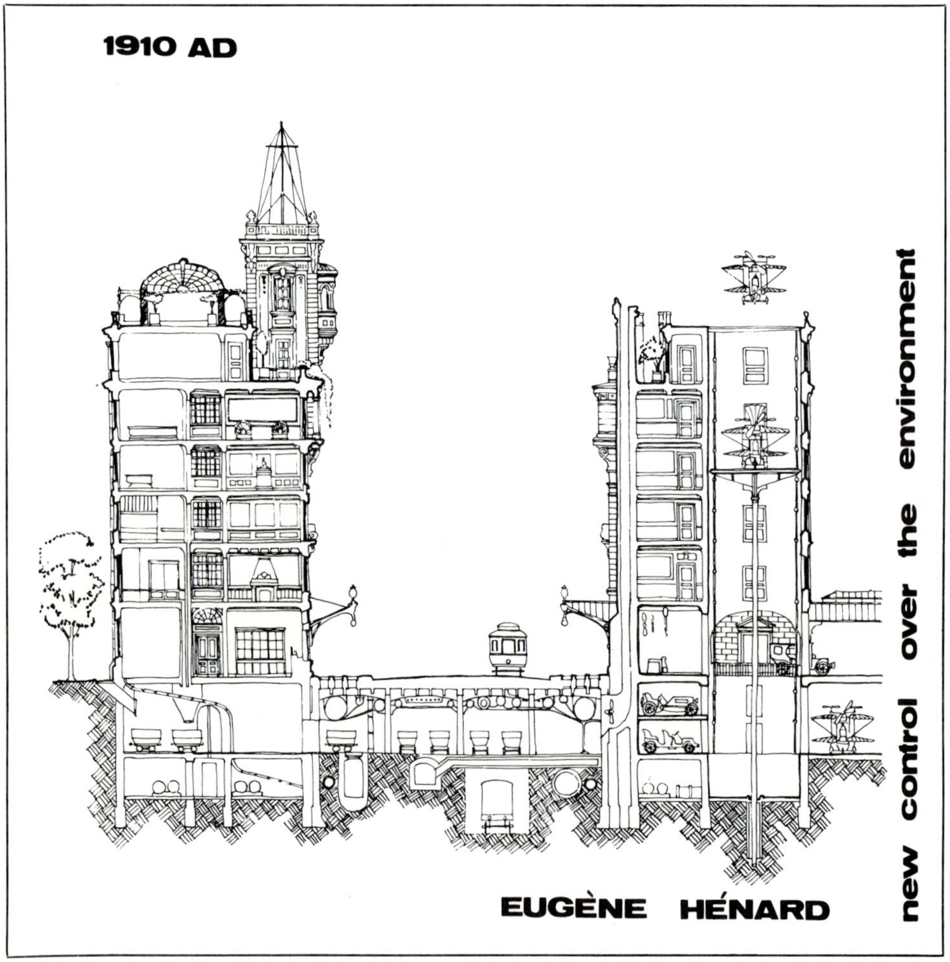

FIGURE 12.17

FIGURE 12.18

resolution, as do the organization of building forms and spaces and the selection of urban textures and colors for maintenance and utilitarian function. The various forms of space and the specific building forms, appropriate pedestrian movement, and vehicular traffic patterns must be laid out. At the same time the relationship between the new and the old needs emphasis in a constant monitoring of the total process.[29] Relationships to be given attention in the design process include: (1) probing the relationships between human densities and their effects on public economy, standards of maintenance, and personal environment; (2) using the powers of different land uses in different situations to compel differing intensities and volumes of flow of vehicles or of people at different times; (3) seeking the optimum for securing the following environmental conditions (a) a safe, quiet environment for working, (b) lively, tempting conditions for selling, and (c) fast absorption of pedestrians from public transport routes. To develop the basic design abilities the planners need to do the following: (1) to see, rather than to draw; (2) to conceive shapes three-dimensionally; (3) to select affinities; (4) to distinguish real differences from apparent differences; (5) to create space by erosion, rather than by construction; (6) to compose spatial orders by erosions and articulations; (7) to experience

FIGURE 12.19

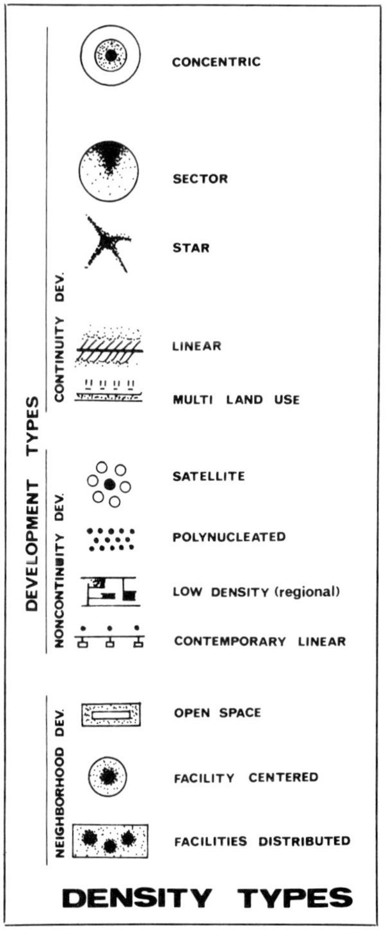

[29]Graeme Shankland, Address at the Annual Conference of the American Institute of Planners, Urban Design Session, August 18, 1964.

Table 12.1 Sketch description of a grid

Ends Goals	Purpose Principles Strategy	Theory Commitment	
Organizing principles	Characteristics Operation Tactics	Methodology	Operational components
Organizing specifics	Environment Place Use	Operational Tools	Empiric knowledge Field research Systems Systems analysis
Components Means	Functional Physical	Social hierarchies Technical	 Model

SOURCE: Ibid.

spatial and other, nonvisual relationships; (8) to recognize and analyze local characteristics; (9) to re-order local character recognizably; (10) to correlate economic, social and physical data with sensuous aspects of surroundings; and (11) to prepare, in the three dimensions of space and in a continuum of time, a succession of environmental changes that progressively redevelop (e.g.) a school area, so that the rate of succession may be accelerated or retarded to adjust to social and economic conditions without abandoning environmental standards.[30]

The designer goes through a procedure that involves abstraction, parameter definition, and the design process. One mechanical procedure for going through this process is called a *grid.* The grid is primarily used for parameter definition. (See Table 12.1.) Its purpose is to illustrate the following principles:

(1) Urban hierarchies in complementarity (physical components in interaction); (2) complementarity of choices [maximization] of opposites; (3) complementarity of organizational principles (intensity-density and tranquility); (4) functional hierarchies in complementarity (public and private interest).[31]

[30]David Thomas, "Education for Assessing, Designing and Cultivating Urban Environment," *Planning Outlook,* no. 2, **11**:48 (1964).

[31]*Advanced Studies in Urban Environments, Toward an Urban Model,* A Study by the Master Class in Architecture at Yale University, Serge Chermayeff, Professor in Architectural Design (New Haven, Conn.: Yale University, 1967), p. 149.

Special attention to the natural characteristics of the environment must be constantly given by the planner. These include climate, light, the various types of interrelationships among the activity systems and adherence to appropriate scale, color, texture and patterns. Attention must be constantly given to the functions to be served, as well as to the aesthetic aspects of the urban design. Statuary, street lights, green strips, broad streets, buildings of historical consequence, sculpture and the appropriate use of natural landmarks within the design environment are necessary for the success of the total design. The designer must put all these characteristics together and come up with an integrated whole. The natural topography, in terms of botanical resources, natural landmarks and the appropriate arrangement of man-made structures within these natural environments, are essential for good educational design. Table 12.2 summarizes the primary data in the composition of a design.

The design process includes four essential activities: defining, analyzing, synthesizing and modifying. The activities occur in that sequence—first, problem definition; second, analysis of the relevant variables; third, the synthesis of relevant variables into a tentative design; and finally, a modification that continues until the final form is agreed on. The above sequence suggests the strong similarity between the planning process and the systems approach to problem solving. They both include a strong reliance on the creative

Table 12.2 Components of design

- **I Materials that are sensed**
  - A Visible materials
    - 1 Surface qualities
      - (a) Color
      - (b) Texture
      - (c) Pattern
      - (d) Rhythm
      - (e) Shape
      - (f) Night effects
- **II Forms**
  - A Single forms
    - 1 Objects (man-made)
      - (a) Utilitarian
      - (b) Artifacts
      - (c) Curiosities
    - 2 Architectural examples
      - (a) Style
      - (b) Important architect
      - (c) Major work
      - (d) Curiosity
  - B Relations of forms
    - 1 Architectural combinations
      - (a) Façades
      - (b) Groups
      - (c) Masses
      - (d) Transitional and boundary forms
    - 2 Land and plant forms
      - (a) Important topographic features
      - (b) Land or planting designs of period or style
      - (c) Land or planting designs of notable practitioners
      - (d) Groups of indigenous plants
      - (e) Unusual plants
    - 3 Viewpoints and landmarks
      - (a) Major prospects
      - (b) Impressive vistas
      - (c) Unusual scenes
      - (d) Forms that usually dominate or symbolize surroundings
    - 4 Open Spaces
      - (a) Square and piazzettas
      - (b) Recreational areas
      - (c) Parks and other
      - (d) Cemeteries
      - (e) Intersections
      - (f) Cul-de-sacs
- **III Expressions**
  - A Past associations
    - 1 Historic sites
      - (a) Locus of single important event
      - (b) Locus of recurrent event or activity
      - (c) Site associated with significant personality
      - (d) Site associated with historic group
  - B Present associations
    - 1 Social activity sites
      - (a) Locus of recurring event or activity
      - (b) Site associated with major group
    - 2 Visual communications
      - (a) Conventional symbols
      - (b) Messages in words

SOURCE: Stephen W. Jacobs, "Design Resources of the City," *Planning for Urban Aesthetics*, Fifth Annual Conference, Organization of Cornell Planners, October 27–28, 1961, Ithaca, N.Y.: Cornell University, pp. 15–16.

input of the analyst or planner, plus a strong technical requirement in both areas. Both activities are analytically oriented, and both activities use repeated modification of the tentative solution.

> . . . One of the key reasons that the systems approach has been so effective is precisely because they have developed such tools, i.e. better modeling techniques which yield more precise evaluations, and which handle problems of rather staggering complexity with great effectiveness. To be sure, these are largely technical problems, or problems involving mostly technical issues. But it is generally erroneous to conclude that in . . . design . . . there are no subjective issues involved. Rather than elimination of subjective issues, the systems approach has helped to more clearly identify these, and to place them in proper perspective with rational issues. If anything, the systems analyst ends with more regard, not less, for man's subjective and intuitive decision-making quality.[32]

The planner, sometimes unknowingly, has borrowed heavily from the concepts of cybernetics or feedback theory. The constant repetition so character-

[32]Gary K. Stonebreaker, "Systems Analysis and Engineering Applications to Building with Special Emphasis on Design," *Handbook on Systems Analysis, Proceedings of the 1967 AIA Student Forum* (April 1968), p. 14.

istic of cybernetics subjects the process to continuous monitoring,

> ... so that by the time a design reaches the prototype stage, the designers not only know how well certain aspects of the design may work; but they also know what they don't know, and thus know what to monitor in real world testing. This, and more, adds up to a well-regulated design process, with excellent feedback control mechanism, and with extraordinary reliability of results.[33]

Thus, it has become increasingly apparent that planners are not only using systems technology more frequently and more effectively, but indeed they are becoming more cognizant of the basic principles of systems work and are in a better position rationally to incorporate those ideas into the design process.

> The design process unfolds something like this: at the beginning, in the design of a device or system ... the designer does not have a very clear notion of what he wants to do. He has only a vague concept, or none at all, of how he will go about accomplishing his task. In this sense, the design process is a learning process during which the designer must learn what the problem is and how to solve it. Within this process of learning there are certain exciting aspects of discovery. But these are interspersed with long tedious periods of rote behaviour—sheer unadulterated dull work— non-creative but necessary. It is appropriate to have computers to do this non-creative work so as to leave the designer free for the activities human beings are good at: innovation—the association of hitherto unrelated ideas. The typically human aspect of the design process is invention: the grasping of schemes that are at the beginning vague, tenuous, dream-like, and solidifying them into something tangible that can be looked at, explored qualitatively, and evaluated quantitatively. To the same schemes one can apply analytical procedures and then, on the basis of these procedures, make more precise judgments. While all activities during the design process up to the application of analytical procedures are humanoid, analytical procedures are essentially not.[34]

Probably all types of planners, whether they are educational, engineering, architectural, graphic, or tool, go through essentially the same process. They begin with a general concept and apply all of their technical and analytical training, in order to produce a specific solution to a problem. They combine utility with aesthetic qualities and use mathematical techniques, mechanical knowledge and technical skills to cut across various disciplines. All of this work is directed toward the creation of an appropriate form out of an idea.

THE EDUCATIONAL DESIGNING PLAN PROCESS

Modern methods provide a sounder base for the whole educational designing process, but the diminution of human craftsmanship could possibly sterilize the planning process. If properly used, however, there should be no danger of modern technology being anything other than another tool to further liberate the creative energies of the educational planner. An overview of the educational designing plan procedure follows:

I The Educational Planning Procedure
- 1 Development of a sketch plan
  - (a) Within a relatively short period—in months, rather than years.
  - (b) To be progressively refined from the first quick reconnaissance survey and the first drafts through later detailed drafts.
  - (c) Making use of existing data and knowledge not involving extensive programs of new research.
  - (d) Through democratic collaboration—participation of informed citizens and outside consultants when needed, cooperation between public and private groups, and between local, state and federal agencies.

II The Educational Planning Method
- 1 Determination of goals—what do the people of the planning area want their area to become in the light of:
  - (a) Its possibilities—what could the area become if proper use were made of its resources—physical, human, economic, social, cultural?
  - (b) Feasible paths of development—what should the area become in the best judgment of those who have made a special study of community problems?

[33]Ibid., p. 15.
[34]Stephen A. Coons, "Computer-Aided Design," *Ekistics* **24**:278 (October 1967).

2 Determination of educational needs—what must be provided in order to reach goals, measuring:
   (a) Existing conditions and facilities?
   (b) Shortages of physical facilities and arrangements and of program of service?
3 Programs of meeting educational needs—how can the necessary changes, facilities, and services be provided in terms of:
   (a) Time schedules—what order of projects and programs should be followed?
   (b) Physical changes—new development, redevelopment of existing arrangements?
   (c) Legislative, administrative and financial means?
   (d) Community organization and public opinion?

III The Educational Plans
1 A Statement of community objectives answering such questions as:
   (a) Size—smaller, larger or stationary population?
   (b) Economic base—the same or broader or narrower base: What existing activities should be retained, expanded, contracted, converted, abandoned? What new activities should be introduced? What relocations should be encouraged?
   (c) Community living—what improvements are needed in the way of facilities, programs of services, kinds of community organizations?
   (d) Physical arrangements—what arrangements in land use, central facilities, neighborhood designs? What areas changed, expanded, conserved?
2 Reports, charts, maps presenting what is to be done, when, by whom and by what means, covering:
   (a) Population estimates—size, characteristics and distribution.
   (b) Program for economic development—steps to achieve maximum employment, with special attention to problems of demobilization, high levels of production, employment stabilization, high standard of living and economic security, programs relating to labor force; recruitment, training, counseling, placement; capital entrepreneurial and managerial requirements; policies for industrialists, businessmen, investors, organized labor groups to follow; programs for private and public development.
   (c) Program for community services in housing, education and cultural activities, recreation, health, welfare, community and organization, and institutional development.
   (d) Programs for physical development—land use, transportation and density, plans, public work, and housing programs; designs for neighborhood units, central business, and other areas.
   (e) Programs of planning action—programs of public and private action; legislative, administrative, financial tools; official and citizen organization.[35]

From this review of the planning process, an almost classical model of the steps in the educational planning process emerges. It can be summarized as follows: projection of future decision-making, identification of the problem, development of desirable alternatives for development, invention of policies and public action to influence desirable development, testing plans for effectiveness and efficiency and choosing from among alternatives a set of policies for initiating still further improvement. Added to the general procedures described above is the concept of a continuous monitoring of the planning guidelines, with resulting modifications whenever the situation dictates, while at the same time having a reasonably clear-cut concept of the goals toward which the educator is constantly striving.

[35]E. Gordon Ericksen, *Urban Behavior* (New York: Macmillan, 1954), pp. 439–440.

Part Four

Evaluating plans

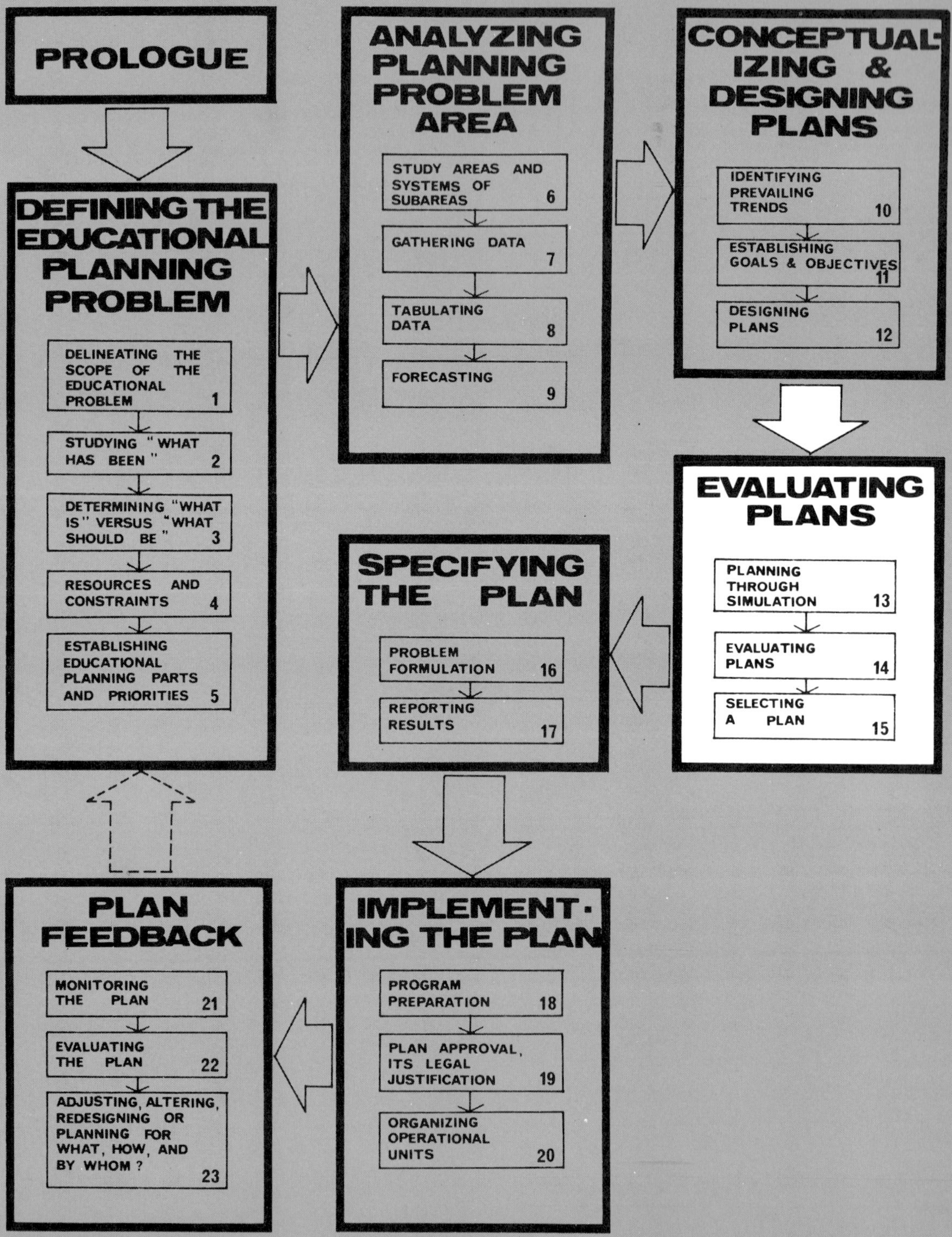

PROLOGUE
DEFINING THE EDUCATIONAL PLANNING PROBLEM
DELINEATING THE SCOPE OF THE EDUCATIONAL PROBLEM 1
STUDYING "WHAT HAS BEEN" 2
DETERMINING "WHAT IS" VERSUS "WHAT SHOULD BE" 3
RESOURCES AND CONSTRAINTS 4
ESTABLISHING EDUCATIONAL PLANNING PARTS AND PRIORITIES 5
ANALYZING PLANNING PROBLEM AREA
STUDY AREAS AND SYSTEMS OF SUBAREAS 6
GATHERING DATA 7
TABULATING DATA 8
FORECASTING 9
CONCEPTUALIZING & DESIGNING PLANS
IDENTIFYING PREVAILING TRENDS 10
ESTABLISHING GOALS & OBJECTIVES 11
DESIGNING PLANS 12
EVALUATING PLANS
PLANNING THROUGH SIMULATION 13
EVALUATING PLANS 14
SELECTING A PLAN 15
SPECIFYING THE PLAN
PROBLEM FORMULATION 16
REPORTING RESULTS 17
IMPLEMENTING THE PLAN
PROGRAM PREPARATION 18
PLAN APPROVAL, ITS LEGAL JUSTIFICATION 19
ORGANIZING OPERATIONAL UNITS 20
PLAN FEEDBACK
MONITORING THE PLAN 21
EVALUATING THE PLAN 22
ADJUSTING, ALTERING, REDESIGNING OR PLANNING FOR WHAT, HOW, AND BY WHOM? 23

Introduction

The fourth phase of this educational planning model deals with the evaluation of plans that were designed in phase three. It also deals with selecting the best plan. One technique of evaluating plans is in the following three steps:

Step 13 Planning through simulation
Step 14 Evaluating plans
Step 15 Selecting a plan

These three steps are elaborated on in Chapters 13 through 15 in Part Four.

13 Planning through simulation

The purpose of simulating an educational plan is to provide a means of observing the potential behavior of the various components of the plan. *Simulation* is a term that applies to models within which notions about relationships are identified.

THE NATURE OF SIMULATION

Simulation is a form of copying the behavior of a system (for instance, an educational plan) that proceeds in true time-sequence. It is a working model that contains a set of variables representing the principal features of the real-life system. It permits decisions that determine how these features might be modified in real time.

The implementation of educational plans is influenced by factors whose effect cannot be foreseen exactly. In many cases, however, relationships can be described in terms of probabilities. For each relationship, a range of possible effects or outcomes can be defined, and with each effect or outcome a certain probability can be defined. When repeated, if possible, such a procedure reproduces the average effect of the plan's components in the conditions assumed. Playing out the events of the plan in a realistic sequence within a probabilistic framework is the function of simulating.

The components used are, to some extent, unpredictable; therefore, some uncertainty is expected in the results. However, if simulation occurs long enough, an adequate answer should be found. In general, simulation runs are broken into a set of periods, the results of which can be taken as independent values. The general problem is then to determine the precision of estimates obtained from a run made up of several successive periods of simulation. In many cases, the successive periods possess some degree of mutual correlation, e.g., the output of a finishing period is the input for the next period. In other cases, however, a natural lull occurs that negates the output of the previous period's having any effect on the activities after the lull.

Frequently, however, correlation exists between periods, especially in educational planning operations. It is possible to allow for the effect of this by using a correction factor or a coefficient based on the degree of correlation.

Three major types of simulation models can be identified. They are: continuously changing models (analogue simulation), fixed-period models, and discrete-event models.

In the continuously changing model, the set of variables is changing continuously with time. This model represents such systems as the electromechanical forces. In the fixed-period model, time is broken up into a set of finite periods, and the variables are allowed to change only at the end of the periods. The variables are continuous quantities whose change is specified by a set of difference equations, for example. The model is used in work such as econometrics, when data are available only on a periodic basis. The discrete-event model's variables are discrete quantities representing states of the entities in the system. Interactions among the entities take place only at discrete points in time and are known as *events*. Time advances from one event to the next, and all changes in the system are made at that time. This model can be applied to a wide range of problems such as the queuing up of students in lunch lines, movement systems, and the interactions of various educational activities.

One problem of mathematically describing a plan, or a portion of a plan, is determining which variables are deterministic and which are probabilistic. The choice and the establishment of their relationships are of extreme importance for mathematical abstraction. The first step, then, for mathematical simulation is that of abstraction, and the second is the attitude that the educational planner takes toward approximating the nature of simulation and the real world as deterministic or probabilistic. As a result, the educational planner can develop the following model types:

1 A deterministic simulation of a probabilistic real world.
2 A probabilistic simulation of a deterministic real world.
3 A deterministic simulation of a deterministic real world.
4 A probabilistic simulation of a probabilistic real world.

An example of a deterministic-deterministic relationship is the study of the routes of school buses. An example of probabilistic-probabilistic relationship is the simulation of a school lunch line. An example of a deterministic-probabilistic simulation is planning an educational program using the city as a classroom. Finally, in a probabilistic real world and deterministic simulation belong statistics, such as the number of student failures.

SOME CONSIDERATIONS IN MODELING

In the simulating of a plan, four fundamental factors must be considered. They are as follows:

1 The role of planning.
2 The model.
3 The measure of the model's effectiveness.
4 The criteria for decisions.[1]

Objectives serve as criteria against which to measure the results of the simulation. This usually means a payoff in terms of the appropriate variables.

Limitations exist in simulation application. Though usually a quantitative procedure, simulation also possesses qualitative factors that must be considered.

[1]Dimitris N. Chorafas, *Systems and Simulation* (New York: Academic Press, 1965), p. 27.

Another limitation of simulation application is that, although objectivity is essential, personal opinions should not be overlooked as a data source. A further limitation concerns the degree of care that is used in forming objectives. The educational planner must not ignore uncertainty and must even take it into account during the simulation operation. Added to the above limitations is the danger of distorting a real situation, such as when the plan of nonlinear relationships is thought of as a linear set of activities. This danger exists, despite the fact that most techniques of the past have conditioned our methods of work on sets of linear equations.

With these limitations in mind, a second concern is related to abstracting, a process already mentioned. Abstracting does not necessarily mean simplifying. What is meant, however, is that the educational planner is able to bring a complex plan into proper perspective by economizing on the use of variables. It is not a matter of going directly from the original plan to reality, but rather taking a detour through simulating the major variables that will have the greatest impact on the activities when they do occur in reality. This is true whether one is using mathematical, physical, graphic or even verbal techniques of simulation. Simulation is not an all-encompassing approach, but is greatly dependent on the planner's skill, patience, creative imagination and the method he selects. Figure 13.1 gives an idea of the process.

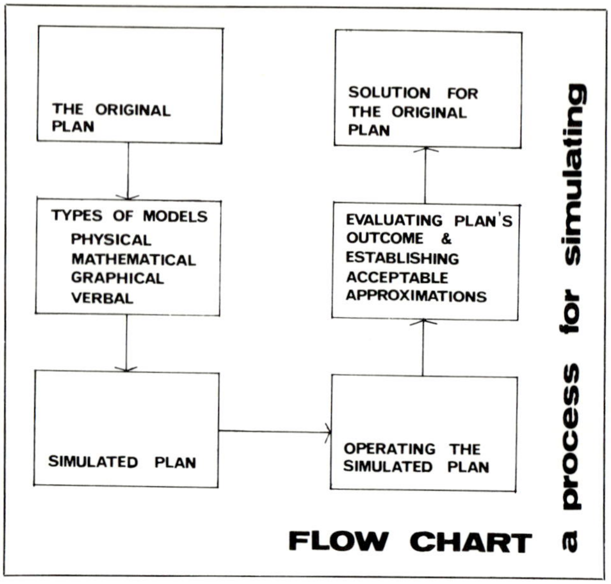

FIGURE 13.1

To carry out the above activities some further considerations are necessary: to what extent shall the level of aggregation be carried, how shall time be treated and how shall the model operate?

The level of aggregation

Perhaps the most important consideration is at what level—macro or micro—shall the data of the plan be assembled. The macro level deals with statistics of mass behavior and their properties. They are likely to be stock flow parameters (linear programming), gravity or potential functions (gravity models) and matrices of transition probabilities. The danger of using these models lies, in large part, in the planner's failure to state the explicit causal structure. Many planning assumptions are based on historical evidence or statistical frequency, when in reality these assumptions will be invalid in the future. It is not easy for the educational planner to fit probable future changes into the environment of educational behavior.

A second danger in macro analysis is the difficulty in financial accounting. This results from failure to specify objectives numerically. Thus, in choosing among alternative educational plans, the objective may be to maximize net social returns for educational financial investments, in place of solely maximizing manpower needs. This may be accomplished with a social model of employment behavior and educational attainment. Such a model may more easily yield relevant data than, for example, an optimizing model, such as linear programming.

Micro models require that the educational planner's preference system be specified in considerable detail. Preparing such detailed specifications is frustrating and, to date, still operationally crude. Lacking the tools, the educational planner is limited to empirically relevant propositions concerning the suitability of education's wares. Concomitant with this state of affairs is the failure to implement a comprehensive educational model embracing the entire range of educational activities that substantially affect the urban activity patterns. If one possesses complete information on the needs of the learner and the resources available, a perfect educational model is simple enough. However, the educational modeler is faced with subtly differentiated individual behaviors, imperfections in communication—e.g., poorly trained teachers or lack of a specific and required resource—and inequities among the various educational decision-makers who are all on the same team. These factors rule out an easy mathematical solution. At present, educational simulation is a crude approximation of the educational model.

Treating time

The model begins at one time and is carried forward to a new time, $t + n$. The way the time dimension is conceived is a matter of considerable significance. One major consideration is how often results are required. Another consideration is the response lag among the variables, and yet another, the educational planner's perception of the self-equilibrating features of the model. Such features represent equilibrium relationships between exogenous (variables outside of the model, but influencing its operation) and endogenous variables (variables within the model). Without self-equilibrating properties, the plan's systems could fluctuate cyclically, explode, or degenerate.

An approach at either end of the spectrum is possible. One focuses on the processes of change, the other on the emergent state of the plan at a specified target date. In the comparative statics approach, the endogenous variables respond quickly and fully to exogenous influences. As a result, the values of exogenous variables require prediction at the target dates, as shown in Chapter 9. How the plan moves from the base year t, to target dates, $t + n$, is unspecified.

Analytical dynamics, on the other hand, require only the plan's structural parameter and the initial values of its variables. Once implemented, all processes are endogenous except time, allowing the plan to be evaluated at any point in time.

As analytical dynamics require complete closures, and comparative statics require strong equilibrium, ". . . most model-builders compromise on recursive progressions."[2] This approach shows the plan's changes over time in lock-step fashion using lagged variables, variables of one time period that bring forward variables of another time period.

The effects of change

Variables considered as changing over time are conceived as *flows* and variables considered as an inventory of items are *stock*. As the size and number of variables in stock change they become flows, and as such they have the same determinants. The existing pattern (initial stock) of schools in a large city reflects locational decisions made over a course of time. During this course of time, the movement system, the numbers and locations of people, the resources available and the patterns of established activities all changed slowly, but cumulatively. If the educational planner organizes his plan around the present characteristics of the above-mentioned stock, the resulting plan may be quite adequate for short-range changes. The model, however, will soon lose its usefulness. To overcome this condition, many planners make use of drift parameters; that is, the structure of stocks is periodically revised to reflect changing environmental conditions.

Operating the model

Four major kinds of simulation are possible. They are: verbal models—e.g., an analogue—the physical or three-dimensional models, long used by physical designers; graphic models including photography; and the logico-mathematical models about which much has already been said.

Illustrative of a verbal model is the comprehensive educational planning process being presented in this book. An example of a three-dimensional physical model is the common architectural wood, cardboard or plastic model showing the building in a greatly

[2]Ira S. Lowry, "A Short Course in Model Design," *Journal of the American Institute of Planners*, No. 2, **31**:161 (May 1965).

reduced scale. A graphic model is an aerial photograph or a drawing. The logico-mathematical model consists of several types.

One type is the tight logical structure, whose functional relationships are uncomplicated by nonlinearities and discontinuities. The set of equations is solved by a direct relationship between the input and relevant output variables. Another type of logico-mathematical model is one lacking complete logical closure. Its method is to assume approximate values for some of the variables and to solve the rest by analytical means. The values obtained for the first pass become the basis for computing the results of the second round, the results of the second round, in turn, serve as the basis for the third, and so on. This converging operation is known as an *iterative approach.*

Still a third mathematical approach is the random operation. A number of possible events and their consequences are indicated with the use of stock variables. A change in the stock has specified consequences that induce new events. New events are also induced by exogenous factors. These are generated in a simulated approach by random choice from a given frequency-distribution of possibilities (Monte Carlo model). This approach is a good simulation test for a real-world plan.

The man-machine simulation is yet another operation. The processing of input data by the computer is periodically stopped, and the readouts are inspected by the planner. He may then adjust the results to correspond with his judgment, as to their inherent plausibility, which is then fed back to the computer as an exogenous change in values. Many of the gaming simulation models use this operation.

Using variables

Data for variables are generally obtained from the U.S. Bureau of Census or special counts or are personally obtained. Because of the many sources, the educational planner must give precise empirical definitions to his variables. This means that the restrictions and qualifications surrounding the data must be carefully examined, so that the data used do not seriously undermine the variables in the model, e.g., aggregating means with medians, equating responses with biases, or choosing sampling techniques that may be inconsistent or without definition.

Sometimes variables may not be directly observable in the real world. Empirical sources may tell one thing, whereas hidden facts or covert influences are the actual characteristics of the data. As a result, it is easy for the educational planner to misinterpret a particular class of data or the data's reliability.

Establishing parameters

Establishing parameters, the measuring of relationships, is a highly developed branch of statistical method. It is necessary, because the precise empirical definition of a variable affects the parameter's value. For example, the educational population participation rate depends on, among other things, whether it is a pool defined for persons between the ages of seven and nineteen or for persons between the ages three and ninety.

A commonly used tool is regression analysis. The simplest case is the linear function of two variables,

$$Y = a + bx$$

From a set of coordinated x and Y values, the educational planner can estimate values for a and b in such a way as to minimize the expected error, if the value of Y is estimated from a set of known x values. (See Figure 13.2.) Another tool receiving wide attention can be described as the *heuristic method.* This approach involves partitioning the equations into smaller systems, so that the parameters of each system can be fitted independently. This approach is prevalent among planners, as it enables them to build large models of the educational system as a single system of equations. Some methods for estimating the parameter values are as follows:

1 An arbitrary but plausible value is assigned.
2 By trial and error methods.
3 By intuitive standards of plausibility based on experience.

FIGURE 13.2

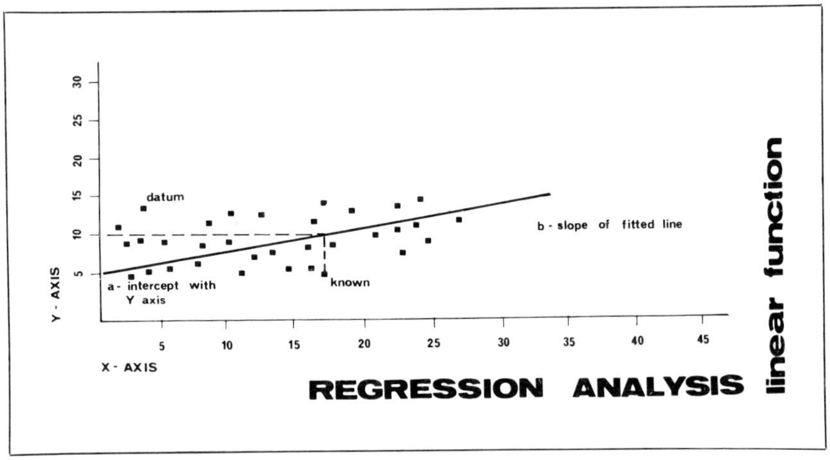

SOME MODEL APPROACHES USED IN SIMULATION

In keeping with our concern for people, places, movements, economics and activities, cited models will be discussed in terms of these five factors. The criteria used for using a model involving two or more components depend on the model's emphasis. If this is lacking, the authors' arbitrary classification will be used. The models selected are by no means the best or the worst, the simplest or the most complex insofar as problems requiring solution are concerned. The models merely indicate possibilities for simulating various aspects of the educational comprehensive plan.

Simulation models for the people's dimension

"Capsburg, U.S.A. (population 39,104) is a typical American City. . . . It includes seven residential districts, two of which offer the sharpest tensions. . . . Such contrasts are not unusual in our times. The unusual thing about Capsburg is the simple fact that it does not exist. . . . Capsburg is an imaginary city, a 'computer city' represented by a deck of punch cards and designed to help investigate the long-range effects of new educational programs on an urban community."[3]

The model was designed by scientists at Philco's Operations Research Division and revised by the Colorado State Department of Education. Its general aim is to predict the effects of various projects, given a certain expenditure, on such factors as the earned income of families in poverty areas, their educational status, and so on. The objective is to achieve the highest return per dollar spent. Returns for the social and economic changes over a two-year period can be obtained via computer in about thirty seconds. Now the model has been expanded to include the metropolitan area of Denver. Data are being gathered for a series of computer runs that will furnish predictions of how various educational changes will affect the economic and social growth of the city.

Another people-oriented model is the Delphi model, a consensus simulation approach. It encourages convergence of opinion by eliciting experts' opinions, without their facing each other. The procedure includes first asking for a list of opinions or facts involving experienced judgment. Second, each expert, in turn, receives a copy of the list and is asked to rate or evaluate each item by a set of criteria. Next,

[3]John Pfeiffer, *New Look at Education* (New York: Odyssey Press, 1968), pp. 1–2.

the list of items with ratings or consensus, if any, is returned to the experts for their revision or reasons, if applicable, for remaining outside the consensus. Finally the list with ratings, consensus and minority opinions is returned to the expert for another round. Generally, this procedure is successful in reaching a convergence of opinion. It is not difficult to understand its application for evaluating the effects of educational policies on educational planning.

A similar technique, but with a different purpose, is METROPOLIS. Developed by Duke University, the game is a scenario with a director and a number of role players. The stage is a land-use map, with the history of the city's socio-economic development. Each scene constitutes a decision-making process that ends with setting a tax rate and determining what goes into the city's capital improvement program. To help improve the decision-making, a plot composed of the recent past rewards and penalties is given. This is derived from the payoffs of the last cycle and reveals the way each player's behavior affects the outcome of the decision. A series of cycles make up an act that terminates with an election. The roles generally involved are of administrators, land speculators, school boards and politicians supported or not supported by the general population. The METROPOLIS simulation is based on game theory. Game theory has certain properties, as follows:

1 There is a finite number of players.
2 Each player has available to him a finite list of possible courses of action.
3 A cycle of the game results when each player chooses a single course of action from the list available to him. The players make their choices simultaneously.
4 The outcome consists of a set of actions, rewards or penalties, which are given to the players.

The general format for a game is shown in Figure 13.3. The game provides the players with a choice of courses of action (strategy) to achieve the maximum expected gain, by maximizing gains and minimizing losses. For further discussion, the reader is referred to the many textbooks on the subject of game theory.

Another model of a mathematical nature that simulates patterns of urban and regional population, employment, and related variables, is the allocation model. One such model is the following one, developed by Donald M. Hill of Traffic Research Corporation in Toronto, Canada:

$$(1) \quad \Delta R_i = \sum_{\substack{j=1 \\ j \neq i}}^{N} a_{ij} \Delta R_j + \sum_{k=1}^{M} b_{ik} (Z_k \text{ or } \Delta Z_k)$$

where:

i or $j = 1, 2, \ldots i, \ldots j, N$: number of the located variable (a total of N equations)

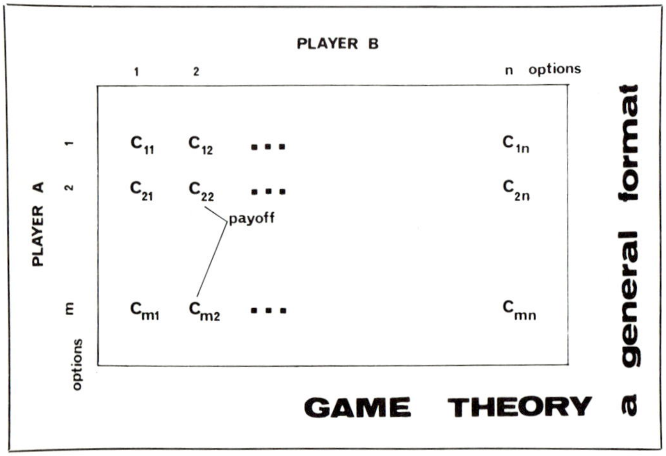

FIGURE 13.3

$k = 1, 2, \ldots, k, \ldots M$: number of the locator variables

$\Delta R_{i \text{ or } j}$ = change in the level of the ith or jth located variable over the calibration or forecast time interval

Z_k = level of locator variable k at the beginning of the calibration or forecast time interval

ΔZ_k = change in the level of the kth locator variable over the calibration or forecast time interval

a_{ij}, b_{ik} = coefficients expressing the interrelationships among variables[4]

The concept is based on patterns of urban activities that are interrelated in a systematic manner and whose development provides a reasonable basis for simulation. The region is divided into a number of subregions whose activities are simulated at the end of a given forecast period. The task of the model is to allocate to the subregions various activities taken from the regional totals at the time specified. The assumption is made that urban activities are related to developmental patterns of one or more variables in a causal manner. The change in the subregional share of urban activities in each subregion is proportional to the change in the subregional share of all other urban activities in the subregion and is proportional to the change in the subregional share of a number of urban activities in the subregion, and is proportional to the value of the subregional shares of other urban activities. These relationships are expressed in Hill's equation.

An example of an application of the cause-and-effect relationships between the subregional growth rates of population and employment is seen in the following breakdown:

1 Resident population participating in white-collar labor force.
2 Resident population participating in blue-collar labor force.
3 Retail plus wholesale employment.
4 Manufacturing employment.
5 All other employment.

[4]Donald M. Hill, "A Growth Allocation Model for the Boston Region," *Journal of the American Institute of Planners,* **31:**113 (May 1965).

This model simulates a distinct residential preference, for example, socio-economic classes of population for different subregions.

An example of models related to people is the psychological simulation, specifically in the area of cognition. One such study was conducted by François Vigier, who used a sequence of photographs of one street scene to select the physical elements that would consistently strike the viewer. Mental-processing strategies were simulated through sensory excitation and by developing a constructional process. Those physical elements appropriate to their degree of importance produce a response-tendency profile.

Simulation models for places

One of the oldest simulation methods is the iconic model used extensively by architects and physical planners to simulate the real world. Its output for the amount of development required is extremely limited. Unless the model possesses kinetic features, it represents one condition at one particular time that does not exist in the real world. Recently, the application of laser beams has made possible halographs whose three-dimensional effects are simulated by the visual ability to move around a building or a group of buildings at a scale much less than life size.

Another recent development is graphic notation for simulating urban form, space and activities. (See Figure 13.4.) Primarily developed by urban designers as a communicative device, graphic notation simulates a wide range of elements. Philip Thiel has developed an alphabet of space notations of plans, sections and elevations that permits the designer to quickly simulate a variety of spatial experiences with varying sizes, positions, numbers, shapes, directions and relationships of spatial sequences.

In contrast to the micro simulation techniques are the macro graphics of paths, edges, nodes, districts and landmarks developed by Kevin Lynch. Applied at city scale, they quickly (with a minimum

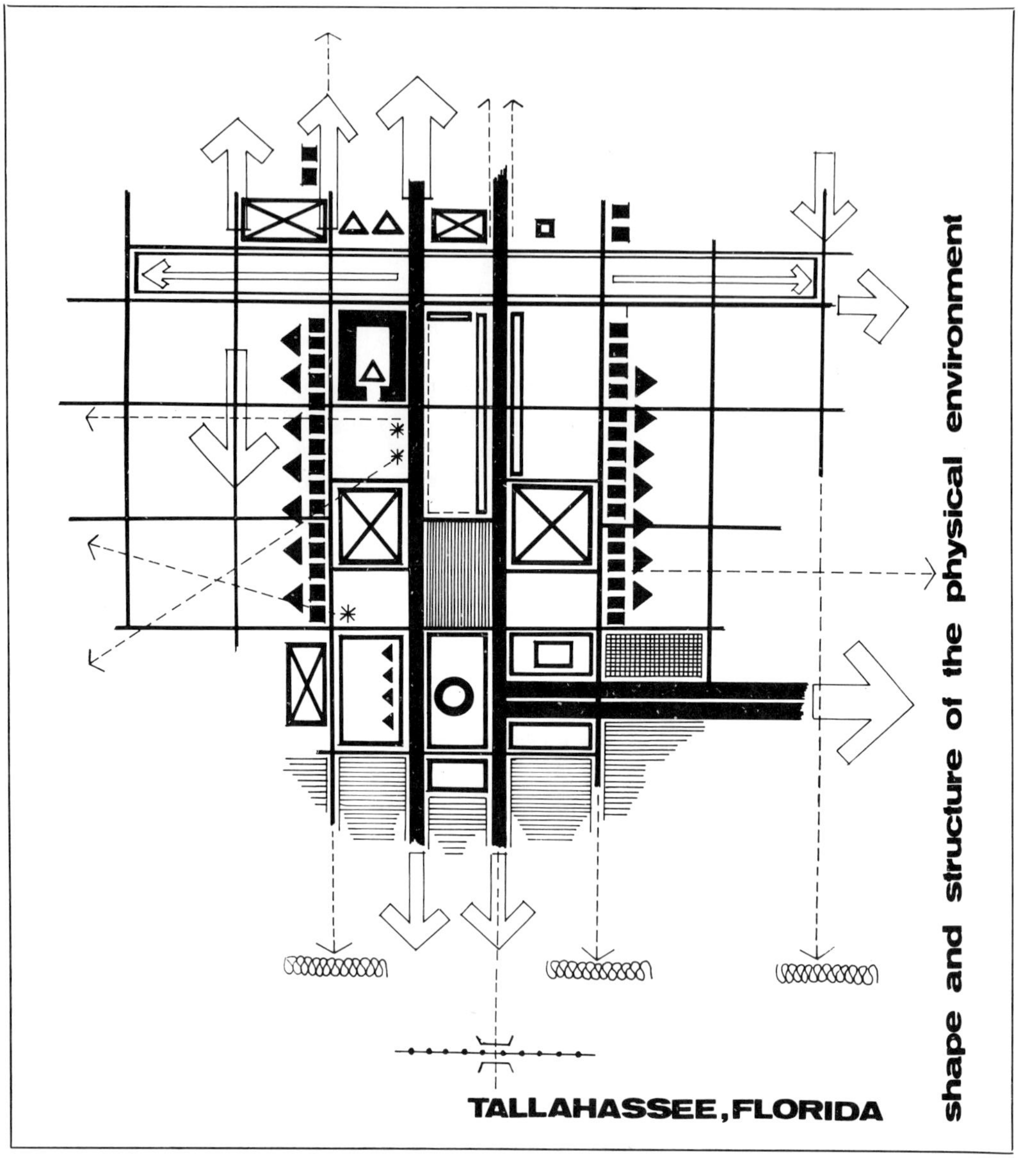

FIGURE 13.4

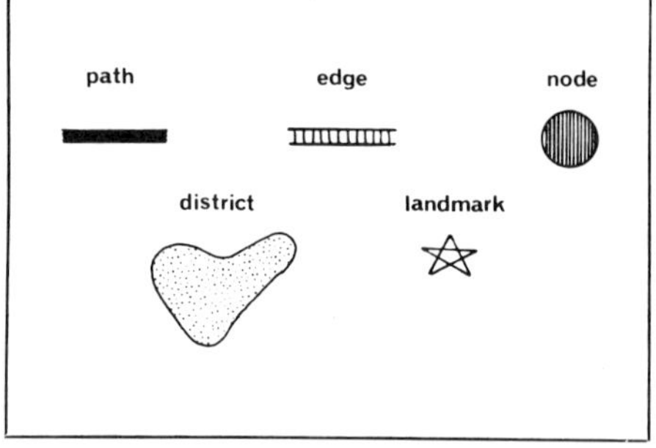

FIGURE 13.5

of elements) simulate the urban form.[5] (See Figure 13.5.)

A recent development by Christopher Alexander et al., at the Center for Environmental Structure, is a pattern language. It is a system of graphic notes illustrating three-dimensional conditions in two-dimensional form. By being cascaded in a hierarchical manner (from the largest to the smallest), by being moved toward details and by clustering, patterns near one another that have parts in common help the designer to simulate a holistic attitude toward his project. These patterns also help the designer to identify the unique features of his project, tell him which patterns to consider first and tell him which patterns go together.

Another simulation technique for places is the photographic matrix. It is composed of selected places contained in a range of landscape contents. The matrix is arranged so that the independent variables can be examined through a wide range of varying relationships. By superimposing one matrix on another, a simulated scene can be created to show what would happen if certain actions were taken with relation to certain other actions.

The use of computers has added a number of simulation techniques. One such program is SYMAP, illustrating in a two-dimensional format of varying densities spatially disposed quantitative and qualitative data. Its sister program, SYMVU, shows the same data in three-dimensional form. Another graphic simulation program is OTOTROL. It produces perspectives that provide a number of views at any scale and seen from any point in space.

In the realm of games are two games used for places. One is POGE, a game dealing with the interactions and competing strategies of planners and real estate speculators. It attempts to change zoning regulations in a previously zoned city.

The second game is CLUG. The rules of the game are a rough analogue of the basic economic forces that shape the growth of the city. A predetermined set of factors, including the location of a major highway network and the location of major points of access to the outside world, are established. In addition, a particular form of real estate taxation to support buildings and the maintenance of various community services are established before the game starts. Money is given the players to enable them to buy land and construct buildings for homes, commerce, and manufacturing. The aim of the game is, first, to observe and participate, through simulation, the effects of simultaneously distributing activities across the urban scope, and second, to simulate the cumulative effects and how to cope with them over time.

Mathematical simulations also exist for places. One such simulation is the rank-size or Pareto distribution,

$$P_r^g = P_1/r$$

Another is the gravity field formulation,

$$T_{ij} = kP_iP_j/d_i^a$$

Yet another simulation is based on gradient values, such as land, densities, incomes, and so on,

$$D_t = D_0e^{-bt}$$

There are also models of attractiveness of centers under competition,

$$S_j = k\sum_i [P_i(E_j/d_{ij})\ (\sum_k E_k/d_{ik})^{-1}]$$

where:

r = rank of city by size
g, a, k, b = constants
i, j = places
P = population
T = interaction, e.g., number of auto trips
d = distance
V = population potential
A = area
D_t = population density at distance t from center of city
D_0 = population density at city center
t = distance from center of city
S = sales
E = measure of attractiveness, e.g., square feet of commercial places

[5]Kevin Lynch, *The Image of the City* (Cambridge, Mass.: M.I.T. Press, 1960), p. 18.

Simulation models for movement

Transportation models are probably the largest source of use for simulation models. One of the largest models, using primarily the linear programming approach, is the Penn-Jersey Transportation Study. It stresses accessibility to opportunities for employment, shopping, and so on as the prime factors governing the pattern of growth of urban housing. By the simulation and, thereby the control of transportation development, the pattern of land use can be controlled to a significant degree. Unfortunately, this model has not been put into effective operation.

Another simulation movement model is the intervening opportunities model. It is based on the assumption that the total travel time from a point is minimized if every destination has a stated probability of being acceptable once considered. The probability of a trip that originates in one zone's finding a destination in another zone is proportional to the possible trip destinations in the other zone and to the number of trip destinations previously considered. The model is as follows:

$$T_{ij} = O_i \left[e^{-LD} - e^{-L(D+D_j)}\right]$$

where:

T_{ij} = trips originating in zone i and destined for zone j
O_i = trip origins in zone i
D = trip destinations considered before zone j
D_j = trip destinations in zone j
L = measure of probability that a random destination will satisfy the needs of a particular trip (an empirically derived function describing rate of trip decay with increasing trip destinations and increasing length of trip)
e = base of natural logarithms (2.71828)

Applications of queuing theory to movement are extensive. Queuing is concerned with the statistical description of the behavior of queues, e.g., the probability distribution of the number of the queue from which the mean and variance of queue length and the probability of queue length exceeding a certain size may be calculated. Queue theory is also concerned with the probability distribution of waiting time for an object or person, or the distribution of the server's busy period. A queuing system is fully specified when the following are obtainable:

1 The arrival pattern of persons or objects.
2 The servicing pattern of those persons or objects.
3 The queue discipline, that is, the order in which persons or objects begin service in relation to the order of their arrival.

The queuing equation may be written as follows:

$$A_i = Q_{i-1} + (\bar{f_i} + ds_{f_i}) - L_i$$

where:

Q_i = number of persons or objects at end of period i
Q_{i-1} = holdovers from preceding period
$(f_i + ds_{f_i})$ = inflow of current period
$\bar{f_i}$ = mean inflow during period
s_{f_i} = standard deviation of the inflow of the current period
d = a stochastic normal deviate with zero mean and unit variance, and
L_i = persons or objects served during current period

Another procedure is simulating human movement as a function of color simulation. With the use of a special device called a *hodometer* developed at the Environmental Research Foundation in Topeka, Kansas, tests conducted by Rajendra K. Srivastava and Thomas S. Pall demonstrated that differences in colors do affect human movement in subtle ways when the human is behaving naturally and is not aware of color *per se*. By establishing a mean of color effects from statistical testing, a simulated environment can be devised to show what effects color will have on movement.

Simulation models used in economics

One ambitious undertaking in economics is the simulation model developed by Jay W. Forrester. Using methods of industrial dynamics developed at MIT, Forrester developed an equilibrium model previewing 250 years of urban growth. Using 156 different

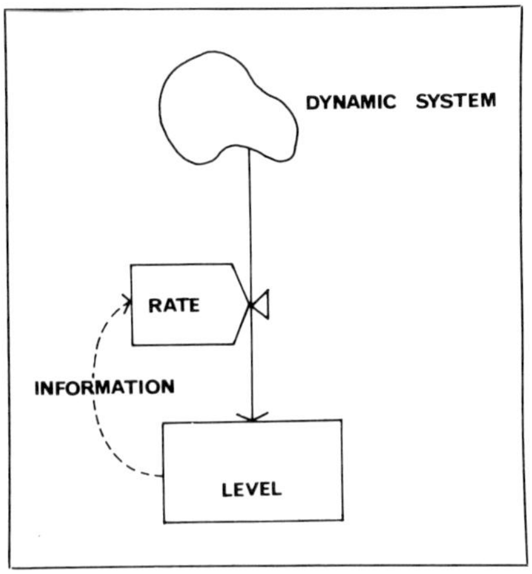

FIGURE 13.6

equations, he simulated effects on city growth using such variables as underemployment, labor and managerial-professional needs, housing densities, family sizes, taxes levied and taxes needed. The behaviors of these various systems are generated from a series of interrelated feedbacks, which become the fundamental building blocks of the simulation model. This feedback is shown in its simplest form in Figure 13.6.

This feedback loop ". . . is the structure within which a decision point—the rate equation—controls a flow or action stream. The action is accumulated (integrated) to generate a system level."[6]

Earlier the terms *stock* and *flow* were used and these are applicable here. Level variables are stock or accumulations and are changed by rates of flow. The rate depends only on information about the stock or level and is determined by the system policies. Each rate equation, therefore, represents "going toward" or "going from" a goal.

There is also a process whereby the observed condition of a system is detected. It is the observed condition, not the true condition, that determines action. Very often in systems the perceived condition of the system is distorted with respect to the true condition. A rate equation states the discrepancy between the goal and the observed condition. And finally, the rate equation states the action that will result from the discrepancy.[7]

[6]Jay W. Forrester, *Urban Dynamics* (Cambridge, Mass.: The M.I.T. Press, 1969), p. 140.
[7]Ibid., p. 14.

This basically is the concept used in simulating urban growth, its stagnation and the policies required to revive its growth.

Another growth-simulated model is the one of T. R. Lakshmanan and Walter G. Hansen. Together, they developed a retail-market-potential model. It asserts that the location or sales potential of a retail center should not be viewed as a function of the purchasing power of an arbitrary spatial slice, but as a function of overlapping competition between shopping centres. This relationship is expressed in the following mathematical form:

$$(1) \qquad S_{ij} = C_i \frac{\dfrac{F_j}{d_{ij}{}^a}}{\dfrac{F_i}{d_{ij}{}^a} = \dfrac{F_j}{d_{ij}{}^a} \cdots \dfrac{F_n}{d_{in}{}^a}} = C_i \frac{\dfrac{F_j}{d_{ij}{}^a}}{\sum_{k=1}^{n} \dfrac{F_k}{d_{ik}{}^a}}$$

where:

S_{ij} = consumer retail expenditures of population in zone i, spent at zone j
C_i = total consumer retail expenditures of population in zone i
F_j = size of retail activity in zone j
d_{ij} = distance (in driving time) between zone i and zone j
a = exponent applied to the distance variable

The above model states the retail center in zone j (F_j) attracts consumer dollars (S_j)

(a) in direct proportion to the consumer expenditures, C_i,
(b) in direct proportion to its size F_j,
(c) in inverse proportion to distance to the consumers ($d_{ij}{}^a$), and
(d) in inverse proportion to competition

$$\left(\sum_{k=1}^{n} \frac{F_k}{d_{ik}{}^a} \right)$$

Equation (1) can be modified to state the consumer expenditures available in all zones of the region that would probably be spent in zone j (retail centers F_j).

$$(2) \qquad S_j = \sum_{i=1}^{n} C_i \frac{\dfrac{F_j}{d_{ij}{}^a}}{\sum_{k=1}^{n} \dfrac{F_k}{d_{ik}{}^a}}$$

where S_j = total sales in retail center F_j.

Equation (2) sums up the sales from every zone at zone j. It implies that there is no trade area boundary but a shopping interaction between all zones, though this may fall off sharply with distance.[8]

Ira S. Lowry, as a part of the economic study of the Pittsburgh region, helped develop the Pittsburgh Model, a model directed toward the development of a general model of urban form. The model, as developed, is a set of simultaneous equations whose solution represents an equilibrium in the pattern of land use and in the distribution of employment and population. The model generates appropriate amounts of retail employment and residential population and distributes employees and households among the subareas of the city. The model is as follows:
for land use,

$$A_j = a_j^u + A_j^B + A_j^R + A_j^H$$

for retail,

$$D^k = a^k N$$ (employment as a function of households in region)

$$D_j^k = b^k \left[\sum_{i=1}^{n} \left(\frac{c^k Ni}{T_{ij}^k} \right) + d^k E_j \right]$$

(market potential based on number of households in surrounding areas and number of persons employed nearby)

$$D^k = \sum_{j=1}^{n} \sum_{j}^{k}$$ (amount of employment for each line of retail)

$$E_j = E_j^B + \sum_{k=1}^{n} E_j^k$$ (total employment for tract)

$$A_j^R = \sum_{k=1}^{m} e^k E_j^k$$ (amount of land occupied by retail)

for household

$$N = f \sum_{j=1}^{n} E_j$$ (number of households as a function of employment)

[8]T. R. Lakshmanan and Walter G. Hansen, "A Retail Market Potential Model," *Journal of the American Institute of Planners*, **31**:135–136 (May 1965).

$$N_j = \Phi \sum_{i-1}^{n} \frac{E_i}{T_{ij}}$$ (number of households in tract as a function of tract's accessibility to employment opportunities)

$$N = \sum_{j=1}^{n} N_j$$ (number of all households)

where:

A = area of land
E = employment
N = population (number of households)
T = index of trip distribution
Z = constraints
U = unusable land
B = basic sector
R = retail sector
H = household sector
K = class of retail establishments
M = number of classes of retail establishments
i, j = subareas or tracts
n = number of tracts

a, b, c, d, e, f, Φ = unspecified functions or coefficients.
Its simplicity, however, negates sophisticated precision. Walter Hansen has also developed a simulation model using a two-pronged approach—the accessibility function and a development ratio. The accessibility function is in the form of a gravity model:

$${}_iA_j = \frac{S_j}{T_{i-j}^x}$$

where:

A = accessibility measurement from zone i to employment activity in zone j
S_j = size of employment activity in zone j
T_{i-j} = travel distance between zone i and j
x = exponent describing effect of travel time between zones

For the development ratio, the expression becomes as follows:

$$D_i = kA_i^x$$

where:

D_i = development ratio for zone i
A_i = accessibility to employment from zone i
k = constant of proportionality

Having both accessibility to employment and, from this, its development ratio, Hansen distributed household population through the city as follows:

$$\frac{P_i}{P_t} = \frac{D_i O_i}{D_i O_i + D_j O_j + \ldots + D_n O_n}$$

where:

P_i = increase in residential population in zone i
P_t = total increase in residential population in city
O_i = developable land in zone i

Possible simulation models for activities

One such simulation for activities is the opportunity model. The spatial distribution of an activity is assumed to be the successive evaluation of alternative opportunities for sites that are ranked in order of travel time from a city center. Opportunities are defined as the product of available land and units of activity per unit land area.

$$A_j = A\,[e^{-\ell 0} - e^{-\ell 0 + 0j}]$$

where:

A_j = the amount of activity to be allocated to zone j
A = the aggregate amount of activity to be allocated
ℓ = probability of a unit of activity being sited at a given opportunity
0 = the opportunities for siting a unit of activity rank ordered by access value and preceding zone j
0_j = the opportunities in zone j[9]

The San Francisco Model outlines a simulated method based on gaming-theory principles and applicable to urban education. Figure 13.7 illustrates the various components of a total urban educational system.

[9]George T. Lathrop and John R. Hamburg, "For Allocating Regional Growth," *Journal of the American Institute of Planners,* **31:**96 (May 1965).

The set of tasks enumerated in Figure 13.7 is broken down into steps, as follows:

1 The inventory of users (learners, teachers, administrators, and others) is divided into groups. Each group reflects similar cultural patterns, life styles, housing preferences, and personal and professional goals.
2 The groups are classified on the basis of the requirements of the education programs in which they will participate.
3 All the groups are then assigned to specific activities, each of which exists in a variety of physical conditions, and are allocated throughout the urban community.
4 It is assumed that public interest and participation will be elicited to build new units or to rehabilitate existing ones, whenever it becomes educationally profitable for them to do so.
5 The "rule of profitability" just described is tied to the variables of social demand, manpower needs, cost of construction or rehabilitation and community educational goals and objectives.

The fundamental unit of learning is the *learning activity unit* (LAU). In order to keep inventories of learning activity units up with other community activities, and to keep the inventory of space in the city within the memory capacity of the computer, a land unit called a *learning tract* (LT) is used. The LT equals approximately two acres. A community is composed of several thousand learning tracts, including various lands available for learning purposes. Transitions in use of space and in schooling (such as new construction), conversions and mergers or changes in the assigned programs to an LT unit occur for one complete LT at a time.

Binary flags, each with a different meaning, are used. Each flag can be turned on or off for each LT. For example, one flag signals that only one learning project composed of several LAU's can be undertaken at the same LT within a specified time module. The LT is not available for another transition in this time module. Another binary flag indicates that the LT is owned by private individuals. A third flag shows whether an LT is available for public occupancy in

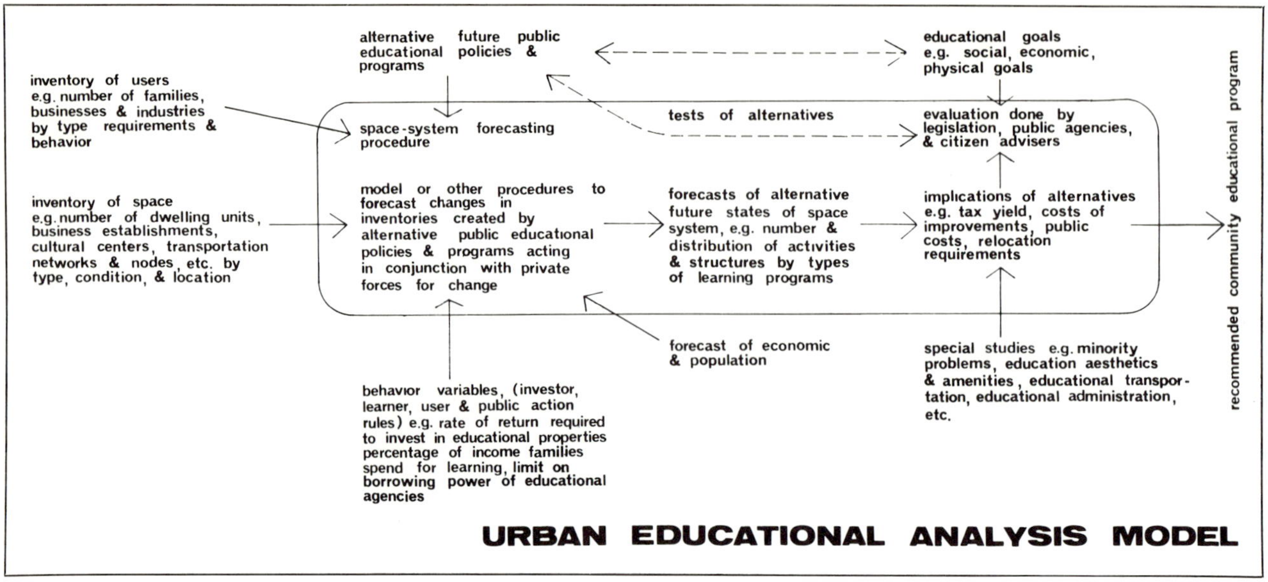

FIGURE 13.7

spite of private ownership. Still another flag shows whether an LT is available for private occupancy in spite of public ownership. Other rules are established to meet the unique needs of the community and the LAU.

The purpose of the model is to simulate the interactions with, and the effects of learning activities on, public policies, programs, other community activities, the investment behavior of the private market and the location decisions of businesses, industries, households, and so on. Existing space can then be matched with the needs of the educational program and the educational users. This process allows for the following adjustments:

1 If the existing supply of space proves inadequate for the needs of the various educational users, the computer makes the necessary changes in the space stock to allow the space needs to be met with the financial resources available.
2 Financial feasibility is determined by a comparison of the cost of making the change in the LT facility or facilities with the yield that can be anticipated from the change. When the comparison indicates profitable circumstances, the computer adds the approximate number of new LT units to the educational inventory.
3 To complete the analysis, the computer is asked to consider what the effects of the additional LT would be on such matters as shifts in rent levels, new space-market values, modification in the tax property base for school support, neighborhood amenities and other public actions.[10]

SUMMARY

The simulation of complex physical and social systems is becoming a valid step in the general comprehensive planning process. Past experiences have shown clearly that the development and testing of simulation models is a long-term process. No one can really claim that school-location models, for example, can provide a mechanically reliable guide for educational planning. However, little doubt exists that the use of simulation

[10]Cyril C. Herrmann, "Systems Approach to City Planning," *Harvard Business Review,* No. 5, **44:**74–76 (September/October 1966).

models in the planning process is an important information feedback source that increases the educational planner's understanding of educational problems within the context of an urban environment. Simulation forces the educational planner to deal explicitly and rigorously with many relationships within the system that he once ignored.

14 Evaluating plans

THE NATURE OF EVALUATION

Evaluating is essentially ascertaining the value of educational planning and its potential results. By necessity, therefore, evaluation should occur throughout the planning process. In some cases partial evaluations are made by the use of quantitative tests or judgments based on experience to reject, modify, combine, or accept results.

The educational planner must know the relative values that are attached to the various objectives established for the plan. Not only must he know the values that are the focus of interest but also those that exist in the backgound, which should not be violated while the stated objectives are being achieved. Because of this, evaluation techniques are not simple.

A key factor is how much a planner is prepared to sacrifice regarding the attainment of certain objectives in order to attain other objectives more fully. Evaluations of this kind are extraordinarily difficult and create difficulties for the educational planners who are not familiar with utility theory.

Some comparative evaluations can be made when a change is caused by an act programmed by the plan. The consequences may be anticipated or unanticipated, but can be evaluated only in relation to the outcome. This, in turn, can be expressed in most instances as benefits or costs. Whether the outcome is a benefit or a cost depends on the public interest involved. The objectives of public interest serve as a single set of ends. In a democracy common interests are likely to be vague, for the plurality may prevail without the individual's sharing its point of view.

In such a state evaluation can occur in three ways. In the utilitarian way the public interest can be determined by gains and losses based on what happens to be most important to the various individuals. The quasi-utilitarian way considers the utility to the individual as a relevant quantity, but a greater value is given to some people's interests than to others. Qualified individualism, on the other hand, considers the ends of public interest as the aggregate of those selected from certain classes that are deemed appropriate.

A mechanism should be selected for evaluating that will create the greatest total satisfaction. First, an evaluation of values must be undertaken. Key terms must be defined, and objectives must be reduced from the abstract to the concrete. Second, a time perspective must be established. If a short-term plan is to be used, the values selected must receive political approval if the plan is to be implemented. If a middle-range plan is contemplated, the selection of values that might be rejected may be overcome with educational or public relations efforts. These values, of course, are assumed to be in the public interest. Long-range planning must be evaluated in terms of whether a standard, new, or radical program of educational activities is what the public desires.

Several methods for identifying the values to be evaluated are available. These include the public opinion polls, anthropological surveys, and public hearings; interviews with informed leaders, press-content analysis, studies of current and past laws, studies of current and past administrative behavior, and studies of current and past school budgets.

Because evaluation permeates the whole educational sequence, a clear notion of objectives lies at the heart of the educational planner's task. The evaluation of these objectives thus must be given primary emphasis in the comprehensive educational planning process.

Much work in the area of evaluation is judgmental and takes place at a highly philosophical level. The practical aspects of educational objectives deal less with the definitions and detailed operational problems of evaluation. The technical methods discussed are gaining in acceptance and increased use by educational planners.

SOME EVALUATION TECHNIQUES

One set of techniques is the cost ratio techniques—cost/effectiveness, cost/benefit, and cost/utility methods.

Cost/effectiveness approaches are used generally in situations in which alternative outputs are designed to yield a high degree of effectiveness relative to cost. The cost/benefit approach differs from the first approach in its application to situations in which the alternative outputs are judged in terms of benefits. The assignment of the cost/utility approach requires the formulation of numerical utility values for specific activities and also the formulation and assignment of specific cost factors to those same activities. *Utility* in this case means the worth or the value of the activity (i.e., personal preference).

Regardless of which of the three approaches is used the aim is to minimize the x/cost ratio ($x =$ effectiveness or benefit or utility). Each relies heavily on quantifiable elements. The following example illustrates a hypothetical situation.

Assume six plan alternatives are possible for satisfying the four objectives established for planning. The objectives are as follows:

(a) To increase the average daily attendance (ADA) of adults in the community from five persons per activity to thirty persons per activity.
(b) To minimize the overall personal travel of the adults involved from home to learning activities.
(c) To increase the number of activity choices through all parts of the city.
(d) To offer a variety of times for participating in the activities.

Beginning with (a) the process begins with the estimation of all costs for increasing attendance, e.g., teachers' salaries, the equipment required, possibly

Cost matrix (1)

Plans	1	2	3	4	5	6
Teachers' salaries						
Equipment costs						
Facility costs						
Etc.						

Cost matrix (2)

Objective Plan	1	2	3	4	5	6
(a)	4	6	1	1	4	3
(b)	5	1	4	4	5	1
(c)	3	1	2	3	4	3
(d)	1	6	4	2	3	5
Sum of rankings	13	14	11	10	16	12

new facilities, the maintenance and operation of space and equipment, and possibly a public relations campaign. The benefits are scaled by the extent of increase in absolute terms or as percentages of the present five persons per activity. Item (b) would include all the costs of increasing the number of learning centers, transportation costs, and other measures taken to minimize travel time. The benefit side of the ratio might be expressed in total person-miles or person-minutes or some other suitable measure. Items (c) and (d) would be càrried out in the same manner, i.e., the estimating of the costs involved, then the listing of the benefits gained.

These objectives in turn are related to each of the six plans. It is necessary to combine these results into a single score. Considering objective (a) the costs for each plan can be compared to the benefits obtained and set out in matrix form (1). The same is done for objectives (b), (c), and (d).

These various matrices are combined into one measure that enables the educational planner to place them in rank order of preference. Combining costs is not difficult as they are expressed in money; the corresponding benefits are generally expressed in different units, making comparability more difficult.

The alternative plans are in rank order from the point of view of each objective as shown in (2). The result indicates that the best alternative is plan 4, then plans 3, 6, 1, 2, and 5. This, of course, assumes that each objective has the same priority. This may not be the case, and, if so, weights can be applied. The table could then read as in (3).

As seen here plan 4, which at first ranked best is now replaced by plan 2, although the differences between them are small and could be completely altered if the weights were varied.

So far, the tabulations have been limited to the

Cost matrix (3)

Objective	Weight	Plan 1	2	3	4	5	6
(a)	1	4	6	1	1	4	3
(b)	4	20	4	16	16	20	4
(c)	3	9	3	6	9	12	9
(d)	2	2	12	8	4	6	10
Weighted sum of rankings		35	25	31	30	42	26
Final rank order		5	1	4	3	6	2

Cost matrix (4)

Objective plan	1	2	3	4	5	6
(a)	3,560	2,150	4,610	2,550	2,670	5,550
(b)	2,450	3,210	3,450	3,460	3,710	4,100
(c)	3,120	4,670	7,610	4,650	3,450	3,200
(d)	4,430	3,220	3,210	2,150	4,210	5,670
Totals	13,560	13,250	18,880	12,810	14,040	18,520

Cost matrix (5)

	Plan 1	2	3	4	5	6
Benefit rank order	5	1	4	3	6	2
Cost rank order	3	2	6	1	4	5
Combined rank order	8	3	10	4	10	7

Cost matrix (6)

	Plan 1	2	3	4	5	6
Total cost	13,560	13,250	18,880	12,810	14,040	18,520
$x =$ weighted sum of rankings index	35	25	31	30	42	26
$=$ final cost/benefit index	47	33	58	38	59	48

Cost matrix, planning balance-sheet method

	Plan 2				Plan 4			
	Benefits		Costs		Benefits		Costs	
	Capital	Annual	Capital	Annual	Capital	Annual	Capital	Annual
Producers								
A	$12,550	M_1	—	$14,550		—	$11,450	$15,550
B	I_1	$5,000	—	—	I_3	I_2	—	—
C	M_1	—	M_3	—	M_3	—	M_4	—
Consumers								
A′	—	11,550	—	13,550	—	8,900	—	—
B′	I_2	I_3	—	—	I_6	—	—	—
C′	M_1	—	M_2	—	M_2	—	M_4	—

benefit side of the ratio and now the cost must be brought into account. For example, these hypothetical costs are estimated for the various objectives as in (4). The matrix shows that plan 4 is the cheapest choice.

Next the relationships between costs and benefits are introduced. Two methods are possible. Rank order can be compared as shown in (5). The other method is the weighted sum-of-ranking (6). The lower the number the greater the benefit score.

In this case plan 2 gives the greatest payoff, closely followed by plan 4.

The planning balance-sheet method, first developed by Nathaniel Titchfield in 1956, helps to examine the effects of alternative plans. Each plan with its producers and consumers or suppliers and demanders is listed. The costs and benefits for each section of the community are estimated. Money or physical terms are used, including intangible costs and benefits.

A, B, and C are groups of producers in the community and A′, B′, and C′ are the same groups but in a consumer role. Dollars, physical items represented by M, and intangible costs and benefits indicated by I are each summed separately for plan 2 and plan 4. The additions are statements of total cost and total benefits for each plan and provide a method for selecting the plan that optimizes objectives with respect to their impacts on production and consumption by people.

OTHER TECHNIQUES USED FOR EVALUATION

A number of evaluative techniques are appropriate for use in the various steps of the comprehensive educational planning process. Some typical techniques follow. First consider a preference matrix.

Technique 1: Preference matrix

Rank	Tabulation	
2	3	1. Cost
3	1	2. Football team
2	3	3. Recreation
4	0	4. Museum
2	3	5. School buses
1	5	6. School

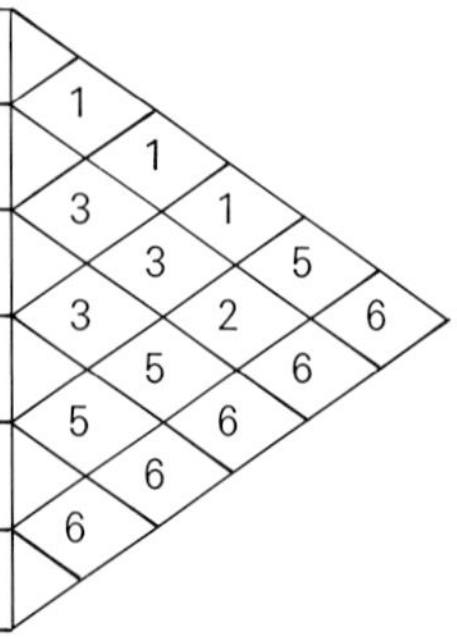

Each factor is given an identifying number. The factors are then compared to all other factors. A priority is thereby established. The number that appears most often in the intersecting box represents the factor of greatest importance. The number appearing the second greatest number of times is ranked second, and so on. Next a ranking chart technique is given.

Technique 2: Ranking chart

	Cost	Football team	Recreation	Museum	School buses	School	Total	Rank
Cost		1	1	1	1	0	4	2
Football team	1		0	1	1	0	3	3
Recreation	0	0		0	0	1	1	4
Museum	1	0	0		0	0	1	4
School buses	1	0	1	1		0	3	3
School	1	1	1	1	1		5	1

The alternatives are placed as above. A binary notation is used to record preferences. If the horizontal factor is preferred to the vertical factor a one is placed and if the vertical factor is preferred to the horizontal a zero is placed in the intersecting box. The binary marks are then totaled for each row and the rank ordering of items is revealed. The following technique illustrates a procedure of weighting a large number of objectives.

Technique 3: Weighting a large number of objectives

The objectives are ranked in terms of preference: O_1, O_2, $O_3 \ldots O_{12}$. By random selection they are subdivided into sets, preferably of equal sizes.

Group A	Group B	Group C
O_4	O_1	O_9
O_{12}	O_{11}	O_6
O_5	O_8	O_1
O_{10}	O_2	O_3

A selection is made at random of one objective from each group. Each is assigned a value by use of the method of weighting objectives.

From Group A	$O_4 = .60$
From Group B	$O_8 = .30$
From Group C	$O_3 = 1.00$

They are replaced in the groups from which they were drawn. This is continued until all objectives have been assigned values. Then they are compared by ranked values from the selection process with the values obtained by the original ranking.

Group A	Group B	Group C
$O_4 = .60$	$O_2 = .9$	$O_1 = 1.20$
$O_5 = .50$	$O_7 = .35$	$O_3 = 1.00$
$O_{10} = .2$	$O_8 = .30$	$O_6 = 0.45$
$O_{12} = .15$	$O_{11} = .10$	$O_9 = .25$

The above values are standardized by the dividing of their totals into each value.

Group A	Group B	Group C
$O_4 = .1$	$O_2 = .1$	$O_1 = .2$
$O_5 = .08$	$O_7 = .06$	$O_3 = .1$
$O_{10} = .03$	$O_8 = .05$	$O_6 = .09$
$O_{12} = .02$	$O_{11} = .1$	$O_9 = .04$

Another common procedure is the ordinal rating scale.

Technique 4: Ordinal rating scale

A three-part process is required. First, a ranking of elements is accomplished by the use of the paired-comparisons method. This establishes a hierarchical order of preference. Second, a notational ranking scale is formed. A conveniently numbered scale of relative distance is established between the elements. Third, an ordinal rating scale is formed. The smallest distance between elements on the notational ranking scale units is marked off. The intervals of the notational scale are superimposed on the ordinal scale with the highest ranked element falling on the highest position of the scale. These units then become the basis of comparison used to rank the elements. The prime advantage of this technique is that it quantifies subjective data with intervals capable of being used for the comparison of various numbers of elements. The evaluation matrix is a preference matrix.

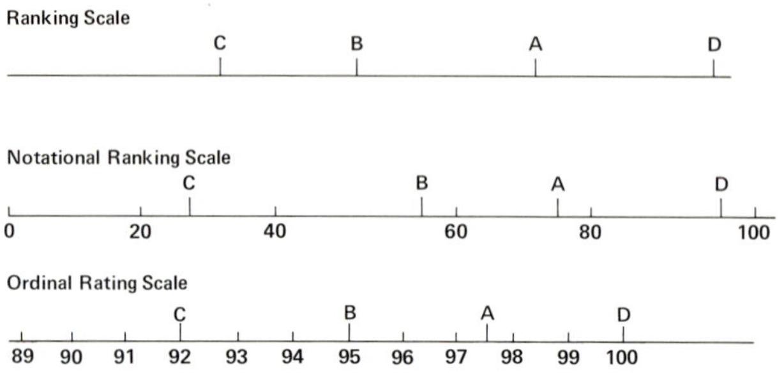

Technique 5: Evaluation matrix

This technique requires a scale of judgment, e.g.:

1 = good
2 = barely good
3 = barely bad
4 = bad

A matrix is then formed as follows and judgments by numbers are applied to the cells.

Evaluation criteria	Alternative plans P_1	P_2	P_3	P_4	P_5	P^9
Football preferred in winter but not in summer	1	4	2	2	3	4
Open-plan school preferred to egg-crate school	3	5	6	1	3	4
Recreation available at all times	2	1	3	6	5	1
Museum available for learning activities at all times	1	4	2	1	3	4
School bus use only from 8 a.m. to 9 p.m. and 3 p.m. to 4 p.m.	1	2	4	1	4	2
	—	—	—	—	—	—
Total	8	16	17	11	18	15
Rank order	1	4	5	2	6	3

A final technique, a ranking and weighting method, follows.

Technique 6: Ranking and weighting method

A list of elements is ranked in order of importance without the assignment of quantitative values.

$O_1 \quad O_2 \quad O_3 \quad O_4$

A tentative value of 1.00 is assigned to O_1, the most valued element, reflecting its value in relation to the others.

O_1	1.00	V_1
O_2	.80	V_2
O_3	.50	V_3
O_4	.30	V_4

A comparison is then made of O_1 to O_2, O_3, and O_4.

O_1 versus (O_2 and O_3 and O_4)

If O_1 is preferred to the sum of the other three, then the value of V_1 is adjusted.

O_1	2.00	V_1
O_2	.80	V_2
O_3	.50	V_3
O_4	.30	V_4

Retaining the values of O_2, O_3, and O_4, assume the new value of O_1 to be 2.00. Assume also that O_2 is not preferred to O_3 and O_4. Further adjustments are necessary.

O_1	2.00	V_1
O_2	.70	V_2
O_3	.50	V_3
O_4	.30	V_4

The values are now consistent with the evaluations. To normalize, divide each value by the sum of all values.

O_1	2.00/3.50	=	.57	V_1
O_2	.70/3.50	=	.20	V_2
O_3	.50/3.50	=	.14	V_3
O_4	.30/3.50	=	.09	V_4
			1.00	

SUMMARY

Several types of evaluation techniques have been discussed that are valuable for plans. The selection, of a multipurpose plan from a range of alternatives is a very complex procedure. In using the above techniques the educational planner must consider them only partial tools for evaluating plans.

15 Selecting a plan

Every plan should accomplish its objectives by integrating all elements so that they come in their natural order without being forced into place. The results should indicate the payoff associated with systematic planning.

Comprehensive educational planning must include the physical, social, and economic elements. In the real world, they are all inextricably related and should be treated as an integrated system.

The various types of planning have been separated in this chapter for explanatory purposes. Their interrelatedness, however, is constantly assumed. The purpose of this chapter, then, is to further clarify the role of comprehensive educational planning and why it should be selected as one efficient way of interrelating people, places, movements, economics, and activities.

The major sections of an educational comprehensive plan—the physical, social, and administrative processes—indicate the requirements for coordination, flexibility, the timing of commitments, and both single and multiple functions. Emphasis should be given to the approaches that fully implement a total solution to the problem, rather than to the incremental, disjointed approach. (See Figure 15.1.)

PHYSICAL PLANNING

Physical planning is concerned with the three-dimensional elements. Physical planning, however, is

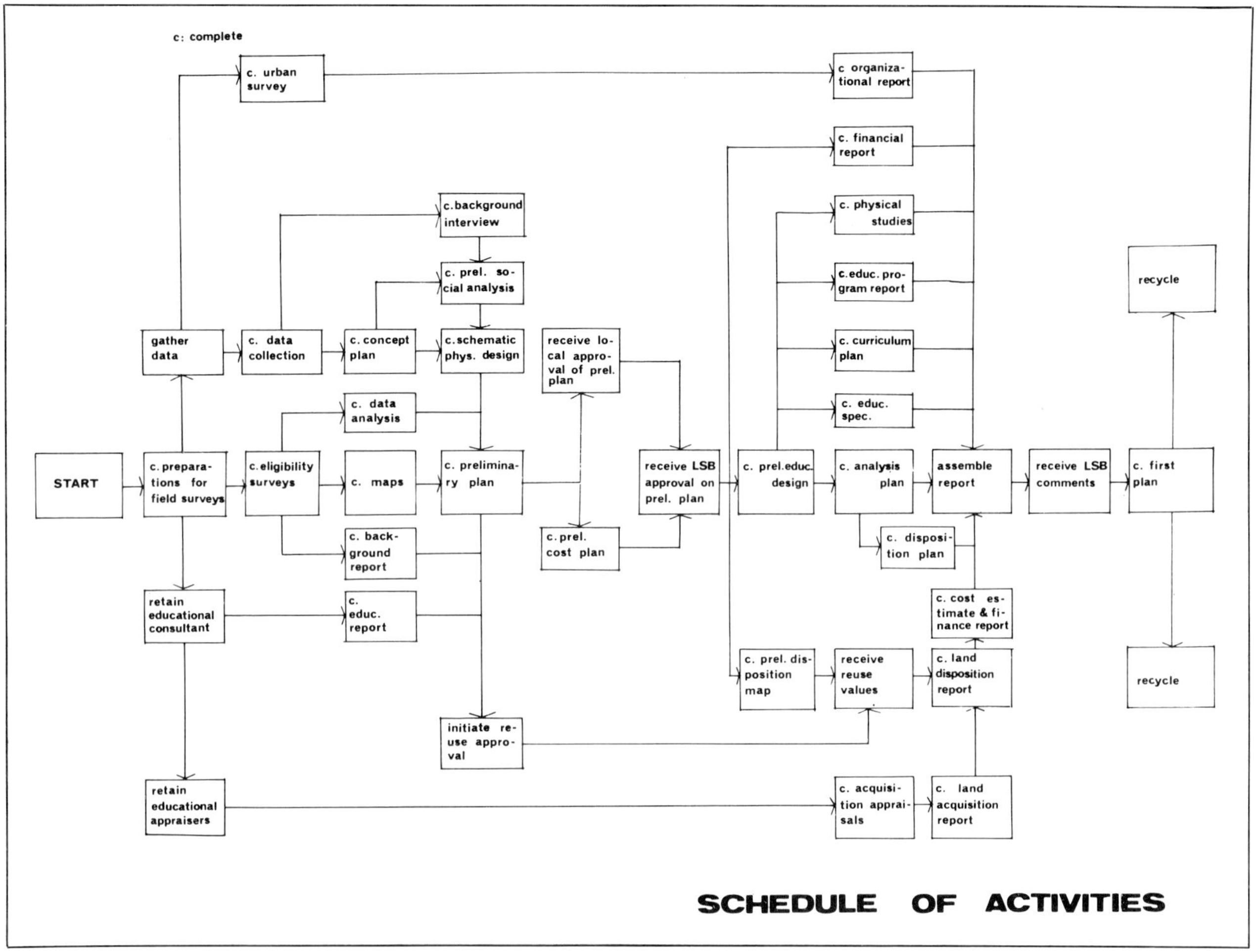

FIGURE 15.1

concerned with more than just the erection of structures. Physical planning, basically, is the "art of shaping and guiding the physical arrangement and structure of towns in harmony with social and economic needs (see Figure 15.2) and in tune with the community's educational attainment."[1] In a true sense physical planning is the physical expression of human needs. Its medium is spatial design, a major tool for urban educational designers.

There are three relatively clear-cut steps to be followed in the process of location planning: "defining the demand for land in terms of people and position of location, measuring and expressing this demand in units and in intensity, and defining these upon the ground and achieving them."[2]

In location planning the educational planner must choose the most appropriate locations for various uses. The classification of uses may be based on an exploration of needs, typical associations, linkages, employment, traffic, generating capacity and the

[1]M. Barley and H. Nuttgens, "The Local Authority," *Living in Towns,* BBC Broadcast, October 1966.

[2]Norman Pearson, "Towards Principles of Land Planning," *Planning Outlook,* no. 2, **4:**19 (1957).

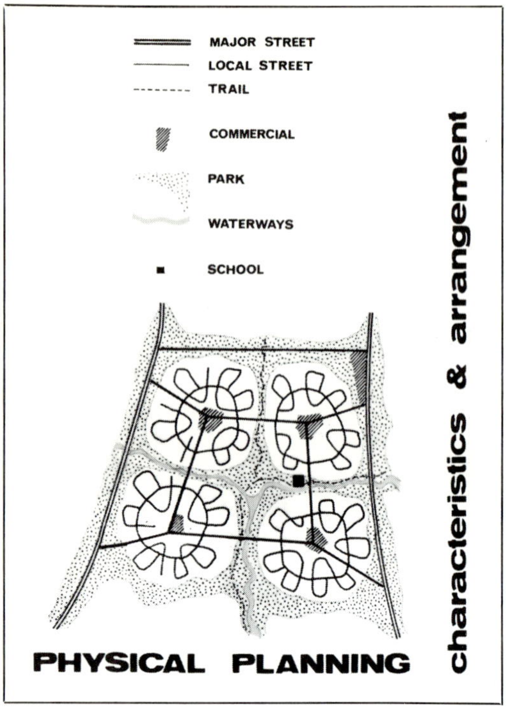

FIGURE 15.2

potential growth factors in relation to the use. An investigation of typically used sites would reveal how the spatial needs of a community and its educational needs are being met, as well as relative efficiency, the effects and impacts and the reactions to certain external happenings that a reassignment of uses would cause. A comparison of the development and growth of these associations would allow the planner to project any climax and decline, successions or displacement and consequences that would result from planning. To complete the study, the educational planner should investigate the areas that require transition and adjustment to adjacent surroundings. "Land planning seeks to guide the evolution of groupings of land use, and it is wise to base such actions on a thorough knowledge of the ecology involved."[3] (See Figure 15.3.)

The following general principles have been suggested as appropriate guides for location planning:

1 "The principles of cultural lag." This denotes the usual inertia within a developed culture and its effects upon change.
2 "The principle of simplicity." This implies the use of present resources, procedures and technology wherever possible.
3 "The principle of unity." This principle is concerned with the totality or comprehensiveness of the plan.
4 "The principle of reasonable modification." The implication here is that the plan must be flexible enough to meet contingencies without being unduly rigid.
5 "The principle of constant satisfactory adjustment." This implies that future needs might require adjustments in the planning process.
6 "The principle of multiple compatible use." This principle is becoming increasingly important in a highly changeable society. It places the burden on planners of physical design to handle the structures with maximum flexibility.
7 "The principle of consistent flexibility." The concept of flexibility is an extension of the idea of modification, but it also implies a continuous flexibility within a clearly established goal.[4]

With these general principles as guides, the procedure for charting the sequence of physical planning can be organized into three phases. The first is the initial spadework. This includes the delineation of study areas and the bringing together of the data needed in the physical-planning analysis of a school system. This area can be classified as the *planning area*, and its subdivisions can be called *subplanning areas*.

The planning area is defined by the population of the school system. Generally, it coincides with the area's jurisdiction as defined by the state. However, combining several districts into one regional planning area may be more effective, because of the interaction of economic, social, cultural, and physical dimensions.

For detailed studies of the subplanning areas, geometric forms of a complex of grid cells in quarter-, half- or square-mile units are more appropriate. The units may be either natural or arbitrarily chosen for analytical purposes. In educational systems with long-established planning programs, the subplanning

[3]Ibid., p. 22.

[4]Ibid., pp. 25–26.

FIGURE 15.3

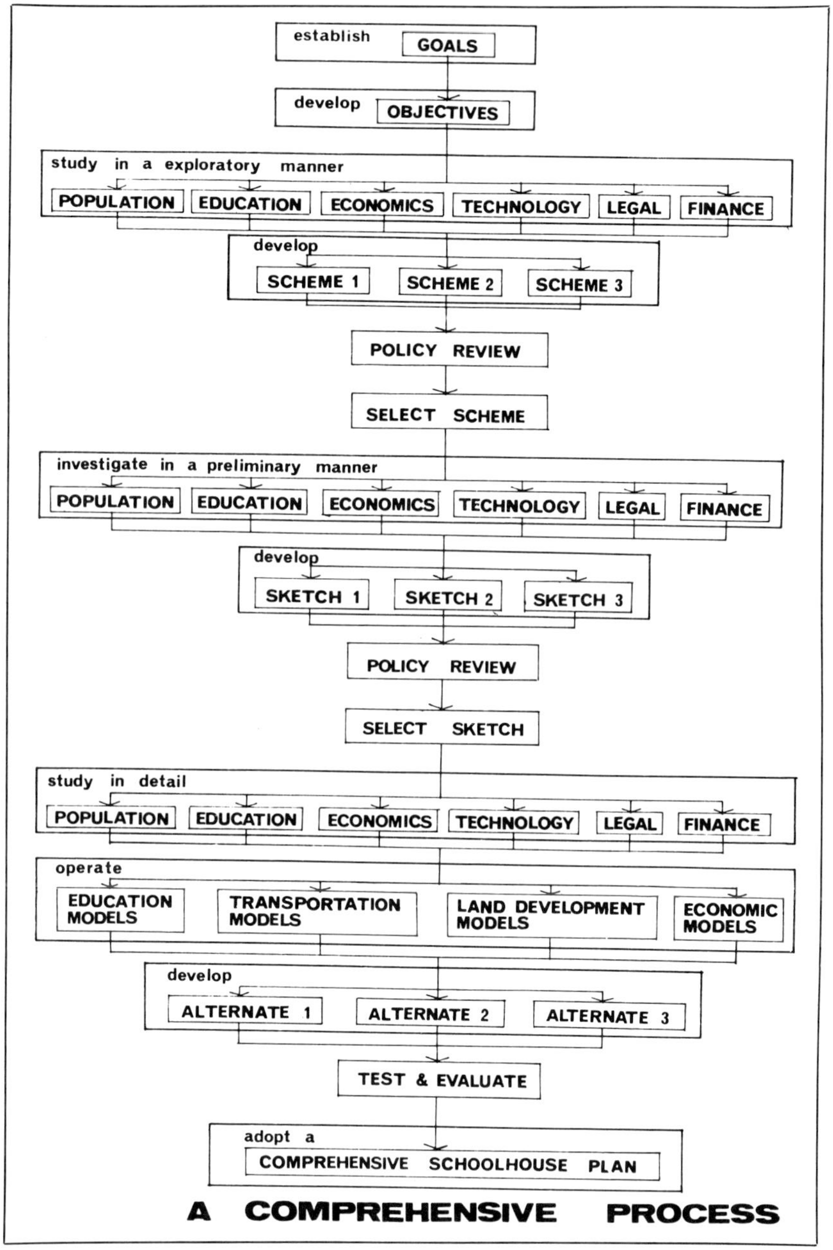
establish
GOALS
develop
OBJECTIVES
study in a exploratory manner
POPULATION
EDUCATION
ECONOMICS
TECHNOLOGY
LEGAL
FINANCE
develop
SCHEME 1
SCHEME 2
SCHEME 3
POLICY REVIEW
SELECT SCHEME
investigate in a preliminary manner
POPULATION
EDUCATION
ECONOMICS
TECHNOLOGY
LEGAL
FINANCE
develop
SKETCH 1
SKETCH 2
SKETCH 3
POLICY REVIEW
SELECT SKETCH
study in detail
POPULATION
EDUCATION
ECONOMICS
TECHNOLOGY
LEGAL
FINANCE
operate
EDUCATION MODELS
TRANSPORTATION MODELS
LAND DEVELOPMENT MODELS
ECONOMIC MODELS
develop
ALTERNATE 1
ALTERNATE 2
ALTERNATE 3
TEST & EVALUATE
adopt a
COMPREHENSIVE SCHOOLHOUSE PLAN
A COMPREHENSIVE PROCESS

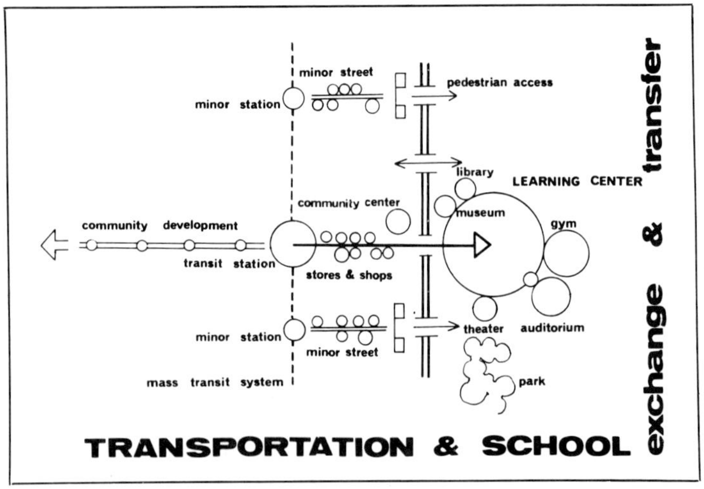

FIGURE 15.4

areas may already exist. In addition, the subplanning-area technique is more appropriate for handling new neighborhoods. Regardless of present or future conditions, the study of the subplanning area aims "... to recognize the service area of an elementary school, but often must be modified according to the number of people or families present and the density of population in relation to the existing school plant and the physical barriers present such as railroads, thoroughfares, watercourses, and large areas of nonresidential use."[5] (See Figure 15.4.) In subareas where no such delineations have been made, a somewhat arbitrary system may be based on census tract boundaries or other small statistical areas, such as traffic zones.

Once a system of subareas is defined, the tooling-up studies previously begun should be completed, based on the following minimum required information:

1 The current and forecast "planning area" population.
2 Current and forecast manufacturing, wholesale and office-related employment-manpower, and social-demand needs.
3 A map and a tabular summary of existing land use that would effect educational land use.
4 Data on the cost-revenue relationships for educational physical development in varying locations, at varying densities and intensities of use and on the general pattern of land values.

The second phase of physical planning is the qualitative and quantitative land use requirements. The qualitative aspect includes "... principles and standards governing the location of individual uses and the relationships between uses."[6] These identify prevailing patterns of interaction between school activities and community activities; trends in activities, e.g., from work to leisure; and the technological effects on the interaction patterns. (See Figure 15.5.)

The quantitative aspect involves the estimation of space requirements. Estimation of the acreage required, of future demands, and of any displacement of existing uses is included and is expressed not only in space dimensions, but in the number of people involved, the dollar value, the structural units, and so on. Regardless of the dimensional unit selected and used, the subplanning area is the scale most appropriate for mapping and summing the data.

The third phase of physical planning is the physical designing phase. A sketch plan is made that best fits the activity patterns, the livability concepts and the

[5]F. Stuart Chapin, Jr., *Urban Land Use Planning* (Urbana: University of Illinois Press, 1965), p. 365.

[6]Ibid., p. 367.

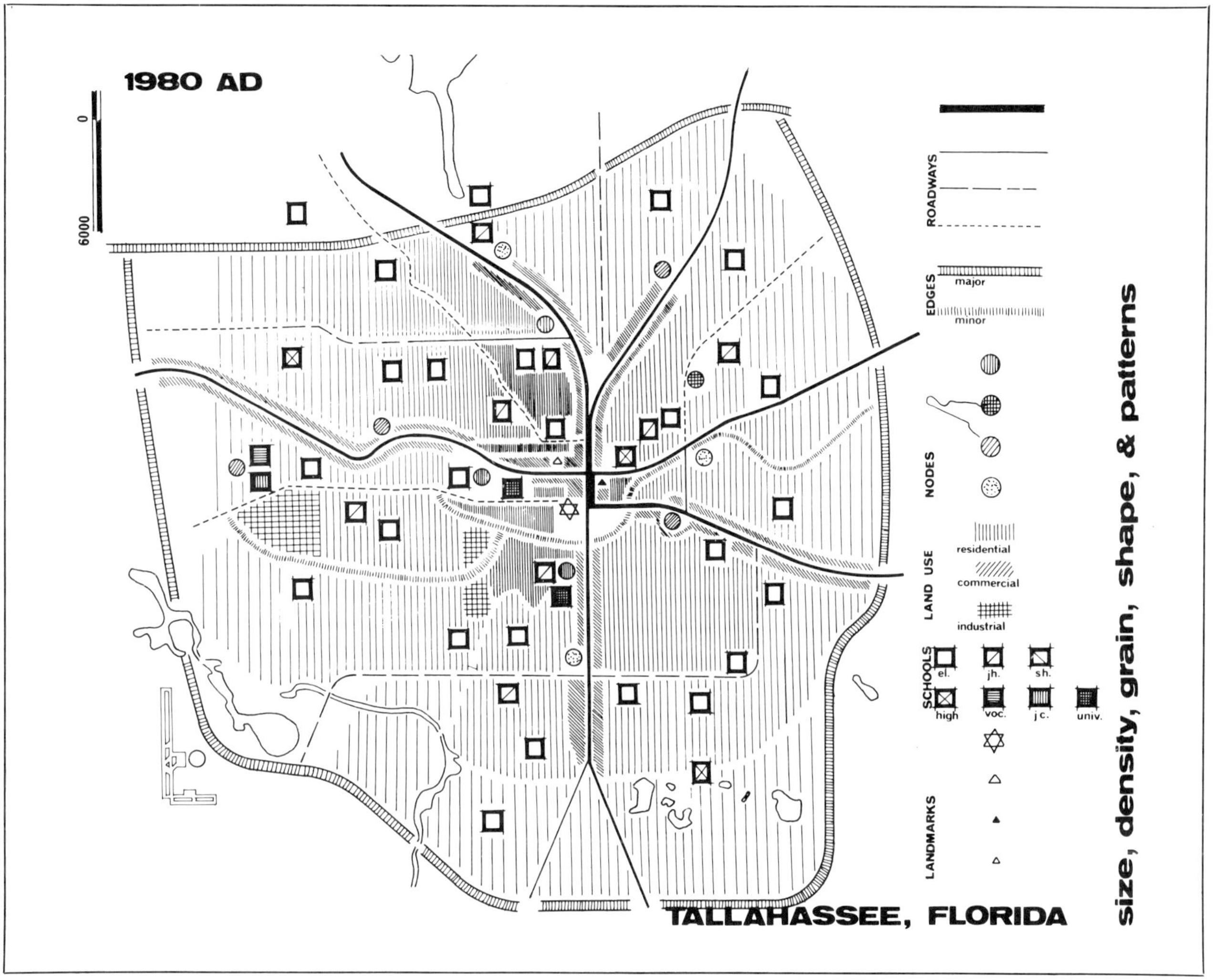

FIGURE 15.5A

cost considerations. (See Figure 15.6.) The sketch plan also collates the previously gathered data into defined-location and formal-distribution patterns. Here, conflicts become apparent, economic feasibility is indicated, new legal standards are determined and various alternatives are created and designed. Out of these, one physical plan—the most economical, the most attractive design for all educational uses, the best topographic fit and an optimal land-use pattern articulated with a workable movement system—can be selected as the best solution.

FIGURE 15.5B

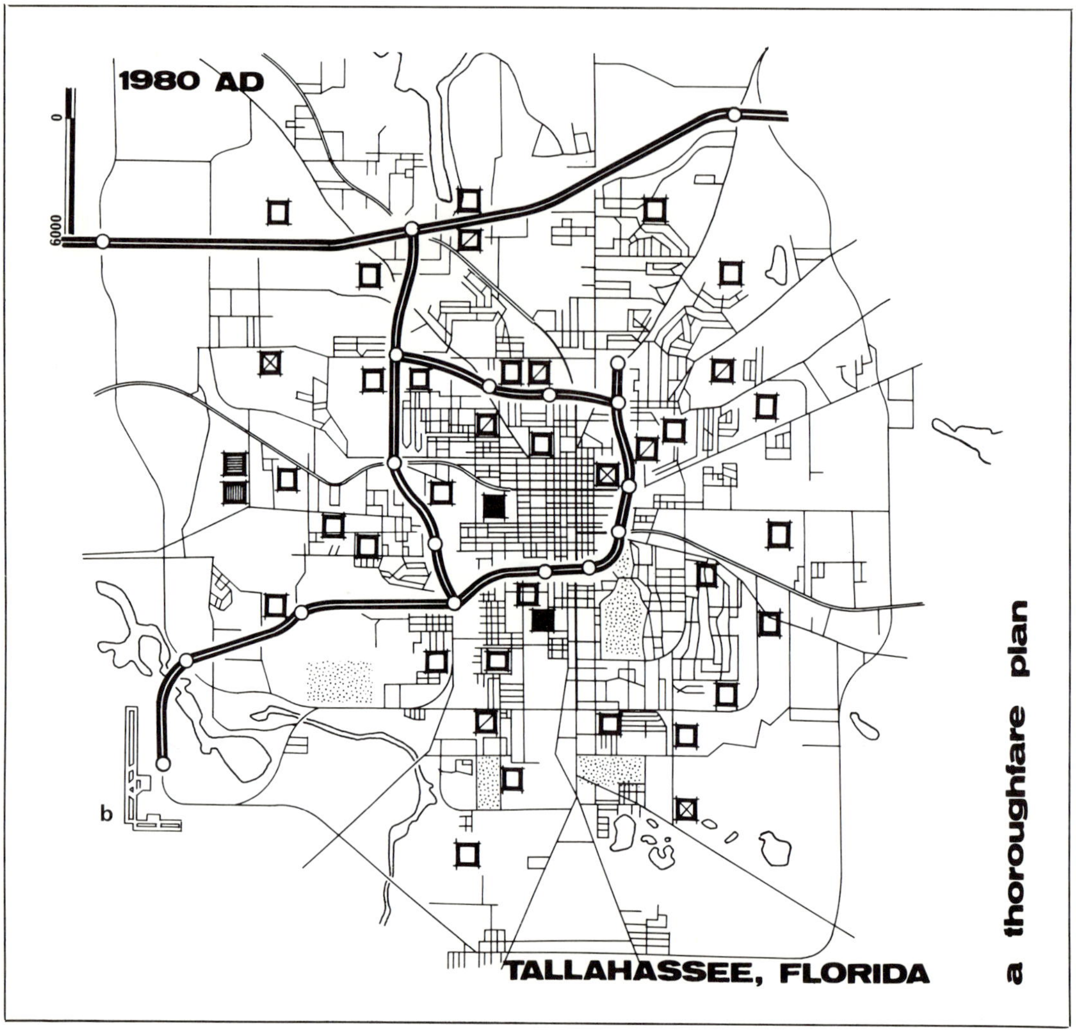

FIGURE 15.5C

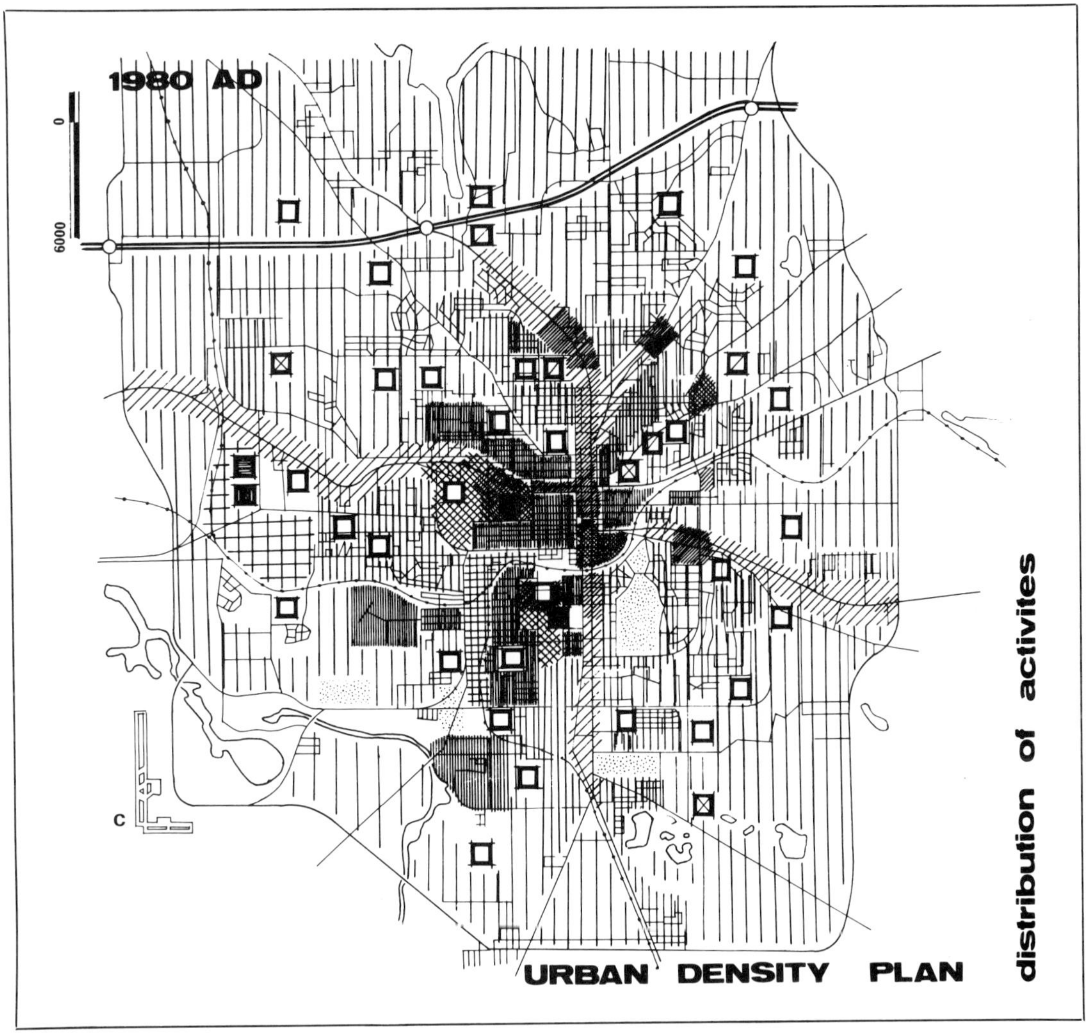
1980 AD
0
6000
C
URBAN DENSITY PLAN
distribution of activites

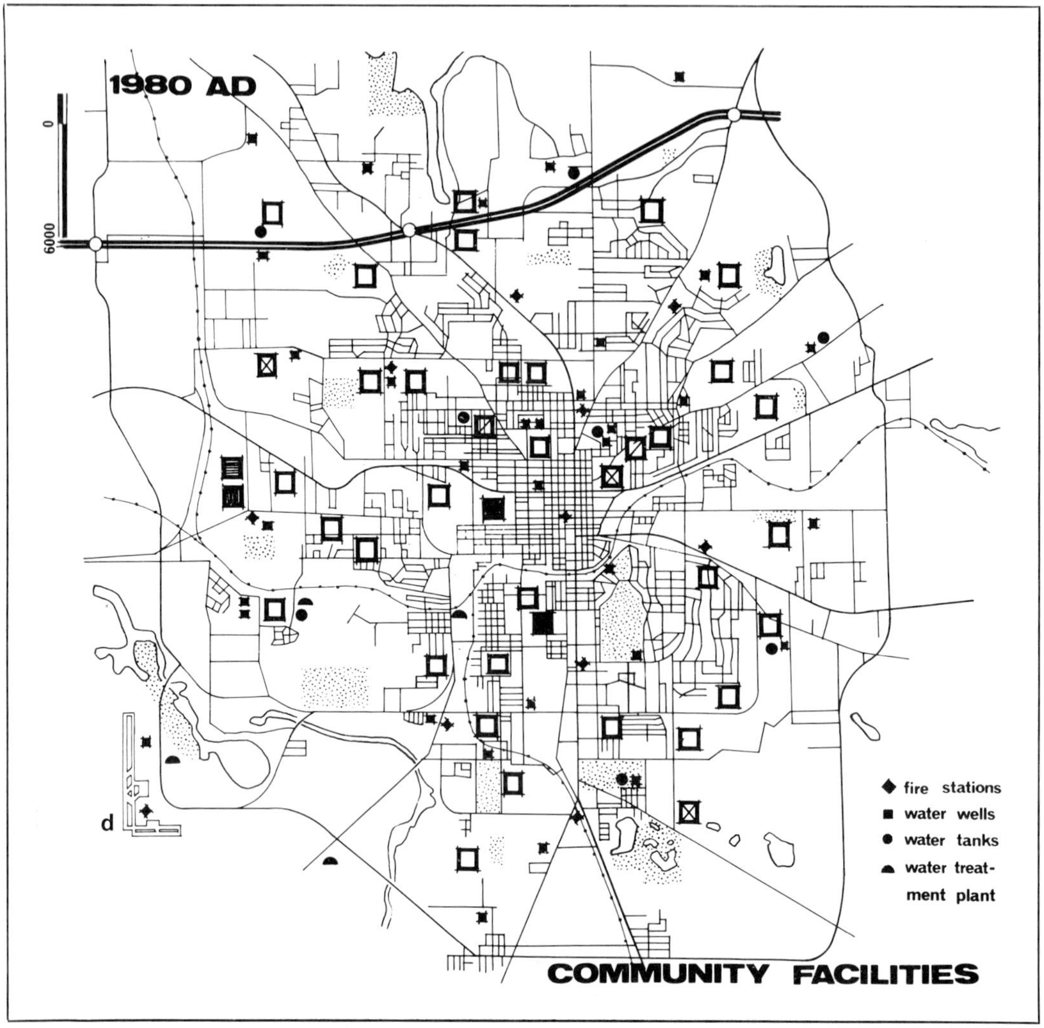
1980 AD
0
6000
d
fire stations
water wells
water tanks
water treat-
ment plant
COMMUNITY FACILITIES

FIGURE 15.5D

FIGURE 15.5E

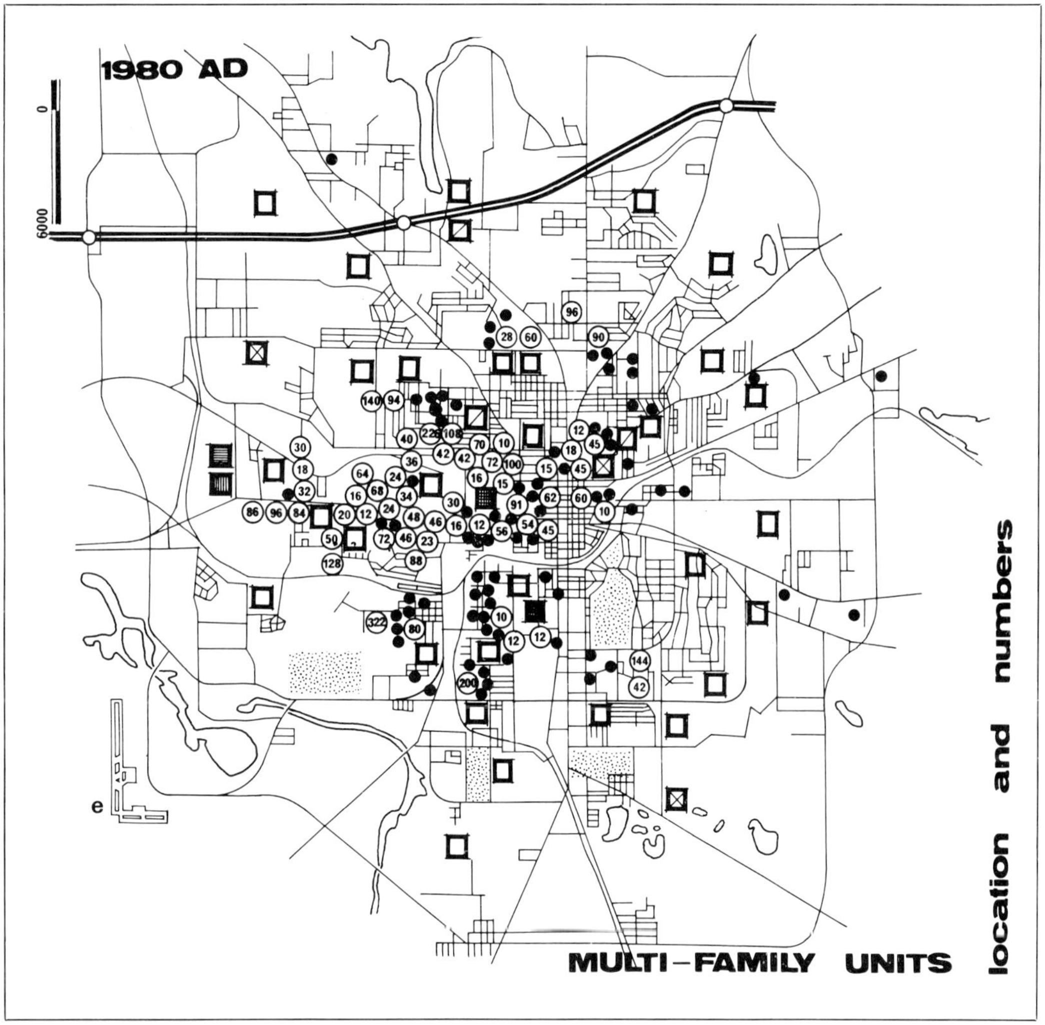

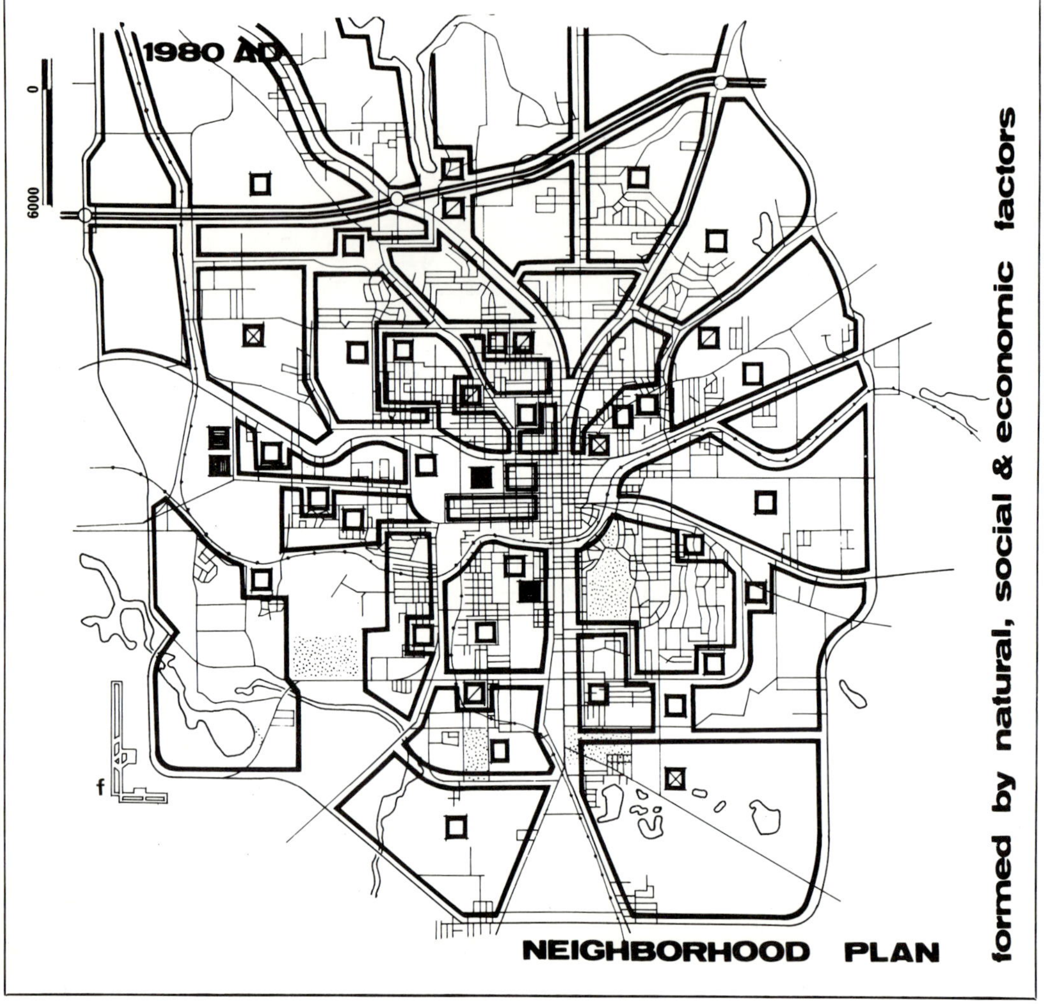
1980 AD
0
6000
f
NEIGHBORHOOD PLAN
formed by natural, social & economic factors

FIGURE 15.5F

FIGURE 15.5G

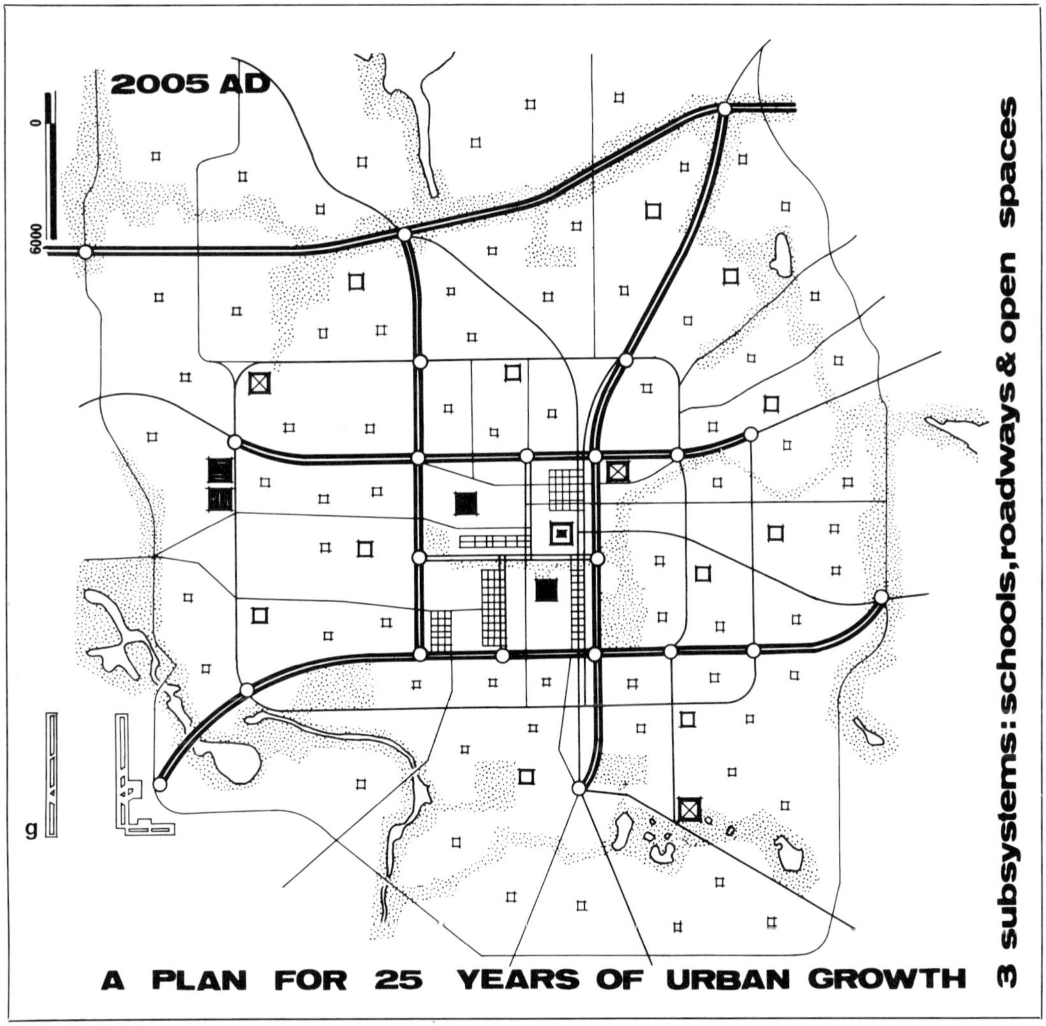

2005 AD
0
6000
g
A PLAN FOR 25 YEARS OF URBAN GROWTH
3 subsystems: schools, roadways & open spaces

FIGURE 15.6

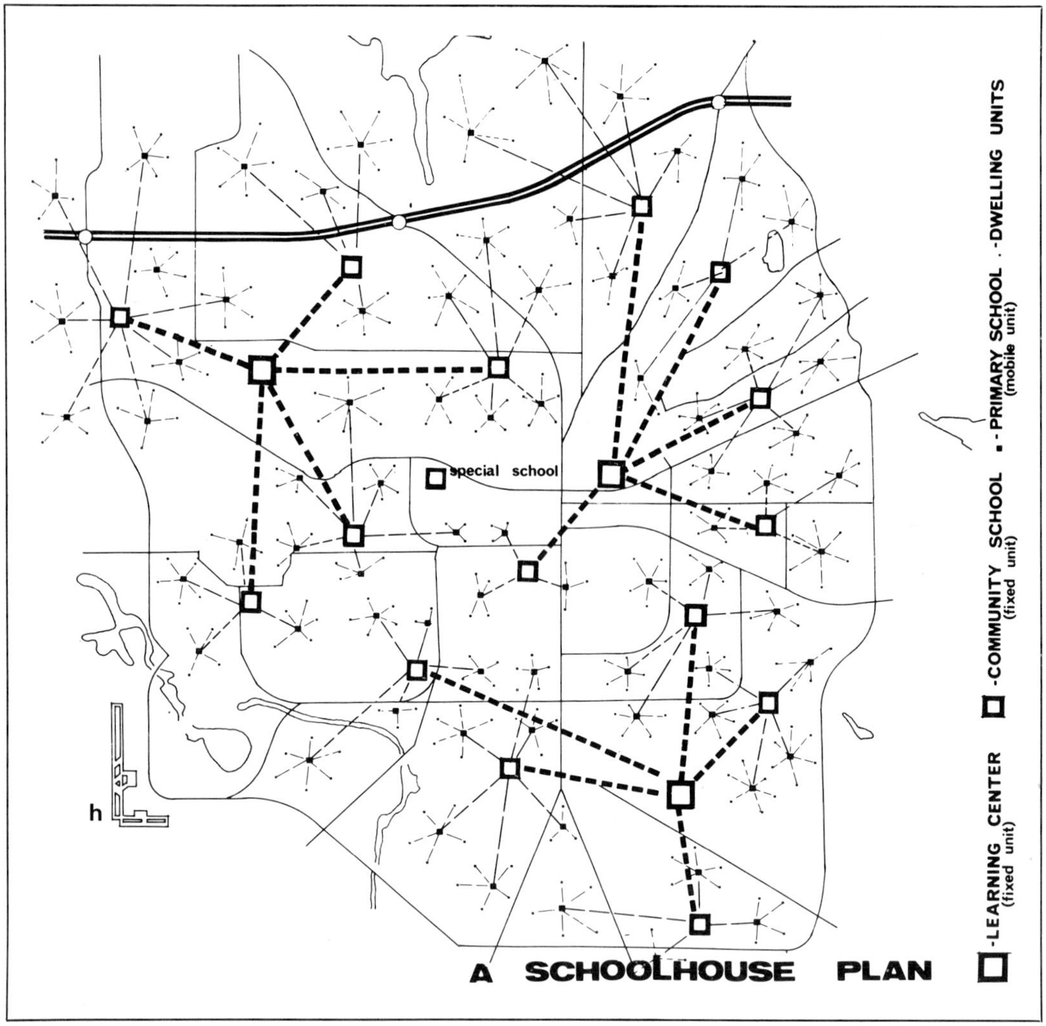

SOCIAL PLANNING

Because educational planning purports to fulfill human needs, no matter what form the planning takes, it influences the social aspects of the situation. Therefore, even if the plan deals only with the physical aspects, it still has social implications. The term *social planning* has no clear-cut boundaries and, hence, carries various connotations. Dealing with such problems as race and poverty, it is sometimes considered a form of social engineering whereby planners manipulate people and their environment. As these change, the social engineering will also have to change its focuses of concentration. Planning would be incomplete if it considered only the physical, social, economic, or educational subgroup without the overall environment. Systems analysts have recognized the problems of suboptimization, where one subgroup functions optimally, but causes the overall system to be neglected or to function badly. Therefore, the problems of poverty and race must be considered within the constraints of the larger system; whatever the objectives of social planning—whether to provide more desirable environments for specific groups or to provide equal opportunity or residential choice—all facets of the society must be considered or attempts be made to consider them all.

Social planning includes both the social and the physical environments in which social systems operate. Liberating the energies of all people and, thereby, furnishing them with an opportunity to contribute their best to society are the primary objectives of social planning. Like other branches of planning, social planning does not dictate or limit behavior, but creates an environment that liberates desirable behavior. Social planners draw up plans for the future action of the social institutions and human resources available and, with these plans, create opportunities for individuals that otherwise may never have existed.[7] Even in the early periods of systematic planning

> . . . it was seen that while the core of social planning consists in a plan for balanced capital investment in industry and agriculture, national plans must also allocate resources for education, health, housing and other kinds of social investment.[8]

"How widespread can planning be?" "How rational can planning be?" Such questions about the specific role of the social planner and the extent of his planning are yet to be answered. Whatever the role, it is apparent that the social planner, like all other planners, must be concerned with the basic fact-finding mission. There is considerable disagreement among social planners about the approach to and scope of social planning. The basic disagreement lies in the philosophical theses contrasting the overall remaking of society with the solution of specific problems within the larger social context. Probably the best characteristic is that the planning process

> . . . is no longer envisaged as a master plan but as a set of incremental or developmental programs that will improve present conditions, formulated so that they can be plugged into the ongoing decision-making processes of city officials. Physical determinism is thus being replaced by a broader systems approach, which seeks to deal with the causes of the problem. In this conception of the planning process, land-use studies are less relevant, and the community renewal planners are turning to surveys of the present behavior and future wants of the populations for whom they are planning, analyses of the quality of opportunities and social services now available to them, and economic as well as political studies to determine the feasibility and the results of the programs and policies they recommended.[9]

Social planning is not merely economically or behaviorally oriented; priority decisions are essentially political decisions that are based on social values and have long-term political effects.[10] Yet these various facets of planning obviously are interrelated.

> The noneconomic part of social planning must, at the present time, largely consist in attempting to foresee some of the ways in which economic decisions will affect social behavior and some of the ways in which social behavior will impede or facilitate the implementation of the economic decisions.[11]

In terms of current social requirements, the educational planning process must be measured against the means available to satisfy them; the social, economic, and technological factors should relate to one another in temporal and spatial matters within a three-dimensional physical plan.

> This process of integration implies a realistic assessment of economic and technological resources required for the realization of the plan, and it also calls for a careful consideration of the plan's social consequences. The resulting new set of social requirements now becomes the starting point for further development.[12]

The technology of educational planning has been somewhat related to the development of quantitative scientific approaches in the field of management.

[7]Charles Madge, "Introduction: Planning, Social," *International Encyclopedia of the Social Sciences,* vol. 12, ed. David L. Selts (New York: Macmillan and Free Press, 1968), p. 125.

[8]Ibid., p. 126.

[9]Herbert J. Gans, "City Planning in America: A Sociological Analysis," *People and Plans: Essays on Urban Problems and Solutions* (New York: Basic Books, 1968), p. 70.

[10]Madge, p. 126.

[11]Ibid.

[12]H. Peter Oberlander, "The Relation of Planning Education to the Planning Process," *Training for Town and Country Planning: Housing, Building and Planning,* No. 11 (New York: United Nations, Department of Economic and Social Affairs, 1957), p. 56.

Harlow Pearson identified four elements in the planning process that are somewhat related to the scientific management movement:

> (1) the definition of the objective of the enterprise, (2) formulation of policies governing its achievement, (3) designing a system of procedures whereby the objective would be achieved precisely and with the minimum waste of energies employed, and (4) in most instances giving initial direction of execution.[13]

Pointing out a similar concept, John Millet felt that planning prepared the administrator for his decisions by working out a specific program according to defined goals. Millet identified three phases in the planning processes: (1) the determination of objectives, (2) the measurement of the existing situation, and (3) the designing of a program for positive action.[14] There is a certain commonality in the various steps, principles, and procedures in these two sets of processes and those of other experts. G. Galloway, for example, perceived planning as a process of five steps:

> (1) determination of objectives to be sought, (2) research to understand the problem, (3) the discovery of alternative solutions, (4) policy making—choosing between alternatives, including the frequent choice of doing nothing, and (5) the detailed execution of the chosen alternative—known in physical planning as layout or design.[15]

However, in looking at other writers who have dealt with the administrator's principles of planning, one finds a considerable amount of overlap among the sets of principles.

What principles exist?

1 The principle of overall planning.
2 The principle of zoning.
3 The principle of neighborhood planning.
4 The principle of traffic segregation.
5 The principle of coordinated utility services.
6 The principle of functional efficiency.
7 The principle of esthetic satisfaction.
8 The principle of social cost.[16]

[13]Mary McLean (ed.), *Local Planning Administration* (3rd ed.; Chicago: International City Manager's Association, 1959), p. 42.

[14]Ibid.

[15]Ibid.

[16]Pearson, pp. 20–21.

Table 15.1 Phases of planning

Phase	Objective
First phase	*Goal formulation:*
	Implication analysis
	Work with public
Second phase	*Data collection:*
	Review
	Analysis
	Evaluation
	Conflict discussion
Third phase	*Synthesis:*
	Development of alternatives
	Synthesis of alternative policies
Fourth phase	*Creative phase:*
	Translation of goals and policies into planning programs
	Physical formulation
Fifth phase	*Persuasion:*
	Public education and review
	Modifications
Sixth phase	*Effectuation:*
	Action based on strategies developed within the planning program
Seventh phase	*Feedback and review:*
	Review based on experience
	Feedback as an activity that takes place at all phases of the planning process

SOURCE: Ralph G. Crouch, "A Study of the Goal Formulation Process." Prepared for the Department of City Planning, Los Angeles, Calif., September 30, 1964, p.57.

Frederick Adams lists goal formulation, survey and analysis, plan preparation, and plan effectuation as the four principles of planning.[17]

The planning may be examined by a close observation of its different components. As an illustration, functional planning focuses on a particular aspect of the total problem. It is essentially segmented in nature, but can be effective when it is coordinated with other planning efforts and forms within the overall long-range planning framework. The model in Table 15.1 reemphasizes the various phases of planning.

There are various alternative variations in any educational planning system. The planning strategy

[17]McLean, p. 41.

FIGURE 15.7

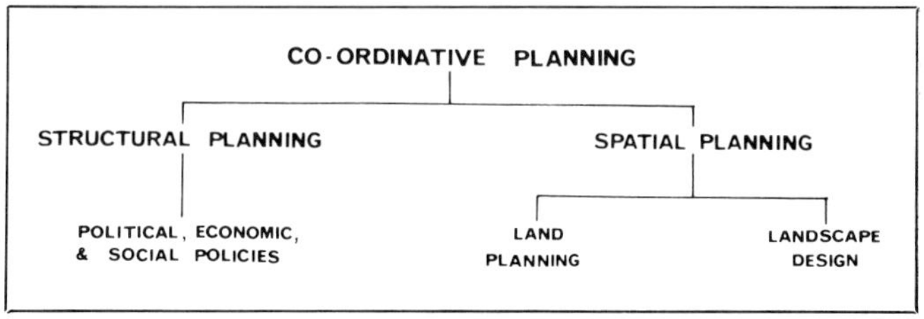

itself may fluctuate from one project to the next. The methods used in one situation may be incongruous in the second situation; in systems analysis alone, the administrator must choose, for example, between a cost/benefit and a cost/effectiveness approach. There are alternative inclusions in the planning content. Any one of the four basic components of planning, that is, strategy, method, techniques, and content, may furnish the appropriate flexibility for the total planning process.

> The Chicago school approached planning as a method of rational programming . . . the essence of planning is the deliberate choice of ends and the analytic determination of the most effective means to achieve these ends, these being means which make optimal use of scarce resources and which, when implemented, are not accompanied by undesirable consequences. [it was argued] . . . that ends are not imposed by planning ideology or by a priori determination of the public interest, but by political and market processes and by other forms of feedback from those affected by planning. According to this view, means and consequences are determined through predominantly empirical analyses, and by other studies that test the fit of means to ends and predict the consequences of these means.[18]

COMPREHENSIVE EDUCATIONAL PLANNING

The comprehensive educational plan is a variation on the general systems approach to planning, involving the total activity systems of education and the community that influences the overall operation, for example, those between the community and school. The emphasis is on the totality rather than on the component parts. In many respects comprehensive planning is easier than setting short-term goals. The objectives and goals are more broadly described and do not require the planner to be as specific as short-term goals require him to be. Edward McClure has listed the following six areas for the development of a comprehensive plan:

1 The creation of a unified set of development goals.
2 Guidance for public decisions.
3 Guarantees that the public regulation of land is done in a fair and unbiased manner.
4 Guidance for the individual citizen.
5 The evaluation of unexpected problem areas or opportunities within the urban area or region.
6 A plan for preserving the resources and amenities of the community or region.[19]

Planning is need oriented and, as a result, is gradually expanding into new areas, such as education, which has been devoid of comprehensive planning. Concurrently with its increased use, comprehensive planning is expanding into larger geographical areas than formerly and is involving, at the same time, broader and more detailed elements of the activity systems. By coordinating activity systems, planning organizes and regulates. Planning, in this light, may be classified into two main branches: structural and spatial planning. (See Figure 15.7.) Structural planning is associated with the activities and the behavior of societies and with land and resources. Structural planning is involved with the consequences of social behavior and the development of policies within which spatial planning can operate. Spatial planning, how-

[18]Gans, p. 134.

[19]Edward McClure, "Planning: Its Method and Process," *The Student in Society*, ed. D. Keith Lupton (Totowa, N.J.: Littlefield, Adams, 1969), p. 201.

ever, is concerned with land-use planning and landscape design.[20]

The characteristics of comprehensive planning include coordination, projective studies, flexibility, time and degree of commitment, the consideration of alternatives, safety factors, single and multiple functions and the optimal allocation of available resources. Because the primary objective of comprehensive planning is the creation of the master plan that guides and coordinates planning efforts, comprehensive planning should have a built-in, inherent evaluative procedure, such as those described in the last chaper. To be analytically sound and practical, planning cannot subordinate existing reality in favor of the ideal. Yet, the inherent principle of comprehensive planning

> . . . can provide the combination of sufficient accuracy and enough flexibility to justify application of the analytical process. But, by its nature, it cannot provide at the same time the highest order of accuracy and flexibility which would be attained for each if they could be considered separately.[21]

With such a constraint, the solution lies only with a specific set of guidelines, which in their makeup must allow some flexibility and which are continuously open to modifications as contingencies arise.

Comprehensive planning projects into the future a systems approach that correlates disparate elements into a design and translates them into useful dimensions. By continuous monitoring, comprehensive planning, with established objèctives, makes possible the conducting of institutional affairs for the attainment of objectives. Productivity may be continuously optimized in this manner. According to Ericksen three justifications of a master plan exist:

> The master plan is designed to keep us from day-to-day accumulation of mistakes which inhibit us from arriving at a goal. A master plan allows the community to observe the repercussions of a change to other factors that enter into the problem. A master plan fosters recognition of the instrumental elements over against the goals. That is, the relationships between means and ends are more visible.[22]

The concept of comprehensive planning, however, is not without its critics. As an impossible ideal, Edward Banfield deplored its

> (1) . . . inability to predict the future much beyond five years at a time, (2) [its] inability to discover the goals of the community on which all can agree, (3) [its] decentralized character of our political system, and (4) [its] lack of knowledge of effective means to achieve ends.[23]

John Friedmann has said, ". . . the notion of comprehensive planning serving the total public interest is incompatible with the narrow interests involved in the competition for power and influence which is characteristic of any political system."[24] Laurence D. Mann suggested ideas along the same line: "Given the character and composition of the decision-making process, the best that the planner can hope for is 'problem solving' or 'opportunity seizing.'"[25]

Alan A. Altshuler also commented, ". . . in reality decision-makers prefer operation at levels where comprehension and prediction are more certain even if this means fragmenting policy choices rather than integrating them."[26] Lowdon Wingo also suggested that

> . . . the comprehensive ideal overlooks the substantial human and social costs of achieving the desired goal. Such a logic implies that the payoff to the community is realized only as the sought-after environment emerges. . . . The critical policy question is not only how much the community is prepared to give up to realize the goals implicit in the master plan, but who gives up how much so that the fruits of the plan can be realized.[27]

To the above, David Braybrooke and Charles Lindblom have added attacks on comprehensive planning ". . . on the grounds of the practical limits of rationality." They questioned one's ability ". . . to deter-

[20]Pearson, pp. 17–18.

[21]Melville Brand and Ira M. Robinson, "Goals and Objectives in Civil Comprehensive Planning," *Town Planning Review,* no. 4, **38:**265 (1968).

[22]E. Gordon Ericksen, *Urban Behavior* (New York: Macmillan, 1954), p. 430.

[23]Richard Bolan, "Emerging Views of Planning," *Journal of the American Institute of Planners,* no. 4, **33:**234 (July 1967).

[24]Ibid.

[25]Ibid.

[26]Ibid.

[27]Ibid.

FIGURE 15.8

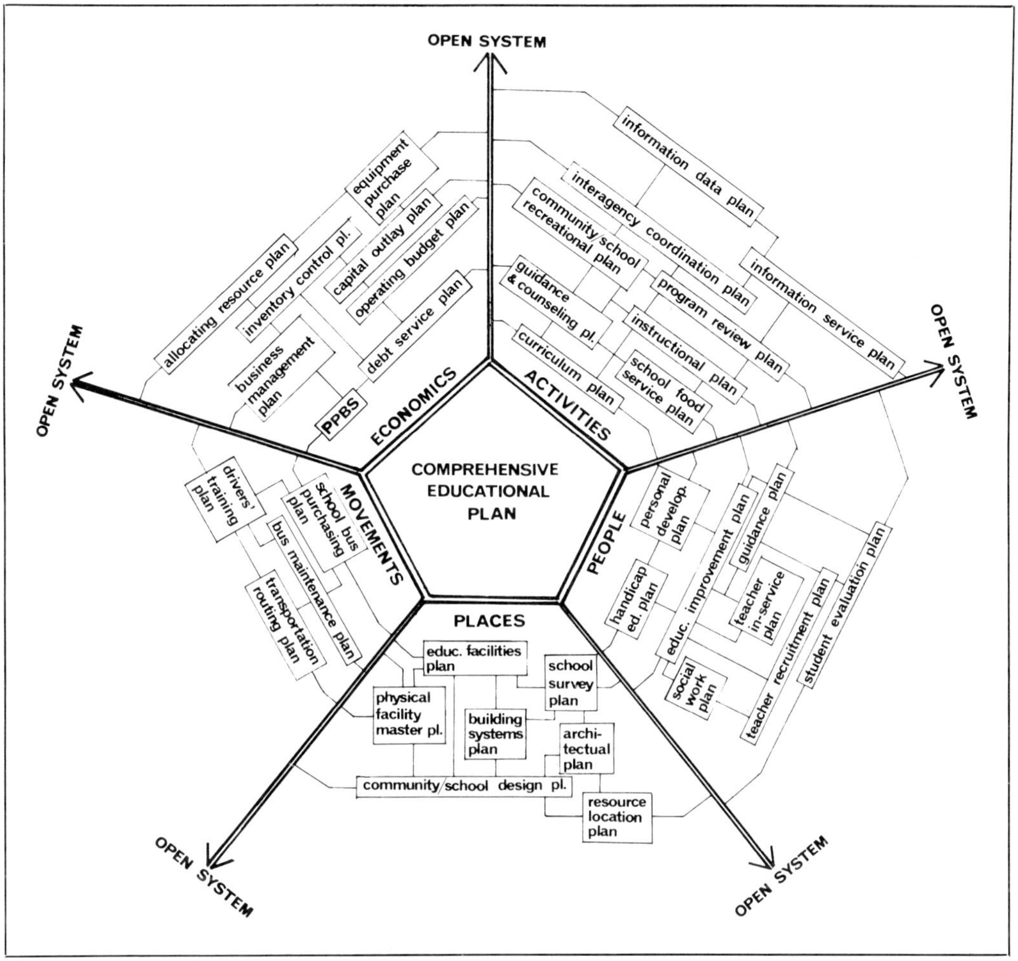

mine goals or values which in any event are always in the state of flux."[28]

The following is a list of limitations of comprehensive policy making:

1 Man's limited problem-solving capabilities.
2 The lack of truly comprehensive information.
3 The costliness of comprehensive analysis.
4 The inability to construct a satisfactory method for evaluating goals or values.
5 The closeness of observed relationships between fact and value.

[28]Ibid.

6 The openness of systems of variables.
7 The analyst's need for strategic sequences of analytical moves.
8 The diverse forms in which policy problems arise.[29]

With such heavy criticism leveled at comprehensive planning, especially within educational systems, it would seem that its processes are doomed to failure. On the other hand, it is difficult to conceive of a planning project without comprehensive planning, particularly in view of the potential help coming from current systems studies. Comprehensive educational

[29]Ibid.

planning allows the educational planner to include all segments of the community's physical and human resources, as they are allocated over time and space and to do so in the most useful way. (See Figure 15.8.)

The comprehensive educational plan represents the components operating within a total school system. Each subplan in the system contains certain general phenomena peculiar to its own operation and by virtue of its own past development. As systems grow, new subplans are added, because no rigid perimeter exists for the educational system: education is by definition an open system. Because it is an open system, changes occur that make some subsystems obsolete.

Subplans are grouped according to their interaction with the environment. Each subplan is related, in some way, to a particular aspect of the educational environment. The processes and results of the subplan have some relationship with other subplans, with the five dimensions—people, places, movements, economics, and activities—serving as interacting focuses. These focuses serve to place the subplans in perspective with other subplans. The resulting state establishes a homeostatic state, according to which certain relationships of the subplans are in balance. The behavior resulting from the subplans is defined in terms of these balanced states.

This approach allows a multidimensional com-

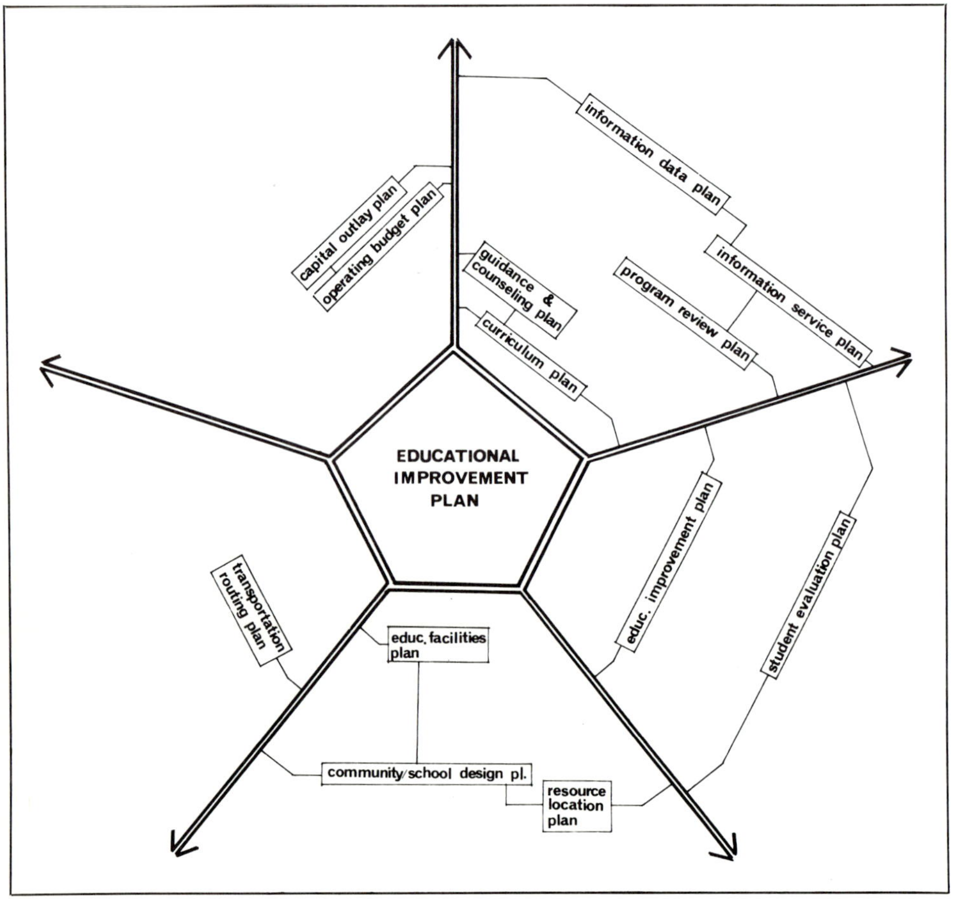

FIGURE 15.9

munication system to replace the standard single-line hierarchical organization now used by most educational systems. The hierarchical type of organization fragments planning into pieces that remain disjointed, because communication channels are not available. The two basic approaches are the linear infrastructure (the form of most educational organizations) and the planar infrastructure (the proposed model above). The linear approach is the weakest form for a communicative system, whereas the planar, with more lines for communicating, should be superior. Structure depends on communication and information processes.

The following example illustrates the operation of a portion of a multidimensional communication model. The scene is a typical city center of mixed activities, with thirty thousand inhabitants. Their educational needs were not being met by the existing school system's educational curriculum. Recently, a comprehensive educational planning division using the planar infrastructure model had reached the operational stage with a number of tested subplanning units. The assignment was to develop a plan that would solve the stated problem. A student evaluation plan was then made, along with a resource location plan and a program review plan. From these studies the data were processed and stored in an information management data unit. At the required times data were made available to those subplanning units involved in the preparation of a comprehensive educational improvement plan. Upon completion of the analysis by the various subunits, a new curriculum plan was made, along with a guidance and counseling plan. Facts were then fed to the educational-facilities-planning and operating-budget-planning units. Based on this feedback new alternatives in the curriculum were required. The new alternatives were fed to the operating-budget-planning unit, which coordinated with the capital-outlay-planning unit to help the educational facility planners make the required modifications. Educational-facility planners communicated with the transportation-routing planners to determine the most feasible points of interactions. These, in turn, were constantly communicated to the community/school-design planners to pick the sites most appropriate for such a program. From this interchange of data an understanding and an appreciation of all the influences on the problem's total environment produced an educational improvement plan. (See Figure 15.9.) The implementation resulted in optimizing the results while minimizing the misallocation of resources

Problems are different in magnitude, causes, and effects. The key to solving them is in communicating the right data to the right place at the right time. This type of sub-planning optimizes the use of resources. It does so by pinpointing and directing planning efforts to needed areas while retaining a comprehensive planning approach.

Part Five

Specifying the plan

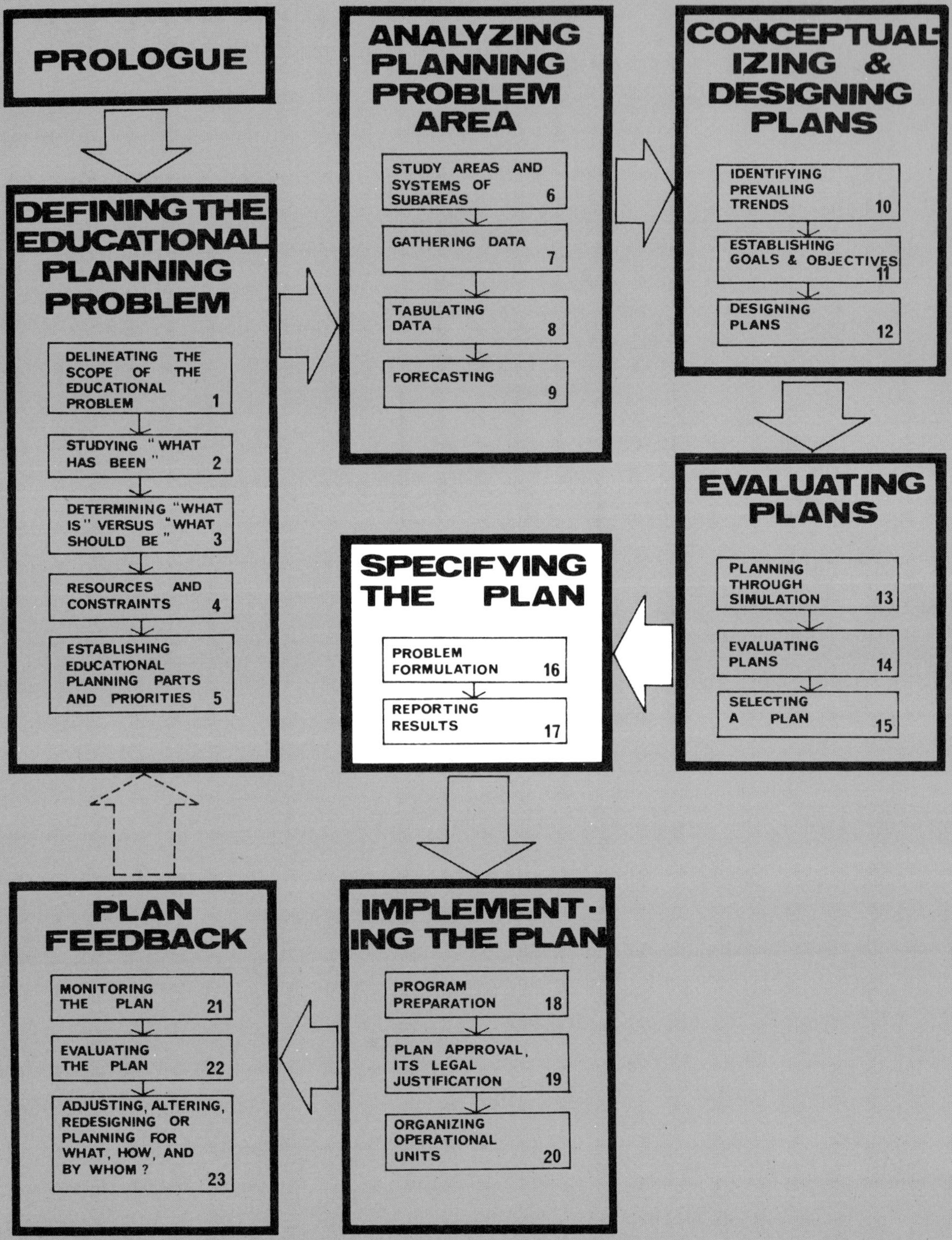
PROLOGUE
DEFINING THE EDUCATIONAL PLANNING PROBLEM
DELINEATING THE SCOPE OF THE EDUCATIONAL PROBLEM 1
STUDYING "WHAT HAS BEEN" 2
DETERMINING "WHAT IS" VERSUS "WHAT SHOULD BE" 3
RESOURCES AND CONSTRAINTS 4
ESTABLISHING EDUCATIONAL PLANNING PARTS AND PRIORITIES 5
ANALYZING PLANNING PROBLEM AREA
STUDY AREAS AND SYSTEMS OF SUBAREAS 6
GATHERING DATA 7
TABULATING DATA 8
FORECASTING 9
CONCEPTUAL-IZING & DESIGNING PLANS
IDENTIFYING PREVAILING TRENDS 10
ESTABLISHING GOALS & OBJECTIVES 11
DESIGNING PLANS 12
EVALUATING PLANS
PLANNING THROUGH SIMULATION 13
EVALUATING PLANS 14
SELECTING A PLAN 15
SPECIFYING THE PLAN
PROBLEM FORMULATION 16
REPORTING RESULTS 17
IMPLEMENT-ING THE PLAN
PROGRAM PREPARATION 18
PLAN APPROVAL, ITS LEGAL JUSTIFICATION 19
ORGANIZING OPERATIONAL UNITS 20
PLAN FEEDBACK
MONITORING THE PLAN 21
EVALUATING THE PLAN 22
ADJUSTING, ALTERING, REDESIGNING OR PLANNING FOR WHAT, HOW, AND BY WHOM? 23

Introduction

The fifth phase of this educational planning model is essentially one of communicating to those interested in the selected plan. Too often selected plans are shelved because their message was not communicated clearly, nor concisely, nor precisely. Two major aspects of the plan will be discussed as shown in the following steps:

Step 16 Problem formulation
Step 17 Reporting results

These two steps are detailed respectively in Chapters 16 and 17.

16 Problem formulation

Today's Society and Educational Tasks
Some Types of Educational Planning

Presenting a comprehensive educational plan requires first a precise statement of the problem. The original situation for most educational planning is filled with uncertainty. Questions have been raised about planning's ability to solve immediate problems. Educational planners themselves disagree on issues so that their efforts may be interpreted as an expression of uncertainty.

Chaos, *crises*, *poverty*, and *stagnation* are only a few of the words heard so frequently about our society and about token efforts to help eradicate them. This argument is superficial. Education has a particular structure with open-ended boundaries. Educational problems are, to a considerable extent, due to a failure to communicate education's role, and, in turn, its failure to interpret a changing society.

It is the educator's main task to formulate solutions to problems on the basis of the various and often contradictory needs that are brought to him.

Many educators dispute the functional problems of education because they disagree on what are the desirable ends of education, or because they fail to understand how the ends may be formulated, or translated into an educational framework.

What is needed is a concise statement of the problem that defines educational tasks and the means of their solution through planning. Formerly these tasks and programs were defined under the "philosophy of education," and somehow tasks and programs were masked in a word. What is needed is a conscious clarification of the problem, a definition of eductional tasks, and an analytical approach to their solution.

TODAY'S SOCIETY AND EDUCATIONAL TASKS

The urban scene might be considered a complex of urban, social, and economic interactions that take place within a physical environment. The urban scene represents a dynamic and continuously changing system. The educational planner must help to develop an appropriate educational form that fits well within the context of the social and economic systems. The urban system represents a complicated communications system of constant interactions through direct and indirect confrontation. The various levels of these confrontations have great relevance for the educational planner. The dynamics of the urban system might be considered in terms of continuous movements or flows of activities from one node to another. Such activities involve social interactions as well as mere physical activities. Somehow the various movements must be integrated into some type of operational system. This is accomplished through appropriate arrangement in time, space, and scale.

The new systems technology is contributing substantially to the planning process. The iterative procedures involve problem definition; the analysis of a problem into its component parts; the synthesis of these relevant variables into a new set of tentative solutions; the evaluation of the alternative solutions in terms of aesthetics, economy, scale, and functionalism; and finally a selection of the best of the alternatives. The iterations pass through this procedure and evaluate each alternative. Continuous modification of the system eventually determines the most acceptable alternative. In evaluating the alternatives weight is attached to various aspects of the problem according to the definition of the problem. Political, social, physical, and environmental factors, and time, cost, and resources are all major considerations in the evaluating of alternatives.

Increasing concern about the environment has created new demands on analytical approaches to studying the environment. This concern has occasioned a greater role for the computer in the area of urban educational analysis.

> The computers, the plotters, system analysis and programming are going to extend greatly the limited problem, display, handling of data, and evaluation capacities inherent in the techniques of drawing and modeling. Cybernetic techniques will solve technical problems far beyond the range of our conscious thinking process. But this simply elevates the level of the problem and solution. Creativity must still act beyond this level in the same way it acts beyond the level of the current techniques. Creativity is the primary ingredient. Techniques makes it evident and useful. Excellence in these techniques is genius.[1]

Modern technology has extended beyond data analysis and processing in the role of the computer and analytical approaches to studying the environment.

> Modern engineering technology can make drastic changes in the environment before we have had time to assess their ultimate results. The top soil it has taken centuries to accumulate can be removed in a few years. A marsh can be drained before anyone weighs the benefit of its increased agricultural production against its recreational value to bird watchers, Sunday walkers and October hunters who utilized it in its present state. On the other hand, left to himself, the biologist or ecologist is likely to become so bemused by the beauty of the balance of nature that he underestimates the importance of human needs or the power of modern engineering technology to compensate for what may at first glance seem to be wanton destruction. The economist and the sociologist are likely to develop too abstract a picture for both man and nature in a pseudo scientific search for order in human affairs. A more balanced view is needed that recognizes man as a part of nature—a somewhat peculiar part since he can modify the direction in which natural forces operate in order to reach objectives different from those which nature might produce if he were not there.[2]

The application of technology to environmental change places great responsibility on the planner. It is necessary to consider all of the side effects that a change in the environment will have. One must

[1]Niels Diffrient, "Form and Circumstance," *Landscape*, **18**:17 (Winter 1969).

[2]Robert S. Morrison, "Education for Environmental Concerns," *Daedalus*, no. 4, **96**:1219 (Fall 1967).

remember that the various components of the system are affected by manipulation of parts of the system. Technology tends to diminish the individual's decision-making capacity as the environment becomes more artificial. The usual standards for evaluating the environment tend to shift more to those artificial cues within the environment and hence make the individual less capable of evaluating the natural environment. "The merits of each technical advance are always so obvious that we hardly ever stop to ask ourselves if the sum total of all improvements may not pass beyond the limits of desirability."[3]

Analytical procedures being derived from such fields as ecology, cultural anthropology, and the behavioral social sciences are all becoming useful to the designer. The computer can handle their data and produce various alternative designs from which the best designs may be selected. This process has placed within man's hands the technical capacity to manipulate his own environment and enhance the chances of his survival. Indeed, man's new control over the environment relieves his dependence on the environment and forces him to rely on artificial necessities that have been derived from the environment. Many believe that although the goal of technology

> . . . should be to provide man with a sheltered environment in which he is protected as completely as possible from any form of traumatic experience, this assumption is dangerous because certain important traits of man's nature cannot develop normally, or remain in a healthy state, without constant stimulation and challenge. Life at constant temperature through air conditioning, learning made effortless through mechanical aids, avoidance of conflicts through social adjustment, are examples of the means by which modern life eliminates or minimizes physiological or psychological effort, but by the same token results in atrophy of man's adaptive mechanisms.[4]

One of the dangers for society that results from increasing technology is the possibility that life will become monotonous and routine. It is imperative that the planner, whether in education or in environmental planning, create a design that will produce a stimulating, viable, and continuously changing environment.

> The stage of scientific and technical development which renders large scale automated process possible also destroys all previous intrinsic value in [physical] resources or properties. From this point on, broadly speaking, all materials are inter-convertible. The only unique resources input is human knowledge—the organized information which programs machine performance. The products are non-unique and expendable, as are the machines and materials acted upon by them. The only part of the whole process which is non-expendable and uniquely irreplaceable is man.[5]

Without the support of the people, technology is almost useless. Fortunately present-day society does recognize the high degree of relevance and payoff in technology. Technology makes possible the enlargement of the physical world and extends our physical environment, ". . . providing a constant stream of moving, fleeting images of the world for our daily appraisal. . . . Through these devices (cinema, radio, TV, magazines, newspapers) we can telescope time, move through history and span the world in a variety of unprecedented ways."[6]

Technology has furnished man with the unique capability to alter his environments and to plan his environment for future activities. It is left up to the planner, especially the educational planner, to determine the most useful way to apply the available technology to the environment. Although it would be extremely shortsighted to develop any long-range educational plans through the decade of the seventies without seriously considering the role of technology in the educational enterprise, it is also necessary to remember and include in the planning process the distinctly human element found within that system. Only by realizing that the individual interacts within the total system of his environment will educational planning be effective. It should be pointed out, how-

[3]Albert E. Parr, "Toward Culture Entropy," *Ekistics,* **24:**15 (November 1967).

[4]René Dubos, "Promises and Hazards of Man's Adaptability," *Environmental Quality in a Growing Economy,* ed. Henry Jarrett (Baltimore: Johns Hopkins Press, 1966), p. 38.

[5]John McHale, "2000+," *Ekistics,* **24:**238 (September 1967).

[6]John McHale, "Education for Real," *Ekistics,* **24:**377 (November 1967).

ever, that the omission of modern technology occurs more often than the exclusion of concern for the psychological aspects of the individual. Indeed, there is increasing evidence that the profession of education has spent too much time and effort on the psychological or behavioral aspects of the educational program. The time is long overdue for giving technology the appropriate place within the educational learning environment in order to reach a balancing order if, as educators, we hope to bridge the gaps between the individual and his group, between nature-made and man-made environments, between human psychological needs and human physical needs, between the social rich and the social poor, between ignorance and knowledge, between ethnic or racial groups and between social cost and physical cost.

Any environmental design requires a relatively clear-cut series of steps, including a detailed analysis of the environment, a clear statement of problem definition, and a concept of the various activity systems, of the interrelations among the various activity systems, and of the nature of the population whose needs are to be served. A combination of the social and the physical goals to be accomplished must be carefully analyzed and integrated.

Man's image of the world in which he lives and his understanding of man's place in the universe are critical in achieving ecological homeostasis. Science can constitute basic facts and ideas about eco-systems. But man's concerns and values also determine the behavior of societies. His conceptual environment has changed through time, a transformation expressed in literature, poetry, music, architecture, and modifications of the landscape. . . . Man's conceptual environment, not science will determine the future of humanity.[7]

Planning is emerging as a participatory activity; that is, those people who are to be served by the environment and who are to be influenced by the environment have a right and an obligation to participate in planning the modification or development of that environment. Such participatory planning should cause the participants to develop a more responsible attitude toward life and the environment.

[7]S. Dillon Ripley and Helmut K. Buechner, "Eco-system Science as a Point of Synthesis," *Daedalus,* **96:**1196 (Fall 1967).

Such a philosophical orientation to planning assumes that value systems should be given high priority. The value system is directly related to the individual use to be derived from the environment. Again this concept emphasizes the interrelationships between the environment and the individual.

Many designers reject the idea that the optimal environment . . . has a single static form. Architect Raymond Studer advocates servo-environmental systems, which respond to changes in behavioral inputs. He feels that design problems phrased in terms of buildings, schools, houses, and neighborhoods, obscure dynamic processes that will change over time.

James Marston Fitch has described a school environment that rejects day-long environmental norms—the ideal temperature of 72 degrees, 50 per cent humidity, 60 foot lamberts at desk tops, and 45 foot decibels of sound. A child needs less heat in the afternoon than in the morning, more oxygen and less humidity by the end of the day, as well as greater sound levels in the afternoon than in the morning.[8]

Why is the influence of the environment on the individual relevant to the educational setting? The individual is profoundly influenced by both the natural and the man-made factors of his environment. This condition makes it incumbent on the educational planner and the environmental designer to consider how best to use all of the resources of an urban area as a part of the educational enterprise. Recreational, cultural, artistic, and economic resources must be incorporated in the educational system to make a usable program of learning activities beneficial to the youth in the community.

Incorporating in an integrative system more of the community's resources could have a dual payoff. First, if one of the primary objectives of the educational system is to achieve the student's better understanding of and interest in his environment, it seems reasonable that the greater the student's involvement in the environment, the greater his understanding and interest will be in the environment. As a result, the student would continually make efforts to improve his environment. The second potential gain to the student and, in turn, to his society would come in

[8]Ibid., p. 149.

his experiencing an assortment of exposed environments. The new and changing offerings in music, art, and the theater, as well as athletic events, would maintain the student's interest over periods of time. By creating environments that encourage students' participation and that emphasize relevance, the educational system will have its greatest effect on the community.

SOME TYPES OF EDUCATIONAL PLANNING

Planning, in a sense, is the preparation of a layout for the construction of something physical; in another sense, planning can be the arrangement of the time of actions, which is a form of program planning. Both are needed in educational planning. Following are types of planning approaches that can be used to accommodate the construction of something physical and to arrange the timing of activities.

Educational planning

Educational planning is a blueprint for future development. It recommends courses of action for the achievement of desired objectives. Some of the ways educational planning is practiced follow.

Adaptive educational planning

Adaptive educational planning takes place in response to an externally induced development. It is problem solving in the narrowest sense. It can be quite simple and quickly understood by most. Its purpose is to maintain the equilibrium of the organization.

Contingency educational planning

Contingency educational planning is an approach aimed at creating conditions whose effects can be deflected or absorbed at minimum cost or inconvenience.

Compulsive educational planning

Compulsive educational planning specifies in great detail what should and is expected to be done. Its major tool is reward if successful and punishment if unsuccessful.

Manipulative educational planning

Manipulative educational planning relies on various types of instruments to gain an advantage. Its tools are deals, trades, and personal inducements.

Indicative educational planning

Indicative educational planning spreads information calculated to give individuals the right signals in the hope that they in turn will take appropriate actions.

Incremental educational planning

Incremental educational planning is planning that takes short steps, correcting mistakes as it proceeds. Such a process, while constituting acceptable short-term adaptability, will accumulate a sufficient body of mistakes to force the planner to take a completely comprehensive approach. On the other hand, such planning, if successful, should accumulate a sufficient body of experience to enable the educational planner to attempt comprehensive planning.

Autonomous educational planning

Autonomous educational planning is planning pursued by itself and not as a part of any other planning.

Ameliorative educational planning

Ameliorative educational planning is designed to restore what was, without any consideration of what could be. Its purpose is to return to a status quo.

Normative educational planning

Normative educational planning is long-range planning, planning for twenty-five to forty years ahead. Its inherent nature is general, and its function is to establish guidelines for the planning to follow. It is comprehensive by nature in that it focuses on the total educational plan.

Functional educational planning

Functional educational planning focuses on a particular aspect of the total problem. Essentially this type of planning is segmented in nature but still functions as a part of the total planning effort.

Educational programming

Educational programming specifies the target groups, the programs required, and the resources needed to achieve a specific objective.

17 Reporting results

Contributions from Land-Use Planning
One Possible Classification Scheme
An Educational-Activity-Planning Format

Statistical and mapping presentations of data are necessary to comprehend the complicated matter of land usage. The general specifications for graphic or statistical presentations include general classifications, such as residence, with a scheme to indicate low, medium, and high intensity; retail businesses; local, central, and regional types of transportation; utilities, communications, and industry groups; and wholesale uses. All of these should be combined to form various groups that can be classified into readable clusters. Traditionally maps have been presented as engineering, topographic, and property-tax charts; aerial photographs; and various miscellaneous maps. Engineering maps are usually in a large, atlas form and resemble detailed engineering drawings. Topographic maps use contour lines to show the various elevations of the physiography and show the broadest possible view of the area. They include such things as rivers and streams, wooded areas, and other geographic characteristics, along with streets, railroads, and principal structures. Property charts usually show a specific piece of property rather than a regional area. Derived from aerial photographs, engineering drawings, and other legitimate sources, they usually show property lines and serve legal purposes. Miscellaneous maps include highway maps, census maps, historical or commercial tracts, and so on.

General-purpose base maps, which are used for generalized displays or rough working-charts, show named streets, corporate limits, railroads, major public buildings, lakes, and streams. They come in three principal sizes: (1) wall-display size (the scale of 2,500 feet equals one inch), (2) table size (the scale of 500 feet to two miles equals one inch), and (3) letter size (the scale of several miles equals one inch). Detailed base maps are prepared in atlas form and represent towns or natural planning areas. They are usually prepared in three sizes: (1) the first one shows right-of-way lines, railroads, water courses, lakes, and civil division lines; (2) the second shows property and easement lines; and (3) the above two maps are combined with a map of the structures in the area to form the third size. The first two maps are used primarily for neighborhood and detailed studies, and the third map is used to maintain records. A relatively straightforward procedure is followed in the preparing of base maps. A typical sequence is to (1) assemble various reference maps; (2) decide on the areas to be mapped; (3) decide on the coverage for the individual sheets of the atlas; (4) prepare the three series of detailed base maps already described; (5) prepare work sheets for the base maps; (6) field-check the work sheets in a walking survey or a driving survey; (7) produce the final drawings in ink form; and (8) set up some type of systematic procedure for updating the maps.

CONTRIBUTIONS FROM LAND-USE PLANNING

Land-use planning has used a relatively standardized set of guidelines for assisting the planner in developing information about urban development. (See Table 17.1.) The usual guidelines furnish the planner with data regarding the basic characteristics of the environment and the basic facts that relate the developmental area to the general urban environment. In addition to the general-characteristics guide, there is usually a directory to assist the planner in analyzing the central city. This directory includes central maps and special overlays that show the traffic pattern movements in the center. Comprehensive development guides furnish the planner with detailed data regarding various activity systems in the parts of the town that require special consideration. The comprehensive guide might include such things as aerial photographs, topographical maps, and specialized sketches. Guides usually include some type of financial profile that summarizes the costs and benefits to be derived from the development plan and that records sources of possible funds for the development program.

Residential areas are treated somewhat differently from the central district; consideration is given to the net density and the most efficient unit for studying residential areas. Projections of future population as well as current profiles of population density are usually examined in the set of plans. Density distance gradients are frequently used in an analysis of the dynamics of residential areas. Future residential patterns are also considered in terms of both the immediate impact on residential areas and the interactions of the population growth with other segments of the urban environment. Land-use planning is concerned primarily with the residential and business structures and the movement of people.

ONE POSSIBLE CLASSIFICATION SCHEME

An appropriate classification scheme is necessary for the urban educational planner, not only to furnish information about current status but also to help derive an appropriate mix of the various land-use factors.

> . . . The arrangement of the set of phenomena involved into a systematically ordered body of separate groups each composed of members having definable characteristics in common in accordance with a principle of classification which reflects the purpose or purposes which the classification is intended to serve is basic to inquiry into every distinct field of study. Yet, when the set of phenomena to be classified involves the uses to which urban land in a community is put, the satisfaction of these basic requirements is generally conspicuous by its absence.[1]

[1] Irving D. Shapiro, "Urban Land Use Classification," *Land Economics,* **35**: 149 (May 1957).

Table 17.1 A chart of general environmental characteristics

Community		A & M			Fair Ground		Golf Club			Lake Bradfd		Lake Jackson			Lincon	Mccosuke			Murat			San Luis				
Neighborhood Number		1	2	3	1	2	1	2	3	1	2	1	2	3	1	1	2	3	1	2	3	1	2	3	4	
Urban Expansion Area																										
Urban Fringe																										
Urban																										
Neighb'd Facilities	Primary school												P													X = Existing
	Park												P													P = Proposed
	Shops												P													XCP = Available
	Bus route																									NP = Not recommended
Community Facilities	Employment center												X													P = Accessible
	Secondary school												P													I = Improvement recommended
	Shopping center												P													
	Health services												X													
	Sport center																									
Travel Pattern	Low-volume road																									
	High-volume road												X													
	Interconnection												X													
Site Charac.	Drainage												X													
	Soil characteristics												X													
	Topography												X													
	Mixed uses												X													
Utilities	Water												X													
	Sewage												P													
	Electricity												X													
	Gas												P													
	Paving												P													
	Street light												P													
Environmental Maintenance	Refuse collection												P													
	Fire protection												P													
	Smoke												X													
	Noise												X													
	Fire danger												X													
	Moral hazard												X													
Housing Characteristics													Excellent													

A considerable amount of ambiguity exists in attempts at urban land classification. Planners seldom agree except on the most commonly defined segments in urban land usage. Classifiers have not stipulated specifically the objectives for which the land is to be used.

Types of activities, types of structures, types of establishments, and legal rights are all lumped together as land uses; the principles of classification used do not operate to group like items, and the classifications themselves do not reflect the prime purpose which they are intended to serve—presumably to act as bases for the land use pattern descriptions of individual communities.[2]

An appropriate classification of land use has been a problem to planners for some time. There are very few distinctions made between such things as industry and commerce; broad generalizations do not specifically pinpoint the precise function being considered. Complications arise in cases in which a particular organization is splintered, with headquarters and branch offices in various sections of the country. However, land-use studies frequently find the main office assigned a land-use function for the entire business rather than for only the fraction of the business that is actually located there. A more functional classification of land use might be by the precise space occupied by an individual, an organization, or a facility at any period of time. This classification would allow the planner to relate the uses to specific kinds of activities rather than to general classification terms. When mapping, one must have reasonably clear-cut definitions of the specific facilities and the various types of activities in which they are engaged. It follows that the planner not only has to determine the location of the various organizations but also has to understand the movement patterns of the activity systems associated with those organizations.

Here is one approach to the classification problem:

Following is material illustrative of this proposed principle of classification—a tabulation of primary types of activities and, for each, a few types of establishments which correspond to it.

[2]Ibid., p. 152.

Primary activity	Corresponding types of establishments
Advising	Accountant
	Consultant, all types
Assembling	Lodge
	YMCA
Buying	Buyer
	Residence buyer
Cleaning	Dry cleaning
	Laundry
Communicating	Broadcasting and receiving station
	Newspaper publishing establishment
Designing and/or drawing	Architects, all types
	Engineers, all types
Dining and/or drinking	Cocktail lounge
	Restaurant
Displaying	Art gallery
	Museum
Dwelling—houskeeping	Family unit
	Trailer camp
Non-housekeeping	Hotel
	Rooming house
Entertaining	
As spectators	Athletic field
	Motion-picture house
As participants	Bowling alley
	Dance hall
Exchanging	Commodity exchange
	Securities exchange
Extracting	Coal mining
	Gravel pit
Financing	Finance company
	Loan company
Instructing	College
	Vocational school
Investigating	Credit rating establishment
	Private investigator
Managing	Courthouse
	Police station
Packaging	Beverage bottling plant
	Tea and spice packaging
Printing	Book publishing establishment
	Printer
Processing and/or fabricating	Auto assembly plant
	Tile manufacturer

Raising and/or developing	Chicken hatchery
	Greenhouse
Repairing and/or maintaining	
People	Dentist
	Physician and surgeon
Things	Auto repair firm
	Watch repair shop
Researching	Laboratory
	Research center
Risk-bearing	Insurance company
Servicing	Employment agency
	Translator
Selling	
Retail	Camera shop
	Stationery dealer
Wholesale	Building materials yard
	Produce dealer
Shipping and receiving	Airport
	Freight depot
Storing	
People	Mental hospital
	Penitentiary
Things	Bank
	Parking lot
Storing	
Refuse	Dumping station
	Refuse dump
Testing	Assayer
	Chemist
Transporting	Railroad trackage
Worshipping	Church
	Synagogue[3]

Land use and studies of land use allow the planner (educational or otherwise) to make appropriate decisions in acquiring and utilizing the real estate in an area. Table 17.2 illustrates one way of studying or presenting land-use data.

[3]Ibid., pp. 154–155.

Table 17.2 Summary of land-use data

Class of use	Total planning area			Inside city limits			Outside city limits		
	Acres	% of total land	% of developed land	Acres	% of total land	% of developed land	Acres	% of total land	% of developed land
All Residential									
One family									
Two family									
Multifamily									
Retail business									
Wholesale and other†									
Industrial‡									
Transportation and utilities									
Streets and railroad rights-of-way									
All Public									
Public									
Military									
Institutional									
Water areas									
Vacant and nonurban									
Total									

SOURCE: F. Stuart Chapin, Jr., *Urban Land Use Planning* (Urbana: University of Illinois Press, 1965), p. 296

† Other refers to plumbing, heating, suppliers, trucking, terminals, amusement parks, race tracks, and so on.

‡ Includes extraction activities.

AN EDUCATIONAL-ACTIVITY-PLANNING FORMAT

Any consideration of urban form must include the human culture and activities that will use the space to be designed. Under these constrictions the planner matches the raw materials of the physical environment and the needs and activity systems of the human element. Form and patterns constitute the basis for urban organization. Proximity to given spaces, the mixture of parts, choice, opportunity, the accessibility of various facilities, and stability are factors of form and pattern. The spatial arrangement of physical structures, and the movement within and the use of space compose the city's form. The common elements in the urban form include such things as spatial organization, the appropriate use of the topography, and the inhabitant's sense of identity and orientation. The basic structure and function of the city, appropriate scale and architectural design, and specific activity systems influence the form of the design.

A meaningful set of physical entities reflects the end product of the process of design and spells out clearly the role of education. The structures include those for housing and business plus broad land uses that allow such various social phenomena as education to function unencumbered with unnecessary constraints such as too small a site, too much noise, too much traffic, traffic that is too fast, or too many people for so few resources.

The systems format is one method for indicating the interactions among activities, the people involved, and the environmental form.

Such a systems format might consist of two classification systems: the blocking system and the coding system.

The blocking system is a graphic reporting of the three major components—activity, participants, and environment. Each contains necessary data for the specific level of planning. The following principles delineate the blocking system's format:

1 The blocking system must be broad enough to permit the classification of every activity, the type and number of participants, and environmental factors.
2 Each block of the blocking system must be clearly defined and mutually exclusive.
3 Each block and its data must be susceptible to systems analysis.

In developing the format one must ask a minimum of three questions:

1 What is the activity and what are its characteristics?
2 Who are the participants?
3 What will be an appropriate environment for the participants while they are engaged in this activity?

Four aspects of the activity must be considered. First is the extraterritorial aspect of interactions. Activities are not necessarily bound to one in-place location. They can begin at one location and end at another miles away. The second aspect is interaction. Very few activities are independent. Most require inputs from other activities for their execution, which in turn makes up the inputs for other activities in other places. Dynamic scale is the third aspect. Activities occur within the entire movement spectrum from very slow to supersonic speed. The fourth aspect is the activity's location. Each activity has certain requirements if it is to be effectively performed.

Planning for the participants involves considering them as a part of a nonstationary, open system that is undergoing continuous interchange with the environment. The participants can be distinguished according to a range of categories, such as the following:

Individuals	Age
	Physical ability
	Emotional ability
	Mental ability
	Experience
	Interests
	Talents
Social	Language
	Ethnic characteristics
	Educational attainment level

Economic	Income level
	Possession patterns
Occupation	Unskilled
	Semiskilled
	Skilled
	Blue collar
	White collar
	Semiprofessional
	Professional
Developmental interests	Past accomplishments
	Current happenings
	Desired goals or objectives

The environment can be described as a complex entity composed of many facets. Some are naturally formed and others man-made, e.g., climate, culture, physical spaces, and energies. These influence and set constraints on as well as offer opportunities for participants and activities. Thus, activities, participants, and environments are in constant interaction. Participants respond to and also change their environments.

The planner's task becomes one of relating the three major components. A set of activities and a set of participants are related to particular environments. By altering the component elements, one can measure the effects on participants within particular environments.

Not all factors will be important. Sorting out the important factors solely by intuitive means would deny that a rational process for planning the best environments exists. By studying a series of subsystems that bring various selected elements into focus, one can determine certain effects. Such a process helps to reveal which environments have the highest potential value for particular participants in certain activities.

The formats and levels of subsystems in Figure 17.1 through Figure 17.5 comprise one model:

The coding system might be used as a systematic method for storing and identifying the various activities. The general principles for developing a coding system are as follows:

1 The code should be easy to use, expandable, and computer oriented.
2 The code should be flexible enough to accept any degree of detail that is important in the planning process.
3 The code must be organized for convenience in updating the data.

The number of digits found in a code indicates the level of detail. The coding explanation is as follows:

1 One-digit numbers denote activity class.
2 Two-digit numbers denote activity type.
3 Three-digit numbers denote the component.
4 Four-digit numbers denote activity element.

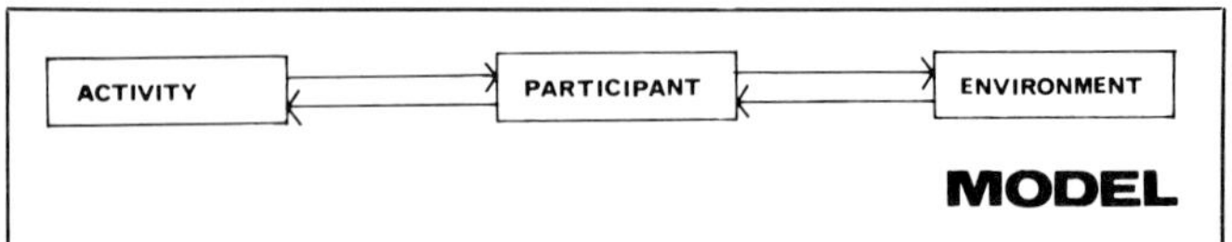

FIGURE 17.1

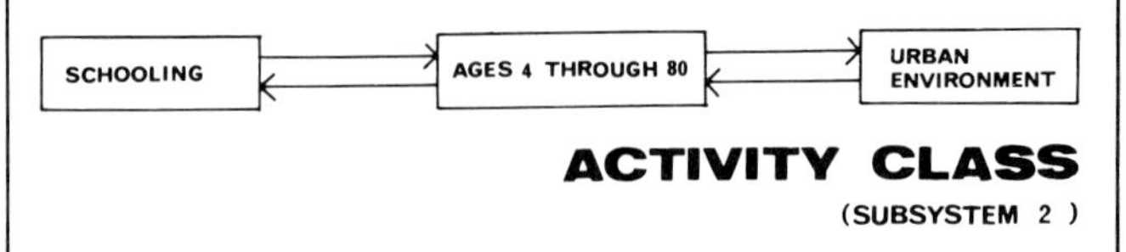

FIGURE 17.2

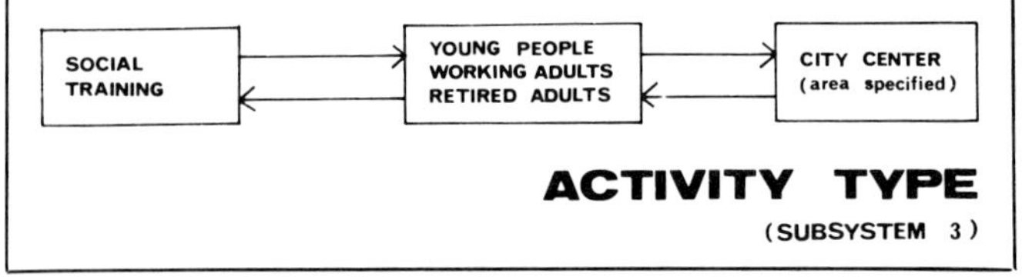

FIGURE 17.3

FIGURE 17.4

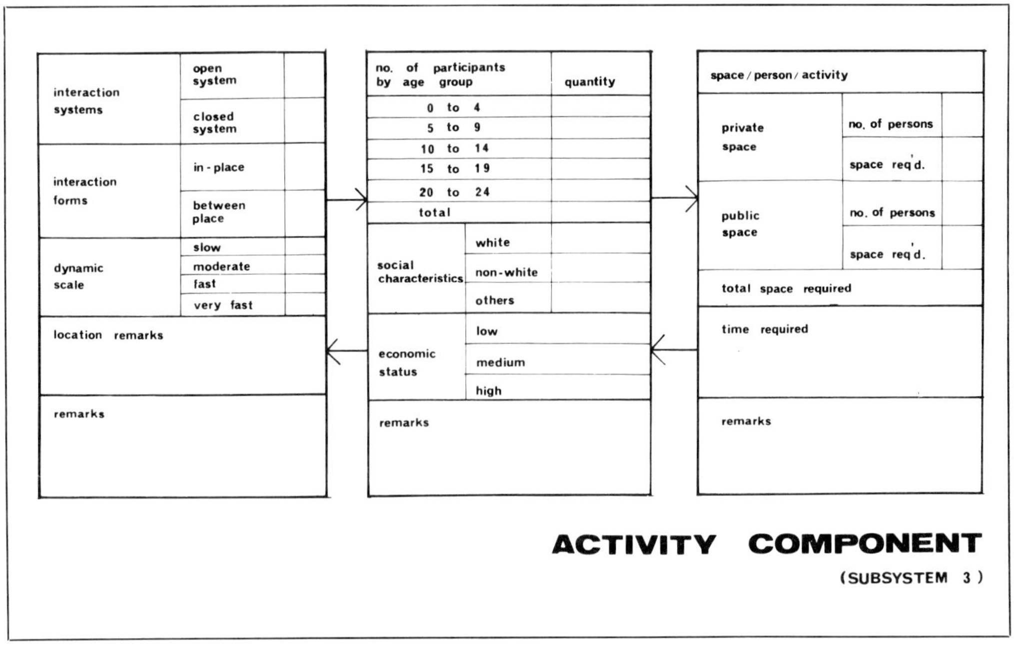

The following example illustrates one breakdown applicable to the study of a community learning center.

Subsystem 1: Activity classes

Code number	*Color codes*	*Activity class*
1	Crimson red	Moving
2	Deep blue	Schooling
3	Purple	Socializing
4	Light olive	Creating
5	Dark olive	Re-creating
6	Yellow	Dwelling
7	Light red	Shopping
8	Orange	Servicing
9	Brown	Maintaining

Moving is an activity requiring an object or person to go from one place over a distance to another place.

Schooling is an activity that requires the participant to acquire, in a formal sense, new knowledge and skills, plus all supporting activities.

Socializing includes activities that involve the company of like-minded friends or equals.

Creating involves a cathartically oriented type of activity whose primary purpose is to create anew, restore, or refresh the participant's imagination or mental outlook.

Re-creating includes activities that require brisk movements, that function freely within prescribed limits, and that usually require the handling or using of an instrument.

Dwelling encompasses activities requiring a place for some time length for individualistic types of activities, such as sleeping, eating, and procreating.

Shopping is an activity that requires the selling and buying of goods for personal, household, or institutional consumption and all kindred incidental services.

Servicing includes a group of activities that are performed for the physical and psychological welfare of the participant or for enhancing his other activities.

Maintaining includes preserving, repairing, prolonging, and supporting activities that keep up the physical facilities, equipment, and all their parts.

FIGURE 17.5A

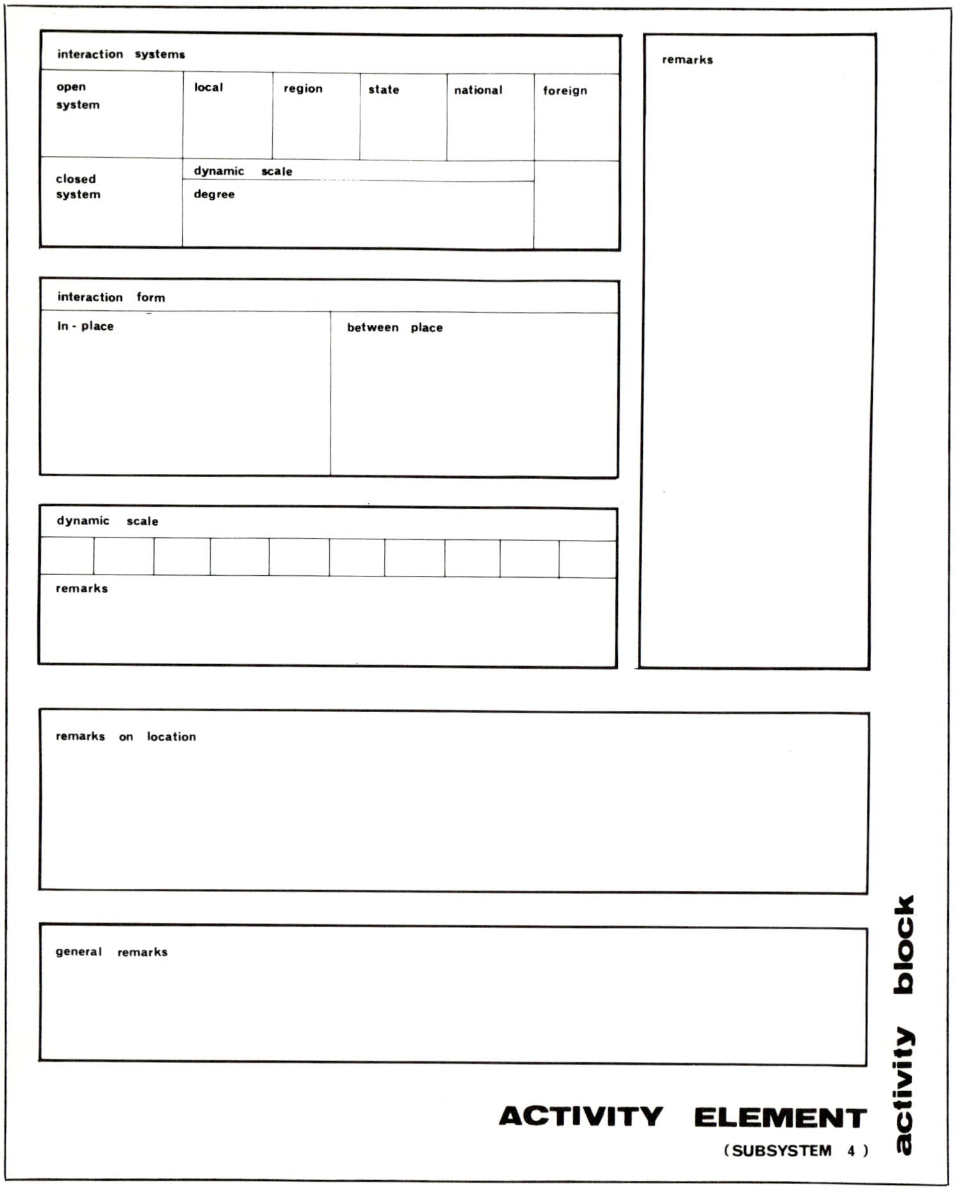
interaction systems

open system | local | region | state | national | foreign

closed system | dynamic scale | degree

interaction form

In - place | between place

dynamic scale

remarks

remarks

remarks on location

general remarks

ACTIVITY ELEMENT

(SUBSYSTEM 4)

activity block

FIGURE 17.5B

number of participants by age group	quantity
0 to 4	
5 to 9	
10 to 14	
15 to 19	
20 to 24	
25 to 39	
40 to 59	
60 to 79	
80 plus	
total	

remarks

characteristics			age range	
sex distribution			educational level	
community relationship		rural	suburban	urban

economic characteristics			
status	low	medium	high
remarks			

occupational status	unskilled	semi-skilled	skilled	blue collar	white collar	semi-profes.	professional

developmental interests		
past	present	future

remarks

general remarks

participant block

ACTIVITY ELEMENT

(SUBSYSTEM 4)

FIGURE 17.5C

atmospheric requirements		
temperature / space		
relative humidity		
outside temperature		
air changes		
air flow		
room air pressure		
air filter efficiency		
odors		
number of participants		

heat gain	source	watts	

visual requirements			
foot candles			
view out	view in	privacy	
daylight	level control		

acoustic requirements					
ambient noise level					
reverberation time					
generated noise level					

mechanical requirements			
cw	hw	steam	gas
air	drain	exhaust	
other			

electrical requirements			
pa	intercom	tape set	telephone
program system		clock system	tv
computer terminal		duct systems	
power			
other			

remarks

notes

ACTIVITY ELEMENT

(SUBSYSTEM 4)

environment block

Subsystem 2: Activity types

Class: moving   Code numbers: 10–19   Color code: Crimson red

Code number:	Activity type:
10	Communicating
11	Person, nonmoving
12	Walking
13	Bicycling
14	Riding
15	Driving
16	Practicing
17	Parking
18	Trucking
19	Non-person-moving

Class: schooling   Code numbers: 20–29   Color code: Deep blue

Code number:	Activity type:
20	Communicating
21	Training
22	Retraining
23	Special training
24	Rehabilitating
25	Researching
26	Practicing
27	Physical training
28	Private schooling
29	Religious training

Class: socializing   Code numbers: 30–39   Color code: Purple

Code number:	Activity type:
30	Communicating
31	Viewing
32	Meeting
33	Entertaining
34	Eating
35	Exploring
36	Practicing
37	Playing
38	Performing
39	Competing

Class: creating   Code numbers: 40–49   Color code: Light olive

Code number:	Activity type:
40	Communicating
41	Designing
42	Drawing
43	Sculpturing
44	Cooking
45	Photographing
46	Practicing
47	Fabricating
48	Gardening
49	Worshiping

Class: re-creating   Code numbers: 50–59   Color code: Dark olive

Code number:	Activity type:
50	Communicating
51	Water playing
52	Single playing
53	Dual playing
54	Team playing
55	Special playing
56	Practicing
57	Physical conditioning
58	Professional playing
59	Attending

Class: dwelling   Code numbers: 60–69   Color code: Yellow

Code number:	Activity type:
60	Informing
61	Child training
62	Sleeping
63	Working
64	Eating
65	Avocating
66	Practicing
67	Playing
68	Occupying
69	Worshiping

Class: shopping Code numbers: 70–79 Color code: Light red

Code number:	Activity type:
70	Informing
71	Browsing
72	Displaying
73	Buying
74	Eating
75	Banking
76	Repairing
77	Delivering
78	Paying
79	Selling

Class: servicing Code numbers: 80–89 Color code: Orange

Code number:	Activity type:
80	Communicating
81	Healing
82	Legal services
83	Counseling
84	Eating
85	Repairing
86	Personal servicing
87	Financing
88	Renting
89	Community servicing

Class: maintaining Code numbers: 90–99 Color code: Brown

Code number:	Activity type:
90	Communicating
91	Cleaning
92	Storing
93	Replacing
94	Rebuilding
95	Repairing
96	Distributing
97	Disposing
98	Landscaping
99	Inspecting

Subsystem 3: Activity elements

Because this subsystem is composed of literally hundreds of elements, only one illustration will be given.

Activity type: training Code number: 21 Color code: Deep blue

Code number:	Specified activity:
210	Home training
211	Preschool training
212	Preadolescent training
213	Adult training
214	Senior-citizen training
215	Military training
216	Vocational training

Subsystem 4: The activity

Again, to give an exhaustive summary would be nearly impossible in the space allotted, but as above, an example will be given.

Activity element: vocational training Code number: 216 Color code: Deep blue

Code number:	Activity:
2162	Architectural training
21620	Architectural drafting I
21621	Architectural drafting II
21622	Structural drafting
21623	Building codes
21624	Analyzing construction
21625	Building utilities
21626	Plane surveying
21627	Materials testing

Of course, the above coding schemes are only illustrations, but they do indicate the detail required for reporting and handling information.

Planners, much like systems analysts, are technical generalists. They must perceive the whole problem but they must have the technical ability to come up with a creative form. Several types of plans include several common ideas.

I The Comprehensive Plan, deeply rooted in an understanding of the community, based on both experience and research, sets forth an interrelated sensitively balanced range of objectives.

II The Functional Plan sets forth the physical organization, on a regional basis, of a manageable number of factors in their primary interrelation with one another.

III The Area Plan sets forth for a limited geographical section of the city, the three-dimensional relationships between the physical factors, correlated with the Functional Plan, which bear on the problems to be solved in order to achieve comprehensive plan objectives.

IV The Project Plan sets forth in explicit three-dimensional terms, the essential nature of the project or projects which are necessary to achieve the objectives of the Area Plan.

V The Architectural Image sets forth in human experiential terms what it would be like to see and to move about in the project when it is complete, providing a powerful impetus toward community understanding and popular acceptance of the plan.

VI The Money Entity, based on cost estimates for the construction of the project, is necessary to give dimensions and reality to the project, to provide a definite issue for public debate, and to provide the unit which seeks to find its place in the flow of the Capital programming process.

VII The Capital Program, really an apportionment of time, sets forth the sequence and dimension of public action for project accomplishment, and so becomes a sensitive regulatory device to set the range of comprehensive plan objectives in their proper relationship in space and time.[4]

Variations of the plans enumerated give form to comprehensive educational planning and permit continuous monitoring as well as the reporting and displaying of results.

[4]Edmund Bacon, "Design as Process," *Ekistics*, **24:**329 (October 1967).

Part Six

Implementing the plan

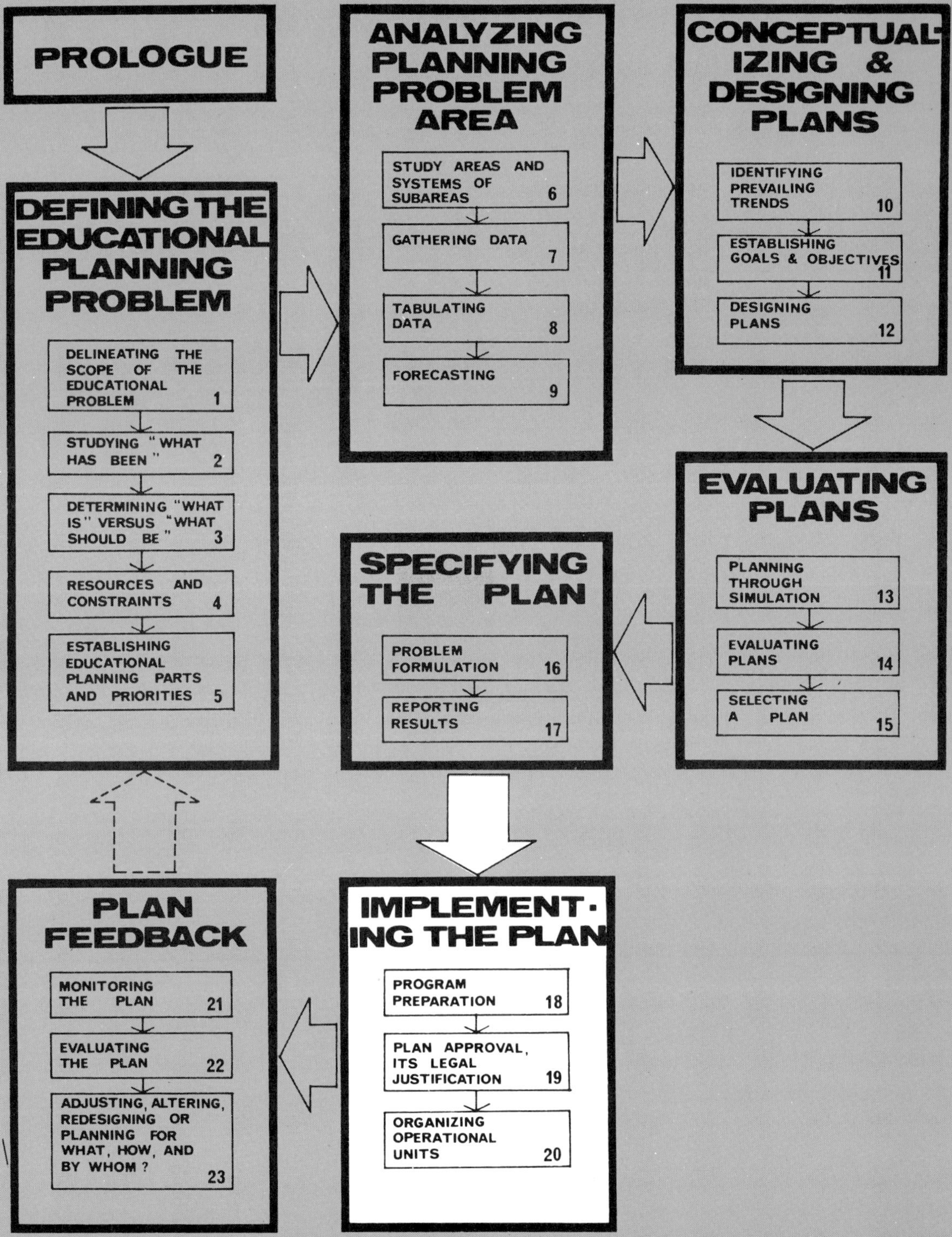
PROLOGUE
DEFINING THE EDUCATIONAL PLANNING PROBLEM
DELINEATING THE SCOPE OF THE EDUCATIONAL PROBLEM 1
STUDYING "WHAT HAS BEEN" 2
DETERMINING "WHAT IS" VERSUS "WHAT SHOULD BE" 3
RESOURCES AND CONSTRAINTS 4
ESTABLISHING EDUCATIONAL PLANNING PARTS AND PRIORITIES 5
ANALYZING PLANNING PROBLEM AREA
STUDY AREAS AND SYSTEMS OF SUBAREAS 6
GATHERING DATA 7
TABULATING DATA 8
FORECASTING 9
CONCEPTUALIZING & DESIGNING PLANS
IDENTIFYING PREVAILING TRENDS 10
ESTABLISHING GOALS & OBJECTIVES 11
DESIGNING PLANS 12
EVALUATING PLANS
PLANNING THROUGH SIMULATION 13
EVALUATING PLANS 14
SELECTING A PLAN 15
SPECIFYING THE PLAN
PROBLEM FORMULATION 16
REPORTING RESULTS 17
IMPLEMENTING THE PLAN
PROGRAM PREPARATION 18
PLAN APPROVAL, ITS LEGAL JUSTIFICATION 19
ORGANIZING OPERATIONAL UNITS 20
PLAN FEEDBACK
MONITORING THE PLAN 21
EVALUATING THE PLAN 22
ADJUSTING, ALTERING, REDESIGNING OR PLANNING FOR WHAT, HOW, AND BY WHOM? 23

Introduction

Once the educational plan package has been prepared, the next phase of a planning process is the implementation of the plan. In this model this phase consists of three distinct activities as represented in the following steps:

Step 18 Program preparation
Step 19 Plan approval: Its legal justification
Step 20 Organizing operational units

The various aspects of each activity will be discussed in Chapter 18 through Chapter 20.

18 Program preparation

Implementing the plan has grown to be the most difficult phase of the planning process. Three reasons may be cited. First, the problem of amassing resources for distribution has never been adequately solved. Second, public policies for implementing plans have never been systematically studied or formulated. Third, support from academic communities, political decision-makers, and educational practitioners has frequently been esoteric rather than a cooperative effort for effective programs of action.

Problems surrounding programs of action rest with our inability or simply our refusal to understand indigenous processes and therefore to generate a meaningful approach for implementing prepared plans. Even before plans are presented to officials for approval, continuous debate gets underway, frequently over educational purposes and methods. In the broadest sense educational politics involves the comprehension of approximately 26,000 school districts, each different and each enormously complex. Thus, a method for implementing plans applicable to all educational political bodies is unlikely.

SOME NORMS THAT REQUIRE ATTENTION

Educational planning must be made an integral part of the whole managerial process of decision-making and implementation, if it is to produce positive results. Educational planning has not been removed from the political arena, regardless of whether the educational planning agencies have a line or staff structure. They are formed in specific circumstances. In Puerto Rico planning activities are expanding from the Central Office down to teachers, school principals, and district superintendents, to forge a new kind of link between the political decision-maker and planners at various levels of the school system. In Iowa, the planner's purpose is to supply the information required to operate educational programs and therefore focuses on the problems faced by educational administrators. In Utah, planners are directly responsible to the state superintendent of public instruction. In other states, the planning agency is a line function on a parallel with other educational agencies. Implementing programs of action, therefore, depends on the mission assigned to educational planning. This is a significant consideration and a vital one.

Differences exist between educational policy planning and educational program planning. Educational policy planning is concerned with developing broad general outlines for action by elected officials. One such example is whether or not to implement comprehensive educational planning and if so for what purposes. Educational program planning is concerned with the preparation of specific plans and with the procedures to be employed by the administration agency within the framework of the existing educational system.

The agency in implementing a program of action must meet three tests:

1 The agency and its plan must have the support of the appropriate decision-makers.
2 The agency must allow the leading decision-makers to participate in drawing up the educational plan.
3 The agency in concert with the leading decision-makers must control the making of crucial decisions at the point of implementation.

In each of the above tests the need for involving various decision-makers in the planning process if educational plans are to be implemented is mandatory. Therefore, a procedure is required to identify the key decision-makers on educational matters. In this procedure there must be specific information related to the educational process; there must be agents who channel pressures to decision-makers; there must be alternative plans available; and the educational planner must fix the boundaries of his planning process in relation to the politics of education.

POINTS TO CONSIDER IN PREPARING A PROGRAM OF ACTION

1. Urban social mobility has obvious relevance to educational processes. The pressures of urban movement on governments in terms of the use of resources, and the attitudes of urban populations with respect to the manner in which resources are used obviously affect programs of action. Real needs are identified from the interaction of people in terms of space, size, density, culture, class structure, ideology, and the income available for expanding educational resources.

Defining the different categories of needs is critical, for it reveals who benefits and who does not benefit from programs of action. As a result many interpretations and reinterpretations of educational needs emerge, each claiming to be the solution to educational problems.

Urban mobility and the resulting needs, however, are not the essence of the problem. How, then, do differences arise in apparently similar communities? According to Edward Banfield the rapid growth of he city has little effect on politics. New schools, and all that goes with them, necessitate political action. Political difficulties occur, however, with disagreement about the providing of resources, making the management of programs for action more difficult.

2. Expressing urban needs has been the educator's dilemma. Articulation of educational needs in terms of goals and objectives has had little success in educational planning. Many urbanites feel alienated from education and have slipped into a state of lethargy when it comes to their own needs for providing for education. As a result, popular action at school board meetings seems to be becoming less and less meaningful.

3. Some claim that urban solutions to educational

problems are made by segregated centers of power, each operating with little knowledge of other educational politics, e.g., interests in primary education and higher education. Wallace Sayre, Robert Dahl, Norton Long, Edward Banfield, and others claim that many actors in many areas are pursuing objectives unknown to each other. Highly fragmented groups are frequently in conflict with each other. In such an environment the implementation of a program of action designed to meet educational needs possesses a high degree of uncertainty.

4. The ordering of priorities in education has not always been based on systematic analysis. If programs are activated it is frequently because pressures have been brought to bear on the educational decision-maker. There are political strategies sufficient to assure public acceptability. A determined minority in command of its own field may quickly push through its own programs of action. These sudden thrusts may appear to solve the problem, but for providing a long-term solution this approach is inappropriate.

5. The role of the educational institution in implementing programs of action has recently been critically analyzed. New questions are being asked about resource allocation, educational strategy, and tactics. Who gains by education and who does not gain? How are educational needs expressed by minorities to government? If these needs are expressed, are genuine attempts made by educational institutions to satisfy those needs? How effective are decision-makers in recruiting the best kinds of people? What do educational offices offer for advancement in educational politics? These questions naturally effect higher levels of educational administration through interbureaucratic negotiations on programs of action.

6. The expanding efforts of education into the suburbs for programs of action have complicated their implementation. The process of articulating, formulating, and expressing needs has become inextricably involved in urban politics. The suburb's size and homogeneity allow the educational political process to become subject to the rule of a few decision-makers, who act, in the main, from civic consciousness to better the education of their own area. Concern with only one area leaves areawide educational problems unsolved.

7. The consequences and the outputs from programs of action are generally the result of stimulation received from outside the educational body or by highly mobilized groups who have successfully separated their own activities from the business of education. What has happened is that the educational resources of local school systems have been subjected to greater demands and the pressures on the local decision-maker have been increased.

Limitations on programs of action are usually associated with educational politics. These limitations are summarized by a good number of political scientists relying on old models for implementing programs of action and will not guarantee implementation. The educational planner must resort to even wider studies in decision-making and political science.

SOME POSSIBLE PITFALLS

A program of action should not be exclusively concerned with one or two aspects of the comprehensive educational plan. The past mistakes in most educational systems have been to isolate one part of the educational program and exclude other educational segments. An example is that of a new school building, which, without reference to the community it serves, is built as a good, maintenance-free educational facility—without reference to the planning of a good educational program of studies. There is great need in urban educational buildings for more personalized and more appealing spaces that are more related to the process of individualized learning instead of the 30 × 30-foot egg-crate spaces now so widely prevalent. To avoid the one-shot approach requires increased motivation and involvement, which will extract from the educational planner and/or educational decision-maker a higher cost in time and effort. Joining the affairs of education together will demand joint use of scarce professional talents.

A program of action in education should be thought of as being economically productive. The resources required for schools, teachers, students, and materials are investments for talents and skills for the private sector. The harmony between public-sector programs and private sector activities has payoffs to both.

A program of action in education must not be so radical or so utopian that it fails to be implemented. Comprehensive educational planning is not meant to dislodge the established segments of education from their positions of service. Rather, the comprehensive educational plan is a network of links that provide the medium across which the various segments of education may communicate and begin to work together. To consider programs of action as new blueprints requiring a new form of educational government before implementation is erroneous. Even though components of the educational system appear to be independent and highly complex, the educational planners should accept them as they work within the educational system as it is constituted. Reforming does not mean that new structures must be invented to carry out new purposes but also that infinitely complicated coalitions of support must work together to better the system as a whole.

19 Plan approval: its legal justification

Comprehensive educational planning affects the property interests of many thousands of landowners and, therefore, comprehensive educational plans must be carried out within the framework of law. Failure to get legislative approval may negate comprehensive educational planning no matter how appropriate and well done the plan might be otherwise.

A comprehensive educational plan is an official public document adopted by a local school government. As a policy it guides the process of decision-making regarding the development of educational programs and the tools for carrying them out. The plan indicates the general way in which the elected decision-makers want the community to develop educationally for the next twenty to thirty years.

In this chapter consideration will be given to legislative matters, the regulatory powers for accomplishing educational planning proposals, and the comprehensive educational plan as "an impermanent constitution."

THE LEGISLATIVE BASES FOR PLANNING

A first step in establishing a comprehensive educational plan is a careful review of the adequacy of existing state enabling acts. The state has authority to pass any legislative act that seems wise. [Fletcher *v.* Peck,

6 Cranch (U.S.) 128, 3 L.Ed. 162.][1] In our form of government, the state legislature does not have to find constitutional authority for its acts, rather it may pass any law relative to education that is not expressly forbidden by the constitution. [Board of Education of City of Chicago *v.* Upham, 357 Illinois 263, 191 N.E. 876, 94 A.L.R. 813.][2] With constitutional prohibitions absent, the ends to be attained and the means to be employed are wholly subject to legislative determination, e.g., educational comprehensive planning for administering the schools.

The principal regulatory powers employed in planning proposals are taxing power, the power of eminent domain, and police power.

Taxing power

The state legislature has plenary power over taxation and may tax to any extent and in any manner as long as it is not arbitrarily done. [Shaffer *v.* Carter, 252 U.S. 37, 40 S. Ct. 221, 64 L.Ed. 445.][3] The school district, therefore, cannot levy taxes for school purposes unless it has the express power to do so. Even then the school tax obtained is not a local school tax but a state tax.

The principal constitutional requirement of due process of law is that the tax to be collected be uniformly applied. Uniformity, however, does not prevent the state from classifying objects for purposes of taxation and applying different rates to different classes; but the state is forbidden to apply an "arbitrary" classification and an unequal assessment, the degree of arbitrariness or unequality being determined by the courts. As a result, the courts have been forced to formulate a theory of education based on public policy. This policy, as a legal theory, is that the public school's primary function is not to confer benefits on the individual, but that the school is a state institution for maintaining a civil society.

Taxing by the state for school purposes, unless restrained by state or federal constitution, can be done in the ways best suited to serve the purposes of state government. The states, therefore, have created in the main quasi corporations and conferred on them the power to tax. [Smith *v.* Board of Trustees of Robersonville Graded School, 141 N.C. 143, 53 S.E. 524 8 Ann. Cas 529.][4] The taxes collected can produce major benefits but only if they are managed with that objective in mind. To do so effectively and efficiently requires planning.

The power of eminent domain

The right to take private property for public use requires legislative action that specifies the occasion and the agency. [Sazarus *v.* Morris, 212 Pa.St. 128, 61 At. 815.][5]

Constitutionally, land may be taken only for public use. Land for school sites is considered by the courts land for public use. This also includes playgrounds, athletic fields, and sites for gymnasiums. [Cousens *v.* School District No. 4, 67 ME. 280; State *v.* Superior Court, 69 Wash. 189. 124 Pac. 484; Sorenson *v.* Christiansen, 72 Washington 16. 129 Pac. 577.][6]

Advance acquisition is also permitted under the above restraints. [Board of Education *v.* Baczevsky, 340 Mich. 265, 268, 65 N.W. 2d 810, 811.][7] In the case cited, the school board proceeded long before a new high school site was needed, in order to save money. This is, by definition, planning.

The taking of property, however, necessitates just compensation to the owner. The taking of property without just compensation is unconstitutional, and the amount to be paid is determined by the fair market value.

The determination of a fair market value depends on all the uses for which the land would be profitably suited. The award is then based on the most profitable use. For example, an owner possessing unzoned land plans to sell it for a filling station site at an appraised

[1]Newton Edwards, *The Courts and the Public Schools* (Chicago: University of Chicago Press, 1955), p. 27.
[2]Ibid.
[3]Ibid., p. 254.
[4]Ibid.
[5]Edwards, p. 314.
[6]Ibid.
[7]Charles M. Haar, *Land-Use Planning* (Boston: Little, Brown, 1959), p. 468.

value of $10,000. Before he is able to do this, a local zoning ordinance restricts the land for sale to residential use only; its value then becomes $3,000. As the zoning is in accordance with the comprehensive plan of the community, the owner is not entitled to the $7,000 difference. This case, however, does not represent all similar cases, as some courts take into consideration the market value diminution as a factor in determining "reasonableness."

Police power

The third regulatory power employed for accomplishing planning proposals is police power, defined broadly by the Supreme Court of the United States as follows:

> It embraces every law which concerns the welfare of the whole people of the state or any individual within it, whether it relates to their rights or duties, whether it respects them as men or citizens of the state, whether it relates to the rights of persons or property of the whole people of the state or of any individual within it.[8]

Police power is the power of the state to limit individual rights to the interest of the social group when considering public health, safety, welfare, or morals. This consideration for public welfare was strongly sustained by the Supreme Court of the United States in a 1954 case as follows:

> The concept of the public welfare is broad and inclusive.... The values it represents are spiritual as well as physical, aesthetic as well as monetary. It is within the power of the legislature to determine that the community should be beautiful as well as healthy, spacious as well as clean, well-balanced as well as carefully patrolled. [Berman v. Parker, 348 U.S. 26.][9]

The preceding case clearly demonstrates the right of the Supreme Court of the United States to review the economic and social legislation of the states. The Court can determine whether the objects to be accomplished and the mode and agency to be used promote public welfare in a reasonable fashion. The state judges the necessity of all police regulations and the guarantee of due process "demands only that the law shall not be unreasonable, arbitrary or capricious, and that the means selected shall have a real and substantial relation to the object to be attained." [Nevvra *v.* New York, 291 U.S. 502, 54 S.Ct. 505.][10]

The state, therefore, is free to formulate and to execute its own educational policies. In Florida the statutes for comprehensive educational planning are cited at several places throughout Florida school laws. For example, in Chapter 229, "Functions of State Educational Agencies," Section .053 (2) (a) and (b),

> The board has the following duties:
> To adopt comprehensive educational objectives for public education;
> To adopt comprehensive long range plans and short range programs for the development of the state system of public education.[11]

On the school district level, the legislation of the State of Florida requires the school board to assemble data and make surveys to help in developing programs, with one phase of the program to be long range and the other an annual program. [Chapter 230, 23, (3).] Another statute is Chapter 318, the Florida Community School Act of 1970, whose purpose is to promote a more efficient use of school facilities through an extension of school personnel, buildings, and equipment to help involve all people of the community in programs designed to fulfill their educational needs. A comprehensive plan for the community school program shall be prepared by the local school board to include, among other activities, activities for preschool-age children, after-school-courses activities for children and adults, continued and remedial education programs for children and adults, and cultural enrichment and recreational activities for citizens in the community.

AN "IMPERMANENT CONSTITUTION"

After an examination of the various educational problems in the light of planning and its legal implications, plan approval procedures can be evaluated.

[8]Edwards, p. 12.
[9]Mary McLean (ed.), *Local Planning Administration* (Chicago: International City Managers' Association, 1959), p. 28.

[10]Edwards, p. 19.
[11]Florida Statutes (1969 ed.), p. 1060.

The question becomes: does comprehensive educational planning, if approved, achieve a more rational allocation of community resources for educational needs? Whatever its accomplishment has been to date, comprehensive educational planning has achieved its first victory, legislative approval. The period in which comprehensive educational planning has been practiced has been too short to reveal its potential impact. As new concepts of educational programs, such as the Valley View 45–15 Plan in Lockport, Illinois (Valley View School District No. 96), where students go forty-five days to school and then have a fifteen-day class vacation, evolve, special attention must be paid to the role of comprehensive planning in providing a guide for the control of educational programs.

The content of educational plans and the procedures for approval and implementation vary widely among the states. Despite these differences certain basic questions require answers. What are the purposes of comprehensive educational planning? What goals and objectives are expressed or implied? For whom are the plans intended—the students, the community's citizens, the teacher, the educational administrator, the school board? Is comprehensive educational planning relative to many of the legal powers for educational control and guidance now at hand? Many problems still remain. One is a fully appropriate legal mechanism for approving and carrying out a legal structure for comprehensive educational planning. This possibility does not require radically new techniques. Rather, the requirements are a better understanding of existing legal instruments and an imaginative exploration of their uses.

Comprehensive educational planning is an "impermanent constitution" whether on the state or the local level. The materials and forces can be arranged to produce major benefits. This arrangement will not occur accidentally.

Comprehensive educational planning, as an "impermanent constitution, is an aggregate of fundamental principles of education. The plan, therefore, should grow out of a functioning whole. Educators cannot plan for schools, students, teachers, and resources without considering how they relate to each other, and how they relate to activities, e.g., taxation, communication, insurance, and community facilities. Educational services cannot be provided effectively and efficiently without some coordinating instrument such as a comprehensive educational plan.

The precedents for approving comprehensive educational plans have been established. A need exists for a system of technical and administrative channels of information. A legal justification is required for purposes of approval, implementation, and review, all integrated within a cybernetic framework. Periodic examinations of interrelationships are required.

20 Organizing operational units

Because no single form of planning has emerged, no single form of implementation or organization exists that will assure agency effectiveness. The infinite number of unique planning problems preclude a definitive model of planning and hence of implementation and organization. Hence the planner is forewarned regarding possible pitfalls. However, some techniques for carrying out and organizing an operational plan are relatively well established. Attention should first focus on organizing operational units and then on carrying out plans.

ORGANIZING OPERATIONAL UNITS

Three forms of operational units exist. They are the strong chief executive (for example, a state superintendent of education or a board of public instruction's superintendent), an independent agency with a weak executive, or a combination of the two.

Where a strong chief executive exists it generally seems advisable to have the planning unit attached to his department. But where he is weak and the planning proposals are generally controversial, the organization is often not a key factor in assuring agency effectiveness. Past results have proved that when both types are incorporated into an organization many disagreements occur between the planning process and the political process.

Comprehensive educational planning is a part of

the political system. In fact, comprehensive educational planning is itself a growing political force. As a result, one objective of organizing operational units is to achieve a level of accommodation between the forces of planning and those of politics that will permit plan implementation and hence significant educational achievement.

Politics is the activity of negotiating, arguing, discussing, applying force, persuading, or one of many other activities. Performing these activities makes the preparation of strategy necessary. Very often strategies are developed by educational planners to minimize the number of future conflicts; they attempt to persuade educational officials and others that educational plans should not be influenced by narrow organizational interest but that plans should be influenced by information, criteria, and values that they as educational planners are specifically able to formulate.

In organizing operational units educational planners place themselves squarely in the cross-fire of conflict. Armed with methodological skills, they attempt to span the entire range of educational interests with rational and objective criteria. They involve themselves directly with working out compromises and other bases for settlement of education-related issues. The strategies they select for educational planning have a higher degree of technical validity than the general approach used by many educational politicians and administrators.

Acceptance of these strategies by the educational decision-maker depends, of course, on the content of the plans and on the methods by which they are produced, or on how the operational units for planning are organized. Another important aspect is how the educational plan is communicated. With so many values to consider, educational planners have a wide range of freedom in choosing their strategies. They may even legitimately fight for any values in education that they consider worthy of protection. Most educational planners do exercise this right to some extent but they do not exercise it anew on every plan. They must choose a general posture with relation to the political process and be committed to that position; the bureaucratic planners who serve as advisers to strong executives cannot change their character at will to fight publicly for independent policies. They may do so occasionally but only at the risk of jeopardizing their chosen role.

Planners and politicians are inseparable. This fact has helped convince educational planners that they are ethically justified in playing the political game. Controversies are therefore not all unfortunate. If educational planners put forth plans on which consensus can be achieved, they may serve to divert attention from conflicts. This diversion of attention, however, may serve to intensify a later disruption. Then again, the problem may very well work itself out. No one, unfortunately, can predict for every plan whether or not disruption will occur. This is a problem that educational planners must deal with anew in every case.

The possibility always exists that the plans may give such satisfaction that dissatisfactions will appear less important. Of course, the possibility always exists that when one set of problems is solved another set may result from the plan's implementation.

The uncertainty as to public reactions to educational plans is due in large part to the diverse nature of interest groups influencing the educational process. Consensus on an implemented educational comprehensive plan is usually difficult to obtain. Few educational planners have representatives who perform such a task for them.

Maintaining an educational planning organization is an absorbing task. A great deal of energy, talent, and money is required to maintain the structural merits of an educational plan, to convince others of its merits, to inform others of its accomplishments, and to maintain the plan's viability. When the numbers of an organization increase to perform an increasing number of tasks, a cost is paid in support of that organization by groups within the educational community. A generalization is made that other things being equal, organizations become easier to understand as their jurisdiction becomes smaller, not larger. In organizing for planning, therefore, the size of its various subunits and their disposition play an important part in the eventual success of comprehensive educational planning.

A second factor in the organizing of operations for educational planning is the usual condition that educational planners must work within the existing limits of local educational government powers. In fact, in the majority of cases this condition exists. If planning is new to an organization, planning may also be new to the community in which the educational organization is located. The more articulate the opposition, the more novel and controversial the comprehensive educational planning, the less likely that planning will proceed without controversy.

Some educational planners find it almost impossible to conceive of a comprehensive approach to educational planning because it may run afoul of some provisions of the existing educational laws. An unpopular action is generally challenged in the courts. American courts have in many cases interpreted provisions of educational law with utmost severity on the theory that state legislatures can rectify overstrict interpretations of their intent. As a consequence, some educational officials tend to be concerned more with the legality of the planning proposal than with the wisdom of its planning.

Many educational officials claim that they cannot peruse a comprehensive educational plan until the educational planners assure them that all of their proposals are legal under the educational law. In many cases educational planners do try to remain within the law but are seriously hampered in devising a comprehensive educational plan if in every case they take the narrowest view of the law. Also, if they must take an advisory opinion on every potential point of legal controversy, comprehensive educational planning becomes virtually impossible.

A final restraining factor is the educational planners' own lack of executive authority. Educational planners cannot carry out a plan on their own authority. They are required to persuade the educational decision-makers, who in turn must incur the risks of acting on the comprehensive plan that was presented to them for approval. If educational planners had the authority to execute their own plans they might win some battles by default. It takes more effort to oppose a plan than merely to neglect to act on it.

The typical educational operating agency possesses a point of view and a known constituency. Because educational planners claim to champion a wide variety of values, educational politicians tend to feel that they do better by moving slowly and suspiciously in their efforts to discover what values dominate any particular plan. They feel that they can take the overall view in balancing competing claims. The educational planners believe that they are the more disinterested group and possess a more comprehensive perspective than the educational politician. To overcome this threat the educational politician in many cases defines the planners' specialties as narrowly as possible. Educational planners are considered specialists in such things as school facility planning, curriculum planning, and in maintenance and operation planning. By withholding the authority to do anything without explicit approval, educational politicians keep educational planners within the boundaries of their specialties. If the educational planners do step beyond their boundaries they are exposed to a new host of conflicts that may undermine the potential effects they may have on the educational process.

Given the nature of the operating environment educational planners must develop better operational strategies. Educational planners may have to reach beyond the immediate confines of political support and attempt to win public support for their activities. Educational planners may have to plan on a neighborhood scale, one objective of which might be preserved for the neighborhood school and hence community pride, to gain public support. If successful, the educational politicians are likely to support planning for their own self-interest and survival.

Another strategy involves doing those tasks that no other agency has the time or ability to do. Educational planners can undertake special studies on some problems referred to them by educators. Educational planners also furnish information when asked by school board members, administrators, or other educational groups. There is a danger in this strategy because of its incremental approach, which is disjointed and not conducive to comprehensive planning.

Another possibility is to concentrate on factual analyses. Fact gathering is useful and an acceptable professional procedure. Many types of research are of use to educators. Anyone having frequent dealings with the educational government finds it convenient that educational officials can locate many facts about educational activities. These facts, however, may be only descriptive in nature and may not be used for overcoming the problem.

Another approach for educational planners is to comment on the plans of others. Plans may be developed by various educational agencies' existing staff and then checked for their fitness within the overall comprehensive educational plan. This approach, however, may be perilous. If the agency heads are challenged they in turn may close their minds to future suggestions by the educational planners. Or agency heads may give only lip service to the value of planning. Too often educational personnel accept in principle the interdependence of community and education but in actual practice ignore community inputs when making their decisions.

In considering only facts, educational planners retain their confidence in their own expertness within a defined area of operation and preserve a certain amount of freedom from criticism. Educational planners themselves are not immune to the temptation of retreating behind technology. Unfortunately, educational technology in many school districts is not very highly developed, and when it is, educational planners may not agree on its proper objectives.

Educational planners can do detailed staff work for various educational agencies at their request. Educational planners can establish a position as the school board's or the state agency's factual resource. They can issue general plans that include no specific calls to action. Educational planners can make persuasive points when speaking off the record with other educational officials. Nevertheless, educational planners who seek political approval for a comprehensive educational plan will find it difficult to be completely candid.

Is administrative reorganization necessary for organizing operation units? Many students of American politics advocate this approach. No universal answer can be given, for each school administrative unit possesses its own unique characteristics. The criteria to use depend on the purposes of educational planning. In the case of comprehensive educational planning a central location within an educational governmental structure gives effective planning room. (See Figure 20.1.)

The central position of the planning unit allows educational planners to deal with all facets of the educational program and at the same time allows all existing educational agencies to participate and be actively involved in preparing the comprehensive educational plan.

The planning unit can accept assignments from the chief school officer of the school board. The planning unit can also initiate planning projects. These projects can be recommended to the school officer.

This arrangement separates the operations of planning and administering. This arrangement, however, permits the establishment of a rapport with administrative personnel but does not impinge on an administrator's duties and responsibilities. The diagram illustrates a relationship rather than an organizational chart between the planning unit and other educational administrative agencies. It eases communication between the many necessary educational agencies; it shares personnel between the planning unit and the various educational agencies; and it makes educational planners directly responsible for their planning. More importantly it permits planning to be developed along consistent and comprehensive lines that bridge the gap between the disjointed and ad hoc approaches now prevalent in educational activities. Personnel from throughout the educational establishment can be assigned at various times to the preparation of a comprehensive educational plan.

This arrangement provides (1) a base for planning with full-time educational planners plus many educational specialists from most educational agencies; (2) for intraagency and interagency involvement in comprehensive educational planning; (3) for and assists school boards in formulating educational policies; (4) for a comprehensive approach in that no aspect of educational development is beyond planning's responsibility; (5) a multidiscipline approach to educational planning; (6) a broad perspective and gives substance to short-term decisions;

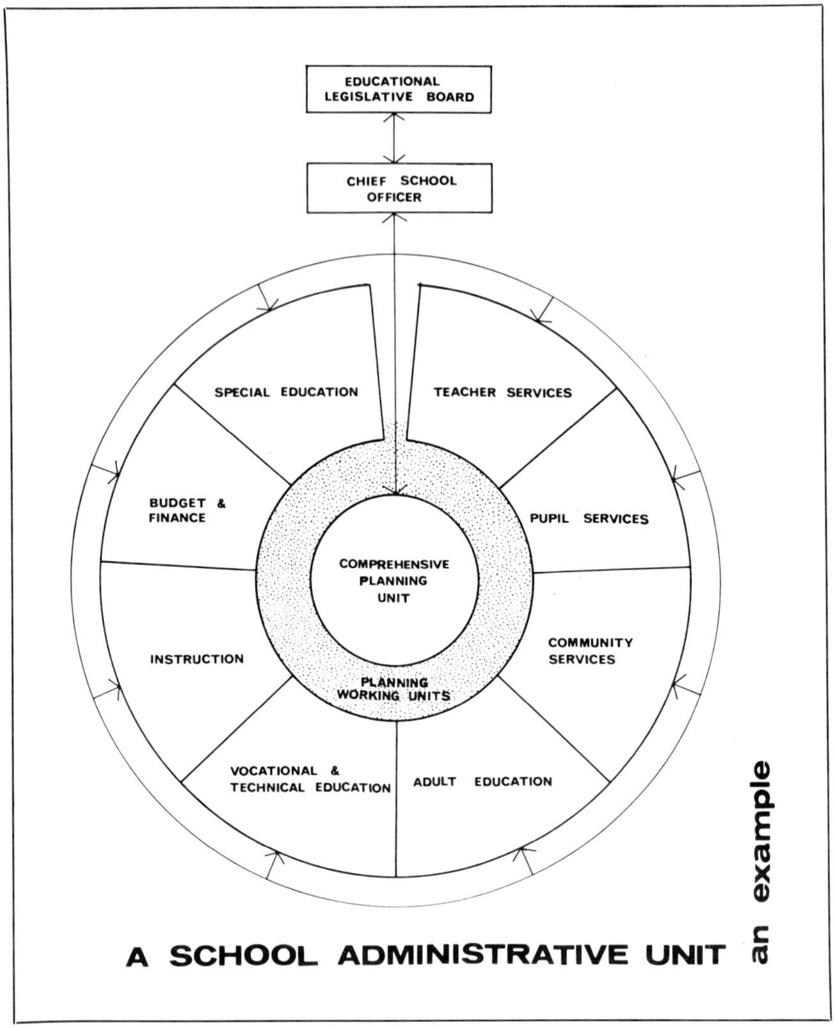

FIGURE 20.1

(7) for and assists with the development of an information system; (8) for the development of short-range, intermediate, and long-range planning; (9) for short-term plans to be measured against the criteria of the comprehensive plan; (10) for leadership in establishing and up-dating goals for education; (11) for and assists the establishment of priorities of needs; (12) for and assists with the implementation of plans, helps to develop strategy, and provides consultants to any educational agency desiring help; (13) for and assists with the assessment of the status of education in relation to the goals established in the comprehensive educational plan; (14) for and allows enrollments, personnel, facilities, and resource needs to be projected; and (15) for the educational planning process to be recycled. It allows for goal changing, for acceptance of new values, for new opportunities, and for unforeseen side effects to enter the educational process.

This approach, however, is not without its difficulties. Required among the new educational participants—the planners—and educators is cooperation, coordination, and controls. Each will be discussed in the light of carrying out the comprehensive educational plan.

COOPERATING ON CARRYING OUT THE EDUCATIONAL PLAN

Cooperating is the act of operating jointly with one another. *Participating* is a key word in educational planning. It helps to sharpen individual responsibility in developing a sense of planned purpose and in making a coherent educational plan.

A plan contains many parts, roles, and actors, and cooperation is necessary for achieving educational goals and objectives. Actions that require cooperation stress the need for a clear-cut meeting of minds before the project begins.

Variations in cooperative situations may be interpreted in terms of our five-dimensional model: those that relate to aspects of (1) people, (2) places, (3) movements, (4) economics, and (5) activities.

Cooperation between people

In education the social elements are probably the most important in terms of cooperative effort. The various social components—student, teacher, principal, administrator, and their activities are included in the system. Both friendly and hostile participants make contact with other systems. The other systems must be included within the comprehensive educational planning process.

In the past, social components have been in the main excluded from considerations related to implementation or have been disregarded as constants that could be neglected for most purposes. The fact that many programs are required by law or are mandated under contractual obligations has minimized private initiatives for cooperation.

Cooperation related to places

The physical environment is an inseparable part of comprehensive educational plans. Every place requires adjustments and adaptations to other aspects of the comprehensive educational plan. By place is meant its location, topography, climate, structures, tools, equipment, and so on. Their effect and their manner of use in large measure dictate the manner of carrying out the comprehensive educational plan.

Cooperation related to movement

From all systems cooperation is mandatory if movement, however slow, is to occur. This cooperation is basic to the reduction of the "friction of space" between activity sites, for it allows movement to take place.

The specialization of educational activities makes it necessary for people to cooperate with each other. The patterns of educational activities represent a large dependent system in which choice of location is made in terms of spatial cooperation with each activity and their interactions. For some this means access to the largest number of persons; for others convenience of movement is adequate; and for still others it means mere proximity.

Cooperation related to economics

Economics receives more attention than any other of the four factors discussed here. No plan can be carried out without revenues and expenditures. Too often the activity to be carried out must be curtailed in order to be economically feasible. This is cooperation in one direction.

Economics holds the key to how and what educational projects are to be carried out. Viewed in this light, economics probably shapes the educational environment more than any of the other four factors. It provides the means for incentives, which are fundamental to conscious efforts to organize. Inadequate incentives may mean failure of cooperation.

Money is an inducement for individuals to accept employment, a compensation for service, and a reward for contribution. Under our money system inducements to cooperation are among the most powerful and the most neglected. In an organization like education the motives are rooted in individual and community satisfactions.

Cooperation related to activities

Cooperation among the activities of various educational agencies is essential if educational objectives are to be achieved. Cooperation justifies itself by overcoming the limitations inherent when only one or a few activities are executed. A limitation is a function of the total number of activities required. If, for example, the school bus failed to bring the students to school, their learning activities would be affected, or if a teacher was ill prepared to teach a certain subject, the students' learning activities would suffer. "Overcoming a limitation is a means to an end; when the limitation cannot be overcome the end must be dropped."[1]

The effectiveness of cooperation is measured in terms of achieving the objectives of cooperative action. Accomplishment is an aim of cooperation as a whole. The degree of success is determined by the amount of action and the number of resources required for the system of cooperation to satisfy the objectives. Its effectiveness rests with the actions of each individual. If the school bus driver, and the teacher, and the principal, and the administrator fail in cooperating with each other in the execution of their activities the effectiveness desired from learning activities may prove to be inadequate.

Cooperation is essential to success. Two considerations must be noted:

1 The interactions among educational agencies must be discovered.
2 The interactions of different educational agencies help to assure the continuing success of the project.

Defects in cooperation arise when one or more activities fail to relate to the overall purpose and when one or more individuals participating in the various activities fail to receive satisfaction from their activities and decide not to cooperate. Cooperation depends on common ends or purposes.

[1]Chester I. Barnard, *The Functions of the Executive* (Cambridge Mass.: Harvard University Press, 1968), p. 24.

COORDINATING THE IMPLEMENTATION OF THE EDUCATIONAL PLAN

Coordination is the process of scheduling activities to eliminate conflicts, so that the objectives may be achieved. The more complex the activities become, the more difficult it becomes to distinguish the more rational points of coordination from the less rational ones.

Coordinating the diverse activities and purposes of the various educational agencies is the essence of comprehensive educational planning. Coordinating activities is also the creative side of organizing. The appropriate combining of educational activities to produce effective educational outputs is the purpose of any educational system.

Coordination is indispensable to the comprehensive educational plan. Some organizational authorities have claimed that at least nine tenths of all organizational activity is based on the responsibility and the authority of those persons who apply personal energies to the final objectives. A common formulation of purposes is required if each person is to contribute effectively his personal specialization, experience, and training.

The objective of coordination is to translate the purpose of comprehensive educational planning into practical programs. By doing so, coordination brings into focus the relevant activities and objectives of each educational agency that shares in improving education. The concerns are for what will work, what the educational community can be induced to do, what specific opportunities exist at any point in time, and what is politically desirable and acceptable.

Therefore, coordination requires a consistent set of policies to serve as guidelines for implementing the comprehensive educational plan. It requires taking advantage of services offered by educational interest groups in the community and finding out how their interests can be tied in with educational purposes. It requires the educators' understanding of and their support for comprehensive educational planning for the future viability of education and hence for the future economic, social, and physical health of the community. It requires a willingness among educators to develop the ability to use new strategies of coordination whenever they appear promising.

CONTROLLING THE EDUCATIONAL PLAN

One of the most exciting developments for the implementing of educational plans can be found in cybernetics, the study of the processes of information transfer, communication, and control. Control relates directly to the work of the plan as a whole.

The problem is one of integrating the whole, of finding the right balance between the requirements for single activities and for the total school-system mission. Control, therefore, is always important and is sometimes critically important to total effectiveness.

Imbalance requires a systems approach such as that provided by a comprehensive educational plan. Answers to the following questions are essential to effective comprehensive planning. Is the type of educational activity proposed consistent with the intentions of the comprehensive educational plan? Are the sizes of activities proposed consistent with the intentions of the comprehensive educational plan (e.g., number of students, volume of courses, volume of equipment, and so on)? Are other characteristics of the proposal consistent with the objectives of the comprehensive educational plan (e.g., adaptable and changeable classrooms, teacher training, and so on)? Is the amount of space required consistent with the comprehensive educational plan (e.g., sufficient classrooms for the number of students present, and so on)? Are the locations of schools consistent with the comprehensive educational plan (e.g., a few centralized learning centers or a decentralized system of neighborhood schools)? Is the use of the classrooms consistent with the comprehensive educational plan (e.g., number of students per instructional unit, number of students per square foot per activity, and so on)? Is the amount of equipment consistent with the comprehensive educational plan (e.g., number of computer terminals for reading assignment, number of school buses for transporting the school population, and so on)? Is the communication equipment consistent with the comprehensive educational plan (e.g., school bus safety, school bus capacity, a workable fire alarm system throughout the school, and so on)? Is the communication among people consistent with the comprehensive educational plan (e.g., between administrators and principals, between principals and teachers, and so on)? Is the educational environment consistent with the comprehensive educational plan (e.g., the school building architectural design, landscape treatment, noise levels, and so on)? Is the scheduling of educational activities consistent with the comprehensive educational plan? Are the locations of activities consistent with the comprehensive educational plan? Are the connections, access points, and juxtapositions of educational activities consistent with the comprehensive educational plan?

Implied in these questions is the concept of systems. Cybernetics, the science of communication and control, has enabled educational planners to postulate the structure of control in the connections among the many parts of an educational system. Control enables the educational planner to determine what is achievable and then to provide comprehensive plans and concomitant strategies that can be used in a variety of cases. These systems can be regarded as servosystems, by which society through its educators seeks to furnish feedback to the education process.

Comprehensive educational plans must be kept under constant observation. Monitoring should include the regular collection of statistics, improved forecasting methods, the review and revision of educational objectives when necessary, and the analysis of educational outputs. Reviews of educational plans are the periodic examinations of the relationships between intentions and actions, a continual step in the whole process of implementation.

Part Seven

Monitoring the plan in action

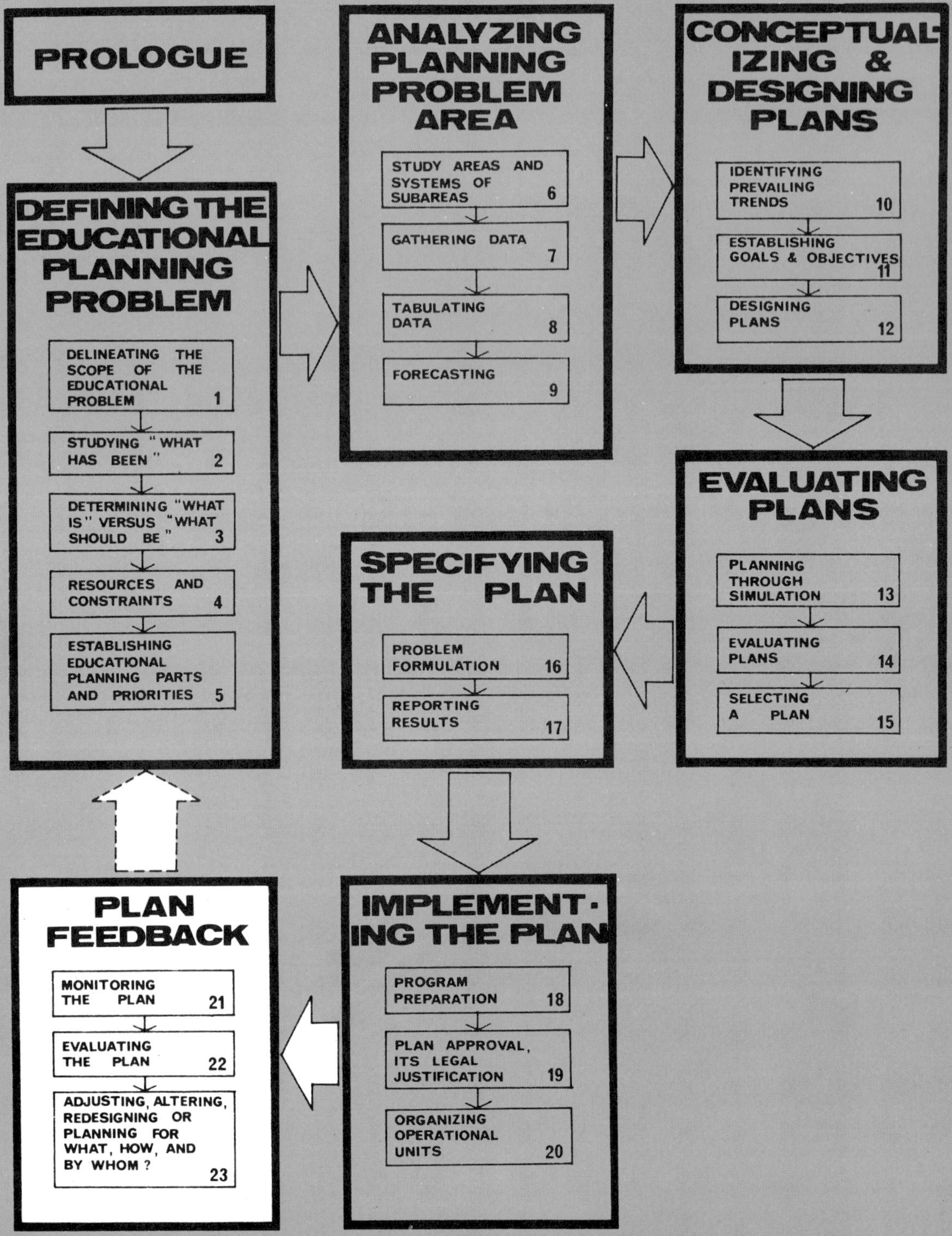
PROLOGUE
DEFINING THE EDUCATIONAL PLANNING PROBLEM
DELINEATING THE SCOPE OF THE EDUCATIONAL PROBLEM 1
STUDYING "WHAT HAS BEEN" 2
DETERMINING "WHAT IS" VERSUS "WHAT SHOULD BE" 3
RESOURCES AND CONSTRAINTS 4
ESTABLISHING EDUCATIONAL PLANNING PARTS AND PRIORITIES 5
ANALYZING PLANNING PROBLEM AREA
STUDY AREAS AND SYSTEMS OF SUBAREAS 6
GATHERING DATA 7
TABULATING DATA 8
FORECASTING 9
CONCEPTUALIZING & DESIGNING PLANS
IDENTIFYING PREVAILING TRENDS 10
ESTABLISHING GOALS & OBJECTIVES 11
DESIGNING PLANS 12
EVALUATING PLANS
PLANNING THROUGH SIMULATION 13
EVALUATING PLANS 14
SELECTING A PLAN 15
SPECIFYING THE PLAN
PROBLEM FORMULATION 16
REPORTING RESULTS 17
IMPLEMENTING THE PLAN
PROGRAM PREPARATION 18
PLAN APPROVAL, ITS LEGAL JUSTIFICATION 19
ORGANIZING OPERATIONAL UNITS 20
PLAN FEEDBACK
MONITORING THE PLAN 21
EVALUATING THE PLAN 22
ADJUSTING, ALTERING, REDESIGNING OR PLANNING FOR WHAT, HOW, AND BY WHOM? 23

Introduction

This last phase is actually the beginning phase for the next cycle of planning and at the same time the end phase of the present cycle. In this model three steps are defined as part of the feedback system. They are as follows:

Step 21 Monitoring the plan in action
Step 22 Evaluating the plan
Step 23 Adjusting, altering, and redesigning the plan

Each step and some of its attributes are discussed respectively in Chapter 21 through Chapter 23.

21 Monitoring the plan in action

Monitoring the plan in action affords a good controlling device in the whole process of implementation. In one case, the outputs are just what the plan predicted. In another, the outputs are significantly off course from what was intended. In the second case, the educational planner has two options. One is to use all the aids at his command to indicate what actions are needed to put the system back on course. The other is to consider the desirability of keeping to the deviant course and thinking afresh about the major objectives of the comprehensive educational plan in the light of unforeseen developments.

Project scheduling is ideally suited to these two options. It can be used to identify every activity to be carried out in the comprehensive approach. It identifies the various stages that are required to schedule the activities to be undertaken by various educational agencies. It also identifies the resources that are available and those that are required within a given period of time for various educational activities. It gives a realistic picture of the amount of time and money necessary for each activity and of the human resources available. It identifies clearly the sequence of activities, i.e., which activities must be ended before another activity can be started. The network of activities and events establishes the critical time-periods for their completion so that the timing of the plan as a whole works.

PROJECT SCHEDULING BACKGROUND FOR MONITORING ACTIVITIES

The technology of project scheduling dates from World War I and originated primarily in the American Ordnance Department of the U.S. Army. During World War I Brigadier General William Crozier, Chief of Ordnance, was responsible for the logistics for the American expeditionary forces serving in Europe. Strange as it may seem, there was no centralized body of control for the management of war production, even in American industry. Because of this lack of regulation, few schedules were met and even fewer records were kept. The uncertainty of deliveries of matériel stimulated the Ordance Department to devise a method for better management control. Within this framework, Gantt Charts were developed to serve primarily as production-control devices. Individual machine-operators were observed, and the production recorded for each day's work. Widespread use of such records soon followed the early work of Gantt.

Scheduling techniques as we know them today evolved much later. The development of computer technology in the fifties initiated the application of more rigorous approaches to the problems of planning and scheduling, and in 1956 the duPont Company began working on computer applications in this area. A result of the early duPont work was the Critical Path Method (CPM), which was developed in 1957 by two engineers, Morgan Walker of duPont and James Kelly, Jr., of Remington Rand. In 1959 Walker and Kelly presented one of the first papers illustrating computerized planning and scheduling, "Critical Path Planning and Scheduling," to the Eastern Joint Computer Conference.

The U.S. Navy Special Projects Office was given the responsibility for developing the nuclear submarine *Polaris* in 1957. The solution to the problem of managing this large, sophisticated weapons system was derived through the cooperation of the U.S. Navy Special Projects Bureau of Ordnance and the consulting firm of Booz, Allen & Hamilton. The technique developed on the *Polaris* project became known as PERT and was published in July 1958, in a technical document entitled *Program Evaluation Research Task Summary Report: Phase I and Phase II.* Although many acronyms have been used in connection with this technology, only two (PERT and CPM) have become widely employed.

PERT AND CPM

The acronyms PERT and CPM are frequently used interchangeably to denote a scheduling procedure. Although both techniques are used in critical path analysis, there are essential differences between them. Table 21.1 summarizes some of the paramount differences, showing that PERT is probabilistic in nature, whereas CPM is deterministic. PERT is used when the prospective management project requires subtasks of considerable uncertainty. This usually occurs when the project involves new types of activities; the *Polaris* missile submarine entailed the completion of many diverse tasks with which no one had had prior experience. Time estimates had to be given under terms of considerable obscurity and major variability. CPM, which is essentially deterministic, is associated with projects where the various subtasks are reasonably well known and where the time estimates for the completion of those tasks can be reasonably ascertained. The construction of a schoolhouse would be a case in point, because many schools have been built. An experienced contractor can predict

Table 21.1 PERT/CPM comparison

PERT	CPM
Probabilistic	Deterministic
Event-oriented	Activity-oriented
Nonexperience-based	Experience-based
Multiple-time estimates	Single-time estimates

quite accurately how long it will take to complete the subtasks of the building.

PERT is event-oriented, whereas CPM is activity-oriented. We will treat this concept in more detail later in our discussion of networking. Suffice it here to say that the distinction is relatively simple. An event is an instant period in time denoting either the beginning (onset) or the completion (terminus) of some activity. Assume two points in time, one indicating the onset of an activity and the other the terminus of that activity. The time elapsing between these two events is known as the activity. In network design the PERT method concentrates on the events, whereas CPM focuses on the activities. PERT is primarily nonexperience-based; it is used on projects that involve new activities. Because the activities are primarily untried, a different approach to time estimation is used. CPM is experience-based. Since the subtasks are familiar, the experienced person can project these times quite accurately.

As a result of the nonexperience base, the PERT technique uses multiple-time estimates, whereas the experience-based CPM uses single-time estimates. The greater uncertainty associated with experimental activities requires that PERT users project three time estimates: an optimistic time, a pessimistic time, and a most likely time. These three time estimates are used in a formula for deriving the expected time required for the completion of a given event. Because of the greater certainty associated with CPM, only one time estimate is made. However, one major advantage of PERT's use of three time estimates is that the calculations can be used in computing probabilities. Since CPM uses only one time estimate, and since no variance occurs with that time estimate, probabilities cannot be calculated.

SCHEDULING DIAGRAMS USED FOR MONITORING ACTIVITIES

The four diagrams discussed here are listed in the order of their evolution, starting with Gantt Charts, and continuing with PERT diagrams, arrow diagrams, and precedence diagrams.

Gantt Charts

Figure 21.1 illustrates a common Gantt Chart. The activities are listed in the left column, and each

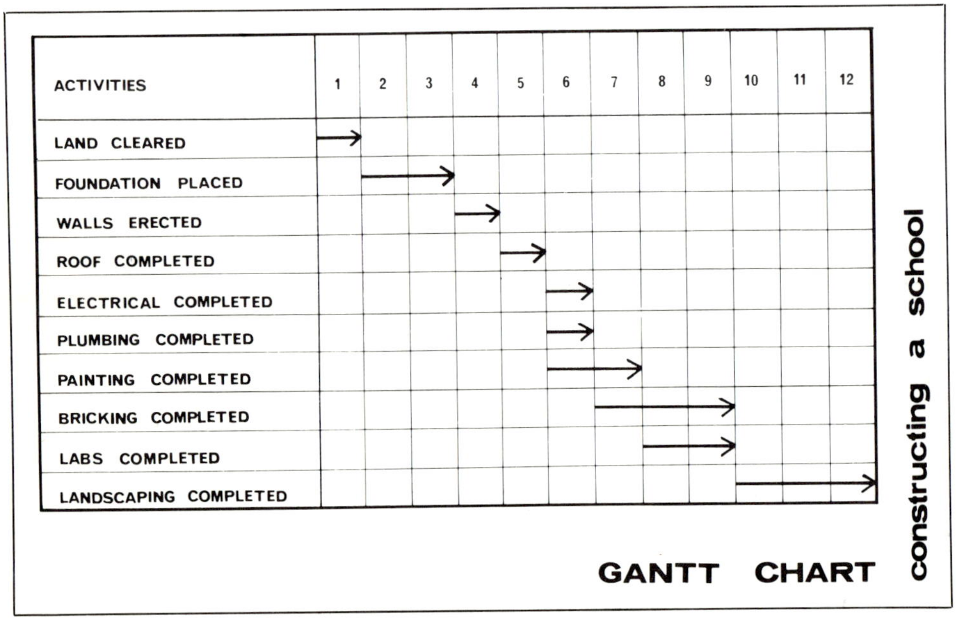

FIGURE 21.1

FIGURE 21.2

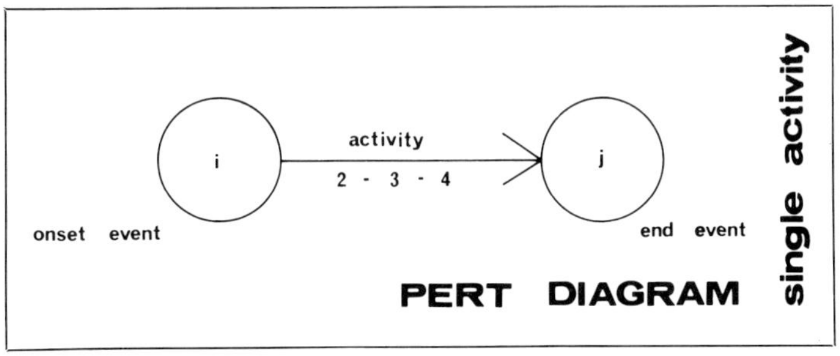

week occupies an additional column. Each activity's completion time is marked off in its respective column. Figure 21.1 shows that one week elapses while the land is being leveled. When the land is leveled, the foundation may be laid, an operation that requires two more weeks. The erection of walls begins after the third week and takes one week. The same is true for the roof. After the fifth day of erecting the walls, electrical work, plumbing, and painting can begin.

One of the problems associated with Gantt Charts involves the interdependency of the various activities. Although the painting is not to be completed until the seventh week, it is not clear from the chart if electrical work and plumbing must be completed by the end of the sixth week or if they may be extended to the middle of the seventh week. Also, the bricking, which starts at the end of the sixth week, runs through the ninth week. Obviously, the labs are started before the bricking is completed. Even though it is not clearly indicated in the diagram, the labs could be started at the end of the sixth week. On the other hand, it may be that the painting must be completed before the labs are completed.

These problems of interdependency require that a more sophisticated procedure be evolved beyond Gantt Charts. The Gantt Charts do give a picture that clearly depicts the scheduling process, but their major shortcoming is their inability to determine the interdependence of the various tasks involved. Later scheduling techniques have overcome this deficiency.

PERT diagrams

PERT diagrams consist of network variations that involve single activities, sequential activities, and parallel activities. Figure 21.2 illustrates the structure of a single activity, which is characterized by an onset event and a end event. These events are symbolized by the nodes labeled *i* and *j*. The arrow connecting the two nodes denotes the specific activity to be completed. The activity begins at the *i* node and ends at the *j* node. As mentioned earlier, an event takes *zero* time; it is simply an instant in time denoting the beginning or the completion of an activity. In compiling PERT networks, events can be identified as either starting times or completion times—either is appropriate so long as the application is consistent throughout the network.

Figure 21.3 illustrates the use of the PERT diagram for sequencing activities. Three events are listed here: Event 2 furnishes the completion time for Activity 1, and Event 3 for Activity 2. Since the

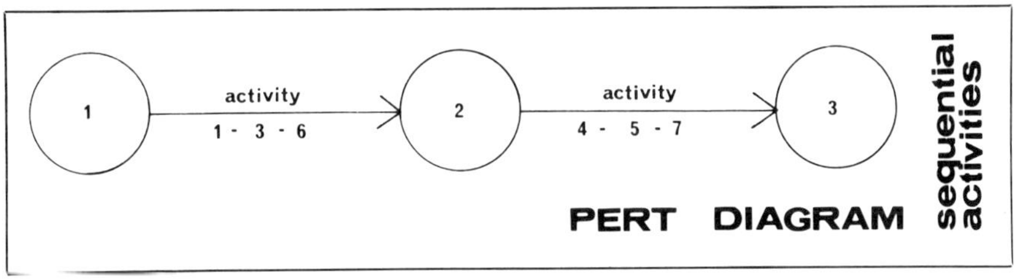

FIGURE 21.3

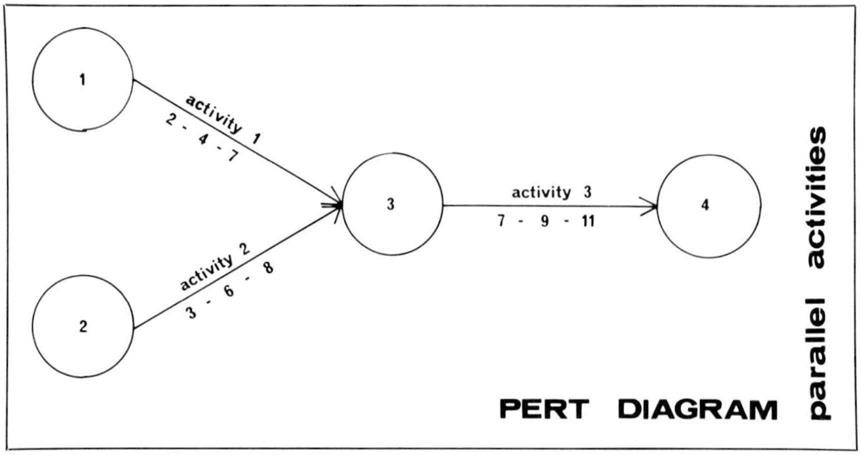

FIGURE 21.4

arrows merely denote logical connections between events, there is no relationship between the length of the arrow and the time it takes for the completion of an activity. The time that the event takes is listed beneath the arrow under the activity description.

Figure 21.4 is an illustration of paralleling activities. Obviously, this is a combination of the single activity and sequential activities. Activity 1 and Activity 2 both feed into Event 3. Activity 1 can require greater, equal, or less time than Activity 2. Event 4 denotes a point in time when Activity 3 is completed. Paralleling is used frequently to shorten the overall time period for the completion of the overall tasks. In Figure 21.4 Activity 1 and Activity 2, if placed sequentially, would equal the time elapsing for the completion of the two activities, or the sum of the two activities. However, by paralleling, the total time elapsing for Activity 1 and Activity 2 is equal to the greater time for either of the two activities. It follows, therefore, that the total completion time from the onset of Event 1 through Event 4 is the sum of the two parallel times, that is, the greater time for Activity 1 or Activity 2, plus Activity 3. If, again, these activities were sequenced, then the total time for Event 1 through Event 4 would include the sum of Activity 1, Activity 2, and Activity 3.

The three diagrams form the basic building blocks on which the PERT network is constructed. As a practical matter, as many activities as possible should be paralleled in order to shorten the overall time lapse between the onset event and the end event. However, one must be cognizant of both cost and time. Frequently, it is possible to parallel activities if additional resources are put into those activities. Decisions to follow such a regimen must be made, and obviously some are more easily determined than others. For example, if penalties are involved for work not completed on time, a comparison of the total cost of the penalties and the total cost of adding resources to certain activities to ensure completion would be made. If the total cost is less than the total penalty, then, of course, the resources should be added to speed up other activities. If, however, the total cost exceeds the penalties, the penalties would be elected rather than the additional resources.

Arrow diagrams

As in the PERT diagrams, arrow diagrams are considered in terms of single activities, sequential activities, and parallel activities. It was noted in discussing PERT that the network was constructed around events. With arrow diagrams, on the other hand, the network is constructed around activities, and the nodes in arrow diagrams are merely logical connectors.

Figure 21.5 illustrates a single activity in an arrow diagram. The nodes are labeled *1* and *2*. Nodes in

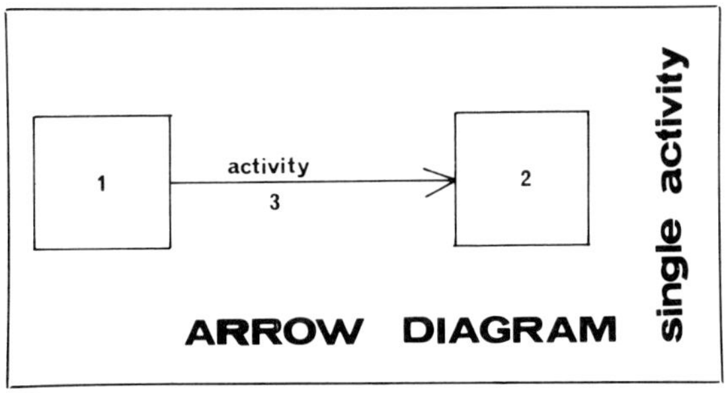

FIGURE 21.5

PERT, arrow or precedence diagrams are nominally numbered, and they need not necessarily be in sequential order. Should the nodes be labeled with letters, the labels could be randomly assigned, as the numerical labels are. In Figure 21.5 an activity begins at node 1 and is completed at node 2; 3 time units are required to complete this activity.

Figure 21.6 shows sequential activities using arrow diagrams. Nodes 1 and 2 designate the beginning and the ending of plastering walls; the time period elapsing is equal to 3 time units. Starting at node 2 and ending at node 3, the activity Paint Walls involves 2 time units. Included in Figure 21.6 is an illustration of how the list of activities is constructed. Under nodes *i* and *j*, node 2 is a *j* node when joined with the activity Plaster Walls, but it becomes an *i* node when joined with the activity Paint Walls. Again it should be remembered that these nodes are merely logical connectors denoting the ending of one activity and the beginning of another. This necessitates the same node's being an *i* node for one activity and a *j* node for another.

Parallel activities with the use of an arrow diagram are shown in Figure 21.7. There are, of course, similarities between the PERT diagram and the arrow diagram. Figure 21.7 shows how Activity A and Activity B are paralleled in order to conserve time; the total time flowing in Figure 21.7 is 13 time units rather than the 17 units required if the three activities are sequenced. In Figures 21.6 and 21.7 only one time estimate is given for each activity, thus suggesting an association with the Critical Path Method instead of the PERT method, which uses three time estimates.

The use of single events, sequential events, and parallel events in either PERT or arrow diagrams will vary according to the expertise of the person constructing the scheduled network. It would be highly unusual if two persons constructing the same network should produce precisely the same result. In other words, there is no one absolute way to construct a network. The design depends on the experience and the ingenuity of the person who constructs it. However, there are varying levels of efficiency in network design. Some built-in factors compel the network constructor to be efficient. An obvious example is the case where a building must be completed within twelve months. If the network constructor schedules the building to be completed within a time interval greater than twelve months, he will have to reevaluate his network in order to reduce the time schedule and thereby create a more efficient network.

FIGURE 21.6

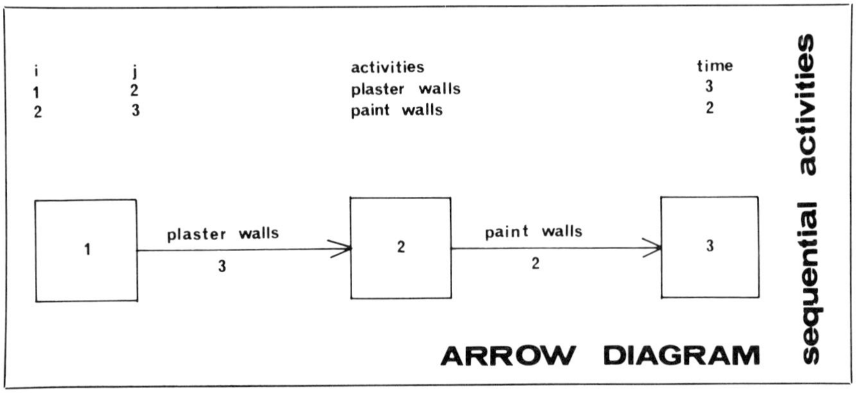

FIGURE 21.7

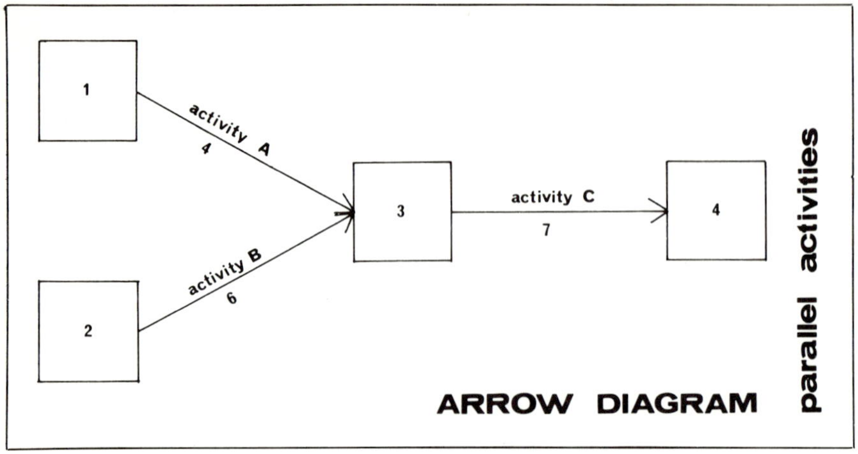

Precedence diagrams

Precedence diagrams use as building blocks the same three basic elements that are used in PERT and arrow diagrams: the single activity, the sequential activity, and the parallel activity. The construction base of precedence diagrams offers considerably more flexibility than either PERT or arrow diagrams. The lines connecting the boxes in a precedence diagram do not symbolize either activities or times; they are used only to demonstrate the logical connections between the boxes.

Figure 21.8 illustrates a single activity diagrammed with a precedence outline. The connector between A and B here does not consist of an arrow like that used in both the PERT and the arrow diagrams. It presents neither any descriptive records nor any time references; it is used solely to indicate the connection between A and B, as predecessor and successor events and activities. Box A in Figure 21.8 shows that Activity A requires 3 time units; Activity B requires 4 time units, as indicated in Box B. Additional information given in Figure 21.8 shows that A is the predecessor event and B is the successor event. This same illustration shows that Activity A must be completed before Activity B can begin. The time elapsing for the completion of Activities A and B is seven weeks.

As an example of sequential activities using precedence diagrams, Figure 21.9 diagrams A as the predecessor to B, and B as the predecessor to C. B is the successor to A, and C is the successor to B. Only the immediately preceding activity is considered a predecessor activity. Also, only the immediately succeeding activity is considered a successor activity. Figure 21.9 shows the completion of three activities: A requiring 2 time units, B requiring 4 time units, and C requiring 5 time units. The total number of time units required for the completion of all three activities is 11. Frequently, because of certain time constraints, it is necessary to reevaluate the sequencing of activities in order to conserve time.

Figure 21.10, which gives a description of paralleling activities using precedence diagrams, illustrates one way of conserving time. Using the same activities employed in Figure 21.9 (Activities A, B, and C), Figure 21.10 shows how B and C might be paralleled in order to conserve time. It was indicated in Figure 21.9 that the total time required to complete C was

FIGURE 21.8

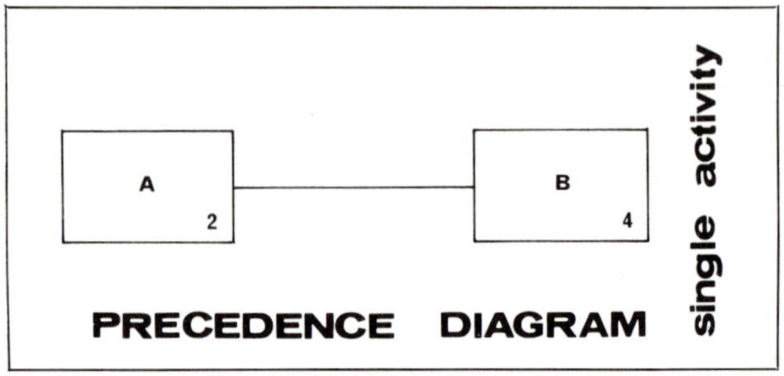

FIGURE 21.9

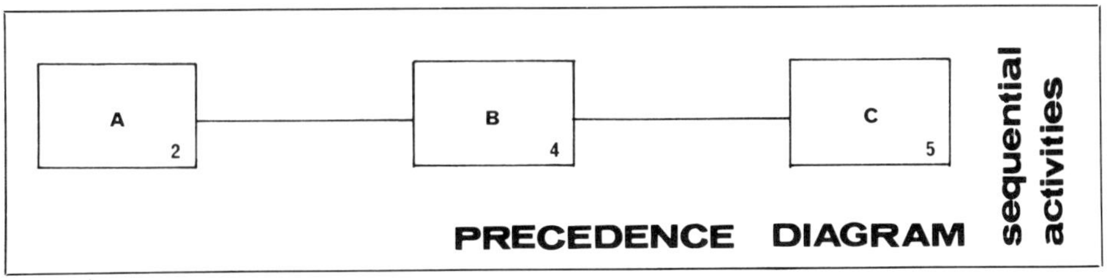

equal to the time for A, B, and C, or 11 time units. If additional resources or better planning will allow the paralleling of activities, substantial time can be saved. Again, in Figure 21.10, Activity A requires 2 units; B, 4 units; C, 5 units; and D, 3 units: the total time required for all four activities is 10 time units. This is possible because the planner was able to parallel activities B and C. The procedure for finding the path to parallel activities is to use the longest path. This may appear to be paradoxical, but it should be remembered that all activities in the network must be completed. Therefore, the earliest time that all tasks could be accomplished would be the time required along the longest path throughout the network. It is this path that turns out to be the Critical Path because conservation of time is possible only if the time can be conserved on the Critical Path. A word of caution should be given here about changing times on the Critical Path. Frequently, one route is eliminated as the Critical Path, and another path assumes that position. Therefore, all network paths must be computed each time any changes are made.

Miscellaneous diagrams

In the preceding pages we have considered the three basic components of network construction: the single activity, the sequential activity, and the parallel activity. Various other diagramming techniques are available to make the network more efficient: dummy activities, restraint activities, splitting procedures, and looping.

FIGURE 21.10

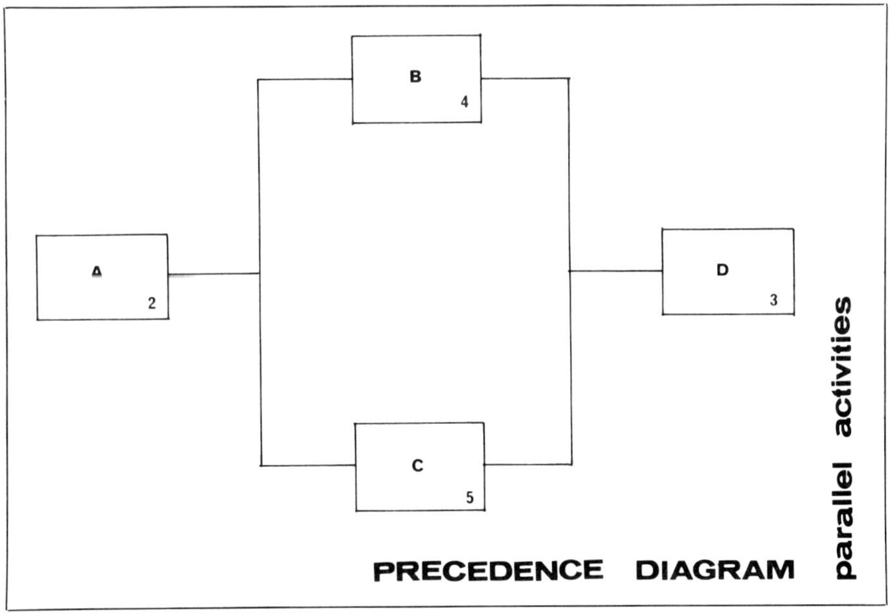

FIGURE 21.11

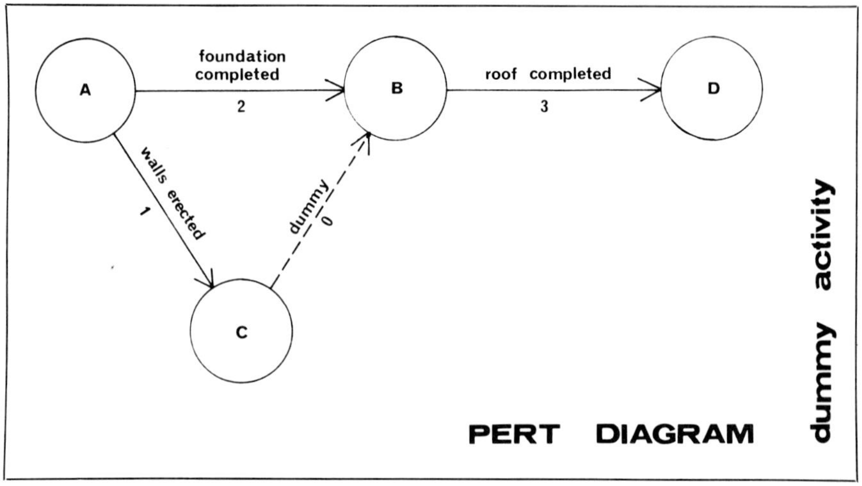

Every activity must have unique nodes showing onset and completion times. The uniqueness of identification nodes frequently requires that a dummy activity time be used. For example, in Figure 21.11, nodes A and B identify only the activity Foundation Completed; nodes A,C identify the activity Walls Erected; nodes B,D identify the activity Roof Completed; nodes C,B represent a dummy activity that requires no time and is symbolized by a broken arrow. Again, the primary purpose of the dummy activity is to retain the unique identification of a specific activity. If, for example, the dummy activity in Figure 21.11 were eliminated, nodes A,B would denote both Foundation Completed and Walls Erected. Since this is obviously impossible, the dummy activity is required.

Frequently, a network contains a restraint activity with a time completion constraint that is independent of the sequential listing of activities. For example, in Figure 21.12 the restraint activity A,C stalls the completion of C to ten weeks because of the delay in delivery of laboratory equipment. Painting Completed requires four weeks and Laboratory Completed requires five weeks, suggesting that only nine weeks would be needed if the restraint activity of laboratory equipment were excluded.

FIGURE 21.12

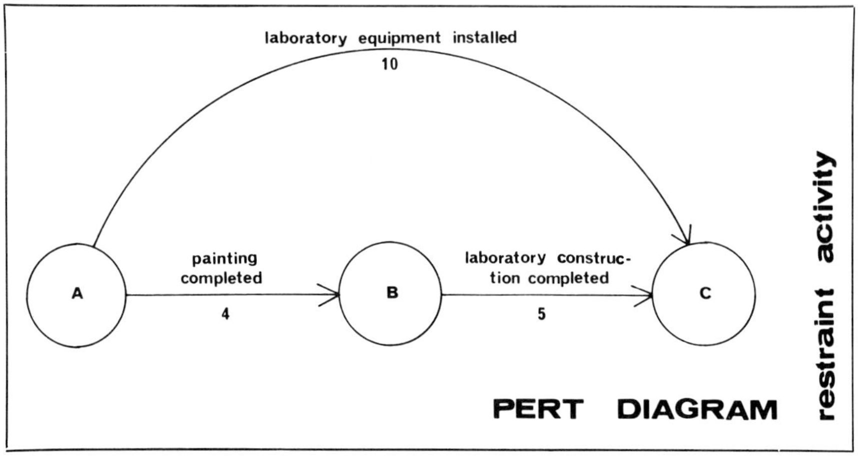

FIGURE 21.13

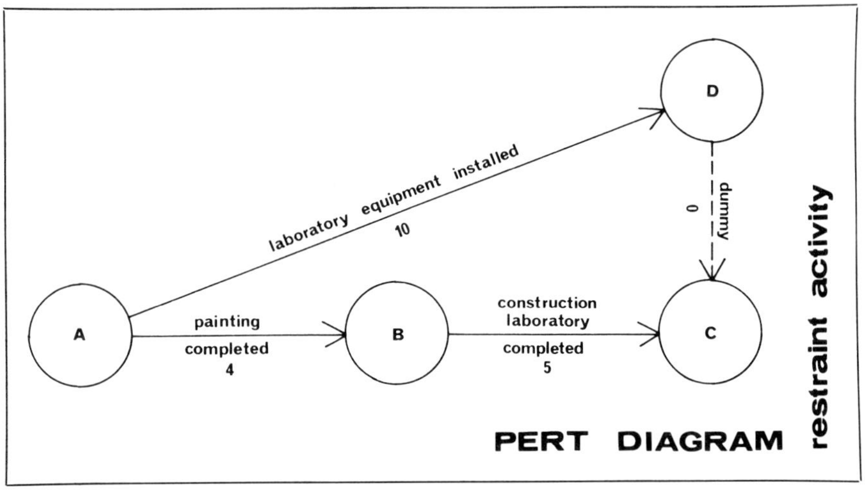

The restraint activity as illustrated in Figure 21.12 is permissible, but it is frequently possible to diagram more clearly by using the dummy activity as shown in Figure 21.13. In Figure 21.13 Laboratory Equipment Installed has unique identification nodes, A and B, which prevent any confusion in the network diagram. In Figures 21.12 and 21.13 all three activities will be completed: laboratory equipment will be installed, the painting completed, and the laboratory finished. Node C shows the completion of that portion of the project in ten weeks. From this, it is evident that the use of a dummy activity, as shown in Figure 21.13,

FIGURE 21.14

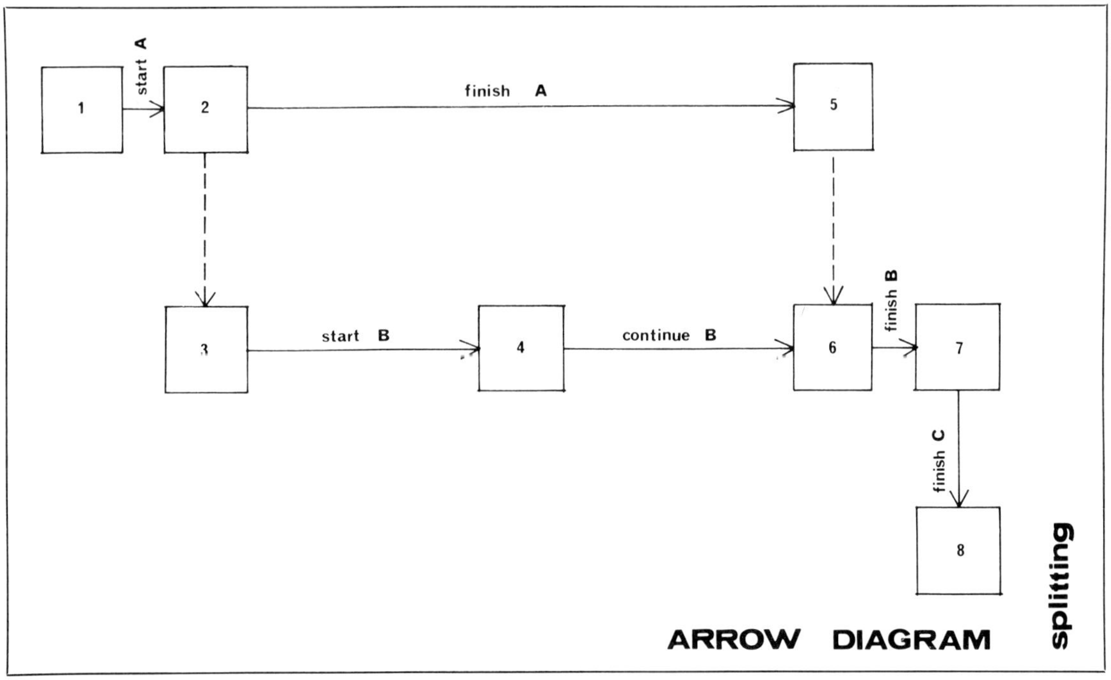

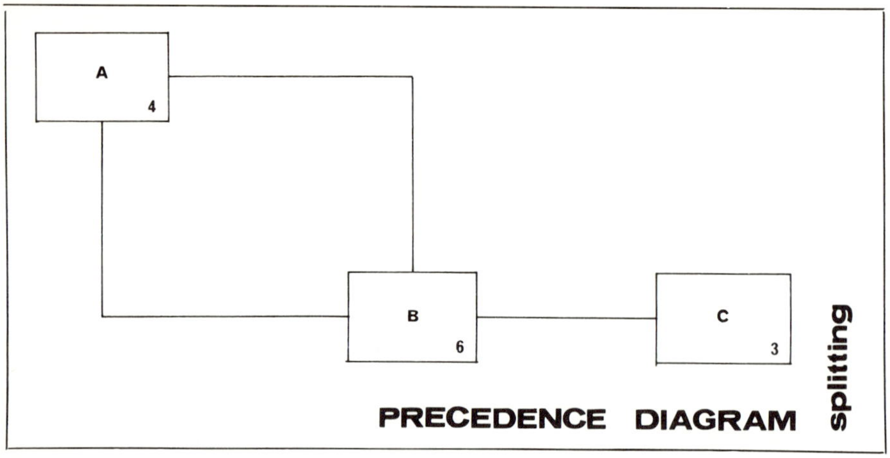

FIGURE 21.15

provides unique nodal identification for a given activity.

Figure 21.14 illustrates a splitting operation using an arrow diagram. Nodes 2,3 and 5,6 are the two dummy variables used. Nodes 1,2 in Figure 21.14 show the Start A activity and nodes 2,5 indicate the Finish A activity. Since B can start before A is finished, we have an activity Start B with nodes 3,4, Continue B with nodes 4,6, and Finish B with nodes 6,7 plus Finish C at nodes 7,8.

An advantage of the precedence diagram in illustrating a splitting procedure is pictured in Figure 21.15. B starts approximately midway between the start and completion times of A, and A is finished about one third of the way between B's start and finish times. C begins after B has been completed. The advantages of precedence diagramming seem obvious when one considers the activities shown in Figures 21.14 and 21.15. The diagram in Figure 21.16 is a precautionary one; such a diagram should not be used, especially with the computer, because this procedure would never go beyond node 2, but, instead, would merely continue to run around this particular loop.

SCHEDULING NETWORKS

The PERT network, the arrow network, and the precedence network are all examined in this section. Figure 21.17 shows the PERT network with the events labeled A, B, C, . . . K. Three time estimates are given for each activity time. To determine the expected time (T_E) for each activity, one should apply the formula:

$$T_E = \frac{A + 4M + B}{6}$$

These T_E's must be evaluated for each activity time throughout the network before the Critical Path can be specified. It is possible to calculate probabilities when the PERT network is used. A simplified formula is used for computing standard deviations. Since the standard deviation of 3 above and 3 below the mean includes almost all of a normal distribution, the standard deviation of the distribution is found by subtracting A from (B) and dividing by 6. This formula is an activity standard deviation (σ_A). In order to compute the event standard deviation, the following formula is used:

$$\sigma E = \sqrt{\left(\frac{B_1 - A_1}{6}\right)^2 + \left(\frac{B_2 - A_2}{6}\right)^2 + \cdots \left(\frac{B_N - A_N}{6}\right)^2} \qquad (1)$$

This event standard deviation is used in the denominator of the t-test, or students' distribution. The numerator of the t-test is the difference between the latest allowable time and the earliest expected time.

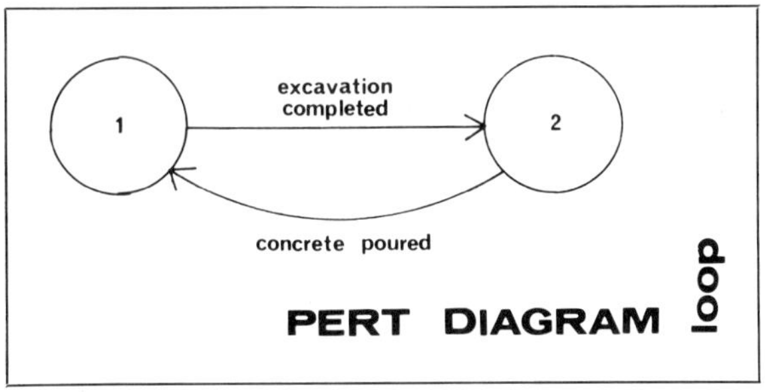

FIGURE 21.16

$$t = \frac{T_L - T_E}{\sqrt{\left(\frac{B_1 - A_1}{6}\right)^2 + \left(\frac{B_2 - A_2}{6}\right)^2 + \ldots \left(\frac{B_N - A_N}{6}\right)^2}} \quad (2)$$

Figure 21.18 is an example of the arrow network and shows the visual similarities between the two networks. However, the activities are now labeled on the arrow. Although the connectors are labeled, they only show the logical connections between activities. To repeat, the PERT network is event oriented and probabilistic in nature, whereas the arrow network is activity oriented and deterministic.

Figure 21.19 is a precedence network in which the rectangles include the activity's label, description, and time. Since a precedence network is a greatly simplified network, it offers the scheduler a considerably greater degree of flexibility, than other networks. In all three networks—PERT, arrow, and precedence—the Critical Path is calculated by determining the

FIGURE 21.17

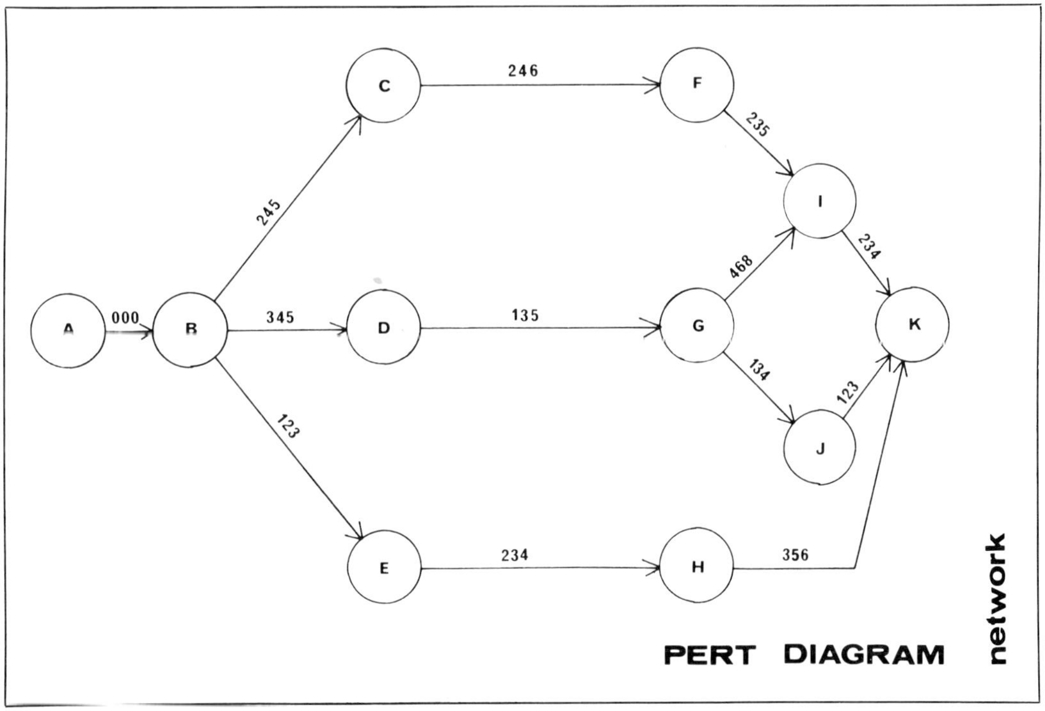

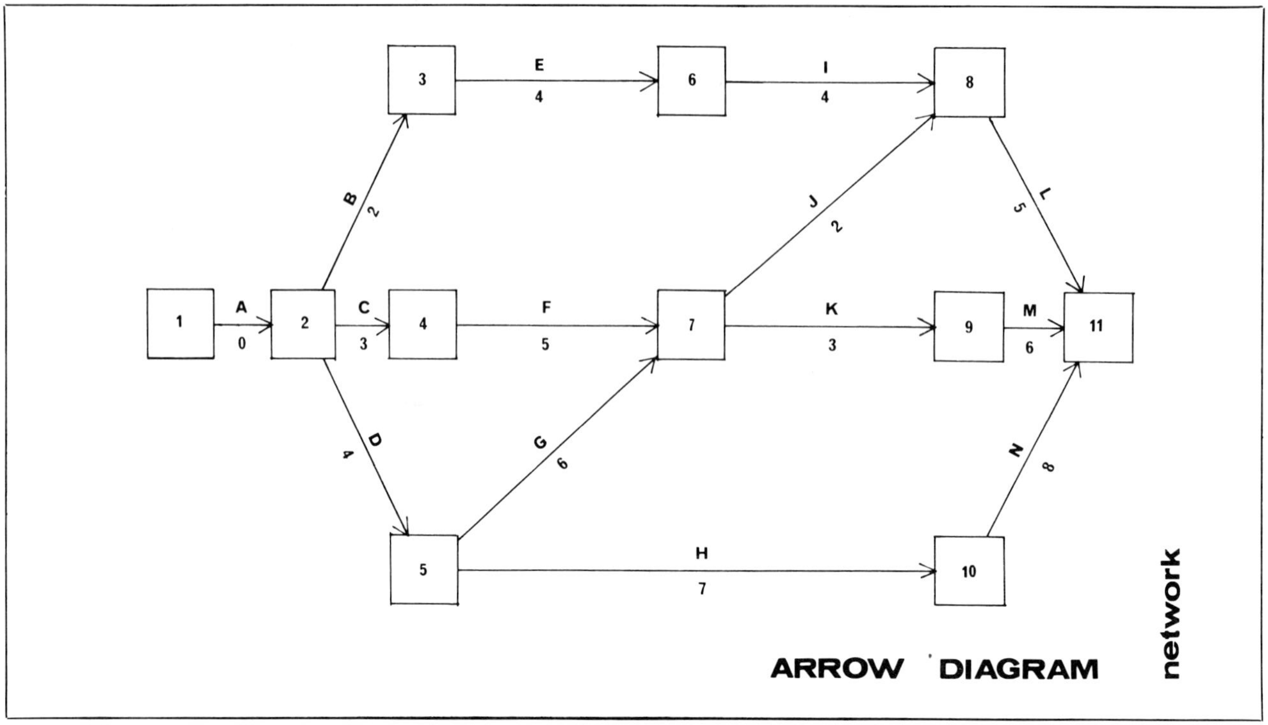

FIGURE 21.18

FIGURE 21.19

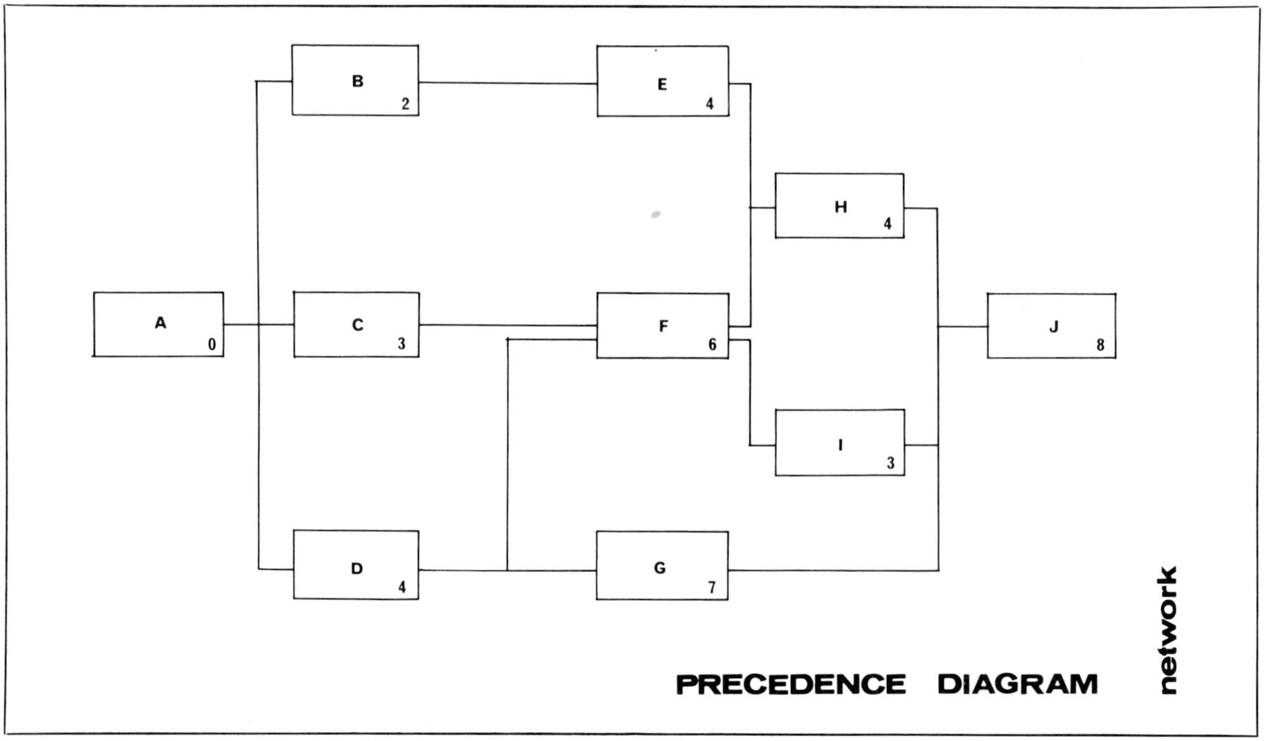

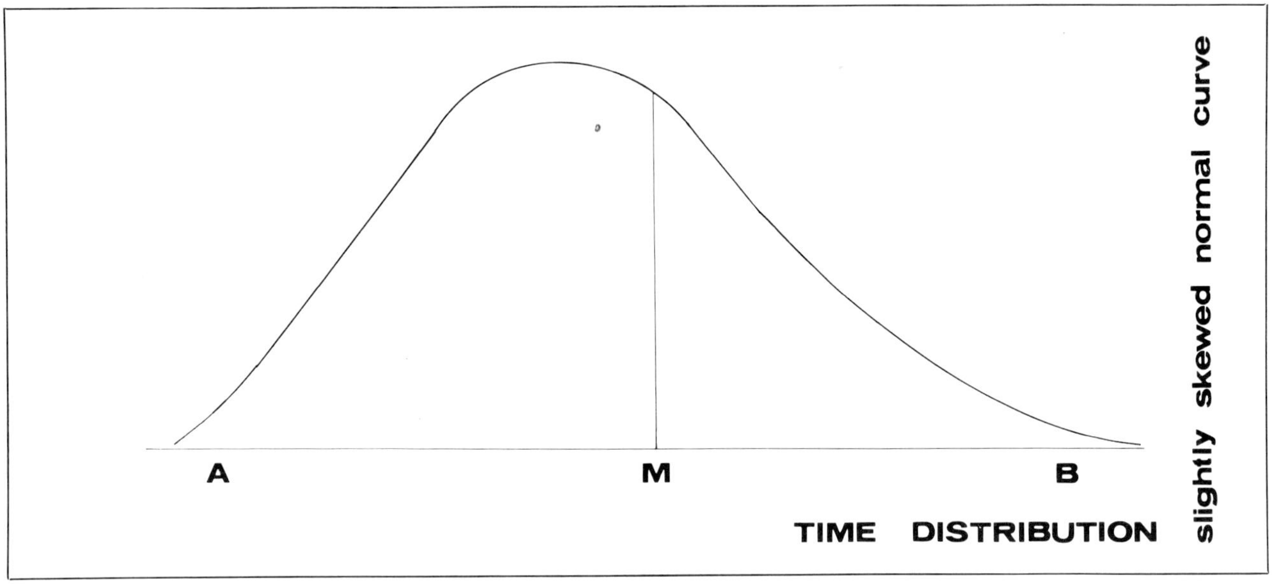

FIGURE 21.20

maximum amount of time required to go from the first activity to the last activity.

TIME CALCULATIONS

Since CPM uses only one time estimate, in the following discussion on time, variability is applied only to PERT. Three time estimates are made: (1) the most optimistic time, A; (2) the most pessimistic time, B; and (3) the most likely time, M. The most optimistic time suggests that every activity will occur under almost ideal conditions; the most pessimistic time suggests that Murphy's law holds; that is, if anything can go wrong, it will. The most likely time suggests that a normal amount of trouble, but no major problems, will occur. These precepts assume that the completion times are distributed as a Beta function. The Beta function is similar to a slightly skewed normal curve (see Figure 21.20). All three numbers, A, B, and M, are estimates. The expected time, T_E, is calculated as follows:

$$T_E = \frac{A + 4M + B}{6}$$

M is given the weight of 4. Since 6 weights are used, the sum must be divided by 6.

The latest allowable time, T_L; earliest expected time, T_E; and slack time, T_S; are some other important time elements. Their calculations are shown in Figure 21.21. To determine T_E proceed from left to right, accumulating the times as they are listed. Since it takes one week to complete B after A is completed, T_E (B) is 1. The time needed to complete C after B has been finished is three weeks. When the 3 is added to the cumulated time of B, T_E becomes 4. As this method is continued, if two or more routes lead to the same event, the greater of the two sums should be used. Where the path from A to G passes through B and D, the time units are equal to 6. On the other hand, the path from A to G that reaches B and then E requires 7 time units. In this instance $G = 7$ is used.

To estimate, T_L, proceed from right to left, accumulating the times, in much the same way as T_E was estimated. Unless there is a good reason to the contrary, assign $T_L = T_E$ for the end event. Calculate slack time, T_S, by finding the difference between the earliest expected time and the latest allowable time ($T_L - T_E$). Throughout the network calculate the slack periods by finding the differences between the

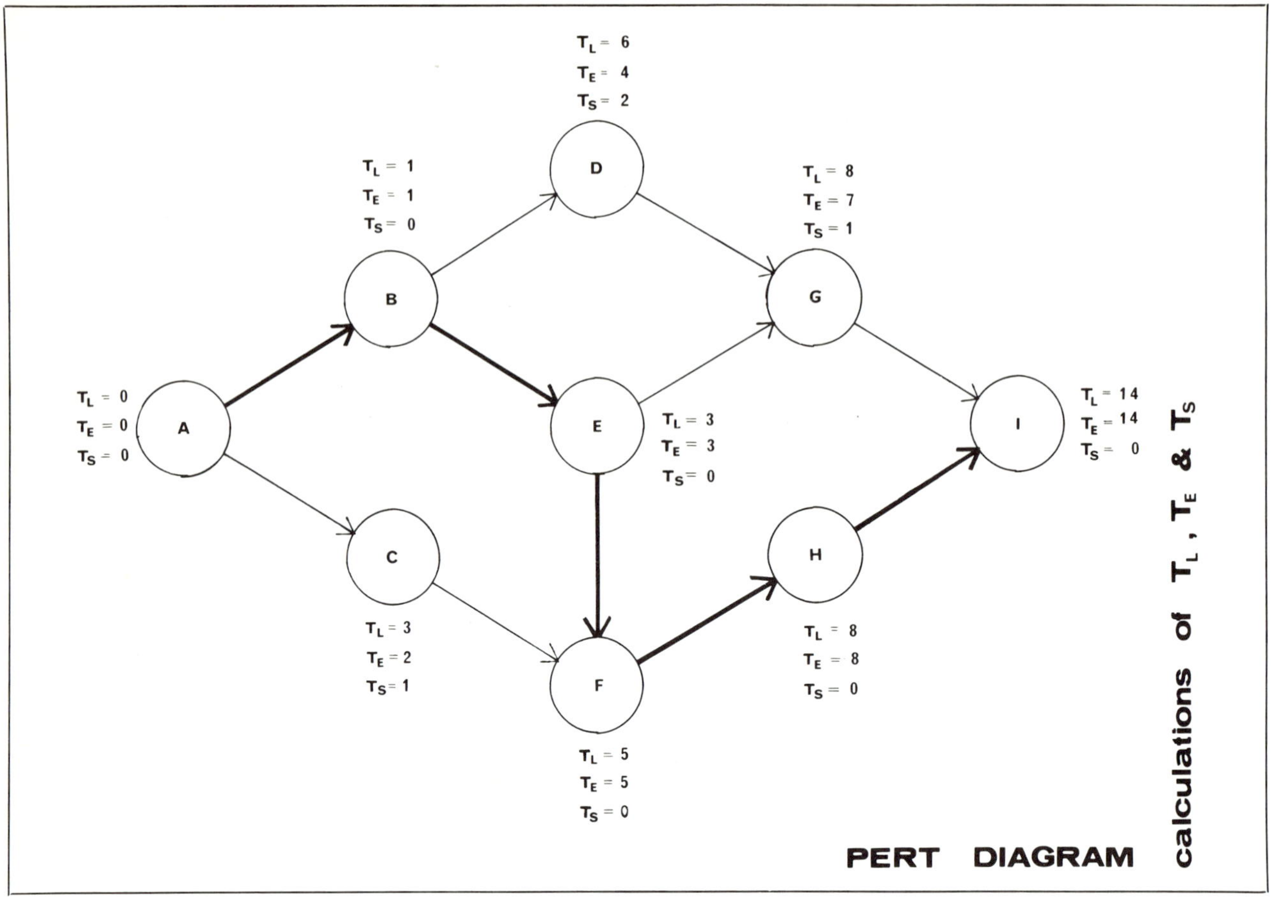

FIGURE 21.21

earliest expected time and the latest allowable time. If the final T_L equals the final T_E, slack periods will be zero for all events on the Critical Path. This suggests that, if time is to be conserved, the route must be shortened by the use of the Critical Path. It will do little good to shorten the 4 units of slack time of an activity not located on the Critical Path, since the total time taken for the completion of all tasks will not be influenced.

Table 21.2 is a tabulation of the basic data that are connected with the problem and that are used for the construction of networks. The "label" column identifies the specific activities to be completed, and the "time" column shows the time required for each. The predecessor and successor columns provide the logical sequence of the various activities. For example, A is the first activity to be completed, taking two time units. There are no predecessors, since it is the first activity, but its successors are B and C. Activity B requires three time units, and its predecessor is A.

Figures 21.22 and 21.23 illustrate calculated networks based on arrow diagrams and precedence diagrams, respectively.

SUMMARY

In the discussion of the background of project scheduling, its evolution from Gantt Charts through PERT, arrow, and precedence networks is described. The

FIGURE 21.22

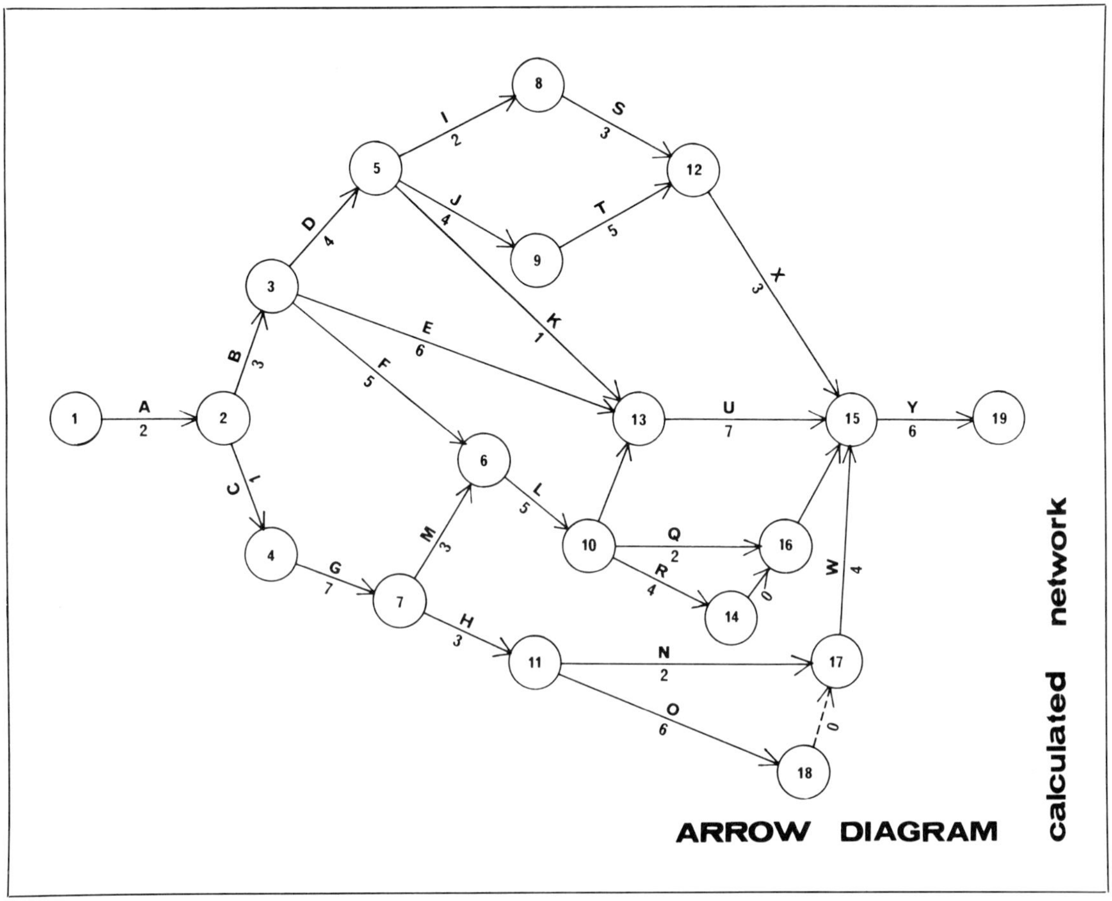

Table 21.2 Scheduling events

Label	Time	Predecessors	Successors	Label	Time	Predecessors	Successors
A	2	—	B,C	N	2	H	W
B	3	A	D,E,F	O	6	H	W
C	1	A	G,H	P	8	L,M	U
D	4	B	I,J,K	Q	2	L,M	V
E	6	B	U	R	4	L,M	V
F	5	B	L	S	3	I	X
G	7	C	M	T	5	J	X
H	3	C	N,O	U	7	E,K,P	Y
I	2	D	S	V	6	Q,R	Y
J	4	D	T	W	4	N,O	Y
K	1	D	U	X	3	S,T	Y
L	5	F	P,Q,R	Y	6	X,U,V,W	—
M	3	G	P,Q,R				

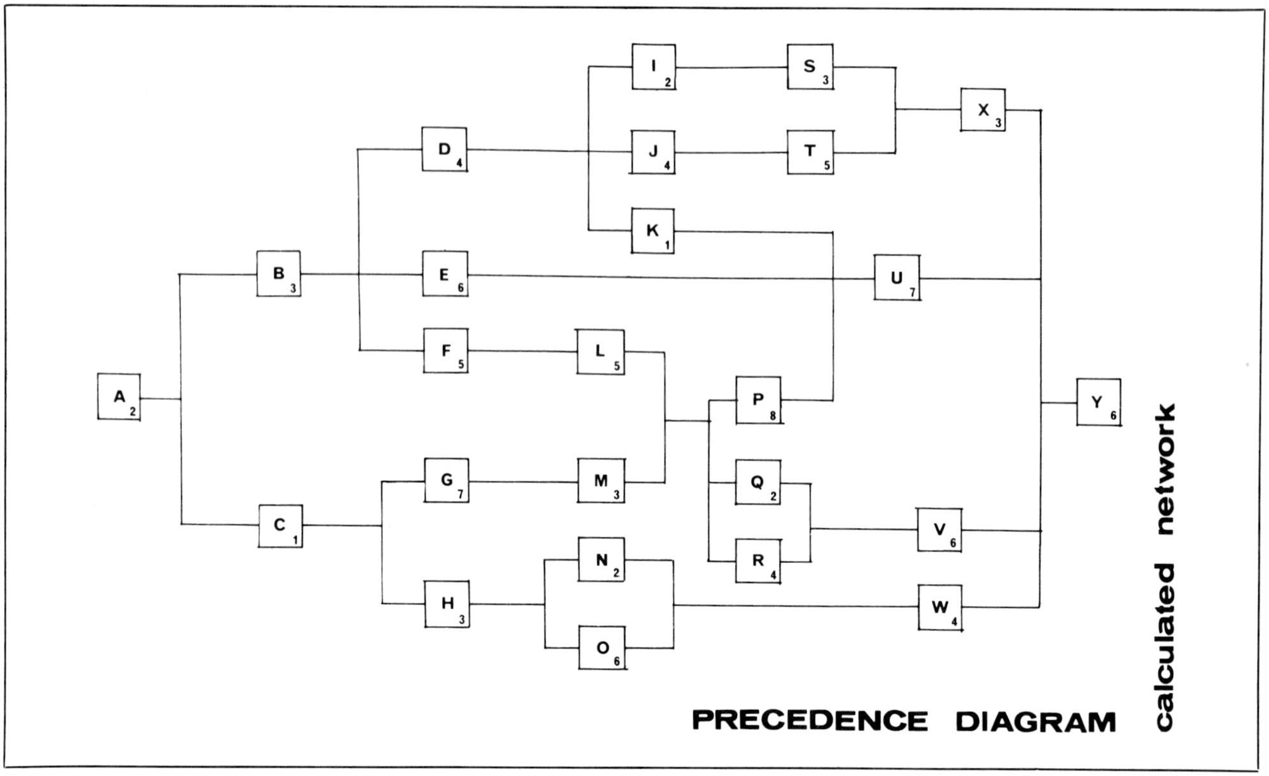

FIGURE 21.23

basic modules for network construction—single, sequential, and parallel activities—along with variations of activity diagrams, such as dummy and restraint activities, splitting, and loop variables—are discussed. Diagramming procedures are illustrated with detailed networks of Gantt Charts, PERT, and precedence diagrams in terms of single, sequential, and parallel activities. Time estimates are presented in terms of optimistic, pessimistic, and most likely times; the expected time; the latest allowable time; the earliest expected time; and slack times. Finally, a detailed illustration is given in an arrow network and a precedence network based on a problem.

It is shown that in order to make a sound project schedule, an educational planning agency will need more information on students, teachers, and so on. The agency will be dealing with more information about the nature of education, and more precise timetables from other participating educational agencies. The agency will have to take stock of its resources for monitoring its services within the described framework. Doing so will result in greater clarification of objectives than has normally been the case in the monitoring stage. It will also make evident the fact that the disposition of resources among the various educational agencies can never be treated as a finished activity but rather as actually a continuing process. Consideration of these facts and the questions that arise in the actual execution of the plan makes project scheduling a valuable tool for monitoring educational activities while they are under way.

22 Evaluating the plan

Evaluating the plan in action completes the cycle of the educational planning process. Evaluating is essentially a control activity where positive intervention is possible. It examines the direction taken and evaluates the results or deviations from the plan. But that is not the only point at which evaluation occurs. From time to time evaluation occurs at many points in the planning process. Quantitative tests and judgments based on prior experiences serve as means of evaluating the various steps within the planning process.

The educational planner is in a difficult situation. His job is to consider the costs and benefits of each alternative. The difficulty arises when he must evaluate the effects that the allocation of resources for education will have in the public interest. In this evaluation the educational planner must be comprehensive and on this point alone his evaluation is open to attack. He can be questioned on his ability to determine educational objectives or values, which are always in a state of flux. The limits on his ability to evaluate are many. Some of these limitations follow.

Educational planners may have limited problem-solving capabilities.

Educational planners may lack truly comprehensive information about the many facets of education.

Educational planners may not have the financial resources for comprehensive evaluation.

Educational planners may not have the ability to construct a satisfactory method for evaluating the objectives or the degree of success in their accomplishment.

Educational planners may be too close to observe the relationships between fact and value of each and every educational activity.

Educational planners may evaluate the various educational systems as closed systems.

To help counter these limitations the following discussion of activities, environments, and utility furnish the educational planner with an evaluation plan.

EVALUATING EDUCATIONAL ACTIVITIES

Five factors are important in any educational activity. They are as follows:

1 The place in which the activity is done.
2 The time at which the activity is done.
3 The people involved in the activity.
4 The resources required for the activity.
5 The process by which the activity is done.

It is impossible to avoid geographical specialization. An activity must be done somewhere, not everywhere. Because an activity or a series of activities is a system of efforts of individuals who have a physical location, such a system is so obvious that frequently its evaluation escapes attention. Thus, if two educational activities are identical but are located in two different areas, their evaluation must be different. The difference is often not significant, but sometimes it is. The evaluation of the same kind of activity is always different when the location is different. For example, teaching a second-grade class of children from a middle socio-economic class of families in one part of town may appear to be the same kind of work as teaching a second-grade class in another part of town, and hence requires the same kind of evaluation. But a good teacher knows that the evaluation may be radically different, and, moreover, that effective and efficient work may depend on a specialized knowledge of the location from which the pupils come. The educational planner in his evaluation, therefore, must consider the characteristics of the location. The limitations of the endurance of individuals is another factor.

Specialization of activities with respect to time is one of the aspects for evaluation. The scheduling of activities is among the most complex requiring evaluation. Because the methods required by the activities seem the same in most cases in different hours of the day, week, or season, time has been much overlooked in the general process of evaluating. Yet the necessity to adhere to time-schedule assignments is one important basis of evaluating individuals.

The individuals involved in the activity, their experience, the type of organization, housing, formal and informal grouping, and the communication between individuals or groups, as well as the individual's interest, loyalty, prestige, pride, and responsibility, are all important in evaluation.

Objectives of activities must be evaluated. In many cases this evaluation can focus on the materials to be used. In other cases the evaluation may center on the

FIGURE 22.1
Combining information for new experiences

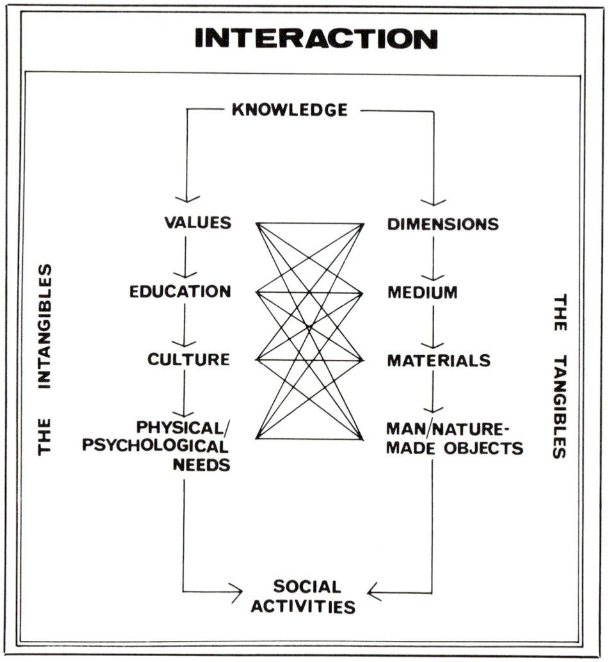

FIGURE 22.2
A structure for content and purpose

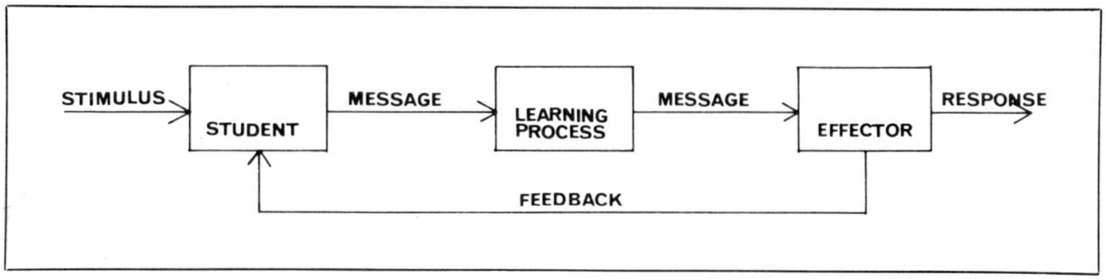

ends to be accomplished, especially where services are to be performed. In either case, there are usually some implications of differences in the process of evaluation. The emphasis depends on the evaluator.

EVALUATING EDUCATIONAL ENVIRONMENTS

The environment must allow the student to find his own discipline. The success of this objective can be evaluated. The school environment should establish a clearly defined range of opportunities for the student to explore and experience. The environment should include the chance to understand the needs and hopes of people, the chance to understand the choices that are provided, and the continuing opportunity to try new ways of combining basic information to create new experiences. (See Figure 22.1.)

Evaluating educational environments requires consideration of three basic questions. What does the everyday physical environment do to students, that is, what are its consequences for learning? What do students do to their everyday physical environment, that is, what are the learning antecedents of environmental transformations? How do students comprehend the everyday physical environment?

All three questions center on the stimulus properties of the environment and on their symbolic manifestations. René Dubos

> . . . comments on the fact that man has a tendency to symbolize everything that happens to him and then to react to the symbols as though they were the environmental stimuli. He suggests that, as a result, the actual effects which the environment has on man, bear little if any resemblance to the direct effects to be expected from the physical nature of the stimulus. The body reacts not only to the stimulus itself, but to all the symbols associated with the experience of the past and expectations of the future—symbols which are converted into effective stimuli. Symbols are used to structure information from the environment which otherwise would become unmanageable due to its fantastically rich sensory bombardment. Symbols do this by increasing the redundancy or predictability by increasing the number of connections between elements and groups of elements, and by reducing the number of elements through selection. Selection involves choice and hence value judgments which are based on images and schemata.[1]

Evaluating an infinite array of environments without a structure is impossible. An elementary evaluative scheme can be constructed from Figure 22.2. In this manner each aspect of the interaction, i.e., student, stimulus, message, learning process, effector, and response plus feedback, can be evaluated and cross-referenced to help educational planners plan effective learning environments.

Too often evaluation has been limited to measuring the cost without measuring the value of an alternative. The evaluation is simple because the device for measuring values is money. It is not a perfect device but it is hard to find a better one that will allow educational planners to compare a large number of alternative ways of doing things. However, criteria for evaluating the utility of one course of action against another at the least cost should be developed.

One method for evaluating uses utility theory. It aids evaluation by using more responsible, educated,

[1]Raphael O. Nystrand, "The Study of School-Community Relationships in Urban Settings: A Discussion of the Methods Employed in the Cincinnati, Columbus, Detroit and Washington, D. C. School Surveys." Paper presented at the Annual Meeting of the American Educational Research Association, Los Angeles, February 5–8, 1969.

and rational judgments through setting down in order the criteria being used for evaluating.

CONCEPT OF EVALUATING WITH UTILITY

The concept of utility implies subjective judgment. Specifically utility is a personal preference. The subjective nature of utility has no doubt retarded systematic investigation of the nature of utility.

Paradoxically the field of utility theory is grounded in mathematics. A mathematical treatment of utility is possible because of the order axiom. Indeed, the order axiom is the foundation of any quantitative treatment of utility, and hence evaluation.

Consider two alternatives a_1 and a_2. How can a_1 and a_2 be expressed in terms of personal preferences? Clearly one of three conditions must prevail; a_1 is preferred to a_2 or a_2 is preferred to a_1 or a_1 is preferred equally with a_2.

These preferential relationships form the basis for ordering alternatives.[2]

These relationships can be extended to composite alternatives. Consider the following set of alternatives: a_1, a_2, a_3, a_4, and a_5. Relative strengths can be established as follows.

Either

$a_1 > a_2 + a_3 + a_4 + a_5$ (see Figure 22.3)

or

$a_1 < a_2 + a_3 + a_4 + a_5$ (see Figure 22.4)

or

$a_1 = a_2 + a_3 + a_4 + a_5$ (see Figure 22.5)

Let

$a_1 > a_2 + a_3 + a_4 + a_5$ (see Figure 22.3)

Assign numerical values to a_1 so that the above inequality holds

$100 > 40 + 20 + 10 + 5$

where

$a_1 = 100, a_2 = 40, a_3 = 20, a_4 = 10, a_5 = 5$

continue as follows

$a_2 > a_3 + a_4 + a_5$ (see Figure 22.6)

$40 > 20 + 10 + 5$

$a_3 > a_4 + a_5$ (see Figure 22.7)

$20 > 10 + 5$

$a_4 > a_5$ (see Figure 22.8)

$10 > 5.$

If at any time the inequality does not hold, adjust the left side of the inequality.

$a_1 = 65, a_2 = 40, a_3 = 20, a_4 = 10, a_5 = 5$

$65 \ngtr 40 + 20 + 10 + 5$

adjust

$a_1 = 80$

$80 > 40 + 20 + 10 + 5$

After all adjustments have been made, normalize the values as follows:

$a_1 = 100$

$a_2 = 40$

$a_3 = 20$

$a_4 = 10$

$a_5 = 5$

$\sum a_i = 175$

Divide each a_i by the $\sum a_i$

$a_1 = 100/175 = .57120$

$a_2 = 40/175 = .22848$

$a_3 = 20/175 = .11424$

$a_4 = 10/175 = .05714$

$a_5 = 5/175 = .02856$

The results (normalized values) furnish a basis for

Text continues on page 412.

[2]Frank W. Banghart, *Educational Systems Analysis* (London: Macmillan & Co., 1969), p. 207.

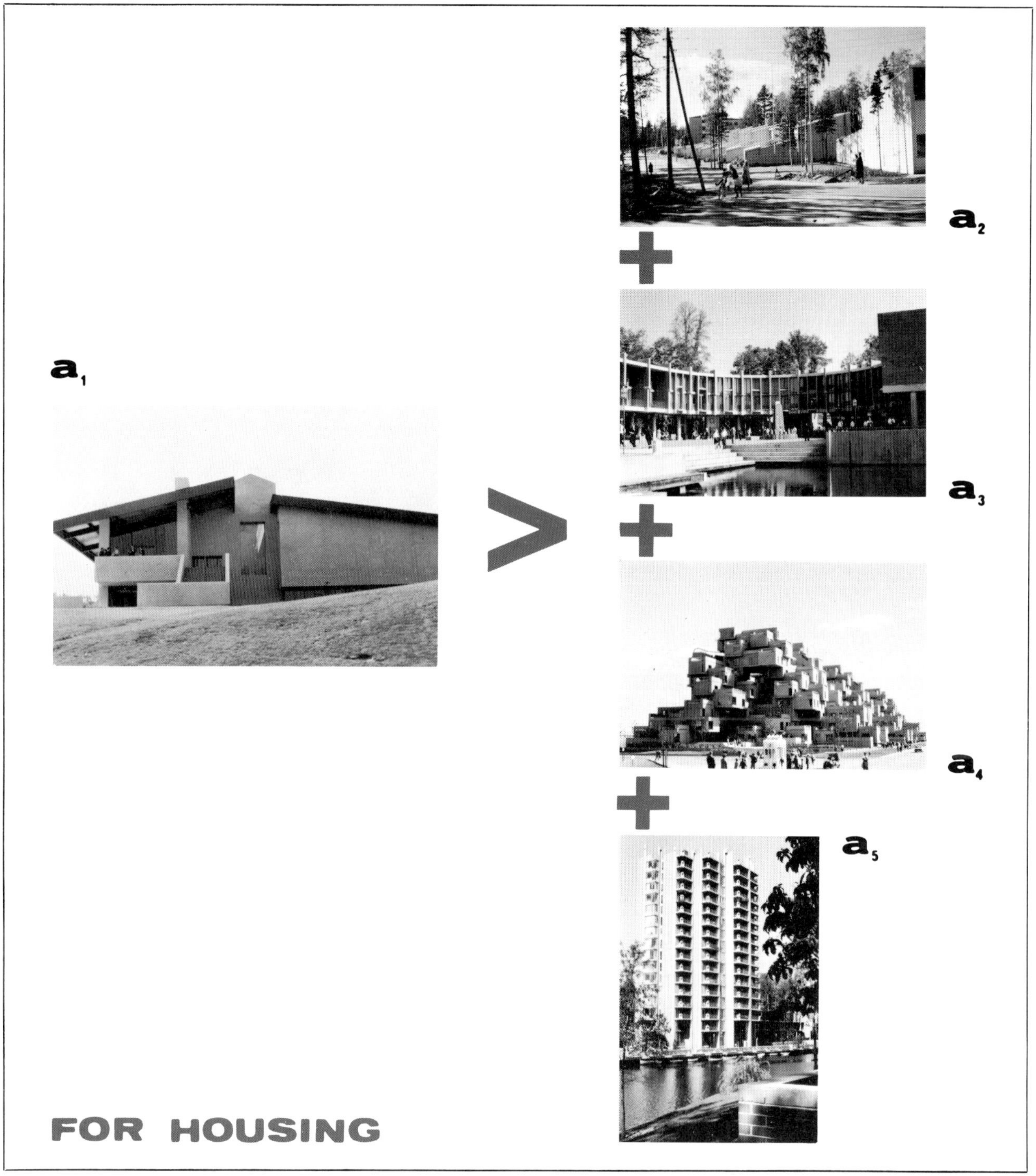

FIGURE 22.3

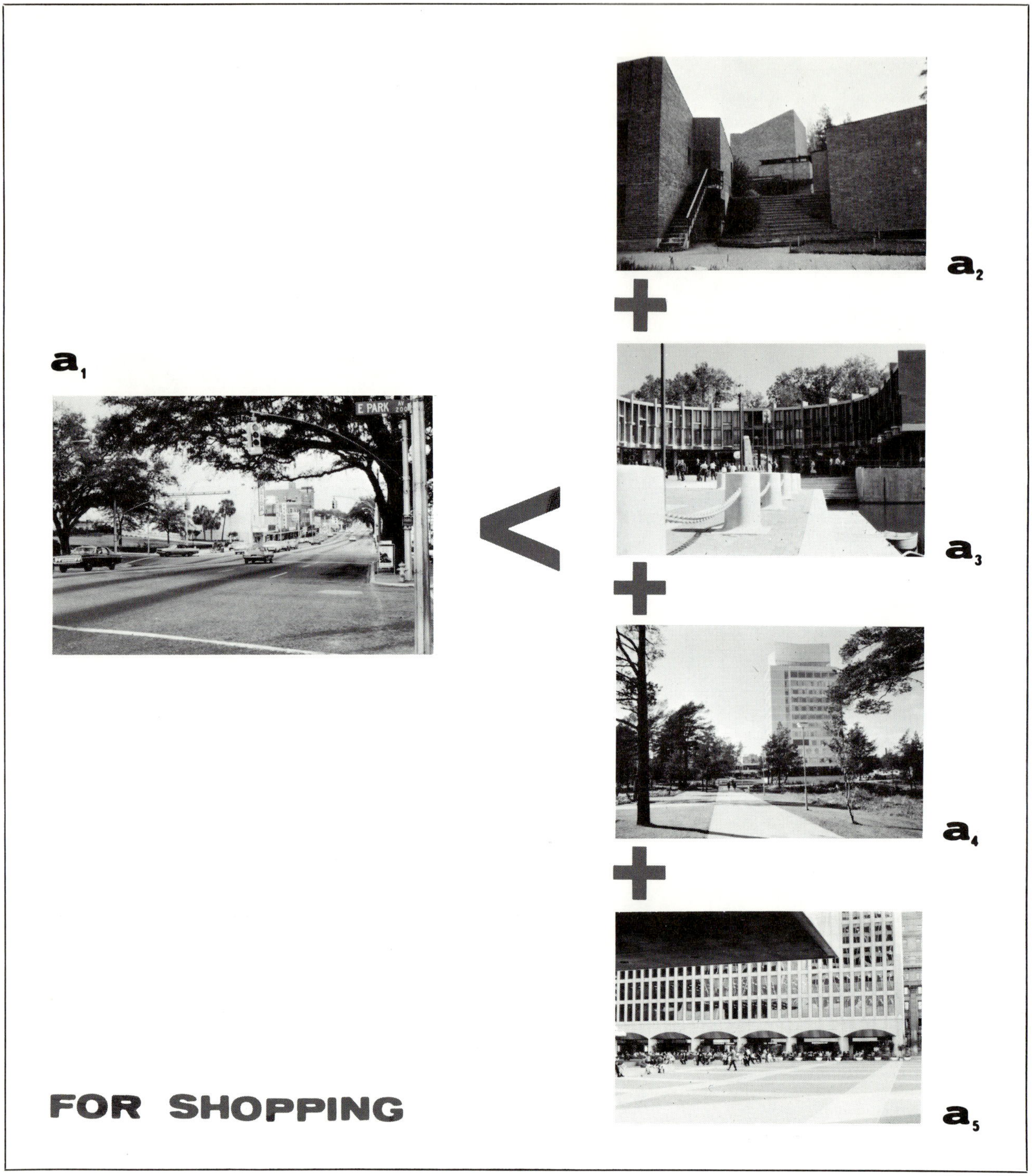

FIGURE 22.4

FIGURE 22.5

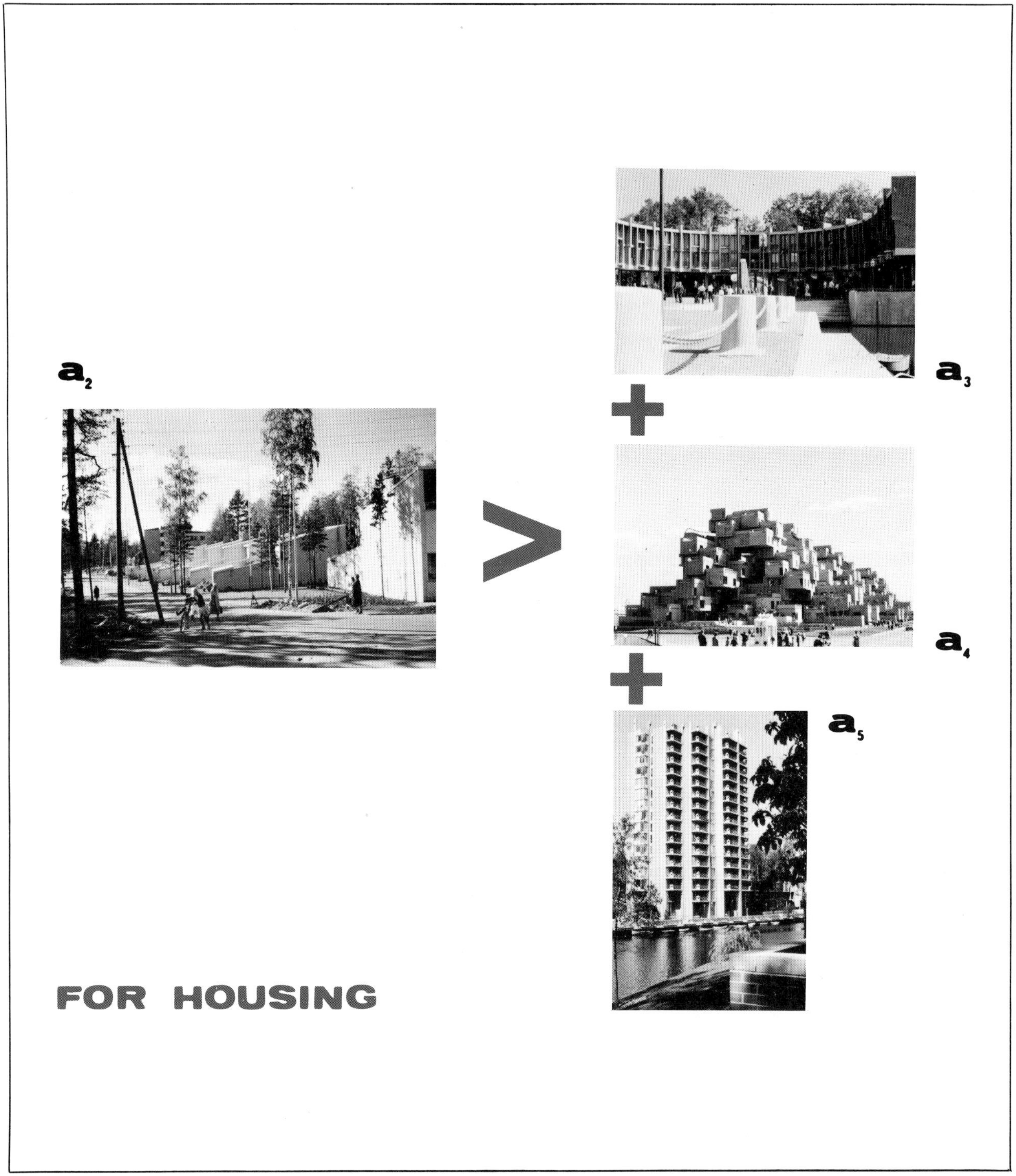

FIGURE 22.6

FIGURE 22.7

FIGURE 22.8

making a quantitative evaluation even though the original a_i's were subjective judgments.

The concept of utility implies three characteristics: (1) the expression of personal preference from (2) among a set of possible alternatives through (3) the appropriate allocation of resources based on the relative utilities.

Educational planners and educational planning procedures overcome many indecisive evaluations with the use and concept of utility. It is an evaluation tool that can determine the unique value associated with each educational planning project.

Definitions of utility

For almost a century and a half professionals have attempted to define utility. The resulting definitions have reflected the subjective nature of utility. Jeremy Bentham in 1823 wrote

> By the principle of utility is meant that principle which approves or disapproves of every action whatsoever, according to the tendency which it appears to have to augment or diminish the happiness of the party whose interest is in question: or what is the same thing in other words, to promote or to oppose that happiness.[3]

Clearly happiness is a personal and subjective state. (See Figure 22.9.) Adam Smith interjected value into the definition of utility.

> The word *value* it is to be observed, has two different meanings, and sometimes expresses the utility of some particular object, and sometimes the power of purchasing other goods which the possession of that object conveys. The one may be called "value in use"; the other, "value in exchange." The things which have the greatest value in use have frequently little or no value in exchange; and on the contrary, those which have the greatest value in exchange have frequently little or no value in use. Nothing is more useful than water: but it will purchase scarce anything: scarce anything can be had in exchange for it. A diamond, on the contrary, has scarce any value in use: but a very great quantity of other goods may frequently be had in exchange for it.[4]

[3]Jeremy Bentham, "An Introduction to the Principles of Morals and Legislation," *Utility Theory: A Book of Readings*, ed. Alfred N. Page (N.Y.: Wiley, 1968), p. 3.

[4]Adam Smith, *The Wealth of Nations* (New York: Modern Library, 1937), p. 28.

Smith's treatment of utility is oriented toward economics. His understanding of the concept of utility is not entirely reflected in the quotation, but his treatment of the difference between intrinsic and extrinsic values is relevant to utility.

Irving Fisher's treatment of utility is distinctively modern. The emphasis in Fisher's definition is on the subjective preference of the individual. Inherent value (utility) is irrelevant according to Fisher. Fisher's concept of utility is, however, embedded in economic thinking.

> It has occurred to me that the term really needed may be built on the good old economic term "want." Long before the days of "marginal utility" economists spoke of "human wants." Wants include wants for purposes of ornamentation as well as for purposes of real utility; wants for what is trivial or useless as well as for what is important, useful, and desirable; wants for evil as well as for good purposes. So far as the influence on price is concerned the essential fact is that an object is actually wanted or rather that it is capable of being actually wanted under stated circumstances, whether it ought to be wanted, or whether it is wanted for a proper purpose is immaterial. It must merely have the capacity for being wanted, it must be wantable, it must have wantability.[5]

Jules Dupuit (1844) extended the concept of utility to the modern concept of demand curves.

> Assume that all like commodities whose general utility one wishes to determine are subjected to a tax which is increased by small steps. At each increase, a certain quantity of the commodity will no longer be purchased. The utility of this commodity in terms of money will be the quantity multiplied by the tax. By increasing the tax until all purchases cease, and adding the partial products, one will obtain the total utility of the commodity.[6]

Heinrich Gossen (1854) combined the qualitative approach of the past with a semiquantitative approach in discussing the concept of marginal utility: "A person maximizes his utility when he distributes his available money among the various goods so that he obtains the same amount of satisfaction from the last

[5]Irving Fisher, "Is 'Utility' the Most Suitable Term for the Concept It Is Used to Denote?," *American Economic Review*, **8**:335–337 (June 1918).

[6]Jules Dupuit, *De l'utilité et de sa mesure* (Torino: Les Filforma Sociale, 1924), p. 50.

FIGURE 22.9

unit of money spent upon each commodity."[7] (See Figure 22.10.)

Therefore

$$\frac{MU_1}{P_1} = \frac{MU_2}{P_2} = + \ldots + = \frac{MU_i}{P_1}$$

"We can conceive of the magnitudes of various pleasures only by comparing them with one another, as, indeed, we must also do in measuring other objects."[8]

Notations for evaluating with the utility approach

The following notation illustrates the basic utility relationships that may exist among alternatives.

1 x may be preferred to y: i.e., xPy.
2 x may be indifferent to y: i.e., xIy.
3 x may be preferred to or indifferent to y: i.e., $x0y$.
4 If x has a utility value this utility is expressed as $U(x)$. (See Figure 22.11.)

Assumptions for evaluation with the utility approach

The following assumptions express relationships between preferences and utilities.

1 If x is preferred to y then the utility of x is greater than the utility of y: i.e., $xPy \Rightarrow U(x) > U(y)$.
2 If x is indifferent to y then the utility of x is equal to the utility of y: i.e., $xIy \Rightarrow U(x) = U(y)$.
3 If x is indifferent to or prefers x to y then the utility of x is equal to or greater than the utility of y: i.e., $x0y \Rightarrow U(x) \geq U(y)$. (See Figure 22.12.)

[7]Heinrich Gossen, *Entwicklung der Gesetze des menschlichen Verkehrs* (3rd ed., Berlin: Prager, 1927), p. 93.
[8]Ibid., p. 123.

A CITY'S RESOURCES
DISTRIBUTED FOR

GARDENING

RECREATION

URBAN RENEWAL

NEW CITY HALL

SCHOOL

FIGURE 22.10

FIGURE 22.11

P

I

O

FIGURE 22.12

These assumptions are all related to the order axiom and are necessary consequences of that axiom.

Preference/utility relationships

The following utility relationships are implied from the associated preference relationships. (See pages 420–435.)

1 Either x is preferred to y, y is preferred to x; or x is indifferent to y. This preference relationship implies that the utility of x is greater than, lesser than, or equal to y: i.e., xPy, yPx, or $xIy \Rightarrow U(x) > U(y), U(x) < U(y)$, or $U(x) = U(y)$.

2 If x is equal to y then x is indifferent to y and the utility of x is equal to the utility of y; i.e., if $x = y$, then xIy and $U(x) = U(y)$.

3 If x is indifferent to x, then $U(x)$ is equal to $U(x)$: i.e., $xIx \Rightarrow U(x) = U(x)$.

4 If x is preferred to y and y is preferred to z, then x is preferred to z implies that if $U(x) > U(y)$ and $U(y) > U(z)$, then $U(x) > U(z)$.

5 If x is preferred to y and y is indifferent to z, then x is preferred to z implies that if $U(x) > U(y)$ and $U(y) = U(z)$ then $U(x) > U(z)$.

6 The relationship if xPy and xIz then zPy implies that if $U(x) > U(y)$ and $U(x) = U(z)$, then $U(z) > U(y)$.

7 If xIy then yIx implies that if $u(x) = U(y)$, then $U(y) = U(x)$.

8 If xIy and yIz, then xIz implies that if $U(x) = U(y)$ and $U(y) = U(z)$, then $U(x) = U(z)$.

9 If P_i equals the probability of x_1 and $p_1 + p_2 + \ldots + p_n = 1$, then $U(p_1x_1 + p_2x_2 + \ldots + p_nx_n) = p_1U(x_1) + p_2U(x_2) + \ldots + p_nU(x_n)$.

Relationship number nine above implies that utilities are additive. If xPy and yPz and x, y and z are not independent then the individual might select a proportionate amount of x, y, and z. If so then the total utility relationship would be

$$U(t) = U(x) + U(y) + U(z)$$

(See Figure 22.13.)

Measuring utility for evaluating

The measurement of utility involves determination of the strength of personal references in evaluating. By definition utility is subjective. However, if the concept is to be helpful in decision-making it must be measurable.

There are two basic approaches to the measurement of utility. One involves the difficulty of choice; the other involves consistency of choice. Assume a choice between alternatives a_1 and a_2. Recall, also that utility is meaningful primarily in relative terms: i.e., a_1 has utility in relation to one's preference of a_1 to a_2. One measure of the utility of a_1 is the degree of difficulty for an individual to choose between a_1 and a_2. The degree of difficulty could range from an unquestionable preference for a_1 or a_2 to the predicament of the proverbial ass, which stood between two identical bales of hay and starved to death because it could not choose between them.

The other approach to measurement of utility involves consistency. If an individual selects a_1 over a_2 80 per cent of the time, the inference is that a_1 has greater utility than a_2 for that individual.

Both *difficulty* and *consistency* of choice involve the order axiom. Such ordering permits quantification of previously qualitative information as suggested in the section on the concept of utility. Combining the ability to quantify prior qualitative information with composite utilities (discussed in same section above) and with choice difficulty and consistency, one can derive a reasonably comprehensive system of utility measurement for evaluating.

Total and marginal utility

Total utility might be defined as the total psychological benefit derived from acquiring things or services.

Consider, for example, the graph in Figure 22.14.

The relationship that exists between total utility and the quantity of x is shown in Table 22.1.

Text continues on page 436.

Preference/utility relationships

The charts on pages 420–435 illustrate the statements listed in the left column of page 418.

1

if

P

or

P

or

I

u  > u 

u  < u 

u  = u 

2

if

=

then

|

&

3

if

|

=

u  = u 

u  = u 

4

if

p

&

then

p

implies

&

u

> u

then

P

u

> u

u

> u

5

if

P

&

then

P

implies

&

u

= u

then

6

if

P

&

then

P

then

&

u

= u

then

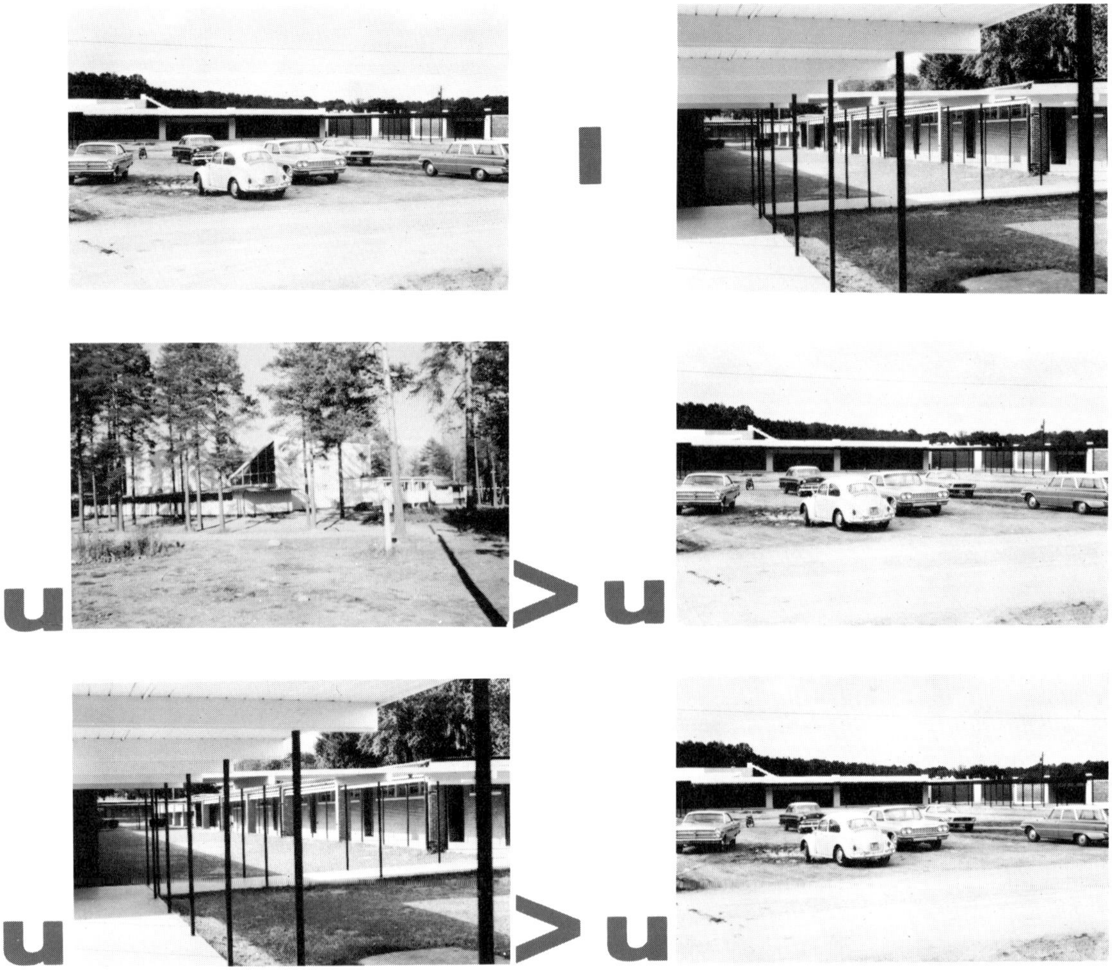
I
u > u
u > u

7

if

I

then

if

u

= u

then

I

u

= u

8

if

I

&

then

I

if

&

u = u

then

I

u

= u

u

= u

9

if $p_i = p$  $_1$

$u\Big(p_1$  $_1 \; + \; p_2$  $_2$

$p_1 u$  $_1 \; + \; p_2 u$  $_2$

$p_1 + p_2 + \cdots + p_n = 1$ **then**

$+ \cdots + p_n$  $_n \Big) =$

$+ \cdots + p_n u$  $_n$

FIGURE 22.13

FIGURE 22.14

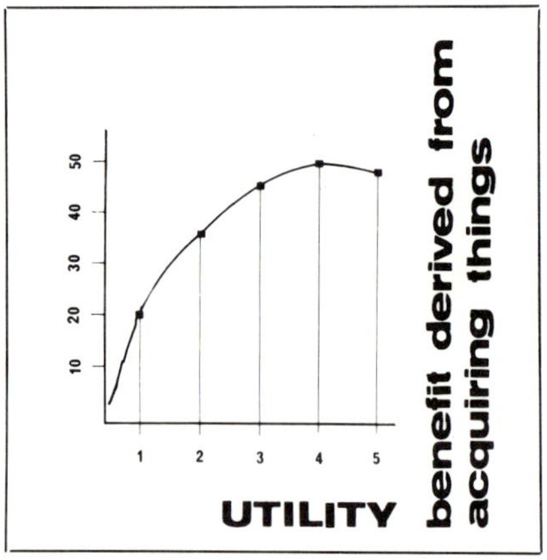

From Table 22.1 it is evident that a point of satiation exists at $x = 4$. That is, the utility of x increases up to four units of x, and beyond four units the utility begins to decrease. One can eat only so much of a good meal and beyond that the benefits derived decline.

Figure 22.14 shows the curve to be a decelerating one and shows the incremental increase of utility per increase in x.

Marginal utility has an established place in evaluation. In terms of costs for teacher time, for example, the marginal cost for adding one student to a class of twenty-nine is not the same as adding one student to a class of two if one teacher is required for each class.

Table 22.1 Relationship between total utility and quantity x

x	TU
1	20
2	35
3	45
4	50
5	48.5

Evaluating by maximizing utility

One attempts to maximize utility by appropriate mixtures of alternative sources of satisfaction.

Consider Table 22.2, for example.

Assume that A has five units of x and two units of y and that B has four units of x and two units of y. The question is—is there a basis for a trade? If B trades A one unit of y for one unit of x, B will give up seven MU_y but receive ten MU_x—clearly a gain of $3MU$.

From the point of view of A, if A gives up one unit of *x* for one unit of *y*, A will give up $4MU_x$ but will receive $6MU_y$—clearly a gain of $2MU$.

As a result of the trade, obviously both A and B benefit because both are better off than before the trade.

For educational planning purposes consideration of total and marginal utility and the distinction between the two is very important in evaluating alternatives. Educational planners should always consider the problem when evaluating the allocation of resources. The concept of marginal utility plays an important role in helping the decision-maker to evaluate the resource allocations and when he is likely to reach a point of diminishing returns.

Table 22.2 Maximizing utility

g_x	MU_x	g_y	MU_y
1	65	1	53
2	60	2	50
3	57	3	48
4	52	4	45
5	48	5	43
6	45	6	40
7	42	7	38
8	40	8	36
9	38	9	32
10	35	10	30

Evaluating with indifference curves

Indifference curves are considered by some planners to be superior to utility curves for evaluating preferential behavior. Indifference curves represent the combination of two quantities that are equally satisfying or various combinations of such quantities to which the chooser is indifferent.

Assume that one could buy one unit of *x* for one dollar and one unit of *y* for one dollar.

Reference to Table 22.2 would suggest that for the first unit bought one would receive $65MU$ (sixty-five marginal units) from *x* and $54MU$ from *y*. One would, therefore, take *x* first. Next, one would receive $60MU$ from *x* and $53MU$ from *y*. The second unit would also be *x*. Third, one would receive $57MU$ from *x* and $53MU$ from *y*. One would again select *x*. Fourth, one would receive $52MU$ from *x* and $53MU$ from *y*. The fifth unit would be selected from *y*. One would continue comparing *x* and *y* throughout the table until one's resources were extended or the supply of *x*'s and *y*'s was exhausted.

Evaluating by trading off

In practically all allocation problems the possibility of trades exists. Examine Table 22.3 to gain some insight into trades. The combinations of x and y in Table 22.4 represent pairs of things to which the individual is indifferent.

The plotting of the information from Table 22.4 results in Figure 22.15. Any combination of x and y on the curve in Figure 22.16 is equally satisfying to the individual.

Indifference curves, such as the one in Figure 22.11 never intersect, they are convex from the origin and their slope is negative.

Greater preference is expressed by the moving away from the origin in a family of indifference curves illustrated in Figure 22.11. In Figure 22.11, B shows greater preference than A, and C shows greater preference than B. On any curve—A, B, or C—the preference mixtures of x and y are equal.

The curves of A, B, and C in Figure 22.11 show an index of substitutability for x and y. As the curve approaches a straight line the substitution tends toward one for one.

Table 22.3 Prospect of trades

A				B			
g_x	MU_x	g_y	MU_y	g_x	MU_x	g_y	MU_y
1	12	1	1	1	14	1	9
2	10	2	(7)	2	13	2	(7)
3	9	3	6	3	12	3	6
4	6	4	5	4	(11)	4	5
5	(4)	5	4	5	10	5	4
6	3	6	3	6	8	6	2

Table 22.4 Satisfying quantities

x	y
1	20
2	8
5	4
8	2
12	1

FIGURE 22.15

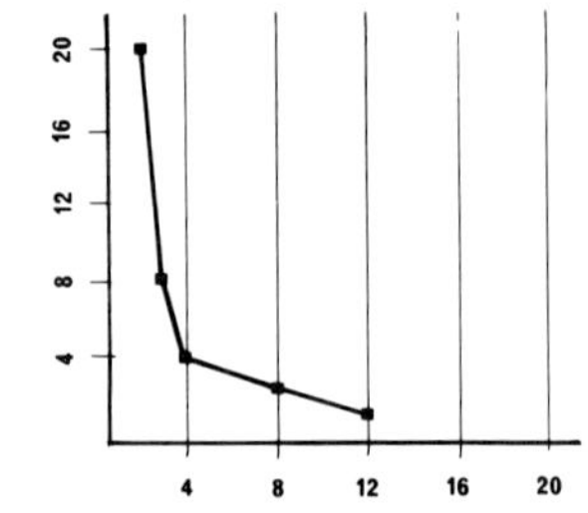

INDIFFERENCE CURVE

FIGURE 22.16

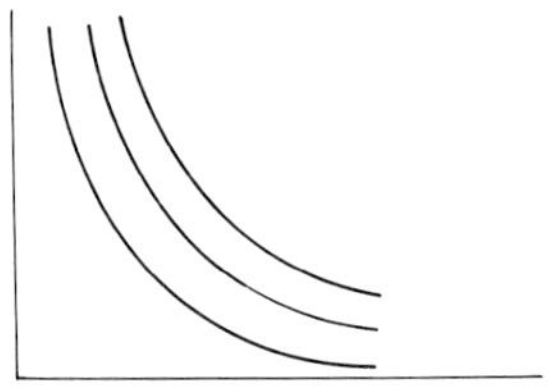

INDIFFERENCE CURVES

FIGURE 22.17

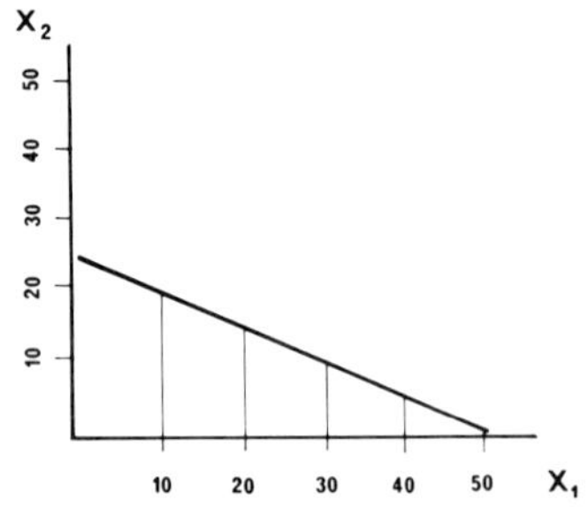

CONSTRAINT LINE

FIGURE 22.18

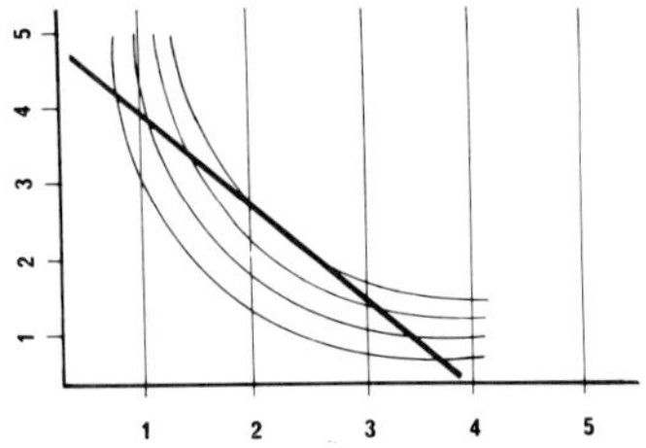

INCOME ALLOCATION

In situations where money is concerned, the level of satisfaction will depend on the price of x and y and the individual's income.

This constraint is shown by the equation

$$p_1x_1 + p_2x_2 = I$$

where:

p_1 = price of x_1

p_2 = price of x_2

I = income

The graph of the constraint function is given in Figure 22.12, where $p_1 = 2$, $p_2 = 4$, and $I = 100$. That is, one's indifference curves must lie below the line $2x_1 + 4x_2 = 100$ in Figure 22.17.

Consider Figure 22.18, which consists of four indifference curves and the appropriate line of attainable objectives. In order to allocate one's income between x and y so that the maximum satisfaction can be derived within one's income, one moves to that indifference curve just tangent to the line of attainable objectives. In that way one can evaluate the most desirable and the most attainable and select the point at which they converge.

Evaluating using demand curves

A demand curve reflects the different quantities of consumption expressed as a function of price; i.e., $g = f(p)$. Consider Figure 22.19. The line in Figure 22.19 has a negative slope, indicating that the quantity of x increases as the price decreases; i.e., as p moves away from the origin, x moves toward the origin, and vice versa. The changing price and quantity factors generate the demand curve shown in Figure 22.19.

Variations in the price, with utility and income held constant, lowers the quantity one can purchase and hence changes the line of attainable objectives.

Consider Figure 22.20. Obviously the change in price of x from p_{x_1} to p_{x_2} shifts the line of attainable objectives from I/p_{y_1}, I/p_{x_1} to I/p_{y_1}, I/p_{x_2} At the points where indifference curves are tangent to attainable objectives lines, a new curve appears. This new curve is called a *price consumption* curve. This curve reflects the combinations of x and y that maximize satisfaction at various price levels for x.

Evaluating using Engel curves

An Engel curve reflects the different quantities of consumption at different income levels. Assume that the utilities and the prices of x and y remain constant.

Figure 22.21 shows that the quantities of both x and y change as functions of income. The indifference curves tangent to the changing lines of attainable objectives generate a new curve called an *income consumption* curve.

Both demand curves and Engel curves help the decision-maker to evaluate the different behavior patterns expected for different individuals and different things.

FIGURE 22.19

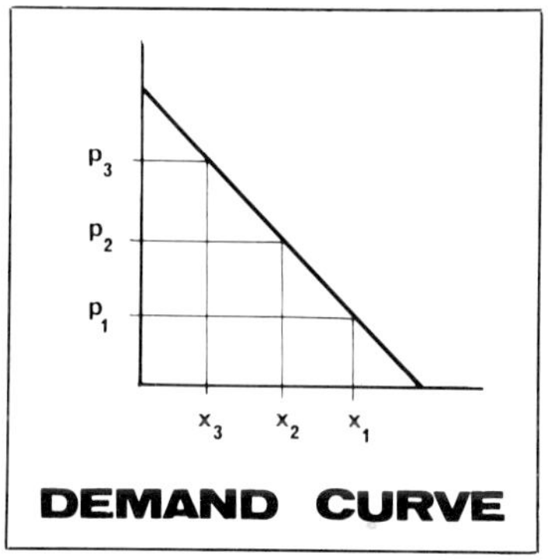

FIGURE 22.20

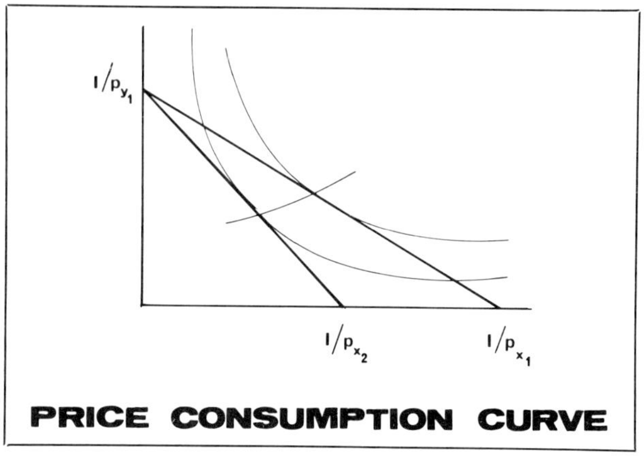

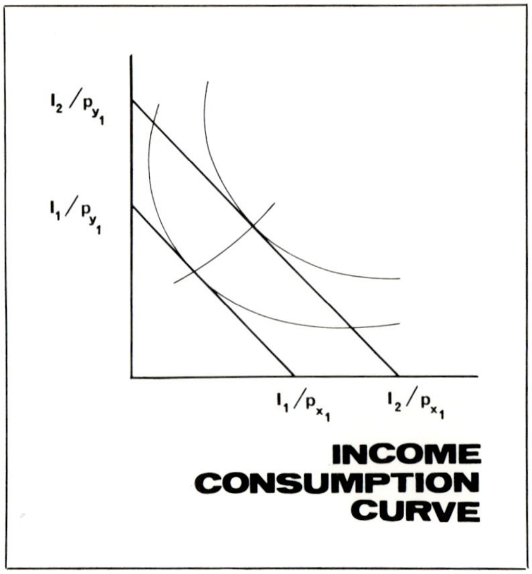

FIGURE 22.21

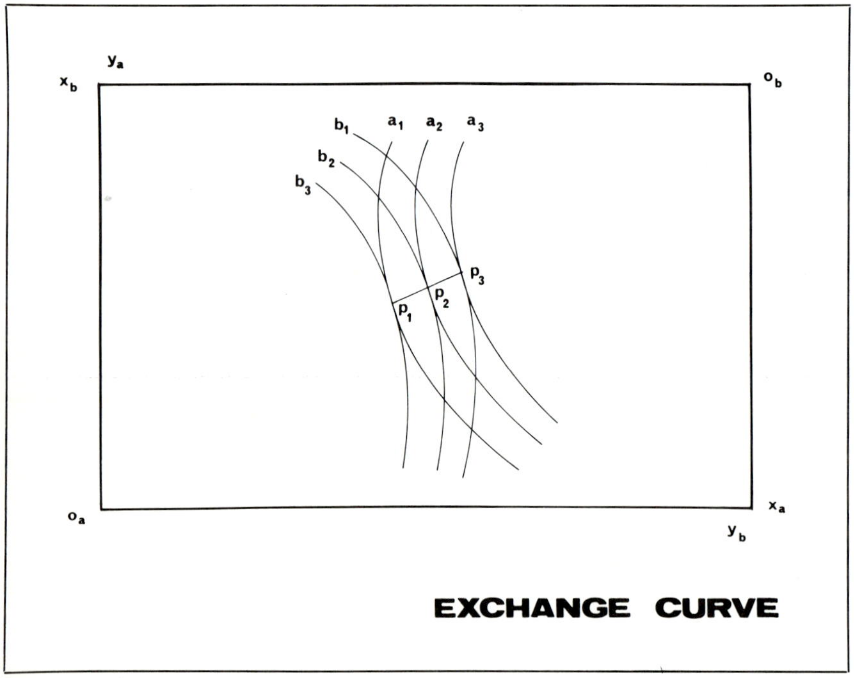

FIGURE 22.22

In Figure 22.22, the indifference curves for A appear on the usual axes. The indifference curves for B are rotated and superimposed on A. Any point within the rectangle is a possible mixture point.

If rotated 180° the origin of B O_b and x_b and y_b would overlay the origin of A O_a and x_a and x_b, respectively.

By definition the mixtures of x_a and y_a are equal at any place on the curve a_1. The same holds true for a_2 and a_3. B's situation is analogous. The ranking of utility for A is given by $U(a_3) > U(a_2) > U(a_1)$. The ranking of utility for B is given by $U(b_3) > U(b_2) > U(b_1)$. These rankings imply that for A $U(p_3) > U(p_2) > U(p_1)$. But for B the reverse is true, i.e., $U(p_3) < U(p_2) < U(p_1)$ because each step away from the origin denotes greater utility. Assume a point p_o for A and B; i.e., the intersection of a_1 and b_2.

The mixture of x and y can traverse the indifference curves a_1 or b_2. Because B wishes to maximize his utility by moving away from O_b he would prefer to move along a_1 to p_1 moving from b_2 to b_3. The change leaves A's utility unaltered because his utility remains the same at any place on the indifference curve a_1. However, A would prefer to move along b_2, because his utility would move from p_1 to p_2.

The curve p_1, p_3 is called a *contract curve* because it is on this curve that bargains can be struck.

The trade-off curves derived from indifference curves or trade-offs represented by earlier allocation problems both suggest the mutual benefits derived from trades. Such evaluation is central to all allocation planning.

The above approach to the evaluation of educational activities differs from traditional educational research. Traditional research has been based on the hard sciences experimental paradigm, i.e., dependent and independent variables. Educational planning evaluation seems to be more amenable to the techniques associated with operations research and systems analysis.

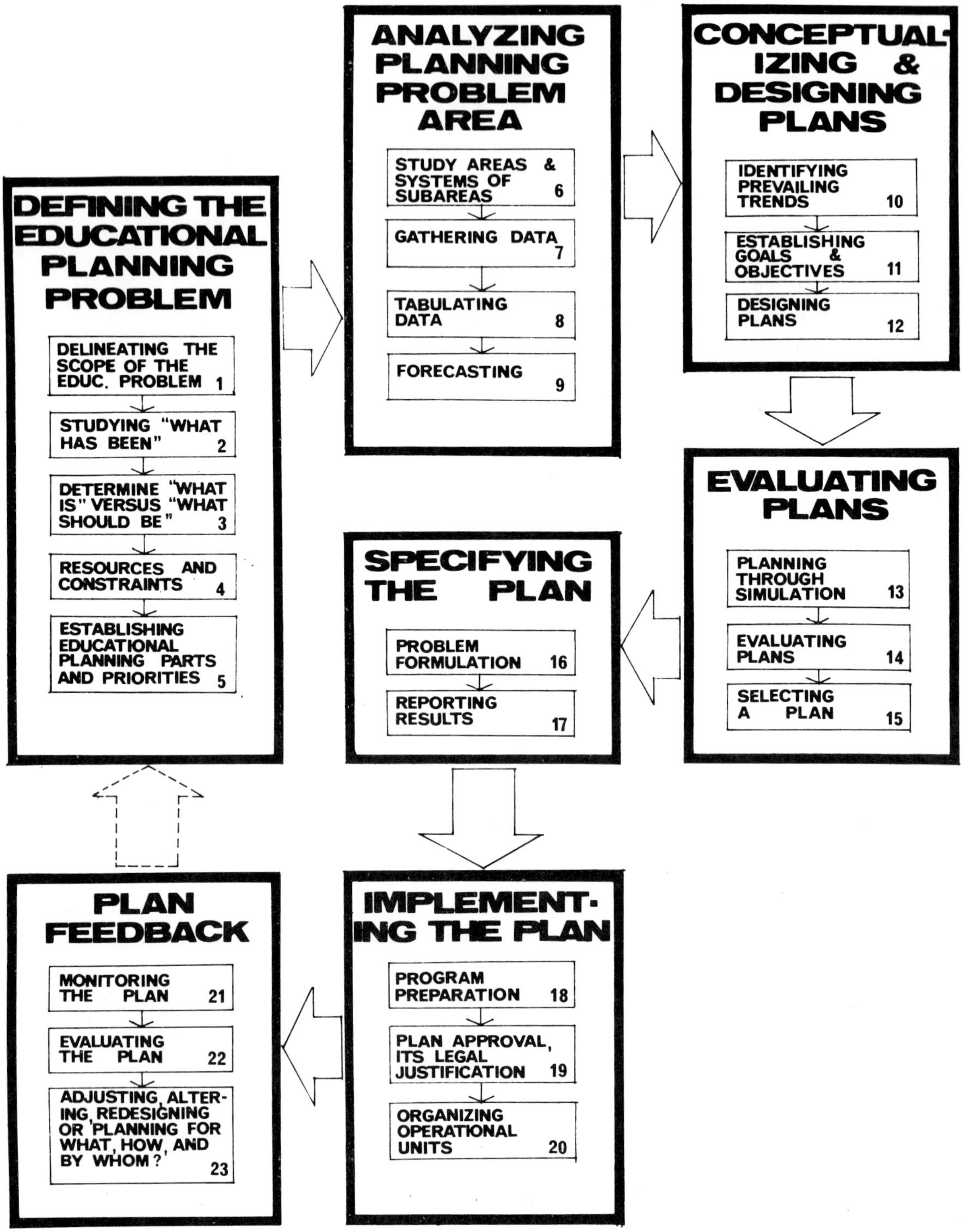
DEFINING THE EDUCATIONAL PLANNING PROBLEM
DELINEATING THE SCOPE OF THE EDUC. PROBLEM 1
STUDYING "WHAT HAS BEEN" 2
DETERMINE "WHAT IS" VERSUS "WHAT SHOULD BE" 3
RESOURCES AND CONSTRAINTS 4
ESTABLISHING EDUCATIONAL PLANNING PARTS AND PRIORITIES 5
ANALYZING PLANNING PROBLEM AREA
STUDY AREAS & SYSTEMS OF SUBAREAS 6
GATHERING DATA 7
TABULATING DATA 8
FORECASTING 9
CONCEPTUAL-IZING & DESIGNING PLANS
IDENTIFYING PREVAILING TRENDS 10
ESTABLISHING GOALS & OBJECTIVES 11
DESIGNING PLANS 12
EVALUATING PLANS
PLANNING THROUGH SIMULATION 13
EVALUATING PLANS 14
SELECTING A PLAN 15
SPECIFYING THE PLAN
PROBLEM FORMULATION 16
REPORTING RESULTS 17
IMPLEMENT-ING THE PLAN
PROGRAM PREPARATION 18
PLAN APPROVAL, ITS LEGAL JUSTIFICATION 19
ORGANIZING OPERATIONAL UNITS 20
PLAN FEEDBACK
MONITORING THE PLAN 21
EVALUATING THE PLAN 22
ADJUSTING, ALTER-ING, REDESIGNING OR PLANNING FOR WHAT, HOW, AND BY WHOM? 23

23 Adjusting, altering, and redesigning the plan

The chapters of this book are the steps in a seven-phase comprehensive educational planning process. Examining them in the light of planning history, planning techniques, and legal implications provides a guide for adjusting, altering, or redesigning plans for education. This means, of course, planning for what, how, and by whom? Each of these questions is discussed in light of the seven phases of our comprehensive educational planning model.

PLANNING FOR WHAT?

Comprehensive educational planning is being used more and more to shape the ever-widening range of community activities. There are many problems, for example, questions about the role of education in the community, and about the lack of legal means for carrying out planning policies more efficiently. The educational planner must also blend familiar and traditional ideas with the many innovations of today.

Originality and ingenuity are required in the shaping of appropriate legislative and administrative ideas for educational planning. And there are other questions: How wisely and democratically will planning tools be used? Will they be used intelligently, with a proper balance between daring and restraint?

The organization and distribution of resources are in large measure dictated by opinion, the established laws and the determined action of a few educators.

FIGURE 23.1
Major elements of a comprehensive educational planning process

FIGURE 23.2
Inputs from the environment

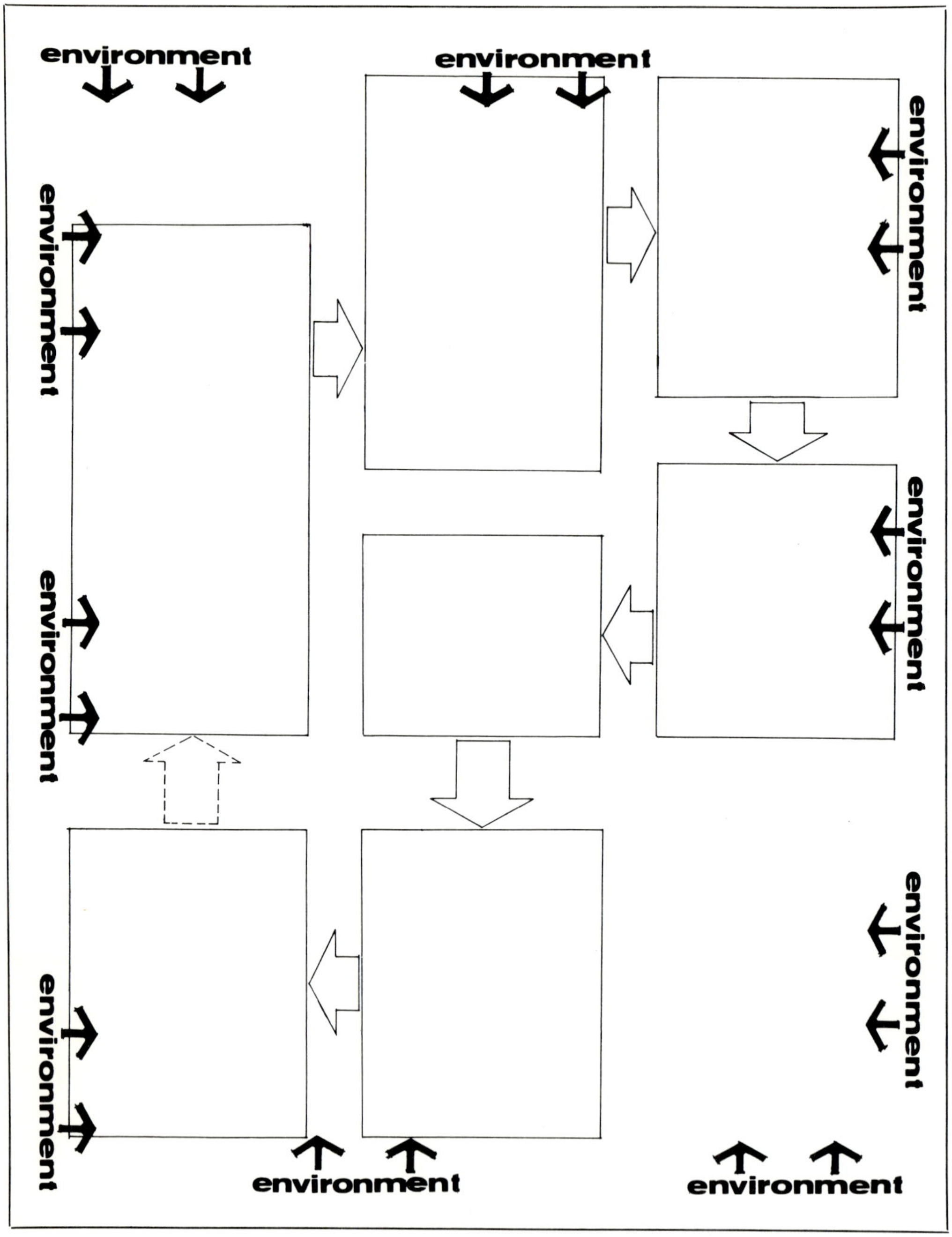

Regardless of the pace and structure of changes these educators will affect the minds of students and eventually the behavior of society.

Education requires constant readjustments to political, economic, and social conditions and must be responsive to changing public opinion. Many plans fail because the planner has not taken public opinion into account.

Comprehensive educational planning should show the patterns of progress being made by education.

The major elements of the comprehensive planning process have been outlined. Each element relates to education, each is conceived as a subpart of the larger urban planning process, and each can be graphically displayed, as in Figure 23.1.

The plan must not crystallize into a static form. As plans cease to be elastic and adaptable to changing opportunities their effectiveness is decreased. With an open-ended orientation the educational planner is more able to accomplish his task. With frequent points of reference to the environment, the objectives of planning are more effectively achieved. (See Figure 23.2.)

A comprehensive educational plan may include the following:

1 Careful surveys and studies of existing conditions and the probable future growth of education at the local level, the school district level, the intermediate level (substate), and the state level.
2 Maps, charts, and descriptive material presenting basic information, locations, and the extent and character of any of the following:
   a. History of educational growth and philosophy, community characteristics, and so on.
   b. School plant and site use, including all the physical characteristics of both private and public structures.
   c. Curriculum planning, including mental, intellectual, physical, and social development.
   d. Instructional planning, including strategies, media, equipment, supplies, and so on.
   e. Manpower and social planning.
   f. Student-profile planning, including location of residence, age, attendance standing, grade standing, employability, aptitude, interest, promotion, graduation, and so on.
   g. In-service training for all members of the educational community.
   h. Community social and physical profile.
   i. Administrative planning.
   j. School and site use plan.
   k. Building maintenance and operation planning.
   l. Special-education planning, including for the handicapped, for rehabilitation nongrading, for adults, for vocational and technical training, and for community college programming.
   m. Student transportation planning.
   n. Scheduling, including course offerings, teacher placements, student assignments, module structures, and so on.
   o. Community resources, including museums, zoos, gardens, theaters, city halls, courthouses, department stores, fire stations, libraries, newspapers, and so on.
   p. Student guidance service plan.
   q. Student health service plan.
   r. Community service plan, including recreation programs, library service, exhibitions, concerts, and so on.
3 Reports, maps, charts, and recommendations setting forth plans for the development, redevelopment, improvement, extension, and revision of education to accomplish the objectives of state and local legislation and the parents of the community.
4 A long-range development program of educational projects based on the recommendations of educational commissions, advisory boards, or the legislature for the purpose of eliminating unplanned, untimely, and extravagant educational projects and with a view to stabilizing education to incorporate cultural and technological changes and the yearly revision of such plans to keep them up to date.
5 A short-, intermediate, and long-range financial program of educational expenditures, kept up to date for the best possible use of the available public funds.

PLANNING HOW?

How can comprehensive planning be accomplished? One way is to base educational planning on five basic dimensions—people, places, movements, economics, and activities—in accordance with the following assumptions:

1 A student occupies a necessary, fixed space for his activities. However, he can move to another space.
2 A student, at times, belongs to a group. His group is defined by the communications used, their meaning and the amount of communication between the members.
3 A student needs to maintain an equilibrium between his external and his internal environments. Some modification of environmental elements might become necessary.

These interrelated assumptions cover almost any educational planning activity. Furthermore, the five basic dimensions of educational planning can be organized into two groups—continuous and discontinuous.

Students can be continuously organized in a graded system or organized into separate groups. *Places* can be organized in a continuous way as an "everywhere school" or in a discontinuous way as the predominant "neighborhood school." *Movement* can be centralized (a student going to a specific place for a particular course) or movement can be decentralized and a student can get the same instruction at a number of places. Economic budgeting can be annual budgeting or continuous budgeting like that required by the program planning budgeting system (PPBS). Activities can be centralized as the educational park or learning center concepts or decentralized as the Parkway School of Philadelphia. Figure 23.3 illustrates the ideas of continuity and discontinuity.

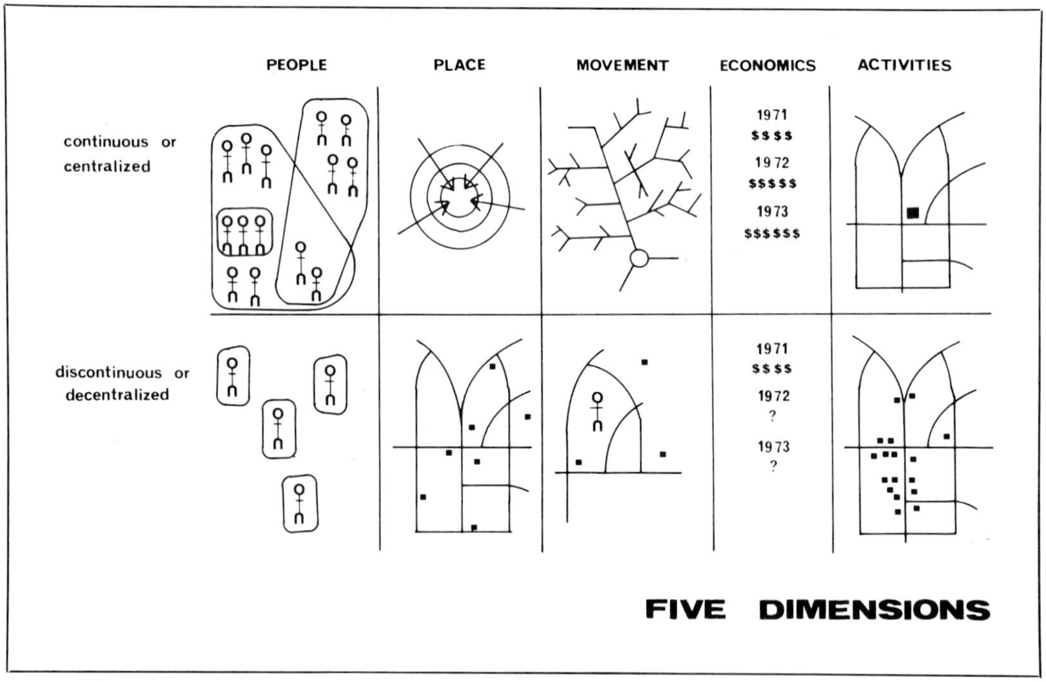

FIGURE 23.3

PLANNING BY WHOM?

Educational planners are a new kind of educator. They are not just curriculum planners, physical facility planners, media experts, or administrators. They are educators assembled in a planning unit and they represent a variety of skills, competencies, and experiences.

The educational planner, a technical generalist, is an expert in educational research and in systems design who can provide direction by applying the techniques of systems analysis and the new management tools such as PERT, CPM, and PPBS.

Educational planners may also be experts in communication. They are able to perceive and analyze the significance of information received for the purpose of validating the plan's input data. They are experts in descriptive and inferential statistical techniques, procedures for data handling and computer techniques. They may be expert in the knowledge and interpretation of educational laws. As members of the planning team they know about the social, political, and economic needs of their community, and they are vital to the formation of comprehensive plans for education.

Educational planners have at least one common trait. They all look to the future. As a vital, new part of education, the educational futurist associates with problems that center around trend analysis.

SUMMARY

The comprehensive educational planner is concerned with the full scope of educational activities, and, consequently, with cooperation, coordination, and communication. Educational planning requires team effort and the participation of every person concerned with the business of education: they must work not only in their areas of specialization but also in the overall planning.

Comprehensive educational planning is concerned with the activities of the community at large and with the cooperation of such professionals as urban planners, transportation planners, social planners, land-use planners, and educational consultants.

Comprehensive educational planning should exist at all levels of educational activities, e.g., local school district, substate regions, and the state. Thus, the local planning units or regional units or state units can work cooperatively for the mutual educational advantage of all. This cooperation affords educators an opportunity to act rather than react to problems. As new socio-economic or political units affect education, these units can be easily considered and incorporated into educational programs, because liaison has been maintained at all levels of the community structure.

Comprehensive educational planning must deal with an environment in transit, not one that is starting from zero. The task for comprehensive educational planning is to improve, not necessarily to make perfect. Comprehensive educational planning should not impose a new world on the community. Rather, comprehensive educational planning should put the art and science of planning at the service of learners, providing environments that help them to learn more about their environment and themselves.

References

Index

References

Chapter 1
Delineating the Scope of the Educational Problem

Campbell, Ronald, Lucy Ann Marx, and Raphael O. Nystrand, eds. *Education and Urban Renaissance.* New York: John Wiley & Sons, Inc., 1969.

Carr, Stephen, and Kevin Lynch. "Where Learning Happens." *Daedalus,* no. 4, **97** (Fall 1968), 1277–1291.

Coombs, Philip H. "The Challenge to Education Planning," *International Development Review,* no. 2, **10** (June 1960), 6–9.

Gittell, Marylyn, ed. *Educating and Urban Population.* Beverly Hills: Sage Publications, Inc., 1967.

Handler, A. Benjamin. "What Is Planning Theory." *Journal of the American Institute of Planners,* no. 3, **23** (1957), 144–150.

Lecht, Leonard A. "Strategic Variables in Planning." *Planning and Effecting Needed Changes in Education.* Ed. by Edgar L. Morphet and Charles O. Ryan. New York: Citation Press, 1967.

Lee, James E. "The Role of the Planner in the Present." *Journal of the American Institute of Planners,* **24** (1958), 151–157.

Montagu, Ashley. "To think and To Feel." *Introduction to Education: A Comparative Analysis.* (Ed. by Donald K. Adams. Belmont, Calif.: Wadsworth Publishing Company, Inc., 1966), p. 13.

Peterson, William. "On Some Meanings of Planning." *The Journal of the American Institute of Planners,* **32** no. 3, (May 1966), 130–142.

Chapter 2
Studying "What Has Been"

Barnard, Henry. *Practical Illustrations of the Principles Of School Architecture.* Annual Report ·to the General Assembly, May Session, 1850.

Branch, Melvin C. *Comprehensive Urban Planning: A Selective Annotated Bibliography with Related Material.* Beverly Hills: Sage Publications, 1970.

Cubberley, Ellwood P. *The History of Education.* Boston: Houghton Mifflin Company, 1920.

Handlin, Oscar, and John Burchard. *The Historian and the City.* Cambridge, Mass. The M.I.T. Press, 1966.

Mohaly-Nagy, Sibyl. *Matrix of Man.* New York: Frederick A. Praeger, Inc., 1968.

Mumford, Lewis. *The City in History: Its Origins, Its Transformations, and Its Prospects.* New York: Harcourt, Brace and World, Inc., 1961.

Scott, Mel. *American City Planning Since 1890.* Berkeley: University of California Press, 1969.

Chapter 3
Determining "What Is" Versus "What Should Be"

Bereday, George Z. F., and Joseph A. Lauwerys, eds. *Educational Planning, The World Year Book of Education 1967.* London: Evans Brothers Limited, 1967. Chapters 1–4.

Fisher, G. W. *A Conceptual Framework for School System Planning.* Ann Arbor, Mich.: University Microfilms, 1969.

Friedman, John. "Comprehensive Planning as a Process." *Journal of the American Institute of Planners,* **31** (1965), 195–197.

Lauwerys, Joseph A., and David G. Scanlon, eds. *Education in Cities, The World Year Book of Education 1970.* London: Evans Brothers Limited, 1970. Chapter 1–3.

Loeks, C. David. "The New Comprehensiveness." *Journal of the American Institute of Planners,* **33** (1967), 347–352.

Chapter 4
Resources and Constraints

Davidson, Paul. "The Valuation of Public Goods." *Social Sciences and the Environment: Conference on the Present and Potential Contribution of the Social Sciences to Research and Policy Formulation in the Quality of the Physical Environment.* Ed. by Morris E. Garnsey and James R. Hebbs. Boulder: University of Colorado Press, 1967. Pp. 125–163.

Ehrlich, Paul R., and Anne H. Ehrlich. *Population/Resources/Environment: Issues in Human Ecology.* San Francisco: W. H. Freeman and Company, 1970.

Maslach, George J. "The Reorganization of Educational Resources." *Daedalus,* no. 4, **96** (Fall 1967), 1200–1209.

Morison, Robert L. "Education for Environmental Concerns." *Daedalus,* no. 4, **96** (Fall 1967), 1210–1225.

Schultz, Theodore W. "Investment in Human Capital." *The American Economic Review,* no. 1, **51** (March 1961), 1–17.

Chapter 5
Establishing Educational Planning Parts and Priorities

Gittell, Marylyn. "Participants and Participation: A Study of New York City School Policy. *The Urban Review* (March 17, 1967), 4–12.

Kermoian, S. B. *Urban Community Maturation and School Plant Planning.* Ann Arbor, Mich.: University Microfilms, September 1956.

Morphet, Edgar L., and Charles O. Ryan, eds. *Designing Education for the Future, No. 3: Planning and Effecting Needed Changes in Education.* New York: Citation Press, 1967.

Organization for Economic Cooperation and Development. *Budgeting, Programme Analysis and Cost-Effectiveness in Educational Planning.* Paris, DECD: Education and Development-Technical Reports, 1968.

Chapter 6
Study Areas and Systems of Subareas

Bor, Walter, and Milton Keynes. "The First Stage of the Planning Process." *Journal of the Town Planning Institute,* **54** (1968), 203–208.

Chapin, Jr., F. Stuart, and Henry C. Hightower. "Household Activity Patterns and Land Use." *Journal of the American Institute of Planners,* **31** (August 1965), 221–231.

Doxiadis, Constantinos A. *Ekistics: An Introduction to the Science of Human Settlements.* New York: Oxford University Press, 1968.

Fletcher, H. *Speech and Hearing in Communication,* 2nd ed. Princeton, N.J.: D. Van Nostrand Company, Inc., 1953.

Haggett, Peter. *Locational Analysis in Human Geography.* London: Edward Arnold, 1970.

Harris, C. M. *Handbook of Noise Control.* New York: McGraw-Hill Book Company, 1957.

Journal of the Acoustical Society of America.

Knudsen, V. O., and C. M. Harris. *Acoustical Designing in Architecture.* New York: John Wiley & Sons, Inc., 1950.

McLoughlin, J. Brian. *Urban and Regional Planning: A Systems Approach.* New York: Frederick A. Praeger, Inc., 1969.

Parkin, P. H., and H. R. Humphreys. *Acoustics, Noise and Buildings,* 2nd ed. London: Faber & Faber, Limited, 1963.

Chapter 7
Gathering Data

Campbell, Robert D., and Hugh C. Le Blanc. *An Information System for Urban Planning*. Washington, D.C.: Government Printing Office, 1965.

Clawson, Marion. *Land Use Information*. Baltimore: The John Hopkins Press, 1965.

Cook, Robert C., and Jane Lecht. *People! An Introduction to the Study of Population*. Washington, D.C.: Columbia Books, Publishers, 1968.

Rapoport, Anatol. "The Promise and Pitfalls of Information Theory." *Modern Systems Research for the Behavioral Scientist*. Ed. by Walter Buckley. Chicago: Aldine Publishing Company, 1968.

Richert, John E., and Sandra L. Hals, eds. *Urban and Regional Information Systems: Past, Present, and Future*. Papers from the Eighth Annual Conference of the Urban and Regional Information Systems Association. Center for Urban Regionalism, Kent State University, 1970.

Webber, Melvin M. "The Roles of Intelligence Systems in Urban-Systems Planning." *Journal of the American Institute of Planners,* **31** (November 1965), 289–296.

Chapter 8
Tabulating Data

Hearle, Edward, F. R., and Raymond J. Mason. *A Data Processing System for State and Local Governments*. Englewood Cliffs, N.J.: Prentice-Hall, Inc., 1965.

Jay, Lesilie S. *The Development of an Integrated Data System*. London: Town Planning Institute, 1967.

Passoneau, Joseph H., and Richard Saul Wurman. *Urban Atlas: 20 American Cities: A Communication Study Notating Selected Urban Data at a Scale of 1:48.000*. Cambridge, Mass. The M.I.T. Press, 1966.

Rogers, Andrei. "Matrix Methods of Population Analysis." *Journal of the American Institute of Planners,* **32** (1966), 40–44.

Werdelin, I. "A School Enrollment Model." *Educational and Psychological Interactions,* no. 12. Department of Educational and Psychological Research, School of Education, Malmo, Sweden, April 1966.

Chapter 9
Forecasting

Boyliss, D. *Some Recent Trends in Forecasting*. London: Center for Environmental Studies, September 1968.

Bruck, H. W. "Problems of Planning for the Future." *1966 National Transportation Symposium*. New York: The American Society of Mechanical Engineers, 1966.

de Cani, John S. "On the Construction of Stochastic Models of Population Growth and Migration." *Journal of Regional Sciences,* no. 2, **3** (Winter 1961), 1–13.

Ivankhnenko, A. G., and V. G. Lapa. *Cybernetics and Forecasting Techniques*. New York: American Elwevier Publishing Company, Inc., 1970.

Sonenblum, Sidney, and Louis H. Stern. "The Use of Economic Projections in Planning." *Journal of the American Institute of Planners,* **30** (1964), 110–123.

Chapter 10
Identifying Prevailing Trends

Bolan, Richard S. "Emerging Views of Planning." *Journal of the American Institute of Planners,* **33** (July 1967), 233–245.

Childs, Dereck Rigby. "Trend, Countertrend or Counterdrift." *The Architects' Journal*. no. 3, **139** (January 15, 1964).

Elam, Stanley, and William P. McLure, eds. *Educational Requirements for the 1970's*. New York: Frederick A. Praeger, Inc., 1967.

Erber, Ernest, ed. *Urban Planning in Transition*. New York: Grossman Publishers, Inc., 1970.

Fabun, Don, ed. *Dynamics of Change*. Englewood Cliffs, N.J.: Prentice-Hall, Inc., 1967.

McLoughlin, J. Brian. "Notes on the Nature of Physical Change." *Journal of the Town Planning Institute,* **51** (1965), 397–400.

Webber, Melvin M. "Comprehensive Planning and Social Responsibility." *Journal of the American Institute of Planners,* **29** (1963), 232–241.

———. "The Role of Intelligence Systems in Urban-Systems Planning." *Journal of the American Institute of Planners,* **31** (1965), 289–296.

Wiener, Anthony J. "The Rocky Road to Utopia." *The Futurist,* no. 1, **3** (February 1969).

Chapter 11

Establishing Goals and Objectives

Altschuler, Alan. "The Goals of Comprehensive Planning." *Journal of the American Institute of Planners,* **31** (August 1965), 186–195.

Bloom, Benjamin S., ed. *Taxonomy of Educational Objectives, The Classification of Educational Goals, Handbook I: Cognitive Domain.* New York: David McKay Company, Inc., 1969.

Branch, Melville C., and Ira M. Robinson. "Goals and Objectives in Civic Comprehensive Planning," *The Town Planning Review,* **38** (January 1968), 261–274.

Crouch, Ralph G. *A Study of the Goal Formulation Process.* Prepared for the Department of City Planning, Los Angeles, September 30, 1964.

Simard, Jacques, "Fundamentals of Planning: Planning Ideals and Objectives." *Planning 1965.* American Society of Planning Officials, November 1965. Pp. 99–105.

Young, Robert C. "Goals and Goal Setting." *The Journal of the American Institute of Planners,* no. 2, **32** (March 1966), 76–85.

Chapter 12

Designing Plans

Alexander, Christopher. *Notes on the Synthesis of Form.* Cambridge, Mass.: Harvard University Press, 1967.

Castaldi, Basil. *Creative Planning of Educational Facilities.* Chicago: Rand McNally & Company, 1969.

de Chiara, Joseph, and Lee Kappleman. *Planning Design Criteria.* New York: Van Nostrand Reinhold Company, 1969.

Fantini, Mario D., and Milton A. Young. *Designing Education for Tomorrow's Cities.* New York: Holt, Rinehart and Winston, Inc., 1970.

Guttenburg, Albert Z. "A Multiple Land Use Classification System." *Journal of the American Institute of Planners,* **25** (1959), 143–150.

Lewin, P. H. "The Design Process in Planning." *Town Planning Review,* **37** (1966), 5–20.

Michelson, William. "Urban Sociology as an Aid to Urban Physical Development: Some Research Strategies." *Ekistics,* no. 144, **124** (November 1967), 401.

Parr, A. E. "Psychological Aspects of Urbanology and the Child in the City." *Ekistics,* no. 152, **25** (June 1968), 399–403.

Stonebreaker, Gary K. "Systems Analysis and Engineering Applications to Building with Special Emphasis on Design." *Handbook on Systems Analysis.* Ed. by Raymond L. Gail. American Institute of Architects, State and Chapter Affairs, April 1968.

Wolfe, M. R., and R. D. Shinn. *Urban Design Within the Comprehensive Planning Process.* Seattle: University of Washington, April 1970.

Chapter 13

Planning Through Simulation

Churchman, Charles W., Russell Ackoff, and E. Leonard Arnoff. *Introduction to Operation Research.* New York: John Wiley & Sons, Inc., 1957.

Duke, Richard D. *Gaming-Simulation in Urban Research.* East Lansing: Michigan State University, 1964.

Forrester, Jay W. *Urban Dynamics.* Cambridge, Mass.: The M.I.T. Press, 1969.

Garrison, William L. "Towards Simulation Models of Urban Growth and Development." *Land Studies in Geography. Series B,* 1962, pp. 92–108.

Harris, Britton. "Urban Development Models: New Tools for Planning." *Journal of the American Institute of Planners,* **31** (May 1965), 90–95.

Lowenstein, Louis K. "On the Nature of Analytical Models." *Urban Studies,* **3** (1966), 112–119.

Lowry, Ira S. *A Model of Metropolis*. Santa Monica, Calif.: The Rand Corporation, 1964.

———. "A Short Course in Model Design." *Journal of the American Institute of Planners,* **31** (1965), 158–166.

Meier, Richard L., and Richard D. Duke. "Gaming Simulation for Urban Planning." *Journal of the American Institute of Planners,* **32** (January 1966), 3–17.

Voorhees, Alan M. "The Nature and Uses of Models in City Planning." *Journal of the American Institute of Planners,* no. 2, **25** (May 1959), 57–61.

Chapter 14
Evaluating Plans

Blecher, Earl M. *Advocacy Planning for Urban Development: With Analysis of Six Demonstration Programs,* New York: Frederick A. Praeger, Inc., 1971.

Cripps, Eric, and David Foot. "Evaluating Alternative Strategies." *Official Architecture and Planning,* **31** (1968), 928–941.

Hill, Morris. "A Goals-Achievement Matrix for Evaluating Alternative Plans." *Journal of the American Institute of Planners,* **34** (1968), 19–29.

Kaplan, Marshall. *The Model Cities Program: The Planning Process in Atlanta, Seattle, and Dayton.* New York: Frederick A. Praeger, Inc., 1970.

Chapter 15
Selecting a Plan

Altshuler, Alan A. *The City Planning Process: A Political Analysis.* Ithaca, N.Y.: Cornell University Press, 1965.

Crewson, Walter. "Characteristics of an Adaptable School System." *Planning for Education in Litchfield Park 2000 A.D.* Ed. by Harold Moore. Tempe, Ariz.: Bureau of Educational Research and Services, 1967.

"Education in Pittsburgh." A Report of the Center for Field Studies, Harvard Graduate School of Education, Cambridge, Mass., 1966.

Lamp, Robert G. "Educational Parks for Twentieth Century Schools." *The Education Digest* (January 1967), 23–25.

Organization for Economic Co-operation and Development. *Mathematical Models in Educational Planning.* Paris: OECD, Education and Development, Document-Technical Report, 1967.

Chapter 16
Problem Formulation

Cantanese, Anthony James, and Alan Walter Steiss. *Systemic Planning: Theory and Application.* Lexington, Mass.: D. C. Heath and Company, 1970.

Chadwick, George F. "A Systems View of Planning." *Journal of the Town Planning Institute,* **52** (1966), 184–186.

Harris, Britton. "The Uses of Theory in the Simulation of Urban Phenomena." *Journal of the American Institute of Planners,* **32** (September 1966), 258–273.

Morse, Philip M., ed. *Operations Research for Public Systems.* Cambridge, Mass.: The M.I.T. Press, 1967.

Chapter 17
Reporting Results

Appleyard, D., K. Lynch, and J. Myer. *The View from the Road.* Cambridge, Mass.: The M.I.T. Press, 1964.

Bell, Daniel. "The Idea of a Social Report." *The Public Interest,* no. 15 (Spring 1969), 72–84.

Cox, Shankland, and Associates. *Expansion of Ipswich.* London: Her Majesty's Stationery Office, 1966.

Meyerson, Martin, and Edward C. Banfield. *Politics, Planning and the Public Interest.* New York: The Free Press, 1955.

Nystrand, Raphael O. "The Study of School-Community Relationships in Urban Settings: As Discussion of the Methods Employed in the Cincinnati, Columbus, Detroit, and Washington, D.C. School Surveys." Paper presented at the Annual Meeting of the American Education Research Association, Los Angeles, February 5–8, 1969.

The Planning of a New Town. London: Greater London Council, 1965.

Chapter 18
Program Preparation

Brown, Maurice. "The Time Element in Planning." *Journal of the Town Planning Institute.* **54** (1968), 209–213.
Gakenheimer, Ralph A. "Introduction to Process Planning: Symposium on Programming and the New Urban Planning." *Journal of the American Institute of Planners,* **31** (November 1965), 282.
Page, David A. "The Federal Planning-Programming-Budgeting System." *Journal of the American Institute of Planners,* **33** (July 1967), 256–259.
Robinson, Ira M., Harry B. Wolfe, and Robert L. Barringer. "A Simulation Model for Renewal Programming." *Journal of the American Institute of Planners,* **31** (May 1965), 126–134.
Studer, Raymond G., and David Stea. "Architectural Programming, Environmental Design, and Human Behavior." *The Journal of Social Issues,* no. 4, **22** (October 1966), 127–136.

Chapter 19
Plan Approval; Its Legal Justification

Babcock, Richard F. *The Zoning Game: Municipal Practices and Policies.* Madison: The University of Wisconsin Press, 1966.
Finey, Walter. *Law and Economy in Planning.* Austin: University of Texas Press, 1965.
Green, Philip R., Jr. *Cases and Materials on Planning Law and Administration.* Chapel Hill: Institute of Government, University of North Carolina, 1962.
Haar, Charles M. *Land-Use Planning: A Casebook on the Use, Misuse, and Re-Use of Urban Land.* Boston: Little, Brown and Company, 1959.
———. *Law and Land: Anglo-American Planning Practice.* Cambridge, Mass.: Harvard University Press and The M.I.T. Press, 1964.
Heap, Desmond. *An Outline of Planning Law.* London: Sweet and Maxwell Ltd., 1963.
Lefcoe, George. *Land Development Law: Cases and Materials.* Indianapolis: The Bobbs-Merrill Company, Inc., 1966.
Mandelker, Daniel R. *Managing Our Urban Environment: Cases, Text and Problems.* Indianapolis: The Bobbs-Merrill Company, Inc., 1966.
Milner, J. B., ed. *Community Planning: A Casebook on Law and Administration.* Toronto: University of Toronto Press, 1963.
Urban Law Annual, 1971. Seattle: The School of Law, Washington University, 1971.

Chapter 20
Organizing Operational Units

Barnard, Chester I. *The Functions of the Executive.* Cambridge, Mass. Harvard University Press, 1968.
Beeby, C. E. *Planning and the Educational Administrator.* New York: UNESCO, 1970.
Beer, Stafford. *Cybernetics and Management.* New York: John Wiley & Sons, Inc., 1964.
Etzioni, Amitai. *Modern Organizations.* Englewood Cliffs, N.J.: Prentice-Hall, Inc., 1964.
Getzels, Jacob W., James M. Lipham, and Roald F. Campbell. *Educational Administration as a Social Process: Theory, Research, Practice.* New York: Harper & Row, Publishers, Inc., 1968.
Griffiths, Daniel E. *Behavioral Science and Educational Administration: The Sixty-Third Yearbook of the National Society for the Study of Education Part II.* Chicago; The University of Chicago Press, 1964.

Chapter 21
Monitoring the Plan in Action

Gittell, Marylyn, and T. Edward Hollander. *Six Urban School Districts.* New York: Frederick A. Praeger, Inc., 1968.
Isard, Walter. *Methods of Regional Analysis.* Cambridge, Mass.: The M.I.T. Press, 1960.
Lynch, Kevin. *The Image of the City.* Cambridge, Mass.: The M.I.T. Press, 1960.

Rabinovitz, Francis F. *City Politics and Planning*. New York: Atherton Press, 1969.
Wallace, David A., and William C. McDonnel. "Diary of a Plan." *Journal of the American Institute of Planners,* **37** (January 1971), 11–25.

Chapter 22
Evaluating the Plan

Chapin, F. Stuart, Jr. *Urban Land Use Planning,* 2nd ed. Urbana: University of Illinois Press, 1965.
Goodman, William I., ed. *Principles and Practice of Urban Planning*. Washington, D.C.: International City Manager Association, 1968.
Lichfield, Nathaniel. "Cost-Benefit Analysis in Plan Evaluation." *Town Planning Review,* **35** (1964), 159–169.
Sanoff, Henry. *Techniques of Evaluation for Designers.* Raleigh: Design Research Laboratory, School of Design, North Carolina State University, May 1968.

Chapter 23
Adjusting, Altering, and Redesigning the Plan

Ashley, W. Ross. *An Introduction to Cybernetics*. New York: John Wiley & Sons, Inc., 1956.
Meier, Richard L. *A Communication Theory of Urban Growth*. Cambridge, Mass.: The M.I.T. Press, 1962.
Wiener, Norbert. *Cybernetics; or Control and Communication in Animals and the Machine*. New York: John Wiley & Sons, Inc., 1948
———. *The Human Use of Human Beings: Cybernetics and Society*. Boston: Houghton Mifflin Company, 1954.

Index

F

G

H

I

K

L

No class of fact or academic
division of knowledge is
the copyrighted property
of one profession –
the field of a profession
is not an area set apart.
It is the bringing to bear
of a certain plexus of
knowledge and skill
on some accomplishment
humanly desirable.

HENRY V. HUBBARD